GREAT EVENTS
FROM
HISTORY II

GREAT EVENTS FROM HISTORY II

HISTORY II

Human

Rights

Series

Volume 3
1960-1971

Edited by

FRANK N. MAGILL

SALEM PRESS

Pasadena, California   Englewood Cliffs, New Jersey

Library of Congress Cataloging-in-Publication Data
Great events from history II. Human rights series / edited by Frank N. Magill.
    p.   cm.
Includes bibliographical references and index.
    1. Human rights—History—20th century—Chronol-
ogy. I. Magill, Frank Northen, 1907-   .

K3240.6.G74   1992
341.4'81'0904—dc20
ISBN 0-89356-643-8 (set)   92-12896
ISBN 0-89356-646-2 (volume 3)   CIP

LIST OF EVENTS IN VOLUME III

GREAT EVENTS
FROM
HISTORY II

CANADIAN BILL OF RIGHTS PROHIBITS SEXUAL DISCRIMINATION

Category of event: Women's rights
Time: August 4, 1960
Locale: Ottawa, Ontario, Canada

The 1960 Canadian bill of rights marked a first step toward the constitutional protection of women's rights and civil liberties in Canada

> *Principal personages:*
> JOHN DIEFENBAKER (1895-1979), the prime minister of Canada whose party placed the bill of rights before the Canadian parliament
> JEAN LESAGE (1912-1980), the leader of the Liberal government in Quebec at the time the bill of rights became law
> LESTER PEARSON (1897-1972), the leader of the opposition Liberal Party at the time the bill of rights passed

Summary of Event

On July 1, 1960, the Canadian House of Commons began debate on a bill titled "Act for the Recognition and Protection of Human Rights and Fundamental Freedoms." A little more than one month later, on August 4, 1960, the House of Commons unanimously approved the legislation. The "Canadian bill of rights," as this piece of legislation came to be known, guaranteed Canadians fundamental freedoms regardless of race, national origin, color, religion, or sex. Numbered among these freedoms were the rights to individual life, liberty, and security, the enjoyment of property, equality before the law, the protection of the law, freedom of religion, freedom of assembly and association, and freedom of the press.

These rights and freedoms were far from unique to Canada; they were those commonly associated with advanced industrialized democracies. What made the Canadian bill of rights an important milestone in the history of human rights was its place in the evolution of formal legal protection for women and minorities. To understand its significance—as well as its limitations—one must examine three aspects of Canadian political history.

First, unlike either the U.S. Declaration of Independence or the U.S. Constitution, the Canadian constitution, the British North America (BNA) Act of 1867, did not begin with rhetorical flourishes extolling the virtues of that document ("to form a more perfect union") or setting forward high ideals ("life, liberty, and the pursuit of happiness"). The BNA Act was written simply as an act of the British parliament. Its purpose was not to separate Canada from Great Britain over Britain's objections but rather to bring together the existing British colonies of Canada, Nova Scotia, and New Brunswick into one country. Moreover, the concern for checking power and protecting individual rights so evident in the U.S. Constitution and Bill of Rights are nowhere to be found. Parliament's powers are defined in terms of making laws for the "Peace, Order, and good Government of Canada."

In large measure, the differences between the two constitutions on this point can be traced to the respective political cultures of Canada and the United States. "Political culture" refers to the way in which a country's people think about politics. Political culture in the United States is characterized as liberal, while that of Canada is seen as conservative. Central to liberalism are a distrust of power, an emphasis on popular sovereignty, and individualism. Canadian conservatism emphasizes respect for and deference to power and a sense of collective responsibility for societal welfare. Thus, where Americans stress the role of private entrepreneurs and the cowboy in "taming" the West, for example, Canadians speak of the role of the government (through the activities of the Royal Canadian Mounted Police, land-grant programs, and the Canadian railroad) in "settling" the West. From a human rights perspective, therefore, the passage of the bill of rights marked a major modification in the long-standing political culture of Canada.

All constitutions set out the basic rules by which the game of politics is played within a state, but not all constitutions are alike in their form, structure, or distribution of powers. The polar extremes are represented by the British and American constitutions. The British constitution is an "unwritten" constitution in which the British parliament is supreme. It is unwritten in the sense that no formal document exists that can be identified as the British constitution. Rather, the British constitution is generally considered to be an amalgam of several documents, most notably the Magna Carta (1215), the Petition of Right (1628), and the Habeas Corpus Act (1679). The British parliament has no rival or independent executive branch to deal with; prime ministers and their cabinets are drawn from its members. No court can declare its laws unconstitutional, and no parliament can tie the hands of a future parliament by denying it the right to make any laws it sees fit to enact.

The U.S. Constitution is a written constitution in which the principles of separation of powers and federalism hold center stage. The separation-of-powers doctrine limits what any one branch of the national government may do. The judiciary, for example, may declare laws to be unconstitutional. Federalism limits the reach of the national government by allocating certain powers to the states and placing them off-limits to national authorities.

The Canadian constitution is a hybrid of these two types of constitutions. No single constitutional document exists, as in the United States, yet far fewer documents make up the Canadian constitution than the British one. In terms of structure, Canada is a parliamentary and a federal system. As in Great Britain, the parliament is supreme. Consequently, the Canadian judiciary was formerly limited, in its ability to protect human rights and civil liberties, to ruling whether a decision fell within the jurisdiction of the legislative body (provincial or federal) that passed the law.

For the overwhelming part of Canadian history, any concerns that human rights and civil liberties might be trampled on by parliament proved unfounded. In this sense, the Canadian constitution successfully incorporated the unwritten spirit of the British constitution into its core. The fact remained, however, that because of the unlimited nature of parliamentary powers and the grant of jurisdiction on civil rights matters to the provinces, human and civil rights in Canada lacked the type of legal protection associated with civil rights in the United States. The 1960 bill of rights was an important first step in the direction of placing human and civil rights off-limits to policymakers. The full realization of this objective, however, did not come until the passage of the Canada Act, with its Charter of Rights and Freedoms, in 1982.

Under the BNA Act, the national government was given authority over trade and commerce, defense, and foreign affairs. The provinces were given jurisdiction over education and welfare. Neither of these were important policy areas at the time the document was signed. According to the act, provinces were also given the exclusive power to make laws concerning "property and civil rights in the province." This provision has been especially important for the province of Quebec and the efforts of its leaders to maintain a separate sense of Quebec identity through the structure of its education and legal system. Quebec leaders have considered Quebec to be one of the two "founding nations" of Canada and deserving of a special place in its laws and political system.

The year 1960 was important in the political history of Quebec because it marked the political awakening of Quebec. The passive and defensive Quebec nationalism that Canadians were accustomed to seeing was replaced by an assertive and aggressive brand of nationalism in which Quebec sought to protect and extend its provincial powers. The "Quiet Revolution," as this transformation came to be known, represented a major challenge to the federal government.

One of the principal forms that this challenge took was a heated political debate over the process of amending the constitution. Because the BNA Act was passed as an act of the British parliament, the British considered themselves entitled to alter it. An understanding between the two countries had been reached on how the amendment process should work: The British parliament would pass amending legislation only when asked to by Canada. The key question facing Canada was the proper role of the provinces in amending the constitution. Could the national government in Ottawa act unilaterally to amend the constitution, or must it have the consent of the provinces? If it needed the consent of the provinces, what voting formula should be used?

It was in this context that the Progressive Conservative government of John Diefenbaker sought to pass a bill of rights. As proposed, the bill of rights applied only on the federal level—one of the major arguments used against it. As noted, the central problem facing the Diefenbaker government was that the BNA Act had given the provinces jurisdiction over human and civil liberties. It was widely accepted that their approval was necessary before any changes could be made in these rights. Jean Lesage, who only recently had become the head of the Quebec government and who was a major force in the Quiet Revolution, was particularly concerned with protecting Quebec's provincial rights. He responded to Diefenbaker's initiative by calling for a provincial-federal conference to establish an amending formula for the constitution. Once this was settled, the question of what rights might be protected could be taken up. A meeting between Diefenbaker and provincial leaders was held in late July on the feasibility and desirability of holding such a conference. Although no agreement was reached on an amending formula (and none would be for more than two decades), Diefenbaker announced that the conference had reached agreement on the bill of rights legislation. That accomplished, the Canadian House of Commons unanimously approved the legislation within one week.

Impact of Event

Textbooks on Canadian politics no longer spend much time discussing the 1960 bill of rights but focus instead on the 1982 Charter of Rights and Freedoms. The latter document is considered to be part of the Canadian constitution and applies at both the provincial and federal levels.

The limitations of the bill of rights were recognized at the time. It was passed as a normal piece of federal legislation and not as a constitutional amendment. It applied only to the federal level, and the War Measures Act took precedence over it, although the bill of rights did modify the procedure for invoking these emergency powers. Given these considerations and the continued federal-provincial impasse over an amending formula, Canadian courts were reluctant to consider the bill of rights as the basis for decisions to overturn legislative or executive-branch decisions.

The limited impact of the Canadian bill of rights on women's rights, and the need for protections and guarantees more deeply rooted in the Canadian constitution, can be seen by looking at a series of Canadian court rulings. On the whole, the Canadian Supreme Court was unwilling to make major human rights decisions based on this piece of legislation. In 1963, a majority opinion of the court stated that the Canadian bill of rights did not deal with "human rights and fundamental freedoms" in an abstract fashion but only as they existed in Canada at the time that the legislation was passed. This narrow view of the reach of the Canadian bill of rights was modified by a 1970 decision extending its reach to previous legislation. The case in point centered on the legality of legislation that denied Canadian Indians equality before the law. In 1974, the Canadian Supreme Court seemed to backtrack on this position. Again the issue centered on Indian rights, but it also entered the area of women's rights. The matter under contention was that a Canadian-Indian woman who married a white man lost her status as an Indian, but a Canadian-Indian man who married a white woman retained his legal status as an Indian, and his wife also legally became an Indian. The court argued that this provision remained valid and was not in violation of the 1960 Canadian bill of rights.

Offsetting the inconsistent way in which the Canadian Supreme Court viewed the provisions of the Canadian bill of rights was the positive contribution that the passage of the bill of rights played in prompting the provinces to pass their own (although generally more limited) human rights legislation. It also kept attention fixed on the lack of constitutionally guaranteed civil rights in Canada and thus contributed to public pressure for the passage of the Charter of Rights and Freedoms. The protections contained in the charter applied to both federal and provincial laws and were embedded in the Canadian constitution, giving them an added aura of importance in judicial decision making.

Bibliography

Bell, David, and Lorne Tepperman. *The Roots of Disunity: A Look at the Canadian Political Culture.* Toronto: McClelland and Stewart, 1979. An examination of Canadian political culture that distinguishes between ideology and culture. Provides an excellent treatment of the theories of fragmented societies and formative events.

Dion, Leon. *Quebec: The Unfinished Revolution.* Montreal: McGill-Queens University Press, 1976. Consists of a series of translated articles and speeches that appeared in French-language media. Brings home the ideologies and sense of nationalism that underlay the Quiet Revolution.

Flanz, Gisbert. *Comparative Women's Rights and Political Participation in Europe.* Dobbs Ferry, N.Y.: Transnational, 1983. Does not have a section on Canada but provides important comparative focus. Chapters are organized geographically (Scandinavia, Western Europe, Southern Europe, and Eastern Europe) and chronologically.

Granatstein, J. L. *Canada, 1957-1967: The Years of Uncertainty and Innovation.* Toronto: McClelland and Stewart, 1986. Written in a very readable style, this book serves as valuable reading for those interested in understanding the nature of Canadian politics at the time the bill of rights became law.

Landes, Ronald. *The Canadian Polity: A Comparative Introduction.* Scarborough, Ontario: Prentice-Hall, 1983. Contains a chapter comparing the American, British, and Canadian constitutions. Has a discussion of the Canadian bill of rights.

McWhinney, Edward. *Quebec and the Constitution, 1960-1978.* Toronto: University of Toronto Press, 1979. Examines two decades of constitutional debate, politics, and developments in the relationship between Quebec and Ottawa. Focus is on Quebec's demands for social, economic, linguistic, and political self-determination.

Tarnopolsky, Walter. *The Canadian Bill of Rights.* Rev. ed. Toronto: McClelland and Stewart, 1975. An important reference and resource because it is one of few book-length studies on this topic.

Van Loon, Richard, and Michael Wittington. *The Canadian Political System: Environment, Structure, and Process.* 3d ed. Toronto: McGraw-Hill, 1981. This edition was written before the passage of the Canada Act and therefore contains a good discussion of the bill of rights. It also has references to relevant court cases.

Glenn Hastedt

Cross-References

The United Nations Adopts the Universal Declaration of Human Rights (1948), p. 789; Congress Passes the Civil Rights Act (1964), p. 1251; The U.N. Covenant on Civil and Political Rights Is Adopted (1966), p. 1353; Canada Invokes the War Measures Act Against Separatists in Quebec (1970), p. 1543; The Canadian Charter of Rights and Freedoms Is Enacted (1982), p. 2158.

CYPRUS GAINS INDEPENDENCE

Category of event: Political freedom
Time: August 16, 1960
Locale: Cyprus

Following a bloody four-year guerrilla war against British colonial rule, Cyprus became an independent state for the first time in its long, turbulent history

Principal personages:
ARCHBISHOP MAKARIOS (1913-1977), the president of Cyprus (1960-1977), a Greek Cypriot religious and political leader
FAZIL KUTCHUK (1906-   ), the vice president of Cyprus (1960-1973), a Turkish Cypriot political leader
GEORGE GRIVAS DIGHENIS (1898-1974), the founder and leader of EOKA, and a Greek Cypriot officer of the Greek army
KONSTANTINOS KARAMANLIS (1907-   ), the prime minister of Greece (1955-1963 and 1974-1980)
ADNAN MENDERES (1899-1961), the prime minister of Turkey (1950-1960)
HAROLD MACMILLAN (1894-1986), the prime minister of Great Britain (1957-1963)

Summary of Event

Cyprus was colonized by the Greeks during the second millennium B.C. The Turks settled on the island during Ottoman rule, which lasted from 1571 to 1878. By the time Great Britain took control in 1878, the Cypriot society's biethnic character had been formed and consolidated. In 1960, when Cyprus became independent from British colonial rule, its population of 570,000 consisted of 78 percent Christian Greek Cypriots, 18 percent Muslim Turkish Cypriots, and 4 percent other minorities. Great Britain granted independence after giving way to pressure from three directions. First, there was a bloody Greek Cypriot anticolonial rebellion led by Archbishop Makarios and Colonel George Grivas Dighenis, the founder and leader of the underground EOKA (*Ethnike Organosis Kyprion Agoniston*—the National Organization of Cypriot Fighters). Second, global pressure resulted from internationalizing the Cyprus issue in the context of the broader African and Asian self-determination and decolonization movements. Third, American pressure was applied to Great Britain, Greece, and Turkey to seek a solution to the Cyprus question and heal the Greek-Turkish "festering sore" within the North Atlantic Treaty Organization (NATO).

Under British colonial administration, life in Cyprus was typical of that of a colony. Human rights and political freedom were limited by the very nature of colonial rule. Both Cypriot communities enjoyed considerable autonomy on educational, religious, and cultural matters, but any ideas and movements advocating self-determination were adamantly resisted by the colonial power. The anticolonial guerrilla war, which was carried out by the Greek Cypriots from 1955 to 1959, caused trouble and bloodshed that made the administration of the island difficult and costly. Curfews, riots, arrests, deportations, imprisonments, and executions became part of everyday life. Archbishop Makarios and his closest advisers were arrested and sent to a year-long exile in the Seychelles. Thousands of political activists were arrested under emergency decrees. Nine members of EOKA were sentenced to death and hanged. Hundreds of people were killed and thousands wounded during the fighting. Collective and individual civil and political human rights were severely restricted and violated. In sum, life on the island was anything but normal.

A settlement of the colonial problem was eventually sought through diplomacy. Early in 1959, talks were held in Zurich among Great Britain, Greece, and Turkey. On February 19, an agreement providing for independence was reached in London by prime ministers Harold Macmillan, Konstantinos Karamanlis, and Adnan Menderes. Archbishop Makarios and Dr. Fazil Kutchuk signed the agreements on behalf of the two Cypriot communities, although they had not participated in the negotiations. In effect, the problem was settled between Greece and Turkey under British directorship. The biethnic character of the Cypriot society, ethnic bonds with Greece and Turkey, and British military interests defined the context and determined the content of the settlement.

The London and Zurich settlement resulted in a series of treaties that were formally signed in Nicosia on August 16, 1960, and went into effect the same day to establish the Republic of Cyprus. These treaties laid the foundations for the domestic political structure of the new state and its relations with the former colonial power and the two ethnic groups' motherlands. The treaty of establishment was aimed at safeguarding British military interests. It provided for two sovereign military bases of ninety-nine square miles and extensive use of other island facilities. The treaty of alliance was a defense pact between Greece, Turkey, and Cyprus. It provided for permanently stationing Greek and Turkish contingents in Cyprus of 950 and 650 soldiers, respectively. With the treaty of guarantee, Cyprus undertook to ensure its independence and prohibit any activity likely to promote, directly or indirectly, either union with any other state or partition of the island. This provision was aimed at mutual abandonment of the conflicting ethnopolitical goals of *enosis* (union with Greece) or *taksim* (partition into Greek and Turkish sections). In effect, that meant that Cypriots were no longer allowed to pursue political objectives and engage in political activities supportive of either *enosis* or *taksim*. Great Britain, Greece, and Turkey were named guarantor powers and reserved the right to take action, jointly or unilaterally, to protect the political independence and territorial integrity of the republic.

The basic provisions of the Cyprus constitution were also laid down in the Zurich and London agreements and provided for a bicommunal system of government. The two communities were recognized and distinguished with reference to their ethnic origin, language, cultural traditions, and religion.

Communal dualism, which was inherited from the colonial era, was institutionalized in all branches of government and public life. In essence, Cyprus was not a unitary state based on the democratic principle of majority rule. In the executive branch, the president was a Greek Cypriot and the vice president a Turkish Cypriot, each elected separately by his or her community. The cabinet was composed of seven Greek Cypriot and three Turkish Cypriot ministers appointed separately by the president and vice president. Legislative power was exercised by a biethnic house of representatives and two communal chambers. The two ethnic groups elected their representatives separately. The judicial system was also based on ethnic dualism. The composition of courts was determined by the disputants' communal membership. The supreme court was composed of a Greek Cypriot, a Turkish Cypriot, and a neutral judge who could not be a citizen of Cyprus, Great Britain, Greece, or Turkey. Separate municipalities would be created in the five largest towns with mixed population. Participation of the two communities in the public service, police, and armed forces would be at fixed disproportionate ratios favoring the Turkish Cypriot minority.

The two ethnic groups were granted the right to celebrate respectively the Greek and Turkish holidays and use the flag of the republic or the Greek or Turkish flag without restriction. The two ethnic groups were also free to establish separate "special relationships" with their motherlands on educational, religious, cultural, and athletic matters.

Finally, the constitution provided that provisions incorporated from the Zurich and London accords could not "in any way, be amended, whether by way of variation, addition, or repeal." All the features presented above were among the basic articles that could not be amended, as were the treaties of alliance and guarantee. Thus, the Republic of Cyprus was created by international agreements reached in the absence of the Cypriot people. The constitution was imposed on Cyprus and never submitted to a referendum or otherwise approved by the Cypriots. Limitations were imposed on the independence, sovereignty, and territorial integrity of the island, and foreign powers were granted the right to station military forces on its territory and interfere in domestic affairs.

In essence, the political and administrative foundations of the newborn republic were based on the bicommunal character of the society and fragmented features and practices inherited from the past. Perfect coincidence of linguistic, ethnic, religious, cultural, and political cleavages made it difficult to develop crosscutting national bonds, overarching loyalties, patriotism, or political culture supportive of a common country. With the declaration of independence, the stage was set for ethnopolitical polarization and paralysis of the newborn state.

Impact of Event

The declaration of independence on August 16, 1960, ended colonial rule but did not bring about institutions and conditions favorable to a peaceful political transformation. The two communities disagreed on issues affecting political participation and interpretation of ethnic, civil, and political rights. Archbishop Makarios and

Fazil Kutchuk, the Cypriot representatives who had signed the London and Zurich agreements, were elected the first president and vice president. One of the first tasks of their government was to build the new public institutions. This proved to be difficult. The Greek Cypriots were reluctant to implement some of the constitutional provisions that they regarded as unjust and unrealistic. The Turkish Cypriots, on the other hand, were unwilling to negotiate any of their disproportional minority rights, safeguards, and privileges. Some of the major sources of tension were the provision on the 70:30 ratio of Greek to Turkish Cypriots in public service, the separate majority vote of the representatives of the two groups in the parliament, establishment of separate ethnic municipalities, and the vice president's right to veto certain decisions of the cabinet and legislature. Because of repeated ethnically colored legal and political controversies at both the elite and grass-roots level, no branch of the government could function properly. The Greek Cypriot majority was tempted to seek changes of the status quo created by independence, while the Turkish Cypriot minority made extensive use of its legal and political safeguards, avoided negotiations, and sought autonomy and secession. At the personal level, the underlying dynamics of majority-minority relations added temptations, fears, and uncertainty. Protracted impasses and frustration reinforced mutual mistrust. Ethnicity dominated politics, and the two groups looked upon each other as ethnopolitical enemies.

On November 30, 1963, President Makarios made a last attempt to break the deadlock by proposing thirteen amendments to the constitution that would make Cyprus a more unitary state. The Turkish Cypriots and Turkey rejected the proposal as completely unacceptable and insisted that Cyprus remain a bicommunal state or else that complete separation of the two ethnic groups should occur through partition. After three years of simmering tension, what seemed to be inevitable came on December 22, 1963, when heavy fighting broke out. The flareup brought a complete breakdown of intercommunal relations, and physical separation of the two communities started. The Turkish Cypriots began moving into enclaves that emerged in various parts of the island. Turkish Cypriot leaders and public servants withdrew from the government and established a separate administration. This was the final blow for what had proved to be an inappropriate settlement of the colonial problem of Cyprus. Independence had ended British colonial rule but did not resolve ethnic differences. Instead, open ethnic conflict became the dominant problem. Hostilities continued throughout 1964 with Greece and Turkey becoming increasingly involved. Another crisis in November, 1967, once again brought the two countries to the brink of war. Following a Greek coup against Makarios, Turkey invaded Cyprus in 1974 and occupied 37 percent of the island. Turkey continued to maintain an occupation army in the north, where the Turkish Cypriots set up their own administration. The Greek Cypriot government controlled two-thirds of the island and was the only internationally recognized government on Cyprus. There was no interaction between the two ethnic groups, and crossing the one-hundred-mile-long dividing line was not allowed. Prospects for unification seemed slim, but efforts were made by the United Nations for a settlement based on a bizonal federal state.

Bibliography

Averoff-Tosizza, Evangelos. *Lost Opportunities: The Cyprus Question.* New Rochelle, N.Y.: Caratzas, 1986. As Greece's minister of foreign affairs, the author played a primary role in the handling of the Cyprus colonial problem in the 1950's. He was an instrumental participant in the negotiations that led to the Zurich and London settlement and the independence of Cyprus. In this volume of memoirs, he writes about events and personalities in an informative and revealing manner.

Crawshaw, Nancy. *The Cyprus Revolt: An Account of the Struggle for Union with Greece.* London: Allen & Unwin, 1978. Provides an account of the events that led to the independence of Cyprus in 1960. The *enosis* movement and EOKA revolt receive the most extensive coverage. Concludes with a presentation of the Zurich and London settlement and its breakdown.

Hill, George. *A History of Cyprus.* 4 vols. Cambridge, England: Cambridge University Press, 1940-1952. A monumental scholarly work of unsurpassed value. The most comprehensive and detailed history of Cyprus ever written, probably the most well known and most widely quoted work on Cyprus. Greatly respected for its precision, objectivity, and documentation. The fourth volume, which covers the periods of Ottoman and British rule, provides an excellent historical background to the Greek-Turkish conflict over the island.

Joseph, Joseph S. *Cyprus: Ethnic Conflict and International Concern.* New York: Peter Lang, 1985. Examines the ethnic problems of Cyprus since independence. Both the domestic and international aspects of the conflict are presented and discussed in a scholarly and analytical manner. The discussion revolves around the failure of the 1960 settlement of the colonial problem, the eruption of ethnic violence, and the unsuccessful search for a peaceful settlement.

Markides, Kyriacos. *The Rise and Fall of the Republic of Cyprus.* New Haven, Conn.: Yale University Press, 1977. The work of a political sociologist. Provides a good background on the contemporary history and society of Cyprus. Focuses on the negative impact that ethnic, ideological, and social fragmentation had on the Cyprus republic that was created in 1960.

Mayes, Stanley. *Makarios: A Biography.* New York: St. Martin's Press, 1981. An extensive biography of Makarios, probably the best. Tells the story of a man with charisma, talent, and vision who dominated the political life of Cyprus from 1950 to 1977. Provides a good overview of the critical years, major events, and turning points in Cyprus' modern history.

Purcell, Hugh D. *Cyprus.* London: Ernest Benn, 1989. A history handbook on Cyprus. Especially good are the chapters on the period of British colonial rule, the early years of independence, and the eruption of ethnic violence in 1963. A good introductory book for the reader with a general interest in the island and its colonial and ethnic problems.

Stephens, Robert. *Cyprus: A Place of Arms.* New York: Praeger, 1966. A brief history of Cyprus in which the author argues that the destiny of the island has been determined by imperial rivalries in the region. An informative and readable book with a detached approach.

Xydis, Stephen G. *Cyprus: Conflict and Conciliation, 1954-1958*. Columbus: Ohio State University Press, 1967. An excellent book on the colonial and ethnic problems of Cyprus and their internationalization through the United Nations in the 1950's. Provides a detailed account of the five Greek appeals to the U.N. General Assembly from 1954 to 1958 asking for self-determination on Cyprus. A revealing work on the use of diplomacy and international forums for the promotion of national goals.

Joseph S. Joseph

Cross-References

The Young Turk Movement Stages a Constitutional Coup in Turkey (1908), p. 98; Armenians Suffer Genocide During World War I (1915), p. 150; The Balfour Declaration Supports a Jewish Homeland in Palestine (1917), p. 235; The United Nations Adopts Its Charter (1945), p. 657; Riots Erupt as Katanga Province Secedes from the Congo (1960), p. 1068; The United Nations Intervenes in the Congolese Civil War (1960), p. 1074; The Nonaligned Movement Meets (1961), p. 1131; Greek and Turkish Inhabitants of Cyprus Clash over Political Rights (1963), p. 1218; A United Nations Peace Force Is Deployed in Cyprus (1964), p. 1236; A Greek Coup Leads to a Military Dictatorship (1967), p. 1359; Ethnic Riots Erupt in Armenia (1988), p. 2348; Ethnic Unrest Breaks Out in Yugoslavian Provinces (1988), p. 2386.

THE TAMIL FEDERAL PARTY AGITATES FOR GREATER LANGUAGE RIGHTS

Category of event: Racial and ethnic rights
Time: February, 1961
Locale: Jaffna, Sri Lanka (then called Ceylon)

In an effort to stem the erosion of language rights for the minority Tamils, the Federal Party in 1961 organized a civil disobedience movement as a way of pressuring the government

Principal personages:

S. J. V. CHELVANAYAKAM (1898-1977), the founder of the Federal Party, a charismatic figure who fought for Tamil rights through parliamentary means

S. W. R. D. BANDARANAIKE (1899-1959), the founder of the Sri Lanka Freedom Party, a former prime minister of Sri Lanka

J. R. JAYAWARDENE (1906-   ), a former prime minister and first president of Sri Lanka

Summary of Event

When the multiethnic island of Sri Lanka gained independence from Great Britain in 1948, it was hoped that the Sinhalese majority and the Tamil minority would be able to coexist peacefully. Such hopes were, however, dashed. Sinhalese politicians soon revealed little hesitation to use communalism for political mobilization of their constituencies.

The polarization of the two communities worsened over time to the point that in the 1980's the country was engulfed in open warfare. Many events led to this disaster, with one of the key turning points coming in 1961, when it became clear to the main Tamil political party, the Federal Party (FP), that more serious action had to be taken to stem the erosion of the rights of Sri Lanka's Tamil minority, which made up about 20 percent of the island's population. In order to understand the significance of the massive 1961 civil disobedience and its impact, it is essential to look at developments preceding it.

The most obvious differences between the Sinhalese and the Tamils were in terms of language and religion, with the former predominantly Sinhala-speaking Buddhists and the latter largely Tamil-speaking Hindus. The Tamil population was concentrated in the northern and eastern provinces of the island. The Sinhalese and Tamil areas represented distinct cultural entities and for most purposes had all the characteristics of separate nations.

Although Tamil concerns came to encompass the entire spectrum of economics, politics, and culture, it was on the language issue that the first clash occurred. The question of language had come to the forefront soon after independence under the imperative of meeting demands to replace English, which was identified with the erstwhile colonial masters. This, however, raised the sensitive point of how to treat the two indigenous languages. All the important Sinhalese parties across the political cal spectrum had begun by advocating parity for Sinhala and Tamil, but this equality proved to be illusory.

The Sri Lanka Freedom Party (SLFP), formed in 1951 by S. W. R. D. Bandaranaike, was the first to appeal to Sinhala-Buddhist nationalism as a way to counter its main opposition, the United National Party (UNP), formed in 1946 and led by the anglicized elite. To that end, the SLFP in 1955 led the fray in advocating primacy for Sinhala as the sole official language in place of English. One factor lurking behind this move was the Sinhalese apprehension regarding the potential relationship between the fifty million Tamils in neighboring India and the Sri Lankan Tamils. From the viewpoint of the minority Tamils, however, it represented a dangerous and chauvinistic move at their expense. In reaction, the Tamil Federal Party, which had been formed in 1949 by S. J. V. Chelvanayakam based on notions of the loose federation of Tamil areas with Sinhalese, now stated its resolve to defend the status of the Tamil language and culture—including the creation of an autonomous Tamil linguistic state if necessary.

The Federal Party's stand became more compelling as the SLFP won at the polls in 1956 and within twenty-four hours passed the "Sinhala only" legislation. This Official Languages Act did provide the Sinhalese masses with a voice, but in doing so it threatened to shut out that of the Tamils. The FP responded with a peaceful sit-in before Parliament but was met with violence from Sinhalese mobs and a lack of government protection. In a conciliatory meeting after months of negotiations, the ruling SLFP leadership and the FP finally entered into what appeared to be a good-faith agreement designed to stave off rising ethnic tensions.

This agreement, the Bandaranaike-Chelvanayakam Pact, recognized the validity of major Tamil grievances and conceded the position of Tamil as the national language of administration in the north and the east. It also agreed in principle to devolve regional autonomy and end Sinhalese colonization of Tamil areas. Had the pact been implemented, much of the later bloodshed between the Tamils and Sinhalese might have been avoided. As it was, the out-of-power UNP fanned communal flames and jeopardized progress. J. R. Jayawardene, a top UNP official who was to later become the country's leader, and a group of extreme Buddhist monks staged a "pilgrimage" on behalf of a Sinhala-Buddhist polity, marking the beginning of outright chauvinistic political plays by the two key Sinhalese parties, with Tamils as the most convenient political targets.

Revocation of the pact in 1958 was viewed by Tamils as a terrible betrayal. The only recourse for the FP was seen as direct action, and at the party convention in May, 1958, plans for mass civil disobedience were discussed. Sinhalese extremists disrupted the convention, however, and what began as stoning of buses and trains carrying Tamil delegates ended in the random massacre of Tamils in many areas, especially in Colombo, the country's capital. Tamil businesses and properties were ransacked and set on fire. Worse, Tamils were singled out in buses and cars, in many instances by their inability to read Sinhala or recite a Buddhist hymn, and killed. This historically unparalleled violence led to the flight of nearly twelve thousand Tamil refugees from their homes in the south to safe havens in the north and east. The 1958 riots demonstrated graphically how fragile communal harmony had become.

The FP still held a final shred of hope that its demands could be met through regular parliamentary means, especially because at the time it held a potential swing role. In the March, 1960, elections, it briefly appeared that the FP's votes would be critical enough for the SLFP, which won only a plurality, to resurrect the provisions of the dormant pact. Potential Tamil influence was quickly undercut, however, when fresh elections were announced and the SLFP won a landslide victory. The turn of events was to prove ominous in terms of Tamil political clout; in general elections after 1965, the two largest Sinhalese parties managed to garner sufficient votes within the majority community to take away the Tamil minority's power as a true political force.

The new SLFP government failed to recognize Tamil as a regional language and decreed that Sinhala would be the language of administration even in Tamil areas. Legislation making Sinhala the language of the courts was also introduced despite Tamil protestations. At the same time, the government declared that the main teacher-training college would be reserved for Sinhalese teachers. An extreme but influential group of Buddhist monks even called for postponing public examinations for persons educated in English or Tamil for a period of ten years.

These moves constituted a blow not only to the cultural rights of Tamils but also to their basic welfare. The language issue was a volatile one because of its impact on education and therefore on employment. The Tamils traditionally had concentrated on highly competitive professions such as teaching, engineering, law, and civil service. They chose this route because of lack of viable alternatives—the terrain of the north was arid and extremely unproductive, and capital for business purposes was in short supply in the Tamil community.

This was the general backdrop to the largest Tamil civil disobedience movement since independence, the *satyagraha*, launched in February, 1961. The immediate catalyst was the Official Languages Act's coming into full force in January, 1961. The FP had been preparing for such an eventuality since the abrogation of the Bandaranaike-Chelvanayakam pact. For example, volunteers had been recruited to teach nonviolent protest techniques, and classes had already started. The movement managed to draw in the other Tamil parties on the political scene as well.

The overwhelming majority of Tamil public servants stopped working in the "official" language in response to individual letters appealing for a boycott of its implementation. Beginning in Jaffna, the principal city in the north, the civil disobedience campaign spread to every town in the two Tamil provinces. The movement expanded to embrace alternative public services, such as a postal system. Plans were also drawn up to distribute public lands and organize a police force.

This peaceful show of resistance failed to bring the central government to the negotiating table; rather, it responded with strong force. Tamil leaders were arrested, and the FP was banned. On April 18, the government declared a state of emergency. Members of army units that were rushed to Jaffna harassed and assaulted peaceful demonstrators and innocent bystanders. The FP leaders were released only in October. The emergency itself lasted 743 days, during which time the Tamils of Jaffna experienced army rule for the first time.

Impact of Event

The crackdown on the peaceful agitation and the two-year emergency led to no progress in negotiations and to a false lull in ethnic tensions. Anti-Tamil passions were rising dramatically among Sinhalese, giving the government less room to negotiate, even half-heartedly. For example, in 1966, when the UNP-dominated government attempted to implement limited concessions on the official languages matter, the attempt led to bloodshed. In that case, three thousand Sinhalese protesters led by Buddhist monks rallied outside Parliament against even the smallest reforms being proposed. For the third time since independence, a state of emergency was declared, and the government's promises to the FP were swept aside.

The central government appeared to give up even the semblance of communal impartiality when it shepherded a new constitution through Parliament in 1972. The new constitution made Sinhala the sole official language and conferred a special role on Buddhism, with the state obliged to protect and foster the religion. This explicit constitutional privilege for the majority religion served to highlight the potential vulnerability of the other three religions on the island—Hinduism, Christianity, and Islam. The government also introduced a "standardization" scheme in education whereby students studying in Sinhala required a lower academic standard for admission to college than did their counterparts being taught in Tamil.

In addition to these affronts, Tamils received an unexpectedly rude reminder of their vulnerability in January, 1974. The World Tamil Congress, an international conference on Tamil language and culture, was held in Jaffna, with scores of eminent writers, scholars, and artists in attendance. On the last day of the meeting, many of the participants mingled with the thousands of interested persons gathered on the esplanade outside the conference hall. With shocking impunity, the police charged the crowd with tear gas and batons, citing unauthorized public assembly. In the melee, nine people were killed.

This unprovoked attack on the cultural gathering outraged the Tamil community and proved to be a turning point in terms of political tactics. Thus far, despite the odds, the leading Tamil politicians had been trying to strike parliamentary deals with the SLFP and UNP, threatening at most civil disobedience when spurned. A new generation of disillusioned Tamil youths who had grown up in the increasingly communalized country and whose futures were at stake viewed the FP as ineffective. Arguing that a more revolutionary approach using guerrilla tactics was needed to pressure the Sinhalese government, they formed the Tamil New Tigers, the forerunners of the Liberation Tigers of Tamil Eelam, who fought for a separate state.

The government reacted with unprecedented repression, intensifying it over time to include harsh measures such as the Prevention of Terrorism Act (PTA) of 1979. The terms of the PTA included such provisions as incommunicado detention for up to eighteen months and admission of confessions obtained through torture. The International Commission of Jurists concluded that, in comparison with other countries, only the South African law against terrorism came close to Sri Lanka's.

The cycle of violence between the Tamils and Sinhalese in many ways can be traced to the successive Sinhalese-led Sri Lankan governments' inability or lack of desire to provide reasonable concessions to the Tamil minority within the parliamentary setting. In retrospect, the 1961 Tamil disobedience movement was a signal event, in that it revealed the inevitable limitations of such measures in a country where communal passion and its manipulation had become a fact of the political system.

Bibliography

Kearney, Robert. *Communalism and Language in the Politics of Ceylon.* Durham, N.C.: Duke University Press, 1967. Although the author's rather optimistic outlook for political coexistence on the island has been disproven by events, this book is valuable for its detailed exposition of language as the key dividing issue between Sinhalese and Tamils. The politics of language is carefully linked up to the broader question of cultural identities. Includes bibliography and index.

Manogaran, Chelvadurai. *Ethnic Conflict and Reconciliation in Sri Lanka.* Honolulu: University of Hawaii Press, 1987. This is a well-documented work covering historical, economic, and political changes. Although written by a geographer, it is very good on economics and politics. Contains bibliography and index.

Ram, Mohan. *Sri Lanka: The Fractured Island.* New Delhi: Penguin Books, 1989. A highly readable book by a foreign correspondent who has covered Sri Lanka for more than a decade. Provides a sweeping overview of the roots of the Sri Lankan conflict and explains the various issues that will have to be worked out before there can be lasting peace. Bibliography and index.

Sivanandan, A. "Sri Lanka: Racism and the Politics of Underdevelopment." *Race and Class* 26 (Summer, 1984): 1-37. Written in a rather polemical style. The author provides sharp criticism of the government's role in the ethnic conflict. Focuses on the interconnections between political and economic aspects of the conflict. Bibliography and index.

Tambiah, Stanley J. *Sri Lanka: Ethnic Fratricide and the Dismantling of Democracy.* Chicago: University of Chicago Press, 1986. Written in easily accessible fashion, this slim volume tends to emphasize the ideological and political aspects of the ethnic conflict. Attempts to link the political violence with twentieth century notions of nationalism in the context of democratic, pluralistic politics. Includes index.

Vittachi, Tarzie. *Emergency '58: The Story of the Ceylon Race Riots.* London: A. Deutsch, 1959. A firsthand account of the key 1958 ethnic violence, written in journalistic style. Provides detailed descriptions and evidence of the atrocities that occurred.

Wilson, A. J. *Politics in Sri Lanka, 1947-1973.* London: Macmillan, 1979. A comprehensive book covering history, politics, economics, administration, and foreign policy. Useful as an introductory text to Sri Lankan politics. Includes bibliography and index.

Wriggins, W. Howard. *Ceylon: Dilemmas of a New Nation.* Princeton, N.J.: Princeton University Press, 1960. Intriguing for the author's early insights into the use of communalism for political purposes and its expected effects on the country's unity. Bibliography and index.

Deepa Mary Ollapally
G. Anandalingam

Cross-References

The Paris Peace Conference Includes Protection for Minorities (1919), p. 252; Gandhi Leads a Noncooperation Movement (1920), p. 315; India Gains Independence (1947), p. 731; Sri Lankans Promote Nationalism (1971), p. 1590; Tamil Separatist Violence Erupts in Sri Lanka (1980's), p. 2068; Amnesty International Adopts a Program for the Prevention of Torture (1983), p. 2204; Government-Supported Death Squads Quash JVP Insurrection in Sri Lanka (1987), p. 2315; Kashmir Separatists Demand an End to Indian Rule (1989), p. 2426.

THE NATIONAL COUNCIL OF CHURCHES
SUPPORTS BIRTH CONTROL

Category of event: Reproductive freedom
Time: February 24, 1961
Locale: Syracuse, New York

Continuing in its liberal tradition and recognizing changing world events such as the population explosion, the National Council of Churches issued a proclamation supporting married couples' use of birth control

Principal personages:
THE REVEREND ROY G. ROSS (1898-1978), the general secretary of the National Council of Churches beginning in 1960
THE REVEREND J. IRWIN MILLER, the president of the National Council of Churches from 1960 to 1963
THE REVEREND WILLIAM H. GENNE (1910-   ), the director of sexuality and family ministries in education for Christian life and mission in education and ministry
RICHARD M. FAGLEY (1910-   ), one of the committee members and a consultant to the United Nations Economic and Social Council

Summary of Event

In 1961, the National Council of Churches (NCC), a federation of twenty-five major Protestant denominations and eight Eastern Orthodox communions representing more than thirty-nine million people, made a startling announcement. Married couples, under certain conditions, would be allowed to utilize artificial birth control in order to foster responsible parenthood and strong, viable Christian families. The forms of birth control condoned included occasional abstinence, which is the method of choice for the Eastern Orthodox churches; periodic abstinence (rhythm method) and artificial contraception were approved by the Protestant church members. In both cases, the means were to be acceptable to both partners and noninjurious to health. The NCC proclamation stated that the rhythm method was not morally superior to other methods as in the Protestant view; motives, not methods, form the moral basis for family planning. Voluntary sterilization was condoned primarily for reasons of health or other obligations of parenthood. Abortion or any life-destroying method was declared absolutely unacceptable except when the life and health of the mother are at risk.

The stated reasons for family planning included the right of a child to be loved, cared for, educated, and trained in Christian principles. The needs of existing children were to be considered in a couple's decision to have or not to have another child. Possible genetic or other defects the parents might transmit to the child, as well as the mother's need to safeguard her health by spacing her children's births, were also listed as appropriate reasons for using contraception. World conditions such as overpopulation and its negative consequences also qualified as justification for birth control. The overriding purpose of the proclamation was that of providing a Christian doctrine of parenthood which would be relevant to husbands and wives in contemporary society.

The document noted that contraception requires the services of the medical community and other family-serving professionals. Therefore, any laws which prohibit giving birth control information, technology, or counsel to married couples violate that couple's civil and religious rights. Furthermore, in the light of the fact that aid given by the United States was in part responsible for the global population problem, individual Christians and government and voluntary agencies have a moral duty to assist those less developed countries (LDCs) requesting assistance in alleviating their overpopulation problems. Material conditions in these countries, the document states, must be improved so that their people can achieve human dignity, freedom, justice, and peace.

The points made in the NCC proclamation were radical for their time. Birth control had long been a controversial issue in the United States. In 1903, Theodore Roosevelt stated that "race suicide" was occurring, as the birthrate of Anglo-Saxons had dropped precipitously. He considered the new immigrants from Europe to be an inferior and immoral "race." "Race suicide" became a rallying cry against contraception. In Roosevelt's opinion, families were to be servants to the state, and their duty was to rear many children. Birth control to improve a family's standard of living was considered to be selfish, egotistical, immoral, and indolent by Roosevelt.

In the late 1910's, Margaret Sanger, a nurse and major crusader for contraception in the United States, argued that birth control should be allowed for the unfit and to alleviate the suffering of overly prolific and poverty-stricken immigrants. This was a variation of Roosevelt's view, and it attracted middle-class reformers who were drawn to the idea, called eugenics, of biologically regulating and thereby improving society. Sanger argued during this period that many social problems—feeble-mindedness, crime, poverty, and degeneracy—could be eliminated if birth control were legal and available. All welfare programs could be dismantled if, through scientific management, only the fit could breed. The eugenics movement remained strong throughout the 1920's.

Birth control was equated by some with racism, in that the immigrants from Southern and Eastern Europe were considered to be members of inferior races who were making America's cities uninhabitable and who were taking jobs from native workers. This reactionary branch of the eugenics movement supported contraception for the inferior races and the unfit. They believed that America had to be kept "pure."

From the beginning, there was opposition to birth control. Margaret Sanger's First American Birth Control Conference (November, 1921) was halted by the police at the request of Catholic clergy, who stated that clean and right-minded people never talked about such things in public. Proponents of birth control persisted.

In 1925, Will Durant, speaking at the Sixth International Neo-Malthusian and

Birth Control Conference, stated that the United States should dispense birth control information to Asian countries where the unchecked birth rate was endangering international peace. A problem with this suggestion, however, was that under the Comstock Law, pushed through Congress in 1873 by Anthony Comstock and his Society for the Suppression of Vice's lobbying efforts, any form of birth control information was defined as obscene and lewd and therefore could not be sent through the U.S. postal service.

The National Woman's Party, which had a feminist orientation, had no plank on birth control in 1927. Such a platform, it was feared, would split the party and alienate possible supporters. In 1929, the National Broadcasting Company refused to carry any speeches on birth control; it was considered too controversial a topic. The League of Women Voters declined a resolution in 1930 that called for a study on birth control; it too feared that such a resolution would split the group.

It has been estimated that in 1938 American women spent more than $200 million on birth control products (labeled as "feminine hygiene" products to avoid the censors) purchased from magazine ads and department store catalogs. Most of these products had no medical backing or proof of efficacy. In 1937, the American Medical Association (AMA) officially endorsed contraception; by 1940, physicians were beginning to accept the idea of voluntary family planning at the individual's discretion. Before this, physicians would provide contraception only for pathologic conditions such as tuberculosis or pelvic deformity. Social and economic considerations regarding contraception had been declared social, not medical, issues in 1917 by the AMA.

The director of the Department of Labor in June, 1942, told the director of the Children's Bureau that the bureau could lawfully (based on several Supreme Court cases) release its funds for the establishment of a state maternal and child-health service plan incorporating family planning. The White House supported family planning during the war years, as war industries desperately needed female workers. Contraception for women in the war industries was controlled by physicians and overseen by the government. After World War II, the Federal Council of Churches (FCC), which became the NCC in 1950, counseled Christians to have large families if they could afford them. This was a strong procontraception statement for the group at the time.

Impact of Event

The FCC, officially formed in December, 1908, emerged from a long and sometimes turbulent history of conflict with the evangelical churches, which held to a stricter, more Calvinistic theology. The churches that came together as the FCC had a liberal view: Human nature is essentially good, and evil in society is essentially attributable to environmental factors that can be ameliorated through proper Christian interventions. The mission of Christian churches was, in part, to improve the society's social conditions, and this mission could be achieved best through a union of churches working together.

The FCC's philosophy and theology closely paralleled the ecumenical movement in Europe that resulted in the formation of the World Council of Churches (WCC) on August 23, 1948. The FCC's and NCC's activities in the United Nations are a reflection of this larger, proactive world view. The NCC's 1961 statement on the responsibility of Christians to assist the world's downtrodden and to do something about overpopulation is an extension of this liberal theology.

The ecumenical movements in Europe and the United States have long supported advances in technological knowledge that improve health, food production, and the general quality of life. Missionary activities by individual denominations, work within the United Nations, and work by bodies of the FCC, NCC, and WCC reflect this.

In 1929, a leading gynecologist at Johns Hopkins Medical School stated that research showed that there was no "safe period" in a woman's menstrual cycle in which pregnancy could not occur. The medical community was still very reluctant to enter the arena of contraception either in research or in the counseling of patients. By 1936, only half of America's medical schools gave their students any training in contraception. The world's population was beginning to expand at a more rapid rate; after World War II, it exploded as a result of improved medical, hygiene, and food production technologies. The medical community remained reluctant to enter seriously into contraceptive work. Governments also were hesitant to develop family planning programs. The FCC, NCC, and WCC, however, were becoming proactive in this area. In their missionary work and in the accumulating statistics gathered by the United Nations, they saw the misery and degradation which too many children could bring to a family, a community, or a society.

By 1961, people in the United States of all religious persuasions were practicing family limitation. The number of children couples stated that they wanted and the number they actually had was a close match, and survey research indicated widespread support of family planning among Protestant, Catholic, and Jewish husbands and wives. In many states, however, these couples found it difficult to receive birth control information or devices, as dispersal of such information, even by a physician to a lawfully married couple, was illegal.

The NCC's 1961 pronouncement was a culmination of a long, liberal, proactive history and theology. The pronouncement focused on the civil and religious rights of couples to make their own determination of proper family size. Accordingly, the state had no right to interfere. The 1961 declaration was also a reflection of current events and the actual behavior of married couples. The NCC validated birth control for couples who had long been practicing it. The declaration took birth control out of its secretive, sometimes guilt-ridden closet. In 1964, the Supreme Court, in the *Griswold v. Connecticut* case, ruled that state bans on contraception were unconstitutional.

Bibliography

Duff, Edward. *The Social Thought of the World Council of Churches.* New York: Association Press, 1956. Duff writes in a difficult, stilted style. Contents deal with the ecumenical movement's critique of economic, political, and contemporary international developments. Good background material; references provided.

Eerdmans' Handbook to Christianity in America. Grand Rapids, Mich.: Wm. B. Eerdmans, 1983. Good compilation of historical events and religion in America. See in particular the chapter "Christianity in a Secular Age: From the Depression to the Present." College-level reading.

Jacobson, Jodi L. *Planning the Global Family.* Washington, D.C.: Worldwatch Institute, 1987. A pamphlet-sized book containing international data on birthrates, family planning, and maternal death rates. References provided.

Kennedy, David M. *Birth Control in America: The Career of Margaret Sanger.* New Haven, Conn.: Yale University Press, 1971. Excellent source of information on birth control and family planning before 1945. Sanger is the "mother" of the birth control movement. College-level reading. References provided.

Pratt, Henry J. *The Liberalization of American Protestantism: A Case Study in Complex Organizations.* Detroit: Wayne State University Press, 1972. Factual analysis of the NCC's organization and policies. The NCC's development is compared with that of other liberal organizations. Good background material. College-level reading. References provided.

Rosten, Leo, ed. *Religions in America.* New York: Simon & Schuster, 1963. Contains synopses of studies, opinion polls, and data on religion in America. Has information on desired number of children, contraception, and variations in fertility patterns by religion. Each study is cited; no bibliography as such. College-level reading.

Singer, C. Gregg. *The Unholy Alliance.* New Rochelle, N.Y.: Arlington House, 1975. Written by a fundamentalist who does not identify himself as such. Gregg does not like the NCC or its policies. One of few books that discusses the NCC family planning document. Material documented but very slanted. College-level reading. References provided.

Wilkinson, L. P. *Classical Attitudes to Modern Issues.* London: William Kimber, 1978. Compilation of lectures presented at University College in London in January, 1976, on population and family planning, women's liberation, nudism in deed and word, and homosexuality. Wilkinson compares Greek and Roman thought and practice with contemporary thought and practice in these areas. Fun and enlightening reading. No references. College-level reading.

Dixie Dean Dickinson

Cross-References

The Pankhursts Found the Women's Social and Political Union (1903), p. 19; Sanger Opens the First Birth-Control Clinic in the United States (1916), p. 184; Sanger Organizes Conferences on Birth Control (1921), p. 356; The United Nations Children's Fund Is Established (1946), p. 689; The United Nations Adopts the Declaration of the Rights of the Child (1959), p. 1038; The Supreme Court Rules That State Laws Cannot Ban Contraceptives (1965), p. 1290; The United Nations Issues a

Declaration on Equality for Women (1967), p. 1391; *Roe v. Wade* Expands Reproductive Choice for American Women (1973), p. 1703; A U.N. Declaration on Hunger and Malnutrition Is Adopted (1974), p. 1775; A U.N. Convention Condemns Discrimination Against Women (1979), p. 2057; Prolife Groups Challenge Abortion Laws (1989), p. 2443; The National Organization for Women Sponsors an Abortion Rights Rally (1989), p. 2489; The United Nations Adopts the Convention on the Rights of the Child (1989), p. 2529.

THE UNITED STATES PEACE CORPS IS FOUNDED

Category of event: Humanitarian relief
Time: March 1, 1961
Locale: Washington, D.C.

The Peace Corps was formed as an independent overseas volunteer program of the United States government that translated idealism into practical contributions

Principal personages:
SARGENT SHRIVER (1915-　　　), the first director of the Peace Corps and the Office for Economic Opportunity
JOHN F. KENNEDY (1917-1963), the thirty-fifth president of the United States, committed to making his "New Frontier" programs a reality
HUBERT H. HUMPHREY (1911-1978), the senator from Minnesota; vice president of the United States under President Lyndon B. Johnson
WILLIAM JAMES (1842-1910), an influential American philosopher of the early 1900's

Summary of Event

Even though the Peace Corps became a reality during the early 1960's, the idea did not originate with the Kennedy Administration. Through the centuries, similar concepts have been considered by those who wanted to end the atrocities of war by converting a country's military might into a force for peace. More than two thousand years ago, Alexander the Great sent peace missions to the Orient. A little more than a century before Kennedy's Peace Corps, the British writers Thomas Carlyle and John Ruskin proposed the formation of "industrial regiments" to make England more habitable for its citizens. Their attempt to implement their idea by using Oxford professors and students to build a road, however, was doomed to failure.

The source of the first truly successful peace corps can be traced to the writings of the American philosopher William James. His essay entitled "The Moral Equivalent of War" (1910) was inspired by the example set by the Spanish-American War veterans who had stayed behind in the Philippines to teach and work. In this essay, which grew out of a speech that he had given to the Universal Peace Conference in Boston, James suggested that young men be drafted not to destroy but to build underdeveloped nations. H. G. Wells, influenced by James's views, outlined a plan for replacing soldiers with an army of scientists and teachers whose prime directive would be to heal the wounds of the world.

James's proposal was not taken seriously in the United States, though, until the Great Depression. Alarmed by the fact that nearly fourteen million workers were unemployed, President Franklin D. Roosevelt started his three-pronged youth resources effort: the Civilian Conservation Corps (CCC), the Works Progress Administration (WPA), and the National Youth Administration (NYA). Since nearly 30 percent of the unemployed workers were between the ages of sixteen and twenty-four, these programs were an effective means of mobilizing the youth of the United States. Most of the projects that were undertaken by these programs, however, such as planting tree seedlings and constructing dams and bridges, were only temporary measures.

The federal work programs of the 1930's followed James's proposal to the extent that they enlisted the services of the country's youthful citizens; on the other hand, they were much more limited in scope than the programs that James had envisioned, focusing primarily on national, not international, recovery. Actually, various churches and private voluntary agencies had been sending help abroad long before the Great Depression forced the United States to find ways to help the disadvantaged. The American Friends Service Committee, for example, is renowned for its contributions to programs of refugee resettlement and of community development. Financed by both private contributions and by government grants, these programs sent thousands of men and women abroad to teach illiterate peasants to read and write, to impress them with the importance of sanitation, and to show them better ways to farm.

In fact, probably the closest forerunners of the Peace Corps were two of these private organizations. The International Voluntary Services was founded in 1953 and run by a board of Catholic and Protestant representatives. Like the Peace Corps, this group worked mostly in rural areas, concentrating on crop and horticultural experimentation, animal husbandry, public health, and housebuilding. Beginning in 1958, a private agency called Operation Crossroads gave college students the opportunity to spend a summer working on community projects in Africa.

At approximately the same time that these private agencies were capturing the world's attention with their humanistic enterprises abroad, interest was being generated in the United States for a government-sponsored youth service. In 1954, Heinz Rollman, a North Carolina industrialist and candidate for Congress, wrote a book entitled *World Construction*. In this book, which he mailed to government leaders throughout the world, Rollman proposed sending a "Peace Army" composed of three million draftees to work in underdeveloped nations.

Three years later, Representative Henry S. Reuss of Wisconsin visited Cambodia to see how the country was using the foreign aid that it had received from the United States. Although Reuss was appalled by a $30-million highway that was practically devoid of motorists, he was impressed by an elementary school that had been founded by four young schoolteachers from the United States. After Reuss returned to Cornell University, he devised a plan for the Point 4 Youth Corps, which would provide technical assistance on a lower level than many underdeveloped nations were receiving. In 1960, he submitted a bill to Congress calling for a government study of the Point 4 Youth Corps. Partially as a result of the interest that had been generated by Dr. Thomas Dooley's work in Laos, the bill passed. Reuss's proposal was adopted in 1960 by the Organization of Young Democrats and the National Student Association, which promoted it on college campuses throughout the United States.

One of the supporters of the Point 4 Youth Corps, Senator Hubert Humphrey, tired of reading studies and longed for action instead. In the spring of 1960, Humphrey's foreign relations adviser, Peter Groethe, determined that five thousand youths could be sent into the field within four or five years. Encouraged by Groethe's report, Humphrey submitted Senate Bill 3675 on June 15, 1960, asking for the development of "a genuine people-to-people program in which talented and dedicated young American men would teach basic agriculture, industrial techniques, literacy, the English language and other school subjects, and sanitation and health procedures in Asia, Africa, and Latin America." The number of letters received concerning the Peace Corps indicated that it dwarfed both the U-2 incident and Fidel Castro in interest. Nevertheless, Humphrey's bill was virtually ignored because the Senate was about to adjourn.

Although the Peace Corps died in the Senate, it became a major issue in the presidential campaign of 1960. After John F. Kennedy won the Democratic nomination, Peter Groethe brought the Humphrey proposal to the attention of Archibald Cox, Chester Bowles, and other members of Kennedy's brain trust. Even though Kennedy knew little about Humphrey's bill before meeting with his advisers, he readily adopted the idea as part of his platform. Kennedy expanded the Humphrey-Reuss plan to include women and older people and to offer a draft exemption to volunteers.

After President Kennedy took office in 1961, he set about creating the Peace Corps. First, Kennedy asked Dr. Max Millikan, director of the Center of International Studies at the Massachusetts Institute of Technology, to prepare a report on such an international youth service. Encouraged by the findings of Millikan's report and by a January Gallup Poll showing that 71 percent of Americans favored the Peace Corps, President Kennedy then asked his brother-in-law, Sargent Shriver, to explore the possibility of setting up the Peace Corps immediately. After meeting with a group of advisers in a Washington, D.C., hotel room for a month, Shriver submitted a plan of action to Kennedy. On March 1, 1961, two days after receiving the news from Shriver that the Peace Corps could be created by executive order, the president issued an order that established the Peace Corps on a trial basis.

On March 4, 1961, Sargent Shriver was appointed director of the Peace Corps. Shriver's first task as director was to persuade Congress that the Peace Corps should be authorized by law. Shriver was assisted by Vice President Lyndon B. Johnson, who not only secured congressional approval but also shaped the Peace Corps into a workable organization. On September 22, 1961, Congress established the Peace Corps by law and appropriated money to support it.

Although the plan for the Peace Corps was praised by many as a "happy inspiration," it did face some opposition both at home and abroad. Some people jokingly referred to it as "Kennedy's Kiddie Corps" and "A Crewcut Crusade." The Soviet Union called the Peace Corps "a super-spy organization." Nevertheless, the first detachment of forty-nine American teachers arrived in Ghana in the summer of 1961, and they were followed later by hundreds of other volunteers to other countries, all determined to make the concept of unselfish service a reality.

Impact of Event

From the outset, the Peace Corps established itself as the embodiment of the idealism expressed by Kennedy. Through the years, the Peace Corps has offered Americans the opportunity to realize Kennedy's dream of brotherhood in practice. Never before had any nation sent so many of its citizens to work and live among the inhabitants of underdeveloped countries. The impact of the Peace Corps can best be determined by assessing the success with which the Peace Corps has met its goals.

The most tangible effects of the Peace Corps on the world can be attributed to its first goal—providing technical assistance to less-developed countries. In the first twenty-five years of its existence, the following projects had direct impact on the lives of nearly one million people: fifteen hundred volunteers provided technical assistance in agricultural and rural development projects; more than six hundred renewable-energy and appropriate-technology volunteers worked on energy-conserving stoves, charcoal production, solar food drying, and biogas production; two hundred volunteers served as planners and supervisors of the construction of small dams, spillways, and irrigation canals; and one thousand volunteers worked on health education and community health organizations.

The effects of the Peace Corps' second goal—to develop a better understanding among foreign peoples—are not as evident as the technical achievements, but they are just as important. Peace Corps volunteers have shown the world a different type of American from the one that is on view in the news or in television shows. Through the work of the Peace Corps volunteers, people-to-people relationships have been formed that have cemented friendships between nations.

Finally, the activities of the volunteers in other countries have met the Peace Corps's goal of changing the attitudes of Americans back home. The more than 100,000 former Peace Corps volunteers who have returned to America were forever changed by the Peace Corps experience. The report of the Commission on Security and Economic Assistance noted that Peace Corps volunteers have an active interest in international affairs and have, in some ways, "provided the nucleus around which a broader-based information system could form." In a Louis Harris poll of former volunteers, 81 percent reported feeling very different from others their ages. Nearly 60 percent of all volunteers have furthered their education after returning home. In addition, almost 15 percent of the returning volunteers are working with government organizations both at home and abroad, thereby realizing the founders' hope that the Peace Corps would provide a steady supply of experienced personnel for the Foreign Service and the Department of State.

On the whole, then, the Peace Corps made a difference, sometimes where massive transfers of foreign aid to Third World countries had not. Individual lives and towns and villages around the world have benefited immensely from the knowledge and concern that volunteers have brought to their countries. At the same time, the Peace Corps has provided young Americans with an opportunity to broaden their horizons.

Bibliography

Adams, Velma. *Peace Corps in Action.* Chicago: Follett, 1964. Written by a Peace

Corps volunteer who admits in the preface that she "couldn't take it," this book depicts the volunteers as a "special breed." Because it is based on interviews with people working in the field, this collection of anecdotes provides a fascinating and realistic glimpse into the day-to-day life of a Peace Corps volunteer.

Ashabranner, Brent. *A Moment in History: The First Ten Years of the Peace Corps.* Garden City, N.Y.: Doubleday, 1971. Written by the man who served as deputy director of the Peace Corps from 1967 to 1969, this book traces the development of the Peace Corps, illustrating its achievements with scores of examples. Even though the author confesses to a lack of complete objectivity, the book does a fine job of explaining the problems that the Peace Corps brought on itself through years of uncontrolled growth.

Hapgood, David, and Meridan Bennett. *Agents of Change: A Close Look at the Peace Corps.* Boston: Little, Brown, 1968. This book is the most objective of the books about the Peace Corps that were based on interviews with workers in the field, probably because it was written by two men whose job it was to evaluate the success of the Peace Corps.

Luce, Iris, ed. *Letters from the Peace Corps.* Washington, D.C.: Robert Luce Publishers, 1964. These letters, written by the first wave of volunteers, contain lively descriptions of training procedures and of the problems of eating, staying healthy, and breaking down barriers of language and custom. Although the letters have been selected to present a predominantly favorable attitude toward the Peace Corps, they do show that not all applicants were motiviated by blind idealism.

McGuire, Edna. *The Peace Corps: Kindlers of the Spark.* New York: Macmillan, 1966. McGuire's book is primarily an inspirational account of the activities of the Peace Corps. The interviews with actual Peace Corps volunteers support the author's view that the goal of the Peace Corps is not just better dams or highways but better people. The book's interest level is enhanced by the photographs that are interspersed throughout the volume.

Madow, Pauline, ed. *The Peace Corps.* New York: H. W. Wilson, 1964. This text is a collection of descriptions of the Peace Corps, its origins, its operations, and its accomplishments, written by government officials and other experts in foreign affairs. The authors represented include those figures who were most instrumental in establishing the Peace Corps, including President John F. Kennedy, Henry S. Reuss, and Sargent Shriver. The book's usefulness is limited by its early publication date.

Wigenbach, Charles. *The Peace Corps: Who, How, and Where.* New York: John Day, 1961. This early book, prepared with the assistance of Hubert Humphrey and Henry Reuss, is essentially an insider's view of the operation of the Peace Corps. Even though the author overstates opinions in places, this book provides the best history of the founding of the Peace Corps that is currently available.

Alan Brown

Cross-References

The First Food Stamp Program Begins in Rochester, New York (1939), p. 555; The International League for Human Rights Is Founded (1942), p. 590; The Marshall Plan Provides Aid to Europe (1947), p. 706; The United States Airlifts Supplies to West Berlin (1948), p. 771; The United Nations Creates an Agency to Aid Palestinian Refugees (1949), p. 814; Schweitzer Is Awarded the Nobel Peace Prize (1953), p. 907; Mother Teresa Is Awarded the Nobel Peace Prize (1979), p. 2051; The United Nations Responds to Problems of the Homeless (1982), p. 2174; The Stewart B. McKinney Homeless Assistance Act Becomes Law (1987), p. 2326.

EICHMANN IS TRIED FOR WAR CRIMES

Categories of event: Atrocities and war crimes; accused persons' rights
Time: April-August, 1961
Locale: Jerusalem, Israel

Adolf Eichmann, the man most responsible for executing six million Jews in con-
centration camps during World War II, was captured by Israeli agents in Argentina
and tried in Israel

Principal personages:
ADOLF EICHMANN (1906-1962), the commander of the Reich Security
Head Office, in charge of Nazi extermination camps during World
War II
ISSER HAREL (1912-   ), the head of the Mossad, the Israeli Central
Bureau of Intelligence and Security
ROBERT SERVATIUS (1896-   ), Adolf Eichmann's attorney
GIDEON HAUSNER (1915-   ), the attorney general of Israel and pros-
ecuting attorney at the trial of Adolf Eichmann
MOSHE LANDAU (1912-   ), the Israeli Supreme Court justice who pre-
sided at the trial of Adolf Eichmann

Summary of Event

Headlights blinded the slightly built, middle-aged man as he began walking the
short distance from the bus stop to his rented house in a suburb of Buenos Aires.
Suddenly three men grabbed him, forced him into a car, and sped away. The kidnapped man was Adolf Eichmann. As commander of the Reich Security Head Office, he was indirectly responsible for the deaths of several million Jews during World
War II. He had been living in Argentina under the name of Ricardo Klement. His
sons, however, still used the name Eichmann. His wife had remarried, but her second marriage was to her first husband under his assumed name.

For fifteen years Israeli agents had sought the whereabouts of this most notorious
war criminal and were quite sure he was in Tucumán or in Buenos Aires. Early in
1960, when Eichmann's father died, the obituary listed Vera Eichmann as a daughter-
in-law, not Vera Klement. The surveillance team watching the Klement house noticed
Mrs. Klement's husband bringing her a bouquet of flowers on March 21, 1960, the
twenty-fifth anniversary of her original marriage to Adolf Eichmann. This confirmed
what their photographs and other information already indicated. The decision was
made to arrest Eichmann, without the knowledge of the Argentine government, and
to take him to Israel to stand trial. The kidnapping was timed to coincide with an
Israeli state visit to Argentina. While the Israeli government delegation was in Buenos
Aires, the Israeli Mossad, or Central Bureau of Intelligence and Security, used the

Israeli airplane to transport Adolf Eichmann to Israel.

The El Al plane landed in Israel on May 22, 1960. The news of its arrival electrified the world. For many months, the Eichmann trial would be prime-time news around the world. Eichmann was taken to the prison in Ramla under elaborate security precautions. He was allowed to choose his own legal counsel and selected Robert Servatius, an attorney from Cologne, Germany, who had experience in defending other war criminals at the Nuremberg trials in 1945. Israel paid $30,000 in legal expenses for the accused.

Eichmann gave a fluent and detailed statement that took 3,564 typewritten pages to transcribe. He demonstrated an incredible memory except regarding his actions in the Holocaust. The Israeli investigation of his statement took eight months to complete. Finally, on April 11, 1961, Adolf Eichmann's trial began at Beit HaAm, a large public auditorium in Jerusalem with six hundred foreign correspondents in attendance. The prisoner's dock was enclosed in bulletproof glass. The three judges, two of whom were born and educated in Germany, were all members of the Israeli Supreme Court. The presiding judge, Moshe Landau, read the indictment accusing Eichmann of causing the deaths of millions of Jews between 1939 and 1945. He was the person responsible for the extermination of Jews by the Nazis in their "final solution" to what they saw as "the Jewish problem."

Eichmann's defense attorney offered two preliminary objections: The judges should be disqualified because they had preconceived opinions about the case, and the court had no jurisdiction over Eichmann since he had been kidnapped from Argentina. Servatius further claimed that Israel's Nazi Law had no validity because it had been enacted after the historical events had occurred.

The court spent six days discussing the matter and citing legal precedents, especially from British and American court decisions. The court held that the judges should be fair, but they could not be expected to be neutral. As for Eichmann's kidnapping, the manner in which a defendant was brought within the jurisdiction of a national state had no bearing on the state's competence to try him in a court of law. Finally, the Nuremberg trials were cited as precedent for the Eichmann trial. Those trials had also involved accusations of acts that had been declared crimes only after their occurrence.

The attorney general of the state of Israel, Gideon Hausner, was the chief prosecuting attorney. In recounting Eichmann's crimes, Hausner cited age-old condemnations of murder, antedating even the Ten Commandments. "Murder is murder," Hausner proclaimed. "And even if one shouts, *'Der Führer befahl, wir befolgen'* ('The Führer has ordered, we obey'), even then, murder is murder, oppression is oppression and robbery is robbery." In his eight-hour introductory address, the attorney general dramatically accused Eichmann:

When I stand before you, O Judges of Israel, to lead the prosecution of Adolf Eichmann, I do not stand alone. With me here are six million accusers. But they cannot rise to their feet and point their finger at the man in the dock with the cry *"J'accuse"* on their lips. For they are now only ashes—ashes piled high on the hills of Auschwitz and the fields of Treblinka and strewn in the forests of Poland. Their graves are scattered throughout Europe. Their blood cries out, but their voice is stilled. Therefore will I be their spokesman. In their name will I unfold this terrible indictment.

From April until August, there followed an incredible parade of witnesses from all over Europe who recounted Eichmann's role in the crimes of the Nazis. After 114 sessions, the trial ended on August 14, 1961, and the court adjourned for four months. When it reconvened on December 11, Eichmann was found guilty on all fifteen counts and sentenced to death by hanging.

A Protestant clergyman was given the task of ministering to Eichmann's spiritual needs. The clergyman sought to persuade Eichmann to repent. Eichmann's reply was, "I am not prepared to discuss the Bible. I do not have the time to waste!" Nevertheless, with the noose literally around his neck just before execution, Adolf Eichmann said, "I have lived believing in God and I die believing in God." The clergyman later commented that Eichmann was "the hardest man I ever saw."

On May 31, 1962, at midnight, Adolf Eichmann was hanged on the gallows. His body was later cremated. Early in the morning of June 1, a police launch carried his remains beyond the three-mile territorial limit and scattered his ashes into the Mediterranean Sea.

Impact of Event

The arrest, trial, and execution of Adolf Eichmann dramatically demonstrated that there are people in the world determined to bring to justice those responsible for horrible violations of basic human rights. Neither time nor national barriers prevented justice from being meted out to the commander of the Holocaust.

It is significant that world opinion was solidly behind what Israel sought to achieve. West Germany, as well as Britain and the United States, cooperated in the investigation and trial. West Germany had issued an arrest warrant for Eichmann in 1956, but there was no extradition treaty with Israel, and the West German government did not request Eichmann's extradition. Argentina's sovereignty had been violated by the Israelis, and Argentina, of course, protested. The matter was discussed in the United Nations, and Argentina eventually accepted Israel's apology.

Besides bringing an exceptionally notorious war criminal to justice, this trial also demonstrated that no matter how terrible the crime, the accused still possessed certain basic human rights that were inviolate. He did not possess the right to avoid public trial, but his personal safety and decent conditions of incarceration were paramount. Eichmann was not tortured or physically abused, and he was protected from those who would harm him. He had adequate living conditions and food, and the ability to communicate with friends and family. Not only was he given legal counsel of his own choosing, but the Israeli taxpayers paid his legal fees. The Jewish people, whose own human rights had been so viciously violated by Germany during the war, demonstrated that human rights are more significant than raw power. The meticulous care for fairness, judicial process, and systematic gathering of evidence in the trial in Israel contrasted sharply with the Gestapo methods familiar to Adolf Eichmann.

The German people knew all this. There was outrage in Germany when, on November 20, 1961, the *Stuttgarter Zeitung* reported a statement by Eichmann's defense attorney that "every German could have found himself in Eichmann's situation." They knew that this was not true. His crime was that of mass murder, not that of being a German or even a member of Hitler's military command.

Ironically, the Eichmann trial fostered a new understanding and a greater empathy between West Germany and Israel. West German loans, at favorable interest rates, were made to Israel. German investments in Israel increased considerably, and German arms shipments to Israel were made at a time of critical need in Israeli history. During the 1960's, West Germany was one of Israel's chief markets, and exports to West Germany rose sharply during the decade.

The intense worldwide publicity surrounding the trial of Eichmann educated a new generation on the atrocities of the Nazi regime. This was particularly true of the many young Germans who were horrified to learn details of the Holocaust. They had been kept in virtual ignorance of these details and felt a sense of betrayal for the silence surrounding these events. Twenty thousand German youths visited Israel between 1961 and 1967 to help in the work of building the young nation. The "final solution" to those Germans and Israelis was mutual respect and service.

Bibliography

Bar-Zohar, Michel. "The Man Who Captured Eichmann." In *The Avengers*. New York: Hawthorn Books, 1967. The story of Isser Harel, the head of the Mossad, and how he managed the capture of Eichmann in Argentina.

Dawidowicz, Lucy S. *The War Against the Jews, 1933-1945*. New York: Holt, Rinehart and Winston, 1975. Recounts in detail Hitler's "final solution" and Adolf Eichmann's key role in bringing it about.

Deutschkron, Inge. *Bonn and Jerusalem: The Strange Coalition*. Philadelphia, Pa.: Chilton Book Company, 1970. A study of the post-World War II relationships between Germany and Israel. Valuable for charting the diplomatic effects of the trial of Adolf Eichmann on Germany and Israel.

Harel, Isser. *The House on Garibaldi Street*. New York: Viking Press, 1975. Isser Harel was the head of the Mossad and made the key decisions involved in the capture of Eichmann. His account is limited to the capture and removal of Eichmann to Israel.

Pearlman, Moshe. *The Capture and Trial of Adolf Eichmann*. New York: Simon & Schuster, 1963. This is a lengthy and full account of the entire Eichmann episode, but most of the book is a detailed account of the trial: the arguments and counterarguments, conclusions, sentence, and final days of Adolf Eichmann.

William H. Burnside

Cross-References

Legal Norms of Behavior in Warfare Formulated by the Hague Conference (1907), p. 92; Hitler Writes *Mein Kampf* (1924), p. 389; Nazi Concentration Camps Go into Operation (1933), p. 491; Nazi War Criminals Are Tried in Nuremberg (1945), p. 667; The United Nations Adopts a Convention on the Crime of Genocide (1948), p. 783; The United Nations Sets Rules for the Treatment of Prisoners (1955), p. 935; The United Nations Issues a Declaration Against Torture (1975), p. 1847; Israel Convicts Demjanjuk of Nazi War Crimes (1988), p. 2370.

POPE JOHN XXIII ISSUES "MATER ET MAGISTRA" AND "PACEM IN TERRIS"

Category of event: Peace movements and organizations
Time: May 15, 1961, and April 11, 1963
Locale: Vatican City

In "Mater et Magistra" and "Pacem in Terris," Pope John XXIII redefined the Roman Catholic perspective on justice and peace and assumed a position of moral leadership in the world

Principal personages:
  JOHN XXIII (1881-1963), the pope of the Roman Catholic church from 1958 to 1963
  LEO XIII (1810-1903), the Roman Catholic pope elected in 1878, author of the first social encyclical, "Rerum Novarum"
  PIUS XI (1857-1939), the Roman Catholic pope elected in 1922, author of the social encyclical "Quadragesimo Anno"

Summary of Event

An encyclical is a letter written by the pope and intended for dissemination to the entire Roman Catholic church. Encyclicals deal with matters of pastoral concern and may address doctrine or morals, including social problems. The first of the social encyclicals was "Rerum Novarum," issued by Pope Leo XIII in 1891. This document upheld the rights of labor. "Quadragesimo Anno," issued by Pope Pius XI, appeared on the fortieth anniversary of "Rerum Novarum." "Mater et Magistra" appeared on the seventieth anniversary, in 1961, with "Pacem in Terris" appearing shortly thereafter in 1963. Although they were not the first social encyclicals of the Roman Catholic church, "Mater et Magistra" and "Pacem in Terris" marked a turning point in Catholic social philosophy as well as the emergence of that philosophy into a position of global status.

That this occurred can no doubt be attributed to Pope John XXIII, who in only five short years as pope changed the entire perspective of the Roman Catholic church. As many cardinals shook their heads, wondering how they would ever be able to undo the "mistakes" of John XXIII's pontificate, he proceeded with assurance to point the church in new directions and to make friends in places where the Roman Catholic church had only had enemies. While many people, Christian and non-Christian, loved this charismatic and congenial pontiff who showed such great concern for common people, very few, perhaps none, understood the depth of his vision while he was alive. This son of landless peasants who had traveled about the world in the diplomatic corps of the Holy See had a vision of the Catholic church as being in the service of all humanity. It was this vision that came to fruition in his two great social encyclicals, "Mater et Magistra" and "Pacem in Terris."

Undergirding both encyclicals is a new understanding of human rights and human dignity. In these two documents, the claim is advanced that individual human beings should be the foundation, the end, and the subject of all social institutions. Human beings are endowed by nature with certain rights and responsibilities that are universal, inviolable, and inalienable. Since many ideologies have made use of the concept of human rights, it may not be obvious initially how innovative this social philosophy is. What is different about the social philosophy espoused in "Mater et Magistra" and "Pacem in Terris" is perhaps best explained through some examples from the encyclicals.

The issues addressed in "Mater et Magistra" are the results of the process of socialization, referring to the progressive increase in social relations, both within nations and internationally. This process has been driven by scientific and technical progress, the globalization of the media, and the internationalization of economics. This process is neither the bane of the world, as individualistic capitalists would have us believe, nor a boon, as perceived by socialists and Marxists, because it is not the product of natural forces working in a deterministic way. It does not shape human beings, for good or ill, turning them either into automatons, as in the negative view, or demigods, as in the positive. It is rather the creation of free and intelligent human beings, whose responsibility it is to draw from it the advantages that it contains while removing or restraining its negative aspects. The amount of creativity, responsibility, and dignity ascribed to persons in this social philosophy is breathtaking by comparison with that of its competitors. Human beings are not the product of the play of social forces but rather their creators and determiners.

Insofar as socialization is a result of the human tendency to band together to attain a good that cannot be attained independently, it is to be welcomed. Farmers joining to lobby for fair prices or laborers establishing a voice for themselves through the International Labour Organisation (ILO) are positive aspects of socialization. In certain cases, John XXIII was even willing to welcome government intervention. Since, as "Rerum Novarum" had already established, work is not only a commodity but an expression of the human person, its remuneration ought not to be left to the mechanical play of market forces. Public authorities should intervene, when necessary, in the interest of justice and the common good. In other words, John XXIII did not wish to see the state stand by impotently in the face of exploitation, unemployment, or poverty. On the other hand, one of the negative results of socialization is the tendency for national governments to assume an ever-increasing role for themselves. "Mater et Magistra" encourages control of this negative aspect by application of the "principle of subsidiarity," which was formulated by Pope Pius XI in the encyclical, "Quadragesimo Anno." This principle states that larger and higher organizations should not take upon themselves functions that can be performed efficiently by smaller and lower bodies.

"Mater et Magistra" does not consider wealth to be an exclusively economic consideration. The encyclical describes the wealth of a nation as lying in its people and their full development as human persons rather than merely in an accumulation of material goods. The wealth of a nation requires not only increases in productivity but also, and more important, the redistribution of goods in accordance with justice. The encyclical does not, however, downplay the importance of economic development, acknowledging that the just distribution of an amount of material goods insufficient to sustain life with human dignity amounts to no more than a sharing of poverty. Economic development and social progress must go hand in hand.

"Mater et Magistra" goes on to state that justice demands even more than the redistribution of wealth. Justice demands the active participation of employees in decisions that regulate their activity. If the structures of an economic system systematically blunt individual responsibility or constitute an impediment to personal initiative, the system is unjust. This social philosophy, contending that human rights must include the right to exercise all endowments, including the power of intelligence, goes far beyond the more conventional listings either of basic necessities, such as food and shelter, or of basic liberties, such as freedom of speech and the right to vote.

The dignity of the human person is also the guiding thread in "Pacem in Terris." This encyclical states that the dignity of the human person requires that people should enjoy the right to act freely and responsibly. This implies that each person should act on his or her own decisions, from a consciousness of obligation, without being moved by external force or by pressure. The encyclical states that any society established on relations of force is to be regarded as inhuman, because the personality of its members is being repressed or restricted when in fact it ought to be developed and perfected.

One of the areas of concern in "Pacem in Terris" is disarmament. The encyclical states that in order for disarmament to occur, thinking about the way to establish and maintain peace must change. Peace among nations depends not upon equality of arms but upon mutual trust. John XXIII believed that relations between nations, as between individuals, should be regulated by the light of reason rather than by the force of arms. He defined reason as the rule of truth, justice, and active and sincere cooperation.

Many people would say that these are unattainable ideals. Such people contend that if force and the fear that accompanies it are eliminated from the political arena, what will be established is not trust but trouble. Many would ask whether refusal to defend oneself does not give others the "right" to take advantage of a person. Such would be the likely criticisms by liberal democracies, in which human rights are interpreted along the lines of individual freedoms and not along the lines of mutual responsibilities.

In contrast to liberal democracies, the Catholic human rights tradition sets human rights into a moral context that includes a linkage of rights with duties. In "Pacem in Terris," John XXIII illustrated this linkage with the following examples: Every person has a right to life, but each also has the duty to preserve it; every person has a right to a decent standard of living, but each also has the duty of living life in a becoming manner; every person has a right to seek the truth freely, but each also has the duty to pursue it with complete commitment. The basis for this correlation of rights and duties is a recognition that there are goods that are essential to human life and dignity. Consequently, individuals are not in a condition of pure liberty and discretion with regard to these goods; they remain under moral obligation. The practice of claiming and exercising rights is not merely an instrument for protecting and advancing self-interest. In saying that those rights that are essential to human dignity are not optional, either for oneself or in the case of others, the Catholic understanding of human rights steers between the extremes of self-sacrifice and self-interest.

Impact of Event

As David Hollenbach, a professor of moral theology, has pointed out, it is a remarkable development that human rights should have emerged as such a central concern for contemporary Roman Catholicism, since the Catholic church was a vigorous opponent of both the democratic and socialist revolutions that were the chief proponents of civil and social rights. The change in attitude toward human rights came about when the church became aware of itself as a transnational, transcultural community in a pluralistic world. Hollenbach connected this change in awareness with the Second Vatican Council. It is even more remarkable, then, that these two encyclicals should express this view so strongly, as "Mater et Magistra" predated the council and "Pacem in Terris" closely followed it.

In one sense, the Roman Catholic church was only following a pattern set by other transnational organizations. The United Nations, the International Commission of Jurists, and Amnesty International all employed a doctrine of human rights as the normative basis for their activities. Indeed, human rights seem a natural basis for social justice in any situation that is pluralistic in terms of cultures and political ideologies.

On the other hand, the Roman Catholic understanding of human rights as it is expressed in these two encyclicals is unique. In its very originality, it may have something to contribute to the political leaders of the world and to other religious organizations. The Roman Catholic understanding of human rights differs from that of classical Anglo-American liberalism in its mistrust of individualism and its emphasis on community. The Catholic approach also has more moral restraints upon the exercise of freedom in society. The Roman Catholic approach differs from that of authoritarian political leaders in its distrust of force and its emphasis on free decisions of conscience. It differs from capitalist economic systems in its distrust of the free play of the market as a guarantor of human rights and in its belief that human beings, not the impersonal market, are responsible for what happens in society. It differs from Marxist economic systems in its defense of private property and freedom of choice in market situations, provided that freedom is exercised with due regard for the common good. Finally, it differs from Protestant approaches in its reliance on philosophical rather than theological or biblical bases for dealing with political and social issues.

Neither "Mater et Magistra" nor "Pacem in Terris" has been adopted as a blueprint for action by any nation. At least part of the reason for this neglect in practical terms is that nations are divided along lines of liberal democracies and totalitarian regimes or capitalist economies and socialist economies, divisions that the encyclicals seek to overcome. While a transnational organization such as the Catholic church can issue theoretical statements drawing on the best of opposing political ideologies, it is more difficult for national bodies identified with one side or the other of those opposing ideologies to adopt such statements and put them into practice.

The impact of these encyclicals upon the Roman Catholic community is much more evident. The Catholic peace movement of the Vietnam years and beyond, as well as the establishment and growth of Pax Christi USA, owes much to "Pacem in Terris." Catholic social action continued to be nourished by the principles set forth in "Mater et Magistra."

Bibliography

Catholic Church. *Mater et Magistra: An Encyclical Letter.* Chicago, Ill.: Discoverers Press, 1962. A thoroughly readable English translation of "Mater et Magistra."

Cronin, John F. "Mater et Magistra: Catholic Social Teaching Updated." *Social Order* 11 (September, 1961): 289-295. A short summary of the encyclical's main themes, spiced with commentary.

Fitzgerald, Mark J., ed. *Proceedings of the Symposium on Mater et Magistra (Christianity and Social Progress) by Pope John XXIII.* South Bend, Ind.: Notre Dame Press, 1962. The proceedings of a conference on "Mater et Magistra," held at the University of Notre Dame on May 5, 1962. Explanations of various parts of the encyclical, with explorations of their application to the American context.

_____. *Symposium on Pacem in Terris by Pope John XXIII.* South Bend, Ind.: Notre Dame Press, 1965. The proceedings of a conference on "Pacem in Terris," held at the University of Notre Dame on May 8, 1965. Explanation and discussion of the encyclical by Notre Dame faculty.

Hehir, J. Bryan. "Human Rights and the National Interest: According to Catholic Social Theory, Human Rights Must Be Factored into All Foreign Policy Equations." *Worldwide* 25 (May, 1982): 18-21. This article shows how the philosophical principles outlined in "Pacem in Terris" can be translated into public policy decisions.

Hollenbach, David. "Global Human Rights: An Interpretation of the Contemporary Catholic Understanding." *Perkins Journal* 39 (October, 1986): 1-10. Describes the contemporary understanding of human rights in the Catholic church and argues that the impetus for the rapid development of the church's position on global human rights came from the Second Vatican Council. This fundamental shift in the church's understanding of its social and institutional place in a pluralistic world came about under the leadership of Pope John XXIII.

Langan, John. "Human Rights in Roman Catholicism." *Journal of Ecumenical Studies* 19 (Summer, 1982): 25-39. A very fine analysis of "Pacem in Terris."

Newman, Jeremiah. *Principles of Peace: A Commentary on John XXIII's Pacem in*

Terris. Oxford, England: Catholic Social Guild, 1964. This is an excellent commentary on "Pacem in Terris," thorough and erudite. If it has a drawback, it would be that its tone is a bit too academic for the general reading public. It does not, however, require specialized knowledge.

Niebuhr, R., and J. C. Bennett. "Pacem in Terris: Two Views." *Christianity and Crisis* 23 (May 13, 1963): 81-83. Two well-known Protestant scholars discuss "Pacem in Terris." Bennett gives a far more positive appraisal of the encyclical than does Niebuhr.

Pope John XXIII. "Pacem in Terris: Human Rights and Duties in Natural Law." *Journal of Church and State* 7 (Winter, 1965): 91-104. The English text of "Pacem in Terris." Does not include a commentary on the text.

Ann Marie B. Bahr

Cross-References

The International Labour Organisation Is Established (1919), p. 281; Social Security Act Establishes Benefits for Nonworking People (1935), p. 514; The Atlantic Charter Declares a Postwar Right of Self-Determination (1941), p. 584; The United Nations Adopts Its Charter (1945), p. 657; Mao's Great Leap Forward Causes Famine and Social Dislocation (1958), p. 1015; Chávez Forms Farm Workers' Union and Leads Grape Pickers' Strike (1962), p. 1161; The Organization of African Unity Is Founded (1963), p. 1194; The International Labour Organisation Wins the Nobel Peace Prize (1969), p. 1509; Soviet Farmers Are Given Control of Land and Selection of Crops (1989), p. 2471.

AMNESTY INTERNATIONAL IS FOUNDED

Categories of event: Accused persons' rights and prisoners' rights
Time: May 28, 1961
Locale: London, England

Reading of the imprisonment of two Portuguese students who toasted freedom, Peter Benenson was inspired to found Amnesty International, the world's largest human rights organization

Principal personages:
PETER BENENSON (1921-   ), the wealthy English lawyer who founded Amnesty International
ERIC BAKER (1920-   ), a cofounder of the initial "Appeal for Amnesty 1961" and interim secretary-general after Benenson's forced resignation in 1967
SEÁN MACBRIDE (1904-1988), a chair of Amnesty International's executive committee and recipient of the Nobel Peace Prize
ANTÓNIO DE OLIVEIRA SALAZAR (1889-1970), the longtime military dictator of Portugal

Summary of Event

In the fall of 1960, Peter Benenson read a news item while on a London-bound train. There was nothing unusual about the item; in fact, it was a routine report of a human rights violation. Two Portuguese students had been sentenced to seven years' imprisonment by the military dictatorship of António Salazar for raising their glasses in a toast "to freedom" at a restaurant. Salazar had exercised power since 1932 in Portugal in a manner typical of dictatorships—repressing democracy and human rights. What was unusual was that Benenson, a wealthy and successful English lawyer, decided at that moment that ordinary citizens must find some effective way to raise their collective voices on behalf of these students, and the thousands of others like them who were imprisoned for the peaceful exercise of their human rights.

Benenson, who had already founded "Justice," an organization of British lawyers working on behalf of the Universal Declaration of Human Rights, immediately began discussing his idea with Eric Baker, a prominent British Quaker, and Louis Blom-Cooper, an internationally prominent lawyer. Through Benenson's friendship with David Astor, editor of the liberal London Sunday newspaper *The Observer*, they were given free space for an "Appeal for Amnesty 1961" on May 28, 1961. The date, Trinity Sunday, was deliberately chosen by Benenson, a Catholic (of Jewish ancestry). To open a newspaper any day of the week, Benenson wrote, is to read of someone imprisoned, tortured, or executed because "his opinions or religion are unacceptable to his government." The article, immediately reprinted in major newspapers around the world, identified eight "Forgotten Prisoners."

Among the eight prisoners was Dr. António Neto, an Angolan poet and one of few Angolan physicians, who later became the first president of Angola. Three religious leaders were also included: the Reverend Ashton Jones, an American imprisoned for his involvement in the Civil Rights movement; Archbishop Josef Beran of Prague, previously imprisoned by the Nazis; and Cardinal Mindszenty, primate of Hungary. The other political activists who peacefully criticized or organized opposition to their governments were Constantin Noica, a Romanian philosopher; Patrick Duncan, a white South African; Tony Abiaticlos, a Greek communist and trade unionist; and Antonio Amat, a Spanish lawyer.

If the "sickening sense of impotence" most readers feel "could be united into common action," Benenson concluded, "something effective could be done." He therefore proposed the creation of a "Threes Network." Each group of human rights activists would adopt three prisoners—one each from the West, the Communist bloc, and the Third World. Their strategy would be to write letters to the prisoners, comfort their families, and harass the governments which imprisoned them. This scheme later evolved into Amnesty's Prisoner of Conscience program. At Benenson's request, British artist Diana Redhouse designed a logo which would become the internationally recognized Amnesty symbol, a candle encircled by barbed wire. She created it as an illustration of the aphorism, "It is better to light one candle than to curse the darkness."

The response was tremendous. Within six months of the "Appeal for Amnesty 1961," Amnesty International emerged as a permanent organization coordinating the Adoption Groups for Prisoners of Conscience which sprang up throughout Western Europe. (Amnesty defines Prisoners of Conscience as those detained for their beliefs, color, sex, ethnic origin, language, or religion, who have neither used nor advocated violence.) In addition to demanding the immediate release of all Prisoners of Conscience, Amnesty's official mandate also included two other points: the prompt and fair trial of all political prisoners and the absolute prohibition of the use of torture or the death penalty.

Although Amnesty was on its way to becoming the 1977 recipient of the Nobel Peace Prize as the world's largest and best-known human rights organization, it nearly collapsed in its early years from internal conflict. A crisis was instigated in 1966 by Benenson, who had long considered it a serious problem that Amnesty was not based in a neutral country. Few in Amnesty shared this concern. Benenson was suspicious that British intelligence and Central Intelligence Agency money had compromised the organization. When a strongly critical Amnesty report on British activities in Aden (Yemen) was delayed, Benenson took it upon himself to release the report. He then asked longtime friend Seán MacBride, chair of Amnesty's executive committee, to authorize and oversee an investigation.

The inquiry, however, led to Benenson's ouster. Apparently without the knowledge of London headquarters, Benenson himself had taken money from the British government for the purpose, he later explained, of aiding the families of Prisoners of

Conscience in Rhodesia (Zimbabwe). This was regarded in MacBride's report as one of the many examples of Benenson's one-person rule, which was characterized by his reliance on personal connections, haphazard organization, and sloppy record keeping. The result, according to MacBride (who earned both the Lenin Peace Prize and the Nobel Peace Prize), was a tendency of Benenson to act through "unilateral initiatives" which resulted in "erratic actions."

Benenson's resignation was accepted, and his position of president was abolished. Eric Baker, one of the organizers of the initial "Appeal for Amnesty 1961," acted as interim secretary-general for a year. Baker took the organization from the edge of self-destruction to a stable and professional organizational foundation. Martin Ennals followed up Baker's critical stabilization with twelve years of sustained growth and the crystallization of Amnesty's international reputation for credibility, impartiality, and accuracy. His tenure as secretary-general was highlighted by the organization's attainment of the Nobel Peace Prize in 1977.

The international organizational structure is based in Amnesty's London headquarters, which verifies all information and authorizes all campaigns. London headquarters collects and analyzes information from newspaper accounts, journal articles, governmental bulletins, reports from lawyers and human rights organizations, and prisoners themselves. Factfinding missions by leading experts are also used to investigate and gather evidence. Amnesty notes in every publication its responsibility for the accuracy of all information and states its willingness to correct any errors. Amnesty rigorously maintains ideological neutrality and does not accept money from governments. Perhaps its most well-known and widely used work is *Amnesty International Reports* (published annually), which reviews the human rights record of every country in the world. In it, Amnesty never ranks governments but reviews each country's record, discussing specific individuals about whom Amnesty has verified information.

Amnesty's growth has been remarkable. At the close of its first decade following the "Appeal for Amnesty 1961," Amnesty had generated one thousand Adoption Groups in 28 countries. By the time of its Nobel Peace Prize in 1977, this had grown to more than 165,000 active members in more than one hundred countries. At its thirtieth birthday celebration on May 28, 1991, Amnesty claimed nearly 700,000 members in 150 countries and more than four thousand Adoption Groups in more than 60 countries. The research department of the international secretariat employed a staff of two hundred people, comprising some thirty nationalities. At that time, Amnesty remained largely based in the constitutional democracies of the West, however, with the United States providing nearly one-third of its membership.

Despite the welcome crumbling of the Berlin Wall and the end of the Cold War at the close of the 1980's, Amnesty noted that two out of three people in the world still lived in the nearly 130 countries of the world that imprisoned unjustly, tortured, or killed their own citizens. Therefore, the work begun in 1961 continued with a thirtieth birthday campaign on behalf of thirty Prisoners of Conscience whose fate Amnesty pledged to publicize until all were released.

Impact of Event

A new attention to human rights violations by the international community followed in the aftermath of the public exposure of the terrible atrocities committed during World War II, especially those committed in the name of Nazism. The Nuremberg Trials, the Universal Declaration of Human Rights, and the numerous treaties which followed were all aimed at eroding the state sanctuary of "domestic jurisdiction."

International law traditionally has upheld the inviolability of domestic jurisdiction—a state's exclusive authority over its own people and territory. A state's prerogatives regarding domestic jurisdiction clash with the ideal of a citizen's universal human rights. Because states are recognized as sovereign, the most effective way to breach domestic jurisdiction is through treaty agreements by which the states bind themselves under international law to human rights standards. Enforcement remains problematic.

Because human rights have honorific status, states unfailingly posture as champions of human rights. For example, virtually all states endorse the Universal Declaration of Human Rights. Governments, however, often suppress human rights to stay in power. As Amnesty noted in its twenty-fifth anniversary celebration, this leaves a wide gap between commitment and reality. Because of this hypocrisy, nongovernmental human rights organizations such as Amnesty International have a crucial role to play.

As the most prominent independent, impartial international watchdog for human rights, Amnesty International can embarrass states by spotlighting flagrant violations. Public opinion can be brought to bear and thereby affect the conduct of sovereign states, which may well conclude that holding an individual prisoner is not worth the negative publicity being generated by Amnesty.

The power of states often leads to the conclusion that one person's actions do not matter, but Amnesty International's format provides an opportunity for individuals to make a difference. Amnesty International was organized by the inspiration of one man, Peter Benenson, on the premise that an organization can bring together numbers of such people to create an international citizens' lobby on behalf of human rights. In such an organizational form, it is an effective participant in international politics.

Perhaps the most significant and poignant confirmation of Amnesty's impact is that more than thirty-eight thousand individuals for whom Amnesty has worked from 1961 to 1991 have been released. A released Prisoner of Conscience from the Dominican Republic testified to Amnesty's effectiveness this way:

> When the first two hundred letters came, the guards gave me back my clothes. Then the next two hundred letters came, and the prison director came to see me. When the next pile of letters arrived, the director got in touch with his superior. The letters kept coming and coming: three thousand of them. The President was informed. The letters still kept arriving, and the President called the prison and told them to let me go.

Bibliography

Amnesty International. *Amnesty International Reports.* London: Amnesty International Publications, annually. Each country is evaluated in terms of individual human rights cases and violations. Appendices discuss Amnesty's fact-finding missions and news releases throughout the year and offer relevant international documents. An introduction summarizes Amnesty's work throughout the year.

_____. *Political Killings by Governments.* London: Amnesty International Publications, 1983. Different types of political killings by governments are examined, along with international legal standards and potential remedies. Some specific countries are discussed. Introduction by Theo van Boven, former Director of the U.N. Division of Human Rights.

Drinan, Robert. *Cry of the Oppressed: History and Hope of the Human Rights Revolution.* San Francisco: Harper & Row, 1987. Good general introduction to human rights, including the Nuremberg Trials, United Nations efforts, and American foreign policy. The chapter on nongovernmental human rights organizations focuses on Amnesty. The author was part of an Amnesty mission to Argentina in 1976. Index and bibliography.

Larsen, Egon. *A Flame in Barbed Wire: The Amnesty International Story.* New York: W. W. Norton, 1979. An accessible, anecdotal presentation of the history of Amnesty International, including its origins, torture in various countries, the death penalty debate, the stories of numerous individual prisoners, and evaluations of Amnesty's work. Index, no bibliography, many illustrations.

Power, Jonathan. *Amnesty International: The Human Rights Story.* New York: McGraw-Hill, 1981. Excellent coverage of the founding and development of Amnesty International, including its attainment of the Nobel Peace Prize in 1977. Describes Amnesty's mandate, organizational arrangements, and campaigns on torture, the death penalty, and children. The records of the Soviet Union, the People's Republic of China, Nicaragua, and Guatemala are examined. Controversies are frankly discussed. Many illustrations; no index or bibliography.

Stephenson, Thomas. "Working for Human Rights." *Bulletin of Atomic Scientists* 37 (August/September, 1981): 54-56. Good general description of Amnesty. The author gives an excellent picture of the work of an Adoption Group by explaining his own and its work on behalf of prisoners in Guatemala and Romania.

Youssoufi, Abderrahman. "The Role of Non-Governmental Organizations in the Campaign Against Violations of Human Rights, Apartheid, and Racism." In *Violations of Human Rights.* Paris: UNESCO, 1984. Good background on nongovernmental human rights organizations. The author explains what they are and how they operate. Offers concrete discussions of their activities on behalf of human rights, using Amnesty in illustration. Appendices include the final report of a U.N.-sponsored conference on individual and collective action to stop human rights violations.

Nancy N. Haanstad

Cross-References

Nazi War Criminals Are Tried in Nuremberg (1945), p. 667; The United Nations Adopts the Universal Declaration of Human Rights (1948), p. 789; The U.N. Covenant on Civil and Political Rights Is Adopted (1966), p. 1353; A Medical Group Helps Gather Evidence of Torture in Greece and Chile (1974), p. 1747; The Helsinki Agreement Offers Terms for International Cooperation (1975), p. 1806; Soviets Crack Down on Moscow's Helsinki Watch Group (1977), p. 1915; Amnesty International Is Awarded the Nobel Peace Prize (1977), p. 1955; The National Commission Against Torture Studies Human Rights Abuses (1983), p. 2186; Amnesty International Adopts a Program for the Prevention of Torture (1983), p. 2204; Argentine Leaders Are Convicted of Human Rights Violations (1985), p. 2280; Amnesty International Exposes the Cruelty of the Death Penalty (1989), p. 2414; Demonstrators Gather in Tiananmen Square (1989), p. 2483.

THE BERLIN WALL IS BUILT

Category of event: Political freedom
Time: August 13, 1961
Locale: Berlin, East Germany

The Berlin Wall, erected to halt the debilitating exodus of East Germans to West Germany and to assert definitively the permanence and legitimacy of the East German regime, in fact attested to the failure of that regime

Principal personages:

KONRAD ADENAUER (1876-1967), the leader of the Christian Democrats, chancellor of the Federal Republic of Germany (West Germany) from 1949 to 1963

WILLY BRANDT (1913-   ), the mayor of West Berlin from 1957 until 1966, when, with his Social Democratic Party, he entered into a national coalition government

JOHN F. KENNEDY (1917-1963), the president of the United States (1961-1963)

NIKITA S. KHRUSHCHEV (1894-1971), the first secretary of the Communist Party from 1953, actual leader of the Soviet Union from 1955 until his dismissal in 1964

WALTER ULBRICHT (1893-1973), the Communist leader of the German Democratic Republic (East Germany) from 1949 to 1971

Summary of Event

Berlin became a focal point for East-West tensions after the breakdown of cooperation between the former World War II Allies. As the Western occupying powers, led by the United States, amalgamated their zones of occupation and began the process of organizing an indigenous government for West Germany, the Soviets responded with their blockade of West Berlin from June, 1948, until May, 1949. A strong response by the Americans and the British preserved the liberty of West Berlin, and the Federal Republic of Germany was proclaimed in the western portion of Germany. The Soviets responded by organizing the German Democratic Republic in the eastern sector, which was under their control. The regime was imposed upon the East German population, whose distaste for the repressiveness and relative material deprivation which characterized it was born out in desperate uprisings in East Berlin and other cities of East Germany in June, 1953.

Although the Soviets lifted the blockade of Berlin, they continued to exert pressure upon it during the Cold War crisis. The Soviets were concerned by the linkage of a rearmed West Germany to the North Atlantic Treaty Organization in 1955. In 1958, the Soviets applied pressure on Berlin in an effort to obtain a European security agreement which would recognize the status quo in Germany. On November 10,

1958, Soviet leader Nikita Khrushchev announced that the Soviet Union was reconsidering its position on the four-power control of Berlin and might hand over control of East Berlin to the East Germans. On November 27, he called for West Berlin to be transformed into a demilitarized free city and for the two German states to be united in a confederation. He threatened to turn over all Soviet rights to the East German regime if the Western powers had not worked out an agreement within six months.

West Berlin, linked to the West, was both an embarrassing symbol of freedom and prosperity and a breach through which the disaffected people of East Germany could escape to the West. By 1958, approximately 2.3 million East Germans, fifteen percent of the East German population, had fled to the West. The majority of these people were of working age, and their emigration constituted a serious drain on the talent and skill of the German Democratic Republic. Unless the hemorrhage could be stopped, the stability and even viability of the East German regime would be threatened. The Soviet Union was concerned not to lose its control of East Germany, which, in addition to having great military importance, was vital economically to the Soviet Union and to the Eastern Bloc. The economy of East Germany, with a level of technological quality superior to that of the rest of the Soviet bloc, had been structured to provide for the needs of the Soviet Union rather than its own people.

At Geneva meetings of the foreign ministers of the four occupying powers in May and July, 1959, the Soviets repeated their demands that the occupation of West Berlin be ended and the city transformed into a "free city." Rebuffed by the West, the Soviets allowed the East Germans to seize the initiative. This tactic was geared to reinforce the sovereignty of the German Democratic Republic and add a new source of pressure. The Soviet Union's principal concern was to gain definitive recognition of the division of Germany. When the East Germans and the Soviets began harassing communications with the city in August, Willy Brandt, the mayor of West Berlin, vigorously defended the rights of the city's inhabitants. In response to suggestions that West Berlin was untenable as a Western enclave, he prophetically asserted that a free West Berlin was indispensable if hope for freedom was to be nurtured in Eastern Europe.

Following a momentary thaw in relations between the Soviet Union and the United States, capped by the Camp David meeting between Khrushchev and President Dwight D. Eisenhower, a Paris summit in May, 1960, fell apart after the Soviets shot down an American spy plane. Sensing Western irresolution on Berlin, Khrushchev tightened the screws on West Berlin to pressure the West and simultaneously to bolster his client regime. In August, the Soviet sector of the city was temporarily closed to West German citizens. On September 8, the East Germans insisted that West German visitors have visitor permits. On September 13, they announced that they would no longer recognize West German passports as legal documentation for West Berlin visitors. The trade agreement between the two parts of Germany was suspended by the East Germans on January 1, 1961.

An overbearing Khrushchev met the new American president, John F. Kennedy, in Vienna on June 3 and 4, 1961. He threatened to sign a separate peace treaty with

East Germany and give it control of Berlin communications if a general peace and an independent status for West Berlin had not been effected within six months. On June 15, Walter Ulbricht, the East German leader, stated that West Berlin would have to stop accepting refugees from the East and cease being a source of propaganda beamed to the East. Kennedy responded in a July 25 "Report to the Nation" that he was determined to support West Berlin. Kennedy discouraged Khrushchev from additional pressure on West Berlin, but his report, by avoiding references to East Berlin, was interpreted as relinquishing any rights there to the Soviet Union. Konrad Adenauer, the chancellor of West Germany, was never overwhelmingly interested in East Berlin and also limited his concerns to maintaining the status of West Berlin.

Unable to pressure West Berlin, Khrushchev decided to take advantage of Western acquiescence to shore up his client state. Births exceeded deaths in East Germany by only eight thousand annually, and 250,000 East Germans were leaving each year. Many of the departing were very difficult to replace. In the seven years before August, 1961, they included five thousand doctors, seventeen thousand teachers, and twenty thousand engineers and technicians. Nineteen thousand refugees crossed over to the West in June, 1961, and more than thirty thousand emigrated in July. In early August, the rush turned into a flood. By August 11, sixteen thousand East Germans had crossed to West Berlin. On August 12, twenty-four hundred crossed, more than had ever done so in a single day.

Ulbricht had requested Khrushchev's permission to block off West Berlin in March. Khrushchev had hesitated then, but now he gave his permission. Just after midnight on the morning of August 13, the Berlin Wall, in the form of barbed wire, began to go up, sealing West Berlin off from East Berlin. At 1:00 A.M., the East German press agency announced that the border had been closed. Thirty Soviet and East German divisions stood ready to counter any armed intervention by the West. Brandt demanded immediate diplomatic pressure to protest this violation of the four-power agreements on Berlin, but, to his great disappointment, the response of the West was too slow and too weak to deter the construction of the barrier. Adenauer, who was engaged in an electoral contest against Brandt, was particularly remiss in his tardy and ineffectual reaction. The dispatch of fifteen hundred American reinforcements and the return of General Lucius Clay, the hero of the blockade, bolstered the morale of the West Berliners as did visits by U.S. Vice President Lyndon Johnson and President Kennedy. The Berlin Wall, however, continued to grow, as did the death and misery it brought. The Basic Treaty between the Federal Republic and the German Democratic Republic, signed on December 21, 1972, and ratified in June, 1973, again granted West Germans the right to travel to East Germany and enter East Berlin, but the Berlin Wall was not genuinely open to free access until November 9, 1989.

Impact of Event

Before the construction of the Berlin Wall, people could move fairly freely through both parts of Berlin. East Berliners could visit family and friends in the evening and on weekends in West Berlin. They had access to the Western press and entertainment. Nearly sixty thousand East Berliners daily took trams to work in factories and shops in West Berlin. The Berlin Wall put an end to this as well as to the permanent movement of East Germans to the West.

The Berlin Wall was eventually elaborated into an impenetrable barrier one hundred miles long, encircling all of West Berlin. Escape was relatively easy at first. Some jumped across barbed wire; others climbed out of second story windows of buildings which formed part of the new frontier. Eventually the windows were bricked over and a genuine wall was erected, fortified by 238 watchtowers and 132 gun emplacements. It was set off by an exposed "death strip" and guarded by twenty thousand East German police. On the Friedrichstrasse, Checkpoint Charlie, the only crossing point open to the Allied occupation forces, was permanently guarded on both sides by armored vehicles facing a fifty-yard slalom-like barrier designed to thwart motorized escape attempts.

The Berlin Wall was the brutal product of a regime willing to employ repression and deadly force against its own citizens. From 1961 until the Berlin Wall was opened on November 9, 1989, seventy-seven people were killed trying to escape through it. Another 114 people were killed trying to cross the increasingly deadly fortified border that divided East Germany from the remainder of West Germany. Observers in the West saw the failed escape attempts and witnessed the refugees being dragged back, sometimes wounded, to the East. One young victim, Peter Fechter, was shot by the East German police in August, 1962, and allowed to lie in view of horrified West Berliners as he bled to death. In 1974, Erich Honecker, Ulbricht's successor, in an effort to further intimidate the East German people, made his regime's practice explicit by issuing a shoot-to-kill order.

The Berlin Wall, in the short term, was perhaps a success of sorts. It stopped the flow of East Germans to the West, and it also played a role in the formation of Brandt's policy of *Ostpolitik*, which resulted in the recognition of East Germany by West Germany. Accepted as a legitimate entity, the German Democratic Republic became, along with the Federal Republic, a member of the United Nations in 1973. Brandt feared that, as a result of the Berlin Wall, the two German states and their people would grow progressively estranged. He also believed that the prospect of German reunification in the near future was remote. When he became chancellor in 1969, he presided over an effort to bring the two Germanies together through small steps. He was greatly concerned with lessening the burden on families created by the separation of the Berlin Wall. The Basic Treaty of 1972, however, did not bring an end to the paranoia of the East German regime. In 1980, to discourage excessive contact between its people and Germans from the West, the East German regime increased the visa fee and the daily foreign exchange requirement for visitors to East Germany. This created a formidable impediment for elderly pensioners wishing to visit relatives in East Berlin.

In the long term, the Berlin Wall was a dismal failure. Psychologically, it further damaged the credibility of the East German regime, which was seen as having to wall in its own citizens. When Mikhail Gorbachev, who became president of the Soviet Union in 1985, lifted the threat of violence, the support of the East German regime disappeared. As East Germans in 1989 fled to West Germany through Hungary and Czechoslovakia, the demand for change in the German Democratic Republic became irrepressible. Honecker was forced from office and, on November 9, 1989, in a prelude to German reunification, the Berlin Wall was breached by the new East German government.

Bibliography

Binder, David. *The Other German: Willy Brandt's Life and Times.* Washington, D.C.: New Republic Book Company, 1975. A thorough biographical treatment of Brandt from his attainment of the chancellorship in May, 1974, through his retirement. Binder provides a much more complete treatment of Brandt's youth and exile and his early political life in Berlin than does Terence Prittie. Although admittedly positive toward Brandt, the author is objective in his treatment. There are photographs.

Griffith, William E. *The Ostpolitik of the Federal Republic of Germany.* Cambridge, Mass.: MIT Press, 1978. Griffith provides an excellent survey of the development of West German policy toward the East and, in particular, toward East Germany. Griffith provides a very sound and clear analysis of the origins of Brandt's *Ostpolitik*, an explanation of its substance, and a solid short-term evaluation of its results.

Merritt, Richard L., and Anna J. Merritt, eds. *Living with the Wall: West Berlin, 1961-1985.* Durham, N.C.: Duke University Press, 1985. This book provides a collection of articles on the history of the wall and its impact upon the inhabitants of Berlin.

Prittie, Terence. *Willy Brandt: Portrait of a Statesman.* New York: Schocken Books, 1974. This well-written and interesting book provides a comprehensive biography of Brandt. It provides a good account of the construction of the Berlin Wall, Brandt's reaction to it, and the impact of the wall upon Brandt's subsequent foreign policy.

Waldenburg, Hermann. *The Berlin Wall Book.* London: Thames and Hudson, 1990. This book provides a pictorial history of the wall.

Whetten, Lawrence L. *Germany East and West: Conflicts, Collaboration, and Confrontation.* New York: New York University Press, 1980. Whetten places the wall in the context of East-West German relations. According to Whetten, because of the wall and the subsequent development of détente, Brandt believed that West Germany had to pursue a different policy toward the East. Brandt hoped that improving relations with the Soviet Union and East Germany would gain acceptance by the East of the status of West Berlin, improve conditions for the East Germans, and preserve the identity of the German nation.

Wyden, Peter. *Wall: The Inside Story of a Divided Berlin.* New York: Simon &

Schuster, 1989. A detailed history of the wall from its construction to the year that it was finally breached. The book was completed too early to include the events of November 9, 1989.

Bernard A. Cook

Cross-References

Soviets Take Control of Eastern Europe (1943), p. 612; The United States Airlifts Supplies to West Berlin (1948), p. 771; Hundreds of Thousands Leave East Germany for the West (1949), p. 795; The Helsinki Agreement Offers Terms for International Cooperation (1975), p. 1806; Gorbachev Initiates a Policy of *Glasnost* (1985), p. 2249; The Berlin Wall Falls (1989), p. 2523; Gorbachev Agrees to Membership of a United Germany in NATO (1990), p. 2589.

THE NONALIGNED MOVEMENT MEETS

Categories of event: Peace movements and organizations; political freedom
Time: September 1-5, 1961
Locale: Belgrade, Yugoslavia

Tito (Josip Broz), the leader of Yugoslavia, invited countries that were not members of the North Atlantic Treaty Organization or the Warsaw Pact to attend a convention of neutrals in Belgrade

> *Principal personages:*
>
> TITO (1892-1980), the president of Yugoslavia, the host of the first non-aligned conference in 1961
>
> GAMAL ABDEL NASSER (1918-1970), the president of Egypt and the United Arab Republic
>
> JAWAHARLAL NEHRU (1889-1964), the prime minister and foreign minister of India, whose policies inspired the Nonaligned Movement

Summary of Event

Following World War II, the United Nations established a system of international security and administration that was heavily oriented toward Europe. Although the U.N. General Assembly contained representatives from all countries on an equal basis, real power rested in the Security Council, whose five permanent members were Great Britain, France, the United States, the Soviet Union, and China. In 1949, when the Communist forces of Mao Tse-tung took control of most of China, the United Nations, under the influence of the West, kept China's seat in the hands of the Republic of China, which was confined on the island of Formosa. This reduced the power of non-European countries even further.

Moreover, in the late 1940's, the Cold War between Western powers and the Soviet Union turned the United Nations into an arena of constant political confrontation between the two superpowers and their allies. In Europe and North America, the superpowers created two opposing alliance systems—the North Atlantic Treaty Organization (NATO) in the West and the Warsaw Pact in the Soviet Bloc. The two sought allies throughout the globe.

The Cold War prevented the United Nations from giving its full attention to the problems that Third World countries had hoped would be foremost on its agenda. Most Third World countries were extremely poor, although they had great resources. Most were emerging from the grip of European imperialism, and most had problems with rapidly growing populations that they could not care for or feed. Disease was rampant. Infant mortality was high. Hunger and famine were endemic. These issues, not superpower confrontation, were the matters that the Third World wanted addressed.

In Asia and Africa, the first two decades after World War II witnessed the end of the great European empires and the formation of many new nations that wished to loosen the subservient ties they had had with the mother countries. Many of their leaders wanted to ensure that the democratic principles of government and the best of the European ideologies remained. All wished to keep Western technology. Most believed that the European and North American world owed them economic assistance to get started, in much the same way that the United States had helped Europe recover from the devastation of World War II with the Marshall Plan. This tension between the Third World and the West over the terms of dissolution caused confrontations between former colonies and former imperial powers.

In a number of countries, liberation struggles brought anti-Western leaders to the forefront, including some who adopted the Marxist ideology of the Soviet Bloc. Many other Third World politicians played both sides in the Cold War against each other in attempts to get foreign aid. Economic chaos added to the political strains, and quite often the new countries found themselves under military or civilian dictatorships.

Moreover, in the international politics of the 1950's the face-to-face confrontations between the superpowers often precluded any room for compromise. This policy was called "brinkmanship" because such face-offs held the threat of the use of atomic and nuclear weapons and were based on the strategy of forcing confrontations to the brink of war before serious negotiating began. Neutral countries felt the danger and imprudence of this policy the most. They realized that they would suffer in a third world war along with the combatants, and many Third World statesmen, anxious to alleviate the situations, became outspoken advocates of peace and disarmament.

The origins of nonalignment can be traced to the years before World War II, as a reaction to the failures and Eurocentrism of the League of Nations. World War II accelerated the desire for independence in the colonies of the European empires, but there was a general feeling of frustration over the need for small, new, struggling nations to depend on larger powers. To many such nations, all the choices of patrons appeared to be repugnant, including the fascist bloc, with its inherent racial prejudices, the totalitarian Soviet Union, and West European governments, with their imperialist histories.

Attempts after World War II, principally among the non-Europeans, to form a bloc of neutrals began with President Jawaharlal Nehru's policies of Indian neutrality. Nehru included these in a foreign policy program announced in the spring of 1954 called *Panchsheel* (five points); the program called for sovereign territorial integrity, nonaggression, noninterference in domestic affairs, equal and mutual beneficial relationships, and peaceful coexistence. Nehru also maintained that international relations of all countries should be directed toward dissolving colonial bonds, promoting national and individual liberty, and eliminating racism, hunger, want, disease, and ignorance. Although many derided Nehru as an unrealistic idealist and an overbearing moralist, he continued to pursue his lofty principles in the international arena.

At about the same time as the promulgation of his *Panchsheel* program, Nehru attended a conference of the Asian subcontinent countries in Colombo, Ceylon (now called Sri Lanka). The conference delegates acknowledged Nehru as the unofficial spokesman for emerging former colonies and agreed to hold a broader conference of Asian and African nations in Bandung, Indonesia, in April, 1965, where his ideas would be discussed.

Although no nonaligned organization or program of action resulted from the Bandung conference, Nehru, with the aid of Chou En-lai, the delegate of the Communist People's Republic of China, was able to have his *Panchsheel* principles adopted as a guide for nonalignment. The opinions of the superpowers were mixed. John Foster Dulles, the American secretary of state and the father of brinkmanship, publicly stated that neutralism was immoral. On the other hand, the Soviet leadership sought to ingratiate itself with the former colonies of the European empires, a policy that it had been following since the 1917 revolution, and praised Nehru's program. Communist China, for its part, despite its presence at Bandung, was skeptical of the movement.

Ironically, the person who proved to be the catalyst for the creation of an alliance of nonaligned nations was not a Third World leader but a European, and a Marxist at that. The post-World War II Nonaligned Movement (NAM) began at a conference convoked by Marshal Tito, the leader of Yugoslavia, in Belgrade in June, 1961.

The government of Yugoslavia had fallen under the control of Tito's Marxist League of Communists in 1945. Tito was among the first to realize the need for independence from both East and West. He did not wish Yugoslavia to be a pawn of the Soviet Union and broke with Stalin in 1948. Furthermore, while the West was willing to support him in his struggle with their common enemy, he was still a committed Marxist and mistrusted the Western Europeans and Americans. Thus in 1961 he invited the leaders of the neutral and former colonial countries of Africa and Asia to join him in a conference in Belgrade, the capital of Yugoslavia, to establish a nonaligned movement. A preliminary meeting was convened in Cairo and was hosted by Egyptian President Gamal Abdel Nasser.

Representatives of about twenty countries attended. Much discussion over whom to invite occupied the organizers of the conference. They established five principles of nonalignment: an independent foreign policy, belief in the principle of peaceful coexistence, support for national liberation movements, no agreements with the superpower blocs, and no military ties with the superpowers. In practice, these criteria were applied very loosely, and many countries involved in the NAM had links with the United States or the Soviet Union. In the end, all who wished to attend the conference did so. There were twenty-five delegations led by heads of state, including some of the most important figures of the twentieth century. Besides Tito, the two most outstanding figures present were Nehru and Nasser. Other delegates included Haile Selassie of Ethiopia, Kwame Nkrumah of Ghana, Habib Bourguiba of Tunisia, Sukarno of Indonesia, Fidel Castro of Cuba, and Archbishop Makarios of Cyprus.

Delegations attending the Belgrade conference included seven from sub-Saharan Africa (Congo, Ethiopia, Ghana, Guinea, Mali, Somilia, and the Sudan), seven from Asia (Afghanistan, Burma, Cambodia, Ceylon, India, Indonesia, and Nepal), eight from the Arab Middle East (Algeria, Iraq, Lebanon, Morocco, Saudi Arabia, Tunisia, the United Arab Republic—as the joint state of Syria and Egypt was called at the time—and Yemen), two from Europe (Cyprus and Yugoslavia), and one from Latin America (Cuba). Three other Latin American countries sent observers (Bolivia, Brazil, and Ecuador).

The Belgrade conference successfully started a vital Third World bloc detached from the superpowers. The nonaligned countries would now be able to play a major role in international affairs, both for promoting world peace and for raising the resources for elevating the standards of living in their own countries.

Impact of Event

The Belgrade conference established the Nonaligned Movement on a permanent basis. Later conferences were held in Cairo (1964), Lusaka (1970), Algeria (1973), Colombo (1976), Havana (1979), New Delhi (1983), and Harare (1986). More and more countries joined the movement as they won their independence and witnessed the influence that the movement had in world affairs. By the time of the Harare conference, the NAM had 101 members. The movement's ability to accomplish its goals was mixed. While it consistently stood as a voice for general peace and the prevention of war, especially nuclear war between the superpowers, the individual countries were not averse to using war to settle their own difficulties.

In a general way, peace was inimical to another program of the movement, the liberation of subject peoples. Thus, for example, the Muslim members consistently favored the Palestinians in their disputes with Israel. Even Nehru's India used force to "liberate" and annex neighboring Goa from Portugal in 1961. Cuba sent soldiers to fight in wars of national liberation in Africa. Furthermore, many of the nonaligned leaders were guilty of maintaining themselves in power through dictatorial, undemocratic, or corrupt means. Tito's Yugoslavia was a one-party Communist state, Nkrumah was a dictator who permitted no opposition, and Sukarno's corruption was the scandal of southeast Asia.

Disputes among the nonaligned nations also flared up at the conferences. Because of the anti-imperial origin of the movement, there was a bias against the West. Most of the leaders, however, did not completely trust the Soviet Bloc either. Some members, such as Saudi Arabia and Indonesia, favored the West. In the most famous row, Tito and Castro squared off against each other at Havana when the Cuban leader wanted to push through a resolution stating that the movement should favor Moscow.

The greatest success of the movement was giving a source of united political power to those countries that were caught between the superpower struggles. The movement also made significant contributions to the movement for nuclear disarmament. During the Belgrade conference, the Soviet Union began testing nuclear bombs in the atmosphere. The United States was already testing underground. The conference sent delegations to both countries to persuade them to end testing and begin serious talks on disarmament. One result was the inclusion of nonaligned and neutral nations at disarmament talks, such as those begun at Geneva in March, 1962. In any case, after Belgrade, the NAM became a force in international politics.

Bibliography

Alimov, Yuri. *The Rise and Growth of the Non-aligned Movement.* Moscow: Progress Publishers, 1987. Translated from Russian. Since it was written during the *glasnost* era, however, it is less propagandistic than previous Soviet works. Contains a detailed history and very favorable description of the NAM. No index; bibliography, some footnotes.

Crabb, Cecil V., Jr. *Elephants and the Grass: A Study of Nonalignment.* New York: Praeger, 1965. Although written before the later nonaligned conferences, this is one of the few comprehensive studies of the movement. Very well researched, it examines the nonaligned movement from different perspectives. The title comes from an old African proverb: "When elephants fight, it is the grass that suffers." Endnotes, index.

Edwards, Michael. *Nehru: A Political Biography.* New York: Praeger, 1971. A biography of the Indian leader for the general reader. Contains passages dealing with Nehru's role in the NAM. Index, some documentation, illustrated. No bibliography.

Jackson, Richard L. *The Non-Aligned, the UN, and the Superpowers.* New York: Praeger, 1983. A balanced, comprehensive, scholarly work analyzing the NAM by a career foreign service officer who served with the United States mission to the United Nations. Argues that the NAM is not inherently anti-American. Index, bibliography, glossary, and appendices.

Jansen, G. H. *Non-Alignment and the Afro-Asian States.* New York: Praeger, 1966. A scholarly analysis of nonalignment in the Third World. Examines steps leading up to the Belgrade conference. Documentation and bibliography.

Kardelj, Edvard. *The Historical Roots of Nonalignment.* Edited by Nikolaos A. Stavrou. Washington, D.C.: University Press of America, 1980. Kardelj was one of Tito's closest political and ideological advisers. This is a reprint of his article that appeared in the Yugoslav journal *Socialist Thought and Practice* in 1975; it is a valuable primary source tracing the development of Yugoslavia's conception and role in the NAM. Stavrou's excellent introduction provides useful information about Yugoslavia, nonalignment, and Kardelj himself. Documented and illustrated, includes an index.

Singham, A. W., and Shirley Hune. *Non-Alignment in an Age of Alignments.* Westport, Conn.: Lawrence Hill, 1986. An excellent scholarly study of the NAM. Contains both the history of the movement and a thorough political analysis. An appendix contains a list of members. Index and bibliography.

Frederick B. Chary

Cross-References

The League of Nations Is Established (1919), p. 270; Soviets Take Control of Eastern Europe (1943), p. 612; The United Nations Adopts Its Charter (1945), p. 657; The Marshall Plan Provides Aid to Europe (1947), p. 706; Palestinian Refugees Flee to Neighboring Arab Countries (1948), p. 749; Castro Takes Power in Cuba (1959), p. 1026; Cyprus Gains Independence (1960), p. 1084; Algeria Gains Independence (1962), p. 1155; The Organization of African Unity Is Founded (1963), p. 1194; Palestinian Refugees Form the Palestine Liberation Organization (1964), p. 1241.

THE EUROPEAN SOCIAL CHARTER IS SIGNED

Categories of event: Civil rights and international norms
Time: October 18, 1961
Locale: Turin, Italy

The signing of the European Social Charter marked a major step forward in the guarantee of economic and social rights in Europe

Principal personages:
> LODOVICO BENVENUTI (1899-   ), the Italian diplomat who was secretary-general of the Council of Europe during the final years of the preparation of the European Social Charter
> GUY MOLLET (1905-1975), the French political leader who was president of the Constituent (now Parliamentary) Assembly of the Council of Europe during the early development of the Social Charter (1954-1956)
> FERNAND DEHOUSSE (1906-   ), the Danish political figure who was president of the Constituent Assembly from 1956 to 1959

Summary of Event

The European Social Charter is a convention created by the Council of Europe as a logical extension of the commitment of its members to human rights. The twentieth century showed an increase in concern for human rights, which led to a series of international covenants intended to define and safeguard a wide range of rights. More concern, however, has often been given to political and civil rights than to economic and social rights. The European Social Charter was an attempt by the Council of Europe to rectify this imbalance.

A first step toward development of international standards for human rights was taken by the young United Nations when it issued the Universal Declaration of Human Rights in 1948. This was the first international declaration to list social and economic rights, such as the right to work and the right to organize, as being among the rights of the individual. Since it was merely a declaration, however, and not a treaty, the nations of the world had to negotiate agreements that would actually bring about the enactment and protection of these rights.

In Europe, the need for international cooperation to rebuild economies destroyed by World War II and concerns about security produced by the onset of the Cold War combined to produce the Council of Europe. The council was founded on May 5, 1949, by ten Western European states: Belgium, Denmark, France, Ireland, Italy, Luxembourg, The Netherlands, Norway, Sweden, and the United Kingdom. Its purpose was to facilitate and coordinate agreements among its member states in the fields of economic, scientific, social, legal, and administrative matters. It was also intended to aid in the protection and advancement of human rights and freedoms.

The European Social Charter was created to assist in the achievement of that purpose.

The Council of Europe has two major governing bodies. The first is the Consultative (or Parliamentary) Assembly, made up of representatives of the parliaments of the member states. It has only the power to make recommendations to the other governing body, the Committee of Ministers. Composed of the foreign ministers of the member states, the Committee of Ministers has the ability to make recommendations to member nations and also supervises the numerous committees and commissions of the council.

The Council of Europe created two treaties aimed at protecting and increasing human rights in Europe. The European Convention for the Protection of Human Rights and Fundamental Freedoms, signed in 1950, sought to protect political and civil rights, while the European Social Charter, signed in 1961, sought to protect economic and social rights. Originally, the council had intended to include economic and social rights in the 1950 human rights convention. Disagreement over which economic and social rights should be included, however, led to the decision to write a separate convention dealing only with economic and social rights. The disagreements stemmed from the relative newness of the idea of fundamental economic and social rights, from the difficulty of defining these rights clearly, and from the differing social structures of the member states.

The process of creating the social charter began in 1953, when the secretariat of the council suggested that a European social charter should be created. After much discussion and the passing of many memoranda among bodies of the council, the parliamentary assembly's committee on social questions drew up the first draft of the charter, which it submitted on October 26, 1955. This first draft set forth general principles that did not directly establish particular rights but that were intended to form a basis for a common social policy among member nations. It also set forth legal obligations for the signing governments and called for the creation of a European economic and social council to enforce the charter.

Further drafts of the charter followed, resulting in a completed document in October, 1956. It called for a European convention on social and economic rights, listed essentially the same rights as previous drafts, and called for the creation of a European commissioner for social affairs and a European social chamber. The long debate in the assembly reflected the conflict between those who wanted a treaty that was binding on its signers and those who preferred a mere statement of goals. At that point, the draft dealt mainly with the rights of workers. The assembly passed this draft to the Committee of Ministers, which delegated the refining of the draft to its social committee.

The social committee had already been working on a draft charter prior to its receipt of the assembly's draft. Its efforts had been geared toward a simple statement of goals rather than a binding treaty. It was instructed to end that approach, however, and begin working on a treaty that would be binding in some manner on the signatory states. In February of 1958, it completed its draft; late that year, the draft was submitted it to a tripartite conference in Strasbourg. In April of 1959, the draft treaty was sent to the assembly, which referred it to its social affairs committee. After some work, the treaty was returned to the assembly, which adopted the draft on January 21, 1960, by a vote of seventy-three to one, with sixteen abstentions. The draft then went back to the social affairs committee to be given its final form. The end product of this long process strongly reflected standards adopted by the International Labour Conference of the International Labour Organisation.

The European Social Charter was signed in Turin, Italy, on October 18, 1961, and came into effect on February 26, 1965. It was originally ratified by Austria, Cyprus, Denmark, the Federal Republic of Germany, France, Iceland, Ireland, Italy, Norway, Sweden, and the United Kingdom. Later, Greece, Malta, The Netherlands, and Spain also ratified the charter.

Part I of the charter established nineteen fundamental economic and social rights: to work; to just working conditions; to safe working conditions; to fair pay; to organize; to collective bargaining; to work abroad; to vocational guidance; to vocational training; to health protection; to social security; to social and medical care; to benefit from social welfare services; of the disabled to vocational training; of the family to social, legal, and economic protection; of children to protection; of employed women to protection; of mothers and children to social, legal, and economic protection; and of migrant workers and their families to protection and assistance. Part II of the charter specified the specific obligations that these rights created for signatory states. Each article of Part II detailed the specific obligations associated with a particular right.

Part III of the charter permitted nations to ratify the treaty without accepting all of its provisions. Signatory states were required, however, to accept at least five of the seven fundamental articles of Part II. The fundamental articles dealt with the rights of workers to organize and bargain collectively, of migrant workers, of the family to protection, to work, to social security, and to social and medical assistance. In addition, a ratifying state had to accept a total of ten of the nineteen articles or forty-five of the seventy-two numbered paragraphs from Part II. A state could later ratify articles not originally accepted.

Part IV of the charter set up procedures for overseeing the execution of the other provisions. Each ratifying nation was asked to submit biennial reports on its application of the articles it had ratified and could also be asked to submit reports on the articles it had not ratified.

The treaty designated four bodies that participate in the oversight process. A seven-member committee of independent experts, appointed by the Committee of Ministers, studies the reports from signatory nations and determines to what extent obligations have been met. The governmental committee on the European Social Charter in turn receives the report of the expert committee. This committee is made up of representatives of the contracting states. Up to two international organizations of workers and two of employers can participate as observers at its meetings. The governmental committee presents reports to the Parliamentary Assembly, which reports to the Committee of Ministers. The governmental committee also submits reports directly to the Committee of Ministers. The Committee of Ministers takes the final step of making recommendations to the signatory states on actions they should take to further their implementation of the charter. Recommendations must be approved by a two-thirds majority of the Committee of Ministers.

The European Social Charter created an international framework designed to encourage the states signing it to achieve certain minimums in economic and social rights. Although the social charter conferred no truly coercive powers on the bodies charged with its implementation, it was the first effort at an international level to guarantee some standard of social and economic rights. When the difficulties faced by an effort to achieve an international consensus on the content of economic and social rights are considered, the European Social Charter becomes a much more impressive achievement.

Impact of Event

Since its signing in 1961, the European Social Charter has had a substantial impact on economic and social rights. Of the Council of Europe's twenty-four member states in 1990, nineteen had signed the charter, and fifteen of these had ratified it. Only France, Italy, and Spain, however, had ratified every article. The Netherlands ratified all articles but made an exception in Article 6, because it did not recognize the right of civil servants to bargain collectively. The other eleven ratifying states only ratified portions of the treaty; the rights to work, to safe working conditions, and of the disabled to vocational training were the only rights that had been universally accepted by the ratifying states.

Since the Council of Europe has no coercive powers over the ratifying states, actual progress in implementing accepted rights has varied. The Committee of Ministers has repeatedly had to inform states that they have failed to meet the standards set by the articles they have accepted. This necessity is complicated by the process used to evaluate the reports submitted by the states. First, the reports often omit necessary information, which causes delay in an already slow process. Second, the language of the treaty is often ambiguous, and many articles require interpretation of their application to actual situations. Third, while the committee of independent experts has proven ready to condemn states for violations of the articles, the governmental committee has been much more reluctant to do so. Not surprisingly, governmental committee members, as agents of the member governments, have been reluctant to condemn their employers. Problems with reports, the ambiguity of the treaty, and politics within the council have made the implementation of the treaty more difficult than its framers imagined.

Despite the difficulties, the number of violations has declined over time, and the ratifying states have made progress in advancing social and economic rights. Moreover, other international agreements have followed. In 1968, the European Code of Social Security entered into force, as did the European Convention on Social Security in 1977. In 1988, an additional protocol, extending rights, was added to the social charter. Although it has not been able to guarantee compliance with its terms, the European Social Charter has facilitated the expansion and protection of economic and social rights in Europe.

Bibliography

Betten, Lammy, David Harris, and Teun Jaspers. *The Future of European Social Policy.* Deventer, The Netherlands: Kluwer Law and Taxation Publishers, 1989. A collection of papers and commentary by some of the leading experts on the charter at a conference on the future of European social policy at the University of Utrecht in 1989. Provides a European perspective on the functioning of the charter. Most of the papers are footnoted, but there is no comprehensive bibliography.

Council of Europe. *Twenty-fifth Anniversary of the European Social Charter: Origin, Operation, and Results of the Charter.* Strasbourg, France: Council of Europe, Publications Section, 1986. This brief booklet gives a good history of the writing of the charter and how it functions. It also provides a table of which states have ratified which articles and a list of available documents on proceedings resulting from the charter. No other reference features.

"The European Social Charter and International Labour Standards." Parts 1-2. *International Labour Review* 84 (November/December, 1961): 354-375, 462-477. A detailed contemporary discussion of the provisions of the social charter and comparison with corresponding international labor standards.

Harris, D. J. *The European Social Charter.* Charlottesville: University Press of Virginia, 1984. This thorough book examines, article by article, the degree of implementation of the charter by ratifying states. It is quite lengthy and detailed, which makes it complete but sometimes tedious. It has a bibliography, an index, and the text of the charter.

Jaspers, C. M., and L. Betten, eds. *Twenty-five Years, European Social Charter.* Deventer, The Netherlands: Kluwer Law and Taxation Publishers, 1988. A collection of articles by legal experts in those states that have ratified articles of the charter. Each article reports on that state's degree of adherence to the charter. It is quite useful for information on a particular state's performance. No reference features.

John W. Biles

Cross-References

The International Labour Organisation Is Established (1919), p. 281; Roosevelt Outlaws Discrimination in Defense-Industry Employment (1941), p. 578; The World Health Organization Proclaims Health as a Basic Right (1946), p. 678; The United Nations Adopts the Universal Declaration of Human Rights (1948), p. 789; The European Convention on Human Rights Is Signed (1950), p. 843; The European Court of Human Rights Is Established (1950), p. 849; The United Nations Adopts the Abolition of Forced Labor Convention (1957), p. 985; The Inter-American Commission on Human Rights Is Created (1959), p. 1032; The United Nations Adopts the

LUTULI IS AWARDED THE NOBEL PEACE PRIZE

Categories of event: Racial and ethnic rights; peace movements and organizations
Time: December 10, 1961
Locale: Oslo, Norway

As leader of the nonviolent struggle against the systematic oppression of non-whites in South Africa, Zulu chief Albert John Lutuli received world recognition in the Nobel Peace Prize

Principal personages:
ALBERT LUTULI (1898-1967), a Zulu chief and president of the African National Congress
NELSON MANDELA (1918-   ), an attorney and fellow freedom fighter
OLIVER TAMBO (1917-   ), an attorney, fellow freedom fighter, and Lutuli's successor
GUNNAR JAHN (1883-1971), the chairman of the Norwegian Nobel Committee

Summary of Event

On December 10, 1961, on the sixty-fifth anniversary of the death of Alfred Nobel, the Norwegian Nobel Committee awarded the Peace Prizes for 1960 and 1961. The 1960 award, which had been postponed the previous year, was given to Albert John Lutuli, Zulu chieftain and leader of the nonviolent struggle against the policy of racial separation, or apartheid, in South Africa.

Lutuli was born in 1898, descended from a line of Zulu chiefs including his grandfather Ntaba and his uncle John. Educated at a missionary school near Pietermaritzburg, Lutuli was graduated from Adams Mission Station College in 1921 and remained there teaching Zulu history and literature and leading the college choir. In 1927, he married a fellow teacher, Nokukhanya Bhengu. A devout Christian, he was active in church organizations, held offices in the Durban and District African Football Associations, and in 1933 became president of the African Association of Teachers.

In 1936, after fifteen years of teaching, Lutuli was chosen chief of a Zulu community in Groutville. His duties included civil administration, adjudication, and presiding over tribal ceremonies; as leader, he sought to preserve Zulu culture, promote Christian values, and improve social and labor conditions. He attended the International Missionary Conference in Madras, India, and toured the United States lecturing on missions, through the North American Missionary Conference.

Power in South Africa was concentrated among the white descendents of European settlers. Blacks, descended from African natives, formed the national majority; descendants of Asian immigrants, especially Indians, and Afrikaners of mixed European and African blood were systematically deprived of rights. In 1936, Afrikaner men were disenfranchised in Cape Province, the only province that allowed them the vote, and in 1948 the government instituted an official policy of apartheid, regulating and limiting the rights and movements of nonwhite populations.

In 1944, in response to growing inequities, Lutuli joined the African National Congress (ANC), an organization founded in 1912 to work for Africans' civil rights. In 1951, he was elected president of the ANC's Natal division. The government ordered Lutuli to choose between his ANC position and his tribal leadership, but Lutuli balked at the ultimatum. The government, as final authority over the Zulus, deposed him as chief. Lutuli's firm stand earned for him respect among the ANC membership and Africans in general.

Meanwhile, a Joint Planning Congress of African, Indian, and Afrikaner groups led to a Day of Defiance, June 26, 1952, that began a campaign of civil disobedience based on the techniques employed by Mohandas Gandhi in the quest for Indian independence. People throughout the country ignored unjust, restrictive laws; the government responded with violence, arrests, and the Criminal Law Amendment Act, allowing for the lashing of protesters. When ANC president-general J. S. Moroka dissociated himself from nineteen codefendants in court, Lutuli was elected the organization's national leader.

Lutuli provided a balance between extremists supporting a militant, purely African agenda, and conservatives seeking cooperation with other groups and the government. He served as president of the ANC from 1952 until his death in 1967, working with such key figures as Nelson Mandela, Oliver Tambo, Walter Sisulu, and Z. K. Matthews. Mandela, Tambo, and Sisulu had founded the ANC Youth League in the early 1940's. Mandela, himself restricted to Johannesburg, was Lutuli's deputy and ANC Transvaal president. Sisulu and Tambo succeeded Mandela as deputies, and Tambo eventually became acting ANC president in exile and Lutuli's official successor. These men formed the core of the ANC.

As a result of his involvement in the Defiance Campaign, Lutuli was banned from political activities for one year. Nevertheless, he strove to continue the nonviolent struggle, which included creative implementation of the 1949 Programme of Action and a greater effort to involve masses of South Africans. He declared June 26, 1953, a day to light candles as symbols of freedom and to recount to the nation's children the history of the struggle. In July of 1954 he was banned for two more years, restricted to the Lower Tugela magisterial district in Natal. There he presided over a joint meeting of the ANC, the South African Indian Congress, the Colored People's Organization, and the Congress of Democrats, where a plan was drafted to poll the populace and create a "Freedom Charter" expressing its beliefs and demands. This led to the historic Congress of the People in Kliptown, near Johannesburg, in June, 1955, where more than twenty-eight hundred delegates established the Congress Alliance and adopted the Freedom Charter. Lutuli, still banned, was not present to witness the event or accept the Isitwalandwe Seaperankoe, the highest ANC honor. After the congress, he hosted an executive committee meeting to mediate between the "Africanists," who opposed the Freedom Charter and demanded black exclusiveness in creating a black-dominated South African State, and the "Charterists."

The government used the 1950 Suppression of Communism Act to suppress not only communists but any agitators. In December, 1956, its Operation T brought simultaneous arrests of 156 alleged conspirators nationwide, including Lutuli, Tambo, Sisulu, Mandela, Matthews, and other ANC and Communist leaders. They were all brought to Johannesburg and charged with treason on the grounds that the Freedom Charter was a subversive document. The arrests, while deactivating the leadership, ironically brought it together as never before. Seated alphabetically, Lutuli became close with Communist leader Moses Kotane. Lutuli was detained for a year and then released with sixty others in December, 1957. In late 1958, charges were dropped against another sixty-four, leaving thirty-one defendants to come to trial. Although he was banned again in 1959, Lutuli spent much time in Pretoria at the treason trial, testifying to the nonviolent foundations of the ANC. The trial dragged on through March, 1961, with Mandela eventually leading the defense. In the end, all defendants were acquitted.

Meanwhile, well-publicized incidents in Zeerust, Sekhukhuneland, Cato Manor, and Pondoland from 1957 to 1960 over the imposition of Bantu authorities, pass regulations, and cattle culling invoked increasingly repressive measures from the government and increased anger among the repressed. Lutuli was elected to his third term as ANC president in 1958 and oversaw a constitutional revision aimed at rejecting the movement's growing racialism, which sought to exclude non-Africans and favored rule explicitly by black majority. Lutuli opposed all racial, sexual, and religious discrimination, but dissent within the ANC led to the formation of the Pan-Africanist Congress (PAC), with exclusionary and afrocentric goals, under the leadership of Robert Sobukwe. Lutuli steadfastly maintained his belief in nonviolence, but a growing voice of frustration called for armed resistance.

A turning point came in March, 1960, when a mass demonstration against pass regulations at Sharpeville led to a police assault. Sixty-nine people were killed, 180 were wounded, and more than eleven thousand were arrested. The government declared a state of emergency. Lutuli publicly burned his pass in solidarity with the victims and proclaimed a national day of mourning, prayer, and noncompliance. Both the ANC and the PAC were outlawed. Lutuli called for a national convention to determine the will of the people and helped to set up a consultative conference of activist leaders. In May, 1961, a convention in Maritzburg of more than fourteen hundred people, many of whom had traveled for days and slept in fields, elected a National Action Council to organize mass demonstrations and strikes and demanded that the government call a national convention. A May, 1961, stay-home campaign was a test of the banned ANC against the government.

It was in this atmosphere of growing militancy, which Lutuli both approved of and feared, that news came to him in Groutville that he had won the 1960 Nobel Peace Prize. The South African government decried the award; then, under international pressure, it granted Lutuli a passport to travel for ten days only, to Norway only, to receive it. Garbed in full tribal attire, he accepted the prize from Gunnar Jahn, chairman of the Norwegian Nobel Committee. In his Nobel lecture, he spoke on the emergence of Africa and concluded, bringing his wife on stage, with a Zulu national song.

Ironically, on December 16, 1961, days after Lutuli was honored for his commitment to nonviolent resistance, Umkonto We Sizwe (Spear of the Nation), a newly formed armed wing of the ANC, triggered its first series of sabotage explosions in three cities, marking the initiation of armed struggle.

Impact of Event

The award of the 1960 Nobel Peace Prize had effects on Lutuli personally, on the development of the Peace Prize, and on the struggle against apartheid in South Africa.

Lutuli's life, on the surface, did not change, for he remained under bans, limited to the Groutville mission, farming, reading, writing, walking, and spending time with friends and family. He maintained what contact he could with his compatriots in the struggle. Tambo had left the country surreptitiously in March, 1961, and led the ANC's External Mission, and Mandela traveled through Africa as Lutuli's representative, seeking the support of African leaders, until his capture and imprisonment by South African authorities in 1964. It was the Peace Prize that gave Lutuli recognition around the world and brought him respect and congratulations from South Africans of all colors. Robert Kennedy, attorney general of the United States, arrived by helicopter on the sands of Groutville to meet with the Nobel laureate. In the year following the Peace Prize, Lutuli was nominated to be president of the South African Coloured People's Congress and elected honorary president of the National Union of South African Students and rector of Glasgow University. His autobiography, *Let My People Go*, written in 1960 and 1961 and published in 1962, further spread his fame and philosophy.

His award marked a new period in the history of the Nobel Peace Prize. Only once before had the honor been given to a non-European or North American—the 1936 prize to Carlos Saavedra Lamas of Argentina—and never before had a non-Westerner, an African or Asian, been recognized. After Lutuli, awards were given to individuals from Vietnam, Japan, the Soviet Union, Israel, Egypt, India, Mexico, Poland, South Africa, Costa Rica, Tibet, and Burma (Myanmar). Equally important, through recognition of Lutuli, the Norwegian Nobel Committee broadened the concept of peace, previously viewed more in terms of government leaders, disarmament, and the prevention of war, to include struggles over basic human rights, struggles that are often more specific and localized in scope. Lutuli's award set the precedent for recognition of others whose work lay in efforts to guarantee equality, respect, and compassion as fundamental conditions for world peace. Later recipients in this tradition included Martin Luther King, Jr. (1964), Seán MacBride (1974), Andrei Sakharov (1975), Amnesty International (1977), Mother Teresa (1979), Adolfo Pérez Esquivel (1980), Lech Wałęsa (1983), Bishop Desmond Tutu (1984), Elie Wiesel (1986), and Aung San Suu Kyi (1991).

Finally, though Lutuli's contribution to the struggle against apartheid cannot be quantified, it is immeasurable. It is true that eventually Lutuli's comrades and successors in the ANC and the PAC chose to abandon the insistently nonviolent path that he forged, yet it was his leadership in the 1950's that tested the limits of that approach against the resilience of South Africa's white minority. Lutuli's work helped to push the government to increasingly repressive measures, bringing the crime of apartheid to the attention of the international community and invoking the approbation of other governments, the United Nations, and antiapartheid movements among the people of many nations. Lutuli knew that the struggle would be difficult and would likely outlast him. Through the 1960's, 1970's, and 1980's, it continued, under Tambo's leadership and spurred by the image of Mandela in prison. As the century entered its last decade, the changes that Lutuli had envisioned began to materialize, with the emancipation of Mandela and the gradual dismantling of apartheid.

Bibliography

Abrams, Irwin. *The Nobel Peace Prize and the Laureates: An Illustrated Biographical History, 1901-1987.* Boston: G. K. Hall, 1978. Abrams gives a detailed discussion of the conception of the prize, the selection process, the award ceremony, and the Nobel Committee. He examines the laureates one by one, with a general discussion combining personal and professional information, facts, and anecdotes. Appended charts break down the laureates by decade, type of achievement, gender, and age.

Foster, Don, Dennis Davis, and Diane Sandler. *Detention and Torture in South Africa.* New York: St. Martin's Press, 1987. This densely researched volume examines the historical, legal, and psychological aspects of repression in South Africa through statistical analysis and case studies. Specific in focus, it provides a clear understanding of the institutionalized structures and processes that Lutuli spent his life fighting.

Frederikse, Julie. *The Unbreakable Thread: Non-Racialism in South Africa.* Bloomington: Indiana University Press, 1990. Frederikse interviewed hundreds of people from the struggle against racialism for this book, which traces the nonracialist tradition and movement from the seventeenth century to the 1980's. Full of quotes, excerpts, photos, and illustrations. It has the feel of a documentary film.

Kuper, Leo. *An African Bourgeoisie: Race, Class, and Politics in South Africa.* New Haven, Conn.: Yale University Press, 1965. Kuper, a member of South Africa's Liberal Party, provides a thoughtful profile of the nation's African elite in terms of occupation, organization, class structure, and political activity. Necessarily and effectively woven into the study are events and developments from the antiapartheid movement.

Luthuli, Albert John. *Let My People Go.* New York: McGraw-Hill, 1962. Written before his Nobel Peace Prize. Lutuli chronicles his own personal and political struggles through the 1950's. This autobiography reveals Lutuli's wisdom, patience, and passion for nonviolence. Appended are the Freedom Charter and two of Lutuli's public statements.

Meer, Fatima. *Higher than Hope: The Authorized Biography of Nelson Mandela.* New York: Harper & Row, 1990. Meer, wife of a leader of South Africa's Indian movement and a good friend of Lutuli and Mandela, narrates Mandela's life story with an effective combination of personal recall, sensitivity, and journalistic historicity. Includes much information about Mandela's personal life, some of his prison letters, a chronology, and a family tree, but no index.

Meli, Francis. *South Africa Belongs to Us: A History of the ANC.* Harare, Zimbabwe: Zimbabwe Publishing House, 1988. This compendium of facts, quotes, conversations, and other documentary material, written by the editor of the ANC journal, is an insider's view of the ANC from its origin into the 1980's. Rich with detail and extremely well documented, the book has ample appended material, including an exhaustive chronology.

Tambo, Oliver. *Preparing for Power: Oliver Tambo Speaks.* New York: George Braziller, 1988. The longtime ANC president gives, through speeches interwoven with historical narrative by his wife Adelaide, a resounding articulation of the concerns and attitudes of the ANC. Fascinating and passionate reading from Lutuli's heir-in-exile.

Barry Mann

Cross-References

Gandhi Leads a Noncooperation Movement (1920), p. 315; South Africa Begins a System of Separate Development (1951), p. 861; The Organization of African Unity Is Founded (1963), p. 1194; The United Nations Issues a Declaration on Racial Discrimination (1963), p. 1212; The United Nations Votes to Suppress and Punish Apartheid (1973), p. 1736; Students in Soweto Rebel Against the White Government (1976), p. 1882; Biko Is Murdered by Interrogators in South Africa (1977), p. 1887; The United Nations Imposes an Arms Embargo on South Africa (1977), p. 1937; The United Nations Issues a Declaration on South Africa (1979), p. 2008; Tutu Wins the Nobel Peace Prize (1984), p. 2244; Black Workers in South Africa Go on Strike (1987), p. 2304; Mandela Is Freed (1990), p. 2559; De Klerk Promises to Topple Apartheid Legislation (1991), p. 2606.

THE COUNCIL OF FEDERATED ORGANIZATIONS REGISTERS BLACKS TO VOTE

Categories of event: Racial and ethnic rights; voting rights
Time: 1962-1965
Locale: Mississippi

Through its massive Mississippi voter-registration project, the Council of Federated Organizations (COFO) played an important role in the struggle of Mississippi's African-American population to achieve voting rights

Principal personages:
ROBERT MOSES (1935-   ), a veteran civil rights activist who directed the COFO registration project
DAVID DENNIS (1940-   ), a veteran grass-roots community organizer who worked as COFO's assistant director
AARON HENRY (1922-   ), the president of the Mississippi NAACP, a symbolic 1963 candidate for governor
EDWIN KING (1936-   ), a Tougaloo College chaplain and civil rights activist who ran for the office of lieutenant-governor in the 1963 Freedom Vote Campaign
ALLARD LOWENSTEIN (1929-1980), a liberal lawyer, educator, and civil rights activist who helped COFO to recruit many of its white college volunteers
MICHAEL SCHWERNER (1939-1964), a Congress of Racial Equity (CORE) worker who was murdered by Ku Klux Klansmen in Neshoba County
JAMES E. CHANEY (1943-1964), a CORE worker who was lynched with two other civil rights workers in Neshoba County
ANDREW GOODMAN (1943-1964), a student volunteer murdered in 1964 in Neshoba County.
FANNIE LOU HAMER (1917-1977), a former sharecropper and activist who worked in the COFO-organized Mississippi Freedom Democratic Party

Summary of Event

During the 1960's Civil Rights movement, Mississippi was perhaps the most difficult and dangerous arena in which activists worked. Essentially a closed society on racial issues, white Mississippi fought tenaciously, often violently, to maintain a way of life based on white supremacy. While some civil rights groups sought to eliminate the state's dual society by pushing to desegregate schools and public accommodations, others worked to open up Mississippi through black political enfranchisement. One organization that played an important role in this effort was the Council of

Federated Organizations (COFO).

COFO was a unique coalition of the major civil rights groups operating in Mississippi. The council included the Student Nonviolent Coordinating Committee (SNCC), the Congress of Racial Equality (CORE), the National Association for the Advancement of Colored People (NAACP), and the Southern Christian Leadership Conference (SCLC). Initially formed in 1961 to assist jailed freedom riders in Jackson, COFO was revitalized in 1962 to increase the number of black registered voters. An additional purpose was to eliminate interorganizational competition over the distribution of foundation funds administered through the Voter Education Project (VEP). Neither the NAACP nor the SCLC played significant roles in COFO, although Mississippi NAACP head Aaron Henry served as its president. The SNCC, which supplied COFO with most of its staff and much of its operating funds, dominated the coalition. Robert Moses, a soft-spoken Harvard graduate student and able veteran SNCC community organizer, served as voter project director; he was assisted by CORE's David Dennis, another activist skilled in grass-roots voter-registration projects.

Few informed COFO staffers were unaware of Mississippi's history on black voting issues. This history had clearly indicated little white support for black political involvement. The first southern state to disfranchise its black electorate constitutionally, Mississippi had bolstered its legal impediments with extralegal efforts whenever it felt the status quo sufficiently threatened. Years of disfranchisement had combined with economic dependence, grinding poverty, rigid segregation, and educational deprivation to trap black Mississippians in an oppressive condition that often worked against direct challenges to white domination.

Significant challenges occurred. Influenced by the landmark *Brown v. Board of Education* Supreme Court decision (1954), in 1955 black Mississippians launched a major voter-registration drive. It ended in failure. Economic reprisals took their toll on many applicants, but the physical violence targeted against the leadership proved more effective. The year 1955 was especially bloody. Black Mississippi was convulsed by the murder of the city of Belzoni's NAACP president and voting-rights champion, George Lee, the near-assassination of his activist friend Gus Court, and the daylight murder of Brookhaven farmer and civil rights supporter Lamar Smith. Operating in such a repressive atmosphere, COFO's task would be difficult at best.

In 1960, African Americans composed 42 percent of Mississippi's population; when COFO began its registration campaign, however, only 5.3 percent of the eligible black population had surmounted the discriminatory laws to qualify as voters. Primarily involved in registering rural community blacks, particularly in the sharecropping delta counties, the organization encountered stiff white resistance and considerable black apprehension. Election officials devised ingenious harassment and delaying tactics against applicants. When such maneuvers or economic intimidation failed to dissuade black interest, violence again came into play. It raged in 1963 in key locations in the delta registration drive. Moses himself barely escaped being assassinated in Greenwood; however, he remained undaunted in his efforts.

Coalition leaders believed that only with federal intervention could any reasonable amount of success be expected, but little help or encouragement came from Washington. COFO did achieve greater success in disproving white myths about black voting indifference. The highlight of the organization's 1963 activities was its registration of black voters for its so-called Freedom Election. Eighty mostly white college students from Yale and Stanford universities were recruited by veteran activist Allard Lowenstein to assist COFO staffers in the campaign. They helped to register eighty-two thousand persons for a mock election that coincided with the regularly scheduled gubernatorial election. Voters could cast ballots for the official candidates or the representatives of a "freedom slate," consisting of gubernatorial candidate Aaron Henry and his running mate, the Revered Edwin King, a white Tougaloo College clergyman. Mississippi officials took little interest in the symbolic Henry-King victory, but the election demonstrated that black Mississippians were clearly interested in acquiring equal political rights and representation.

Moses and COFO organizers were encouraged by the Freedom Election. Its outcome added importance to a campaign announced by Dennis for a massive 1964 voter-organizing project dubbed "Freedom Summer." The project called for a large influx of mostly white college students to assist COFO staffers in registering black voters, establishing community centers, and organizing freedom schools to teach educationally deprived youths basic subjects and to teach adults voting techniques. Project plans also included the establishment of a new political organization, the Mississippi Freedom Democratic Party (MFDP). The party was to serve as an effective alternative to the all-white state Democratic Party and to challenge its delegation in the 1964 national convention.

Freedom Summer clearly bore the influence of Moses, who insisted that whites not be excluded from participating. Dennis agreed. The two leaders reasoned that exposing the children of prominent and affluent whites to the daily terror experienced by blacks would dramatize effectively the need for federal protection and intervention in the Mississippi movement. It was a calculated motive upon which many SNCC staffers frowned, but one which later circumstances partially justified.

After a week of orientation and training in an Oxford, Ohio, women's college, hundreds of idealistic youth came to Mississippi to work in the summer project. Mississippi hastily mobilized to combat this "invasion," increasing the size of the highway patrol and enacting legislation designed to curb the project. Jackson's enlarged police force heavily armed itself and even purchased an armored tank. The Ku Klux Klan and similar extremist groups grew in numbers and influence.

The reality of conducting civil rights activity in the South's most racially oppressive state quickly confronted the volunteers. Numerous workers were falsely arrested, assaulted, or shot at; the homes and churches of many COFO partisans were bombed and burned; and election officials redoubled their efforts not to make concessions in administering Mississippi's discriminatory registration laws. The reign of terror struck fear in the hearts of workers and prospective black registrants.

Clearly, the greatest disruptive event of the summer project was the tragic disappearance of COFO workers James Chaney, Andrew Goodman, and Michael Schwerner. An intensive manhunt uncovered their bodies in Neshoba County on August 4, six weeks after the search began, in an earthen dam near Philadelphia. Their kidnapping and assassination by Klansmen shocked the nation, partially bringing to reality COFO leaders' cynical prediction of government intervention if white youths became murder victims.

That intervention did not occur to the extent desired or expected by COFO workers. Still generally unprotected, the volunteers persisted in their activities, although their registration efforts remained largely ineffective. Throughout the rest of 1964, COFO's energies centered primarily on MFDP affairs, particularly on seeking the party's recognition as a vital political force. By the beginning of 1965, the coalition and the registration drive had essentially ended; COFO officially disbanded in 1966.

Impact of Event

Nothing affected the COFO's registration activities as much as the increased violence they generated. The repercussions were widespread, affecting staff members and registrants, Mississippians and non-Mississippians alike. Violence had always been used by racial extremists against those who sought to undermine Mississippi's white supremacy, but at the height of the registration campaign its usage became more tenacious and its results more deadly. During Freedom Summer alone, in addition to the well-publicized Neshoba County lynchings, at least four other deaths occurred that were related to the state's accelerated civil rights activities. Slightly less grave were the more than one thousand arrests, thirty-five shootings, and eighty beatings, and the bombing or burning of sixty-five homes, churches, and other buildings.

The ever-present terror and the reluctance of the federal government to protect project workers and black registrants influenced the effectiveness of COFO in achieving its objectives. For working-class blacks, the fear of physical reprisal often interacted with the reality of economic reprisal, creating a high price to pay for registering to vote. When added to the force of the state's discriminatory registration procedures, the results were discouraging. In the two years from 1962 to 1964, when COFO was functioning at its highest level, black voter registration increased by only 1.4 percent. Mississippi's 1964 registration rate of 6.7 percent for blacks was the lowest in the nation. This lack of significant progress in Mississippi caused the Voter Education Project in late 1963 to divert its financial contributions from COFO to more promising voter projects.

Still, COFO persisted. The various campaign obstacles had a sobering effect on all involved, but the project also produced positive signs. The 1963 Freedom Election was convincing evidence of black voting aspirations, and it helped to stimulate interest across the state. This expanded interest continued into the summer project. Despite the summer's terrorism, some seventeen thousand blacks were convinced to seek registration in their county courthouses, although only sixteen hundred actually succeeded.

Additionally, the motivation translated into real grass-roots political action in the form of the MFDP. The party did not gain recognition as the legitimate representative of Mississippi Democrats. Through the efforts of such personable and magnetic individuals as Fannie Lou Hamer, however, black Mississippians' political plight received further national exposure.

Perhaps COFO's greatest contribution in the voting-rights struggle was its role in dramatizing the inhumanity of Mississippi's resistance to black political involvement. In so doing, it aided immeasurably the national call for a greater federal role in southern voting practices. COFO's project eventually thus achieved one of its deeper aims. Martin Luther King, Jr.'s Selma voting-rights campaign clearly influenced congressional passage of the 1965 Voting Rights Act, but COFO's Mississippi project was also significant.

Ultimately, COFO aided in opening Mississippi society and shaping its participatory political culture. In 1991, Mississippi had more black elected officials than any other state in the nation. With the country's largest percentage of African Americans in its population, Mississippi had achieved the meaningful political empowerment that many COFO idealists envisioned.

Bibliography

Belfrage, Sally. *Freedom Summer.* New York: Viking Press, 1965. One of the best personal accounts to come out of the 1964 Summer Project. Belfrage's book covers her training and orientation in Ohio and the ordeal of the white resistance in Mississippi.

Cagin, Seth, and Philip Dray. *We Are Not Afraid: The Story of Goodman, Schwerner, and Chaney and the Civil Rights Campaign in Mississippi.* New York: Macmillan, 1988. A detailed account of the murders of the three civil rights workers and the COFO Summer Project. The authors do much to correct the often-repeated suggestion that the Federal Bureau of Investigation played a significant role in protecting the volunteers.

Carson, Clayborne. *In Struggle: SNCC and the Black Awakening of the 1960s.* Cambridge, Mass.: Harvard University Press, 1981. One of the best civil rights organizational histories available. Comprehensively treats the student group, its difficulties and successes, and its evolution from nonviolence to militancy in the mid-1960's. The coverage of Mississippi voting rights and COFO matters is especially good. Notes and index.

Dittmer, John. "The Politics of the Mississippi Movement, 1954-1964." In *The Civil Rights Movement in America*, edited by Charles W. Eagles. Jackson: University Press of Mississippi, 1986. A good analysis of the black Mississippi struggle. Dittmer understandably focuses much attention on the COFO project. Notes.

Holt, Len. *The Summer That Didn't End.* New York: William Morrow, 1965. The personal account of a black Washington, D.C., lawyer who came to Mississippi to work in the 1964 Summer Project. Holt focuses on the Philadelphia murders and the individual COFO projects. Appendix and index.

Lawson, Steven F. *Black Ballots: Voting Rights in the South, 1944-1969.* New York: Columbia University Press, 1976. A comprehensive study of the black voting-rights struggle.

McAdam, Doug. *Freedom Summer.* New York: Oxford University Press, 1988. A sociohistorical study of the COFO volunteers and what influenced them. McAdams claims that the project forever changed these liberal whites, radicalizing them in ways that appeared in their post-1964 summer reform efforts. Appendix, notes, bibliography, and index.

Meier, August, and Elliot Rudwick. *CORE: A Study in the Civil Rights Movement, 1942-1968.* New York: Oxford University Press, 1973. The most comprehensive and scholarly treatment of the Congress of Racial Equality. Includes much discussion of CORE's involvement in the Mississippi voting-rights struggle. References, notes, and index.

Silver, James W. *Mississippi: The Closed Society.* New York: Harcourt, Brace & World, 1964. The classic indictment of Mississippi and its reluctance to address change in its racial order. The book's genesis was primarily the violent white reaction to the integration of the University of Mississippi.

Zinn, Howard. *SNCC: The New Abolitionists.* Boston: Beacon Press, 1964. Although not a formal history, this book is a penetrating analysis of the SNCC by one of its first historians, who was also its adviser. Although dated, it remains essential reading for understanding this organization, which formed the largest part of the COFO coalition.

Robert L. Jenkins

Cross-References

The Congress of Racial Equality Forms (1942), p. 601; Meredith's Enrollment Integrates the University of Mississippi (1962), p. 1167; The Twenty-fourth Amendment Outlaws Poll Taxes (1964), p. 1231; Three Civil Rights Workers Are Murdered (1964), p. 1246; Congress Passes the Civil Rights Act (1964), p. 1251; Martin Luther King, Jr., Leads a March from Selma to Montgomery (1965), p. 1278; Congress Passes the Voting Rights Act (1965), p. 1296; The Civil Rights Act of 1968 Outlaws Discrimination in Housing (1968), p. 1414; Congress Extends Voting Rights Reforms (1975), p. 1812.

ALGERIA GAINS INDEPENDENCE

Category of event: Revolutions and rebellions
Time: July 5, 1962
Locale: Algeria

Algerian independence ended 132 years of brutal French colonialism in which European settlers were granted citizenship and the majority of Algerian Muslims were denied civil and political rights

   Principal personages:
   AHMED BEN BELLA (1918-   ), a founding member of the Front for National Liberation (FLN) and the first president of the Algerian Republic (1962-1965)
   CHARLES DE GAULLE (1890-1970), the president of France (1958-1969), negotiated peace and Algerian independence
   FERHAT ABBAS (1899-1985), the first premier of the provisional government of Algeria (1958-1961), a fervent nationalist since the 1920's
   HOUARI BOUMEDIENNE (1927-1978), second president of Algeria (1965-1978), who overthrew Ben Bella, head of the unified general staff of the FLN during the war for independence
   HOCINE AIT AHMAD (1926-   ), a founding member of the FLN and cabinet member in the first independent government

Summary of Event

The struggle for independence in Algeria, one of the most bitter and protracted independence movements, was also the one involving the largest measure of Arab-world support. First occupied by the French in 1830, Algeria endured more than a century of brutal domination in which Algerian land was appropriated and assigned to European settlers, the majority of Algerian Muslims were denied political and human rights, the masses were impoverished, and those seeking political reform were imprisoned. Unlike other French "colonies," Algeria under settler domination acquired a special status as a "department," an integral part of the French Republic. This status meant full citizenship for Europeans only. In the post-World War II era of decolonization and national independence movements, the special privileges of the European minority collided sharply with the desire for self-determination by the five-sixths of the population that was Algerian.

The key event in Algeria which affected the course of future Franco-Algerian relations was a demonstration in Sétif on May 8, 1945. Marchers carrying signs proclaiming "Long Live Free Algeria" and "Free Messali Hadj" (an imprisoned nationalist) clashed with police, setting off a spontaneous, uncoordinated country-wide insurrection. The brutally suppressed uprising resulted in many deaths (somewhere between the official French tally of fifteen hundred and the Algerian claim of forty-five thousand), forty-five hundred arrests, the banning of Algerian political parties, and the postwar generation's belief that violence was the only road to independence.

This idea gained credence when the French concession to Algerian political participation, the Organic Statute of September 20, 1947, granted French citizenship to Algerians who renounced their Muslim status. The law also created a Muslim electoral college alongside a European one, recognized Arabic as an official language, and abolished military rule in the Algerian Sahara. Muslims and settlers alike opposed this statute, the former because it fell short of expectations and the latter because it went too far. In the 1947 municipal elections, Messali Hadj's proindependence MTLD (Movement for the Triumph of Democratic Liberties) won a sweeping victory, frightening the settlers. Their leaders proceeded, through fraud and intimidation, to rig the first Algerian Assembly elections in 1948, increasing Algerian bitterness.

The lack of Algerian political self-determination was compounded by economic inequality. Algeria's wealth in manufacturing, mining, agriculture, and trade was controlled by *grand colons* (rich settlers). They also owned the most fertile land, producing wine, citrus, olives, and vegetables for the French market system. Undernourished Algerian Muslims were largely confined to subsistence cereal production and poorly paid manual labor. Contributions of Muslim taxpayers were disproportionately greater than the benefits they received. Muslims composed 90 percent of the population and produced 20 percent of the national income but paid 70 percent of the direct taxes, as settlers were exempt from many of them. Less than 1 percent of Muslims belonged to the middle class. In Algiers, the capital city, Muslims were largely confined to the overcrowded shantytowns on the city outskirts, while *colons* lived in gardened, whitewashed villas or handsome apartment buildings. Inadequate health care for Algerians meant that diseases bred by crowded living conditions and malnutrition were common, including tuberculosis, trachoma, pneumonia, diphtheria, scarlet fever, malaria, and polio.

France controlled all aspects of Algerian life, and through a policy of cultural imperialism worked to destroy Algerian cultural identity and reshape the society along French lines. Explicit French policy, to "civilize" by imposing French culture and language, reduced literacy. Algerian Arabic became a "street" language, and schooling in classical Arabic ceased. Education was French, aimed at preparing students for French exams and creating a small, indigenous elite who would compete with colonists for jobs in the modern sector. These few were disproportionately Berber-speaking Kabyles favored in school and jobs by the French "divide and rule" policy.

No longer content with concessions short of majority rule, in 1948 young men from MTLD chapters formed the Organisation Secrète (OS), a group aimed at building a resistance force and destroying the myth of French Algeria. Ahmed Ben Bella emerged as the dominant personality among its collective leadership. By October, 1954, the OS core, along with nationalists from other groups, formed the Front for

National Liberation (FLN) and chose November 1, 1954, to begin a revolution. That day was marked by seventy synchronized attacks on French facilities, an invitation to Algerian Muslims to join the National Liberation Army (ALN), and a public call for the French to negotiate peace, recognize Algerian independence, and allow settlers to remain as Algerian citizens. Taken by surprise, France sent reinforcements of soldiers and arrested 160 known activists. Soon, indiscriminate repression by the French army—destruction of villages and mass arrests—galvanized the Algerian masses to support the rebellion.

By February, 1956, France's new prime minister, socialist Guy Mollet, ordered more than 400,000 French soldiers to achieve victory. Army tactics included population deportation and resettlement, the destruction of FLN suspects' homes, and systematic torture during interrogation of suspects. The FLN also carried out terrorist acts—selected assassinations of French officials and Algerian collaborators, and bombings at cafes and nightclubs. In France and abroad, much publicity and protest was given to torture victims such as Djamila Bouhired, a young, educated Algerian woman active in the urban resistance who refused to reveal the names of her associates even after being raped and tortured in jail.

By 1957, signs that the French government was losing the propaganda war were evident, as French intellectuals, including French anthropologist Germaine Tillion and authors François Mauriac, Jean-Paul Sartre, and Simone de Beauvoir, mobilized public opinion against the repression. Tillion visited Algeria to protest rights abuses in June, 1957, as a member of the International Committee Against the Regime of Concentration Camps. International protests against French human rights abuses escalated after October, 1956, when the French forced a commercial Air Maroc plane to land at Algiers instead of Tunis, taking four FLN leaders hostage—Ben Bella, Hocine Ait Ahmad, Rabah Bitat, and Muhammad Khider.

Fearing international pressure, settlers backed by French generals occupied the governor general's office in 1958. In this tense atmosphere, Charles de Gaulle offered his services and became premier on June 1, 1958, believing he could control the uprising. De Gaulle's policy centered on checking extremists amongst the settlers and the army, ignoring the FLN, and infusing money to induce moderate Algerians to negotiate. The FLN responded by intensifying guerrilla action, extending terrorist raids to France, and, with the encouragement of President Abdel Nasser of Egypt, forming in September, 1958, a Provisional Government of the Algerian Republic (GPRA), a representative coalition with Ferhat Abbas, a moderate, as the president.

Locked between settler-army intransigence and growing international pressure, de Gaulle moderated, telling the United Nations in September, 1959, that Algeria could soon choose its status—secession, federation, or union. Widespread demonstrations during a December, 1960, visit to Algiers convinced him of mass FLN support. With a January, 1961, French referendum showing 75 percent of French voters favoring Algerian independence, France's policy shifted. The Secret Army Organization (OAS) of diehard settlers, however, began a reign of terror, ensuring the departure of 90 percent of the Europeans. The OAS shot Muslims in public, killed European and Algerian teachers in classrooms, assassinated patients in hospitals, and burned the University of Algiers library. Their goal of provoking a Muslim counterattack to prevent independence failed because of FLN and public restraint.

Negotiations between the French and the GPRA opened at Evian on May 20, 1961, after the release of Ben Bella and other FLN leaders. Negotiations foundered on two French requests: special status for settlers and separate sovereignty of the oil- and gas-rich Sahara. Eventually the French yielded on both, signing an accord on March 18, 1962, ending hostilities and agreeing to independence. French voters approved the accords in April, as did 99.7 percent of Algerians on July 1, 1962. Independence became official on July 5, 1962.

Impact of Event

The Algerian struggle for independence produced important global as well as national consequences. For Algerians, the war had proved tragically costly: 1 million dead, 2 million in regroupment camps, 300,000 refugees in neighboring Morocco, Tunisia, and Libya, and 150,000 persons in detention camps. The immediate transition from revolution to the socialist development sought by the FLN was fraught with problems that precluded any immediate improvement in living standards: devastation of agriculture, a shortage of capital, and especially the flight of 90 percent of the Europeans. The latter left Algeria without doctors for victims of the last bombs and without typists, civil servants, or secretaries. On Independence Day, the Oran telephone exchange had one operator doing the job of two hundred. Factories, farms, offices, and transport facilities were destroyed by departing settlers. Close to 70 percent of the work force faced unemployment. A new Algerian bureaucracy tried for months to restore basic public services. The state limped along with foreign loans.

An internal power struggle ensued, eliminating much of the early FLN leadership from power and slowing reconstruction. A few fortunate Algerians claimed abandoned property—houses, apartments, and farms—as their own. Workers' self-management of factories quickly became a grass-roots effort recognized by the state in 1963. Workers elected managers who directed production and marketing. In the March (1963) Decrees, President Ben Bella declared all property previously operated by Europeans vacant, legalizing state confiscation. State ownership of agriculture, industry, mining, transport, utilities, banks, and retail stores laid the basis for Algerian socialism. Gradually, public enterprises were organized into state corporations that participated in every aspect of the country's life. Agriculture, however, languished, and farmers suffered from a lack of machinery, seeds, and credit because of bureaucratic mismanagement.

Algeria's 1963 constitution declared the state to be an integral part of the Maghrib, the Arab World, and Africa. Freedom of religion was guaranteed, but Islam became the state religion and Arabic the official language. Education became a top priority, and enrollments jumped from 750,000 in 1963 to 1.5 million in 1967 and to 3 million by 1975. Girls remained about one-fourth of all students. Public health gradually improved, and so by 1974 a system of free national health was available to all. Social welfare was extended to all Algerians, including farmers. Housing shortages continued after independence, fueled by high population growth and capital shortages.

The Algerian constitution of 1963 outlawed torture but not detention, and Article 12 specified that "both sexes shared the same rights and duties," although women's rights have not been implemented in law or custom. Article 24 invested power in a sole party, the FLN, which in turn controlled the action of the national assembly. The president, nominated by the party, was elected by universal suffrage to a five-year term, but Ben Bella was ousted in June, 1965, in a bloodless coup led by Colonel Houari Boumedienne, thereby negating popular choice. Political freedom in the form of a multiparty system was not produced.

The costs of the Algerian War (1954-1962)—$1 billion annually and one-half million soldiers—mobilized French public opinion against maintaining an empire. Indeed, France succumbed to Moroccan and Tunisian independence in 1956 and granted independence to nearly all of its African colonies by 1961. A new Arab-world unity and Third World politics also emerged from the Algerian struggle, which new Third World nonaligned states supported.

The Algerian people had finally achieved three long-sought goals: independence, citizenship, and validation of an Algerian Arab Muslim identity. Moreover, access to education, civil service, medicine, and other services was opened to all. Full political choice and a higher standard of living proved more elusive. Like all cultures and economies emerging from colonial domination, Algeria faced tremendous obstacles and challenges en route to political and economic democracy. After three decades of state capitalist industrialization and a decade of political liberalization, the search for a better future continued.

Bibliography

Abun-Nasr, Jamil M. *A History of the Maghrib.* New York: Cambridge University Press, 1975. A complete history of North Africa, including Algeria. Useful as an in-depth examination, from a Maghribi viewpoint, of the historical evolution of Algeria and its brutal colonial experience. Thorough bibliography.

Aroian, Lois, and Richard P. Mitchell. *The Modern Middle East and North Africa.* New York: Macmillan, 1984. A standard, readily available text. This work contextualizes the Algerian struggle for those seeking to understand it as part of the Arab world's modern history. Adequate reference and index sections.

Barakat, Halim, ed. *Contemporary North Africa: Issues of Development and Integration.* London: Croom Helm, 1985. A useful anthology for evaluating the lingering political and economic problems of colonialism in Algeria and the Maghrib. Especially good on U.S.-Maghribi relations, but poorly referenced.

Entelis, John P. *Algeria: The Revolution Institutionalized.* Boulder, Colo.: Westview Press, 1984. A critical study of independent Algeria under FLN rule, this contains descriptive analysis of the political culture and the difficulties of industrialization in a postcolonial economy.

Horne, Alistair. *A Savage War of Peace: Algeria, 1954-1962.* New York: Viking Press, 1978. An eminently readable and dramatic account of the Algerian war for independence. Useful for its thoroughness and richness in detail. Especially graphic about French, FLN, and OAS violence. Well referenced and indexed.

Ottaway, David, and Marina Ottaway. *Algeria: The Politics of a Socialist Revolution.* Berkeley: University of California Press, 1970. A somewhat sympathetic examination of the first eight years of FLN rule and the effort to create socialist development. Helpful for understanding Algerian "state capitalism/Arab socialism."

Quandt, William B. *Revolution and Political Leadership in Algeria, 1954-1968.* Cambridge, Mass.: MIT Press, 1969. A critical study of Algerian political leadership which traces the evolution of political thinking among liberals, radicals, and revolutionaries. Contains an excellent reference list and analysis of the postwar political conflict between intellectuals and the military.

Kathleen K. O'Mara

Cross-References

The Atlantic Charter Declares a Postwar Right of Self-Determination (1941), p. 584; The French Quell an Algerian Nationalist Revolt (1945), p. 651; The Nationalist Vietnamese Fight Against French Control of Indochina (1946), p. 683; India Gains Independence (1947), p. 731; Riots Erupt as Katanga Province Secedes from the Congo (1960), p. 1068; The United Nations Intervenes in the Congolese Civil War (1960), p. 1074; Cyprus Gains Independence (1960), p. 1084; Amnesty International Is Founded (1961), p. 1119; The Nonaligned Movement Meets (1961), p. 1131; The European Social Charter Is Signed (1961), p. 1137; The Organization of African Unity Is Founded (1963), p. 1194; Zimbabwe's Freedom Fighters Topple White Supremacist Government (1964), p. 1224; Leftists Rebel in France (1968), p. 1425.

CHÁVEZ FORMS FARM WORKERS' UNION AND LEADS GRAPE PICKERS' STRIKE

Category of event: Workers' rights
Time: September 30, 1962
Locale: Fresno, California

The National Farm Workers Association (NFWA) was a predecessor to the United Farm Workers of America (UFW), the first permanent agricultural workers' union in the United States

Principal personages:
CÉSAR CHÁVEZ (1927-   ), the charismatic, nonviolent leader of the United Farm Workers of America
DOLORES HUERTA (1930-   ), a cofounder and vice president of the United Farm Workers of America
ERNESTO GALARZA (1905-1984), a farm worker, labor organizer, scholar, teacher, and civic leader
EUGENE NELSON (1930-   ), a free-lance writer and son of a Modesto grape rancher; helped organize farm workers in California and Texas

Summary of Event

Throughout the twentieth century farm workers have struggled to organize themselves against a politico-agribusiness complex that has been rather successful at resisting them. Only since the mid-1960's have working conditions for farm workers begun to improve substantially. Improvements in income and working conditions are direct results of the termination of the bracero program as well as the struggles for union recognition and collective bargaining by the United Farm Workers of America (UFW) and its organizational predecessors, the National Farm Workers Association (NFWA) and the United Farm Workers Organizing Committee (UFWOC).

The September, 1962, founding of the NFWA in Fresno, California, by César Chávez, Dolores Huerta, and others signaled a new era in the efforts by farm workers to unionize and bargain collectively with their employers, mostly large agricultural growers. In 1966, Chicanos and *Mexicanos* in the NFWA and Filipino farm workers in the Agricultural Workers Organizing Committee (AWOC), an affiliate of the American Federation of Labor-Congress of Industrial Organizations (AFL-CIO), merged organizations to form the UFWOC. In February of 1972, the UFWOC became a full-fledged affiliate of the AFL-CIO and formed the UFW. In 1975, struggles by the UFW culminated in the passage of the Agricultural Labor Relations Act (ALRA) by the California legislature.

Led by César Chávez and Dolores Huerta, the NFWA brought years of community organizing experience to bear on the problems of farm workers. These problems included economic hardship, general powerlessness against employers, and the lack of adequate facilities in the fields. The NFWA was established as an independent, service-oriented, Chicano farm workers' labor organization that provided credit, burial, and other family services. It sought to organize farm workers one by one.

Prior to the 1960's one important factor hindering the unionization of farm workers was the bracero program, which was established under the Emergency Labor Program of 1942 to ease the labor shortage brought on by World War II. The bracero program supervised the recruitment of Mexican nationals to meet U.S. growers' demands for labor. It was continued by Public Law 78 after the end of World War II and was maintained until 1963, when PL 78 expired. During the 1950's, Mexican braceros greatly influenced the unionization of U.S. farm workers. By serving as alternate sources of cheap labor, they often were used as strikebreakers by growers.

In 1947, the newly founded National Farm Labor Union (NFLU) led a strike against the powerful Di Giorgio Fruit Corporation at Arvin, California. The union demanded an increase in wages, seniority rights, grievance procedures, and recognition of the union as sole bargaining agent. Robert Di Giorgio refused the demands and launched an assault on the NFLU. He used braceros as strikebreakers and manipulated both the press and politicians in his favor. The U.S. Senate Committee on Un-American Activities set upon investigating the union. In 1949, a special subcommittee of the House of Representatives' Education and Labor Committee held hearings on the Di Giorgio strike. The committee supported the growers and Di Giorgio won the strike.

This particular strike taught Ernesto Galarza, one of the strike leaders, an important lesson in the struggle between farm workers and growers. In his view, farm workers could not be organized until growers' access to exploitable immigrant labor groups was halted. Braceros, as international migrant workers, were more exploitable than American workers. If they tried to organize, they were labeled as communists and deported. Those braceros seen by growers as causing unrest among farm workers were often reported to the Immigration Service, the Department of Labor, and the Department of Justice, each of which would investigate the "leaders" for violations of U.S. laws. Consequently, during the 1950's, there was not a single strike by braceros, although the NFLU continued to organize strikes among other farm workers. In 1960, when the NFLU surrendered its charter, the Agricultural Workers Organizing Committee (AWOC) replaced it. The AWOC was the AFL-CIO's new organizational effort to organize farm workers.

The AWOC, with the aid of the United Packinghouse Workers (UPH), quickly initiated farm workers' strikes in the lettuce fields of the Imperial Valley in California. The AWOC-UPH effort was based on the enforcement of federal regulations that prohibited the use of braceros on ranches where there were strikes. Although these initial strikes were successful, competition from the International Brotherhood of Teamsters led to the demise of the AWOC-UPH effort. In the period following these strikes, AWOC membership declined as a result of disillusionment, leaving only a group of Filipino agricultural workers as members.

By 1962, the year the NFWA was founded, economic conditions for farm workers had worsened as a result of increased mechanization on farms and the continued negative impact of the bracero program on unionization efforts. In 1965, farm workers in Tulare County, California, lived in dilapidated labor camps condemned by the Tulare Housing Authority. The labor camps had been built by the U.S. Farm Security Administration near the end of the Great Depression to provide temporary shelters for Dust Bowl migrants. Condemnation led to rent increases meant to yield the necessary revenue to build new housing. Late in the summer of 1965, the NFWA led rent strikes among farm workers.

The rent strike at Woodville, one of the labor camps, evolved into an employment strike at the nearby J. D. Martin Ranch. Strikers complained about low pay, the lack of toilets in the fields, and a peeping crew boss. The strike failed. Within two weeks, however, the NFWA became involved in a strike for higher wages initiated by the Filipino membership of the AWOC local at Delano. On September 16, 1965, the NFWA formally joined the Delano Grape Strike. Four days later NFWA picket leaders asked farm workers to walk off the fields. The AWOC-NFWA strike spread throughout the Delano-Earlimart-McFarland area, affecting approximately thirty ranches and involving several hundred farm workers.

Hundreds of college students, civil rights workers, and religious groups joined the farm workers within days of the onset of the strike. Civil rights organizations quickly sent members of their staff to help with the strike. In October, under the charismatic leadership of César Chávez, the NFWA launched a grape boycott. Supporters quickly started picketing stores and piers throughout California. In response, growers began to bully picketers, often in the presence of law enforcement officials who did nothing to stop them. Growers also resorted to spraying sulfur near the picket lines. The strike continued to gain momentum, and within two weeks nearly four thousand farm workers were out of the fields. Many growers were not economically hurt because they were able to import workers from neighboring cities who were willing to cross picket lines to work. Strike leaders began to spread word of the strike to farm workers in neighboring areas.

In March, 1966, the U.S. Senate Subcommittee on Migratory Labor conducted public hearings in Delano and other nearby cities. At the Delano hearings, Senator Robert F. Kennedy, a member of the subcommittee, reminded the local sheriff to brush up on the rights of all people, including farm workers. In 1966, some growers slowly began to settle with the strikers; others continued to hold out, turning instead to the International Brotherhood of Teamsters Union for "sweetheart contracts." The strike continued through the years 1966 and 1967. In 1968, the union, now called the United Farm Workers Organizing Committee (UFWOC), extended its boycott to include every California grower of table grapes. Slowly, more individual growers agreed to recognize the union, but many powerful others continued to hold out.

Finally, in July of 1970, UFWOC scored the largest victory in the history of farm-labor organizing when several of the most powerful growers agreed to the union's demands, thereby officially ending the strike. Several other victories by the UFWOC followed during the next several months. Farm workers had finally achieved union recognition among growers and begun to participate in the collective bargaining process. Conflict with the Teamsters, however, continued to thwart the union, which had again changed its name and was known as the United Farm Workers of America (UFW). In 1975, the UFW was instrumental in the passage of the Agricultural Labor Relations Act (ALRA) in California. The ALRA brought some order to the rivalry between the UFW and the Teamsters.

Impact of Event

The major consequences stemming from the founding of the National Farm Workers Association in 1962 were the eventual establishment of a permanent farm workers' labor union and passage of the ALRA in California. The farm workers forced growers to recognize their union and to agree to collective bargaining. This meant improvements in wages and working conditions for farm workers. The ALRA eliminated "sweetheart contracts," permitted union organizers on the property of employers, and established a California Agricultural Labor Relations Board that, among other things, conducted elections, determined bargaining units, and investigated unfair labor practices. The ALRA also prohibited secondary boycotts, which stop the delivery of goods from primary employers (growers) to secondary employers (retail stores), but permitted unions to organize consumer boycotts by discouraging the public from trading with stores. Within a few months of the passage of the ALRA, over four hundred union representation elections were held.

Mexican immigrants, Chicanos, and other poor groups have provided a steady supply of cheap labor to agribusiness, especially in the Southwest. In order to maintain access to cheap labor and to thwart unionization efforts, growers have generally been highly supportive of unrestricted immigration from Mexico. Efforts by farm workers to organize unions and bargain collectively have been brutally suppressed by growers, who often have had local criminal justice systems and federal immigration agencies on their side during periods of labor disputes. Growers' use of sheriffs, police officers, judges, strikebreakers, and private armies against farm workers were common. Indeed, the U.S. government itself, through the bracero program, was a "labor contractor" for growers.

The NFWA brought the plight of the farm workers to the forefront of America's conscience and highlighted the suffering and indignities farm workers were forced to endure. It also marked the inception of the farm workers' first permanent, broad-based organization. Chicano and Filipino farm workers, long neglected by labor legislation and traditional trade unions, organized their own independent labor union and assumed their rights to organize and bargain collectively with their employers. The Delano Grape Strike, begun in September of 1965, propelled César Chávez and the NFWA to the front of the civil and labor rights struggles.

Chávez turned the strike into a crusade by promoting the view that farm workers are human beings who deserve respect and a living wage. In 1968, he fasted for twenty-five days in order to gain support for the farm workers' struggle. He ended the fast by "breaking bread" with Senator Robert Kennedy, then a candidate for the U.S. presidency. Chávez's nonviolent approach and charismatic qualities brought dignity and strength to the farm workers and greatly influenced the consciousness of Americans. Through use of the consumer boycott, farm workers were able to involve the American public in their struggle for human and union recognition. As a result, Americans "discovered" the farm workers, who through their own efforts affirmed and reclaimed their humanity. Their struggles have not ended, however. Pro-grower politicians and bureaucrats regularly pose problems, and widespread use of toxic pesticides by growers continues to affect the health and well-being of farm workers.

Bibliography

Acuña, Rodolfo. *Occupied America: A History of Chicanos.* 3d ed. New York: Harper & Row, 1988. This text provides a general history of Chicanos. It includes detailed sections on Chicano agricultural labor organizing, tracing Chicano labor struggles to the turn of the century. It also details labor struggles in other sectors of the economy. The book is well referenced and has an excellent index.

Dunne, John Gregory. *Delano.* Rev. ed. New York: Farrar, Straus & Giroux, 1971. This book provides an extensively detailed description of the events leading up to the formation of the United Farm Workers of America. It also describes the union's organizing efforts during the 1960's. The book includes a section of photographs of the strike but no index.

Galarza, Ernesto. *Merchants of Labor: The Mexican Bracero Story.* Charolette, Calif.: McNally & Loftin, 1964. This book provides an excellent historical analysis of the bracero program from its inception up to 1960. Examines the structure of control affecting the lives of Mexican nationals and American agricultural workers in the fields. Contains some photographs, references, and index.

Kushner, Sam. *Long Road to Delano.* New York: International Publishers, 1975. Provides a class analysis of the development of agribusiness in California. It describes farm workers' working conditions and their struggles against exploitation. There is a chapter on the organizing efforts of the Communist Party in the 1930's among farm workers. The foreword is by Bert Corona, a major Chicano community leader since the 1940's. No index.

Nelson, Eugene. *Huelga: The First Hundred Days of the Great Delano Grape Strike.* Delano, Calif.: Farm Worker Press, 1966. This short book provides an account of the events that led up to the Delano Grape Strike and details the activities up to December, 1965. Written by one of the organizers of the strike, the book captures the mood and views of the farm workers. Contains several photographs, including some of law enforcement officials and strikebreakers. No index.

Taylor, Ronald B. *Chávez and the Farm Workers: A Study in the Acquisition and Use of Power.* Boston: Beacon Press, 1975. Provides a sympathetic description of the Chávez-led farm workers' struggles during the 1960's and early 1970's. In particular, the book details some of the struggles the farm workers had with the Teamsters union. Contains some photographs, including one of Chávez and Kennedy. Includes an excellent index.

Rubén O. Martinez

Cross-References

"Palmer Raids" Lead to Arrests and Deportations of Immigrants (1919), p. 258; Steel Workers Go on Strike to Demand Improved Working Conditions (1919), p. 293; Congress Establishes a Border Patrol (1924), p. 377; The Wagner Act Requires Employers to Accept Collective Bargaining (1935), p. 508; Zoot-Suit Riots Exemplify Ethnic Tensions in Los Angeles (1943), p. 624; The Civil Rights Act of 1957 Creates the Commission on Civil Rights (1957), p. 997; Three Civil Rights Workers Are Murdered (1964), p. 1246; Congress Passes the Civil Rights Act (1964), p. 1251; Congress Enacts the Bilingual Education Act (1968), p. 1402; Chávez Is Jailed for Organizing an Illegal Lettuce Boycott (1970), p. 1567.

MEREDITH'S ENROLLMENT INTEGRATES THE UNIVERSITY OF MISSISSIPPI

Categories of event: Racial and ethnic rights; educational rights
Time: October 1, 1962
Locale: Oxford, Mississippi

Following a fifteen-month legal battle, James Meredith, under the protection of federal troops, became the first black to attend a white university in Mississippi

Principal personages:
> JAMES MEREDITH (1933-   ), a native of Mississippi, grandson of a slave, and Air Force veteran; would later become an important civil rights figure
> Ross R. BARNETT (1898-1987), the governor of Mississippi, a staunch segregationist
> JOHN F. KENNEDY (1917-1963), the thirty-fifth president of the United States (1961-1963)
> ROBERT F. KENNEDY (1925-1968), the attorney general of the United States, brother and close adviser of the president
> HUGO L. BLACK (1886-1971), a United States Supreme Court justice
> CONSTANCE B. MOTLEY (1921-   ), an attorney for the National Association for the Advancement of Colored People (NAACP) Legal Defense Fund.

Summary of Event

Desegregation became a national imperative after the 1954 United States Supreme Court decision in *Brown v. Board of Education.* In its decision, the Supreme Court declared that racial segregation was a violation of the Fourteenth Amendment's requirement of "equal protection of the law." The court's decision, however, had an immediate effect only on those districts that were parties to the cases decided in *Brown.* When other schools or universities did not voluntarily desegregate, individual court suits were required. Noncompliance was the norm throughout the South.

In January, 1961, James Meredith, an African American, applied for admission to the all-white University of Mississippi, challenging the state to comply with the seven-year-old court ruling. Mississippi had by law established separate schools for blacks and whites. Black institutions, which were poorly funded, generally could not give students the same educational opportunities as those provided at white institutions. Without changing the educational system, blacks had little hope of competing equally with whites. Saying he had long "felt a personal responsibility to change the status" of black Americans, Meredith had been waiting for the appropriate time to attempt a change. Events surrounding desegregation in other states, such as the use of federal troops in 1957 to enforce court-ordered integration in Little Rock, Arkansas, led Meredith to believe that he would need the support of the federal government. In 1960, John F. Kennedy, an advocate of civil rights, was elected president of the United States. Meredith, hoping for assistance from the Kennedy administration, believed that the time was right for change. He was also ready personally. A nine-year veteran of the Air Force, he was a student at Jackson State College, a black institution.

Meredith knew his application for admission to the University of Mississippi would create numerous problems. The racist attitude prevalent among white supremacists and segregationists made it dangerous for blacks to attempt to challenge the white community. For example, Clyde Kennard, a black man who had attempted to enroll at the University of Southern Mississippi in 1959, was sentenced to seven years in prison as an accessory in the supposed theft of twenty-five dollars worth of chicken feed. In order to protect himself and his family, Meredith wrote to the National Association for the Advancement of Colored People (NAACP) and the United States Justice Department, notifying them that he had made application to the University of Mississippi.

The first communication Meredith received from the university was positive. When Meredith informed the registrar that he was black, however, he received a telegram notifying him that registration for the semester was closed. Meredith, undaunted, applied for admission for the summer session, which was to begin on June 8, 1961. Word of Meredith's challenge to the status quo made him and his family targets for harassment. Neighbors were questioned, and local police trailed Meredith, hoping for an excuse to arrest him. Warnings of the dire consequences of racial mixing fueled the indignation of those opposed to integration.

On May 25, 1961, Meredith received notification that he had been denied admission to the university. By this time, the NAACP's Legal Defense Fund had assigned Constance B. Motley to the case. Meredith had accumulated ninety hours of college course work and was a fully qualified applicant. Motley swiftly filed a civil suit on behalf of Meredith, hoping for legal action which would allow Meredith to attend the term beginning in June. The court, however, upheld the decision of university officials.

The appeals process cost Meredith another year. On June 25, 1962, the United States Fifth Circuit Court of Appeals ruled that Meredith should be admitted to the University of Mississippi. The state of Mississippi, however, did not give up easily. Through a variety of legal maneuvers, the case ended up in the United States Supreme Court. Justice Hugo L. Black, after consultation with other members of the Supreme Court, upheld the ruling of the Court of Appeals. Upon hearing the decision of the high court, Ross R. Barnett, governor of Mississippi, issued a proclamation. Claiming state sovereignty in matters of public education, Barnett directed university officials to defy the orders of the Supreme Court. Eager to find another means of stopping Meredith, the state of Mississippi charged him with the crime of moral turpitude. Calling a special session of the legislature, the governor obtained passage of a bill on September 20, 1962, the very day Meredith was to register, denying admission to institutions of higher learning to anyone charged with such a crime. The governor was then declared registrar of the University of Mississippi, and Meredith was warned that he would be arrested when he appeared to register.

The actions of the governor did little to calm those opposed to integration. In Oxford, home of the university, several thousand angry people awaited the arrival of Meredith. Newspapers across the state had encouraged citizens to support the governor as Mississippians literally prepared to fight another Civil War.

In Washington, D.C., President John F. Kennedy had been closely monitoring events. Although reluctant to use federal troops, Kennedy was nevertheless prepared to do so if the situation worsened. The attorney general, Robert Kennedy, was no less determined than the president: Meredith would be admitted to the university. Hearing of the unrest and plans to arrest Meredith, Robert Kennedy telephoned Barnett. The governor agreed not to arrest Meredith but refused to allow him to register.

The scenario of Meredith appearing to register and being turned away was repeated three times. Before Meredith reached the university on September 27, his fourth attempt, a nervous Barnett asked the federal government to call it off. The crowds gathered at the university had become uncontrollable. Meredith and his federal escorts returned to Memphis, their temporary base.

A show of force by the federal government appeared to be the only solution. On September 30, President Kennedy issued an executive order authorizing the secretary of defense to call in the military in order to enforce justice in Mississippi. That same evening, hundreds of United States marshals, Mississippi National Guards and members of the regular military lined the front of the administration building. As crowds began to gather, James Meredith was quietly installed, unseen, in a dormitory. As Meredith studied and slept, a riot that left two dead and hundreds injured raged on the university campus.

At 8:00 A.M. the following day, Meredith was registered as a student at the University of Mississippi. At 9:00 A.M., with tear gas still hanging in the air, he attended his first class.

Impact of Event

James Meredith had been victorious, but the costs were great. More than twenty-five thousand federal troops had been needed to allow his enrollment. As a student at the University of Mississippi, Meredith was constantly accompanied by federal escorts. Five hundred troops were maintained at the university to ensure his safety. The university suffered as well. In the aftermath of the riot, forty professors resigned, and many students left to pursue degrees elsewhere.

In June, 1963, Cleve McDowell became the first black to be admitted to the law school at the university. McDowell was intimidated by the fact that the troops on campus to protect Meredith would be leaving in August and asked permission to carry a gun. His request denied, McDowell nevertheless carried the weapon. Late for class one day, he dropped the gun and was summarily dismissed from the university.

When Meredith was graduated in August, 1963, two lives had been lost, and the federal government had spent nearly $5 million. The fall of 1964, however, saw two black students enroll at the University of Mississippi with little fanfare.

The Civil Rights Act of 1964 further encouraged integration. Under Title VI of this act, federal aid would be denied to any public institution discriminating against students on the basis of race. By January, 1966, all but one of the public institutions of higher learning in Mississippi had signed an agreement to comply with the stipulations of Title VI. Desegregation formally had become accepted.

James Meredith continued his struggle to achieve equal opportunity for blacks. While leading a march to encourage blacks to register to vote in June, 1967, Meredith was shot twice in the back but survived. Aubrey Norvell, Meredith's assailant, spent eighteen months in jail for his crime.

In 1982, Meredith returned to the University of Mississippi to commemorate twenty years of integration. That same year, the university elected its first black cheerleader, who also provoked controversy by refusing to carry the Confederate flag, a long-standing symbol of the institution. In an effort to compromise, university officials agreed to break with tradition. Only one cheerleader, not all, would carry the flag. The Ku Klux Klan responded with a protest march through Oxford, carrying Confederate flags. There had been many changes in Mississippi, but Meredith was reluctant to comment on how much of it could be called progress. James Meredith's views also evolved. In 1989, at odds with the Civil Rights movement, he became a staff assistant to archconservative United States Senator Jesse Helms.

Bibliography

Lord, Walter. *The Past That Would Not Die.* New York: Harper & Row, 1965. This intriguing text reads more like a novel than a work of historical fact. The author does an excellent job of explaining the historical background that proved fertile ground for the Meredith incident. Complete with index and guide to source material relevant to the Meredith case.

Meredith, James. *Three Years in Mississippi.* Bloomington: Indiana University Press, 1966. A definitive account of events surrounding Meredith's enrollment and his subsequent education at the University of Mississippi. An objective, insightful retelling of his experiences. Allows the reader to understand Meredith's goals, courage, and intelligence. Includes documentation and letters.

Miller, Norman, and Marilynn B. Brewer, eds. *Groups in Contact: The Psychology of Desegregation.* Orlando, Fla.: Academic Press, 1984. This compilation of empirically based studies of desegregation is useful for students in the social sciences concerned with the implications of race relations. Although quite statistical in orientation, the text provides insight into the psychological effects of desegregation. Includes charts, graphs, bibliography, and index.

Preer, Jean L. *Lawyers v. Educators: Black Colleges and Desegregation in Public Higher Education.* Westport, Conn.: Greenwood Press, 1982. Especially useful for students of law and policy, this text examines the legal background and contemporary legal issues surrounding desegregation. Contains list of cases and statutes, index, and bibliography.

Silver, James W. *Mississippi: The Closed Society.* New York: Harcourt, Brace & World, 1964. Written by a professor at the University of Mississippi during the Meredith incident, the book provides a detailed look into the racist environment of Mississippi in the 1960's. Supplements Meredith's work with a perspective from inside the university. Includes index.

United States Commission on Civil Rights. *Justice in Jackson, Mississippi.* New York: Arno Press, 1971. A good introduction for the general reader not familiar with the intensity and immediacy of the Civil Rights movement of the 1960's. The direct testimony provides a dialogue which is educational and insightful as to the mood in the South during this era. Extensive appendix and index.

Wiggins, Samuel P. *The Desegregation Era in Higher Education.* Berkeley, Calif.: McCutchan, 1966. A product of studies conducted at Southern universities during the most active stages of desegregation from 1954 to 1966. Although the data are somewhat old, the information is useful for comparison with present-day situations and for explaining the impact of desegregation on university policy and students. Contains charts, graphs, and notes.

Laurie Voice
Robert E. Biles

Cross-References

Japan Protests Segregation of Japanese in California Schools (1906), p. 81; The Congress of Racial Equality Forms (1942), p. 601; CORE Stages a Sit-in in Chicago to Protest Segregation (1943), p. 618; *Brown v. Board of Education* Ends Public School Segregation (1954), p. 913; Eisenhower Sends Troops to Little Rock, Arkansas (1957), p. 1003; Greensboro Sit-ins Launch a New Stage in the Civil Rights Movement (1960), p. 1056; The United Nations Issues a Declaration on Racial Discrimination (1963), p. 1212; Congress Passes the Civil Rights Act (1964), p. 1251; The Civil Rights Act of 1968 Outlaws Discrimination in Housing (1968), p. 1414; The Supreme Court Endorses Busing as a Means to End Segregation (1971), p. 1628; The Supreme Court Rejects Racial Quotas in College Admissions (1973), p. 1697; Southern Schools Are Found to Be the Least Racially Segregated (1975), p. 1786.

1172

THE EQUAL PAY ACT BECOMES LAW

Categories of event: Workers' rights and women's rights
Time: 1963
Locale: Washington, D.C.

After several legislative attempts, the Equal Pay Act was passed in an attempt to end wage discrimination against women

   Principal personages:
      JOHN F. KENNEDY (1917-1963), the United States president (1961-1963) who signed the Equal Pay Act
      EDITH GREEN (1910-1987), the Democratic representative from Oregon who championed and authored the act
      WAYNE LYMAN MORSE (1900-1974), the Republican senator from Oregon who cosponsored a similar measure in 1946
      CLAUDE PEPPER (1900-1989), the representative from Florida who co-sponsored a similar measure in 1946

Summary of Event

The legislative struggle that resulted in the 1963 Equal Pay Act began in the United States after World War II. During the war, with male labor in short supply, women were in demand in the labor market. When the veterans returned, however, a protective attitude toward female workers returned with them. Both legislative and judicial opinions tended to allow discrimination against women in the labor market, on the grounds that their unique function in society was to bear children. Even in cases involving single women or in which no children were involved, this special attitude remained, resulting in a body of state and federal laws referred to as protective legislation. State laws, for example, set minimum-wage and maximum-hour laws for women and barred women from jobs that might harm them—those that required lifting weights, for example, or those that might place them in moral jeopardy, such as bartending. Even when they could work, women were not paid the same wages as men for their labor because they were perceived to be weak and dependent.

The battle to gain rights for women in the workplace equal to the rights of men began before World War II and has continued into the early 1990's. The specific legislative fight at the federal level to gain equal wages for equal work took about seventeen years. By the mid-1960's, 36 percent of the American labor force was female, adding a certain urgency to the matter.

As with any piece of legislation, many groups were involved in the formulation, advocacy, proposal, and final passage of the Equal Pay Act. Organized labor was in favor of such a bill, which would prevent employers from lowering the wage scales in general by hiring lower-paid female workers. Several women's groups were in favor of the bill, including the American Association of University Women, the

National Council of Catholic Women, the National Council of Jewish Women, and the National Federation of Business and Professional Women's Clubs. As early as 1946, two members of Congress, Senator Wayne Lyman Morse of Oregon and Representative (later Senator) Claude Pepper of Florida, unsuccessfully sponsored an equal pay for women act. Several subsequent attempts were made to pass a similar equal pay bill, but they also failed. Business organizations, such as the National Association of Manufacturers and the Chamber of Commerce of the United States, opposed such bills. While agreeing that the principle was good, they objected to the intrusion of federal agents into private business. Not until 1963, with the support of President John F. Kennedy, did such an act finally pass. One of the most powerful women in Congress in those days, Edith Green, was instrumental in authoring and championing this major victory for women's economic rights.

The Equal Pay Act was intended to ensure that women would get paid the same wages as men for equal work. It was carefully written to raise women's wages, not to lower men's. Salesclerks in department stores, for example, had to be paid the same wages no matter what kind of merchandise they were assigned to sell. Bank tellers, lab technicians, inspectors, machine operators, nurse's aides, and orderlies were some of the other workers covered by the act, as males and females performed essentially the same tasks in their work. Exceptions to the law were acknowledged: In cases of seniority or merit, in systems measuring earnings by production, or when differences in pay were based on factors other than sex, wages could be different.

Women filing suit under the Equal Pay Act could win up to two years of the wages they would have earned had they been paid equally with men. Discriminating employers could also be required to pay that same amount again as punishment, in addition to reimbursing successful claimants for the costs of hiring an attorney and court charges.

Unfortunately, the act contained loopholes. One phrase from the act, for example, referred to men and women working in the same "establishment," interpreted to mean the same physical space, such as the same building or the same location. Employers wishing to circumvent the act could move female workers to another building separate from male workers and continue to pay the women less. The stickiest point in the act is the definition of "equal work." The Equal Pay Act stipulated that the jobs of men and women must require equal skill, equal effort, and equal responsibility, each factor to be examined separately, for the jobs to be covered by the act. There was no provision that women must have access to the same jobs as men. As an American Civil Liberties Union handbook on women's rights in the early 1970's pointed out, an employer could give assembly-line work only to men and clerical work only to women and then pay the men twice as much without violating the Equal Pay Act.

In subsequent years, several other actions bolstered the rights of female workers. In 1964, the Civil Rights Act was passed. At first, this major piece of legislation, which in part prohibited employment discrimination on the basis on race, color, religion, or national origin, did not include protection for women. Accounts of the

political maneuvering suggest that the Southern congressman who proposed including the word "sex" as a joke, Howard Smith of Virginia, intended to torpedo the
entire piece of legislation. It passed, however, and its broader language helped close
some of the loopholes of the Equal Pay Act and further advance the rights of female
workers. Title VII of the Civil Rights Act did not allow employers to deny jobs to
women because of their sex. Thus it became illegal to manipulate jobs so that women
would be excluded from those with higher pay. The Equal Employment Opportunity
Commission (EEOC) was created to enforce this new employment right.

Two executive orders (presidential orders to the executive branch of government
requiring certain actions) helped in the battle to stop employment discrimination
against women. President Lyndon B. Johnson issued Executive Order 11246, requiring that employers contracting for work with the federal government not discriminate
on the basis of race. Executive Order 11375, which became effective in October, 1968,
added a prohibition against sex discrimination to the previous order. The two together are generally referred to as the Equal Employment Opportunity (EEO) Clause.
President Richard Nixon later issued Executive Order 11478, forbidding the federal
government itself from discriminating. The Equal Employment Opportunity Act of
1972 empowered the EEOC to bring charges, thus adding more bite to the legislative
will.

Impact of Event

The immediate impact of the 1963 Equal Pay Act was salutary. Many women
reported instances of wage discrimination to the Wage Standards Division of the
Department of Labor, which was charged with looking into violations. According to
one source, in the first decade that the act was in force, from June 10, 1963, to June
30, 1973, the department found that 142,600 workers, overwhelmingly women, were
owed $65.6 million. Because it had the power to file suits against employers and
because its employees could visit sites to investigate compliance with the act, the
Department of Labor was able to resolve more than 95 percent of complaints through
voluntary compliance, although it also brought suit against recalcitrant employers.
The act was a firm and much-needed step in the direction of attaining equality for
women in the workplace. The vigorous efforts of the Department of Labor made it,
for a while, an effective one.

On the other hand, the limited and specific legislative victory symbolized by this
act also had to be pursued vigorously in court for it to be enforced in practice.
Because it contained so many loopholes and because it attacked a narrowly defined
type of wage discrimination, the Equal Pay Act helped female workers in only a
limited way. It took an amendment in July, 1972, for example, to extend its protection to executive, administrative, and professional workers.

The Equal Pay Act proves how long it can take between passage of even a well-
intentioned bill through Congress and the actual improvement of the lives of the
citizens it is intended to help. Some scholars on the state of employment discrimination against women have noted that although the Equal Pay Act was extremely nar-

row in what it covered, the efforts of the Department of Labor proved productive in enforcing its provisions. Title VII of the Civil Rights Act of 1964 was much broader and potentially much more effective in improving the employment situation for women, but the EEOC, which took over enforcement in 1979, seems not to have been as effective as was the Department of Labor.

The difference between the two acts is instructive. The Equal Pay Act was in some ways easier to enforce because wage discrimination is often blatant. Wages, as numbers, are easy to spot. Other forms of discrimination are much harder to detect, let alone prove, and the more highly skilled the employment opportunity (with proportionally higher financial stakes), the harder it is to prove discriminatory practices.

In conjunction with the 1964 Civil Rights Act and its broader language, and with the moral support given by the executive orders of President Johnson, the Equal Pay Act must be viewed as a major victory for the human rights of female workers. If nothing else, its long legislative history showed the emerging national will, expressed through the executive and legislative branches of government, to attack long-standing inequitable attitudes toward women in the workplace.

Bibliography

Babcock, Barbara Allen, et al. *Sex Discrimination and the Law: Causes and Remedies.* Boston: Little, Brown, 1975. A hefty volume intended as a law school text. Authored by a law professor, two attorneys, and the chair of the Commission on Human Rights. Includes many cases, statutory materials, popular magazine articles, and notes, as well as historical, economic, and sociological information. Excellent resource for a detailed study of the Equal Pay Act and legal cases arising from it. Index.

Baer, Judith A. *The Chains of Protection: The Judicial Response to Women's Labor Legislation.* Westport, Conn.: Greenwood Press, 1978. Concentrates on aspects of labor legislation common to all states. Follows the judicial history of protective legislation from the beginning of the twentieth century to the late 1970's, with one chapter covering the Equal Pay Act and the Civil Rights Act of 1964. Bibliography, index of cases, and subject index.

Kanowitz, Leo. *Women and the Law: The Unfinished Revolution.* Albuquerque: University of New Mexico Press, 1969. A study which sets out to identify those areas of the law that discriminate on the basis of sex. This is a good introductory volume, even if dated. Particularly useful as a resource for the Equal Pay Act and Civil Rights Act of 1964. Appendices, notes, and indexes by case, subject, and author.

Kirp, David L., Mark G. Yudof, and Marlene Strong Franks. *Gender Justice.* Chicago: University of Chicago Press, 1986. Organized to deal with the question of whether the government should be asked to change society or instead change its processes so that individuals can help themselves. The first part of the book includes a historical overview and paradigms of behavior. The second part examines specific cases.

McGlen, Nancy E., and Karen O'Connor. *Women's Rights: The Struggle for Equality in the Nineteenth and Twentieth Centuries.* New York: Praeger, 1983. Approaches the topic in the context of social movement theory. Details the history of various women's rights movements in politics, economics, and the family. Analyzes the failure of the Equal Rights Amendment as symptomatic of remaining difficulties in gaining women's rights. Tables, figures, appendices, and index.

Ross, Susan D. *The Rights of Women: The Basic American Civil Liberties Union Guide to a Woman's Rights.* New York: Discus Books, 1973. A practical guide for women about their rights. Question and answer format on employment education, mass media, and a host of other issues. Although dated, it is an accessible source for understanding practical issues implicit in the Equal Pay Act. Appendix and charts.

Shakuntala Jayaswal

Cross-References

Supreme Court Disallows a Maximum Hours Law for Bakers (1905), p. 36; The Bern Conference Prohibits Night Work for Women (1906), p. 75; Massachusetts Adopts the First Minimum-Wage Law in the United States (1912), p. 126; The American Civil Liberties Union Is Founded (1920), p. 327; The Nineteenth Amendment Gives American Women the Right to Vote (1920), p. 339; Congress Passes the Civil Rights Act (1964), p. 1251; Congress Passes the Equal Employment Opportunity Act (1972), p. 1650; The Supreme Court Upholds an Affirmative-Action Program (1979), p. 2029.

SOVIET JEWS DEMAND CULTURAL
AND RELIGIOUS RIGHTS

Categories of event: Religious freedom; racial and ethnic rights
Time: 1963-1970
Locale: Union of Soviet Socialist Republics

The Jewish population of the Soviet Union became more active in demanding that the Soviet state permit religious freedom, respect minority rights, and allow free emigration

> *Principal personages:*
> LEONID BREZHNEV (1906-1982), the successor to Nikita Khrushchev
> HENRY "SCOOP" JACKSON (1912-1983), a senator with presidential ambitions
> NIKITA S. KHRUSHCHEV (1894-1971), the premier and first secretary of the Communist Party of the Soviet Union
> RICHARD M. NIXON (1913-   ), the president of the United States (1969-1974)
> ANDREI SAKHAROV (1921-1990), a leading dissident and spokesperson for human rights
> JOSEPH STALIN (1879-1953), the dictator of the Soviet Union from 1924 until 1953; a noted anti-Semite

Summary of Event

As the old Russian Empire expanded into Eastern Europe in the eighteenth and nineteenth centuries, increasing numbers of Jews fell under Russian control, with the total at one point reaching five million. Jews were subject to persecution by czarist authorities: They were confined by law to the Pale of Settlement, a strip of territory along Russia's western border; restricted from entering certain trades and professions; made subject to forcible religious conversion; forbidden to write or teach in Yiddish or Hebrew; and on occasion made the target of spontaneous or even government-sponsored pogroms (massacres and evictions). The intensity of persecution waxed and waned according to the degree of tolerance and enlightenment of the ruling czar or provincial governor. Despite decades of religious and cultural oppression aimed at their assimilation and "Russification," Jews maintained a rich religious life and vibrant cultural independence, if only in the sanctuaries of their homes and the enforced segregation of their ghetto communities.

After the March, 1917, revolution and the fall of Czar Nicholas II, the new provisional government repealed most laws discriminating against Jews. The few remaining discriminatory regulations were abolished by the Bolsheviks after they took power in Russia in November, 1917. For a brief period, Jews were able legally to practice their religion in the renamed Soviet Union. After a short spring of emancipation,

Jews fell victim to two major forces, one old and one new. First, anti-Semitism in the lands of the old Russian Empire had deep roots among the Orthodox population and with certain national groups. Despite the change in legal status, in everyday life Jews still encountered discrimination, persecution, and at times even lynchings and pogroms. Second, the Bolshevik ideologues in charge of the Soviet state harbored a deep animosity toward organized religion of any kind, and they soon embarked on a general campaign to suppress religious belief which swept up Jews along with Orthodox, Catholics, Protestants, and others. Finally, the Jews presented a special problem to the Soviet authorities, as they formed not simply a religious community but a distinct national group without a specific national territory. During the 1920's an attempt was made to create a Jewish region (Birobidzhan) along the desolate Chinese-Soviet border, but fewer than one hundred thousand Jews chose to relocate.

With Joseph Stalin's ascent to full dictatorial power in 1928, Jews faced a whole new level of persecution and terror. Like millions of other Soviets during the 1930's, the years of Stalin's great purges, Jews were subject to persecution, imprisonment, and execution both as individuals and as Jews, for in addition to being paranoid and cruel, Stalin was a hardened anti-Semite. Soviet policy in general aimed at breaking down Jews' separate sense of religion and culture: Yiddish once again was banned; synagogues, schools, and Talmudic academies were closed; Jewish literary and artistic expression was attacked as anti-Soviet; and under the labor code Jews were forced to work on the Sabbath. The average Jew, for survival's sake, had to maintain an outward appearance of conformity with Stalinism.

Then came the Holocaust, in which Soviet and other Jews were singled out from the general population for "liquidation" by the Nazis. The Holocaust had a great effect on Soviet Jews, as it did on Jews everywhere, by impressing many with the reality that assimilation was no barrier to persecution. Germany's Jews had been among the most assimilated in Europe. The Holocaust gave rise to a new consciousness of Jewish identity, spurred by the fact that not even the Nazi genocide led average Soviets to question anti-Semitism, in part because their leaders suppressed information about the Holocaust.

The State of Israel came into existence in 1948. That had two lasting effects: It stimulated a fierce pride among Jews and raised hopes of escape from persecution by emigration to Israel. It also led to a new round of persecution, as Stalin denounced Zionism as a form of imperialism and accused Jews of being potential traitors. At the time of his death in 1953, Stalin was about to launch a large-scale purge of Jews as a way of distracting the public from his foreign and domestic policy failures.

Nikita Khrushchev took power and modified the excesses of Stalinism in the 1950's but failed to attack the sources of anti-Semitism in Soviet society. In 1961, he too began to blame Jews for the failures of the Soviet centrally planned economy. Between 1961 and 1964, official propaganda about "economic crimes" blamed Jews for impeding economic progress. In some areas, such as the Ukraine, Jews were arrested, tried, and often executed in greatly disproportionate numbers. Khrushchev's successor, Leonid Brezhnev, also was personally prejudiced against Jews, especially after Israel humiliated the Soviet Union's Arab allies in the 1967 Arab-Israeli war. That conflict created a surge of pride among Soviet Jews, who began to demand that their religious and ethnic rights be respected and that emigration to Israel be permitted. Efforts were made to revive fluency in Yiddish and Hebrew, to start up religious schools, and to reopen synagogues and Talmudic academies. Soviet leaders responded swiftly: Jewish activists and other dissidents were arrested; some were sent to labor camps and others to mental institutions on the ground that their religious belief was evidence of mental disorder. The activism of Soviet dissidents caught the attention of foreign observers and of foreign Jewish communities in Israel and the United States. From 1967 on, Soviet persecution of Jews was subject to increasing criticism from foreign human rights groups, both Jewish and non-Jewish, and to growing pressure from the United States.

In the early 1970's pressure began to build in the United States to tie *détente* with the Soviet Union to the treatment of dissidents, and especially to free emigration for Jews. President Richard Nixon and his National Security Advisor, Henry Kissinger, at first resisted linkage between human rights, emigration, and *détente*, although they pressured Brezhnev in private. Between 1972 and 1974, however, majority support developed in Congress for the Jackson-Vanik amendment to a trade bill, named for its sponsor Senator Henry "Scoop" Jackson, a man with presidential ambitions and hopes for strong support from the American Jewish community. The amendment linked free Jewish emigration and religious rights to expanded trade with Moscow. A critical moment came on October 21, 1974, when Andrei Sakharov, a leading Soviet dissident and founder of the Moscow Human Rights Committee, threw his support behind the amendment in an open letter to Jackson and Kissinger. Congress soon passed the amendment, but it quickly backfired: The Soviets proclaimed outrage that their internal policy was being questioned and immediately cut off all Jewish emigration. With the complete collapse of *détente* the following year, Jewish religious rights and especially emigration became hostage to larger currents in Soviet-American relations and remained tied to other issues for the rest of the 1970's and most of the 1980's.

Impact of Event

The impact of rising demands from the Soviet Jewish community for greater respect for religious and minority rights had a profound effect on hundreds of thousands of lives. On the positive side, many Jews discovered or rediscovered a personal cultural and religious identity that had been unknown or forgotten under the influence of Soviet daily life and antireligious education. There was a renaissance of Yiddish and Hebrew literature, an increase in participation in religious ceremonies and observance, and a new sense of community both within the Soviet Union and with respect to the larger Jewish world, most notably in Israel and the United States. On the other hand, this revival provoked a fresh round of persecution which adversely affected thousands. Well-known Jewish dissidents such as Yuri Orlov and

Anatol Scharansky were imprisoned for long periods of time but eventually were released and expelled, after the West applied pressure. Less well-known activists, or ordinary people who applied to emigrate to Israel, quickly found that they lost their jobs, their apartments, and often their freedom. In the worst cases, and there were many of these, Jews were sent to prison camps or to mental institutions, away from Western eyes. Even when a trickle of emigration was permitted, the wait for an exit visa could be as long as five to seven years, and then the request might be refused, with no reason given. That situation continued in spite of the fact that the Soviet Union in 1975 signed a comprehensive human rights agreement that was included in the Helsinki Accords on European peace and security.

On a larger plane, the conditions under which Soviet Jews lived were determined by both the Arab-Israeli dispute and also the Cold War, as Arabs lobbied Moscow to curtail emigration and the United States lobbied for an increase. Soviet leaders turned the emigration tap on and off according to the changing stakes of foreign policy, greatly disrupting individual lives and families. By the mid-1980's, however, Jews began to benefit from the enormous changes convulsing Soviet society with the beginnings of *glasnost* and *perestroika* under Mikhail Gorbachev. As the Cold War drew to a close and a severe Soviet need for Western aid and trade became clear, the new Soviet leadership moved away from persecution and toward free Jewish emigration. After 1988, hundreds of thousands of Jews left the Soviet Union, so many that Israel had difficulty housing them. Housing problems placed new pressures on the occupied territories, thereby complicating the Arab-Israeli dispute. Within the Soviet Union there developed more official tolerance for religious belief and practice. By the early 1990's, however, an old pattern started to repeat itself, as the desire of Jews to emigrate was seen by some Soviets as evidence of disloyalty. Incidents of open anti-Semitism increased in number and talk was even heard from *Pamyat*—a reactionary nationalist group opposed to *glasnost* and *perestroika*—of a pogrom against the Jews of Moscow and Leningrad. Although government policy had entered a more liberal phase, Jews still faced the daily reality of deeply rooted anti-Semitism among large segments of the Soviet population.

Bibliography

Amnesty International. *Prisoners of Conscience in the USSR: Their Treatment and Conditions.* London: Author, 1980. A well-documented account of general conditions and individual cases. Photographs and index.

Cohen, Roberta. "The Soviet Union: Human Rights Diplomacy in the Communist Heartland." In *The Diplomacy of Human Rights*, edited by David Newsom. Lanham, Md.: University Press of America, 1986. A useful, short introduction to the problems of outside powers attempting to influence Soviet human rights behavior.

Cullen, Robert. "Soviet Jewry." *Foreign Affairs* 65 (Winter, 1986/1987): 252-266. A readable overview of the problems faced by Soviet Jews up to the point when Gorbachev's reforms began to cause dramatic changes.

Kahan, Arcadius. "Forces for and Against Jewish Identity in the Soviet Union." In

Essays in Jewish Social and Economic History, edited by Roger Weiss. Chicago: University of Chicago Press, 1986.

——————. "Religion and Soviet Policy." In *Essays in Jewish Social and Economic History*, edited by Roger Weiss. Chicago: University of Chicago Press, 1986. These two articles are interpretive rather than documentary and serve as good complements to the drier presentations of Amnesty International and Joshua Rubenstein.

Low, Alfred D. *Soviet Jewry and Soviet Policy.* New York: Columbia University Press, 1990. A good introduction to the history of Jews in the Soviet Union. Particularly useful for its discussion of the interrelationship between anti-Semitism and Marxist-Leninist theory. Select bibliography and index.

Pospielovsky, Dimitry. *The Russian Church Under the Soviet Regime, 1917-1982.* 2 vols. Crestwood, N.Y.: St. Vladimir's Seminary Press, 1984. Important for an understanding of the larger question of the Soviet attitude toward organized religion and of Orthodox attitudes toward Jews.

Rubenstein, Joshua. "Zionists and Democrats." In *Soviet Dissidents: Their Struggle for Human Rights.* Boston, Mass.: Beacon Press, 1980.

——————. "Detente and the Dissidents." In *Soviet Dissidents: Their Struggle for Human Rights.* Boston, Mass.: Beacon Press, 1980. These two articles provide detail on individual cases as well as a general overview of the connections and tensions between Zionist and dissident movements. Full index.

Cathal J. Nolan

Cross-References

Bolsheviks Deny All Rights to the Russian Orthodox Church (1917), p. 202; Lenin and the Communists Impose the "Red Terror" (1917), p. 218; Lenin Leads the Russian Revolution (1917), p. 225; Nazi Concentration Camps Go into Operation (1933), p. 491; Stalin Begins Purging Political Opponents (1934), p. 503; Stalin Reduces the Russian Orthodox Church to Virtual Extinction (1939), p. 561; Israel Is Created as a Homeland for Jews (1948), p. 761; Israel Enacts the Law of Return, Granting Citizenship to Immigrants (1950), p. 832; Khrushchev Implies That Stalinist Excesses Will Cease (1956), p. 952; The Moscow Human Rights Committee Is Founded (1970), p. 1549; The Helsinki Agreement Offers Terms for International Cooperation (1975), p. 1806; Sakharov Is Awarded the Nobel Peace Prize (1975), p. 1852; Soviets Crack Down on Moscow's Helsinki Watch Group (1977), p. 1915, Gorbachev Initiates a Policy of *Glasnost* (1985), p. 2249.

GIDEON V. WAINWRIGHT ESTABLISHES DEFENDANTS' RIGHT TO AN ATTORNEY

Category of event: Accused persons' rights
Time: March 18, 1963
Locale: United States Supreme Court, Washington, D.C.

The Supreme Court's decision in Gideon v. Wainwright *held that the Sixth Amendment's right-to-counsel provision required free provision of a lawyer to any defendant in a state criminal trial who could not afford an attorney*

Principal personages:
EARL WARREN (1891-1974), the chief justice of the United States
HUGO L. BLACK (1886-1971), the author of the majority opinion in *Gideon v. Wainwright*
CLARENCE EARL GIDEON (1910-1972), a drifter and petty criminal; appealed a conviction on the ground that lack of counsel violated his constitutional rights
ABE FORTAS (1910-1982), the court-appointed lawyer for Gideon's appeal
OWEN J. ROBERTS (1875-1955), the author of the decision in *Betts v. Brady* (1942)
GEORGE SUTHERLAND (1862-1942), the Supreme Court justice who first suggested that free provision of counsel was required in at least some circumstances

Summary of Event

The evidence is convincing that the provision in the Sixth Amendment to the U.S. Constitution guaranteeing that "the accused . . . [i]n all criminal prosecutions . . . shall enjoy the right . . . to have the Assistance of Counsel for his defence" meant, at the time of its adoption, no more than the right of a defendant to employ an attorney. This provision was in advance of the practice in contemporary England, where the assistance of counsel was allowed only in misdemeanor, but not in felony, cases, except for treason. Congress required by statute, starting in 1790, that the federal courts appoint counsel at the defendant's request in treason and other capital cases. In state criminal prosecutions, practice varied from state to state. The United States Supreme Court would not define the meaning of the right-to-counsel clause even at the federal level until 1938. As for its application to the states, the generally accepted view before the Civil War—affirmed by Chief Justice John Marshall in *Barron v. Baltimore* (1833)—was that the first eight amendments applied only to the federal government and not to the states. The adoption of the Fourteenth Amendment reopened the question, but the Supreme Court balked at extending any of the provisions of the Bill of Rights to the states via the Fourteenth Amendment until 1925, when the Court ruled that states must protect the freedom of speech. A majority of the justices continued to resist extending the criminal law provisions of the Bill of Rights to states.

The first suggestion that a defendant had a constitutional right to be offered counsel if he or she could not afford an attorney came in 1932, in *Powell v. Alabama.* That decision was an outgrowth of the famous Scottsboro boys case, in which seven black youths had been convicted in Alabama of the rape of two white women. The case against the boys rested on dubious testimony. Speaking for the Supreme Court in overturning the convictions, Justice George Sutherland rested the decision not upon the Sixth Amendment but upon the due process clause of the Fourteenth Amendment, which barred the states from depriving "any person of life, liberty, or property, without due process of law." Due process, Sutherland reasoned, required a fair hearing. Failure to provide the Scottsboro boys with lawyers denied them a fair hearing. Sutherland carefully limited the scope of his holding to the facts in the case: Due process required a state court to provide effective assistance of counsel "in a capital case, where the defendant is unable to employ counsel, and is incapable adequately of making his own defense because of ignorance, feeble-mindedness, illiteracy, or the like."

The Supreme Court did not give its definitive interpretation of the meaning of the Sixth Amendment's right-to-counsel clause until 1938, in *Johnson v. Zerbst.* Ignoring the historical evidence regarding the provision, Justice Hugo L. Black wrote in his opinion that the Sixth Amendment required the appointment of counsel for poor defendants in federal criminal trials. Although the defendant could waive the right to have counsel assigned, the trial judge had the duty to make sure that the defendant fully understood the right to have legal assistance and had knowingly and intelligently waived that right. Did the same rule apply to state criminal trials via the Fourteenth Amendment? The issue came before the Supreme Court in 1942 in *Betts v. Brady*, a case involving a conviction for robbery, a noncapital felony. At his trial in state court, the defendant, an unemployed farm laborer described by the Supreme Court as a person of "ordinary intelligence," had requested appointment of counsel, but his request had been denied. In the trial itself, the defendant had actively participated by examining his own witnesses and cross-examining the prosecution's. Justice Hugo L. Black strongly argued that the Fourteenth Amendment had been intended to incorporate as limits upon the states all the provisions of the Bill of Rights. Even apart from the Sixth Amendment, he held that due process required provision of counsel for those too poor to retain their own. Justice Owen J. Roberts, for the six-to-three majority, held that the Fourteenth Amendment did not incorporate the Sixth Amendment as such. It was only "in certain circumstances, or in connection with other elements" that denial of a specific provision of the Bill of Rights was a violation of the due process of law guaranteed by the Fourteenth Amendment. He went on to conclude that there was nothing in history or contemporary practice to justify holding that due process required the appointment of counsel in every state criminal trial. Rather, the question in each case was whether, in the totality of circumstances, appointment of counsel was required to assure "fundamental fairness." Given the relatively simple issues involved in the case before the Court, the majority ruled that the lack of counsel had not denied the defendant a fair trial.

In the years that followed, the Court overturned most state convictions appealed because of a failure to assign counsel but shied from laying down a blanket rule requiring the appointment of counsel. The one exception was the requirement of appointment of counsel in all capital cases, laid down in *Bute v. Illinois* (1948). By the early 1960's, the Court had turned against the totality-of-circumstances approach. There was growing unhappiness in the legal community with the lack of uniformity in the practices of different states. Many state judges and prosecutors complained about the uncertainty resulting from lack of a clearly defined rule. A majority of Earl Warren's Supreme Court was committed to extending most of the provisions of the Bill of Rights to the states and to promoting a larger degree of egalitarianism in American life. At the beginning of the Court's 1961 term, Warren instructed his law clerks to look through the petitions for review for a suitable right-to-counsel case that would give the Court an opportunity to reverse *Betts*. The petition selected was from Clarence Earl Gideon.

Gideon was a fifty-one-year-old drifter who had previously served four prison terms for felonies. He was charged in 1961 with breaking and entering the Bay Harbor Poolroom in Panama City, Florida, and stealing a pint of wine and some coins from a cigarette machine. When he went on trial in the Circuit Court of Bay County, Florida, on August 4, 1961, he asked the judge to appoint a lawyer for him because he could not afford to retain one himself. The judge refused because Florida law provided for such appointment only in capital cases. After his appeal had been turned down by the Florida Supreme Court, Gideon submitted from prison a petition, handwritten in pencil on lined paper, to the United States Supreme Court. He argued that his conviction had violated the due-process guarantee of the Fourteenth Amendment because of the trial judge's refusal to appoint counsel. The Constitution, he wrote, required that "all citizens tried for a felony crime should have aid of counsel."

The Supreme Court granted review on June 1, 1962, and explicitly instructed counsel to discuss whether *Betts v. Brady* should be "reconsidered." In response to a follow-up petition from Gideon asking that the court appoint an attorney to argue his case, Warren suggested—and his fellow justices agreed—that Abe Fortas, one of Washington, D.C.'s foremost lawyers (whom President Lyndon B. Johnson would later appoint to the Supreme Court) be named. The justices were unanimous in reversing Gideon's conviction and overruling *Betts*. Separate concurring opinions were written by Justices William O. Douglas, Tom C. Clark, and John Marshall Harlan. In a symbolic gesture, Chief Justice Warren picked Justice Black, who had angrily dissented in *Betts v. Brady*, to write the majority opinion. In his ruling, handed down on March 18, 1963, Black held that the right-to-counsel provision of the Sixth Amendment was "subsumed" in the Fourteenth Amendment, and thus its requirement of assignment of counsel for poor defendants applied to state criminal trials. "The right of one charged with crime to counsel may not be deemed fundamental and essential to fair trials in some countries," he concluded, "but it is in ours."

Impact of Event

At his retrial in Florida after the Supreme Court overturned his conviction, Gideon was acquitted. Thereafter, he stayed clear of the law except for a vagrancy arrest. Ten years after his death in 1972, the American Civil Liberties Union arranged for a stone to mark his grave in Hannibal, Missouri, where he had been born. Gideon was not the only one freed by the Supreme Court ruling. The new *Gideon* rule was applied not only prospectively to future criminal trials but also retrospectively to persons in prison who had been tried without counsel.

Before *Gideon v. Wainwright*, in most instances when the court assigned counsel the attorney so named received no, or at most minimal, compensation. The result was that the lawyers typically assigned were beginners or hacks. Worse, they lacked the resources for presenting the most effective defense (for example, pretrial investigations). *Gideon* gave a powerful stimulus to improving this situation. Congress, in the Criminal Justice Act of 1964, instituted a system of compensated legal assistance in the federal courts. Many states and localities established or expanded tax-supported public-defender or legal-aid offices.

Gideon was one of the Warren Court's most popular criminal law decisions. There was wide support for guaranteeing poor defendants minimal legal assistance in criminal trials. More controversial were the court's extensions of the *Gideon* principle. Although the opinion in *Gideon* did not explicitly limit the ruling to felony trials, that was the general assumption. Accordingly, many states did not provide for appointment of counsel for so-called petty offenses (typically where the punishment was no more than six months imprisonment). The Court, in *Argersinger v. Hamlin* (1972), ruled that an unrepresented defendant could not be jailed for any term unless he or she had waived counsel at the trial. In *In re Gault*, the Court recognized a right to counsel in state juvenile court delinquency proceedings.

A second area of extension was to post-trial situations. *Douglas v. California* (1963) upheld the right to appointed counsel for appeal from a conviction; *Mempa v. Rhay* (1967) extended that right to a post-conviction deferred sentence or probation revocation proceeding. What most provoked attack was the extension of *Gideon* to the pre-trial area. *Escobedo v. Illinois* (1964) barred the police from preventing a suspect from consulting with a lawyer until interrogation had been completed. *United States v. Wade* (1967) and *Gilbert v. California* (1967) held that suspects had the right to counsel, retained or appointed, at a police line-up because of the danger of faulty identification. A series of decisions—among them *Massiah v. United States* (1964), *Brewer v. Williams* (1977), and *United States v. Henry* (1980)—appear to have taken the position that the government could not approach a defendant for evidence of his guilt in the absence of counsel any time after the initiation of judicial proceedings by an indictment or other in-court proceedings. Most controversial was the five-to-four decision in *Miranda v. Arizona* (1966) requiring state and federal officers to advise suspects before any questioning of their right to remain silent, to consult with a lawyer, to have that lawyer present at the interrogation, and to have a lawyer provided.

The backlash against what many people thought was too much protection for the criminal at the expense of society led the Supreme Court, beginning in the 1970's, to move back from some of the extensions of *Gideon.* In *Scott v. Illinois* (1979), the Court sustained the conviction of an unrepresented defendant facing prosecution for an offense punishable by fine and/or imprisonment who received only a money fine. *Ross v. Moffitt* (1974) held that the right to assigned counsel was limited to the first-level appeal and did not extend to discretionary appeals in the state courts or applications for review to the United States Supreme Court. *Gagnon v. Scarpelli* (1973) held that counsel need not be appointed at a hearing for revocation of probation or parole unless special circumstances required legal assistance; *Lassiter v. Department of Social Services* (1981) applied the same rule to indigent mothers in proceedings to terminate their parental rights. A series of rulings have chipped away at the *Miranda* protections regarding the questioning of suspects in the absence of counsel, and the Court has largely rebuffed appeals challenging the effectiveness of counsel.

Bibliography

Allen, Francis. "The Judicial Quest for Penal Justice: The Warren Court and the Criminal Cases." *University of Illinois Law Forum*, no. 4 (1975): 518-542. A generally sympathetic appraisal of the Warren Court's criminal law decisions.

Beaney, William M. *The Right to Counsel in American Courts.* Ann Arbor: University of Michigan Press, 1955. An excellent historical account of the development of the right to counsel that examines its antecedents in English history and in practices in the American colonies. Discusses its treatment in the federal and state courts from the adoption of the Bill of Rights to the date of the book's publication.

Braeman, John. *Before the Civil Rights Revolution: The Old Court and Individual Rights.* New York: Greenwood Press, 1988. A survey of the Supreme Court's decision making in the area of civil liberties and civil rights up to the post-1937 revolution in constitutional law.

Cook, Joseph G. *Constitutional Rights of the Accused.* 2d ed. 3 vols. Rochester, N.Y.: Lawyers Co-operative, 1985-1986. A comprehensive guide to current constitutional law regarding criminal procedure. Right-to-counsel issues are dealt with primarily in volume 2.

Graham, Fred P. *The Self-Inflicted Wound.* New York: Macmillan, 1970. This volume by *The New York Times*'s Supreme Court correspondent is the fullest and most balanced account of the Warren Court's criminal law decisions.

Israel, Jerold. "Criminal Procedure, the Burger Court, and the Legacy of the Warren Court." *Michigan Law Review* 75 (June, 1977): 1319-1425. Concludes that complaints that the Court under Chief Justice Warren Burger was guilty of reversing the criminal law decisions of the Warren Court have been grossly exaggerated.

_____. "Gideon v. Wainwright: The 'Art' of Overruling." In *The Supreme Court Review, 1963*, edited by Philip B. Kurland. Chicago: University of Chicago Press, 1963. A critical appraisal of Justice Black's opinion in *Gideon* as failing to offer a persuasive rationale for overruling *Betts* "consistent with the accepted image of judicial review."

Kamisar, Yale. "*Betts v. Brady* Twenty Years Later: The Right to Counsel and Due Process Values." *Michigan Law Review* 61 (December, 1962): 219-282. A critical appraisal of the unfairness and problems resulting from the totality-of-circumstances approach.

Lewis, Anthony. *Gideon's Trumpet.* New York: Random House, 1964. A slickly written journalistic account of Gideon's challenge to his conviction. Marred by Lewis' gushing, exaggerated description of Gideon as a dedicated lover of justice and his even more uncritical admiration for the Warren Court and its works.

Schwartz, Bernard. *Super Chief: Earl Warren and His Supreme Court, a Judicial Biography.* New York: New York University Press, 1983. A look at the behind-the-scenes workings of the Supreme Court, based upon the private papers and notes of many of the justices and interviews with court members and their law clerks. Its weakness is the author's worshipful admiration for Warren.

John Braeman

Cross-References

The American Civil Liberties Union Is Founded (1920), p. 327; The United Nations Sets Rules for the Treatment of Prisoners (1955), p. 935; *Miranda v. Arizona* Requires Police to Tell Arrested People Their Rights (1966), p. 1343; The Supreme Court Extends Protection Against Double Jeopardy (1969), p. 1474; The United Nations Issues a Conduct Code for Law Enforcement Officials (1979), p. 2040.

CIVIL RIGHTS PROTESTERS ATTRACT INTERNATIONAL ATTENTION

Categories of event: Racial and ethnic rights; civil rights
Time: April-May, 1963
Locale: Birmingham, Alabama

Protests by civil rights demonstrators in Birmingham, Alabama, were met with police dogs and fire hoses, focusing world attention on the Civil Rights movement and winning for it much support

Principal personages:
> FRED L. SHUTTLESWORTH (1922-   ), the founder of the Alabama Christian Movement for Human Rights
> MARTIN LUTHER KING, JR. (1929-1968), the leader of the Southern Christian Leadership Conference, in Birmingham to lead a campaign against segregation
> T. EUGENE "BULL" CONNOR (1897-1973), the commissioner of public safety in Birmingham and leader of segregationist forces in the city
> SIDNEY SMYER (1928-   ), a Birmingham businessman and a leading white moderate
> JOHN F. KENNEDY (1917-1963), the president of the United States (1961-1963)

Summary of Event

In the early 1960's, Birmingham, Alabama, was one of the most industrialized cities in the South and boasted a population of 340,000, forty percent of which was African American. Reputed to be the most segregated city in the United States, Birmingham had a rocky history where race relations were concerned. In 1961, the freedom riders had been violently attacked in the city—with the apparent connivance of city authorities—and more than fifty unsolved bombings had earned the city the nickname of "Bombingham" among southern blacks. Birmingham's reputation and the extent of its segregation made it at once an obvious target and formidable obstacle for the Civil Rights movement.

The origins of the protest movement that shook Birmingham in the spring of 1963 were both local and national. Already in place was a Civil Rights movement that had proved its resilience by surviving and periodically protesting during the years since the 1955 Montgomery bus boycott. Its leader was an outspoken Baptist minister, the Reverend Fred L. Shuttlesworth. After the Alabama legislature effectively outlawed the National Association for the Advancement of Colored People (NAACP) in the state in 1956, Shuttlesworth had organized the Alabama Christian Movement for Human Rights (ACMHR), and it had grown to be the largest civil rights organization in the state. Although some black leaders disliked Shuttlesworth's combative style, he had proven to be a dynamic leader as well as a survivor: Bombs had twice failed to silence him. Shuttlesworth, however, realized that the forces of segregation were too strong to be overcome with strictly local resources. The ACMHR was an affiliate of the Southern Christian Leadership Conference (SCLC), a church-based civil rights organization led by Martin Luther King, Jr. In late 1962, Shuttlesworth invited King to come to Birmingham and lead a comprehensive campaign, one that would confront not only segregation but also the economic discrimination faced by Birmingham's African-American citizens.

Although well aware of Birmingham's intimidating reputation, King saw two advantages in challenging such a bastion of segregation. The SCLC had recently waged an unsuccessful campaign against segregation in Albany, Georgia, and a victory was badly needed to restore the morale and resources of the Civil Rights movement. King also saw that segregation was unlikely to be defeated throughout the South without a greater degree of federal involvement. A well-orchestrated and well-publicized campaign in Birmingham could be the means to force intervention from the Kennedy Administration, whose support for civil rights had thus far been lukewarm. Shuttlesworth and King met in February, 1963, at the Dorchester Center in Georgia to work out the details for what was labeled Project C (for "confrontation").

The campaign's start was originally scheduled to coincide with the Easter shopping season, in order to maximize the impact of its planned economic boycott. Municipal politics in Birmingham, however, delayed the campaign's beginning. Two years earlier, a group of Birmingham businesspeople had agreed to African-American demands to obey a court order to desegregate the city's parks and swimming pools. Birmingham's commissioner of public safety, T. Eugene "Bull" Connor, however, had thwarted the agreement by closing down the park system.

At that time, Birmingham had a commission form of government with three elected commissioners, each of whom had specific responsibilities. As public safety commissioner, the staunchly segregationist Connor controlled the fire and police departments. He was, as well, the dominant personality on the commission. To many businesspeople, who were increasingly aware of the economic consequences of Birmingham's image problems, Connor's actions seemed likely to tarnish further the city's reputation.

Sidney Smyer, a prominent Realtor and president of the city's chamber of commerce, and other moderates in the business community decided that the best way to get rid of Connor was to alter the city's form of government. In 1962, they launched a campaign to replace the commission form with a mayor and council plan. The campaign was successful, and in March, 1963, mayoral elections were held. Their inconclusive results necessitated a run-off, on April 2, between Connor and the more moderate Albert Boutwell. On April 2, Boutwell won the run-off.

King and Shuttlesworth had postponed the beginning of Project C until after the run-off, lest an upsurge in civil rights activity create a backlash in Connor's favor. On April 3, the SCLC and ACMHR began a large-scale, nonviolent campaign of protest marked by sit-in demonstrations, marches, and a well-organized economic boycott against downtown retail establishments. Connor meanwhile attempted to overturn the election results by filing a suit arguing that the whole changeover in the city's government was illegal. He refused to relinquish control of the public safety department until the issue was resolved by the Alabama Supreme Court. Although the court eventually ruled against Connor (on May 22, 1963), the short-term result was a confusing situation in which the city's new government was unsure of its powers and Connor was left in control of the machinery of law enforcement.

The Birmingham protests were among the largest ever launched by the Civil Rights movement. For sixty-five consecutive nights, rallies were held in various black churches, while during the day direct action protests continued. On April 11, Connor obtained an injunction in state court against further demonstrations. Some Project C leaders urged that the protests be abandoned until the injunction was overturned in a higher court. King believed that the momentum had to be maintained, however, and he openly defied the injunction. On April 12, Good Friday, King and a number of other demonstrators were arrested. It was while in jail that King wrote his famous "Letter from a Birmingham Jail" as a response to a published letter from some local white clergy who questioned his timing and tactics. Originally penciled in the margin of a newspaper, the letter became a classic indictment of the moral injustice of segregation and a justification for the urgency of the Civil Rights movement.

Although King was released after eight days, more and more demonstrators went to jail. Running short of adult protesters, in early May, King pressed children from the public schools into service. Up until this time, Connor had been fairly restrained in his handling of the protests. Infuriated by the continuation of the protests, he now attempted to shut down the demonstrations by using greater force, including police dogs and fire hoses. At the peak of the demonstration on May 6-7, approximately two thousand protesters had been arrested and the state fairgrounds had been pressed into service as a temporary jail.

By this time, Birmingham was the nation's leading news story, and pictures of young protesters being attacked by dogs and drenched by hoses were flashing around the country and overseas. On May 7, some young blacks had vented their anger and frustration by battling with police and other whites in the downtown area. Many, including some in the Kennedy Administration, began to fear a major race riot was imminent. Many of Birmingham's white elite were appalled at Connor's tactics.

Abandoning the position that they would not negotiate while the demonstrations were in progress, white and black leaders began serious talks. The key figure in the white community was Sidney Smyer, who earlier had secretly established contact with Fred Shuttlesworth. Added pressure came from Washington, D.C., where the Kennedy Administration was worried about the effects that events in Birmingham might have abroad, especially in Africa and Asia. Assistant Attorney General Burke Marshall had been dispatched to the city and was pressuring both sides to come to terms. During the final stages of negotiations both the president and his brother the attorney general were busy on the telephone.

On May 8, the demonstrations were suspended, and two days later a formal agreement was signed. Downtown merchants agreed to desegregate lunch counters, drinking fountains, and other facilities, and to hire at least some African Americans in clerical jobs. In addition, a permanent biracial committee was to be established, and those demonstrators in jail were to be released. The agreement occasioned a heated argument between King and Shuttlesworth (who thought the terms too open to evasion), but its terms defined the final accord. Segregationist extremists made a last-ditch attempt to disrupt the agreement by bombing the Gaston Motel, which had served as Project C's command center, and the home of the Reverend A. D. King, Dr. King's brother. Despite a night of rioting, the agreement held.

Impact of Event

The "Battle of Birmingham" was one of the most dramatic confrontations of the Civil Rights movement. The newspaper and television pictures of nonviolent protesters—some of them no more than six years old—being bitten by police dogs or swept off their feet by high pressure fire hoses provided the movement with some of its most powerful images. In the battle for public opinion, the opponents of segregation won a decisive victory. President Kennedy's remark that Bull Connor had done as much for the Civil Rights movement as had Abraham Lincoln contained an ironic truth.

The victory was more than a moral one. Events in Birmingham made it easier for the SCLC and other Civil Rights movement organizations to raise funds. The protests in Birmingham inspired African Americans across the South; about two hundred communities experienced direct action campaigns in 1963. The enthusiasm generated made it easier to organize the "March on Washington" that summer.

Events in Birmingham also succeeded in achieving King's goal of promoting a greater federal role in dismantling segregation in the South. Shifting public opinion in the North made it less risky for politicians there to support greater federal intervention. There were, to be sure, other dramatic events that helped in this direction: Governor George Wallace's confrontation with federal authorities over the integration of the University of Alabama and the assassination of Medgar Evers in Mississippi, both in June, 1963. When President Kennedy addressed the country on June 12, 1963, he clearly aligned his administration for the first time on the side of the Civil Rights movement and called for a new and more comprehensive civil rights bill. He had first ordered the drafting of such a measure in early May, at the height of the Birmingham protests. The landmark Civil Rights Act of 1964 would not pass for another year, but much of its groundwork was laid by the events of 1963.

The events of April-May, 1963, also had a lasting impact on Birmingham itself. The agreement that ended the demonstrations was implemented more slowly and less fully than many had hoped.

Nevertheless, it marked a break with Birmingham's uncompromising past. Racial hatred remained a feature of the city's life, however, and on September 15, 1963, a bomb exploded at the Sixteenth Street Baptist Church, killing four African-American girls. The church had been a starting point for the marches of early May. It was this tragic epilogue, perhaps, more than the spring campaign itself, that brought home to many of the city's whites the need to improve race relations. Eight years later, progress in this area won for Birmingham *Look* magazine's "All-American City" designation.

Bibliography

Abernathy, Ralph David. *And the Walls Came Tumbling Down.* New York: Harper & Row, 1989. The memoirs of King's second-in-command and successor at the SCLC. A prominent participant in the Birmingham protests, Abernathy provides a first-hand account of Project C from the vantage point of its leadership. Index but no bibliography.

Branch, Taylor. *Parting the Waters: America in the King Years, 1954-63.* New York: Simon & Schuster, 1988. A large-scale history of the Civil Rights movement up until the Kennedy assassination, stressing the underlying role of the African-American church. Contains three detailed but highly readable chapters on Birmingham. Bibliography and index.

Brauer, Carl M. *John F. Kennedy and the Second Reconstruction.* New York: Columbia University Press, 1977. The most comprehensive treatment of the Kennedy Administration and civil rights. Sees Birmingham as the point at which Kennedy moved to more active support of the Civil Rights movement. Takes a more positive view of the administration's contributions to the movement than some historians have. Index and bibliography.

Corley, Robert. "In Search of Racial Harmony: Birmingham Business Leaders and Desegregation, 1950-1963." In *Southern Businessmen and Desegregation*, edited by Elizabeth Jacoway and David P. Colbourn. Baton Rouge: Louisiana State University Press, 1982. Details the meager efforts at interracial dialogue in Birmingham before the demonstrations. Essays on other southern cities in the volume provide comparative context.

Fairclough, Adam. *To Redeem the Soul of America: The Southern Christian Leadership Conference and Martin Luther King, Jr.* Athens: University of Georgia Press, 1987. The Civil Rights movement as seen from the SCLC. Sees events in Birmingham as constituting an important breakthrough for the organization and as laying the foundations for subsequent legislation. Detailed endnotes but no bibliography. Index.

Garrow, David. *Bearing the Cross: Martin Luther King, Jr., and the Southern Christian Leadership Conference, 1955-1968.* New York: William Morrow, 1986. The fullest study of King's career from 1955 to 1968, by an author who has written two other books on King. Sees Birmingham as the event that cemented King's stature as the nation's preeminent civil rights leader. Bibliography and index.

_____, ed. *Birmingham, Alabama, 1956-1963: The Black Struggle for Civil Rights.* Brooklyn, N.Y.: Carlson, 1989. Contains three useful and previously unpublished studies on Birmingham in this period: on the ACMHR, by Glenn T.

Eskew; on Fred Shuttlesworth, by Lewis W. Jones; and on the 1963 confrontation, by Lee E. Bains, Jr. The studies are placed in context by William D. Barnard's introduction. Bibliographies and index.

King, Martin Luther, Jr. *Why We Can't Wait.* New York: New American Library, 1964. King's own account of events in Birmingham, written in the fall of 1963. Written to persuade and inspire, it contains the famous "Letter from a Birmingham Jail."

Morris, Aldon. *Origins of the Civil Rights Movement: Black Communities Organizing for Social Change.* New York: Free Press, 1984. Covers the history of the movement through 1963, emphasizing its organizational features. Contains a good chapter on Birmingham. Morris argues that the confrontation in Birmingham was primarily local and economic in origin. Bibliography and index.

Raines, Howell. *My Soul Is Rested: Movement Days in the Deep South Remembered.* New York: G. P. Putnam's Sons, 1977. An oral history of the Civil Rights movement. The section on Birmingham includes interviews with Fred Shuttlesworth, Sidney Smyer, participants in the demonstrations, and Birmingham police officers. No bibliography, but does include an index.

William C. Lowe

Cross-References

Brown v. Board of Education Ends Public School Segregation (1954), p. 913; Parks Is Arrested for Refusing to Sit in the Back of the Bus (1955), p. 947; The SCLC Forms to Link Civil Rights Groups (1957), p. 974; The Civil Rights Act of 1957 Creates the Commission on Civil Rights (1957), p. 997; Eisenhower Sends Troops to Little Rock, Arkansas (1957), p. 1003; Greensboro Sit-ins Launch a New Stage in the Civil Rights Movement (1960), p. 1056; Meredith's Enrollment Integrates the University of Mississippi (1962), p. 1167; Martin Luther King, Jr., Delivers His "I Have a Dream" Speech (1963), p. 1200; Three Civil Rights Workers Are Murdered (1964), p. 1246; Congress Passes the Civil Rights Act (1964), p. 1251; Martin Luther King, Jr., Wins the Nobel Peace Prize (1964), p. 1257; Martin Luther King, Jr., Leads a March from Selma to Montgomery (1965), p. 1278; Congress Passes the Voting Rights Act (1965), p. 1296; Martin Luther King, Jr., Is Assassinated in Memphis (1968), p. 1419.

THE ORGANIZATION OF AFRICAN UNITY IS FOUNDED

Categories of event: Peace movements and organizations; revolutions and rebellions
Time: May 25, 1963
Locale: Addis Ababa, Ethiopia

The Organization of African Unity aimed to eradicate European political power in Africa but accepted European-imposed boundaries on African states and avoided discussion of infringements on human rights by African states

Principal personages:
KWAME NKRUMAH (1909-1972), the president of Ghana (1960-1966)
ABUBAKAR TAFAWA BALEWA (1912-1966), the first prime minister of Nigeria (1960-1966)
GAMAL ABDEL NASSER (1918-1970), the leader of the United Arab Republic (1954-1970)
HAILE SELASSIE I (1891-1975), the emperor of Ethiopia (1930-1974)
LÉOPOLD SENGHOR (1906-   ), the president of Senegal (1960-1980)
AHMED SÉKOU TOURÉ (1922-1984), the president of Guinea (1958-1984)
JOMO KENYATTA (c. 1894-1978), the president of Kenya (1964-1978)
JULIUS NYERERE (1922-   ), the president of Tanganyika (1962-1964) and president of Tanzania (1964-1975)
WILLIAM V. S. TUBMAN (1895-1971), the president of Liberia (1943-1971)
DIALLO TELLI BOUBACAR (1925-1977), the administrative secretary-general of the Organization of African Unity (1964-1972)

Summary of Event

The Organization of African Unity (OAU) is an attempt by African countries to achieve harmony and cooperation on the African continent. This group operates on a 1963 charter which exudes idealism. Pragmatism, however, restricts that idealism.

The Organization of African Unity evolved from African hostility to the European seizure of the so-called "Dark Continent." This opposition sprang not only from the soil of Africa itself but also, interestingly, from the "African diaspora." That phenomenon resulted from the centuries-long export of slaves to the Americas and the resulting reaction to it by people of African descent in the so-called "New World." This response resulted in the movement of pan-Africanism, which had as its slogan Africa for the Africans. This slogan implies the casting aside by Africans of subservience to foreign masters and the Africans' confident assertion that African interests are paramount.

Pan-Africanism sprang from two realms, the literary and the political. The former constituted a movement of ideas and emotions. These were deep feelings of dispossession, oppression, persecution, and rejection by people of African descent. Such expression came from poets Claude McKay, Langston Hughes, Raphael Ernest

Grail Armattoe, Aimé Césaire, Léopold Sédar Senghor, and Léon Dalmas, and also prose writers Majola Agbebi, John Edward Bruce, and Edward Blyden. The political stream of pan-Africanism preached African emancipation, black colonization in Africa, and an end to Europe's scramble for control of Africa. The literary and political streams of pan-Africanism were united by the rivals Marcus Garvey and William Edward Burghardt Du Bois. In New York City, Garvey founded the Universal Negro Improvement Association, which trumpeted "Back to Africa" to the black masses of the New World. Opposed to that idea, Du Bois urged regeneration of blacks in the lands of their residence and in association with a freed, independent African continent.

Another foundation of pan-Africanism was the black American churches, notably the African Methodist Episcopal Zion. That body's Bishop Alexander Walters became the chief collaborator with H. Sylvester Williams of Trinidad in calling the first Pan-African Congress in 1900. Present at that London conference was Du Bois, who led the second Pan-African Congress in Paris in 1919. The second conference insisted that "the natives of Africa must have the right to participate in the Government as fast as their development permits." Du Bois led three more pan-African congresses in 1921, 1923, and 1927. The sixth Pan-African Congress, convening in Manchester, England, in 1945, featured Africa's young leaders. They included Jomo Kenyatta, the poets Raphael Armattoe and Peter Abrahams, and Kwame Nkrumah, who owed much to Garvey's ideas. This congress demanded independence for Black Africa.

Pan-Africanism was transplanted organizationally to Africa itself. At the Manchester Congress, Nkrumah organized the West African National Secretariat. The latter in 1946 began promoting a West African Federation as a basis for a United States of Africa. The Egyptian Revolution in 1952 propelled Gamal Abdel Nasser into a leading role in pan-Africanism. The Bandung Conference in 1955, with its insistence on fundamental human rights, also influenced pan-African thinking.

April, 1958, marked the formal launching of pan-Africanism by individual states. Except for South Africa, all the independent states—Egypt, Ethiopia, Ghana, Liberia, Libya, Morocco, Sudan, and Tunisia—sent representatives to Accra, Ghana. The conference condemned colonialism, South Africa's racism, and France's occupation of Algeria. The conference favored a "fundamental unity" between African states on foreign questions.

Pan-Africanism received impetus from three All African Peoples Conferences. The first, a nongovernmental conference of political parties at Accra in December, 1958, proposed a commonwealth of free African states. It also favored Africa's independence and the principle of equal representation of citizens in government.

The movement for African unity received a severe setback in 1960-1961. Meeting at Abidjan, Ivory Coast, in 1960, twelve states—Cameroon, the Central African Republic, Chad, Congo (Brazzaville), Dahomey, Gabon, Ivory Coast, Madagascar, Mauritania, Niger, Senegal, and Upper Volta—formed the Brazzaville Group. It favored Mauritania's independence, mediation in the Congo (Kinshasa), and peace in Algeria by 1961. In January, 1961, eight states—the Algerian Provisional Government, Ceylon, Ghana, Guinea, Libya, Mali, Morocco, and the United Arab Republic—established the Casablanca Powers. They favored Morocco's acquisition of Mauritania, recognition of Antoine Gizinga's government in the Congo (Kinshasa), and immediate independence for Algeria. In May, 1961, the twelve Brazzaville states joined Ethiopia, Liberia, Libya, Nigeria, Sierra Leone, Somalia, Togo, and Tunisia in the Monrovia States. This organization carried on the Brazzaville Group's program. Neither the Monrovia States nor the Casablanca Powers called for political union in Africa.

In May, 1963, the Organization of African Unity (OAU) debuted. It was a merger of the Monrovia and Casablanca blocs (minus Ceylon) and Burundi, Congo (Kinshasa), Rwanda, Sudan, Tanganyika, and Uganda. Hosted by Emperor Haile Selassie I, the meeting at Addis Ababa featured Kwame Nkrumah, Abubakar Tafawa Balewa, Gamal Abdel Nasser, Ahmed Sékou Touré, Julius K. Nyerere, and William V. S. Tubman. A long debate occurred over the institution's name, but Malagasy's insistence on inclusion of its name failed. Arguments ensued over the frequency of holding the summit Assembly, the majority vote for an Assembly decision, the rules for the general secretariat and for the Commission of Mediation, Conciliation, and Arbitration, the working languages of the OAU, ratification of the charter, and admittance and withdrawal of states from the OAU.

The charter of the OAU consists of a preamble and thirty-three articles. The preamble is a ten-point statement outlining the convictions, hopes, and ideals of the member states. Its first sentence, beginning "We, the Heads of African States and Governments . . . ," emphasizes that the OAU is an organization of governments, not of peoples. The preamble stresses the inalienable right of all people to control their own destiny. As will be noted, the application of this noble principle is a different matter entirely. The preamble recognizes the territorial integrity of all African states. Thus, it ratifies the European establishment of boundaries despite the arbitrary methods by which the borders were determined. Self-determination by peoples thus seemed to receive short shrift from the self-styled African defenders of human rights.

The OAU charter established four main institutions. The first, the Assembly of Heads of State and Government, makes and coordinates policy and reviews all activities of the OAU. It has yearly scheduled meetings and can convene extra sessions if necessary. Each member state has one vote, and a quorum is two-thirds of the OAU's total membership. The Council of Ministers consists of the foreign ministers or other persons designated by members. It implements decisions of the Assembly, prepares conferences, and coordinates inter-African cooperation. Meetings are twice yearly or as needed in extraordinary session. Each member state possesses one vote, and a quorum is two-thirds of the OAU's total membership. The General Secretariat is directed by the administrative secretary-general, who is appointed by the Assembly on the recommendation of the Council. A fourth body, the Commission of Mediation, Conciliation, and Arbitration, is intended to settle disputes by peaceful means. A separate agreement among the members would later define its composition, responsibilities, and functions.

The founding fathers of the Organization of African Unity overwhelmingly believed that their creation promised to advance pan-Africanism. Events that followed would show successes and failures.

Impact of Event

The Organization of African Unity (OAU) sprang forth in 1961 from pan-Africanism, a movement characterized by its slogan, Africa for the Africans. Indeed, the OAU became the concrete manifestation of the spirit of pan-Africanism. It is an institution featuring successes and failures in the realm of human rights in Africa. Certain of its actions reveal its idealism balanced against cynical pragmatism.

The OAU charter pledges the member states "to eradicate all forms of colonialism from Africa." Thus, action should spring against vestiges of European imperialism. The OAU did little in the liberation from Britain of Botswana, Gambia, Kenya, Lesotho, Malawi, Mauritius, Swaziland, Zambia, and Zanzibar, nor of Equitorial Guinea from Spain. Collective pressure from the OAU likewise was insignificant in freeing Angola and Mozambique from Portugal. The OAU included Malawi, which had cordial relations with Portugal and Ian Smith's Rhodesia, and eventually established diplomatic relations with South Africa. In 1965, Haile Selassie I's Ethiopia, the OAU's host, led twenty-one of the thirty-three member states in not severing diplomatic relations with the United Kingdom over the question of Rhodesia's unilateral declaration of independence.

The OAU has a checkered history concerning interstate strife. Emperor Haile Selassie I of Ethiopia and President Modibo Keita of Mali represented the OAU in the successful mediation of an Algerian-Moroccan border dispute. The OAU failed, however, in solving the long Chadian-Libyan confrontation and the bitter Ethiopian-Somalian conflict. In the latter situation, the OAU proved ineffective in dealing with two successive Ethiopian regimes, the conservative government of Haile Selassie I, a founding father of the OAU, and the radical state of Mengistu Haile Mariam, whose capital, Addis Ababa, continued as the OAU's seat.

The Organization of African Unity could not end three significant bloody engagements. One was the Eritrean people's desire to end their subordination to Ethiopia, which Emperor Haile Selassie I had effected in 1962. The Eritreans fought for independence, first against Haile Selassie I's feudal monarchy and then against his Marxist republican successor. The OAU found it politically expedient to refuse to recognize the conflagration as a war of liberation, and the Eritreans fought on. Another episode featured the Nigerian civil war of 1967-1970. The Ibo people attempted secession from Nigeria by establishing Biafra. The OAU, acting through Emperor Haile Selassie I of Ethiopia and others, failed to end the Ibo breakaway. Moreover, member states of the OAU split. Thirty-seven favored the Nigerian government, which eventually crushed Biafra. Four members of the OAU—Gabon, Ivory Coast, Tanzania, and Zambia—backed Biafra. An acrimonious problem for the OAU has been the Western Sahara. Spain, which had begun to occupy the region in 1885, relinquished control in 1975, and King Hassan II of Morocco claimed it. An indigenous institution of the Western Sahara, Polisario, rose up to proclaim the Saharawi Arab Democratic Republic. Clashes between it and Morocco began in 1975. The OAU failed at mediation and in 1984 admitted the Saharawi Arab Democratic Republic to its membership; Morocco then renounced membership in the OAU.

The Organization of African Unity chose to ignore human rights violations in many states. Examples are atrocities by Idi Amin (Uganda), Eddine Ahmed Bokassa (Central African Empire), Francisco Macias Nguema (Equatorial Guinea), Mengistu Haile Mariam (Ethiopia), Muhammad Siyad Barrah (Somalia), Mobutu Sese Seko (Congo [Kinshasa]), and Samuel Doe (Liberia).

Bibliography

Addona, A. F. *The Organization of African Unity.* Cleveland: World, 1969. Readable, popular account of the formation of the Organization of African Unity and its charter. Lists the founding fathers of the OAU. Interesting illustrations, helpful index, limited bibliography. Discussion of the OAU's problems is limited, as the book was published in 1969.

Binaisa, Godfrey L. "Organization of Africa Unity and Decolonization: Present and Future Trends." *Annals of the American Academy of Political and Social Science* 432 (July, 1977): 52-69. Succinct description of the creation of the Organization of African Unity. Impartial discussion of the OAU's achievements and failures up to early 1977. Some documentation.

Cervenka, Zdenek. *The Organization of African Unity and Its Charter.* Praha, Czechoslovakia: Academia Nakladateslvi Ceskoslovenské Akademie Ved, 1968. Brief, clear telling of the founding of the Organization of African Unity. Good political and legal analysis of the OAU charter and a concise discussion of the OAU-United Nations relationship. Excellent annotation. Introduction by Diallo Telli, the first secretary-general of the OAU.

Legum, Colin. *Pan-Africanism: A Short Political Guide.* Rev. ed. New York: Praeger, 1965. Excellent, balanced narrative of pan-Africanism. Lucid account of the early Organization of African Unity. Praiseworthy documentation, including poetry. Many first-rate appendices, including declarations, charters, protocols, and resolutions. Good index.

Neweke, G. Aforka. "The Organization of African Unity and Intra-African Functionalism." *Annals of the American Academy of Political and Social Science* 489 (January, 1987): 133-147. Stresses the Organization of African Unity as a product of compromise between advocates of continent-wide political union and proponents of functional cooperation as a building block for an African sociopsychological community. Happenings in African states and international politics frustrated functional cooperation within the OAU. Profuse notes.

Tekle, Amare. "The Organization of African Unity at Twenty-five Years: Retrospect and Prospect." *Africa Today* 35 (1988): 7-19. Objectively assesses the Organization of African Unity's achievements and failures within the context of its original mission and historical constraints. Calls for reform in the OAU's charter and decisionmaking framework. Unannotated.

Wolfers, Michael. *Politics in the Organization of African Unity*. London: Methuen, 1976. Scholarly, detailed story of the formation of the Organization of African Unity's charter. Estimable history of the OAU from 1963 to 1973 and some narration of events between 1973 and 1976. Has a well-documented, select bibliography, a map of the OAU's membership in 1975, and an adequate index.

Erving E. Beauregard

Cross-References

The Statute of Westminster Creates the Commonwealth (1931), p. 453; Riots Erupt as Katanga Province Secedes from the Congo (1960), p. 1068; The United Nations Intervenes in the Congolese Civil War (1960), p. 1074; The Nonaligned Movement Meets (1961), p. 1131; Lutuli Is Awarded the Nobel Peace Prize (1961), p. 1143; Algeria Gains Independence (1962), p. 1155; Zimbabwe's Freedom Fighters Topple White Supremacist Government (1964), p. 1224; The OAU Adopts the African Charter on Human and Peoples' Rights (1981), p. 2136; Namibia Is Liberated from South African Control (1988), p. 2409.

MARTIN LUTHER KING, JR., DELIVERS HIS "I HAVE A DREAM" SPEECH

Category of event: Racial and ethnic rights
Time: August 28, 1963
Locale: Washington, D.C.

The "I Have a Dream" speech, delivered during the 1963 March on Washington, D.C., encapsulated the social vision of the nonviolent movement and elevated it in American and world consciousness

Principal personages:

MARTIN LUTHER KING, JR. (1929-1968), the president of the Southern Christian Leadership Conference

ASA PHILIP RANDOLPH (1889-1979), a labor leader and civil rights activist; a major organizer of the 1963 March on Washington

JOHN LEWIS (1940-   ), the Student Nonviolent Coordinating Committee leader who made a controversial speech during the 1963 March on Washington

JOHN F. KENNEDY (1917-1963), the thirty-fifth president of the United States (1961-1963); introduced the package of reforms that led to the 1964 Civil Rights Act

Summary of Event

The setting for Dr. Martin Luther King, Jr.'s best-remembered speech was a massive March on Washington, D.C., in late August, 1963. On August 28, he delivered the partly extemporaneous address from the steps of the Lincoln Memorial to more than 200,000 march participants and, through radio and television, to millions of others around the world. To many, it was his clearest expression of his vision for America's future. His rhythmic repetition of "I have a dream" between each major point of the speech accounts for the title and reflects the measured optimism he sought to project.

At the time of the March on Washington, both King and the nonviolent Civil Rights movement were under intense pressure from several directions. The settlement effected on May 10, 1963, after the massive Birmingham campaign was considered inadequate by some critics. Birmingham officials and business leaders had made substantial concessions, including hiring and promoting more black personnel and desegregating public facilities, but there was little assurance that living conditions for African Americans would improve substantially. Violence also continued in Birmingham, beginning with the bombing of the home of King's brother Alfred Daniel the day after the May 10 agreement.

Furthermore, King's image among the more militant black activists was waning. His post-Birmingham national tour brought him in June, 1963, to Harlem, where

Black Muslims threw rotten eggs at his car. This troubled King and prompted his belief that they were transferring their frustrations to him unfairly. The Federal Bureau of Investigation was beginning to spy more extensively on King and his aides, and its director, J. Edgar Hoover, was more candidly criticizing King.

In key ways, the Birmingham campaign had been a success. Certainly it had made the public more aware of racial problems in the United States. Scenes of police using fire hoses and dogs against demonstrators, including children, were televised across the nation, heightening public awareness of the plight of blacks and the entrenched resistance to even minimal desegregation in the South. Offsetting this to some degree was the reluctance of President John F. Kennedy's administration to meet black leaders' demands for a more direct role in mandating desegregation. Kennedy did introduce a civil rights bill in late May, 1963, but because of his narrow election in 1960 that had required support by conservative Southerners who opposed integration, he was politically restricted. On May 30, King requested a conference with the president after having consulted several times by telephone with white supporter Stanley Levison about such a meeting. Levison had suggested that civil rights leaders threaten a march on Washington to dramatize the need for reform, just as labor leader Asa Philip Randolph had done in 1941.

Since late 1962, Randolph independently had been discussing the possibility of such a march, and in March, 1963, he proffered the idea to the board of his Negro American Labor Council in New York. Randolph was interested in collaborating with King's Southern Christian Leadership Conference and other organizations in implementing the march, originally scheduled for May, 1963. The SCLC's activities in Birmingham precluded that march, but planning continued in various circles over the following three months. By late June, King and the SCLC were ready to support Randolph's general plan and to play a key role in preparing for a massive march in August. Some fourteen civic and civil rights organizations spearheaded the campaign that they hoped would bring more than 100,000 people to the nation's capital.

There were detractors. President Kennedy opposed the idea of a march on Washington because it might jeopardize the pending civil rights legislation. Militant black leaders considered it histrionic and accommodating to the white establishment. There was little that could be done about the latter, but march planners agreed to avoid any direct political attacks on Kennedy in order not to weaken his leverage or his support. There was some concern when it was learned that Student Nonviolent Coordinating Committee (SNCC) leader John Lewis was planning to deliver a speech critical of the administration's civil rights bill. It was released to the press on August 27, the day before the March on Washington, but was toned down somewhat before delivery and had little impact. Generally, the march was orderly and the speakers avoided direct attacks on the Kennedy Administration.

Many speakers, including Asa Philip Randolph, National Association for the Advancement of Colored People (NAACP) leader Roy Wilkins, labor leader Walter Reuther, Lewis, and others, spoke to the crowd of more than 200,000 that rallied near the Lincoln Memorial on August 28. It was a hot, sunny Wednesday afternoon, and the crowd was tiring when King came to the microphone. He had been introduced by the march's prime mover, Randolph, who had dreamed of this kind of massive display since 1941. King began slowly and deliberately, noting that he was happy to join with the marchers "in what will go down in history as the greatest demonstration of freedom in the history of our nation."

King spoke of the Declaration of Independence and its recognition of the rights of all citizens, as well as President Abraham Lincoln's Emancipation Proclamation of 1863. "But one hundred years later," King said, "the Negro still is not free." Instead, "the Negro lives on a lonely island of poverty in the midst of a vast ocean of material prosperity." Black Americans were in Washington to "cash a check"—to demand their rights as American citizens. The "promissory note" of the founding fathers had never been paid to the nation's black citizens, the SCLC president averred.

King paid respect to those who had suffered in the quest for racial justice, noting that many had been jailed, beaten, and otherwise "battered by the storms of persecution." In the midst of such difficult times, King affirmed, "I still have a dream." With that, the crowd became excited. Repeating the "I have a dream" phrase, King outlined his fundamental hopes for the future. "It is a dream deeply rooted in the American dream. I have a dream that one day this nation will rise up and live out the true meaning of its creed, 'We hold these truths to be self-evident, that all men are created equal.'"

From there, King proceeded through several of his specific dreams. One was that "one day on the red hills of Georgia, sons of former slaves and the sons of former slave owners will be able to sit down together at the table of brotherhood." For his own children, he dreamed of the day when they would not be judged "by the color of their skin, but by the content of their character."

In Alabama, Tennessee, and Georgia, and across the nation, King hoped, racial discrimination and tension would cease. Drawing upon Old Testament prophecy, as he often did, King cried out:

> I have a dream that one day "every valley shall be exalted and every hill and mountain shall be made low. The rough places will be made plain and the crooked places will be made straight, and the glory of the Lord shall be revealed, and all flesh shall see it together."

The ending was dramatic and similarly charged with moral emphases. "So let freedom ring from the prodigious hilltops of New Hampshire; let freedom ring from the mighty mountains of New York. . . ." In his panoramic survey of the mountains of America, he included Stone Mountain of Georgia and Lookout Mountain of Tennessee, and "every hill and molehill of Mississippi. From every mountain side, let freedom ring." If that happened, said King, Americans could speed up the day when all people, regardless of race, religion, or creed could "join hands and sing in the words of the old Negro spiritual: 'Free at last. Free at last. Thank God Almighty, we are free at last.'"

By then, the huge throng of marchers was electrified. King walked quickly to a car provided by President Kennedy and met with the president, along with several other civil rights leaders, at the White House. The high emotion of the rally now had to give way to the reasoned discourse of political realities of the civil rights bill. No one was sure on August 28 whether it would pass, despite King's warmly received address.

Impact of Event

The initial impact of the "I Have a Dream" speech was to lift the spirits of the participants and to give the March on Washington a tone of historical importance. King's speech was to become his most famous, epitomizing for many people the essence of the nonviolent movement's social vision. It was heard, directly and indirectly, by millions of people, including hundreds of Representatives and Senators. One of them, Senator Hubert Humphrey, watched and heard the speech with some 150 other members of Congress and remarked that although it probably did not change anyone's vote on the pending civil rights bill, it was "a good thing for Washington and the nation and the world." That was generally the feeling among supporters. There were detractors as well, many of whom considered the whole affair histrionic and unrelated to the actual power struggle for civil rights reform.

There is little doubt that the march and the King speech contributed to support for civil rights reform, although resistance to the administration's bill continued for months and was not overcome until well after Kennedy's assassination in November, 1963. President Lyndon B. Johnson, Kennedy's successor, steered an enlarged version of the Kennedy bill through Congress in the spring of 1964, and on July 2 signed it into law. Most of the resistance was from Senators. House passage on February 10, 1964, was much easier than the months-long process that led to a favorable Senate vote, seventy-three to twenty-seven, on June 19. The role played by the march and King's speech in that legislative struggle was to provide the example of a basically orderly demonstration and an articulate statement of blacks' demands set in a traditional American value structure.

That the speech did not change attitudes widely is also evident. Violence and racial tensions continued. On September 15, 1963, just days after the speech, four young black girls were killed by dynamite hurled into a window of the Sixteenth Street Baptist Church in Birmingham. In St. Augustine, Florida, and several other cities, there were other manifestations of racial violence in the months immediately following the events in Washington. On balance, however, the speech did have significant impact on attitudes. In the address, King had retained continuity with his previous speeches and sermons on human relations. He understood that the task of building bridges between races and social classes would not be easy. That he emphasized the economic plight of African Americans and poor people in the United States assured that there would be controversy, but it also signaled one of the principal emphases of the movement in the period after passage of the Civil Rights Act of 1964 and the Voting Rights Act of 1965.

The address was highly moral and religious in tone, while linked clearly to the

American constitutional tradition. This important aspect of the "I Have a Dream" speech made it adaptable to a variety of uses in churches and civil rights campaigns and in the political processes of civil rights reform. For the SCLC, it became the major symbol of its future programs. Keeping the dream alive was the prevailing theme of King's organization in his last years and well beyond.

Bibliography

Ansbro, John J. *Martin Luther King, Jr.: The Making of a Mind.* Maryknoll, N.Y.: Orbis Books, 1982. This is the best study to date of the intellectual and spiritual life of Martin Luther King, Jr. What it lacks in awareness of the controversy about King's personal life it makes up for with a profound study of King's education, ideology, and faith. It is indispensable for examining this area of King's career. Contains notes and index.

Garrow, David J. *Bearing the Cross: Martin Luther King, Jr., and the Southern Christian Leadership Conference.* New York: William Morrow, 1986. Despite its exposure of King's personal flaws, Garrow's account is basically sympathetic and contains useful information on almost all aspects of King's career. It is relatively short on analysis and probing of the moral dimensions, but it has a detailed summary of events leading to the March on Washington and King's role in it. Carefully documented, with a detailed index.

Gentile, Thomas. *March on Washington: August 28, 1963.* Washington, D.C.: New Day Publications, 1983. Published in the twentieth anniversary year of the 1963 March on Washington for Jobs and Freedom, Gentile's account is detailed, illustrated with photographs, and valuable for both its historical information and its capture of the spirit of the large crowd that marched on the nation's capital in August, 1963. Gentile treats it as a grass-roots movement given shape and purpose by key national organizers such as Asa Philip Randolph, various labor leaders, and civil rights advocacy organizations. Includes illustrations, some notes, and an extensive bibliography.

Lewis, David Levering. *King: A Biography.* 2d ed. Urbana: University of Illinois Press, 1978. A reissue of his 1970 work, this study is more valuable than some of the more recent, better documented works in probing the inner meaning and motivations of the nonviolent movement. It has a particularly good section on the March on Washington and King's "I Have a Dream" speech. Contains selected bibliography, notes, and index.

Peake, Thomas R. *Keeping the Dream Alive: A History of the Southern Christian Leadership Conference from King to the 1980's.* New York: Peter Lang, 1987. This comprehensive study of the SCLC focuses in many places on the moral and religious dimensions of the nonviolent Civil Rights movement and has a detailed analysis of the setting and content of the "I Have a Dream" speech. Contains chronological charts, bibliography, text of the speech, notes, and index.

Schulke, Flip, ed. *Martin Luther King, Jr.: A Documentary, Montgomery to Memphis.* New York: W. W. Norton, 1976. Although basically a pictorial account of King's career from the Montgomery bus boycott until his assassination, Schulke's fascinating survey also reflects the inner spirit of the nonviolent movement and the King mystique. For the March on Washington, it is particularly valuable in showing the interracial nature of the march, the political contacts with the Kennedy Administration, and the reactions of the crowd to King's speech. Contains extensive explanatory text and excerpts from speeches and sermons by King, including the "I Have a Dream" speech.

Watley, William D. *Roots of Resistance: The Nonviolent Ethic of Martin Luther King, Jr.* Valley Forge, Pa.: Judson Press, 1985. A brief but useful study of the ethical content of King's nonviolent concepts, this book examines the role of the black religious experience, evangelical liberalism, and personalism in shaping King's ideas. Watley also focuses on the Albany, Birmingham, and Selma campaigns as contributing factors and concludes with what he calls the six principles of King's nonviolent ethic. Watley's account is a sympathetic study but one which retains a sense of balance. Contains bibliography, notes, and index.

Thomas R. Peake

Cross-References

The SCLC Forms to Link Civil Rights Groups (1957), p. 974; The Civil Rights Act of 1957 Creates the Commission on Civil Rights (1957), p. 997; Pope John XXIII Issues "Mater et Magistra" and "Pacem in Terris" (1961), p. 1113; Meredith's Enrollment Integrates the University of Mississippi (1962), p. 1167; Civil Rights Protesters Attract International Attention (1963), p. 1188; The Twenty-fourth Amendment Outlaws Poll Taxes (1964), p. 1231; Congress Passes the Civil Rights Act (1964), p. 1251; Martin Luther King, Jr., Wins the Nobel Peace Prize (1964), p. 1257; Martin Luther King, Jr., Leads a March from Selma to Montgomery (1965), p. 1278; The U.N. Covenant on Civil and Political Rights Is Adopted (1966), p. 1353; Martin Luther King, Jr., Is Assassinated in Memphis (1968), p. 1419.

LEGISLATION USHERS IN A NEW ERA OF CARE
FOR THE MENTALLY DISABLED

Category of event: Disability rights
Time: October 31, 1963
Locale: Washington, D.C.

Congress enacted legislation to extend grants to aid construction of facilities for research and treatment of the mentally ill and retarded

> *Principal personages:*
> WILBUR D. MILLS (1909-   ), a Democratic representative from Arkansas
> ABRAHAM A. RIBICOFF (1910-   ), a Democratic senator from Connecticut and floor manager for the bill in the Senate
> JOHN F. KENNEDY (1917-1963), the president of the United States (1961-1963)
> LYNDON B. JOHNSON (1908-1973), the president of the United States (1963-1969)

Summary of Event

Little attention had been given to the problems and needs of the mentally ill until the 1960's. During that time, there were an estimated 5.4 million people in the United States who were mentally ill in varying degrees. Developmentally disabled individuals for many years were not assured the basic rights afforded nondisabled people. Mentally ill people were relegated to the status of second-class citizens, and therefore few services were provided to aid in improving their daily lives.

Children who were mentally ill were assigned to "special" schools because they were identified as being unable to learn. Their only hope was that they could be "trained," rather than educated, to become functioning adults. They were also presumed to need teaching in morals and ethics, since this was not considered inherent in their natural abilities. Many special schools were located far from children's homes, thus removing them from concerned family and friends.

Usually, the mentally ill and retarded adults were involuntarily placed in institutions, where they could be hidden from public view. These institutions on the whole had very poor conditions. Most were overcrowded, unsanitary, and extremely unpleasant. There was little in the way of education or training for the residents. School programs designed to teach turned into rote exercises administered by drill masters; the training programs, which focused on farm and garden activities and laundry and kitchen skills, became unpaid institutional maintenance assignments instead of programs teaching skills to help patients integrate into the community. Many residents of these institutions spent their days on a variety of drugs intended to calm them and keep them from causing trouble. Some states spent as little as two dollars per person per day on the care of the mentally ill; the average was only four dollars. Charges of mistreatment and neglect of the residents of these institutions became more and more frequent.

Part of the problem was that the specific causes of mental illness and retardation were unknown. Often, the mentally ill were neglected because their illnesses were misunderstood and clouded by superstitions and irrational fears. Developmentally disabled people were stereotyped as unstable, temperamental, and morally deficient. Further, because mental illness was an inherent defect, it was thought that medicine probably would not help its victims. The only "cure" was to perform surgery.

As more scientific research was completed in the area of mental illness, people began to realize that mental disease was often the result of chemical imbalances rather than of uncontrollable factors. As more of the causes of mental illness began to come to light, the population of needy people received more attention. It was recognized that, in many ways, these people simply needed more help than others throughout their entire lives. Their needs included special education, health maintenance, legal protection, daily care, and sometimes community services. It was also recognized that their needs, to a great extent, depended on age and degree of mental illness.

During the 1950's and 1960's, the plight of the mentally ill in the United States began to get more recognition. Individual states began to recognize the needs of this special population. For example, New York passed the first state-county mental health law, which provided state financing to county programs. The law's goal was to spend as much money outside state hospitals as inside.

The federal government also began to get involved. President Dwight Eisenhower signed the Mental Health Study Act of 1955, through which the federal government provided one-quarter of a million dollars, to be matched in private funds, to invest in a national study. The study was set up to investigate the human and economic problems associated with mental illness, to assess current methods for dealing with them, and to recommend improvements and new programs. The final report was given to then-President John F. Kennedy.

President Kennedy was a major supporter of the rights of the mentally ill. Part of the reason was that Kennedy had a sister, Rose, who was mentally retarded. Kennedy's father, Joseph P. Kennedy, was also a supporter of the rights of the mentally ill. In 1964, he established a foundation named after Joseph P. Kennedy, Jr. The foundation gave out a yearly award to persons or organizations that performed research, service, or leadership in the field of mental retardation.

President Kennedy recognized that the problems of mentally ill Americans were a "most urgent need in the area of health improvement." He acknowledged that mental illness was a problem that occurred frequently and caused suffering not only for its victims but also for victims' families. Mental illness was recognized as a cause of both emotional suffering and economic hardship. In Kennedy's opinion, the nation could save money by helping the mentally ill population learn how to work in society and lead productive lives outside institutions.

Kennedy appointed a special panel to study the mentally retarded. The panel examined many facets of mental illness, including questions of program development. It found, among other things, that only a small percentage of the mentally ill people in the United States were so severely afflicted that they required constant care or supervision. This and other specific recommendations formed the primary basis of Kennedy's message to Congress, which in turn formed the basis of the Community Mental Health Centers Construction Act.

On February 5, 1963, Kennedy gave a speech to Congress on mental illness and mental retardation. In it, he called for a "bold new approach" to the problem by federal, state, and local governments. In the message, he requested that federal funds be transmitted to states so that they could detect, treat, and rehabilitate those identified as mentally ill. He said he wanted to get away from simply institutionalizing those who were mentally ill, a practice that was a burden on both the government and the individual families involved.

President Kennedy made a series of recommendations about mental illness. He recommended that a matching-grant program be instituted to allow states to build community health centers. He requested federal grants for maternity and child health services to combat the problem of mental retardation. He supported special education programs for retarded children and increased teacher training, including improved vocational training. Finally, Kennedy supported federally financed research into the causes and prevention of mental illnesses.

After the message of February 5, hearings were held in the Senate on two separate bills directly relating to the recommendations proposed by Kennedy. The bill's floor manager was Senator Abraham A. Ribicoff, a Democrat from Connecticut. A few weeks later, similar hearings began in the House of Representatives. The floor manager was Representative Wilbur Mills, a Democrat from Arkansas. The bill had tremendous support in both the House and the Senate. Supporters of the bill believed that the concept of community health centers could lead to the treatment of many mental patients in their homes and decrease the populations of state mental hospitals.

The bill became law on October 31, 1963, when Kennedy signed the bill. A few weeks later, Kennedy was assassinated, and Lyndon Johnson became president.

Impact of Event

The Mental Retardation Facilities and Community Mental Health Centers Construction Act authorized construction of research centers. Between 1965 and 1967, $27 million was expended to establish twelve centers. A Mental Retardation Branch and the National Institute of Child Health and Human Development were developed to administer the research centers' policies. University Affiliated Facilities, or UAFs, were built as part of the act. Between 1965 and 1971, $38.5 million was allocated to eighteen UAF sites.

A Community Facilities Construction Program was also part of the act. This helped individual states build specially designed facilities for the diagnosis, treatment, education, training, and personal care of mentally ill people. The program received

$90.2 million between 1965 and 1970. The centers were small, centrally located buildings that provided a wide range of psychiatric programs. These included inpatient and outpatient facilities, day and night care services, emergency services, precare, aftercare follow up, rehabilitation clinics, halfway houses, and foster care. There were facilities for training and research and for the evaluation of programs.

These programs were located within communities, thereby increasing the availability of psychiatric services to community residents. In this way, mental illness could be detected and treated before hospitalization was necessary. If hospitalization became necessary, separation from family and community would be minimized.

This was the first time the federal government took a leadership role in the field of mental illness. In his speech of February 5, President Kennedy had recognized that the United States had not seen much progress in understanding, treating, and preventing mental disabilities. Kennedy also recognized the importance of the role of the federal government in assisting, stimulating and channeling public energies to help address the problem. Kennedy wanted to return a large proportion of the mentally ill to useful lives and, through research, cut the number of new cases down. After Kennedy's assassination, President Johnson and the Congress continued to support the initial goals set forth by Kennedy.

The first federal grant to finance on-the-job training for mentally retarded youth was given to a New York company. The money was used to train ninety mentally retarded and handicapped youths for a variety of jobs. These jobs included key-punching, typing, and glass etching. It was expected that, after the training, the youths could obtain private employment.

The Johnson Administration continued to fund research programs associated with the new law. Money was allocated for many research grants to qualified personnel to investigate the causes and treatments of mental illness. Other groups also became involved in seeking appropriate solutions to the issues surrounding mental health. For example, the American Medical Association held a series of conferences to seek ways to speed up the attack on mental illness.

Mental health institutions changed as well. They began to include private institutions with cottages containing social rooms, classrooms, extensive playgrounds, and arts and crafts centers built to meet current recommended standards in the field. The goal was to encourage students to participate actively in the community. The goal no longer was to hide these people from society, but rather to prepare those with mental illness to lead productive lives with little help from others, if possible.

On a broader level, sponsors of the bill hoped it would change the way Americans thought about and treated mentally ill people. Until this attention was given, most Americans were uninformed about the problems the mentally ill faced. The bill helped remove a large number of mentally ill persons from institutions and helped to integrate them into society, where they were no longer a financial burden on their families or the nation.

The bill was also successful in creating a society that was more accepting of those who suffered from mental illness. It allowed such people to take part in society. It also sent mentally ill people a message that they no longer had to be dependent on others, but that they could have greater participation in community life and greater control over their own lives.

Bibliography

Birenbaum, Arnold, and Herbert J. Cohen. *Community Services for the Mentally Retarded*. Totowa, N.J.: Rowman & Allanheld, 1985. Focus on community treatment programs for the mentally ill: what services have traditionally been provided and some future trends based on past research. Includes information on the politics surrounding legislation involving mental retardation and the legal rights of the mentally ill.

Crissey, Marie S., and Marvin Rosen. *Institutions for the Mentally Retarded*. Austin, Tex.: PRO-ED, 1986. Focuses on the role of the residential institution in the lives of mentally ill people. Institutions can play valid roles in educating and training the mentally ill for productive lives and can also be used as research centers to learn more about the problems and concerns of the mentally ill.

Evans, Daryl P. *The Lives of Mentally Retarded People*. Boulder, Colo.: Westview Press, 1983. Contains an overview of mental retardation, including the causes of mental illness, how mental illness has been viewed throughout history, and the current definitions of some relevant terms. Also gives some information on the legal rights of the mentally disabled and how they have been viewed by the courts. Other social issues, such as the mentally ill in the workplace, in education, and in marriage, are also included.

Krishef, Curtis H. *An Introduction to Mental Retardation*. Springfield, Ill.: Charles C Thomas, 1983. After a brief history of mental retardation is presented, the rights of the mentally ill are discussed. Other topics, such as residential institutions, counseling, and vocational training for the mentally ill are also presented.

Ludlow, Barbara L., Ann P. Turnbull, and Ruth Luckasson. *Transitions to Adult Life for People with Mental Retardation: Principles and Practices*. Baltimore, Md.: Paul H. Brookes, 1988. These authors present useful strategies for developing the independent skills of mentally ill adults, including independent living and productive employment. Some legal issues related to providing community services for the disabled are provided.

Stroud, Marion, and Evelyn Sutton. *Expanding Options for Older Adults with Developmental Disabilities*. Baltimore, Md.: Paul H. Brookes, 1988. Focuses on the needs of elderly persons with mental disabilities. A "hands-on" source that is useful in helping provide mentally ill older adults with the same opportunities that are available to others.

Summers, J. A. *The Right to Grow Up*. Baltimore, Md.: Paul H. Brookes, 1986. Summers presents a comprehensive introduction to topics related to adults with mental illness. Some nontraditional issues are addressed, including the need for sexual expression, friendship, and self-choice.

Nancy E. Marion

Cross-References

Congress Passes the Civil Rights Act (1964), p. 1251; The United Nations Declares Rights for the Mentally Retarded (1971), p. 1644; Congress Passes the Equal Employment Opportunity Act (1972), p. 1650; Congress Responds to Demands of Persons with Disabilities (1973), p. 1731; Congress Enacts the Education for All Handicapped Children Act (1975), p. 1780; An APA Report Discusses the Homeless Mentally Ill (1984), p. 2226.

THE UNITED NATIONS ISSUES A
DECLARATION ON RACIAL DISCRIMINATION

Categories of event: Racial and ethnic rights; civil rights
Time: November 20, 1963
Locale: United Nations, New York City

The Declaration on the Elimination of All Forms of Racial Discrimination was adopted in 1963 to expedite the elimination of apartheid, segregation, and other forms of racial domination

Principal personages:
ADLAI E. STEVENSON (1900-1965), the United States ambassador to the United Nations during the John F. Kennedy and Lyndon B. Johnson administrations
PHILIPPE DE SEYNES (1910-   ), the undersecretary of the U.N. Department of Economic and Social Affairs, represented the French delegation during the 1950's and 1960's
U THANT (1909-1974), the United Nations secretary-general from November, 1961, to December, 1971

Summary of Event

After World War II, for the first time in history, the fundamental rights of individuals became an international concern. Before that time, the rights of individuals had been a matter exclusively of domestic jurisdiction of a state. With the exception of certain categories of persons such as diplomats, aliens, and refugees, international law and international organizations dealt directly only with nation-states. The massive inhuman treatment and torture of people at the hands of Nazis and Fascists both before and during World War II made the protection of rights derived from the inherent dignity and equality of a human person a matter of universal concern. Thus, the human rights of individuals were to find a place in the agenda of the newly established United Nations.

The United Nations took a major initiative by adopting the Universal Declaration of Human Rights on December 10, 1948. The declaration served as the basic document providing guidelines and goals about the rights of individuals before the community of nations. The Universal Declaration was adopted in the General Assembly with forty-eight nations voting in its favor, none against, and eight abstaining. Although it lacked legal binding force over member states, it served as a model to be emulated, inspired the inclusion of guaranteed protections for individuals in many constitutions all over the world, and provided a yardstick against which the conduct of nations could be judged.

The Universal Declaration formally stipulated human rights of an individual related to liberty and spiritual integrity, political freedoms, and social, economic, and cultural independence. It became the basis for the adoption of a number of important U.N.-sponsored declarations and covenants in subsequent years. The spirit of this declaration was violated in varying measures by most members of the United Nations; however, despite frequent practices to the contrary, no government has ever publicly admitted the disregard of the declaration's provisions.

The United Nations' declarations are formalized statements of general principles. The United Nations Declaration on the Elimination of All Forms of Racial Discrimination of 1963 was an offshoot of the 1948 Universal Declaration. It received its main impetus from dual sources: the entry of a host of African and Asian states into the United Nations championing the cause of self-determination of nations and the policy of apartheid, which extolled racial discrimination and racial superiority, practiced in South Africa. The racial problems in the United States, particularly the practice of segregation in the South, also provided impetus to the declaration.

The groundwork for the declaration on racial discrimination of 1963 was prepared as early as 1947, when the U.N. Commission on Human Rights established a subcommission to study and report on discrimination against and protection of minorities. A number of organs and procedures for the supervision of human rights were established by the United Nations in the following years. In 1963, the Subcommission on Prevention of Discrimination and Protection of Minorities, the Commission on Human Rights, the Economic and Social Council, and the General Assembly of the United Nations considered the question of the elimination of all forms of racial discrimination. After considerable debate and several amendments, on November 20, 1963, the General Assembly unanimously adopted the Declaration on the Elimination of all Forms of Racial Discrimination.

The purpose of the United Nations Declaration on the Elimination of All Forms of Racial Discrimination was to expedite the elimination of racial discrimination, which, despite international efforts, had continued to manifest itself in many parts of the world in the form of "apartheid, segregation and separation, as well as by the promotion and dissemination of doctrines of racial superiority and expansionism in certain areas." Under the provisions of the declaration, the practice of discrimination between human beings on the grounds of race, color, or ethnic origin was declared to be a denial of the principles of the charter of the United Nations, a violation of human rights, and an obstacle to friendly and peaceful relations among nations and peoples within nations. States, institutions, groups, and individuals were all barred from practicing racial discrimination and the use of police powers and violence to oppress individuals on racial and related grounds. Moreover, prescription was made to adopt positive measures at the state level for the adequate protection of individuals belonging to certain racial groups in order to ensure their full enjoyment of human rights. The declaration on racial discrimination suggested speedy governmental action in reversing public policies of racial segregation and the policies of apartheid. It advocated effective steps to be taken by governments to promote teaching, education, and information, with the intent of eliminating racial discrimination and prejudice and promoting understanding, tolerance, and cooperation.

The General Assembly requested all states to undertake all necessary measures to implement fully, faithfully, and without delay the principles contained in the declaration. It also requested governments and nongovernmental organizations to publicize the text of the declaration as widely as possible. The U.N. secretary-general and specialized U.N. agencies were given the responsibility of circulating the declaration in as many languages as possible.

The most important immediate outcome of the declaration on racial discrimination was the adoption of a resolution by the U.N. General Assembly to give absolute priority to the preparation of a Draft Convention on the Elimination of All Forms of Racial Discrimination to be considered by the General Assembly in 1964. The Convention on the Elimination of All Forms of Racial Discrimination was later adopted by the General Assembly in 1965, and by August, 1991, it had been adopted by 129 states. A committee on the elimination of racial discrimination was also established to review the information placed before it by the convention's signatory states and to report directly to the General Assembly once a year.

The Declaration on the Elimination of All Forms of Racial Discrimination was to have a strong impact on the future U.N. instruments related to human rights, which included the two International Covenants adopted by the U.N. General Assembly in 1966, the 1968 convention on the nonapplicability of statutory limitations to war crimes and crimes against humanity, the Convention on the Suppression and Punishment of the Crime of Apartheid (1973), the Convention on the Elimination of All Forms of Discrimination Against Women (1979), the Declaration on the Elimination of All Forms of Intolerance and of Discrimination Based on Religion or Belief (1981), the Declaration on the Rights of All People to Peace (1984), and the Declaration on the Human Rights of Individuals Who Are Not Nationals of the Country in Which They Live (1985). Moreover, the General Assembly declared the period of 1973-1983 to be the "Decade Against Racial Discrimination." The declaration on elimination of racial discrimination also gave a boost to the activities of nongovernmental watchdog agencies such as Amnesty International in bringing to light the violation of human rights of racial and ethnic minorities within states.

On a limited scale, despite the approval of only a very few states, the committee on the elimination of racial discrimination deals with communications directly from individuals within these states. It comments upon particular situations involving racial discrimination and prepares proposals and recommendations regarding such acts. Although its jurisdiction is advisory in nature and without any legal force, the committee plays an important role in focusing world attention on racial issues and mobilizing worldwide public opinion.

Impact of Event

The Declaration on the Elimination of All Forms of Racial Discrimination of 1963 considerably increased worldwide public awareness of the human rights of individuals regardless of their race, color, or ethnicity. The declaration generated moral, rather than legal, pressure in the society of states, and thus, despite their record of violations, all governments pay lip service to the doctrine and deny its disregard.

The declaration on racial discrimination suffered from an inherent limitation. As a result of the sudden emergence of a multitude of Asian and African states as the new majority at the United Nations in the 1960's, the Universal Declaration of Human Rights was expanded by adding the right of self-determination of nations to its list, a right which had been conspicuously absent from the original list. The rights of racial groups or individuals began to be perceived in terms of the self-determination of nations and an ideological framework opposed to Western colonialism and Western imperialism. The rights of people within these postcolonial societies and elsewhere in the international state system continued to be regarded as a matter of state jurisdiction and sovereignty.

Furthermore, Cold War bloc politics and the superpower rivalry complicated the situation. The Soviet Union, as the leader of the communist countries and a friend of the nonaligned Third World, and the United States, as the leader of the Western Bloc and an ally of the Third World Western-aligned or anticommunist states, introduced the system of bloc voting at the United Nations, a system that seriously undermined the cause of human rights. Political expediency caused the United States to vote with its allies on the side of such countries as South Africa to maintain the solidarity of the Western Bloc. The United States' criticism and negative vote during the deliberations on the draft proposal of the 1963 declaration on racial discrimination related mainly to technical grounds and the use of certain phrases in the proposal. The declaration in its final form was unanimously adopted by the General Assembly.

The Soviet Union and other communist countries, as well as most of the Third World countries, continued to violate the human rights of racial and ethnic minority groups within their respective states to varying degrees. Their rhetoric indicated a discrepancy of perceptions caused by their focus on colonialism and imperialism as the exclusive manifestations of racism.

The issue of racial discrimination at the United Nations remained heavily focused on South Africa, which represented a unique, formally created political-legal system of racial discrimination. Israel, too, became a main target. As a result, racialist practices in the Western world, particularly in the form of institutional racism, escaped receiving similar criticism or denouncement. For example, in 1963, the year in which the declaration was made, the Civil Rights movement in the United States began to protest the practice of segregation in the South and violation of human rights of black Americans. Practices in the United States did not become a controversial issue at the United Nations.

The powers of the U.N. Commission on Human Rights have gradually expanded. The role of nongovernmental watchdog organizations, which closely collaborate with the U.N. agencies, has been impressive. These include Amnesty International, the International Commission of Jurists, the International League of Human Rights, the International Federation of Human Rights, and the World Council of Churches. In promoting their efforts and others, the U.N. Declaration on the Elimination of All

Forms of Racial Discrimination played an important role within the structural limitations of its parent organization.

Bibliography

Baehr, Peter R., and Leon Gordenker. *The United Nations: Reality and Ideal.* New York: Praeger, 1984. Reviews and provides a critical summary of the history of the United Nations. Attempts to evaluate the functioning of the United Nations to ascertain if the organization has developed according to expectations.

Donnelly, Jack, and Rhoda E. Howard, eds. *International Handbook of Human Rights.* New York: Greenwood Press, 1987. This reference work provides an excellent summary and review of the progress made in the area of human rights in the post-World War II years. A critical analysis is made of the academic, political, and cultural complexities surrounding the problem of adherence to human rights standards.

Mower, Glenn A., Jr. *The United States, the United Nations, and Human Rights.* Westport, Conn.: Greenwood Press, 1979. This book is a survey of American foreign policy and the issue of human rights at the United Nations, and how at times the United States has appeared to be working at cross purposes as a result of the pressures of domestic politics.

Riggs, Robert E., and Jack C. Plano. *The United Nations: International Organization and World Politics.* Chicago: Dorsey Press, 1988. Written from the perspective of international politics, this book traces the evolution of the United Nations and its structure, form, and activity. Describes the structure and processes of human rights rule-making.

United Nations. *Yearbook of the United Nations, 1963.* New York: Columbia University Press in cooperation with the United Nations, 1965. A good source for detailed technical information about United Nations proceedings and texts of documents.

United Nations. Office of Public Information. *The United Nations and Human Rights.* New York: United Nations, 1973. A documentary work about the activities of the United Nations in the area of human rights development and promotion since its inception. Also a systematic compilation of declarations, covenants, and other related documents.

Indu Vohra

Cross-References

Roosevelt Approves Internment of Japanese Americans (1942), p. 595; The Indian Government Bans Discrimination Against Untouchables (1948), p. 743; The United Nations Adopts the Universal Declaration of Human Rights (1948), p. 789; China Initiates a Genocide Policy Toward Tibetans (1950), p. 826; China Occupies Tibet (1950), p. 837; The U.N. Covenant on Civil and Political Rights Is Adopted (1966), p. 1353; Conflicts in Pakistan Lead to the Secession of Bangladesh (1971), p. 1611;

GREEK AND TURKISH INHABITANTS OF CYPRUS CLASH OVER POLITICAL RIGHTS

Category of event: Racial and ethnic rights
Time: December, 1963
Locale: Cyprus

Ethnic violence between Greek Cypriots and Turkish Cypriots led to segregation of the two communities and the disintegration of the Republic of Cyprus

Principal personages:
    ARCHBISHOP MAKARIOS (1913-1977), the president of Cyprus (1960-1977),
        a Greek Cypriot religious and political leader
    FAZIL KUTCHUK (1906-   ), the vice president of Cyprus (1960-1973),
        a Turkish Cypriot political leader
    GEORGE GRIVAS DIGHENIS (1898-1974), a Greek Cypriot officer of the
        Greek army
    GEORGE VASSILIOU (1931-   ), the president of Cyprus beginning in 1988
    RAUF DENKTASH (1924-   ), the president of the self-proclaimed Turk-
        ish Republic of Northern Cyprus beginning in 1983

Summary of Event

Among the many successive rulers of Cyprus since antiquity, only the Greeks and Turks had a sizable demographic impact. The Greek Cypriots are descendants of Greek colonizers from the second millenium B.C. The Turkish Cypriots are the descendants of soldiers and settlers who moved to Cyprus during Ottoman rule from 1571 to 1878. Great Britain took control of the island, with consent of the Ottoman sultan, and then formally annexed it in 1914. In 1960, following a bloody four-year guerrilla war, Britain granted independence to Cyprus, thus ending the colonial relationship. From 1960 to 1963, Cyprus went through a transformation, and ethnic conflict emerged as the dominant problem. The causes and dynamics of the ethnic conflict can be understood better if seen against the background of the fragmented historical and social foundations of the newborn Cypriot republic.

At the time of independence, Cyprus had a population of 570,000, consisting of 78 percent Greek Cypriots, 18 percent Turkish Cypriots, and 4 percent other minorities. There were purely Greek, purely Turkish, and mixed villages in all regions. The Greek and Turkish groups were divided along linguistic, historical, ethnic, cultural, and religious lines. The Greek Cypriots spoke Greek and identified with the Greek nation, culture, and classical heritage, and with the Byzantine Empire. Almost all of them were members of the Orthodox church of Cyprus. The Turkish Cypriots spoke Turkish and identified with the Turkish nation and culture and with the Ottoman Empire heritage. Virtually all were Sunni Muslims.

Despite four centuries of coexistence and considerable geographic intermingling, the two communities remained separate and distinct ethnic groups. A partial physical separation occurred with the eruption of ethnic violence in December, 1963. An almost complete separation occurred with the 1974 Turkish invasion of Cyprus.

Certain factors helped the two ethnic groups preserve their national identities throughout centuries. The Orthodox church, which maintained a dominant position among the Greek Cypriots, helped them remain Greek Orthodox. When the Ottomans took Cyprus from the Venetians in 1571, they destroyed the Roman Catholic church and restored the Cypriot Orthodox church. The autonomy of the church was reconfirmed and the archbishop was recognized as ethnopolitical leader. The church became a symbol of political and ethnic unity, as most political, social, cultural, and intellectual life was associated with religious organizations.

The Ottoman *millet* administrative system separated the two communities on the basis of religion and ethnicity. Administration and tax collection were carried out with the help of religious institutions. Under British rule, the two groups retained control over religion, education, culture, personal status, and ethnic institutions.

The segregated and divisive educational system perpetuated ethnic distinctiveness by transferring conflicting ethnic values from generation to generation. The two communities had separate schools which were largely controlled by their religious institutions. Throughout the Ottoman period and the early years of British rule, the teachers were mostly local Orthodox or Muslim religious leaders. During the British period, curricula were almost identical to those in Greece and Turkey and emphasized religion, national heritage, ethnic consciousness, and the longtime Greek-Turkish rivalry.

The two communities had antagonistic loyalties to Greece and Turkey. Each community honored the national holidays, played the national anthem, and used the flag of its mother country. Cypriots from both ethnic groups returned to the mainland and fought as volunteers on opposite sides during the 1912-1913 Balkan Wars, World War I, and the 1919-1923 Greek-Turkish War. Attachment to two rival and often belligerent countries promoted ethnic chauvinism and prevented development of unifying patriotic bonds and cohesive Cypriot nationalism.

The two groups held conflicting views about the island's political future. Throughout the British period, *enosis* (union of Cyprus with Greece) was the most persistent and rigid Greek Cypriot goal. It was part of the wider Panhellenic movement of *megali idea* (the great idea), which aimed to reconstruct the Byzantine Empire under Greek hegemony. As a counterforce, the Turkish Cypriots advanced the idea of *taksim* (Cyprus partition into Greek and Turkish sectors). The two movements were strongly supported by Greece and Turkey, respectively. Attachment to the conflicting goals of *enosis* and *taksim* led to political polarization.

The British colonial policy of "divide and rule" maintained and reinforced ethnic, administrative, and political separation. The British colonial administration made no effort to create a unified native Cypriot consciousness. The two communities were treated as separate groups, and antagonism between them was stirred up. Maintenance of a psychological gap between the two groups was used to ensure British control.

Against the background of these historical and sociopolitical realities, the Republic of Cyprus emerged on August 16, 1960, as a bicommunal state. Greece and Turkey had, in effect, negotiated a settlement in Zurich and London under British auspices. The political institutions of the newborn state formalized and reinforced ethnic differences through divisive structures and practices. The two communities were treated as distinct ethnic groups, and the Turkish minority was given extensive privileges and guarantees, including disproportional participation in the government, public service, army, police, legislative process, and handling of foreign affairs. Ethnic dualism was institutionalized in all sectors of public life. Although the ethnopolitical goals of *enosis* and *taksim* were formally ruled out by the constitution, no measures were taken to promote integrative practices and unifying bonds cutting across ethnic lines. Old controversies revolving around ethnopolitical goals and differences (including *enosis* and *taksim*) and conflicting loyalties remained part of private and public life on both sides. Ethnic segregation in large towns, ethnic division in the administration of justice, and the hiring of government employees on the basis of disproportionate ethnic quotas favoring the minority were some of the more controversial issues that were never resolved.

On November 30, 1963, after three years of intensifying ethnic and legal controversies, the Greek Cypriot president, Archbishop Makarios, proposed to the Turkish Cypriot vice president, Fazil Kutchuk, a thirteen-point amendment of the constitution that would make Cyprus a more unitary state and bring the two communities closer together. The Turkish Cypriots rejected the proposal because they were afraid it would take away some of their privileges and safeguards. They were especially concerned about their right to disproportionate participation in the armed forces and public service, as well as their right to veto legislation on defense and foreign affairs. All attempts to find common ground for negotiation failed, and heavy fighting broke out on December 22, 1963.

Despite peace efforts and mediation by Britain, the United States, and the United Nations, the fighting spread and intensified. Greece and Turkey also became involved in military operations, and international concern shifted from the Cypriot setting to the imminent danger of a Greek-Turkish war. A United Nations peacekeeping force was sent to Cyprus in March, 1964. In early June, a Turkish invasion and Greek-Turkish war were averted through the adamant insistence of U.S. president Lyndon B. Johnson that there would be no war between two North Atlantic Treaty Organization (NATO) allies. Another major crisis erupted in August, 1964, when Greek and Greek Cypriot forces launched an attack against the Turkish Cypriot enclave in the Tylliria region. Turkey was using that enclave, the only one with access to the sea, to smuggle soldiers, arms, and supplies into Cyprus. Turkey responded by launching large-scale air attacks on military and civilian positions in the region. Napalm bombs were used during the air raids.

In November, 1967, another crisis brought Greece and Turkey to the brink of war and caused intensive diplomatic intervention by the United States, NATO, and the United Nations. The Greek military government, which was largely responsible for the crisis, satisfied most Turkish demands, including withdrawal from Cyprus of ten thousand Greek troops and the removal of General George Grivas Dighenis from the position of commander of Greek Cypriot forces. Uneasy peace was established, but a settlement of the broader ethnopolitical conflict was never within sight.

On July 15, 1974, the military regime in Athens staged a bloody coup against President Makarios. Turkey reacted by invading Cyprus five days later. Turkish forces took control of 37 percent of the island and established the "Attila line" dividing Cyprus into north and south sectors. Greek Cypriots living in the north were forced to move to the south and Turkish Cypriots were transferred to the north. The forced population movement completed the physical separation of the two communities that had started in December, 1963. Despite international condemnation and several U.N. resolutions, the Turkish army continued to occupy the island's northern part until at least the early 1990's.

Impact of Event

The outbreak of ethnic violence in Cyprus in 1963 marked the beginning of violent disintegration of the Republic of Cyprus and physical separation of Greek Cypriots and Turkish Cypriots. Twenty years later, on November 15, 1983, the Turkish Cypriots, under the leadership of Rauf Denktash, unilaterally declared the independence of the "Turkish Republic of Northern Cyprus." Turkey, which militarily occupied northern Cyprus, was the only country to recognize the Turkish Cypriot "state." The rest of the world, through U.N. resolutions and otherwise, has repeatedly condemned both the Turkish occupation and the unilateral declaration of independence. Although Cyprus was still internationally recognized as one country in 1991, its people were completely segregated along ethnic lines. Prospects of unification were not good, but efforts were made by the United Nations to negotiate a lasting settlement.

The impact of ethnic violence on the people of Cyprus has been devastating. The protracted armed confrontation undermined not only the republic but also the prospect of reuniting the Cypriots under one flag and one administration. As a result of hostilities, thousands of people, including civilians, were killed and wounded. Following the Turkish invasion of 1974 and the forceful physical separation of the two ethnic groups, one-third of the population became refugees. This painful demographic surgery was accompanied by extensive damage to the economic structure and resources of the island and an enduring trauma of the Cypriot psyche—Greek and Turk alike. The southern Greek sector showed signs of economic expansion, but Turks in the north did not live up to their economic potential. The two groups remained separated not only by a widening economic gap but also by trenches, minefields, and columns of tanks and cannons that neither side could cross. Interaction across the dividing line became almost nonexistent after 1974.

Several rounds of talks between President George Vassiliou and Turkish Cypriot leader Rauf Denktash, under the auspices of U.N. secretary-general Javier Pérez de

Cuéllar, created a spirit of optimism but gave no results. A sense of pragmatism has emerged on both sides, however, favoring rapprochement and a settlement based on bizonal federalism. Given the realities of Cyprus—geography, economy, size, distribution of natural resources, demography, and the traumatic experiences of the past—this seems to be a feasible and promising solution.

Bibliography

Attalides, Michael A. *Cyprus: Nationalism and International Politics.* New York: St. Martin's Press, 1979. A good presentation and analysis of the Cyprus issue in the context of national movements, societal changes, and international politics. The relationships of the two Cypriot communities with their motherlands are discussed extensively. The book has a contemporary focus but also provides a brief historical background.

Ehrlich, Thomas. *Cyprus, 1958-1967: International Crises and the Role of Law.* New York: Oxford University Press, 1974. A scholarly work with a legal perspective. It looks for the origins and major elements of the problem in the legal structure surrounding the creation of the Republic of Cyprus. Major decisions and crises on Cyprus are examined from the viewpoint of international law.

Hitchens, Christopher. *Hostage to History: Cyprus from the Ottomans to Kissinger.* New York: Noonday Press, 1989. A popular book by a prominent journalist and frequent visitor of Cyprus. It provides a critical analysis of American policy toward Cyprus and argues that the problems facing the island are the result of external interference. Supportive of Greek Cypriot views and critical of Turkish policies and actions on Cyprus.

Joseph, Joseph S. *Cyprus: Ethnic Conflict and International Concern.* New York: Peter Lang, 1985. Examines both the domestic aspects and international implications of the Cyprus problem. Historical, social, cultural, institutional, and political roots of the ethnic conflict are examined. The impact of Greek-Turkish antagonism, superpower politics, and United Nations involvement receive considerable attention. A scholarly work of analysis and interpretation with a detached approach.

Koumoulides, John T. A., ed. *Cyprus in Transition, 1960-1985.* London: Trigraph, 1986. A good collection of eight articles with diverse perspectives and viewpoints. Although each article reflects the interests, expertise, and background of its author, the book as a whole provides a rounded and objective look at the ethnopolitical conflict and its consequences.

Kyriakides, Stanley. *Cyprus: Constitutionalism and Crisis Government.* Philadelphia: University of Pennsylvania Press, 1968. One of the most authoritative works on the constitutional aspects and breakdown of the Republic of Cyprus. The causes and consequences of the 1963 constitutional crisis are examined in the context of domestic Cypriot politics and external interference.

Loizos, Peter. *The Heart Grown Bitter: A Chronicle of Cypriot War Refugees.* London: Cambridge University Press, 1982. The story of Greek-Cypriot inhabitants of a village who became refugees after the Turkish invasion of Cyprus. Very informative and revealing of human attitudes and social conditions; also a good source of information about the huge refugee problem that resulted from the war. Based on field observation and interviews with refugeees.

Markides, Kyriacos. *The Rise and Fall of the Republic of Cyprus.* New Haven, Conn.: Yale University Press, 1977. A widely quoted book on the social aspects of national movements and rivalries among Greek Cypriots. The *enosis* movement, nationalism, and the role of leadership are extensively discussed in the light of ethnic conflict. A good scholarly work with penetrating analysis.

Salih, Halil Ibrahim. *Cyprus: The Impact of Diverse Nationalism on a State.* University: University of Alabama Press, 1978. The work of a Turkish Cypriot who believes that the two Cypriot communities cannot coexist in a united Cyprus. Salih writes about the causes and effects of the ethnic conflict with the intent of proving his point. A good part of the book is made up of several useful appendices.

Volkan, Vamik D. *Cyprus, War and Adaptation: A Psychoanalytic History of Two Ethnic Groups in Conflict.* Charlottesville: University Press of Virginia, 1979. A study of the poor relations and mutually negative perceptions held by the two Cypriot communities about each other. Helpful for the reader who wants to learn more about the causes and consequences of the conflict at both the individual and group levels. An interesting and unique study of the myths and realities that divide the Cypriots.

Joseph S. Joseph

Cross-References

The Young Turk Movement Stages a Constitutional Coup in Turkey (1908), p. 98; Armenians Suffer Genocide During World War I (1915), p. 150; The Balfour Declaration Supports a Jewish Homeland in Palestine (1917), p. 235; Cyprus Gains Independence (1960), p. 1084; The Nonaligned Movement Meets (1961), p. 1131; A United Nations Peace Force Is Deployed in Cyprus (1964), p. 1236; A Greek Coup Leads to a Military Dictatorship (1967), p. 1359; Ethnic Riots Erupt in Armenia (1988), p. 2348; Ethnic Unrest Breaks Out in Yugoslavian Provinces (1988), p. 2386.

ZIMBABWE'S FREEDOM FIGHTERS TOPPLE WHITE SUPREMACIST GOVERNMENT

Category of event: Revolutions and rebellions
Time: 1964-1979
Locale: Zimbabwe (Southern Rhodesia)

Settler colonialism was finally defeated in Zimbabwe's war for liberation when freedom fighters succeeded in their attrition battle against the white supremacist Rhodesian state

Principal personages:

ROBERT MUGABE (1924-   ), the first prime minister of the independent Republic of Zimbabwe

JOSHUA NKOMO (1917-   ), a leading nationalist who headed the Zimbabwe African People's Union (ZAPU)

IAN SMITH (1919-   ), the eighth prime minister of Southern Rhodesia (1964-1978) and the leader of Rhodesia's Unilateral Declaration of Independence (UDI) from Great Britain in 1965

ABEL MUZOREWA (1925-   ), the leader of the African National Council in 1971

NDABANINGI SITHOLE (1920-   ), a political activist who became the head of the Zimbabwe African National Union (ZANU) at its founding in 1963 and later participated in the internal settlement after being ousted by ZANU

JOSIAH TONGORARA (1938-1979), the most popular and effective commander of the military wing of ZANU

HERBERT CHITEPO (1923-1975), the leader of the external wing of ZANU from 1963 until his assassination

KENNETH KAUNDA (1924-   ), the president of Zambia, an outspoken supporter of liberation struggles in Southern Africa

Summary of Event

In 1979, the leaders of the Patriotic Front, the political alliance between the Zimbabwe liberation factions, signed the Lancaster House Agreement ending the war between the white minority government and the Zimbabwean freedom fighters and paving the way for a short transition period to Zimbabwean independence. The agreement called for a new constitution that would institute a parliamentary system and reserve 20 percent representation for whites for seven years. The new government would honor Rhodesia's debts and obligations, protect minority rights, and pay full compensation for any land taken for redistribution. During the brief transition, there would be neutral armed forces to monitor elections and the cease-fire. The negotiation led to Zimbabwe's independence under the newly elected prime minister, Robert Mugabe, and to the end of international economic sanctions against Rhodesia on April 18, 1980.

Several years before two African liberation movements emerged to initiate a guerrilla struggle against the Southern Rhodesian white minority government in 1964, African nationalists had pushed for political reforms that could achieve decolonization and African majority rule. These efforts were complicated by the peculiar political history of the self-governing colony known as Southern Rhodesia.

Southern Rhodesia was the name given to the colony in south-central Africa occupied in 1890 by the British South Africa Company, a private British charter company under the directorship of Cecil Rhodes. In 1923, after several years of company rule, the colony was turned over by Great Britain to its small community of white settlers. From that point, Southern Rhodesia was a self-governing British colony. The settlers instituted a white minority government, which expropriated the best lands, guaranteed preferential employment opportunities for whites, and forced Africans into a low-wage labor market. African dissent was divided and weak. The government used coercion and brutality to keep resistance to a minimum.

The Southern Rhodesian government expanded its influence in 1953 with the creation of the Central Africa Federation (Zimbabwe, Zambia, and Malawi). The federal regime was dominated by Southern Rhodesian settlers, who used their position to spur economic development in the territory at the expense of Zambia and Malawi. When African nationalism in those two states undermined the federation, it also challenged the nature of colonial rule in Southern Rhodesia.

The Southern Rhodesian African National Congress (ANC) emerged as an effective voice of African aspirations in 1957. Under the leadership of Joshua Nkomo, its president, the organization built on the political activism of its predecessor, the Youth League. The ANC worked within the system to seek redress of its grievances—pass law restrictions, labor exploitation, and land policies. It sought the repeal of discriminatory laws and the basis for genuine political participation by the African majority. In 1959, the government banned the organization, arrested most of its leaders, and declared a state of emergency.

A new organization, the National Democratic Party (NDP), was formed in 1960 as successor to the ANC. It too was banned in December of the following year, only to be replaced by the Zimbabwe African People's Union (ZAPU), under Joshua Nkomo's continued leadership. All efforts at achieving internal reforms by working within the system seemed exhausted by 1963. Prominent leaders such as Ndabaningi Sithole and Robert Mugabe raised concerns about Nkomo's effectiveness and his direction for the organization. Nkomo denounced their dissent and moved to expel them. This split was cemented when Sithole formed the Zimbabwe African National Union (ZANU) in 1963. ZANU's focus on political activism within the country seemed in sharp contrast to Nkomo's interest in forming a government-in-exile.

Meanwhile, Southern Rhodesia's white politics suffered political defeats at the hands of the British when the federation came to an end in 1963. A right-wing political party, the Rhodesia Front (RF), assumed a leading position in 1964, under the prime ministership of Ian Smith. Smith wanted to gain independence for his government while subverting African nationalism. He banned both ZAPU and ZANU and jailed most of their leaders, including Nkomo, Sithole, and Mugabe, for the next ten years. When negotiations broke down with Great Britain, he announced the Unilateral Declaration of Independence (UDI) for the state of Rhodesia in November of 1965.

Herbert Chitepo, Zimbabwe's first African attorney, was designated by ZANU to set up an external ZANU wing. By 1965, he had a revolutionary council in operation in exile in Lusaka, Zambia. Chitepo mobilized the Zimbabwe African National Liberation Army (ZANLA) as the means to prosecute a long guerrilla struggle. Jason Moyo represented ZAPU in Lusaka and began forming a military wing, the Zimbabwe People's Revolutionary Army (ZIPRA). The division between the two nationalist parties was now institutionalized with the development of two armies.

The Battle of Chinhoyi on April 28, 1966, between ZANLA forces and the Rhodesian military is often considered to be the beginning of the military struggle for Zimbabwe. Initially, ZANLA trained and mobilized troops with a conventional strategy in mind, but the Chinhoyi experience, together with external influence from China and the liberation movement in neighboring Mozambique, convinced the ZANU leadership that guerrilla warfare with political education for mobilization would be more effective.

Chitepo successfully shifted ZANU's emphasis. By 1968, ZANU cadres were recruiting troops inside Zimbabwe and politicizing the peasantry. Most training took place in camps in Zambia or Tanzania, with some guerrillas receiving training in China. The progress of the liberation movement in Mozambique meant that ZANU was allowed to create staging and training camps in liberated zones in Mozambique after 1972. Their proximity to Zimbabwe made for effective recruitment and deployment of forces throughout the eastern border with Mozambique. ZANLA also benefited from the military leadership of Josiah Tongorara, who earned the chair position of the war council. He built on the strategy of stretching Rhodesian forces throughout the country, attacking white farms, and increasing Rhodesia's economic costs in prosecuting the war.

ZAPU's military wing, ZIPRA, remained small in this period, showing no indication of any willingness to engage the Rhodesian forces in any sustained effort. Instead, ZAPU retained Nkomo's strategy of negotiation while building its military capacity. ZIPRA was trained by Soviet advisers but remained small until the mid-1970's. Even then, ZIPRA demonstrated no inclination to politicize the peasantry in the area in western Zimbabwe where it made incursions. ZIPRA seemed more interested in preparing for conflict with ZANLA at some future date than in attacking the Rhodesians.

The military tactics used by ZANLA and, to a lesser extent, by ZIPRA proved successful in raising the costs to Rhodesia. Although they were crucial to the ultimate victory, the movements benefited considerably from African political pressure both inside and outside the country. The military struggle also gained from economic sanctions against Rhodesia and other forms of international pressure.

The British had rejected the UDI in 1965 and had successfully implemented economic sanctions against Rhodesia through the support of the United Nations. The Smith regime had tried to find a basis for a negotiated settlement with Great Britain, but the sticking point of African acceptance remained to thwart Smith's aspirations. In 1971, Smith made some considerable international progress. The United States openly defied sanctions and purchased strategic minerals, primarily chromium. The British signed a tentative settlement that recognized the validity of the UDI while pledging the Rhodesian government to some form of majority rule in the next century. The one caveat was that African opinion would be sampled to ensure its support for the settlement. The Pearce Commission was formed by the British in 1972 to assess the African response.

Methodist bishop Abel Muzorewa, who had not participated openly in politics, was approached by ZANU and ZAPU representatives to lead the fight against the agreement. In December of 1971, he became head of the African National Council and began to mobilize African public opinion so that the Pearce Commission would know that Africans unequivocally rejected the Anglo-Rhodesian settlement. His success working within the country made him a leading political figure and brought him a substantial international reputation. Although Muzorewa undermined the settlement, he was not ready to support violence to gain Zimbabwe's freedom.

Smith then sought negotiations directly with Muzorewa. During their talks, circumstances changed in southern Africa. A coup in Portugal quickened liberation forces' victory in Mozambique, leading to independence in 1975 and raising concerns about expanding regional conflicts in South Africa. Even though South Africa provided some troop support in Rhodesia, its leadership, under the direction of Prime Minister John Vorster, pressured Smith to seek an agreement. The African front-line states, under the initiative of Zambian president Kenneth Kaunda, pushed Zimbabwean nationalists for unity, which would hasten the war's end. In response to progress in the talks with Muzorewa, Smith agreed to an amnesty for political leaders in jail, and in December, 1974, most were released.

It was then that a coup within the ZANU leadership was disclosed. Robert Mugabe replaced the ousted Sithole as ZANU's head. This move did not enhance efforts at unity, though there was a general recognition of Muzorewa's leadership through the umbrella organization of the African National Council.

International conferences based on initiatives by U.S. secretary of state Henry Kissinger did not prove fruitful. Smith enjoyed some success in broadening the conflict and lessening the pressure in Rhodesia. He organized a resistance insurgency against the newly independent Mozambique and applied military and economic pressure to Zambia.

In 1976, the nationalists countered with the formation of the Patriotic Front, which unified the political wings of ZANU and ZAPU—at least publicly. The following year, the United States repealed the Byrd Amendment, which had provided a loophole in economic sanctions against Rhodesia. As the war heated up, it pushed Smith toward new negotiations. Smith reached an internal settlement with Muzorewa, Sithole, and Chief Jeremiah Chirau in 1978 as a basis for African majority rule.

The internal settlement meant an African prime minister and African parliamentary majority, but it entrenched whites in much of the political and economic leadership of the country. The internal settlement was rejected by the international community and the Patriotic Front. The war continued.

By the middle of 1979, it was clear to the new government and Smith's forces that negotiations with the Patriotic Front under British auspices were necessary to achieve peace. With external pressure on both Smith and the uneasy Mugabe-Nkomo alliance, a new constitution was negotiated at Lancaster House in London. The frontline states, particularly Zambia and Mozambique, which had suffered considerably during the war, celebrated this success. South Africa, which remained concerned about the possibilities of the war expanding on its borders, was relieved by the settlement. Great Britain was finally off the hook for its colonial role in Southern Rhodesia. The white settlers were apprehensive, and though many fled to South Africa, others saw the settlement as entrenching their economic position. For the Africans, independence was finally a reality.

Impact of Event

Zimbabwean independence changed the face of southern Africa. It proved that the white settlers were not invincible and undermined many of South Africa's rationales about its position in Namibia. Although the post-independence era was not without difficulties, Zimbabweans have proved that white settlers and Africans can work together for national development and prosperity.

For Zimbabweans, the victory opened new opportunities through self-determination. The edifice of discriminatory legislation that had underwritten policies of separate amenities, segregated services, movement restrictions, job reservation, and limited access to land was eliminated quickly. Efforts to purchase land for the resettlement of refugees and former combatants became a priority. The new government took the unprecedented step of opening up schools to all prospective students, through high school. The old colonial system, which had promoted considerable wastage from grade to grade, was abolished. Support for new facilities, teachers, and materials was mobilized to meet the new demand.

Integration of the civil service and private companies demonstrated that racial arguments that had kept Africans in inferior positions were preposterous. Independence unfettered a huge supply of untapped talent and bolstered strategies for development. Africans took leading roles in business and labor. Higher education provided mobility for Africans in key professions. Attorneys, physicians, dentists, journalists, professors, teachers, and nurses reflected the changes brought about by majority rule. No longer were their professions exclusively white.

Although Zimbabwe's internal changes have been dramatic since 1979, they also challenged the old order dominated by South Africa's regional power. The end of the war brought greater stability to Botswana and Zambia. Strife continued to bloody Mozambique, however, and South Africa remained willing to send commandos against its neighbors. Zimbabwe showed that it was possible for whites and blacks to prosper side by side. Zimbabwe also demonstrated that the ties of the liberation struggles to the Soviet Union and China did not inhibit independence.

Zimbabwe's role in making the regional economic organization, the Southern Africa Development Coordinating Conference (SADCC), work to its and the front-line states' advantage had made the nation a regional power from the day of its independence. Zimbabwe often spoke of its desire to follow a socialist development path, but it successfully implemented a mixed economy that attracted both foreign and domestic capital. Its leading roles in international agencies like the International Labor Office (ILO) and in the nonaligned movement have brought the former international pariah Rhodesia into a position as one of the most respected developing nations, Zimbabwe.

The significance of the African victory over the white minority regime was best seen in terms of the reaffirmation of human dignity. Zimbabwe's ability to develop and maintain democratic institutions in the face of its colonial legacy and South African subversion and overt attacks provided important inspiration to the people of South Africa who struggled to remove the burdens of apartheid from their society and their spirit.

Bibliography

Hancock, Ian. *White Liberals, Moderates, and Radicals in Rhodesia, 1953-1980.* London: Croom Helm, 1984. This book focuses on the liberal tradition in Rhodesia and the politics surrounding negotiations for the settlement with the African nationalists. It outlines the pressure in white politics to follow Smith's policies.

Martin, David, and Phyllis Johnson. *The Struggle for Zimbabwe: The Chimurenga War.* New York: Monthly Review Press, 1981. This book provides a detailed account of the liberation struggle. It shows how and why the war effort succeeded. It is sympathetic to African aspirations and the socialist model of development.

Moorcraft, Paul. "Rhodesia's War of Independence." *History Today* 40 (September, 1990): 11-17. This article traces the efforts to preserve white minority rule in Southern Rhodesia. It discusses the military strategies and their effectiveness during the war. It also examines the internationalization of the conflict.

Nyagumbo, Maurice. *With the People: An Autobiography from the Zimbabwe Struggle.* London: Allison and Busby, 1980. This volume provides an insider account from the African nationalist perspective. Nyagumbo shows the nature of the commitment to the struggle and the hardships endured to achieve victory.

O'Meara, Patrick. "Zimbabwe: The Politics of Independence." In *Southern Africa: The Continuing Crisis,* edited by Gwendolen M. Carter and Patrick O'Meara. Bloomington: Indiana University Press, 1982. This chapter is a readable overview of the struggle for independence. It recounts the split between ZANU and ZAPU in 1963, the Pearce Commission inquiry in 1972, and the development of the Patriotic Front.

Jack Bermingham

Cross-References

Ho Chi Minh Organizes the Viet Minh (1941), p. 573; The Nationalist Vietnamese Fight Against French Control of Indochina (1946), p. 683; India Gains Independence (1947), p. 731; The Mau Mau Uprising Creates Havoc in Kenya (1952), p. 891; Castro Takes Power in Cuba (1959), p. 1026; Riots Erupt as Katanga Province Secedes from the Congo (1960), p. 1068; The United Nations Intervenes in the Congolese Civil War (1960), p. 1074; The Nonaligned Movement Meets (1961), p. 1131; Algeria Gains Independence (1962), p. 1155; The Organization of African Unity Is Founded (1963), p. 1194; Namibia Is Liberated from South African Control (1988), p. 2409.

THE TWENTY-FOURTH AMENDMENT
OUTLAWS POLL TAXES

Category of event: Voting rights
Time: January 23, 1964
Locale: Washington, D.C.

The poll tax was an arbitrary limitation on voting rights, particularly in the South, where it was often employed to deny the franchise to African Americans and poor whites

Principal personages:

JOHN F. KENNEDY (1917-1963), the thirty-fifth president of the United States, an advocate of legislation to end both the poll tax and literacy tests

LYNDON B. JOHNSON (1908-1973), the thirty-sixth president of the United States, a strong advocate of civil rights who presided over passage of the 1964 Civil Rights Act

MARTIN LUTHER KING, JR. (1929-1968), a civil rights advocate who organized opposition to racial and social discrimination

SPESSARD L. HOLLAND (1892-1971), a conservative Democratic senator from Florida who sponsored the Twenty-fourth Amendment

RICHARD B. RUSSELL (1897-1971), a conservative Democrat from Georgia and leader of the Senate's Southern bloc

MICHAEL H. MANSFIELD (1903-   ), a Democrat from Montana, the Senate majority leader

Summary of Event

On January 23, 1964, the South Dakota senate cast the deciding vote in the ratification process of the Twenty-fourth Amendment to the United States Constitution. The amendment ended the poll tax as a condition of voting in federal elections. The real function of the tax had been to deny civil rights to racial minorities, especially Southern blacks. The Twenty-fourth Amendment, passage of which began in 1962, was only one part of a larger campaign of civil rights reform that came to a head with the Civil Rights Act of 1964.

Civil rights issues were central to the social questions that surfaced during the 1950's and 1960's. Beginning with the *Brown v. Board of Education* case in 1954, which disallowed school segregation, both courts and legislatures were engaged in the resolution of such issues. John F. Kennedy assumed office as president in 1961, at a time when the Civil Rights movement was taking on a direct-action character— undertaking mass demonstrations, civil disobedience, and occasional acts of violence—and opposition to it was being manifested in mass arrests, intimidation, and even murder. This trend convinced the new administration and its liberal supporters in Congress that the time had come to use federal legislation as well as the courts to initiate civil rights reform. The first target was the poll tax.

The poll tax, a uniform, direct, and personal tax levied upon individuals, was not a new phenomenon. It had existed in some states since the early 1900's, and in others, such as New Hampshire, since colonial times, though not as a franchise prerequisite. All states with the poll tax allowed exceptions to it: officers and men on active militia duty, veterans, and persons disabled as a result of gainful occupation and whose taxable property did not exceed $500, for example. The tax was nominal in most cases for those who did have to pay, being only $1.50 or $2.00 per year. The tax was cumulative, however, so that voters who came to register after having not paid the tax for a number of years might find themselves having to pay what for many poor people would be a considerable sum. To civil rights advocates, the poll tax paralleled literacy tests as a device to limit voting rights, and they were determined that both should be abolished. Even in Southern states where the poll tax was no longer used, literacy tests, closed registration lists, and straightforward intimidation were used to prevent blacks from voting.

The process of reform had to begin somewhere, and Northern Democrats, acting upon inspiration from the Kennedy Administration, began with the anti-poll-tax amendment process early in 1962. There was strong opposition from a Southern bloc of conservatives, mostly Democrats led by Richard B. Russell, a Democrat from Georgia, but it was not as strong as might have been expected.

The Senate majority leader was Michael H. Mansfield, a Democrat from Montana, and it was his responsibility to shepherd the legislation through the Senate. The anti-poll-tax amendment itself was sponsored by Spessard L. Holland, a Democrat from Florida, whose role might have appeared surprising, since he was part of the Southern bloc. Holland, however, was no friend of the poll tax in any form and had led a successful campaign to abolish it in his own state in 1937.

The Senate Judiciary Committee, chaired by Senator James O. Eastland, a Democrat from Mississippi and part of the Southern bloc, had conducted hearings on the poll tax and literacy tests for weeks to little avail. On March 14, Senator Mansfield moved for Senate consideration of a bill to establish Alexander Hamilton's New York home as a national monument, to which, it was suggested, the proposed constitutional amendment could be attached. The Senate Judiciary Committee, wherein, according to liberal senators, civil rights issues tended to get lost, was effectively bypassed, and the Hamilton motion, with the expectation of its being linked to the anti-poll-tax amendment, was put before the Senate.

As soon as it appeared on the floor, the Southern conservative bloc began a "friendly" filibuster, so termed because the Southerners did not go all-out to prevent the Hamilton resolution from coming to a vote. It is conceivable that the vote was considered a foregone conclusion, and the filibuster was merely for form's sake. In any event, it endured for ten days, until, apparently, the participants had run out of words. Then Senator Holland introduced the preordained motion to substitute the language of the anti-poll-tax amendment for the language of the Hamilton resolution. This brought Senator Russell to his feet in protest: "We are adopting an absurd, farfetched, irrational, unreasonable, and unconstitutional method to get this amendment," he charged. Others agreed, including Jacob K. Javits, a Republican from New York, who proposed that the Senate should act against the poll tax by simple legislation, and Paul H. Douglas, a Democrat from Illinois, who warned that, the questionable manner of the adoption notwithstanding, using the amendment process could itself prove the downfall of efforts to abolish the tax.

Nevertheless, the Holland motion was put to a vote, and on March 27 it passed the Senate by a margin of seventy-seven to sixteen. An amendment to the Constitution of the United States repealing the poll tax for all federal elections was then forwarded to the House of Representatives, where it was debated, dissected, promoted, and opposed in similar manner, until it passed that chamber in August, 1962. It was then up to the states to ratify the amendment by vote of their legislatures.

It was speculated widely during succeeding months that, on the premise that the poll-tax amendment would pass the states and greatly broaden the base of the Southern electorate, the Democratic leadership would work to break the power of the Southern bloc by promoting candidates who were more loyal to the national party to oppose the bloc's members in the primaries. At least thirteen congressional seats were thought to be on a target list. Needless to say, Republican Party leaders were delighted, convinced by the Southerners' defiant attitude that the Democrats had outsmarted themselves.

Meanwhile, the poll-tax amendment was being considered by the states, and it was an uphill battle. The Arizona house, for example, approved the amendment in 1963, but it died in the state senate. By the end of the year, however, momentum toward ratification gathered, and by January 5, 1964, the amendment needed to be approved by only two more states. A few days later the number dropped to one, and on January 23 South Dakota's senate voted thirty-four to zero in favor of ratification. The Twenty-fourth Amendment to the Constitution was law, requiring then only the further technicality of formal certification by the General Services Administration of the federal government. South Dakota was compelled to race through its vote in order to beat out Georgia as the deciding state. There was an irony in this, as Georgia was the home of Senator Richard Russell, the most outspoken opponent of the amendment in the early days of debate on the motion.

Impact of Event

The poll-tax amendment symbolized the liberal determination to institute civil rights reform. There was, however, opposition of nearly equal intensity. Three political proposals made in 1963 were meant to redress—or so their advocates claimed—the eroding of states' rights by the federal government. In fact, this package aimed at countering the possible effects of impending civil rights legislation, including abolition of the poll tax. The first proposal sought to give the power to redraw congressional districts to state governments. Gerrymandering could then keep power out of the hands of racial minorities, even if minorities came to the polls in greater numbers after the Twenty-fourth Amendment was passed. The second proposal placed the constitutional amendment process in the hands of the state legislatures, bypassing either Congress or a national convention. Under this plan, a two-thirds majority of the state legislatures could propose an amendment, and a three-fourths majority could make it part of the Constitution. The third proposal sought to create a "Court of the Union" that would review Supreme Court decisions on federal-state relations and would be made up of the chief justices of the fifty states. This court would have effectively nullified the Supreme Court as the final arbiter of constitutionality in matters touching upon civil rights, because most such matters touched in turn on federal-state relations.

None of these propositions came to fruition, but the Twenty-fourth Amendment did, abolishing the poll tax in federal elections. Within two months, however, Arkansas, one of the last states to cling to the poll tax, upheld in court the state constitution's requirement of a poll tax for state and local elections. Later, a private election oversight organization found at least seven irregularities in the primary election process in Arkansas, including the fact that unauthorized persons were permitted to help count ballots. The organization discovered that, while the poll tax was no longer required for federal elections, there were many other devices available to skew elections in the way segregationists wanted.

Various avenues were taken to limit the impact of the new amendment even for federal elections. In Mississippi, state officials cracked down on minor violations of little-used aspects of the civil code as a device to intimidate members of the Congress of Racial Equality and others who were involved in voter registration drives among blacks. Violence was used as well when blacks congregated in anticipation of a protest march in Canton, Mississippi, in 1963. In Georgia, support for segregationist presidential candidate George Wallace led to black-white confrontations and violence. In Virginia, on the eve of the 1964 presidential election, a federal court upheld a state law requiring payment of the poll tax for the right to vote in local and state elections. Two years later, however, in *Harper v. Virginia Board of Elections*, the Supreme Court concluded that poll taxes violated the equal protection clause of the Constitution, and the last such tax was swept away.

Abolition of the poll tax was a step in the right direction, but there was a long road still to travel before voting rights for minority groups would be secure at all levels of American politics.

Bibliography

Branch, Taylor. *Parting the Waters: America in the King Years, 1954-63.* New York: Simon & Schuster, 1988. A sweeping, authoritative, well-conceived, and well-written account of the Civil Rights movement, concentrating on Martin Luther King, Jr., and the Southern Christian Leadership Conference. Not an academic treatment in the conventional sense but rather intensely personal.

Kelly, Alfred H., Winifred A. Harbison, and Herman Betz. "Civil Rights and the Constitution." In *The American Constitution: Its Origins and Development.* 6th ed. New York: W. W. Norton, 1983. This chapter discusses in detail the Supreme Court cases and the contents of civil rights legislation, of which the Twenty-fourth Amendment was a part. It is particularly useful on those court cases that either struck down segregation rules or wiped away such voting restrictions as the poll tax and literacy tests.

Kluger, R. *Simple Justice: The History of Brown v. Board of Education and Black America's Struggle for Equality.* New York: Alfred A. Knopf, 1976. A study in depth of the first major step in the civil rights reform era, in which the principle of desegregation of American society was laid down. Thurgood Marshall, later a distinguished Supreme Court justice, played a central role in the developments examined here.

Matusow, A. J. *The Unraveling of America: A History of Liberalism in the 1960s.* New York: Harper & Row, 1984. This volume traces the rise and fall of American postwar liberalism, concentrating on both the successes and the failures of liberal views and policies during the era of civil rights reform.

"Poll Taxes and Literacy Tests." *The Congressional Digest* 41 (May, 1962): 131-137. A careful and detailed explanation of the background of the poll tax and the process and content of the Senate debate leading to passage of the Twenty-fourth Amendment. The article proceeds in a detached and factual manner and lists specifically the nature of poll taxes as they existed in the several states as of May, 1962.

Schlesinger, Arthur M., Jr. *A Thousand Days.* Boston: Houghton Mifflin, 1965. An inside look at the Kennedy Administration with observations on aspects of Kennedy's civil rights policies, including abolition of the poll tax. Schlesinger was part of the Kennedy inner circle and an old-line Democrat. His view of the Kennedy years is not without bias; all the same, this is a masterful work and very useful.

Robert Cole

Cross-References

Brown v. Board of Education Ends Public School Segregation (1954), p. 913; The SCLC Forms to Link Civil Rights Groups (1957), p. 974; The Civil Rights Act of 1957 Creates the Commission on Civil Rights (1957), p. 997; Eisenhower Sends Troops to Little Rock, Arkansas (1957), p. 1003; Martin Luther King, Jr., Delivers His "I Have a Dream" Speech (1963), p. 1200; The United Nations Issues a Declaration on Racial Discrimination (1963), p. 1212; Three Civil Rights Workers Are Murdered (1964), p. 1246; Congress Passes the Civil Rights Act (1964), p. 1251; Congress Passes the Voting Rights Act (1965), p. 1296; The U.N. Covenant on Civil and Political Rights Is Adopted (1966), p. 1353; Marshall Becomes the First Black Supreme Court Justice (1967), p. 1381; Congress Extends Voting Rights Reforms (1975), p. 1812.

A UNITED NATIONS PEACE FORCE
IS DEPLOYED IN CYPRUS

Categories of event: Peace movements and organizations; racial and ethnic rights
Time: March, 1964
Locale: Cyprus

The UNFICYP was established to prevent escalation of the fighting in Cyprus, help restore law and order, and foster peaceful conditions favorable for a negotiated settlement of the problem

> *Principal personages:*
> ARCHBISHOP MAKARIOS (1913-1977), the president of Cyprus, a Greek
> Cypriot religious and political leader
> FAZIL KUTCHUK (1906-   ), the vice president of Cyprus, a Turkish
> Cypriot political leader
> U THANT (1909-1974), the secretary-general of the United Nations

Summary of Event

Cyprus and the human rights of its people became a major issue at the United Nations in the 1950's. From 1954 to 1958, Greece appealed five times to the General Assembly for the termination of British colonial rule and the application of self-determination of the island. The Greek appeals were aimed at internationalization of the issue and the exercise of pressure on Britain to withdraw from Cyprus. The settlement reached in 1959 and the subsequent establishment of an independent Cypriot republic in 1960, however, were not the direct result of U.N. involvement or application of human rights principles. Instead, a settlement was agreed upon in a Western setting through Greek-Turkish negotiations carried out in Zurich and London under British auspices.

The United Nations was asked again to intervene in Cyprus after the eruption of ethnic violence on December 22, 1963. The island was beset by ethnic differences and controversies over the rights of the Greek Cypriot majority and the Turkish Cypriot minority. Following three years of simmering tension and confrontation over constitutional matters, the two communities, with support from their motherlands, resorted to arms. Some ethnic segregation and much human suffering resulted from the hostilities. When fighting broke out, the Cyprus government, headed by Archbishop Makarios, appealed to the U.N. Security Council for help against acts of aggression and intervention in the internal affairs of Cyprus. In Makarios' view, the declared intention of Turkey to intervene in Cyprus by force threatened the sovereignty and political independence of the island, in direct violation of the United Nations' charter and principles. Therefore, his government argued, it was "in the vital interests of the people of Cyprus as a whole, and in the interest of international peace and security" that the Security Council take measures to remedy the situation.

The first Cypriot resort to the United Nations proved abortive, since Makarios agreed, after a short session of the Security Council, to attend a peace conference in London. On February 15, 1964, following the failure of the London conference and further escalation of fighting and suffering, the Cyprus government reactivated its appeal to the United Nations. On the same day, the British government filed a similar request for a Security Council meeting. For the Cypriot government, the problem was the imminent danger of a Turkish invasion. The British appeal stressed the domestic nature of the ethnic dispute and blamed the Makarios government for inability to restore law, order, and internal security.

Two blocs with different positions emerged during the debate. One bloc included Turkey, Great Britain, and the United States, and argued that the problem was basically one of internal conflict and disorder for which the Cyprus government was largely responsible. As the Turkish representative put it, the cause of the problem was Makarios' attempt to bring about changes in the political structure of the Cypriot state at the expense of the Turkish Cypriot minority. A different view was advanced by the Greek Cypriots, who received the full support of Greece and the Soviet Union. They argued that the problem facing Cyprus was one of circumscribed independence caused by the 1960 settlement of the colonial problem, a settlement imposed on Cyprus by outside powers.

The three-week-long acrimonious debate ended with the adoption of Resolution 186 on March 4, 1964, urging all parties to respect the territorial integrity and political independence of the sovereign Republic of Cyprus. The resolution also recommended the appointment of a U.N. mediator and the creation of a U.N. Force in Cyprus (UNFICYP) to preserve international peace and security and to cooperate with the government of Cyprus in restoring law and order. The United States and Great Britain, which for weeks had been arguing for a North Atlantic Treaty Organization (NATO) peace force and resisting any U.N. involvement, in the end decided not to veto the resolution. The West appeared to view the risks of U.N. involvement in Cyprus as less than the risks of delay in getting a peace force there. The most vital and urgent goal of Anglo-American policy was to restore peace and prevent an escalation of the crisis that could lead to a Greek-Turkish war. Developments in the eastern Mediterranean region, including war preparations on both sides of the Aegean, indicated a real threat of military confrontation.

Great Britain had additional reasons for letting the United Nations assume the peacekeeping role. Ethnic violence was directly affecting its extensive military installations on the island, including two important sovereign bases. Moreover, the former colonial power had been trapped into shouldering alone the burden of peacekeeping. As the British delegate put it to the Security Council, his country was not willing to go on policing Cyprus alone for a day longer than was necessary. Escalation of violence on Cyprus was accompanied by threats, charges, and countercharges coming from Nicosia, Athens, Ankara, London, Washington, and Moscow. *The New York Times*, commenting editorially on the imminent danger facing international peace, wrote that Cyprus was threatening "to embroil Europe, the United States, and even the whole world in its petty communal strife."

The creation and deployment of the U.N. peacekeeping force occurred in this setting of spreading violence and increasing ethnic segregation. During the first two months of fighting, hundreds of people were killed or wounded, hundreds were taken hostage, and thousands became refugees on both sides. President Makarios had been the strongest proponent of a U.N. force, and its deployment was a major victory for him. By having U.N. troops on Cyprus, he thought he could eliminate any prospect for the dispatch of NATO troops and also limit the peacemaking role of British troops, which had lost the trust of the Greek Cypriots. Makarios also hoped that a U.N. force would serve as a deterrent against external military intervention and be seen as a multinational shield protecting the island from a Turkish invasion.

On March 6, 1964, U.N. secretary-general U Thant appointed Lieutenant-General Prem Singh Gyani of India as the first commander of the UNFICYP. According to the Security Council mandate, the composition of the force would be decided by the secretary-general in consultation with the governments of Cyprus, Great Britain, Greece, and Turkey. The first Canadian troops arrived on March 13, but the force did not become operational until March 27, when a sufficient number of troops were deployed and able to discharge their functions. The original mandate provided for a three-month stationing, but subsequent consecutive extensions, first for three-month and later for six-month periods, kept the force in Cyprus until at least the 1990's. By June, 1964, the force reached its maximum strength of 6,411. The size and composition of the force have varied. The countries with the largest contingents have been Great Britain, Canada, Finland, Ireland, Sweden, and Denmark. Smaller units were sent by Australia, Austria, and New Zealand.

Impact of Event

The UNFICYP's mission was spelled out in Security Council Resolution 186 (1964) as follows: ". . . in the interest of preserving international peace and security, to use its best efforts to prevent a recurrence of fighting and, as necessary, to contribute to the maintenance and restoration of law and order and a return to normal conditions." Following the Greek coup against Makarios, invasion of Cyprus by Turkey, and division of the island in 1974, the main function of the force was to supervise the hundred-mile-long cease-fire line between Greek Cypriot forces in the south and Turkish and Turkish Cypriot forces in the north.

Like other U.N. peacekeeping operations, the ultimate objective of the UNFICYP was to create and maintain peaceful conditions favorable for a negotiated and lasting settlement of the problem. Besides supervising cease-fires and preventing recurrence of fighting, the UNFICYP was also extensively and actively involved in humanitarian and relief efforts. These efforts were aimed at helping individuals and groups on both sides go about their daily business without disruption by the conflict. Restoring basic civilian services and economic activities was a major concern for the force. Some of the measures taken in that direction included mediation and facilitation of exchange of hostages and prisoners; cooperation with the Red Cross, Red Crescent, and other relief agencies in helping refugees, protecting lives, and minimizing suffering; arranging for the supply of vital utilities, such as water, electricity, and telephone services; providing postal service, public benefits, and medical treatment; escorting people and convoys carrying medicine, food, and other essential merchandise; and enabling farmers to cultivate lands in the buffer zone.

In 1974, during the large-scale hostilities that followed the Turkish invasion, the UNFICYP was instrumental in evacuating thousands of foreign tourists and families of foreign diplomatic missions. Evacuees were first transferred to the British Sovereign Base Areas and then shipped out of Cyprus.

The problem of Cyprus remained unresolved into the 1990's, with the divided island in a state of neither peace nor war. Despite repeated peace efforts and rounds of talks carried out under U.N. auspices, no progress was made, and deep differences remained between the two sides. Although Cyprus was recognized internationally as one state, its people were geographically and politically divided along ethnic lines. The presence of the UNFICYP on the island remained indispensable for maintaining peace and making possible the continuation of peace efforts.

Bibliography

Attalides, Michael A. *Cyprus: Nationalism and International Politics.* New York: St. Martin's Press, 1979. A widely cited book by a Princeton-educated Greek Cypriot. It discusses sociopolitical changes in Cyprus and the role of external factors in shaping the dynamics of the domestic ethnic conflict. United Nations involvement and U.S.-Soviet rivalry are discussed extensively.

The Blue Helmets: A Review of United Nations Peace-Keeping. New York: United Nations, 1985. An overview of a dozen U.N. peacekeeping operations in Asia, Africa, and the Middle East. The chapter on Cyprus includes a narrative on the peacekeeping force as well as other efforts by the international organization to resolve the ethnic conflict. A good source of information on peacekeeping.

Ehrlich, Thomas. *Cyprus, 1958-1967: International Crises and the Role of Law.* New York: Oxford University Press, 1974. The work of a prominent academic with a scholarly and legal perspective. It examines the origin, elements, and consequences of the Cyprus problem from the viewpoint of international law and the U.N. Charter. It focuses on major crises and outside interference during the critical period of the declaration of independence and the eruption of ethnic violence.

Harbottle, Michael. *The Impartial Soldier.* London: Oxford University Press, 1970. The author was commander of the United Nations Force in Cyprus from 1966 to 1968. He provides an insider's account of the role, functions, and problems of peacekeeping.

Joseph, Joseph S. *Cyprus: Ethnic Conflict and International Concern.* New York: Peter Lang, 1985. A work of scholarly analysis and interpretation examining the causes and dynamics of the Cyprus conflict at both the domestic and international levels. United Nations involvement is discussed extensively in the light of repeated efforts to resolve violent crises and reach a peaceful settlement.

Mayes, Stanley. *Makarios: A Biography.* New York: St. Martin's Press, 1981. Perhaps the best and most comprehensive biography of Makarios. An informative and fascinating account of the personal life and political achievements of the charismatic archbishop and first president of Cyprus. It also provides a good overview of United Nations involvement in Cyprus.

Stegenga, James A. *The United Nations Force in Cyprus.* Columbus: Ohio State University Press, 1968. Although it covers only the early years of the United Nations Force in Cyprus, it is still the best work on the topic. It evaluates the role, successes, and failures of the force. Although it focuses on peacekeeping, it also helps the reader understand the issues and complexities of the conflict between Greek Cypriots and Turkish Cypriots.

Stephens, Robert. *Cyprus: A Place of Arms.* New York: Praeger, 1966. A readable book providing a historical background to the ethnic problems facing Cyprus. The author argues that the origins and complexities of the conflict can be traced to regional rivalries and conflicting imperial interests in the eastern Mediterranean region. He concludes with a recommendation for a peaceful settlement based on a truly independent and united Cypriot state.

Xydis, Stephen G. *Cyprus: Conflict and Conciliation, 1954-1958.* Columbus: Ohio State University Press, 1967. A monumental work on the colonial problem of Cyprus and the practice of international diplomacy at the United Nations. It provides an extensive account and thorough analysis of the five consecutive Greek appeals to the General Assembly from 1954 to 1958. It is especially good for the scholar looking for information on events that led to the independence of Cyprus.

Joseph S. Joseph

Cross-References

The Young Turk Movement Stages a Constitutional Coup in Turkey (1908), p. 98; Armenians Suffer Genocide During World War I (1915), p. 150; The Balfour Declaration Supports a Jewish Homeland in Palestine (1917), p. 235; The United Nations Adopts Its Charter (1945), p. 657; Riots Erupt as Katanga Province Secedes from the Congo (1960), p. 1068; The United Nations Intervenes in the Congolese Civil War (1960), p. 1074; Cyprus Gains Independence (1960), p. 1084; The Nonaligned Movement Meets (1961), p. 1131; Greek and Turkish Inhabitants of Cyprus Clash over Political Rights (1963), p. 1218; A Greek Coup Leads to a Military Dictatorship (1967), p. 1359; Ethnic Riots Erupt in Armenia (1988), p. 2348; Ethnic Unrest Breaks Out in Yugoslavian Provinces (1988), p. 2386; Kashmir Separatists Demand an End to Indian Rule (1989), p. 2426.

PALESTINIAN REFUGEES FORM THE PALESTINE LIBERATION ORGANIZATION

Category of event: Indigenous peoples' rights
Time: May, 1964
Locale: The Middle East

The Palestine Liberation Organization was created to voice the nationalist aspirations of the Palestinian people

Principal personages:

YASIR ARAFAT (1929-), the president of the Palestine Liberation Organization and leader of al-Fatah

GEORGE HABASH (1926-), the founder, in 1952, of the Arab Nationalist Movement; he later created the Popular Front for the Liberation of Palestine as part of the PLO

IBN TALAL HUSSEIN (1935-), the third king of Jordan, sponsored the formation of the PLO

GAMAL ABDEL NASSER (1918-1970), the president of Egypt from 1954 until his death, a major force behind the establishment of the PLO

AHMED SHUKAIRY (1908-1980), a Palestinian diplomat who led the efforts that resulted in the formation of the PLO

Summary of Event

A Jewish nation was established on May 14, 1948, in accordance with a resolution of the United Nations General Assembly. The individuals who founded the new state were of various political persuasions but most basically may be termed Zionists. Zionism is both a doctrine and a movement which aims at reuniting Jews into their own state to end centuries of dispersal and persecution. This movement is based on biblical promises and texts but more immediately found support in the wake of Adolf Hitler's genocidal mass murder of European Jewry.

As soon as it was created, the new state of Israel found itself at war with Arab nations. The Arab-Israeli war of 1948-1949 resulted in Israeli victory and tragedy for the Palestinian Arabs. The war forced massive numbers of Palestinians to flee their homes. Moreover, at the end of war, Israel annexed the Arab areas originally set up for Palestinians by United Nations Resolution 181, commonly known as the "partition plan." This left those Palestinians who remained in the areas as citizens of the new Israeli state, albeit citizens forced to carry passes, obey curfews, or endure house arrest for political dissidence. Furthermore, the Israeli government promoted a policy of Jewish settlement within the territory which originally had been set aside for Palestinians. This settlement was often facilitated by forceful confiscation of Arab land.

The result was that by 1950, according to U.N. estimates, about a million Palestinians had become refugees. Although debate surrounds the question as to whether Israel consciously displaced the population of the 369 Arab towns and villages emptied during the 1948-1949 war, it is significant that this was the predominant perception among the Palestinian population. In fact, the belief that Israel systematically seized Arab land and forced Palestinians from their homes was to be a major source of Palestinian nationalism. This belief was strengthened by the Israeli law of "abandoned property" which made possible the legal seizure of Arab land belonging to those who had fled, even if temporarily.

The 1956 War in the Middle East resulted in another defeat for Arab armies. The Gaza Strip, Sinai, and the Suez Canal area were overrun, this time at the hands of not only Israel but also England and France. The involvement of Israel with France and England, both traditional colonial powers in the region, further sharpened the Arab belief that the Jewish state was a pawn of the Western imperialist powers. During the conflict, Palestinian student activists in Cairo formed a commando battalion which fought on the side of Egypt. While of little military significance, this direct involvement of Palestinians in armed conflict against Israel foreshadowed the growing emphasis on armed struggle.

The rapid changes that took place in the Middle East in the 1940's and 1950's included not only the birth of Israel but also the rise of Egyptian president Gamal Abdel Nasser and growing pan-Arab sentiments. In addition, this period saw increasing efforts of Palestinians to regain the land they had lost with the creation of Israel and the Arab-Israeli war which had followed. As early as 1951, Yasir Arafat began organizing Palestinian students in Cairo and recruited several fellow students who agreed with his "Palestine-first" beliefs.

Despite the popularity of autonomous organizations among many Palestinians, the 1950's were a period of frustration for most activists. The Arab nations were often willing to pay lip service to the plight of the Palestinians but equally quick to expel or imprison Palestinian militants who became troublesome. The formation of al-Fatah in 1959 offered an organization committed to the Palestinian cause first and "Arab unity" second.

Al-Fatah was based on five points of unity: a common goal of a liberated Palestine, the need for armed struggle to achieve liberation, Palestinian self-organization and reliance, cooperation with friendly Arab forces, and cooperation with friendly international forces. The new organization faced difficult times, since the predominant mood within the Arab world in the early 1960's was support for pan-Arabism, sponsored by Nasser. This was true even within the Palestinian movement, as witnessed by the stance of Arab Nationalist Movement leader George Habash. In addition, the harsh effects of Palestinian dispersal and the ever-present threat of repression by the Arab states caused many to doubt al-Fatah's ability to effect its goals.

Although al-Fatah envisioned that the establishment of some type of Palestinian organization would be the result of the grass-roots work of the Palestinians themselves, events were to go in quite a different direction. At the first Arab summit, held in Cairo in January, 1964, President Gamal Abdel Nasser of Egypt, King Ibn Talal

Hussein of Jordan, and other Arab leaders discussed Israeli plans for diverting large amounts of water. This would allow further massive settlement of Jewish immigrants on what had once been Palestinian land. Faced with what seemed to them to be increased expansion by an Israel which they had failed to defeat militarily, attendees of the summit decided to back the "liberation of Palestine" and sponsor a Palestinian organization to achieve this goal.

What the role of this new organization was to be was at first unclear. It was, after all, the creation of a diverse coalition of mainly conservative Arab states and developed under the particular influence of pan-Arabist Egypt. Clearly, it was not meant to be independent of Arab government supervision, as many Palestinians such as Yasir Arafat desired. In addition, most pan-Arab groups continued to be wary of any suggestion of Palestinian separatism or any hint of decreased enthusiasm for the cause of Arab unity.

All the same, the concept of an all-embracing Palestinian organization had the official blessing of the leaders of the Arab world, including premier pan-Arabist Abdel Nasser. Thus, opposition to the formation of such an organization was restrained in most quarters. On the other hand, within the Palestinian diaspora there was considerable apprehension that the new organization would be little more than a paper structure attached to Egypt's foreign office.

Ahmed Shukairy, a Palestinian veteran of numerous Arab foreign services, was the man who was to guide the birth of the Palestine Liberation Organization (PLO). An accomplished and tireless speaker, Shukairy was to trek throughout the Palestinian diaspora in preparation for the May, 1964, founding convention of the PLO. Despite reservations, both political and personal, about Shukairy and his mission, al-Fatah chose to cooperate with the newly proposed organization.

Meeting in the Jordanian-controlled East Jerusalem of King Hussein in May of 1964, 422 delegates from the Palestinian refugee communities throughout the world ratified two basic texts sponsored by Shukairy and the interim leadership. These documents were the Palestine National Charter and the Basic Law of the PLO. The charter has often been termed the Palestinian "Declaration of Independence," while the Basic Law could be considered to be a PLO constitution. Both of these were to be altered significantly by the fourth convention of the Palestinian National Council, meeting in Cairo in July, 1968. From its shaky origins, the Palestine Liberation Organization was to become a major factor in the Middle East equation in the years to come.

Impact of Event

In the decades after the formation of the Palestine Liberation Organization in 1964, the PLO established itself, in its own words, as "the sole representative of the Palestinian people." In spite of various political splits and struggles, the PLO clearly established a framework with which most Palestinians could identify. This question of emotional identity was important for the average Palestinian, since Palestinians no longer had a homeland with which to identify.

Moreover, a large number of Palestinians lived under Israeli control, where their self-identity was hardly encouraged by the occupational forces. Even those Palestinians who lived in the Arab world found themselves deprived of their identity. Jordan, for example, was home to an estimated one million or more Palestinians, yet the government in Jordan made no distinction between them and other citizens; those Palestinians traveling abroad were listed in their passports as Jordanian.

In this situation, the PLO became vital not only as a real political force but also as both symbol and prompter of Palestinian national pride and self-awareness. After 1948, Palestinians became dispersed throughout the world. They worked and lived in various communities cut off from one another and lacking common cultural or political institutions. Into this vacuum the PLO injected a concrete framework for political action and cultural identification.

In a sense, what defined a Jordanian, or other citizen of Palestinian origins, as a Palestinian was "belonging" to the PLO. Thus, no matter what nation's passport Palestinians may hold, they may still view themselves as part of another nation, albeit a nation without a homeland. Without an organization such as the PLO, there would have been a very real danger that Palestinian culture and identity would have been lost in the decades of exile and repression.

Nor is the significance of the PLO only emotional or psychological. The organization made a number of specific contributions to the Palestinian nationalist movement. Despite the wishes of Israel, many Arab governments, and the United States, the PLO prevented the plight of the Palestinian people from being forgotten. In a world seemingly overloaded with human tragedy, this was no small accomplishment. It can be argued that if no PLO had been established, the average world citizen might have remained ignorant of the existence of the Palestinian people.

The PLO, by speaking with a single voice, was able to take a geographically dispersed, politically divided group of people and present a relatively unified strategy and program. If it were not for the PLO, there is every reason to think that the various Palestinian nationalist factions would have wasted far more energy in political infighting than they have. Finally, the Palestine Liberation Organization considers itself a "government-in-exile," which allows the possibility of a less painful transition of power when and if a Palestinian state is established. For all of its problems, the PLO has made a tremendous contribution to the struggle of the Palestinian people to maintain their identity and reestablish a homeland.

Bibliography

Cobban, Helena. *The Palestinian Liberation Organization.* Cambridge, England: Cambridge University Press, 1984. An excellent survey of the PLO, with emphasis on the development of its largest component, al-Fatah. Written by a journalist who was based in Beirut from 1976 to 1981. Includes reference notes and bibliography but no index.

Gresh, Alain, and Dominique Vidal. *A to Z of the Middle East.* London: Zed Books, 1990. An invaluable reference source not only for the Middle East in general but for the Palestinian movement in particular, with entries on "Israeli Arabs," "Palestinians," "Palestinian Dissidence," "Palestine Liberation Organization," and "Partition Plan." Contains index and bibliography.

Mussalam, Sami. *The Palestine Liberation Organization: Its Function and Structure.* Brattleboro, Vt.: Amana Books, 1988. Frankly partisan, this volume was written by the director of the office of Yasir Arafat. It is an excellent source for the official structures and positions of the PLO. With reference notes.

Shafir, Gershon. *Land, Labor, and the Origins of the Israeli-Palestinian Conflict.* Cambridge, England: Cambridge University Press, 1989. This stimulating work argues that the Palestinian-Israeli conflict had its origins in the struggle over land and labor during the closing years of the Ottoman Empire. Contains reference notes and bibliography.

Williams, David. *The Palestinian/Israeli Conflict: A Select Bibliography.* Chicago: Chicago Public Library, 1989. An excellent, concise survey of the existing literature on the subject in English.

William A. Pelz

Cross-References

The French Quell an Algerian Nationalist Revolt (1945), p. 651; Palestinian Refugees Flee to Neighboring Arab Countries (1948), p. 749; Israel Is Created as a Homeland for Jews (1948), p. 761; The United Nations Creates an Agency to Aid Palestinian Refugees (1949), p. 814; Arab Terrorists Murder Eleven Israeli Olympic Athletes in Munich (1972), p. 1685; Sadat Becomes the First Arab Leader to Visit Israel (1977), p. 1943; A Lawyers' Union Demands Justice and Political Reform in Syria (1978), p. 1967; Sadat and Begin Are Jointly Awarded the Nobel Peace Prize (1978), p. 2003; Palestinian Civilians Are Massacred in West Beirut (1982), p. 2164; The Palestinian *Intifada* Begins (1987), p. 2331; Iraq Invades and Ravages Kuwait (1990), p. 2600.

THREE CIVIL RIGHTS WORKERS ARE MURDERED

Category of event: Civil rights
Time: June-July, 1964
Locale: Nashoba County, Mississippi

A group of white supremacists attacked and murdered three civil rights workers who had just been released from the county jail

> *Principal personages:*
> MICHAEL HENRY SCHWERNER (1939-1964), a white member of the Congress of Racial Equality; was the principal target of the attack
> JAMES EARL CHANEY (1943-1964), a plasterer from Meridian, Mississippi, a black civil rights field worker
> ANDREW GOODMAN (1943-1964), a white Queens College student from New York
> CECIL RAY PRICE, a deputy sheriff from Nashoba County and a member of the Mississippi Ku Klux Klan
> J. EDGAR HOOVER (1895-1972), the director of the Federal Bureau of Investigation
> ROBERT F. KENNEDY (1925-1968), the United States attorney general

Summary of Event

The struggle for black equality reached its crest in the two years after the August, 1963, March on Washington. During that period, the last elements of legal segregation died. More important, black disenfranchisement, the key to maintaining the old, dual system of life in the South, also ended. The registration and enfranchisement of African Americans came, however, at a heavy cost: Three young civil rights workers were killed for their efforts to give the right to vote to those who had been denied it since the end of Reconstruction in the 1870's. The murders of James Earl Chaney, Andrew Goodman, and Michael Henry Schwerner focused international attention on the Civil Rights movement and brought a commitment from the federal government to bring to justice those responsible for the crime.

After judicial decisions had ended the tradition of separate schools and facilities in the South, civil rights organizations turned their attention to registering African Americans as voters. Believing that access to the ballot box was the key to empowering the dispossessed, organizations such as the Student Nonviolent Coordinating Committee (SNCC) and the Congress of Racial Equality (CORE) sought to organize massive voter registration drives in the Deep South. In particular, leaders targeted the state of Mississippi, the poorest and least literate in the nation. During the winter of 1963-1964, the Council of Federated Organizations (COFO), a confederation of civil rights organizations, planned for the Mississippi Freedom Summer, which had as its goal the registration of as many blacks as possible. More than one thousand white college students volunteered to spend their summer organizing community centers and teaching reading, writing, and civics to rural blacks who wanted to become voters. In the area of Nashoba County, Mississippi, COFO's plans were unpopular with most white citizens. For the first time since the end of Reconstruction, the national Ku Klux Klan organized local klaverns in the area.

Michael Schwerner, a graduate of Cornell University, and his wife had moved to Meridian, Mississippi, during the winter to begin the preparations for the Freedom Summer. A committed believer in racial equality, Schwerner quickly became a target for the white supremacists of Nashoba County. Various plans to eliminate him were discussed in Klan meetings. James Chaney was a native of the area and had become a paid COFO staff member a few months before he was murdered. Andrew Goodman was one of the Freedom Summer volunteers who was scheduled to work in Nashoba County. He arrived in the area on June 20 and was killed one day later.

The events surrounding the murder of the three civil rights workers began on June 16, when a group of armed white men beat the lay leaders of the Mount Zion Methodist Church in Longdale, a small, all-black community in Nashoba County. Later that night, several of the whites returned and set fire to the church, which was to have housed one of the Freedom Schools. On June 21, Chaney, Goodman, and Schwerner drove to Longdale from Meridian to examine the church's remains. On their return from Nashoba County, Deputy Sheriff Cecil Ray Price stopped their car for speeding. After arresting Chaney for driving sixty-five miles per hour in a thirty-five mile per hour zone, Price arrested Goodman and Schwerner for suspicion of arson in the Mount Zion church fire. He then placed the three in the Nashoba County jail, where they remained for more than five hours.

At about the time that the three were placed in jail, COFO was activating its procedures for locating field workers who had not returned or phoned by 4:00 P.M. In addition to telephoning all of the area hospitals, COFO staff placed calls to all the jails. When the Nashoba County jail was called by the Meridian COFO office, however, the person who answered the phone flatly denied having seen any of the three. While Chaney, Goodman, and Schwerner were in the jail, Price, a member of the White Knights of the Ku Klux Klan, notified his Klan superiors and made arrangements for the elimination of the troublemakers. Specifically, leaders of the local klavern located a bulldozer operator and arranged for him to dispose of the three men's bodies even before they were released from jail. Several years later, it became known that the murder plan was finalized before the three were released from the jail that evening.

Sometime after 10:00 P.M., Deputy Price allowed Chaney to pay a twenty dollar fine for speeding and prepared to release all three. None was permitted to make a phone call, and all three knew that a release after dark was dangerous. Price escorted the three to their car and directed them to leave Nashoba County. On the drive back toward Meridian, a high-speed car chase began as Chaney, Goodman, and Schwerner raced for the county line. They did not make it. Price stopped their car again and ordered the three into his car as the rest of the Klan posse arrived. The three cars—Price's, the posse's, and the COFO car, driven by a Klansman—proceeded to a deserted dirt road. Once off the main road, Schwerner and Goodman were pulled from the car and shot through the heart at point-blank range. Before Chaney was killed, he was beaten severely with a blackjack. He was shot three times, with the third shot fired into his brain. The bodies of the three were carried to a remote farm, where a cattle pond was under construction. Chaney's, Goodman's, and Schwerner's bodies were dumped into a prepared hole in the fresh earthen dam, and the COFO station wagon was driven in the opposite direction and burned.

The reaction to the disappearance of the three was swift. On June 22, U.S. Attorney General Robert Kennedy ordered a full-scale inquiry by the Federal Bureau of Investigation (FBI). Following the discovery of the burned car on June 23, President Lyndon Johnson authorized the use of two hundred men from the Meridian naval air station to aid in the search. Within Nashoba County, popular belief held that the three were hiding in an attempt to arouse northern sympathy for their work. Some even argued that COFO was responsible for the arson at the Mount Zion church, using it to complete the hoax effect. J. Edgar Hoover, director of the FBI, flew to the area on July 10, at the president's request, to investigate the disappearances personally. At a press conference in Jackson, Mississippi, Hoover disclosed that the FBI force in the state had been increased to 153 agents—more than ten times the normal number—to protect civil rights workers.

On August 5, the bodies of Chaney, Goodman, and Schwerner were unearthed from the new dam. Despite autopsies that unequivocally showed that Goodman and Schwerner had been shot to death and that Chaney had suffered an "inhuman beating" before dying from three gunshot wounds, a Nashoba County coroner's jury ruled on August 25 that it was unable to determine the cause of death for any of the three.

On December 4, Hoover announced the arrests of nineteen men on federal conspiracy charges in connection with the murders, including Price and his superior, the Nashoba County sheriff. The FBI focused on the role of the Klan in the deaths, and more than sixty agents infiltrated the Mississippi Klan to obtain evidence. More than one thousand Mississippians, including 480 Klan members, were interviewed during the investigation.

Impact of Event

The murders of James Chaney, Andrew Goodman, and Michael Schwerner brought profound changes to the Deep South generally and to Nashoba County, Mississippi, specifically. Eventually, those directly involved were tried and convicted, and the cause for which the three men died, black enfranchisement, became a reality.

When the 1964 Nashoba County Fair opened six days after the bodies had been recovered, the mood was subdued and tense. Arizona Senator Barry Goldwater, the Republican nominee for president, canceled a planned appearance at the event, even though it had been an obligatory stop for politicians in the past. The discovery of the corpses also ended most of the discussions of a COFO-arranged hoax. Instead, the

FBI used the discovery as a lever to secure information from Klansmen who mistrusted each other and feared arrest in the case. Since the FBI learned the precise location of the bodies, it was clear that agents were receiving very reliable information. A number of those involved suspected that more than just the burial location had been passed to the federal government, and the Klan's code of silence was broken as several sought to save themselves by cooperating with the investigation.

Using laws passed as part of the Civil Rights Act of 1870, the federal government obtained grand jury indictments charging those involved with conspiracy to deny Chaney, Goodman, and Schwerner their civil rights. No substantive local investigation of the crime ever took place, and no murder charges were ever filed by the state of Mississippi. On October 20, 1967, a federal jury in Meridian convicted Cecil Ray Price and six codefendants of the charges, marking the first successful prosecution in Mississippi history of white officials and Klansmen for crimes against African Americans or civil rights workers. After unsuccessful appeals, all of the defendants entered federal custody on March 19, 1970, five and one-half years after the three murders.

The impact on the fight for civil rights was less clear. On July 2, 1964, Congress enacted the Civil Rights Act of 1964, which prohibited discrimination in public accommodations, publicly owned facilities, federally funded programs, and union membership. It also created the Equal Employment Opportunity Commission to end discrimination in employment. In November, 1964, Lyndon Johnson won a landslide reelection, capturing 61 percent of the popular vote and 94 percent of the African-American vote. Two million more blacks voted in that election than had in 1960.

Following the discovery of the bodies and the revelation that Chaney had been beaten before his murder, unlike Schwerner and Goodman, the trend toward self-segregation within the Civil Rights movement came to the fore. Some blacks had come to believe that they needed to lead their own fight and that whites could not be part of it. As the 1960's progressed, these differences of opinion within the Civil Rights movement became more acute, and the movement became more diffuse as a result. Some, like Martin Luther King, Jr., rejected the idea of a movement for racial equality practicing segregation within itself. Others, like the leadership of the SNCC, assumed a more radical position and eventually expelled all nonblacks from its projects. By then, enfranchisement for all was no longer a dream but instead a reality, and the Civil Rights movement was a success in ending legal segregation.

Bibliography

Cagin, Seth, and Philip Dray. *We Are Not Afraid.* New York: Macmillan, 1988. This is the best one-volume work on the Mississippi murders, the result of research into oral histories, court transcripts, and investigators' files. Annotated, with a complete index.

Grimshaw, Allen D., ed. *Racial Violence in the United States.* Chicago: Aldine, 1969. One of the most comprehensive anthologies on racial violence. Covers American history beginning with seventeenth century slave revolts and running through the riots of the 1960's. Contains a complete bibliography and index.

Leuchtenburg, William E. *A Troubled Feast: American Society Since 1945.* Boston: Little, Brown, 1973. A valuable, brief volume that provides a balanced introduction to recent American history. The Civil Rights movement is discussed within the context of broader social movements of the era. Contains a list of suggested readings and an index.

Lewis, Anthony. *Portrait of a Decade: The Second American Revolution.* New York: Random House, 1964. One of the seminal books on American race relations in the 1950's and early 1960's, this single volume examines the origins and manifestations of the disagreements over civil rights through analyses and excerpts from both the popular and the scholarly press. Contains an index.

Mars, Florence. *Witness in Philadelphia.* Baton Rouge: Louisiana State University Press, 1977. This first-person account of the events in Nashoba County, as told by a white woman, provides valuable insight into life before, during, and after the murders, the investigation, and the federal prosecution. Although not scholarly, it yields a textured view of the events that is valuable for those who want to understand better how such an event could have happened. Contains annotations, an index, and photographs of those involved in the events.

Sitkoff, Harvard. *The Struggle for Black Equality, 1954-1980.* New York: Hill & Wang, 1981. One of the best books for an overview of the American Civil Rights movement. This volume places the various elements of the movement into an understandable context for nonspecialists. Contains a biographical essay and an index.

E. A. Reed

Cross-References

The Ku Klux Klan Spreads Terror in the South (1920's), p. 298; Martial Law Is Declared in Oklahoma in Response to KKK Violence (1923), p. 367; *Brown v. Board of Education* Ends Public School Segregation (1954), p. 913; The SCLC Forms to Link Civil Rights Groups (1957), p. 974; Eisenhower Sends Troops to Little Rock, Arkansas (1957), p. 1003; Greensboro Sit-ins Launch a New Stage in the Civil Rights Movement (1960), p. 1056; The Council of Federated Organizations Registers Blacks to Vote (1962), p. 1149; Civil Rights Protesters Attract International Attention (1963), p. 1188; Congress Passes the Civil Rights Act (1964), p. 1251; Congress Passes the Voting Rights Act (1965), p. 1296; Race Rioting Erupts in Detroit (1967), p. 1376; Martin Luther King, Jr., Is Assassinated in Memphis (1968), p. 1419.

CONGRESS PASSES THE CIVIL RIGHTS ACT

Category of event: Civil rights
Time: July 2, 1964
Locale: Washington, D.C.

Congress passed comprehensive civil rights legislation giving life to the Constitutional principle of "color blind" equal protection of the law

Principal personages:
EVERETT DIRKSEN (1896-1969), the Senate minority leader, a key individual in coordinating the votes necessary to kill the anti-civil rights filibuster
HUBERT H. HUMPHREY (1911-1978), the Senate majority whip and floor leader of the civil rights bill
LYNDON B. JOHNSON (1908-1973), the thirty-sixth president of the United States
JOHN F. KENNEDY (1917-1963), the thirty-fifth president of the United States, who initiated the original civil rights proposal
EMANUEL CELLAR (1888-1981), the House Judiciary Committee chair
RICHARD RUSSELL (1897-1971), the leader of the Southern Democratic block in the Senate

Summary of Event

After the Civil War, and after ratification of the Thirteenth, Fourteenth, and Fifteenth Amendments to the Constitution, commonly referred to as the "Civil War Amendments," Congress did little to enforce, by statute, the provisions of those amendments, particularly as they applied to voting and equal access to and protection of the law. Although some important advances were initiated by passage of the Civil Rights Acts of 1957 and 1960, most human rights observers agree that most of the provisions found in those laws did little if anything to eradicate the sometimes blatant discrimination suffered by many African Americans prior to 1964.

On February 28, 1963, President John F. Kennedy, perceived by most at the time as being a strong advocate of civil rights, proposed to Congress the need for strengthened civil rights legislation. Although Kennedy was in favor of greater gains for minorities, his civil rights agenda included only minor cosmetic additions to the civil rights laws already on the books. The agenda was conspicuous in its failure to advance fair employment guarantees.

Kennedy understood that a proposal for a stronger civil rights bill would be doomed to failure before ever reaching the floors of the House and Senate for debate. Kennedy recognized the barriers which a bill would have to cross before it came to a roll-call vote in either house of Congress: the House Rules Committee, chaired by long-time civil rights antagonist Howard Smith (D-Va.), and the Senate Judiciary

Committee, chaired by equally inimical James O. Eastland (D-Miss.).

President Kennedy was keenly aware that his foreign policy initiatives regarding Cuba, Berlin, Vietnam, and the Soviet Union required maximum public support and congressional unity. He initially conceded to the powerful Democratic "Southern Bloc" and advanced proposals that would not antagonize its members and therefore jeopardize his foreign policy program in Congress. He hoped that these halfway measures would indicate to his black constituents that he was at least doing something.

Black leaders at the time understandably believed that they had been betrayed. The Black Leadership Conference on Civil Rights suggested that Kennedy had sacrificed domestic civil rights on the altar of foreign relations and re-election politics.

Not long after the president had sent his civil rights message to Congress, the issue of civil rights manifested itself to the American public as an issue involving violations of fundamental human rights. In May of 1963, the Southern Christian Leadership Conference, led by the Reverend Martin Luther King, Jr., began sit-in demonstrations across the South protesting segregation of public facilities and accommodations. The American public, only vaguely aware of the human rights violations taking place in some sections of their own country, were outraged and appalled as they viewed on the nightly news the likes of Birmingham, Alabama, Commissioner of public safety Eugene "Bull" Connor unleashing his dogs and opening up fire hoses to disperse peaceful protesters. America's sense of justice required that President Kennedy take a leadership role to abolish these violations of human rights and to achieve civil rights for all American citizens.

President Kennedy, responding to that mandate as a matter of duty as well as political necessity, commissioned his brother, Attorney General Robert F. Kennedy, to draft a comprehensive civil rights bill to submit to Congress. Sent to Congress on June 19, 1963, the bill was originally referred to the House Judiciary Committee. It was "reported out" to the full House on November 20, 1963, and included, as an amendment, a fair employment proviso, thanks in large part to the leadership of Committee chair Emanuel Cellar and his partner on the committee, Republican William McColloch.

Normally, the next hurdle in the House would be to get the bill past the House Rules Committee, which had killed many past civil rights initiatives before they could come to a vote on the floor. Committee Chairman Smith had promised to utilize that strategy again.

It is difficult to speculate the effect that John F. Kennedy's assassination on November 23, 1963, had on the success of the civil rights bill as it entered the Rules Committee phase. Most analysts concede that this unfortunate accident of history paradoxically set in motion a series of events supportive of the bill. Support might easily have not been as strong had the young president not been killed.

There are two strong arguments to support this theory. First, Lyndon B. Johnson became president. As a Southern Democrat with a questionable civil rights voting record as a member of the Senate, Johnson needed to dispel his "Southern" image among Northern liberals in Congress. In a more general sense, he needed to establish himself as a decisive and compassionate leader to the grief-stricken nation, a nation that would be going to the polls in less than a year. To accomplish these goals, and perhaps because he sincerely believed in the need to pass the civil rights legislation, President Johnson made passage of the civil rights bill his highest priority.

John Kennedy had been martyred, and Congress quickly learned that any legislation introduced "in memory of" the slain president would be tough to vote against in a political sense. When President Johnson addressed a joint session of Congress on November 28, 1963, it was within this context that he appealed for quick passage of the former president's bill.

It was also in this spirit that a majority of the House signed a discharge petition, filed on December 9, 1963, by Judiciary Committee chair Emanuel Cellar. This petition would get the bill to move directly from Howard Smith's Rules Committee to the House floor for debate, without the addition of debilitating features likely to be tacked on by Smith. On January 30, 1963, the Rules Committee, yielding to the pressure of the petition and the president, allowed the bill to be reported out to the floor under an "open debate" rule.

The floor debate took only nine days. On February 10, 1964, with bipartisan support of Republicans and Northern Democrats, the House passed its version of the civil rights bill by a 290-130 roll-call vote.

Following in the footsteps of the House, the Senate put the bill on a fast track. On February 26, 1964, it voted fifty-four to thirty-seven to bypass referring the bill to James Eastland's Senate Judiciary Committee, where it could have been stalled or mortally wounded, and voted instead to place the bill directly on the Senate calendar for debate. It was resolved that the actual debate would commence on March 30, 1964.

In an attempt to kill the measure outright, or at least to gain crippling amendments to the bill, a Southern Democratic filibuster was initiated on March 26, 1964, by Richard B. Russell (D-Ga.), leader of the Southern Democratic coalition. It was Russell's belief that the only way for the bill's supporters to bring the filibuster to a close would be to vote for cloture. This type of cloture required that two-thirds of those present and voting had to vote to end the filibuster.

Russell was confident that the opposition would have to accept the Southern amendments to the bill on his terms. He and his supporters called the bluff of the rest of the Senate and lost.

Behind the bipartisan leadership and political maneuvering of the Senate majority floor leader for the bill, Hubert H. Humphrey, and Senate minority leader Everett Dirksen, a coalition of votes was put together to challenge the "Southern Strategy." On June 10, 1964, the cloture measure came up for a vote. With all one hundred members present, the Senate voted seventy-one to twenty-nine to shut down the civil rights filibuster. For all intents and purposes, any opposition to the civil rights legislation was dead.

After accepting a number of primarily technical amendments by Dirksen dealing with the enforcement sections of the public accommodations and employment provisions, the Senate, on June 19, 1964, passed by a roll-call vote of seventy-three to twenty-seven the so-called "Mansfield-Dirksen" substitute version of the civil rights bill. Fearing a renewed Senate filibuster, House Representatives Celler and McColluch accepted in principle the Senate version of the bill. The House formally agreed to the Senate compromise bill by a roll-call vote of 289-126 on July 2, 1964, thus concluding congressional action on the bill. Later that evening, President Johnson, in the presence of many of the bill's sponsors and civil rights leaders, signed into law the most comprehensive and meaningful piece of civil rights legislation in American history.

Impact of Event

The Civil Rights Act of 1964, the most comprehensive piece of civil rights legislation to be enacted into law in the twentieth century, put statutory "teeth" into the "color blind" language enunciated in the dissenting opinion of *Plessy v. Ferguson* (1896) and the majority opinion of *Brown v. Board of Education* (1954).

Congress invoked its authority to enact civil rights legislation under the commerce clause of the U.S. Constitution rather than the equal protection clause of the same document. This allowed Congress wider authority to eliminate, among other things, discrimination in public accommodations and facilities, the symbolic focal point of the black civil rights movement, and job discrimination, which was viewed as a national problem. The Civil Rights Act of 1964 requires that determinations made within its jurisdiction be made without regard to race, color, religion, sex, or national origin. The major effect of the act has been to cast aside the legal barriers of segregation as they relate to voting, public education, public accommodations and facilities, federally assisted programs, and private employment.

Although it has certainly expanded opportunities of those affected in a legal sense, the Civil Rights Act of 1964 has generated controversy over its enforcement and effects. Civil rights leaders and organizations have held since the inception of the law that the Civil Rights Act is a hollow promise, given that the law has done nothing to dispel the institutional forms of discrimination prevalent in society. Statistical evidence suggests that the employment rate, mortality rate, education level, and living conditions among minorities have in fact worsened since 1964.

On the other hand, nonminorities have become increasingly alienated by what they see as a gross transformation of the intent and letter of the Civil Rights Act. They cite, for example, disregard for a section of the act which expressly holds that preferential treatment in employment cannot be granted for the purpose of balancing a work force by race or sex, and for another section which expressly guarantees that desegregation of schools will not be implemented in order to overcome racial imbalance. It is widely agreed, even in light of these concerns, that the Civil Rights Act of 1964 has gone a long way in guaranteeing the rights of minorities and in advancing the human rights atmosphere within the United States, setting an example for democratic nations worldwide.

Bibliography

Bureau of National Affairs. *The Civil Rights Act of 1964: Text, Analysis, Legislative History.* Washington, D.C.: Author, 1964. Published as an "Operations Manual" on fair employment practices, public accommodations, and federal assistance, this publication is important because it describes the Civil Rights Act as it was understood at the time of its enactment. The book is complete with an extensive legislative history of the act as well as an analysis of each of the major provisions of the act.

Friedman, Joel, and George Strickler, Jr. *The Law of Employment Discrimination: Cases and Materials.* New York: Foundation Press, 1983. A compilation of United States Supreme Court and lower court decisions that relate to the law of employment discrimination, including a large number of landmark cases addressing the issue of discrimination as a violation of the Civil Rights Act of 1964. Valuable in understanding the courts' evolving interpretation of this law. Available in most postsecondary and public libraries.

Garrow, David J. *Bearing the Cross: Martin Luther King, Jr., and the Southern Christian Leadership Conference.* New York: William Morrow, 1986. A comprehensive and sympathetic history of the black Civil Rights movement, centering on the Southern Christian Leadership Conference and its leader, Martin Luther King, Jr. Based on more than seven hundred interviews with key figures in the Civil Rights movement and civil rights bill advocates. Includes a ninety-three page bibliography and ninety pages of notes.

Whalen, Charles, and Barbara Whalen. *The Longest Debate: A Legislative History of the 1964 Civil Rights Act.* New York: Mentor Books, 1986. Written by former Congressman Charles Whalen, this book presents a concise and readable account of the legislative struggle to pass the Civil Rights Act of 1964. Particularly useful for those attempting to understand the procedure and politics of congressional lawmaking, specifically as it related to racial matters in the mid-1960's.

Williams, Juan. *Eyes on the Prize: America's Civil Rights Years, a Reader and Guide.* New York: Viking Press, 1987. A companion piece to the PBS television series of the same name, the book presents an easily read, yet highly informative, appraisal and account of the struggle to ensure basic human rights by enactment of the Civil Rights Act of 1964. Complete with many excellent photos and an epilogue informing the reader of the recent history of the main figures portrayed in the book.

Frank W. Andritzky

Cross-References

Roosevelt Outlaws Discrimination in Defense-Industry Employment (1941), p. 578; The Congress of Racial Equality Forms (1942), p. 601; CORE Stages a Sit-in in Chicago to Protest Segregation (1943), p. 618; *Brown v. Board of Education* Ends Public School Segregation (1954), p. 913; The SCLC Forms to Link Civil Rights Groups (1957), p. 974; The Civil Rights Act of 1957 Creates the Commission on

MARTIN LUTHER KING, JR., WINS THE NOBEL PEACE PRIZE

Categories of event: Peace movements and organizations; racial and ethnic rights
Time: December 10, 1964
Locale: Oslo, Norway

Martin Luther King, Jr., led a nonviolent battle for racial equality in the United States and was rewarded for his efforts with the Nobel Peace Prize

Principal personages:
   MARTIN LUTHER KING, JR. (1929-1968), the Nobel Peace laureate for 1964, a minister and civil rights leader
   CORETTA SCOTT KING (1927-   ), the director of the Center for Nonviolent Social Change, King's wife
   RALPH D. ABERNATHY (1926-1990), a close associate of King and the second president of the Southern Christian Leadership Conference
   ROSA PARKS (1913-   ), the woman in Montgomery, Alabama, who sparked King's first major civil rights campaign
   JESSE JACKSON (1941-   ), the first African American to seek presidential nomination by the Democratic National Committee

Summary of Event

The African American's struggle for civil rights in the United States is not a recent phenomenon. The movement for racial justice in the United States dates to the period between the American Revolution and the Civil War. Some of these early efforts were directed at returning blacks to Africa, and several groups of emancipated slaves did in fact emigrate to West Africa. By the early 1850's, however, the majority of black leaders favored a campaign to stay in the United States and improve the socioeconomic and political conditions for American blacks through racial integration.

Various black organizations sprang up between 1850 and 1900, all with the objective of attaining improved quality of life for African Americans. Among such organizations was the Niagara Movement, founded in 1905 by a prominent black sociologist, W. E. B. Du Bois and later reorganized into the National Association for the Advancement of Colored People (NAACP). Also, Marcus Garvey, a Jamaican educator, provided tough and charismatic leadership for much of the black populace as founder and head of the Universal Negro Association. Unfortunately, his leadership was short-lived as the result of a mail-fraud conviction in 1922 and subsequent deportation.

A major epoch in black-white relations was marked by the 1954 *Brown v. Board of Education* case, argued before the U.S. Supreme Court by NAACP counsel Thurgood Marshall. By fall, 1954, as a result of the Supreme Court's decision on the

Brown case, school systems of eight states, a total of 150 major school districts, were partially desegregated. Thus, the Supreme Court ruling provided an immediate catalyst for the 1950's struggle for racial integration and socioeconomic emancipation. The ruling did not make a major impact on racial integration in public institutions, however, primarily because of a group of southern U.S. senators who vehemently opposed racial integration. One blatant expression of their opposition took the form of a "Southern Manifesto," sponsored by Senator Harry Byrd and signed by one hundred mostly southern state senators, to attack the Court's decision.

Such was the climate when Martin Luther King, Jr., ascended to national prominence: More needed to be done to bring about rapid racial integration within all sectors of American society to combat the violently repressive economic, political, and social atmosphere faced by black Americans. Moreover, African Americans needed leadership to offset a growing sense of apathy, divisiveness, and helplessness.

King, pastor of the Dexter Avenue Baptist Church in Montgomery, Alabama, became visible in black politics on a national level during the Montgomery bus boycott, which began as a minor racial incident on December 1, 1955, when Rosa Parks refused to give up her seat to a white male passenger. The boycott evolved into a major strike by blacks lasting 382 days and resulting in desegregation of Alabama buses. King was elected the first president of the Montgomery Improvement Association (MIA), the organization responsible for leading the boycott. A resistance movement throughout the South grew out of the victory of the boycott, coalescing into the Southern Christian Leadership Conference (SCLC) in 1957. King became the first president of the SCLC, and his voice began to be heard worldwide.

Between 1957 and 1968, King led voter registration drives and protest marches, traveled more than six million miles, and gave more than twenty-five hundred lectures and speeches. A charismatic speaker and scholar well versed in the philosophical works of great thinkers, King valued and embodied religious concepts; he pledged his life as a champion of the downtrodden in society and embraced and inspired nonviolent civil disobedience through direct action as espoused through the life and teaching of Mahatma Gandhi of India. Before the eyes of the world, King led protest marches in which marchers met with police dogs, water hoses, and police brutality. During his own incarceration following a Birmingham protest march, King inspired his followers with his classic treatise "Letter from a Birmingham Jail." He also wrote several books and was jailed many times; his life was threatened often.

As a result of the efforts of King and those who were led by him, other events also took place that helped to transform King and the entire American society. On the national level, the Eisenhower Administration enacted the 1957 Civil Rights Act, which affirmed the rights of all Americans, to vote in all elections. President John F. Kennedy, elected in 1960, received overwhelming support in his election bid from King and his supporters. Following his election, Kennedy pledged support for the Civil Rights movement to support racial equality. One tangible result of Kennedy's pledge was the dynamic cooperation of the Justice Department and the Civil Rights Commission in enforcing neglected voting rights laws. There was a tremendous upsurge in the number of voting rights suits initiated, from six during the entire Eisenhower Administration to fifty-eight by 1963, when Kennedy was assassinated.

On August 28, 1963, King directed the largest demonstration that the U.S. capital had ever seen, the historic "March on Washington" to demand jobs and freedom for all unemployed Americans, especially blacks. Moreover, the march was staged to support a civil rights bill pending in the U.S. Congress and to support the movement's economic goals. King delivered his famous "I Have a Dream" speech at the march.

In 1964, when King was nominated for the Nobel Peace Prize, the plight of the black American had improved on some levels with regard to human rights. There were fewer "whites only" signs throughout the South as more public facilities such as restaurants, movie theaters, schools, and hotels had become desegregated. Unfortunately, less-blatant forms of racial discrimination persisted, as reflected, for example, by the common phrase that black people in America were "the last to be hired and the first to be fired." Thus, the interaction between abject poverty and racial discrimination was identified by King as an enduring destructive force that was crippling the entire society and exacerbating the ordinary survival problems among underprivileged blacks.

The Nobel Prize Committee lauded King not because he had led a racial minority in its struggle for equality but for the way in which he waged his struggle. Martin Luther King, Jr., was the first person in the Western world to show that a struggle could be waged without violence. King called the award a recognition of nonviolence as the answer to the crucial political and moral question of our time—the need for humankind to overcome oppression and violence without the use of oppression and violence. King praised the real heroes and heroines of the freedom struggle and shared his prize money among his various organizations. In his acceptance speech, King reflected upon the problems of humankind worldwide: racial injustice, poverty, and war.

Impact of Event

King's untiring leadership supported the election of President Lyndon B. Johnson, whose administration passed two major civil rights laws, the 1964 Civil Rights Act and the 1965 Voting Rights Act, which provided the nation's minorities legal protection to vote. King perceived, however, that these measures did not go far enough in reversing the hopeless plight of millions of blacks in northern city ghettos who suffered from racism and deprivation.

Through its nonviolent approach, King's movement stirred the conscience of the American people and caused irrevocable changes in American society. Further, King's objectives and principles strengthened and united minorities seeking freedom, justice, and racial integration. The strong foundation laid in the 1960's for minority cohesiveness and political awareness aided Jesse Jackson in his bid for the presidential nomination of the Democratic Party and helped elect numerous mayors and congressional representatives.

Has King's dream for a society of racial equality and justice been realized? *The New York Times* of January 15, 1984, in an editorial commemorating King's fifty-fifth birthday, wrote that King's dream remained alive. The editors pointed out that in the 1980's one-third of all blacks lived below the poverty line; that almost half of black families were female-headed and thus tended to be poor; and that the unemployment rate for blacks was twice that for whites. Moreover, the relative income of blacks had not improved since 1960.

Leadership in black America has changed since the King era. King's widow, Coretta Scott King, founded and served as director of the Atlanta-based Center for Nonviolent Social Change. Ralph D. Abernathy, King's close associate, succeeded him as the SCLC's president until 1977, when he was pressured to step down. Subsequent black leaders seldom possessed the stamina, organizational ability, and charisma of King, and civil rights marches and delegations became sporadic and often did not involve direct participation of the masses.

Additionally, support from the White House waned after the Johnson Administration's "War on Poverty" legislated social programs for combating poverty. During the 1980's, the Reagan Administration cut numerous social and economic programs and made limited progress regarding the race problem in America.

The status of black Americans in the areas of education, standard of living, housing opportunities, earnings, and political participation had regressed relative to whites since the early 1970's, according to a twenty-two-member study commission that began work in 1985. According to the commission, full integration of black Americans into a color-blind society was unlikely, largely because of existing social and economic separation and low rates of intermarriage. Finally, new impediments to racial equality may be harder to erase than legal segregation and discrimination, because subtle racism is less amenable to legal and political pressure for change.

Bibliography

Assensoh, A. B. *Rev. Dr. Martin Luther King, Jr., and America's Quest for Racial Integration.* Ilfrancombe, England: Arthur H. Stockwell, 1987. Testimonies from King's former classmates, close friends, and colleagues. Highlights King's early life and includes an analysis of his moral, political, and social philosophies, an analysis of King's participation in the American movement for racial integration, and an assessment of King as a peacemaker and a nonviolent leader in the struggle for racial integration and justice in the United States. Appendices, bibliography, index. Rare photographs.

Garrow, David. *Bearing the Cross: Martin Luther King., Jr., and the Southern Christian Leadership Conference.* New York: William Morrow, 1986. An extensive chronological documentation, the result of five years of research, the book spans the period from the Montgomery bus boycott to King's assassination. Detailed, scholarly, well written, and easy to read. A valuable contribution, based on several hundred interviews, federal documents, unpublished sermons, and speeches. Extensive bibliography, index.

Hanigan, James. *Martin Luther King, Jr., and the Foundations of Nonviolence.* Lanham, Md.: University Press of America, 1984. Critical and reflective. Seeks to understand exactly what King meant by insisting that nonviolence was an absolute moral imperative of human life, the basis on which he rested his claim, and some implications and problems flowing from the claim. Addresses key questions: What did King hold to be true about reality and human life that led him to embrace nonviolence? What can be said critically about the coherence, meaningfulness, and truth of King's position? Index.

Jaynes, Gerald D., ed. *A Common Destiny: Blacks and American Society.* Washington, D.C.: National Academy Press, 1989. Covers the years 1940 to 1989 and points out remaining impediments to racial equality. Follows the Kerner Commission report of the late 1960's. A twenty-two-member study commission assessed indicators that showed that the status of black Americans relative to white Americans had stagnated since the early 1970's. Includes the story of success as well as the story of hardship in the struggle for equality.

Oates, Stephen B. *Let the Trumpet Sound: The Life of Martin Luther King, Jr.* New York: Harper & Row, 1982. Based on intensive original research using source materials previously unavailable. The first major biography of King, by a professional biographer. In storytelling style, compassionate, rich in modern-day history. A portrait of the public figure and the private individual. Written in ten parts. Photographs, references, index.

B. Mawiyah Clayborne

Cross-References

Parks Is Arrested for Refusing to Sit in the Back of the Bus (1955), p. 947; The SCLC Forms to Link Civil Rights Groups (1957), p. 974; The Civil Rights Act of 1957 Creates the Commission on Civil Rights (1957), p. 997; Civil Rights Protesters Attract International Attention (1963), p. 1188; Martin Luther King, Jr., Delivers His "I Have a Dream" Speech (1963), p. 1200; Three Civil Rights Workers Are Murdered (1964), p. 1246; Discrimination in Accommodations Is Forbidden by the U.S. Supreme Court (1964), p. 1262; Martin Luther King, Jr., Leads a March from Selma to Montgomery (1965), p. 1278; The Civil Rights Act of 1968 Outlaws Discrimination in Housing (1968), p. 1414; Martin Luther King, Jr., Is Assassinated in Memphis (1968), p. 1419; Congress Passes the Equal Employment Opportunity Act (1972), p. 1650.

DISCRIMINATION IN ACCOMMODATIONS IS FORBIDDEN BY THE U.S. SUPREME COURT

Category of event: Racial and ethnic rights
Time: December 14, 1964
Locale: United States Supreme Court, Washington, D.C.

The U.S. Supreme Court endorsed laws forbidding private discrimination by hotels, restaurants, and other places of public accommodation in the case of Heart of Atlanta Motel v. United States

> *Principal personages:*
> TOM C. CLARK (1899-1977), an associate justice of the Supreme Court, considered a moderate during his term on the Court from 1949 to 1967
> LYNDON B. JOHNSON (1908-1973), the president of the United States (1963-1969)
> JOHN F. KENNEDY (1917-1963), the president of the United States (1961-1963); he proposed major civil rights legislation
> ROBERT F. KENNEDY (1925-1968), an attorney general of the United States and a United States senator from New York
> ARCHIBALD COX (1912-   ), a Harvard University law professor and solicitor general of the United States
> STROM THURMOND (1902-   ), a United States senator from South Carolina; he led opposition to civil rights laws

Summary of Event

The Fourteenth Amendment to the United States Constitution was enacted in 1868 to provide protection for the newly freed slaves. After the Civil War, Congress passed several broad statutes aimed at protecting African Americans against racial discrimination in housing and contracts. These laws were needed because, although they were freed from slavery, blacks still suffered from severe discrimination in all aspects of American life. The Supreme Court took a narrow view of congressional power in 1883, however, and issued a decision that prevented Congress from attempting to stop private individuals and companies from engaging in racial discrimination. The Supreme Court said that Congress could enact laws aimed only at governmental discrimination. In effect, the Supreme Court declared that blacks could be victims of blatant discrimination by private entities without any interference from the law. As a result, many blacks' lives changed little from their experience as slaves. They were still forced to work as agricultural laborers because they were not permitted to be trained and hired for other jobs.

Because no federal laws could prevent private discrimination, until 1964 blacks were deprived of many opportunities readily enjoyed by white people. If they wished to travel, black people frequently could not find motels that would accept them or restaurants that would serve them. Blacks were forced to carry their own food if they went on bus trips and often had to knock on doors in black neighborhoods in order to find families that would put them up for the night in private homes. For example, when professional baseball teams had spring training in Florida every year, the white players stayed in hotels while their black teammates rented rooms in the homes of local black families. Similar circumstances arose when northern college sports teams traveled to the South for games. Racial segregation and discrimination were so severe that bus stations had separate waiting rooms, rest rooms, and drinking fountains for black passengers. In many cities, black and white friends could dine together only in black-owned restaurants because blacks were not allowed to eat in white-owned establishments. In sum, it was very difficult for blacks to travel and shop because they were denied access to so many business establishments.

Beginning in the 1940's, members of Congress made repeated attempts to enact antidiscrimination legislation. The structure of Congress, however, gave members power according to seniority. Because southerners had the most seniority, they controlled many of the legislative committees. Thus, by keeping bills tied up in committee hearings, they could prevent Congress from considering proposed legislation. Southern congresspeople were very successful in ensuring that only weak civil rights laws, if any, were enacted by Congress.

Beginning in the 1940's and 1950's, many African Americans organized boycotts, marches, and other protests to challenge racial discrimination. Peaceful protesters were often met by violent mobs of whites or were attacked, beaten, and arrested by all-white police forces. Shortly after highly publicized demonstrations against racial discrimination in Alabama during May, 1963, President John F. Kennedy decided to send a major civil rights bill to Congress. Title II of the proposed legislation that eventually became the Civil Rights Act of 1964 prohibited private discrimination in places of public accommodation, including hotels, motels, restaurants, and theaters. President Kennedy was assassinated in November, 1963, while the bill was working its way through Congress. Upon succeeding to the presidency, Lyndon Johnson made the civil rights bill his major legislative priority. Within days of Kennedy's assassination, President Johnson asked a joint session of Congress to enact the Civil Rights Act as a memorial to the late President Kennedy.

When the Senate held hearings to consider the proposed legislation, questions arose concerning congressional power to outlaw private discrimination. The Supreme Court had clearly stated in 1883 that Congress lacked such power under the Fourteenth Amendment. Attorney General Robert F. Kennedy testified that Congress possessed the power to outlaw discrimination in public accommodations through its constitutional authority to regulate interstate commerce. Kennedy and his assistants argued that racial discrimination in public accommodations hampered the national economy because it prevented blacks from traveling freely. Moreover, it deterred northern companies from expanding into the South because they did not wish to subject their black employees to severe discrimination.

Senator Strom Thurmond of South Carolina, one of the consistent opponents of civil rights legislation, questioned Attorney General Kennedy closely. From the repeated questioning, it was clear that the Civil Rights Act's supporters were not completely certain about precisely which private businesses would be prevented from discriminating under the law. Although a national bus company could clearly be regulated under congressional power over interstate commerce, it was not clear whether establishments such as neighborhood diners and barbershops were subject to federal laws governing commerce. If these small businesses were involved only in the local economy and did not affect interstate commerce, then Congress presumably would be unable to prevent them from engaging in racial discrimination.

When the Civil Rights Act was enacted in 1964, it was immediately challenged by southern businesses that wished to continue engaging in racial discrimination. The Heart of Atlanta Motel claimed that it was not engaged in interstate commerce because it provided services at one location inside Georgia. The motel wished to continue its practice of refusing to rent rooms to black customers, so it filed a legal action seeking to have federal judges declare that the Civil Rights Act was invalid. Although it usually takes several years for cases to work their way through the judicial system in order to reach the Supreme Court, the high court took up the issue of discrimination in public accommodations without delay in late 1964.

In opposition to the motel's arguments, Archibald Cox, the solicitor general of the United States, argued to the Supreme Court that congressional power to regulate interstate commerce should be construed broadly to cover all businesses which affect commerce in any way. Even if a business appeared to be limited to local customers, Cox argued that it would have links to interstate commerce. For example, a neighborhood barbershop's equipment inevitably includes a chair, a pair of scissors, or other equipment that was manufactured in another state.

On December 14, 1964, only two months after hearing oral arguments, the Supreme Court issued a unanimous decision that endorsed congressional power to outlaw private discrimination in public accommodations. The Court's opinion in *Heart of Atlanta Motel, Inc. v. United States*, written by Justice Tom C. Clark, acknowledged that racial discrimination had prevented blacks from enjoying their right to travel. Because the Heart of Atlanta Motel served many travelers from outside Georgia, it was found to affect interstate commerce and therefore to come under the antidiscrimination laws. In this and other decisions concerning Title II of the Civil Rights Act, the Supreme Court interpreted congressional power to regulate interstate commerce so broadly that virtually every private business, no matter how localized in nature, was barred from engaging in racial discrimination. Scholars argue that the Court dispensed with legal arguments concerning technical limitations on congressional power because the justices were committed to endorsing all governmental efforts to combat racial discrimination.

Impact of Event

After the Supreme Court's decision in *Heart of Atlanta Motel*, the United States

Department of Justice initiated hundreds of investigations into racial discrimination complaints concerning places of public accommodation. The Court's decision clearly confirmed the federal government's authority to prosecute businesses that failed to end discriminatory practices.

Through the combined efforts of Congress, the president, and the Supreme Court, African Americans could finally enjoy access to theaters, motels, and restaurants. The deeply entrenched practices of racial discrimination had been dealt a powerful blow by the federal government. As a result, black people who traveled could find motels and restaurants that would serve them. Many proprietors of public accommodations businesses initially resisted implementation of the antidiscrimination law by declining to serve blacks or by being rude to black customers. Over time, however, the American public, including business owners in the South, accepted the idea that all people should have equal access to public accommodations. Only a tiny number of businesses were so opposed to desegregation that they turned themselves into private clubs in order to avoid application of the Civil Rights Act.

Title II of the Civil Rights Act of 1964 is regarded as one of the most effective civil rights laws ever enacted. Unlike laws concerning employment, in which there are controversies concerning proof of discrimination, Title II addresses a very straightforward subject. In the employment context, there might be many legally acceptable reasons why a particular individual did not receive a particular job. Thus, a minority applicant may find it difficult to discover whether illegal racial discrimination played a role in the hiring decision. In public accommodations, the question is much simpler. Were the customers provided with the services that they requested and for which they were willing to pay? Because discrimination in public accommodations, unlike that in employment, is very difficult to disguise, businesses throughout the United States have generally eliminated any vestiges of the formal discrimination that was previously so prevalent. In fact, proprietors of restaurants and other places of public accommodation have discovered that it is good for their businesses to seek African-American customers. Previously, they not only deprived black people of services and the ability to travel but also deprived themselves of customers in a growing segment of the American population. Eventually, racial discrimination in public accommodations was pushed so firmly into the past that many establishments owned or controlled by whites developed advertising campaigns aimed specifically at black consumers.

The Supreme Court's decision in the *Heart of Atlanta Motel* case indicated that all three branches of the federal government were committed to dismantling racial discrimination and segregation. The message sent by this decision not only warned segregationist interests that their power had been diminished but also helped to mobilize and encourage civil rights supporters to pursue actively additional antidiscrimination statutes and favorable judicial decisions in areas such as housing and voting.

Bibliography

Abraham, Henry J. *Freedom and the Court: Civil Rights and Liberties in the United*

States. 5th ed. New York: Oxford University Press, 1988. Thorough review of the Supreme Court's cases interpreting the Bill of Rights and the Fourteenth Amendment. Contains good coverage of the cases and legal issues concerning the interpretation of the Civil Rights Act of 1964.

Cox, Archibald. *The Warren Court: Constitutional Decision as an Instrument of Reform.* Cambridge, Mass.: Harvard University Press, 1968. Discussion of how the Supreme Court's decisions affect social issues. Contains commentary about the design of particular arguments presented to the Supreme Court in the *Heart of Atlanta Motel* case by the lawyer who presented those arguments.

Griffin, John Howard. *Black Like Me.* Boston: Houghton Mifflin, 1961. First-person account by a white writer who had his skin medically darkened in order to travel throughout the South in 1959 as a black man. Describes the discrimination and harassment that faced blacks prior to passage of the Civil Rights Act.

Loevy, Robert D. "'To Write It in the Books of Law': President Lyndon B. Johnson and the Civil Rights Act of 1964." In *Lyndon Baines Johnson and the Uses of Power,* edited by Bernard J. Firestone and Robert C. Vogt. New York: Greenwood Press, 1988. Detailed account of the events leading to the passage of the Civil Rights Act of 1964. Provides insights into the role played by President Johnson in pushing the legislation past opponents in Congress.

Nieman, Donald G. *Promises to Keep: African-Americans and the Constitutional Order, 1776 to the Present.* New York: Oxford University Press, 1991. Discussion of racial discrimination in the United States. Provides a thorough history of the ways in which courts and other government institutions failed to provide blacks with the rights guaranteed by the Constitution.

Christopher E. Smith

Cross-References

Black Leaders Call for Equal Rights at the Niagara Falls Conference (1905), p. 41; The Ku Klux Klan Spreads Terror in the South (1920's), p. 298; Roosevelt Outlaws Discrimination in Defense-Industry Employment (1941), p. 578; The Congress of Racial Equality Forms (1942), p. 601; CORE Stages a Sit-in in Chicago to Protest Segregation (1943), p. 618; Robinson Breaks the Color Line in Organized Baseball (1947), p. 712; Truman Orders Desegregation of U.S. Armed Forces (1948), p. 777; *Brown v. Board of Education* Ends Public School Segregation (1954), p. 913; The SCLC Forms to Link Civil Rights Groups (1957), p. 974; The Civil Rights Act of 1957 Creates the Commission on Civil Rights (1957), p. 997; Civil Rights Protesters Attract International Attention (1963), p. 1188; Congress Passes the Civil Rights Act (1964), p. 1251.

NADER PUBLISHES *UNSAFE AT ANY SPEED*

Category of event: Consumers' rights
Time: 1965
Locale: The United States

Nader's shocking exposé of the American automobile industry made him an American folk hero and led to countless major improvements in product safety and environmental protection

Principal personages:

RALPH NADER (1934-   ), a lawyer known as the founder of the consumer rights movement for his book *Unsafe at Any Speed*

ABRAHAM ALEXANDER RIBICOFF (1910-   ), a U.S. senator who was a strong supporter of consumer protection measures and pollution controls

ROBERT F. KENNEDY (1925-1968), a U.S. senator serving on Senator Ribicoff's subcommittee that approved passage of the Traffic and Motor Vehicle Safety Act of 1966

DANIEL PATRICK MOYNIHAN (1927-   ), the assistant secretary of labor for policy planning who hired Nader as a staff consultant on highway safety

WILLIAM HADDON, JR. (1926-1985), a safety expert who was appointed head of the National Traffic Safety Agency

Summary of Event

The 1960's was one of the most turbulent periods in American history in spite of the fact that it was also a period of unprecedented prosperity. The Vietnam conflict continued to escalate as part of the global Cold War being waged between the United States and the Soviet Union. Many young Americans were disgusted with the complacency of their elders and were looking for something to believe in besides conspicuous consumption. The Beatles and other popular rock and roll musicians of the 1960's expressed the attitude of the younger generation, which was disenchantment with the existing order of things and a yearning for new solutions to the world's critical problems.

Ralph Nader offered a new ideology to many Americans and was in particular an inspiration to America's middle-class youth. He showed them that free enterprise and democracy were not outmoded concepts but were being dangerously subverted by the monopolistic tendencies of big corporations. He also showed them that they could make a difference in their country's and their own futures by following his example and becoming actively involved in the struggle to promote positive change within the existing system. The publication of Nader's *Unsafe at Any Speed: The Designed-in Dangers of the American Automobile* in 1965 did more than expose the problems of the American automobile industry: It began the consumer movement in the United States, a movement that continued to expand and accelerate.

Unsafe at Any Speed is best remembered for its attack on a rear-engine semi-sporty car, the Chevrolet Corvair, developed by a General Motors subsidiary. Nader called it "one of the nastiest-handling cars ever built." He also had harsh words about Ford Motor Company's Mustang and about many other makes and models of American cars. Nader's book was a work of nonfiction and was crammed with facts and statistics; however, he used the techniques of modern article writers to make the book appeal to the widest possible audience. He offered concrete illustrations of the horrible truths he was relating. He told how a woman lost her arm when her car suddenly went out of control and flipped over, and how a small child lost an eye because he was hurled into the dashboard right where a protruding control knob thoughtlessly had been placed by the car's designers.

Incidents such as these reminded readers of their own experiences with automobiles. In 1965, more than fifty thousand people were killed on America's highways and millions more were injured. There was hardly an American who had not suffered physically or emotionally from death or injury, personally or vicariously through a loved one, in an auto accident. Nader claimed that nearly one-half of the automobiles then on the road would eventually be involved in an injury-producing accident, and that one out of every two Americans would be injured or killed in an auto accident. It was his belief that many of these accidents need not have happened and were the fault of the vehicles involved. Other accidents would not have been as serious if the vehicles had been designed for safety rather than style.

Detroit at that time was producing more than eight million automobiles per year. Foreign competition was not yet a serious threat, and because of perceptions of seemingly endless prosperity based on easy credit, American manufacturers could sell all the machines they could build. Factories worked around the clock to turn out gaudy products with dagger-sharp tail fins and other dangerous and totally unnecessary adornments; the speeded-up assembly lines, often staffed with inexperienced workers, turned out slipshod products which gave American automakers a reputation they were still trying to repudiate decades later. With all the cars that were choking the highways, there was pressure on the federal government to provide more and more miles of pavement. This had a snowball effect: More highways created "urban sprawl," which meant more driving to and from places of employment. Suburban expansion led to the proliferation of two-car families, because homemakers refused to be stranded without an automobile.

More cars on the streets and highways would obviously produce more deaths and injuries. Some government leaders, such as Senators Abraham Ribicoff and Robert Kennedy, were concerned about government's passive role. The federal government was being asked to provide billions of dollars for highways but not to interfere in such matters as traffic safety or the growing problem of smog. Larger, gas-guzzling American cars were producing deaths and injuries both directly, through accidents, and indirectly: They were creating deadly air pollution in cities all across the United States. Since so many Americans used automobiles and made their livings directly or indirectly from the automotive industry, legislators were reluctant to interfere with what seemed to be an inevitable trend.

What people admired about Ralph Nader was his fearless aggressiveness. He not only attacked the automakers for their dangerously designed and poorly assembled products but also castigated many other groups that showed inadequate concern for the public safety. He accused the news media of failing to report the truth to their audiences because automobile advertising, with its sumptuous pictorial coverage of shiny new cars, was too lucrative to risk losing. He accused insurance companies of failing to protest against the millions of unsafe cars on the roads because they were able to raise their premiums to offset bodily injury and property damage claims. He accused what he called "the traffic safety establishment"—including the Society of Automotive Engineers, the National Safety Council, the American Standards Association, the Automotive Safety Foundation, and the President's Committee for Traffic Safety—of being in collusion with the automakers and attributing nearly all automobile accidents to "driver error" rather than placing any blame on the vehicles themselves.

In the last chapter of *Unsafe at Any Speed*, Nader made it plain that he favored tougher government controls when he wrote, "Only the federal government can undertake the critical task of stimulating and guiding public and private initiatives for safety." He believed that the democratic process was better equipped to resolve competing interests and determine what science and technology should provide than were automobile firms, with their main focus on profits rather than on public welfare.

Nader's book brought him considerable attention as an individual. People were amazed at his unusual personality. Although he made a large sum of money from the book and was making much more from lecture tours, he lived an ascetic existence. He was unmarried, lived in a cheap rooming house, spent very little on food or clothing, and worked as much as sixteen hours a day, seven days a week, with no vacations. He was totally dedicated to his crusade for consumer rights, and he made it clear that his attack on automobiles was only the beginning. Not since Theodore Roosevelt, the "trust buster," had big business encountered such a formidable foe.

Nader became even more famous as an American folk hero when it came out in a Senate hearing that General Motors had hired private detectives to follow him around and had been harassing him in other ways in an attempt to silence him. In a nationally televised hearing of Connecticut Senator Abraham Ribicoff's subcommittee on executive reorganization in 1966, General Motors president James M. Roche publicly apologized to Nader for his company's behavior. In 1970, the company settled a $16,000,000 lawsuit for invasion of privacy by paying Nader $425,000 out of court.

Impact of Event

Ralph Nader's career has resembled that of the author and human rights crusader Upton Sinclair. Just as Sinclair built his fame on *The Jungle* (1906), an exposé of the American meatpacking industry, and used his prestige and notoriety to attack many other social evils, so Nader has capitalized on the fame he achieved with *Unsafe at Any Speed* to crusade for many years against a wide variety of hazards and abuses. The major difference between Sinclair and Nader is that Sinclair for most of his life pinned his hopes on socialism, while Nader has always believed in strengthening free enterprise through existing democratic means guaranteed by the U.S. Constitution.

Just as Upton Sinclair's *The Jungle* had an immediate effect of expediting passage of the Pure Food and Drug Act of 1906, so Nader's *Unsafe at Any Speed* had the immediate effect of mustering public support for strong federal regulation of the automobile industry. In September of 1966, Ralph Nader was present at the White House when President Lyndon Baines Johnson signed into law two bills which he termed "landmark legislation." They were the Traffic Safety Act, which created a National Traffic Safety Agency under the Commerce Department, and the Highway Safety Act, which provided funds to encourage states to develop their own traffic safety programs. Nader received widespread acclaim for his role in mustering support for this legislation.

Much of the money Nader received from his book and from the settlement of his lawsuit against General Motors went into his Corporate Accountability Research Group, which campaigned for federal rather than state chartering of corporations in order to make it easier for shareholders and watchdog groups to monitor the activities of powerful companies. He also started the Public Interest Research Group (PIRG), which fought for consumer and political reform on the community and college campus level.

In 1971, Nader founded Public Citizen, Inc., a consumer lobbying group, as a means of counterbalancing the enormous influence of corporate lobbies. Public Citizen in turn became the parent organization for the Tax Reform Research Group, the Retired Professional Action Group, and Congress Watch. Nader and his so-called "raiders" were instrumental in the creation of the Environmental Protection Agency in 1970 and in securing passage of the Freedom of Information Act in 1974. They were also instrumental in the creation of the Occupational Safety and Health Administration (OSHA) in 1970.

Unsafe at Any Speed was a prelude to a lifelong career of battling against abuses of the public interest by big business and big government. Nader became a youth hero and was much sought after to lecture on college campuses across the nation. He used the college forum as a double-edged sword: The fees went toward financing his various consumer advocacy organizations, and the lectures themselves urged young intellectuals to get involved in lobbying for government regulation of large corporations.

Nader, a seemingly tireless crusader, gave young Americans both a role model and an ideology. He told one audience, "The most important question that can be asked about any society is how much effort do citizens spend exercising their civic responsibility. We can't possibly have a democracy with 200 million Americans and only a handful of citizens."

Bibliography

Buckhorn, Robert F. *Nader: The People's Lawyer.* Englewood Cliffs, N.J.: Prentice-Hall, 1972. A profile of Ralph Nader as a person and a summary of his activities until 1972. Contains a valuable bibliography of consumer advocacy publications produced or inspired by Nader and a list of the legislation which had resulted from the activities of his organization.

Burt, Dan M. *Abuse of Trust: A Report on Ralph Nader's Network.* Chicago: Regnery Gateway, 1982. A hostile attack on Ralph Nader and his consumer advocacy organization by the president of Capital Legal Foundation, a nonprofit organization concerned with "ensuring a compassionate, fair free market economic system in the United States." The author attempts to show that Nader has selfish motives for his activities. Contains some useful chapter notes.

Gorey, Hays. *Nader and the Power of Everyman.* New York: Grosset & Dunlap, 1975. A heavily anecdotal account of Nader's activities during the first half of the 1970's by a *Time* reporter. It is especially interesting in its revelations of Nader's conflicts with members of President Richard Nixon's administration.

Keats, John. *The Insolent Chariots.* Philadelphia, Pa.: J. B. Lippincott, 1958. This best-seller was one of the earliest attacks on American car manufacturers, criticizing the outlandish designs, inordinate fuel consumption, and planned obsolescence of their products. Enjoyable reading. Imaginative illustrations by Robert Osborn portray American cars of the period as obscenely ostentatious, death-dealing, gas-guzzling, environment-polluting monsters.

Nader, Ralph. *Unsafe at Any Speed: The Designed-in Dangers of the American Automobile.* New York: Grossman, 1965. This book was a best-seller and made Nader a world-famous personality.

Nader, Ralph, Clarence Ditlow, and Joyce Kinnard. *The Lemon Book: How Not to Get Ripped-Off When You Buy a Car; What to Do When You Get Ripped-Off Anyway.* Ottawa, Ill.: Caroline House, 1980. A guide to car ownership with advice on buying, driving, maintaining, and seeking redress for defective workmanship. The book offers hundreds of shocking case histories of unfortunate car owners. Nader and his associates encourage consumers to fight back and explain the various avenues available to the layperson.

Sinclair, Upton. *The Jungle.* 1906. Reprint. New York: Harper, 1951. One of the most influential novels ever published in America. It made a strong impression on the young Ralph Nader, showing him the potential evils of unregulated big business and the power of a single dedicated individual to effect change under a democratic form of government.

Whiteside, Thomas. "A Countervailing Force: I." *The New Yorker* 159 (October 8, 1973): 50-111. Written in the impeccable prose that characterizes the magazine's famous "profiles," this is one of the most interesting and informative magazine articles on Ralph Nader ever published. The author traveled with Nader and interviewed him extensively. As in all profiles in *The New Yorker,* the emphasis is on the subject as a human being.

_____. "A Countervailing Force: II." *The New Yorker* 159 (October 15, 1973): 46-101. The second part of the Nader profile. Nader is one of the rare personalities who has rated a two-part profile in *The New Yorker.*

Bill Delaney

Cross-References

Upton Sinclair Publishes *The Jungle* (1906), p. 46; The Pure Food and Drug Act and Meat Inspection Act Become Law (1906), p. 64; Consumers Union of the United States Emerges (1936), p. 527; The International Organization of Consumers Unions Is Founded (1960), p. 1062; The Motor Vehicle Air Pollution Control Act Is Passed by Congress (1965), p. 1310; Congress Passes the Occupational Safety and Health Act (1970), p. 1585; The World Health Organization Adopts a Code on Breast-Milk Substitutes (1981), p. 2130; New York State Imposes the First Mandatory Seat-Belt Law (1984), p. 2220; Manville Offers $2.5 Billion to Victims of Asbestos Dust (1985), p. 2274.

CIVIL WAR RAVAGES CHAD

Category of event: Atrocities and war crimes
Time: 1965-1980's
Locale: Chad

Intermittent civil war between rival factions in the poverty-stricken Saharan nation of Chad took an awful toll in human lives and suffering

Principal personages:
FRANÇOIS TOMBALBAYE (1918-1975), the first president of Chad (1960-1975)
FÉLIX MALLOUM (1932-   ), the successor to Tombalbaye, overthrown in 1979
HISSEN HABRÉ (1942-   ), a guerrilla leader who seized power in 1979, was replaced in 1979, and regained the presidency in 1982
GOUKOUNI OUEDDEI (1944-   ), a principal rival of Habré who ruled a provisional government (1979-1982)

Summary of Event

Civil war, political brutality, frequent *coups d'etat*, a hostile physical environment, and endemic poverty have plagued Chad's four million inhabitants since shortly after independence from France in 1960. Like those of many other African nations, Chad's boundaries reflect interimperial rivalries (in this case, between France and Italy) rather than social cohesion, so national politics revolve around competition among the myriad social and ethnic groupings of the three arid, predominantly Arab districts of the north; the seminomadic people of the Sahelian central region; and the people of the relatively more arable, densely populated, ethnically diverse south. Backed by Libya, France, and other countries, rival movements have struggled for national power since 1965.

A large, desolate, landlocked territory, Chad was inhabited mainly by nomads and fugitive slaves when it became a colony separate from French Equatorial Africa in 1920. Because of its agricultural potential, the southern region had enjoyed most of the colonial development efforts, including cotton production and social services such as schools and utilities. The first president, François (later Ngarta) Tombalbaye, a member of the minuscule French-educated southern elite, assumed leadership of Chad soon after it was declared a republic with its capital at N'Djamena (formerly Fort Lamy) on August 11, 1960.

Independence brought neither liberation nor peace. Virtually from the beginning, Muslim Chadians from the northern and central parts of the country resisted government efforts to settle nomads and force them to pay usurious rates on government "farm loans." Moreover, they demanded a greater say in the southern-dominated government. The regime responded by outlawing opposition parties in March, 1962, and organizing well-controlled elections. Riots against tax collectors and loan officers broke out in eastern and central Chad in November, 1965, marking the beginning of the civil war. These tax revolts were suppressed by the army, only to erupt again nearby. On June 22, 1966, two or three dissident groups met in neighboring western Sudan to form the *Front de Libération Nationale* (Fronilat). Within a year, the rebellion against imposed sedentarization and heavy taxation spread throughout the north. The army was directed to stop demonstrations and disband the opposition. At least 250 strikers and regime opponents were imprisoned for banditry, and some of them died, disappeared, or were tortured in jail. Amid spreading unrest and even mutiny in 1968, Tombalbaye called on France to support his anti-insurgency campaign. French paratroopers engaged directly in fighting against insurgents and their sympathizers from April, 1969, through mid-1971.

In response to Tombalbaye's strong-arm tactics, the rebellion spread not only throughout the central and northern districts but also to the Sara peoples of his native southern region, where his "authenticity" campaign, which required Sara youth to undergo traditional initiation rites, was resented by more educated Sarans. Pockets of resistance therefore appeared in the south. After Muammar al-Qaddafi's rise to leadership in neighboring Libya in 1969, Libyan aid to Fronilat increased, and the movement became more militantly anti-imperialist and pro-Islamic. Eventually, even Tombalbaye's own top military commanders, including General Félix Malloum, turned against the eccentric, ineffectual, and increasingly hated dictator. Several officers were arrested for plotting against the regime.

After a military coup in 1975 in which Tombalbaye was assassinated, the new president, Malloum, released about 175 political detainees from prison and promoted some reforms. The respite from chaos and repression was, however, short-lived. The rebels controlled rural areas of the central and northern regions and gained on N'Djamena. There was discord within Fronilat, an increasingly motley, diverse, and divided collection of warlord armies. A quarrel between the front's two most prominent leaders, Hissen Habré and Goukouni Oueddei, partly over the treatment of a French archaeologist held hostage by the commandos and exacerbated by al-Qaddafi's efforts to control the movement, split Fronilat. While Oueddei became Libya's favorite client, Habré was brought into the Malloum government as prime minister.

The year 1979 saw countrywide anarchy and chaos, with intercommunal violence as well as military confrontations among the guerrilla groups and with the army. A strike by Muslim students in N'Djamena in February touched off a spate of incidents, some of them reported as massacres, between Muslims and non-Muslims. Within days of the student strike, Habré's forces took the capital from Malloum, who retired under French asylum. Lacking power and water, and prey to Habré's pillaging militia, civilians fled N'Djamena. Meanwhile, as rebel forces fought for control of the provinces, the Organization of African Unity (OAU) sponsored a series of talks leading to a short-lived cease-fire agreement that put Goukouni Oueddei at the head of a "transitional government" with Habré as defense minister. Habré's forces and those of other rebel commandos continued the armed struggle, capturing several towns and besieging the capital.

In 1980 and 1981, direct and indirect foreign intervention further complicated the imbroglio. Fighting broke out in March, 1980, and raged continuously for the rest of the year. After the remaining eleven hundred French forces were recalled to Paris, President Oueddei invited Libya to assist his government in defending the positions under its control against Habré's troops. Anxious also to consolidate Libya's claims to the long-disputed Aozou strip on the Libyan-Chadian border, al-Qaddafi willingly complied, dispatching tanks, helicopters, and mortars south across the desert. By December, they had effectively defeated Habré's forces militarily, and in January, 1981, al-Qaddafi declared Libyan unity with Chad. This prompted the formation of an OAU peacekeeping force and, more important, U.S. and French backing for Habré in the form of both arms and diplomacy. The Libyans withdrew in late summer, 1981, their positions ostensibly being handed over to OAU peacekeepers. Habré's forces gradually took control of the country, entering N'Djamena in June, 1982.

For the next four years, Chad was effectively divided between Libyan-backed, Oueddei-led factions that dominated the northern two-thirds of the country and the western-backed Habré government in the south. Sarans and other southerners resisted military occupation by Habré's army, and soon whole neighborhoods and villages were fleeing before the presidential guard's counterinsurgency campaign. After consolidating his positions, Oueddei began penetrating south in late 1983. This occasioned a new French intervention, including three thousand troops and fighter-bombers, to halt any Libyan advance, allowing Habré's armies to reoccupy some fallen towns. Clashes continued,with Libyan and French support, until a falling out between Oueddei and al-Qaddafi allowed Habré to gain the upper hand in 1986. He gradually conquered the north, and on September 12, 1988, an OAU cease-fire was accepted by all major forces in Chad. The twenty-three year Chadian civil war appeared to be ended, but the country's future was uncertain.

Impact of Event

Throughout the several phases of Chad's civil war, atrocities were committed by all sides. With the number of political, civilian, and combatant deaths numbering in the tens of thousands, staggering infant and child mortality, and the further disastrous effects of drought, famine, and desertification, Chad's rate of population growth was among Africa's lowest. Chadians on the whole were among the most deprived and terrorized people in the world.

The Tombalbaye and Habré regimes in particular, but also other leaders, resorted to execution of rivals and challengers, detention of activists and demonstrators, and heavy military and tax pressure on civilian communities. Dozens of "conspirators" were executed by martial law authorities between 1965 and 1990. Hundreds of students, professionals, civil servants, and peasants were detained at least briefly, and some languished indefinitely without formal charges being brought. The combined forces of climate, unsanitary conditions, and state security methods made disease and death common in detention. All the armies took hostages. For example, in 1983 the Habré and Oueddei forces each claimed to hold at least one thousand captives, an unknown number of whom died or disappeared.

As each region formed its own militias, the strongest men went off to fight, sometimes to die, leaving their families vulnerable to marauding rival armies and a farm economy hard-pressed to function without their labor. Brutal treatment of one clan was likely to provoke retribution, as in April, 1983, when forty villagers in the far south were massacred. Internecine conflict, particularly between Muslims and non-Muslims, helped perpetuate the vicious cycle of violence. Few families remained unscathed.

As in the Sudan, Ethiopia, and other war-ravaged Sahelian countries, more than two decades of widespread conflict also exacerbated an incipient environmental disaster by killing livestock and crops, pillaging grain stores, removing the strongest farmers, polluting or depleting water wells, driving people from their homes, destroying buildings and power stations, and diverting resources from desperately needed development projects. Weakened by the effects of war, the farm economy of central and northern Chad was decimated by the drought of the mid-1980's. Moreover, since the intermediate-rainfall zone in the south was planted mainly in cotton, there was a small domestic food supply. In 1985, approximately one million people, one-fourth of the population, were weakened by famine and in danger of starvation. At least fifty thousand sought refuge in relief camps. With fewer than one hundred paved miles of road amid thousands of miles of desert, and with much less publicity of its plight than Ethiopia had, Chad was in no position to deliver food, medical supplies, and water to the hardest-hit central regions. Well-intentioned humanitarian relief efforts were nowhere near adequate, especially given that the government was bankrupt and continued to be more concerned with state security than with the quality of its citizens' lives.

Some African theorists have argued that in the African context "human rights" might have a different meaning than in the West. In Chad, the human rights conditions from 1965 until at least 1988 were horrible by any criteria. There was no question of freedom of speech, religious communities were at war with one another, martial law was applied by numerous factions, and property rights could not be guaranteed. Beyond these abuses were the terrible loss of and threat to the lives of Chadians, many of whom suffered physical danger and deprivation for years on end.

Bibliography

Collelo, Thomas, ed. *Chad: A Country Study.* Washington, D.C.: Federal Research Division, 1989. This study contains chapters by different authors on Chadian history, society and environment, economy, politics, and national security. The most detailed sections cover ethnic and religious groups and the structure of the army and security forces. Although no explicit argument links these sections to political history, together the various chapters constitute a relatively complete description of the forces contributing to and affected by Chad's civil war.

Lemarchand, René, ed. *The Green and the Black: Qadhafi's Policies in Africa.* Bloomington: Indiana University Press, 1988. Because Chad has been the main focus of Libyan intervention on its southern flank, the entire book is of interest to students of Chadian politics. Lemarchand's chapter on "The Case of Chad" details al-Qaddafi's efforts to annex the Aozou strip, obliterate colonial boundaries, offset Israeli influence in Chad, and manipulate Chad's politics by shifting support for rebel groups.

Mazrui, Ali A., and Michael Tidy. *Nationalism and New States in Africa from About 1935 to the Present.* Nairobi: Heinemann, 1984. Among the many available books on the colonial background and postindependence problems of African states, this one is useful not only for its fairly thorough review of nationalist, interethnic, and political struggles throughout the continent but also for its section on the civil war in Chad. This is currently one of the few studies of Africa to have such a section.

Thompson, Virginia, and Richard Adloff. *The Emerging States of French Equatorial Africa.* Stanford, Calif.: Stanford University Press, 1960. A detailed account of political and economic developments in the four territories of French Equatorial Africa, including a fifty-page chapter on conditions in "Tchad" during the colonial period. Conflicts prior to independence laid the groundwork for civil war.

Whiteman, Kaye. *Chad.* London: Minority Rights Group, 1988. A brief but densely written, information-packed primer on the conundrum of Chadian politics. This study details the events, groups, and leaders that tore Chad apart during the twenty-five years after independence in one of the most embroiled, complex, and violent postcolonial conflicts. Particular attention is paid to civil and political rights and human suffering.

Sheila Carapico

Cross-References

The Sudanese Civil War Erupts (1955), p. 941; Ghana Gains Independence (1957), p. 980; Riots Erupt as Katanga Province Secedes from the Congo (1960), p. 1068; The United Nations Intervenes in the Congolese Civil War (1960), p. 1074; Algeria Gains Independence (1962), p. 1155; The Organization of African Unity Is Founded (1963), p. 1194; Zimbabwe's Freedom Fighters Topple White Supremacist Government (1964), p. 1224; The Secession of Biafra Starts a Nigerian Civil War (1967), p. 1365; Revolution Erupts in Ethiopia (1974), p. 1758; The OAU Adopts the African Charter on Human and Peoples' Rights (1981), p. 2136; Hunger Becomes a Weapon in the Sudanese Civil War (1988), p. 2354; The Kenyan Government Cracks Down on Dissent (1989), p. 2431.

MARTIN LUTHER KING, JR., LEADS A MARCH FROM SELMA TO MONTGOMERY

Categories of event: Racial and ethnic rights; civil rights
Time: March, 1965
Locale: Selma, Alabama, and Highway 80 between Selma and Montgomery

The march from Selma to Montgomery was a significant factor in the passage of the 1965 Voting Rights Act and marked a new and increased emphasis in civil rights reform upon political and economic issues

Principal personages:

MARTIN LUTHER KING, JR. (1929-1968), the president of the Southern Christian Leadership Conference (SCLC), and one of the principal leaders of the march

HOSEA WILLIAMS (1926-), an SCLC field organizer and one of the leaders of the first attempted march on March 7, 1965

JOHN LEWIS (1940-), an activist who, along with Hosea Williams, led the attempted march on March 7

JAMES G. CLARK, the sheriff of Dallas County who was known for adamant resistance to integration and black voting rights

LYNDON B. JOHNSON (1908-1973), the president of the United States (1963-1969)

GEORGE WALLACE (1919-), the governor of Alabama during the Selma campaign, who resisted racial integration and banned the march to Montgomery

Summary of Event

The Selma to Montgomery March of 1965 is often viewed as one of the most decisive events in the history of the American Civil Rights movement. It was marked by considerable violent resistance, a high degree of emotional intensity for those who participated, and political impact not often matched. Its basic purpose was to extend voting rights to black Americans in a period when many southern white leaders adamantly resisted broadening the franchise. The Civil Rights Act signed by President Lyndon B. Johnson on July 2, 1964, did contain provisions for minority voting rights. Its eleven titles spanned the spectrum of basic rights, including equal access to public accommodations, schools, and employment. Title VI gave the federal government the power to cut off funds from state or local authorities that discriminated, but there was little increased authority in the voting rights provisions of Title I. Nor was it certain that any of the desegregation mandates would be respected in the Deep South.

Although Selma was a small city in an essentially rural part of Alabama, it was in the highly segregated Dallas County region that some civil rights leaders believed would be a good place to launch a concerted voter registration drive. In February,

1963, well before the 1964 Civil Rights Act, Student Nonviolent Coordinating Committee (SNCC) field workers such as Bernard and Colia Lafayette, John Love, Worth Long, and others began to work with local black leaders. The results were meager because of intense resistance by the forces of Sheriff James G. Clark and the entrenched white power structure. On the other hand, Clark's roughness provided the kind of focus needed to stir a grass-roots movement. Throughout 1963 and 1964, the SNCC and the Dallas County Voters' League held monthly voter registration clinics and occasional mass rallies. Southern Christian Leadership Conference (SCLC) organizers such as James Bevel, C. T. Vivian, Harry Boyte, and Eric Kindberg participated in some of these activities and began to consider the Dallas County area as a possible target for the SCLC's heightened voter registration drive begun in earnest after the Civil Rights Act.

If voter registration was the chief focus of Dallas County black leaders such as Albert Turner, Amelia Boynton, and Voters' League president Frederick D. Reese, it was by no means the only issue. There was widespread concern among African Americans about police roughness, barriers to school integration, and widespread poverty because of job discrimination. They believed that gaining the vote would open the door to other reforms in the local communities. The Johnson Administration had already introduced a voting rights act in Congress by late 1964, but passage was uncertain and some of its terms were considered weak by the SCLC, the SNCC, the NAACP, and other advocacy groups. Martin Luther King, Jr., the SCLC's president, shared these concerns and came into Selma in January, 1965, to spur the voter registration effort.

King met forceful resistance, as did several others. He was slightly injured when a white detractor attacked him as he tried to integrate Hotel Albert. On January 19, 1965, Sheriff Clark roughly shoved Mrs. Amelia Boynton as she participated in a march to the courthouse on behalf of black voter registration. That incident was pictured in the national and international media and drew the world's attention to Selma, a city in south central Alabama with fewer than thirty thousand residents. It became obvious that voting rights were tied to other basic American constitutional rights. When King, by then a Nobel Peace Prize recipient, was jailed in early February, a new wave of activists poured into Selma to give aid to the effort. Many of them were students, but ministers, workers, and others were also attracted to the increasingly dramatic Selma campaign. Even Malcolm X, just days before his assassination on February 21 in Harlem, went to Selma to support King. The fatal shooting of young Jimmie Lee Jackson by police in nearby Marion added to the determination to continue the voting rights drive and the effort to deal with the various violations of rights that blacks faced. The original plan for a motorcade from Selma to Montgomery was abandoned in favor of a walking demonstration along the rural highway leading to the state's capital. This brought to light a complex pattern of racial segregation that reached all the way to the governor's office and state laws.

The first effort to march from Selma to Montgomery was made on Sunday, March 7, 1965. King and Ralph Abernathy were at their churches preaching. The SCLC's

Hosea Williams and SNCC Chairman John Lewis led a crowd of more than five hundred people out of Brown Chapel to the Edmund Pettus Bridge and toward Montgomery, along Highway 80. Governor George Wallace had banned the march the previous day, and Clark was expected to try to stop it, but no one anticipated the military-like force that waited to confront the marchers. Across the bridge, a large volunteer posse put together by Sheriff Clark waited, along with well-equipped state troopers under Colonel Albert Lingo. As the marchers approached the bridge, they were ordered to stop and told to disband within two minutes.

Before the short warning period had ended, the police began to attack. Some were on horseback, swinging billy clubs and whips that lashed into the marchers' bodies. Tear gas canisters were fired as the crowd began to scatter. Some troopers pursued the fleeing demonstrators as they tried to find refuge. The Selma march had suddenly become a rout that would be remembered as "Bloody Sunday" by many people. About eighty injured people were treated at the Good Samaritan Hospital, seventeen of whom were admitted for more treatment and observation. The "Bloody Sunday" attack was publicized widely, both in the United States and abroad.

King rushed back to the city and prepared for another attempt on Tuesday, March 9, appealing for help from around the nation. Public concern deepened, and within two days about 450 white members of the clergy and a wave of other supporters poured into Selma. This time, a federal injunction prohibited the march, and President Johnson requested a postponement. Local Selma and Dallas County officials disagreed on how to approach any renewed effort to march to Montgomery. Public Safety Director Wilson Baker had opposed the use of force against the first attempted march, and now he urged compromise to avoid a repetition of its violence. Behind the scenes, federal and local officials worked with King and other leaders to arrange a symbolic march across the Edmund Pettus Bridge, with promises that police would let marchers pass. The march would then halt without continuing to Montgomery.

Few people knew of these arrangements, however, so that the March 9 trek caused confusion and some disillusionment. A crowd of about nine hundred people left Brown Chapel once again. The number swelled to more than fifteen hundred as they neared the bridge. King told them, "We must let them know that nothing can stop us, not even death itself." Most assumed that they were on their way to the capital. As the marchers crossed the bridge, the police lines widened to let them pass. The marchers paused to sing "We Shall Overcome," and then the march leaders turned the group around and headed back into town.

Despite this ostensible retreat, the events in Selma were important in the history of civil rights activism in the United States. The week following the second attempted march was filled with significant legal and political moves. A federal court declared the Alabama bans on demonstrations invalid, and President Johnson spoke out forcefully to Congress and the nation on March 15 in support of the effort in Selma. He declared what had happened on March 7 to be "an American tragedy," and said that the Selma campaign was important to all Americans. In Johnson's words, "Their cause must be our cause, too." No president had ever taken this bold a public stand on civil rights. The fact that Johnson ended his address by saying, "And we shall overcome!" won wide applause from black activists.

On March 17, 1965, Judge Frank M. Johnson authorized the march to Montgomery and ordered Governor Wallace not to interfere. The same day, President Johnson sent his completed voting rights bill to Congress. Certain restrictions were placed on the march, such as a limit of three hundred on the number of marchers on two-lane sections of the road, but it would proceed with police protection to its destination. About eight thousand people started out of Selma on Sunday, March 21. It took five days to complete the trip. Along the way, a number of prominent entertainers and political figures participated, among them Harry Belafonte and Leonard Bernstein. King left on Wednesday, March 24, to fly to Cleveland for a speech, but rejoined the march as it entered Montgomery on Thursday. About thirty thousand people had taken part in the march.

There were some violent eruptions in places, but the march proceeded in an orderly way without major incident. After the march, however, a white Michigan housewife and mother, Mrs. Viola Liuzzo, was shot to death in her car as she drove black marchers back home from Montgomery. When the SCLC board of directors met in Baltimore in early April, 1965, they considered a boycott campaign against the state of Alabama in response to that and other violence.

Impact of Event

The Selma march has a significant place in civil rights history. It helped to convince Congress that a voting rights act was necessary. Such a bill was passed by Congress in May, 1965, and signed into law by President Johnson on August 6. It covered all states where screening devices such as literacy tests were used to restrict voting and states in which either fewer than half of the voting-age citizens were registered as of November 1, 1964, or fewer than 50 percent voted in the 1964 presidential election.

In another major sense, this march was historically significant. After Selma, the Civil Rights movement gave more attention to the socioeconomic conditions of racial minorities and poor people in the United States. It seemed imperative after 1965 to exercise the right to vote and thereby seek to bring about some of the reforms that were impossible when black Americans were systematically prohibited from voting. The Selma march was also psychologically important. It boosted confidence and energized new enthusiasm for future changes. King biographer Stephen B. Oates concluded that, "In truth, Selma was the movement's finest hour, was King's finest hour." There is much truth in this estimation. The Selma experience not only effected political changes but also infused the movement with a new confidence. Some scholars see in it the culmination of the trend from nonviolent persuasion to nonviolent coercion, that is, the transition from using marches and other demonstrations to win support to using them to bring higher legal and political authority to bear on local opposition. This distinction is not absolute since, from the beginning, both elements were present.

At the personal level, Selma is remembered as an inspirational experience. Marchers were resisted violently, yet they persisted. Many children and young people who witnessed the March 7 confrontation recalled years later being helped to safety by the adults. Voter registration efforts, furthermore, were thereafter regarded by increasing numbers of individuals as important direct action contributions to social reform in the United States. After Selma, the nonviolent Civil Rights movement in the United States began to venture out of the South into places such as Chicago, Cleveland, and Louisville.

Bibliography

Fager, Charles E. *Selma, 1965.* New York: Scribner's, 1974. Written by a white participant who knew the black leaders involved in the Selma march, this account provides useful insight into the dynamics of the surrounding politics. Fager discusses the tensions between Sheriff James Clark and Police Chief Wilson Baker as well as the differences among Voters' League president Frederick D. Reese and various other voter registration campaign leaders. The book also provides valuable information on the alleged sexual misconduct of participants and shows that this was mostly a myth. Fager also traces the background of the march, its details, and its immediate results. Contains illustrations and an index, as well as some guides to sources.

Garrow, David J. *Protest at Selma: Martin Luther King, Jr., and the Voting Rights Act of 1965.* New Haven, Conn.: Yale University Press, 1978. The most thorough account of the background and development of the Selma campaign. Garrow draws upon a rich array of sources to trace methodically the work of the SNCC, the Dallas County Voters' League, and local politics to show the importance of the Selma experience in forcing Congress to act on the Johnson Administration's voting rights proposals. Garrow's account is a solid, basic study of the campaign and its effects. Contains elaborate notes and index.

Oates, Stephen B. *Let the Trumpet Sound: The Life of Martin Luther King, Jr.* New York: Harper & Row, 1982. The first of the critical analyses of King's life. Oates presents little that is new, but he does take more seriously the charge of King's personal misconduct with women. His treatment of Selma is among the best parts of the book in the sense of capturing both the drama and the significance of the anti-integrationist violence that produced "Bloody Sunday" on March 7, 1965. Contains notes, bibliographical references, and index.

Webb, Sheyann, and Rachel West Nelson. *Selma, Lord, Selma: Girlhood Memories of the Civil Rights Days.* University: University of Alabama Press, 1980. A moving personal account by two women who were small children during the Selma campaign. Part of a growing genre of personal literature that is enriching civil rights studies, this work is warmly presented, very readable, and highly informative on the experience of young blacks during the intense period of civil rights activism. Fears, expectations, and personal views are presented in a refreshing way.

Wolk, Allan. *The Presidency and Black Civil Rights: Eisenhower to Nixon.* Madison,

N.J.: Fairleigh Dickinson University Press, 1971. Although not specifically about the Selma campaign, Wolk's study puts the Johnson Administration in perspective, showing the evolution of the relationship between presidential politics and civil rights issues from the 1950's to the early 1970's. Its chief value in this connection is its information on Johnson's much higher level of involvement in civil rights than any other president of the period covered. Contains a chronological chart of civil rights policies, a selected bibliography, and an index.

Thomas R. Peake

Cross-References

The SCLC Forms to Link Civil Rights Groups (1957), p. 74; The Council of Federated Organizations Registers Blacks to Vote (1962), p. 1149; Martin Luther King, Jr., Delivers His "I Have a Dream" Speech (1963), p. 1200; The United Nations Issues a Declaration on Racial Discrimination (1963), p. 1212; Congress Passes the Civil Rights Act (1964), p. 1251; Martin Luther King, Jr., Wins the Nobel Peace Prize (1964), p. 1257; Marshall Becomes the First Black Supreme Court Justice (1967), p. 1381; Martin Luther King, Jr., Is Assassinated in Memphis (1968), p. 1419; Jackson Becomes the First Major Black Candidate for U.S. President (1983), p. 2209.

HEAD START IS ESTABLISHED

Categories of event: Children's rights and educational rights
Time: May 18, 1965
Locale: Washington, D.C.

Project Head Start has, through federal intervention, helped ensure the rights of disadvantaged preschool children in the United States to adequate health care, nutrition, and education

Principal personages:
> LYNDON B. JOHNSON (1908-1973), the president of the United States who authorized the establishment of Head Start
> R. SARGENT SHRIVER (1915-   ), the first director of the Office of Economic Opportunity and originator of the idea of Head Start
> MICHAEL HARRINGTON (1928-   ), the author of *The Other America* (1962), which heightened President Kennedy's and the nation's awareness of poverty in the United States
> BENJAMIN BLOOM (1913-   ), the author of *Stability and Change in Human Characteristics* (1964), which argued that a child's early years are critical to the learning process
> JOHN F. KENNEDY (1917-1963), the president of the United States who began the federal government's "war on poverty"
> JULIUS RICHMOND (1916-   ), the first director of Head Start

Summary of Event

The United Nations Declaration of the Rights of the Child, enacted in 1959, entitles all children to adequate nutrition, accessible medical services, free education, and lives of freedom and dignity. Project Head Start was inaugurated by President Lyndon B. Johnson in Washington, D.C., on May 18, 1965, and as the first comprehensive federal effort at early childhood intervention stands as a significant contribution to the fulfillment of this declaration.

Head Start is the product of historical, intellectual, political, and personal influences. Many British immigrants arrived in North America in the seventeenth and eighteenth centuries convinced of the importance of education to the political, socioeconomic, and spiritual success of their colonial experiment. A 1642 Massachusetts law, for example, required parents and masters to educate children. By the early nineteenth century, spurred by the rhetoric and ramifications of the War for Independence, education became a birthright of United States citizens. This conviction fueled the common school movement of the 1820's and 1830's. By the end of the century, educational reformers had turned their attention to the early childhood years, hoping that public orphanages, day-care centers, and kindergartens would safeguard the rights of disadvantaged children, especially those of urban immigrant parents.

The first White House Conference on Children, convened by President Theodore Roosevelt in 1909, signaled the first major federal attempt at protecting children's rights. President Franklin Roosevelt's New Deal of the 1930's further addressed early childhood concerns. The Works Progress Administration built nursery schools for low-income children, and the Lanham Act created day-care centers administered by local communities.

The 1950's and early 1960's provided the intellectual foundations for Head Start. Rejecting twentieth century conventional wisdom, J. McVicker Hunt argued that environment, and not heredity, primarily governs human behavior. Oscar Lewis, from his studies of the poor in Latin America, identified a global culture of poverty characterized by matriarchal authoritarian families, early maturation of children, and feelings of helplessness among individuals. Benjamin Bloom concluded that a child develops half of his or her intelligence by age four and eighty percent by age eight. Early education therefore offers a potential escape from poverty.

Journalists joined these scholars in heightening public awareness of the children of the poor. Michael Harrington's *The Other America* (1962) defined poverty as deprivation of minimal levels of health, housing, food, and education. He contended that as many as one in four Americans fit this definition, and that the other three in four largely refused to acknowledge the existence of poverty in an increasingly affluent society.

Dwight Mac Donald's article, "The Invisible Poor" (*The New Yorker*, January 19, 1963), critiqued Harrington's and others' contributions to the emerging literature on poverty. Mac Donald, while finding fault with specific pieces of evidence advanced in these works, nevertheless concurred with their general conclusion that poverty was a dire national problem in need of a prompt national solution. He even forwarded his own antipoverty proposal: a minimum income for all, guaranteed by the federal government.

The 1960's also offered the political opportunity for Head Start. President John F. Kennedy "discovered" poverty in the 1960 West Virginia presidential primary. He coined the phrase "war on poverty" in an August, 1960, campaign speech and presided over the civil rights revolution, which would mobilize many poor people of all races. After reading Harrington's and Mac Donald's indictments of federal inaction toward the poor, he ordered Walter Heller, Chairman of the Council of Economic Advisors, to launch a national antipoverty effort. On November 23, 1963, the day after Kennedy's assassination, Heller presented the martyred president's antipoverty plan to his successor, Lyndon B. Johnson.

Johnson's own background added a personal influence to the creation of Head Start. After working his way through Southwest Texas State Teachers College, Johnson had commenced his teaching career in Cotulla, Texas, at a school for disadvantaged Mexican children.

On January 8, 1964, Johnson resurrected the term "war on poverty" in his State of the Union Address. On January 20, he sent Heller's report to Congress. On February 1, R. Sargent Shriver, the first director of the Peace Corps, agreed to become Johnson's special assistant in the war on poverty and to head a task force to draft antipoverty legislation. The Economic Opportunity Act of August 30, 1964, created the Office of Economic Opportunity (OEO), a federal antipoverty agency whose programs would be directed by Shriver but locally administered by the poor themselves.

The OEO soon incurred criticism for this latter "community action" feature which, by enlisting the poor, often bypassed local administrators. The agency, while furthering the rights of the disadvantaged through work-study, job training, and volunteer programs, overlooked the rights of the children of the disadvantaged. Seventeen percent of the nation's poor, or nearly six million, were under six years old.

Shriver moved to address both of these concerns. He believed that because children were the most tragic victims and the most potentially sympathetic symbols of poverty, a program to ensure their basic human rights would provide a political justification for "community action" and a moral underpinning for the "war on poverty." Building on his experience with his wife, Eunice Kennedy, in early intervention programs for the mentally retarded, Shriver appointed a committee of child-development specialists led by Dr. Robert Cooke, pediatrician-in-chief at Johns Hopkins Hospital, to draft an extensive federal program of early-childhood intervention for the socioeconomically deprived.

On May 18, 1965, President Johnson presented the result of the committee's deliberations. "Project Head Start" (OEO staffer Judah Drob suggested the name) would be a summer program for disadvantaged children who were to enter kindergarten or the first grade in the fall of 1965. It would provide an intellectual, medical, nutritional, and psychological "head start" for children in their lifelong quest for the full enjoyment of their fundamental human rights. It would encourage considerable involvement by parents and community leaders. The OEO would finance up to ninety percent of the cost of the programs; the communities would cover the rest. The first director of the program would be Dr. Julius Richmond, dean of the medical faculty at the State University Upstate Medical Center in Syracuse, New York.

Although Head Start would offer no respite from a summer of civil rights demonstrations and race riots, it would enroll almost 560,000 children at 13,400 centers in 2,500 communities and would provide paid summer employment for about 100,000 people. It engendered such hope that Johnson announced on August 31, 1965, that it would become a year-round program for more than 350,000 disadvantaged preschool children three years old and older. A summer session with follow through programs such as special classes, home visits, and field trips would be available for those children excluded from the year-round classes.

Impact of Event

Preschool children living in poverty are too often the victims of inadequate health services, incomplete immunizations, and uncorrected physical disabilities. They lack communication skills; they have little opportunity to enjoy reading, art, or music; and they instinctively distrust strangers. They reach school age with low self-esteem and little motivation to learn.

Project Head Start has made great progress in attacking these symptoms of early childhood poverty. A teacher in the original summer program on the Texas-Mexico border recalled that Juanita, the middle of nine children living in a small apartment in a housing project, had learned to wait her turn to serve the milk, paint at the easel, and ring the clean-up bell. The director of a Head Start center in Decatur, Georgia, related in the twentieth year of the program that doctors and dentists regularly examined the children there, and that the two full meals which the pupils received at the center were often their only nourishment. A Head Start instructor in Austin, Texas, paused in the twenty-fifth year of the program and her twentieth year of teaching to remember some of her graduates, including the chief of medical records for a noted gynecologist, an airline flight attendant, a bus driver, and a college student.

A 1984 study by the High/Scope Educational Research Foundation vindicated Head Start's faith in early childhood education. It traced the educational and social progress of two groups of African-American children over sixteen years old. One group had received preschool education beginning at age three and one had not. The former group demonstrated substantially higher rates of employment and educational achievement and considerably lower rates of teenage pregnancy and criminal activity than the latter.

Head Start grew to enroll nearly 500,000 children in 24,000 classrooms by 1991. Approximately half of the families served by Head Start in that year had an annual income below $6,000 and the same fraction were headed by a single parent. At least twenty percent of Head Start children are from families with substance abuse problems. President George Bush and Congress, encouraged by studies showing that every dollar spent on Head Start saves six dollars in health care, welfare payments, and crime control, greatly increased the program's funding.

Head Start has suffered setbacks as well. In a widely publicized 1966 case, the OEO revoked its grant to one of the first Head Start centers, the Child Development Group of Mississippi, charging it with misappropriation of funds, politicization of the program, and racial discrimination against white children. OEO restored the grant in 1967, however, under special conditions designed to address these deficiencies.

In 1969, a federal government study conducted by the Westinghouse Learning Corporation and Ohio University concluded that the Head Start program was largely ineffective. It found that children in public primary schools who had experienced Head Start were no more proficient in language development, learning readiness, academic achievement, positive self-concept, desire for achievement, or attitudes toward school, home, peers, and society than those who had not. Critics of the report noted, however, that it evaluated only the intellectual, and not the medical and nutritional, outcomes of Head Start. They also viewed the study as more an indictment of the public schools for dissipating the gains of Head Start than an attack on Head Start. Even the authors of the report advocated reforming, rather than replacing, Head Start.

As of 1991 Head Start enrolled only one in four poor children and suffered from what some believed were inadequate facilities and transportation, poor management, and underpaid teachers. Despite these past and present shortcomings, however, Head Start has won wide acclaim as a significant step in the quest for human rights in the United States.

Bibliography

Bornet, Vaughn Davis. "The Great Society in Law and Practice." In *The Presidency of Lyndon B. Johnson.* Lawrence: University of Kansas Press, 1983. This is the major secondary source on the Johnson presidency. Chapter 10 offers a critical and largely negative assessment of the "Great Society," Johnson's domestic policy of which Head Start was a part. Includes an index and bibliography.

Brauer, Carl. "Kennedy, Johnson, and the War on Poverty." *Journal of American History* 69 (June, 1982): 98-119. This thoughtful revisionist essay argues that the war on poverty was less the product of sociology and politics than the result of Walter Heller's economic analysis, John Kennedy's and Lyndon Johnson's personal convictions, and the unexpected opportunity provided by Kennedy's assassination. Contains references.

Conkin, Paul K. "The Great Society." In *Big Daddy from the Pedernales: Lyndon Baines Johnson.* Boston, Mass.: Twayne, 1986. Chapter 9 of this biography offers a detailed, balanced assessment of Johnson's Great Society, concluding that while its outcomes were not always favorable, its noble intentions deserve more acclaim than derision. Includes bibliography and index.

Gelfand, Mark I. "The War on Poverty." In *Exploring the Johnson Years*, edited by Robert A. Divine. Austin: University of Texas Press, 1981. This study is better at tracing the origins of the war on poverty in the Kennedy and Johnson years than at analyzing its performance ever since. Includes references, index.

Patterson, James T. *America's Struggle Against Poverty, 1900-1980.* Cambridge, Mass.: Harvard University Press, 1981. Patterson presents a comprehensive study of the evolution of policies and attitudes toward poverty in the twentieth century United States. Patterson argues that while public poverty policies have changed, public attitudes toward the poor have largely remained the same. Includes bibliography and index.

Payne, James S., Ruth A. Payne, Cecil D. Mercer, and Roxana D. Davidson. *Head Start: A Tragicomedy with Epilogue.* New York: Behavioral Publications, 1973. A dated, critical, and largely negative assessment of the Head Start program which explores problems of personnel, transportation, and parental involvement and offers suggestions for improvement. Bibliography and index.

Washington, Valora, and Ura Jean Oyemade. *Project Head Start: Past, Present, and Future Trends in the Context of Family Needs.* New York: Garland, 1987. A provocative assessment of Head Start programs and evaluations, and a call to action for Head Start to address changing family trends (feminization of poverty, teen parenting, working mothers, quest for economic self-sufficiency) among the poor, from the perspectives of two African-American female scholars. Bibliography and index.

Zigler, Edward, and Jeannette Valentine, eds. *Project Head Start: A Legacy of the War of Poverty.* New York: Free Press, 1979. A comprehensive history and analysis of the Head Start program's first decade. Includes philosophies, curricula, models, and evaluative criteria of the program. Contains references.

Lawrence J. McAndrews

Cross-References

The World Health Organization Proclaims Health as a Basic Right (1946), p. 678; The United Nations Adopts the Universal Declaration of Human Rights (1948), p. 789; The United Nations Adopts the Declaration of the Rights of the Child (1959), p. 1038; Martin Luther King, Jr., Delivers His "I Have a Dream" Speech (1963), p. 1200; Three Civil Rights Workers Are Murdered (1964), p. 1246; Congress Passes the Civil Rights Act (1964), p. 1251; Congress Passes the Child Abuse Prevention and Treatment Act (1974), p. 1752; A U.N. Declaration on Hunger and Malnutrition Is Adopted (1974), p. 1775; WHO Sets a Goal of Health for All by the Year 2000 (1977), p. 1893; An International Health Conference Adopts the Declaration of Alma-Ata (1978), p. 1998; The United Nations Adopts the Convention on the Rights of the Child (1989), p. 2529.

THE SUPREME COURT RULES THAT STATE LAWS CANNOT BAN CONTRACEPTIVES

Category of event: Reproductive freedom
Time: June 7, 1965 (October, 1964, term)
Locale: United States Supreme Court, Washington, D.C.

The overturning of a Connecticut law banning contraception established the constitutional guarantee of a right of privacy and aided the 1960's sexual revolution

Principal personages:
ESTELLE T. GRISWOLD (?-1981), the executive director of the Planned Parenthood League of Connecticut and codefendant in the case
CHARLES LEE BUXTON (1904-1969), the medical director for the league at its New Haven center; codefendant in the case
WILLIAM O. DOUGLAS (1898-1980), the Supreme Court justice who wrote the Court's decision
MARGARET SANGER (1879-1966), a public health nurse in New York City who campaigned for female emancipation and birth control
ANTHONY COMSTOCK (1844-1915), a rural New Englander who began a campaign to strengthen obscenity laws in the United States
ROBERT LATOU DICKINSON (1861-1950), a surgeon, medical sex researcher, advocate of contraception and marriage counseling, and founder of the Committee on Maternal Health
CLARENCE JAMES GAMBLE (1894-1966), a birth-control researcher who advocated birth-control clinics and projects aimed at teaching the indigent about population control
GREGORY GOODWIN PINCUS (1903-1967), a scientific researcher called "the father of the birth-control pill"
ROBERT OWEN (1801-1877), an English reformer who wrote the first American treatise on birth control in 1831
CHARLES KNOWLTON (1800-1850), the author of the first popular book on birth control written by a physician

Summary of Event

Attempts to prevent conception have existed in human evolution and medical practice for thousands of years. Even in societies scorning birth control and sterility, the desire to control reproduction has existed. Only since the late nineteenth century, however, has there been a planned, organized effort to educate the general population about contraception.

In preliterate primitive societies, abortion and infanticide were the chief practices limiting population growth; contraception was relatively infrequent. When attempts at contraception were undertaken, mixtures of potions, herbs, and powders with supposed magical properties were ingested, or complete abstinence or withdrawal were practiced. Egyptian papyri dating from about 1850 B.C. and 1300 B.C. speak of contraception in the form of combining physical and chemical features to prevent or interrupt pregnancy. The ancient Hebrews also practiced such contraceptive techniques as coitus interruptus and the use of intravaginal spongy substances, potions, and violent movements. The Egyptian and Hebrew techniques were passed on to the Greeks and Romans, whose writers, physicians, and encyclopedists spoke knowledgeably of contraception. Abortion is also mentioned in the Hippocratic oath. Diffusion of information among citizens, however, remained virtually nonexistent. Contraceptive advances in Asian cultures were even less rapid.

Prior to recent developments in birth-control technology, contraception was the primary responsibility of the male. Use of the condom to prevent the spread of syphilis was first described in 1564. By the 1720's, condoms were used for contraception in Europe.

Female contraception historically involved various violent gestures, ingestion of potions with "magical" properties, and the insertion of vaginal plugs and solutions, some with spermicidal effect. Pessaries and sponges were among the oldest contraceptive devices. The cervical cap and diaphragm were developed during the nineteenth century. It was in nineteenth century England, Germany, and France that contraceptive practices spread most rapidly, in part as a result of social changes, attitude shifts, and other forces such as industrialization, urbanization, and "democratization" of contraceptive knowledge. The less privileged in society gained knowledge formerly in the possession solely of the upper class.

The European influence spread to the United States, where such pioneers in birth control and women's rights as Margaret Sanger sought to establish a system of clinics where women could obtain reliable birth-control services. Sanger's clinics also served as educational centers where private medical practitioners were instructed in contraceptive technique, a subject not taught in medical schools at that time. Other important contributions to the birth-control movement in the United States were made by Charles Knowlton, Robert Owen, Robert Latou Dickinson, and Clarence James Gamble. It was through their efforts, individually and collectively, that educational programs on contraception and contraceptive research were created and medical investigation conducted. The birth-control movement reflected the changing social environment and growing emancipation and independence of women.

At the same time, a countermovement condemning contraceptive practice became active. Led by Anthony Comstock, director and organizer of the New York Society for the Suppression of Vice, a relentless and vigorous campaign ensued initially against birth controllers and later against gamblers. In 1873, the United States Congress passed the Comstock Act, which prohibited interstate transport of contraceptive information and devices.

Comstock used the power of his governmental position as special agent of the U.S. Post Office to travel around the country making arrests of those acting in violation of the law. Fear of prosecution inhibited development and dissemination of birth-control knowledge and quelled freedom of expression. Sections of medical treatises containing information on birth-control methods had to be excised. In 1926, twenty-four states had anticontraception laws modeled on the Comstock Act; twenty-two other states' obscenity laws were interpreted to include a ban on contraception. Constitutionality of the act was not questioned, and no clear judicial trend emerged. The act's clause on contraception was not specifically repealed until 1971.

It was in this climate that Estelle Griswold and Charles Lee Buxton sought to challenge a state law of Connecticut that outlawed contraceptives and made their use a criminal offense. Connecticut had not generally enforced its law against individual physicians, sellers, or married couples. The law affected the poor, prohibiting them from receiving the same birth-control information and supplies available to the middle class. Two prior attempts to challenge the law had failed.

The case was instigated on November 1, 1961, when Griswold and Buxton opened their clinic amid maximum publicity. Within ten days, they were arrested for dispensing birth-control information and instructions to a married couple in violation of the General Statutes of Connecticut. The parties were found guilty by the Connecticut state courts and fined one hundred dollars each. They appealed their case to the United States Supreme Court, urging it to declare the Connecticut law unconstitutional. The Court overturned their conviction and caused Connecticut to repeal its birth-control statute (called an "uncommonly silly law" by Justice Potter Stewart). At the same time, the Court for the first time recognized the existence of a constitutional right of privacy and gave it legal protection.

Privacy as a complex and multidimensional legal concept had generally been included in the "liberty" interest guaranteed in the Constitution. It is a personal right whose scope continues to be developed and clarified. Synonymous with freedom, privacy denotes the right "to be let alone" (Justice Louis Brandeis) or the autonomy to make decisions without undue interference from others. Privacy may also mean physical separation from others. Protecting one's reputation from defamatory public disclosure of private facts and control over information about oneself (for example, credit records, bank statements, or tax returns) are other aspects of privacy. Finally, privacy as security from intrusion on the intimacies of life, including family-planning decisions, was the focus of the *Griswold* decision.

In a seven-to-two decision, the Court held that the Connecticut law forbidding use of contraceptives intruded on the right of marital privacy guaranteed under the Constitution. It remained for the Court to define this right, as it is not specifically enumerated in the Constitution. Justice William O. Douglas, writing for the majority, stated that "specific guarantees in the Bill of Rights have penumbras, formed by emanations from those guarantees that help give them life and substance . . . . Various guarantees create zones of privacy." He recognized that the marital relationship at issue lay within a zone of privacy derived from the first, third, fourth, fifth, ninth, and fourteenth amendments to the Constitution and should be protected from state and federal interference. In upholding the sanctity of marriage, Justice Douglas termed it "an association that promotes a way of life." A law forbidding use of contraceptives rather than regulating their manufacture or sale, he concluded, seeks to achieve its goals by means having a maximum destructive impact on that relationship. Such a law was unacceptable and had to be struck down.

Impact of Event

The immediate consequence of the decision was the repeal of birth-control statutes in Connecticut and thirteen other states and a dramatic increase in the number of women who gained access to birth-control devices and counseling. In *Griswold v. Connecticut*, the Supreme Court recognized as a right what had been considered as such by the general populace—a right lying within the spirit of other freedoms expressed in the Constitution even though the right itself is not specified in the Constitution. *Griswold* was confined to traditional notions of contraception of married persons. In 1972, however, the Supreme Court held that the privacy guarantee extended protection to contraception for single persons; in 1977, it was held to cover minors.

These decisions demonstrated a general legal response to a changing social environment. Restrictive birth-control prohibitions were replaced by more flexible regulation or none at all. A general permissiveness ensued in society. The women's movement gained momentum; college dormitories were sexually integrated, and unmarried people openly began cohabiting. The landmark legal concept of a right of privacy in sexual matters was extended in 1973, in *Roe v. Wade*, to encompass a woman's right to choose to terminate her pregnancy through abortion without governmental interference and has also been used in "right to die" or termination of treatment cases. These controversial issues have divided the United States along moral and religious lines. They have also colored political debate. Public demonstrations often surrounded birth control and abortion facilities. Public funding for birth control and greater access to educational information on contraception, family planning, and genetic counseling remained issues of concern.

Birth-control technology and capability have expanded rapidly, with the introduction of methods ranging from the intrauterine device (IUD) and the oral contraceptive ("pill") to injectable contraceptives, subdermal implants, "morning-after" pills, medicated vaginal rings containing steroids absorbed into the bloodstream, and biodegradable systems. The pill, developed by Gregory Pincus and first approved for use in June, 1960, revolutionized contemporary birth-control methods as a result of its accessibility, ease of use, simplicity, and effectiveness. Within twenty years of its advent, an estimated ten to fifteen million American women and eighty to one hundred million women worldwide were using oral contraceptives for birth control.

The principles first articulated in *Griswold* and followed in succeeding related cases suggest that unless the state can demonstrate a compelling interest that outweighs individual human rights, it may not interfere with social mores—a person's marriage, home, children, and life-style. In 1967, a state ban on interracial marriages was repealed; in 1968, state law forbidding private possession of obscene materials in one's home was overturned. When these fundamental privacy interests are invoked, courts will require a state's demonstration of a higher burden of justification or "compelling interest" viewed with "strict scrutiny" before these interests can be abridged.

Bibliography

Dienes, C. Thomas. *Law, Politics, and Birth Control.* Urbana: University of Illinois Press, 1972. Excellent coverage of the period from the latter part of the eighteenth century to the 1970's. Detailed research on Comstock and Sanger, and much information about legal cases. Contains copious primary and secondary source material including cross-references, notes, appendices, and an extensive bibliography. Written in a scholarly manner.

Himes, Norman E. *Medical History of Contraception.* New York: Schocken Books, 1970. Covers historic, anthropologic, economic, and sociologic aspects of contraception. Thorough coverage and meticulous detail. Written for the lay reader.

Knight, James W., and Joan C. Callahan. *Preventing Birth: Contemporary Methods and Related Moral Controversies.* Salt Lake City: University of Utah Press, 1989. An excellent account of contraception and a discussion of its political and philosophical implications. Various chapters discuss human reproductive anatomy, physiology, and endocrinology, as well as giving a detailed overview of the moral debate and social policy concerns surrounding elective abortion. Contains notes and an extensive bibliography.

Reed, James. *The Birth Control Movement and American Society: From Private Vice to Public Virtue.* Princeton, N.J.: Princeton University Press, 1983. Detailed account of contributions of early birth-control crusaders and the entire movement from the nineteenth century to the 1970's. The emphasis is on the role of Margaret Sanger. Written in a clear and direct fashion with numerous notes and bibliographical essays.

Stotland, Nada Logan. *Social Change and Women's Reproductive Health Care: A Guide for Physicians and Their Patients.* New York: Praeger, 1988. Historical and social context of issues of reproduction. Discussion of changing attitudes on controversial topics of sexuality, reproduction, parenting, and medical care, with case examples. Also includes suggested readings. Written in a simple manner.

Tribe, Laurence H. "Right of Privacy and Personhood." In *American Constitutional Law.* 2d ed. Mineola, N.Y.: Foundation Press, 1988. Informative treatise on constitutional law. Locates the concept of privacy within the total scheme of constitutional law. Numerous footnotes and case references. Written for an audience with legal orientation. Also includes material on abortion, death and dying, patients' rights, and association.

Veatch, Robert M., ed. *Population Policy and Ethics.* New York: Irvington, 1977. Collected interdisciplinary essays with varied emphases ranging from traditional American values to legal and political considerations. Useful for research on population problems.

Marcia J. Weiss

Cross-References

Sanger Opens the First Birth-Control Clinic in the United States (1916), p. 184; Sanger Organizes Conferences on Birth Control (1921), p. 356; The National Council of Churches Supports Birth Control (1961), p. 1096; *Roe v. Wade* Expands Reproductive Choice for American Women (1973), p. 1703; Italy Legalizes Abortion (1978), p. 1988; Prolife Groups Challenge Abortion Laws (1989), p. 2443; The National Organization for Women Sponsors an Abortion Rights Rally (1989), p. 2489.

CONGRESS PASSES THE VOTING RIGHTS ACT

Categories of event: Voting rights; racial and ethnic rights
Time: August 6, 1965
Locale: Washington, D.C.

The Voting Rights Act of 1965 was the most significant extension of voting rights to African Americans since the passage of the Fifteenth Amendment to the U.S. Constitution

Principal personages:

LYNDON B. JOHNSON (1908-1973), the president of the United States (1963-1969)

MARTIN LUTHER KING, JR. (1929-1968), a civil rights leader and adviser to President Johnson on civil rights reforms

NICHOLAS KATZENBACH (1922-   ), the U.S. attorney general who drafted the Voting Rights Act

EVERETT DIRKSEN (1896-1969), the Senate minority leader

HALE BOGGS (1914-1972), the majority whip in the House of Representatives

Summary of Event

The Voting Rights Act was the culmination of a ninety-five-year effort to extend voting rights to all Americans regardless of "race, color, or previous condition of servitude." These words are from the Fifteenth Amendment to the U.S. Constitution, which gave Congress the power to pass "appropriate legislation" to ensure voting rights. Although this amendment was ratified on March 30, 1870, it was not until 1965 that the United States Congress exercised that power in a significant fashion. Congress had indeed proposed the Twenty-fourth Amendment, outlawing poll taxes for federal elections, but that measure required ratification by the states. In less than two years, thirty-eight states had ratified this amendment, making it part of the Constitution on January 23, 1964. This action was important but did not reflect the kind of positive congressional response called for by civil rights leaders.

Poll taxes had been merely one of many devices used in the South to discourage blacks from exercising their constitutional right to vote. Literacy tests, examinations, and errors or omissions on applications were also used to deny suffrage to blacks. The Twenty-fourth Amendment had symbolic importance, but it did not provide the kind of sweeping reforms that were needed. This was accomplished by the Voting Rights Act of 1965.

It is hard to pinpoint what brought the voting rights issue into focus in 1965, but it was only one part of the larger civil rights issue. The voting rights sections of the Civil Rights Act of 1964 were among the least controversial aspects of that legislation. In the eyes of most civil rights advocates, greater electoral strength was the appropriate means of allowing black Americans to secure their rights. This was the position of the Mississippi Freedom Democratic Party in 1964. Its actions, together with the 1965 Freedom March from Selma to Montgomery, Alabama, seem to have been pivotal events in the voting rights movement in the United States.

The Mississippi Freedom Democratic Party (MFDP) began as a grass-roots effort to forge a political union among blacks, labor, and poor whites. The party's efforts to participate in regular Democratic party meetings throughout the state met with little success. After meeting with numerous obstacles, the MFDP decided to challenge the all-white delegation that the Mississippi Democrats were sending to the 1964 Democratic convention. Using the rules set by the Democratic National Committee, the MFDP chose forty-four delegates and twenty-two alternates to attend the national convention in Atlantic City.

President Johnson was concerned about the plight of the MFDP, but he wanted to keep as many mainstream southern votes as possible. He attempted to work out a compromise between Mississippi's regular delegation and the MFDP at the convention, but the nationally-televised battle before the Credentials Committee gave many Democratic Party officials a clearer picture of the extent and nature of voter discrimination in the South. In this respect, the actions of the MFDP greatly advanced the cause of voting rights reform.

As soon as his reelection was secured, President Johnson started exploring legislative options for removing obstacles to voter registration and participation. Attorney General Nicholas Katzenbach presented the president with a variety of approaches. One was a constitutional amendment limiting the requirements states could impose for voter registration, including age, residency, felony convictions, and mental stability. The primary objective of this approach was to remove literacy requirements. Another proposal was to create a federal commission to handle registration for all federal elections. Katzenbach also proposed using federal agents to supervise and monitor registration in states and regions where voter discrimination could be verified. As President Johnson pondered these legislative options, others pressed for fast and decisive action.

In early 1965, voting rights activists focused the nation's attention on Alabama. Dallas County was one of the most obvious examples of voter discrimination in America. The population in Dallas County was 57.6 percent black, yet only 335 of its 9,542 registered voters were black. The registration process in Dallas County was one of the most cumbersome in the nation, and there were only two days each month when one could attempt to register. The Student Nonviolent Coordinating Committee (SNCC) led demonstrations on the steps of the courthouse in Selma, the county seat, in order to attract attention. After Jimmie Lee Jackson was killed in a similar demonstration in nearby Marion, the Southern Christian Leadership Conference (SCLC) planned a march from Selma to Montgomery, the state capital. Alabama state troopers turned the marchers back on their first attempt, using violence and tear gas to restrain the marchers. A limited march eventually took place.

The sheer brutality of events in Selma produced a national outcry for swift action to protect the voting rights of all Americans. On March 17, President Johnson, after consulting with Martin Luther King, Jr., submitted a comprehensive voting rights bill to the United States Congress.

President Johnson's bill called for federal monitoring of registration and voting in states with a clear history of discrimination. In the Senate, there were sixty-six co-sponsors to the bill but considerable opposition from some key southerners. One of the most controversial issues during the floor debate in the Senate was whether to ban poll taxes in state and local elections. The Senate passed a version of the bill with the poll tax ban removed on May 26, by a vote of seventy-seven to nineteen.

In the House of Representatives, the Republicans offered a substitute bill which allowed poll taxes but also permitted judicial proceedings when such taxes were found to be discriminatory. Southern Democrats started defending it as the lesser of the evils. On July 9, the House passed the bill by a vote of 333-85. In less than a month, the conference report had passed both houses. On August 6, President Johnson signed the Voting Rights Act of 1965 (PL 89-110).

Impact of Event

Two key provisions in the act were the creation of federal examiners to determine an individual's qualifications to vote and the abolition of literacy tests. An aggressive Justice Department, under Attorney General Nicholas Katzenbach, moved swiftly to implement the new law. On August 7, the department suspended literacy tests and other discriminatory measures in seven states. The entire states of Alabama, Alaska, Georgia, Louisiana, Mississippi, South Carolina, and Virginia were affected. Suspension or investigations occurred within certain counties in Arizona, Idaho, Maine, and North Carolina. By August 9, the first groups of federal examiners were assigned to help blacks register in Alabama, Louisiana, and Mississippi. In fewer than three weeks, 27,385 blacks were added to the voter registration rolls in those three states alone.

From 1964 to 1969, voter registration among blacks in the South rose by almost 30 percent, while registration for whites increased by 10 percent. The most significant change for blacks occurred in Mississippi, where only 6.7 percent of adult blacks had been registered in 1964. By 1969, that figure had risen to 66.5 percent.

The act was not without controversy. South Carolina challenged the constitutionality of the "triggering" provision, which authorized federal examiners for a state or political subdivision if the attorney general determined that there had been discriminatory devices in place on November 1, 1964, and if the director of the census determined that less than 50 percent of the voting-age residents in that area either were not registered or did not vote in the 1964 presidential election. South Carolina argued that such a provision denied the states equal protection, violated the due process clause, constituted a bill of attainder, and violated the separation of powers provision. The United States Supreme Court, in *South Carolina v. Katzenbach* (1966), found the Voting Rights Act to be a logical and consistent expression of the Fifteenth Amendment.

There has been some disappointment over the long-term effect of this act. By the late 1960's and early 1970's, the progress toward enfranchisement had lost its steam. Removing legal barriers was a necessary but not always sufficient means to ensure citizen participation. Attorney General Nicholas Katzenbach observed that the presence of examiners was not enough. Local efforts had to organize registration campaigns actively. Individuals who had been excluded from the political process needed experience and political education before they could exercise their new political clout.

Bibliography

Goldman, Eric. *The Tragedy of Lyndon Johnson.* New York: Alfred A. Knopf, 1969. An insider's discussion of the personal relationships and thoughts that helped shape the development of the Voting Rights Act within the Johnson Administration. A sympathetic yet fair statement of the trade-offs that were taken into consideration by the president as he developed his plan and chose among the different options available.

Katzenbach, Nicholas. "A Lesson in Responsible Leadership." *New South* 21 (Spring, 1966): 55-60. A thoughtful essay that places the limits of federal action in perspective. The author highlights the necessary role of local campaigns to fulfill the goals desired by reformers. Provides insights into the central role citizen participation must play in any reform movement.

King, Martin Luther, Jr. "Behind the Selma March." *Saturday Review* 48 (April 3, 1965): 16-18. A short but concise statement on the expectations of the Freedom March. This piece reveals more than just the thinking that went into this act; it exposes some of the passion behind the entire Civil Rights movement. A tone-setting article with little reference value.

Lawson, Steven. *Black Ballots: Voting Rights in the South, 1944-1969.* New York: Columbia University Press, 1976. A valuable resource on the development of the black suffrage movement. Especially useful to people interested in the obstacles that confronted reform-minded individuals during the two decades preceding the major legislative breakthroughs of the mid-1960's. Contains a complete list of references and a thorough index.

McCarty, Thorne, and Russell B. Stevenson. "The Voting Rights Act of 1965: An Evaluation." *Harvard Civil Rights-Civil Liberties Review* 3 (Spring, 1968): 357-411. This essay provides an insightful early appraisal of the results of the Voting Rights Act. In addition to its analysis, there are some very helpful data which put the issue in perspective. Also addresses the issue of leadership within the black community.

Matthews, Donald, and James W. Prothro. *Negroes and the New Southern Politics.* New York: Harcourt, Brace & World, 1966. A good general resource with an especially helpful bibliography. Chapter 10 has an especially illustrative discussion of some of the frustrations that grew out of the Civil Rights movement after significant legislative successes.

Donald V. Weatherman

Cross-References

Black Leaders Call for Equal Rights at the Niagara Falls Conference (1905), p. 41; The Nineteenth Amendment Gives American Women the Right to Vote (1920), p. 339; The Civil Rights Act of 1957 Creates the Commission on Civil Rights (1957), p. 997; The Council of Federated Organizations Registers Blacks to Vote (1962), p. 1149; Martin Luther King, Jr., Delivers His "I Have a Dream" Speech (1963), p. 1200; The Twenty-fourth Amendment Outlaws Poll Taxes (1964), p. 1231; Congress Passes the Civil Rights Act (1964), p. 1251; Martin Luther King, Jr., Leads a March from Selma to Montgomery (1965), p. 1278; The U.S. Voting Age Is Lowered to Eighteen (1970), p. 1521; Congress Extends Voting Rights Reforms (1975), p. 1812; Congress Requires Bilingual Elections to Protect Minority Rights (1975), p. 1817.

AFRICAN AMERICANS RIOT IN WATTS

Categories of event: Civil rights; revolutions and rebellions
Time: August 11-17, 1965
Locale: Los Angeles, California

Days after the enactment of the Voting Rights Act of 1965, the African-American community in Los Angeles exploded in an orgy of burning, looting, and violence

Principal personages:
> EDMUND G. "PAT" BROWN (1905-   ), the governor of California, a liberal
> SAMUEL YORTY (1909-   ), the mayor of Los Angeles, a conservative
> MARTIN LUTHER KING, JR. (1929-1968), a civil rights leader

Summary of Event

On the evening of August 11, 1965, on one of the hottest days of the year in Los Angeles, California, the black community erupted in what has come to be called the "Watts Riot." Thirty-four people were killed, approximately four thousand were arrested, and more than $40 million in property damage was caused by the riot. It was estimated that ten thousand people participated.

It came as a surprise to many that Los Angeles would be the scene of one of the most violent conflicts in the United States during the twentieth century. Most visitors to the black community in Los Angeles remarked on the fact that the community did not have the physical ugliness and dilapidated conditions of ghettos in the East, Midwest, and South. Moreover, black Los Angeles did not have the tension-ridden history of other areas; for example, by 1741 New York City had experienced two major slave rebellions in which blacks had tried to burn down the entire city and had almost succeeded. Although blacks had participated in the founding of Los Angeles in 1781, an 1880 census showed that there were only about one hundred African Americans in the city. The black population of Los Angeles began to expand dramatically during World War II, when a need for labor in the area led to large-scale black migration. A turning point came when the Japanese-American community was interned; "Little Tokyo" became "Bronzville," and the first black ghetto in Los Angeles was born. Watts itself was known as "Mudtown" and was multiracial until the war, when black migrants from Texas, Oklahoma, and Louisiana particularly began to pour into the city. Although Los Angeles was viewed by some as a sunny paradise, African Americans there encountered restrictive racial covenants that limited their ability to leave the ghetto, police brutality, employment discrimination, and many of the ills that they had hoped to leave behind. The riot itself was a culmination of the accumulated anger, disappointment, and pain encountered by African Americans in Los Angeles.

The riot itself was precipitated by the stopping of Marquette Frye, an African-American male, by the California Highway Patrol. Frye was stopped for speeding and appeared intoxicated. As he was being questioned, a crowd gathered, and the officers decided to call for reinforcements. To that point, Frye had complied with the officers' requests, but then his mother appeared on the scene and began to berate him. Frye then became unruly, and the decision was made to arrest him and take him away.

A highway patrolman—apparently mistakenly—struck a bystander with his billy club. A young African-American woman, who was accused of spitting on an officer, was dragged into the middle of the street. A rumor circulated that a pregnant woman had been attacked by the officers (actually, the woman in question was not pregnant but happened to be wearing a barber's smock).

When the officers departed with the Fryes, the crowd erupted. Rocks and other missiles were hurled at passing cars. White motorists were pulled from their cars and beaten, and their cars were set on fire. Law enforcement authorities reacted hesitantly at first, overwhelmed and stunned by the ferocity of the crowd.

The following day, the area was calm, but that evening the pattern of violence was repeated; however, not until almost thirty hours after the initial flareup did window smashing, looting, and arson begin. These events were concentrated in Watts, two miles from the location of the original disturbance. The looting and arson spread rapidly throughout the black community of Los Angeles, eventually encompassing a 46.5-square-mile region.

The pattern of the riot shifted over time from random attacks on whites to attacks on property, particularly large stores that were viewed as exploiting the community. A number of black-owned businesses escaped damage by conspicuously posting "Blood Brother" or similarly worded signs. A number of small businesses that were not perceived as being exploitative managed to escape damage. It was this pattern that led many in the African-American community to term the events not an inchoate riot but rather a revolt against perceived oppression.

In any event, the combined forces of the California Highway Patrol, the Los Angeles Police Department, and officers dispatched by the Los Angeles County Sheriff were unable to stop the violence. Ultimately, the National Guard was called in; eventually seventeen thousand heavily armed troops were required to subdue the riot—more forces than were used to subjugate the Dominican Republic that same year.

Subsequently, a controversy erupted when Lieutenant Governor Glenn Anderson was accused of temporizing in calling for the National Guard. Governor Edmund G. "Pat" Brown was traveling in Greece at the riot's beginning but flew back immediately upon hearing of the disturbance. Los Angeles Mayor Samuel Yorty was criticized for leaving town during the height of the riot.

Black leaders such as Martin Luther King, Jr., were brought in in an effort to quell the uprising, but to no avail. Indeed, the well-known black activist and performer Dick Gregory was shot in the leg during his attempt to stop what was happening.

Of the estimated thirty-four people who were killed, only two were affiliated with law enforcement and fire authorities; those who were killed and injured were overwhelmingly African Americans. Most of those who died were killed during the evening of Friday, August 13, and the morning of August 14.

By August 17, the riot had dissipated. Governor Brown appointed a commission of inquiry headed by a former director of the Central Intelligence Agency, John Mc-Cone, that included future deputy secretary of state Warren Christopher. In December, 1965, the McCone Commission issued a report that outlined what had happened and suggested why. The commission pointed to unemployment, poor public transportation, general racial discrimination, and inadequate housing as underlying causes of the riot. It also proposed a number of remedies and prescriptions.

Impact of Event

Coming as it did a few days after the signing into law of the Voting Rights Act of 1965, the Watts Riot marked a new stage in the Civil Rights movement. It signaled that all problems of racism were not concentrated in the South and caused Martin Luther King, Jr.—who had been repudiated by rioters—to focus more intently on the North and West. Watts gave rise to new militant trends among African Americans. A Community Alert Patrol was devised to monitor the police, and this led to the formation of the Black Panther Party in 1966. Ron Karenga was inspired by the revolt to devise a "cultural nationalist" program that led directly to the 1960's trend of "Black is beautiful" and the later trend of Afrocentrism.

The riot also was not helpful to the political career of Governor Brown; the riot and the student protests at Berkeley in 1964 were major factors in Brown's defeat at the hands of Ronald Reagan in 1966 in Reagan's first effort to attain political office. Governor Reagan was essential in reviving the conservative movement in the United States, which had suffered what some had seen as a maiming blow when Barry Goldwater was soundly defeated for the presidency in 1964. The Reagan victory in turn underscored the importance of the "crime in the streets" theme as a riveting one for many U.S. voters—a theme that was utilized skillfully by Richard M. Nixon during his victorious presidential campaign of 1968.

The riot also had a significant impact on African Americans in California. A hospital was built in South-Central Los Angeles; the absence of such a facility had been a primary complaint of the area's residents. A shopping center was built so that residents did not have to travel miles simply to buy groceries. Housing units were built. The University of California and the University of Southern California began to admit more African-American students. Local businesspeople and local government initiated programs to address the problem of black unemployment. The riot also highlighted the ongoing issue of police brutality.

The cultural arena may have been most significantly affected by the riot. Budd Schulberg, a well-known screenwriter and novelist and the son of a major film-industry executive, initiated a writers' workshop that helped to produce a number of prominent African-American writers. There was a general cultural renaissance in black Los Angeles that spread across the nation. The fact that the riot took place in Los Angeles meant that the entertainment industry based there was affected. From August, 1965, it was possible to discern an increased employment of African-American actors, technical personnel, and themes in film and television.

Bibliography

Balbus, Isaac D. *The Dialectics of Legal Repression: Black Rebels Before the American Criminal Courts.* New York: Russell Sage Foundation, 1973. Although it ranges broadly, this work does include a useful discussion of the riot.

Bullock, Paul, ed. *Watts, the Aftermath: An Inside View of the Ghetto, by the People of Watts.* New York: Grove Press, 1969. By concentrating on the words of the residents of black Los Angeles, this book provides one of the better views of the motivations and actions of those who participated in the riot.

Cohen, Jerry, and William S. Murphy. *Burn, Baby, Burn! The Los Angeles Race Riot, August, 1965.* New York: Dutton, 1966. This is a journalistic account that includes graphic photographs. It is not, however, a good reference tool.

Conot, Robert E. *Rivers of Blood, Years of Darkness.* New York: Bantam Books, 1967. Although it is a journalistic account and not a helpful reference tool, this remains the best and most complete account of the riot. The author received the cooperation of law enforcement authorities; apparently some of the records he relied on were subsequently lost or destroyed.

Crump, Spencer. *Black Riot in Los Angeles.* Los Angeles: Trans-Anglo Books, 1966. Although thinly documented, this book has the advantage of including highly illustrative photographs. It also reflects a black point of view.

Ridenour, Ron, Anne Leslie, and Victor Oliver. *The Fire This Time: The W. E. B. Du Bois Clubs View of the Explosion in South Los Angeles.* Los Angeles: W. E. B. Du Bois Club, 1965. A partisan and Marxist view of the riot.

Sears, David, and John McConahay. *The Los Angeles Riot Study, the Politics of Discontent: Blocked Mechanisms of Grievance Redress and the Psychology of the New Urban Black Man.* Los Angeles: Institute of Government and Public Affairs, University of California, 1967. A major sociopsychological study of riot participants, focusing on African-American males.

_____. *The Politics of Violence: The New Urban Blacks and the Watts Riot.* Boston: Houghton Mifflin, 1973. A more accessible and less jargon-ridden version of the above-listed study.

Gerald Horne

Cross-References

Zoot-Suit Riots Exemplify Ethnic Tensions in Los Angeles (1943), p. 624; Race Riots Erupt in Detroit and Harlem (1943), p. 635; The Civil Rights Act of 1957 Creates the Commission on Civil Rights (1957), p. 997; Martin Luther King, Jr., Leads a March from Selma to Montgomery (1965), p. 1278; Congress Passes the Voting Rights Act (1965), p. 1296; The Black Panther Party Is Organized (1966), p. 1348; The Kerner Commission Explores the Causes of Civil Disorders (1967), p. 1370; FBI and CIA Interference in the Civil Rights Movement Is Revealed (1971), p. 1595.

INDONESIA'S GOVERNMENT RETALIATES AGAINST A FAILED COMMUNIST COUP

Categories of event: Political freedom; atrocities and war crimes
Time: September 30, 1965
Locale: Indonesia

The Indonesian military came to dominate all aspects of Indonesian life after it successfully defeated the communist coup of September 30, 1965

Principal personages:
> SUHARTO (1921-   ), the president of Indonesia who succeeded Sukarno in 1968
> SUKARNO (1901-1970), a founder of Indonesia, president from 1949 to 1968
> ABDUL HARIS NASUTION (1918-   ), the minister of defense from 1962 to 1966, the chief target of GESTAPU
> SUBANDRIO (1915-   ), the first deputy prime minister under Sukarno, often regarded as his most likely successor
> DIPA NUSANTARA AIDIT (1923-1965), the chair of the Indonesian Communist Party, one of the masterminds of the abortive coup

Summary of Event

After gaining independence from the Dutch in 1949, Indonesia embarked on a program to establish itself as a nation. The formative years, 1949 to 1955, saw a chaotic political situation with numerous political parties vying for seats in the National Assembly and no party having a majority to form a government. Added to the political chaos were inflation, foreign divestments because of the threat of nationalization, and political instability in the forms of strikes by labor unions and student demonstrations.

President Sukarno blamed these problems on the weaknesses and impracticability inherent in Western-style democracy and proposed his own brand of "guided democracy" to save Indonesia. He formed a national advisory council on February 21, 1957, consisting of leaders from the military, communists, nationalists, peasants, and workers. He tried to convince the Indonesians of the advisability of the principle of guided democracy, a government form in which decisions would be made according to Indonesian sensitivities and culture. That is, decisions were to be made by *mushawara* (deliberation) and *gotong royong* (mutual consensus) rather than by debate and majority rule.

Sukarno's personal dictatorship, combined with continued economic, social, and religious turmoil, resulted in several rebellions throughout Indonesia in 1958. In July, 1959, Sukarno reinstated the 1945 constitution, which gave almost unlimited powers to the president. Sukarno introduced a secularist state ideology of *pancasila*, the five principles embracing the belief in God, national consciousness, humanism, social justice, and the sovereignty of the people. The armed forces held the responsibility of safeguarding the integrity of *pancasila* and the 1945 constitution. In order to include Indonesians of all political hues and to satisfy the spirit and concept of guided democracy and mutual cooperation, Sukarno introduced a new symbol, NASAKOM, the acronym for *nasionalisme* (nationalism), *agama* (religion), and *komunisme* (communism), emphasizing his argument that nationalism, Islam, and Marxism were wholly compatible.

After laying the foundation for personal dictatorship, Sukarno concentrated on gaining legitimacy not by striving for the economic and social well-being of the people but by projecting Indonesia and himself as key players in the international arena. He diverted the people's attention from economic needs by encouraging them to join him as the leader of the Newly Emerging Forces (NEF), which aimed to eliminate the neo-colonialism and imperialism of the Old Established Forces (OEF). As proof of Indonesia's leadership of the NEF against the OEF, Sukarno hosted the Asian Games and Games of the New Emerging Forces (GANEFO). Extravagant spending went into building monuments and stadiums. The results were a soaring national debt, double-digit inflation, and reductions of production and exports. The government agencies that were in charge of licensing and taxes resorted to corruption, while honest minor government officials held second jobs to make ends meet. The Indonesian Communist Party (PKI), which by the early 1960's claimed a membership of more than three million, capitalized on the frustration and anger of unemployed youths in the urban areas.

As the PKI grew to be the largest communist party in Asia outside China, the armed forces also gained from military assistance from both the Soviet Union and China. Sukarno encouraged both the PKI and the armed forces to battle the OEF. In March, 1962, Indonesian "volunteers" invaded West Irian, formerly under Dutch control, by ship and by parachute. In June, 1963, West Irian became part of Indonesia. This victory encouraged Sukarno to challenge forces of neocolonialism and imperialism by starting a "Crush Malaysia" campaign in August, 1963. Sukarno received economic and military aid from the Soviet Union because his leadership of the NEF challenged China's leadership role in the region. Dipa Nusantara Aidit, chair of the PKI, and Foreign Minister and First Deputy Prime Minister Subandrio preferred to have closer ties with China.

Sukarno played on the pride of Indonesians as he led the NEF against the OEF, and he controlled the country by balancing the nationalism of the armed forces against the rise of the PKI. The PKI became more powerful as Sukarno became more dependent on Soviet and Chinese aid, which increased tremendously because of the Sino-Soviet dispute. The army leadership was suspicious of the influence of the Russians and the Chinese, and of the possible internal threat as the PKI's political role became legitimized. As the PKI gained strength, it moved to outlaw anti-Marxist student movements and Islamic political parties. The PKI infiltrated labor unions and the armed forces. It also encouraged landless farmers to seize land and squatters to remain on the large former Dutch plantations which were now under army control.

Subandrio and the PKI demanded the creation of a Fifth Force of armed peasants and workers, in addition to the established army, navy, air force, and police. To discredit the army, the PKI spread rumors that renegade Indonesian generals were out to assassinate Sukarno and his army chief of staff. On May 5, 1965, Subandrio produced the "Gilchrist Letter," named after a former British ambassador to Indonesia, to expose a plot by the United States Central Intelligence Agency (CIA) and the pro-Western Council of Generals to take over Indonesia.

Sukarno fell seriously ill on August 4. Jakarta was rife with rumors of an invasion by the American Seventh Fleet, and suspicion and intrigue heightened between the army and the PKI. The final showdown came in the early hours of the morning of September 30, 1965. Several army units, aided by communist volunteers, attempted a *putsch* to rid the army high command of six anticommunist generals. Five of the generals were killed or tortured to death. Their bodies were mutilated and thrown into a well at Halim airbase. The rebel forces then took the radio station and announced to the people that the "September 30 Movement" or *Gerakan Tiga-puluh September* (GESTAPU), consisting of progressive revolutionary officers and political leaders, had successfully defeated a coup by the CIA-sponsored Council of Generals. In support of GESTAPU, PKI-led coups were attempted in Jogjakarta, Surakarta, Semarang, and Bali. Defense Minister General Abdul Haris Nasution, one of the six targeted for capture or death, escaped. Within hours, he rallied loyal troops to fight GESTAPU's Revolutionary Council forces. Together with General Suharto, he regained control of the situation.

The brutal murder of the generals, and other killings by the communists in Central and East Java, resulted in retaliatory slaughter of communists, alleged communists, and sympathizers of the PKI that lasted for several months. The army held mass executions, and Muslim youth organizations took their revenge by killing between 100,000 and 1 million people. By 1969, some 70,000 to 160,000 political prisoners had been taken. Although Sukarno was implicated with the GESTAPU affair, he was never formally charged with the uprising because of fears that his supporters would challenge the new regime of Suharto and start a civil war. While Aidit and most of the leaders of the abortive coup were hunted down and killed, Sukarno was protected by Suharto, the de facto president.

Suharto was made Acting President by the People's Provisional Consultative Assembly, which under Indonesia's constitution was the highest policymaking body and also the body that elected the president. Suharto began his era of New Order as a clean demarcation from Sukarno's "Old Order." Suharto purged the military of communists and other radical influences. To gain national stability and internal security, there was press censorship and the charge for the military to play two roles, as both the protector of national security and law and order and major player in the government.

The multiparty system, which once had nine viable contesting parties, was reshuffled to form three factions. Functional Groups, with the largest representation, consisted of bureaucrats, businesspeople, community leaders, and the military. Next was the United Development Party (PPP), a conglomeration of four Islamic parties. The five others that once represented Christians and nationalists were lumped into the Indonesian Democratic Party (PDI). Suharto was elected to a series of five-year presidencies and was still in power in 1991, with the next election scheduled for 1993.

Impact of Event

President Suharto's government searched for consensus, unity, stability, security, and economic growth. The army after GESTAPU was legitimized to intervene in politics in addition to defending the country. In July of 1976, it invaded East Timor, using a scorched-earth policy which starved to death 100,000 to 200,000 Timorese.

With *pancasila* as a state ideology, journalists were told that they had a duty to provide information which would create national unity and stability. The Command for the Restoration of Security and Order (Kopkamtib) was quick to use force to counter any disturbances. For example, when a new law requiring motorcycle riders to wear helmets was resisted by students in South Sulawesi in four days of rioting, security forces killed fourteen people. When newspapers and magazines provided coverage of university students' protests of this use of force, Kopkamtib, via the Ministry of Information, called in the editors and ordered them not to write about student unrest. Student leaders were told outright that they would be killed if they demonstrated, because Kopkamtib interpreted all such dissent as inspired by communists and provoked by outside forces.

In the 1980's, the licenses of several publications were revoked because articles in them put the military in a bad light. A separatist rebellion in Aceh, North Sumatra, was barely reported because the army restricted any report on clashes between the military and the rebels. In April, 1991, the *Monitor* editor was sentenced to five years in jail for blasphemy when the paper published a popularity poll ranking the prophet Muhammad in eleventh place.

Indonesia continued to suffer from corruption in high places and economic privation for the majority of citizens. Any opposition against Suharto faced charges of being anti-*pancasila* and contrary to the Constitution of 1945. There were periodic student protests, and in May, 1991, forty officers said that they would join the Indonesian Democratic Party to counter Suharto's possible bid to run for the presidency in 1993. The officers' decisions were quickly countered by a charge from the chief of the armed forces, General Try Sutrisno, who warned that they were breaking the officers' code of unity in the guidance of the nation. There was no avenue for peaceful opposition, and unauthorized searches and detention without trial persisted. Political prisoners continued to be taken. The few journalists and members of the Institute of the Defence of Human Rights in Jakarta courageously let the world know of the plight of prisoners and other opponents of the Suharto regime.

Bibliography

Brackman, Arnold C. *Indonesia: The Gestapu Affair.* New York: American-Asian Educational Exchange, 1969. Chapter six emphasizes the major role of the PKI in the GESTAPU affair. Defends the army as not being responsible for instigating the abortive coup.

Crouch, Harold. *The Army and Politics in Indonesia.* Ithaca, N.Y.: Cornell University Press, 1978. The role of the Indonesian army in the political arena during Sukarno's regime and Suharto's New Order government is well documented.

Dahm, Bernhard. *History of Indonesia in the Twentieth Century.* London: Praeger, 1971. Covers the social and economic forces that influenced the political development of Indonesia. Of particular value is Dahm's portrayal of the key personalities of the leaders, the factionalism inherent in the multiparty system, and the patrician role of the army.

Humana, Charles. *World Human Rights Guide.* New York: Facts on File, 1986. Provides good charts and diagrams. Topics include legal rights, personal rights, and personal freedoms.

MacDougall, John J. *Indonesia Faces the Nineties: Pressure for Greater Openness.* Indianapolis, Ind.: Universities Field Staff International, 1989/1990. A good overview of the recent problems and areas where human rights violations can occur.

Viberto, Selochan, ed. *The Military, the State, and Development in Asia and the Pacific.* Boulder, Colo.: Westview Press, 1991. The chapter on military-civilian relations in Indonesia and the probable developments into the next decade is a good up-to-date analysis.

Peng-Khuan Chong

Cross-References

The United Nations Sets Rules for the Treatment of Prisoners (1955), p. 935; Papa Doc Duvalier Takes Control of Haiti (1957), p. 1009; The Chinese Cultural Revolution Starts a Wave of Repression (1966), p. 1332; Brazil Begins a Period of Intense Repression (1968), p. 1468; Marcos Declares Martial Law in the Philippines (1972), p. 1680; An Oppressive Military Rule Comes to Democratic Uruguay (1973), p. 1715; East Timor Declares Independence but Is Annexed by Indonesia (1975), p. 1835; The Argentine Military Conducts a "Dirty War" Against Leftists (1976), p. 1864; Zia Establishes Martial Law in Pakistan (1977), p. 1898; The Kenyan Government Cracks Down on Dissent (1989), p. 2431.

THE MOTOR VEHICLE AIR POLLUTION CONTROL ACT IS PASSED BY CONGRESS

Category of event: Consumers' rights
Time: October 20, 1965
Locale: Washington, D.C.

The Motor Vehicle Air Pollution Control Act of 1965 committed the U.S. government to regulating auto emissions, thereby setting an important precedent for the stricter laws of the 1970's

Principal personages:

EDMUND MUSKIE (1914-   ), a Democratic senator from Maine, a major promoter of the environmental laws of the 1960's and early 1970's

LYNDON B. JOHNSON (1908-1973), the Democratic president (1963-1969) noted for his activist liberal social agenda

OREN HARRIS (1903-   ), the Democratic chair of the House Committee on Interstate and Foreign Commerce

Summary of Event

The United States federal government's first effort to control air pollution was the 1955 Air Pollution Control Act (PL 84-159), which established a program of cooperative research among federal, state, and local governments. As President Lyndon B. Johnson's ambitious domestic programs illustrate, the 1960's were marked by a strong confidence that America's problems could be solved by proper government action. Although less famous than civil rights reforms and the so-called "War on Poverty," various environmental initiatives received attention in the 1960's. Significant air pollution laws were passed in 1963, 1965, and 1967, all receiving bipartisan support in Congress and general promotion or approval by the Johnson Administration. In principle, these laws enhanced the federal government's role as an environmental regulator, although in practice the government was reluctant to place too onerous a burden upon private industry.

The 1963 Clean Air Act (PL 88-206) created a series of steps for national intervention in interstate air pollution problems, with the possibility of federal legal action. Only one prosecution ever occurred under the 1963 act, the shutdown of a Maryland chicken rendering plant in 1970 after a five-year multistage battle in the bureaucracy and the courts.

The 1965 bill focused on a particular part of the air pollution problem, auto emissions, but had broad importance because the law was the first to mandate the establishment of federal standards for pollution production. The 1967 act sought to correct the weaknesses of the previous bills and establish a more systematic federal approach to air pollution regulation. It was superseded by the 1970 Clean Air Act

Amendments before being fully implemented.

The 1965 act (PL 89-272) developed out of hearings held in 1964 by the Special Senate Subcommittee on Air and Water Pollution of the Senate Public Works Committee. Led by Senator Edmund Muskie of Maine, the hearings indicated that two areas of pollution deserved special attention: air pollution and solid waste. The subcommittee report based on these hearings, entitled "Steps Towards Cleaner Air," proposed actions on both air pollution and solid waste disposal. Muskie's subcommittee developed legislation for both problems. From the 1964 hearings all the way through passage of the final 1965 Motor Vehicle Air Pollution Control Act, the matter of solid waste was a companion issue. The significance of the motor vehicle emissions problem was emphasized by the repeated assertion that the country's 82.5 million cars produced up to half of the nation's air pollution.

The committee's report was matched by concern voiced in the media and statements by the secretary of the Department of Health, Education and Welfare (HEW), Anthony J. Celebrezzo. In early 1965, Celebrezzo called for general air pollution remediation and specifically for action on auto emissions. In his February 8, 1965, speech, the so-called "Natural Beauty Message," President Johnson himself referred to his administration's commitment to initiate discussions which could lead to "effective elimination or substantial reduction" of auto emissions. When Muskie introduced the Motor Vehicle Air Pollution Control Act (Senate Bill 306) on January 7, 1965, he had not only nineteen other sponsors but also a very favorable political climate. Predictably, the bill was assigned to Muskie's Special Subcommittee on Air and Water Pollution.

Muskie's subcommittee held hearings on S. 306 from April 6 to April 9, 1965. Hearings in Detroit on April 8 focused on testimony from the auto industry. The original bill proposed three major actions: the establishment by November 1, 1966, of mandatory emission guidelines by HEW, the creation of a federal air pollution control laboratory, and the authorization of a federal program to foster creative solid waste solutions.

Two aspects of the Senate subcommittee hearings deserve particular attention. First, the automobile industry was not adamantly opposed to emissions regulation, although industry leaders testified that the timetable was unreasonable and the new legislation was unnecessary because the secretary of HEW could handle the matter administratively. The auto companies believed that gradual improvement was feasible and that the law was not unacceptably threatening to their interests, although some of the discussed topics and specifics were.

A second interesting aspect of the hearings was the reversal by the Johnson Administration from opposition to support for the bill. On the first day of hearings, the assistant secretary of HEW, James M. Quigley, declared the president's view that a voluntary approach should be attempted with the auto industry before legislation was enacted. The reaction in national newspapers and by the public to Quigley's testimony was overwhelmingly negative. On April 9, Quigley declared that he had been misunderstood and that in fact Johnson supported the Muskie bill, although the president had reservations about the proposed timetable and specific standards. The administration's reversal reflected the political appeal of the issue and the breadth of support for federal intervention in various social problems. The subcommittee modified the bill to relax the deadlines and to leave more areas of regulation to the discretion of the secretary of HEW. The Senate passed the bill on May 18 by a voice vote, with no debate.

In the House of Representatives, the bill was assigned to the Committee on Interstate and Foreign Commerce, chaired by Representative Oren Harris (D-Ark.). The committee weakened the law in three ways. First, the deadlines for required emissions reductions were eliminated. Instead, the secretary of HEW was mandated to establish standards "as soon as practicable" and to enforce compliance in a reasonable period. Second, the committee altered the inspection program, changing it from a factory inspection to an examination of sample cars provided by manufacturers. Finally, the House commerce committee eliminated the provision creating an air pollution control laboratory. The House committee actions were not all negative toward the environmental goals of the Senate bill, however. The committee also provided useful attention to the need to reduce sulfur-oxide emissions and authorized more than $96 million for air pollution and solid waste disposal research for the next four years. Most of these funds were directed toward solid waste disposal initiatives.

With only four opposing votes, the House accepted the commerce committee's bill with only minor alteration on September 24, 1965. On October 1, 1965, the Senate approved the changes made by the House. President Johnson signed the bill into law on October 20, 1965. In his signing ceremony, Johnson referred to the large extent of the problem and claimed that the bill was a step toward rectifying the past and rewriting the history of unhealthy industrialization. Although the law lacked deadlines for when HEW should initiate regulation, the department committed itself to rapid action. Partially because HEW had been working on the problem before the Motor Vehicle Air Pollution Control Act passsed, HEW was able to publish standards for hydrocarbons and carbon monoxide on March 19, 1966. The regulations became effective for cars of the 1968 model year. The speed of the administrative action was increased by the fact that the state of California had similar regulations in place a year before the federal laws. Pushed by the severe air conditions of the Los Angeles area, California continued to lead the country in terms of confronting the problems of auto emissions. The passage of the Motor Vehicle Air Pollution Control Act as well as the Automobile Safety Act of 1965 made the federal government a major regulator of motor vehicles.

Impact of Event

The air pollution laws of the 1960's were generally weak in nature and not aggressively implemented. The fact that these laws all passed by overwhelming majorities hints that they demanded few sacrifices. Evaluating the effects of these laws is complex, since some changes would have occurred anyway because of state and local regulations. The passage of the 1965 law has been attributed to the fact that the auto industry had conceded that emission reductions would be made for the California market. The much stronger air pollution laws of 1970, 1977, and 1990 demonstrated that the needs and political demands for cleaner air became more forceful. Based on these observations, clean air legislation of the 1960's has been criticized as inadequate. Senator Muskie himself was attacked in 1970 in a Ralph Nader study group report asserting that his laws would not provide the standards and actions needed for real environmental improvement.

Some political scientists argue that states and communities would have aggressively regulated pollution had the federal government not acted. Federal action may have preempted more stringent state laws and mandated broader but weaker regulations. For example, the 1965 act prevented states from developing their own stricter emissions requirements, except for California, which was granted independence because of its leadership and unique pollution problem. It is unlikely, however, that many other states would have regulated auto emissions aggressively in the 1960's.

Early environmental laws such as the Motor Vehicle Air Pollution Control Act are probably best evaluated by their indirect effects. Shifts of public attitudes, which early laws reflect and reinforce, significantly affect later environmental policies. Before the government acts on a social condition such as air pollution, the public has to perceive it as a problem suitable for government action. Later, even when the public expects government action, the shift from accepting state or local action to demanding federal action is a major step. Although the laws of the 1960's were weak in substance and enforcement, they reflected a new public sensitivity to pollution and overturned the tradition of leaving environmental regulation to states and localities. Each step of this process is irreversible, and the 1960's saw air pollution evolve from a local matter over which the government's role was uncertain to a problem for which federal action was expected. The environmental acts of the 1960's also fostered research which helped environmental advocates promote stricter laws later. Although the House eliminated the section calling for an air pollution control laboratory, the 1965 Motor Vehicle Air Pollution Control Act forced HEW to research and evaluate the impact of auto emissions, creating data supporting later policy actions.

Automobile emissions continue to be a major environmental problem. The long-term solution probably requires a shift from individualized internal-combustion-driven vehicles as the dominant mode of transportation. In this respect, the 1965 act directed policy down a less promising path than if it had encouraged alternative modes of transportation or reduced the need for such travel. The act sought a technological solution to air pollution without expecting any social change. Although automobile exhausts have been greatly reduced, in the long term more widespread mass transit or bicycle use, for example, would be more environmentally effective. In the 1960's, Congress was unlikely to reconstruct society's basic mode of transportation and, to an extent, the American concepts of freedom and individuality. Even as awareness of how automobiles affect both local and global environmental conditions became much greater, efforts to end dependence on automobiles made little headway. Instead, politicians continued to preserve individualized motorized mobility while reducing its environmental impacts.

Bibliography

Esposito, John C., and Larry J. Silverman. *Vanishing Air.* New York: Grossman, 1970. The 1965 act is part of a pattern of legislation rather than a clearly delineated threshold point. This book by a Ralph Nader study group captures the criticism leveled at the environmental laws of the 1960's and the powerful arguments and sentiments that led to the stronger acts of the 1970's. Very readable descriptions of the air pollution problem and the politics that prevented effective action. The book may overestimate what was politically feasible in the 1960s. The endnotes are largely devoted to articles.

Kneese, Allen V., and Charles L. Schultze. *Pollution, Prices, and Public Policy.* Washington, D.C.: Brookings Institution, 1975. May be too technical for some readers but makes some excellent references to environmental politics of the 1960's. Chapter 3 concisely explains the limited effectiveness of early regulatory legislation. Very interesting as an early primer on the economics of environmental regulation. The few reference notes are very useful, but the book lacks a complete bibliography.

Lippman, Theo, Jr., and Donald C. Hansen. *Muskie.* New York: W. W. Norton, 1971. Obviously written to serve the Muskie presidential campaign, this book still provides an interesting perspective on the 1960's and a man who dominated the environmental legislation movement of the time. Chapter 7, "Mr. Clean" (Muskie's nickname), illustrates how far environmental regulation has come. No useful bibliography or references.

Miller, E. Willard, and Ruby Miller. *Environmental Hazards: Air Pollution.* Santa Barbara, Calif.: ABC-Clio, 1989. The authors call this a "reference handbook." Although making only passing references to the 1965 act, this work provides a comprehensive listing of journals, books, and addresses of organizations and agencies related to air pollution. Any person who wants to delve deeply into the air pollution policy literature should consult this work. Provides the sources for timely and useful movies and other teaching aids.

White, Lawrence J. *The Regulation of Air Pollutant Emissions from Motor Vehicles.* Washington, D.C.: American Enterprise Institute, 1982. Provides a contemporary economic perspective on auto emissions regulation. Should be read with a background on the Clean Air Act Amendments of 1990. Some calculations and theories may confuse readers with little background in economics, but the interesting and useful conclusions of each section may still be understood. Footnotes but no bibliography.

Mark Henkels

Cross-References

The Pure Food and Drug Act and Meat Inspection Act Become Law (1906), p. 64;

Nader Publishes *Unsafe at Any Speed* (1965), p. 1267; Congress Passes the Clean Air Act Amendments (1970), p. 1561; Congress Passes the Occupational Safety and Health Act (1970), p. 1585; Superfund Is Established to Pay for Hazardous Waste Cleanup (1980), p. 2084.

THE BRITISH PARLIAMENT VOTES TO ABOLISH THE DEATH PENALTY

Category of event: Prisoners' rights
Time: November 8, 1965
Locale: London, England

Increasing doubts about the deterrent value and the morality of capital punishment led the British parliament to abolish hanging

Principal personages:

SYDNEY SILVERMAN (1895-1968), a lawyer and Labour member of Parliament (1935-1968) interested in penal reform

SIR ERNEST GOWERS (1880-1966), a civil servant who presided over the Royal Commission on Capital Punishment

JAMES CHUTER EDE (1882-1965), a Labour member of Parliament (1929-1931 and 1935-1964) and home secretary (1945-1951)

HAROLD WILSON (1916-   ), a Labour member of Parliament (1945-1983) and prime minister (1964-1970 and 1974-1976)

Summary of Event

In 1800, there were more than 220 capital crimes on the British statute books, most involving the stealing of property. The chaos produced by the Industrial Revolution together with the lack of an organized police force turned the penal code to harsh punishment as the main deterrent to crime. By 1808, however, with the founding of the Society for the Diffusion of Knowledge Upon the Punishment of Death, demands for reform were heard in public and on the floor of the House of Commons. Sir Samuel Romilly began to agitate for penal reform and in 1808 succeeded in abolishing capital punishment for the crime of picking pockets. This marked the first step in a long series of parliamentary and public struggles that led eventually to the Murder Act of 1965 and the permanent abolition of capital punishment.

Piecemeal legislation during the period 1819-1840 substantially reduced the number of capital crimes, and in 1861 the Criminal Law Consolidation Act reduced capital crimes to four: murder, treason, piracy with violence, and arson in government dockyards and arsenals. A royal commission appointed in 1864 to study the question of capital punishment recommended that the crime of murder be divided into degrees, with the death penalty for only the first degree (murder with malice and murder committed in the perpetration of arson, rape, burglary, robbery, or piracy). No action was taken on the report, and public agitation on the death penalty was dormant until after World War I. Two organizations, the Howard League for Penal Reform and the National Council for the Abolition of the Death Penalty, promoted petition drives, published material designed to influence public opinion, and lobbied members of Parliament against the death penalty. The question was raised in the

House of Commons, but no government during the period, whether Conservative or Labour, supported abolition. A select committee studied the matter in 1929, but its recommendation that capital punishment be suspended for a trial period of five years was ignored. A trial period became the chief plank in the abolitionist platform. In 1938, the government introduced the Criminal Justice Bill, the purpose of which was to consolidate the criminal law. Because the bill retained the death penalty, abolitionists introduced a motion proposing the suspension of the death penalty for a five-year trial period. To their surprise, the motion carried. The government, however, refused to act on the resolution, and the coming of World War II ended consideration of the bill itself.

The end of the war in 1945 also saw the Labour Party come to power, determined to reform British society by creating a humane welfare state. Abolitionists hoped that Labour would be sympathetic to ending the death penalty, but events proved that this was not the case. The Criminal Justice Bill, which Home Secretary J. Chuter Ede reintroduced in 1947, abolished hard labor, penal servitude, and flogging but retained hanging. The abolitionists, led by Sydney Silverman, a left-wing Labour member of Parliament, then proposed a five-year suspension of the death penalty with life imprisonment as the alternative to hanging. Although the government had promised a free vote on the question, it later ordered its ministers either to vote against the clause or to abstain, because the question involved government policy and thus was a matter of collective responsibility. The result of the vote was a serious defeat for the government. Not only did the clause pass, but most of the ministers abstained. The House of Lords, however, rejected both the Silverman clause and a compromise that would have established degrees of murder.

Ede, who wanted to see the long-overdue Criminal Justice Bill pass, convinced the abolitionists to accept the original bill in return for the formation of a royal commission to study the matter. This was done in 1949. The commission, chaired by Sir Ernest Gowers, a recently retired and highly respected civil servant, presented its report in September, 1953. The report proposed that extenuating circumstances should justify modifying death sentences, that the existing rules relating to insanity, malice, provocation, and suicide be revised, and that the statutory age limit for execution be raised from eighteen to twenty-one. By the time that the commission made its report, however, the Conservative Party had again come to power. The government, responding to Tory sentiment, rejected the Gowers Commission's recommendations.

The cause of abolition gained two important converts in the middle 1950's, Gowers and Ede. Gowers' work for the Royal Commission on Capital Punishment had convinced him that the death penalty was counterproductive. His conversion was intellectual in nature. Ede, on the other hand, had become convinced that as home secretary he had sent an innocent man to the scaffold. He had refused to grant clemency to Timothy John Evans, hanged in 1950 for having strangled his child; the notorious mass murderer John Christie later confessed to the murder, however, and Evans was granted posthumous royal pardon in 1966. By 1955, Ede had serious doubts about

Evans' guilt and was ready to come out for abolition.

The abolitionists returned to the fray during the 1955-1956 session of Parliament, when Silverman introduced the Death Penalty (Abolition) Bill. After vigorous debate, the measure passed the House of Commons but was defeated in the House of Lords. Under the British constitution, the measure would become law despite the Lords' rejection if the Commons passed it again in the following session. Wishing to retain the death penalty, the Conservative government refused to give debating time to Silverman's bill and introduced its own measure, the Homicide Bill, in 1956. Lacking time, Silverman's bill died, and the government bill became law. This measure limited the death penalty to murder committed with aggravating circumstances such as murder by shooting, murder while resisting arrest, or murder of a police officer or prison official. So long as the Conservative Party remained in power, the death penalty was retained, but the number of hangings declined to around four per year.

Several troublesome murder cases contributed to the growing disquiet over capital punishment during the 1950's and led to public campaigns for abolition. The Evans case was one. Others were the hanging of Ruth Ellis, a twenty-eight-year-old mother of two children, for shooting her lover, and the Craig-Bentley case. In the latter case, Christopher Craig escaped the death penalty for his crime of fatally shooting a police officer because he was under eighteen. Derek Bentley, a nineteen-year-old accomplice of Craig in the attempted warehouse burglary that led to the shooting, was hanged even though the police had been holding him when Craig fired the fatal shot. Bentley was accused of having incited Craig to shoot the officer. Many people thought that such results were unjust.

In 1964, the Labour Party took office with Harold Wilson as prime minister. Under Wilson's leadership, the government announced that it would permit a free vote on capital punishment and allowed Silverman to introduce the Murder (Abolition of Capital Punishment) Bill in December, 1964. The bill provided that capital punishment would be suspended for a five-year period, during which time convicted murderers would be sentenced to life imprisonment. Although retentionists fought for the death penalty, the bill passed both houses of Parliament and became law on November 8, 1965. Two years later, Parliament voted to make abolition permanent.

Impact of Event

The abolition of the death penalty in Great Britain was the result of a long process related both to changing attitudes toward crime and punishment and to party political rivalries. Originally intended as a deterrent to crime in the absence of an effective police force, the death penalty was reserved for the most serious crimes after such a police force was created in the early and middle nineteenth century. In the twentieth century, however, and especially after World War I, criminologists began to doubt the utility of the death penalty as a deterrent. In the public eye, the "typical" murderer was the premeditated killer who carefully selected his victims for gain or for sexual pleasure. Certainly those were the murderers whose crimes and trials reached the front pages of the newspapers. In real life, however, the "typical" murderer was either the incompetent criminal who killed by accident in the course of a botched crime or the "murderer of passion" whose victim often was a lover or family member and who, many times, was drunk or otherwise impaired in judgment when the crime was committed. It became clear that neither sort of criminal was likely to be deterred by thought of the death penalty. The few premeditated murderers usually were sure that they were too clever to be caught, while the murderers in crimes of passion usually were not thinking at all about their actions. It was the role of outside pressure groups, most notably the Howard League for Penal Reform and the National Council for the Abolition of the Death Penalty, to disseminate these new views about the death penalty's value as a deterrent and to mobilize lobbying efforts in order to influence party leaders and members of Parliament.

The death penalty and its abolition inevitably became political questions, caught up in the rivalry between the Conservative and the Labour parties. Most Conservatives favored retention of the death penalty from personal conviction; their party leaders were willing to oppose abolition as a means of retaining right-wing support. Because the Conservatives were in power during most of the interwar years, abolition had no chance during that time. After 1945, the leadership of the Labour Party, in power from 1945 to 1951, had what it considered more important items on its agenda, and in any case the Labour rank-and-file were divided on the question. The long tenure of power by the Conservatives from 1951 to 1964 again blocked abolition. Things had changed, however, when the Wilson government took over. The Wilson government represented a newer, younger leadership in the Labour Party, a leadership more open to reforms. Moreover, the thinking of both Labour and (to a lesser extent) Conservative members of Parliament had shifted to favor abolition. Thus the abolition of capital punishment must be seen as part of the general opening up of society that characterized the 1960's in Great Britain and the United States.

The abolition of the death penalty did not lead either to the terrible consequences that the retentionists had predicted or to the wonderful results that the abolitionists had anticipated. Retentionists had argued that abolition would lead to an increase in killings and to the eventual arming of the British police. The British police remained unarmed, and although killings increased, they did so in the 1970's, long after the abolition of the death penalty, and because of increased drug use, a reason unconnected with abolition. Similarly, abolitionists had predicted that abolition would lead to a more humane society, one that placed a higher value on the sanctity of human life and that restrained aggressive tendencies. Such a society did not come to pass, as the growth of soccer violence, for example, suggests.

Perhaps the clearest result of the abolition of the death penalty is that some innocent people remained alive who in past years would have been executed. More than half a dozen Irishmen were found guilty in the mid-1970's of bombing a pub in Birmingham and killing several off-duty British soldiers. (It was charged at the time that the Irishmen were terrorists connected with the Irish Republican Army.) In 1991, however, the men were released and completely exonerated after their cases were reviewed. Had the death penalty existed in 1974, the men almost assuredly would have been executed.

Bibliography

Bartlett, C. J. *A History of Postwar Britain, 1945-1974.* London: Longman, 1977. This account of Britain's history since the end of World War II is impartial—an important quality in evaluating a period that in many ways is still "current events"— and understandable. It focuses on political and economic history, however, to the exclusion of social and intellectual history. Includes an extensive bibliography.

Christoph, James B. *Capital Punishment and British Politics: The British Movement to Abolish the Death Penalty, 1945-57.* Chicago: University of Chicago Press, 1962. A scholarly survey of the campaign in Parliament and the debates among criminologists and reformers. Includes an extensive bibliography.

Cooper, David D. *The Lesson of the Scaffold: The Public Execution Controversy in Victorian England.* Athens: Ohio University Press, 1974. Useful for historical background to the twentieth century debate on capital punishment.

Havighurst, Alfred F. *Twentieth-Century Britain.* Evanston, Ill.: Row, Peterson, 1962. This is a straightforward, clearly written general account of British political history from the death of Queen Victoria in 1901 to the end of the 1950's. It provides the context necessary to understand the events of the period.

Hollis, Christopher. *The Homicide Act.* London: Victor Gollancz, 1964. A legal analysis of the measure. Appropriate for more advanced students.

Hopkins, Harry. *The New Look: A Social History of the Forties and Fifties in Britain.* Boston: Houghton Mifflin, 1964. A journalistic study that includes brief accounts of some of the more lurid crimes of the period and that mentions the campaign against capital punishment.

Laurence, John. *A History of Capital Punishment, with Special Reference to Capital Punishment in Great Britain.* London: S. Low, Marston, 1932. An older work, but still useful for the broader historical context.

Tuttle, Elizabeth Orman. *The Crusade Against Capital Punishment in Great Britain.* Chicago: Quadrangle Books, 1961. A scholarly account with an extensive bibliography. Covers the nineteenth century as well as the twentieth century.

D. G. Paz

Cross-References

Capital Punishment Is Abolished in Sweden (1921), p. 345; The Supreme Court Abolishes the Death Penalty (1972), p. 1674; The United Nations Issues a Declaration Against Torture (1975), p. 1847; Khomeini Uses Executions to Establish a New Order in Iran (1979), p. 2013; Sixty-three Persons Are Beheaded for Attacking Mecca's Grand Mosque (1980), p. 2095; Amnesty International Exposes the Cruelty of the Death Penalty (1989), p. 2414.

CANADA DEVELOPS A NATIONAL HEALTH PLAN

Category of event: Health and medical rights
Time: 1966
Locale: Ottawa, Canada

Canadian political leaders developed and implemented a universal national health insurance plan which some experts believe could be used as a model for the United States

Principal personages:
WILLIAM LYON MACKENZIE KING (1874-1950), the prime minister of Canada throughout most of the period from 1921 to 1948
LESTER BOWLES PEARSON (1897-1972), the prime minister of Canada (1963-1968)
WALTER LOCKHART GORDON (1906-), the Canadian minister of finance (1963-1965)
PAUL MARTIN (1903-), the minister of national health and welfare (1946-1957)
JUDY LAMARCH (1924-1980), the minister of national health and welfare (1963-1965)

Summary of Event

Canada's national health insurance program developed piecemeal over the course of the twentieth century. Landmark acts creating the universal program were passed in April, 1957, when a plan to provide hospital care insurance for Canada's citizens was adopted, and in December, 1966, when medical insurance was enacted. Although the Canadian system has its critics, some proponents suggest that the United States policymakers might learn some valuable lessons from the Canadian health care program.

Support for national health insurance emerged in 1919, when William Lyon Mackenzie King, who served as prime minister of Canada for most of the period from 1921 to 1948, proposed that the Liberal Party endorse several social programs, including health care. The need for a health care program was first recognized by policymakers when a large percentage of Canadian men was exempted from service in World War I for medical reasons. In certain areas of Canada, as many as half of the males were excluded from military service because of poor health. Great Britain's adoption of a comprehensive health care plan in 1912 also drew attention to the issue. In the interwar period, the Great Depression illuminated the need for an improved system of medical service delivery, particularly for indigent persons. Many of Canada's displaced workers and others, hit hard by the depression, went without medical attention during this time. Others sought medical treatment but were unable to pay physicians for services rendered.

In the period between 1942 and 1946, Parliament failed to pass a national program, but progress toward that goal was achieved. Canadian political leaders reached consensus on basic aspects of a program and public support for such a plan was strengthened. In 1942, the Interdepartmental Advisory Committee on Health Insurance, headed by Dr. J. J. Heagarty, was appointed by the health minister. The advisory panel created a basic blueprint for Canada's health care program. The House of Commons also held hearings on health care. In recognition of the pressing need for such legislation, the Canadian Medical Association (CMA) endorsed the national health insurance proposals drafted by the Heagarty committee.

Prior to adoption of national health insurance, some of the provinces created their own hospital insurance and medical care plans. For example, in 1947 the provincial government of Saskatchewan set up a pioneer program which provided virtually universal hospitalization coverage. In 1962, Saskatchewan's program was expanded to include physician services. Physicians staged a strike in protest of the new system, withholding for a month all but emergency medical services. A compromise was reached between the government and physicians, allowing the program to be instituted, but physicians were permitted to opt out of the program and to "extra bill" patients at rates higher than those set by the government.

As World War II came to an end, Canadian officials met to carve out programs for postwar reconstruction. The provinces and national government could not reach agreement about a suitable method of financing a national health care program. In 1948, with the strong support of Paul Martin, the new minister of health and welfare, a first step was taken toward adoption of a health insurance plan with passage of the National Health Grants program, which provided federal legislation in support of hospitals. The legislation funded grants for specific purposes such as hospital construction, medical research, and professional training.

By the 1950's, support for national hospitalization insurance grew as many hospitals encountered financial difficulty, medical technology became more sophisticated and expensive, and hospital workers demanded better pay and working conditions. In addition, 60 percent or more of Canadians did not have hospital insurance. With the support of Paul Martin, the Hospital Insurance and Diagnostic Services Act was approved by Parliament in April, 1957. The plan provided for prepaid hospital care for medically necessary services, to be funded by a combination of federal and provincial government contributions. By the early 1960's, all the provinces had joined the hospital insurance program, resulting in coverage of nearly all of Canada's population. Predictions that the legislation would result in a marked increase in hospital use proved to be false. The act has also been credited with increasing availability of accredited hospitals and hospital beds as well as providing all citizens with equal access to hospital care irrespective of their ability to pay.

Additional landmark legislation, which created medical insurance covering physician fees, was passed in December, 1966, during the prime ministership of Lester Bowles Pearson, a Liberal Party member. Pressing for the act were Judy LaMarch, minister of health and welfare, and Walter Gordon, the finance minister. In addition, a report by a Royal Commission on Health Services provided evidence demonstrating that a large number of Canadians did not have medical insurance or had inadequate coverage, that Canada's infant mortality rate was relatively high, and that some provinces lacked the financial capacity to resolve the problems. By 1972, all the provinces had agreed to the program and were receiving federal contributions. Canada's national health insurance program thus took in excess of fifty years to complete.

Canada has a federal system of government, with power divided between a national government and ten provinces. Canada is sometimes said to have twelve health insurance programs, since the plans are administered by the ten provincial and two territorial governments. Provinces, however, must meet certain requirements set by the federal government in order to receive federal funding. The national government grants relatively more federal funding to the poorer provinces and less to richer ones.

The Canadian system is universal, offering coverage to all Canadians. It covers hospital fees and nearly all medical services, including physician visits, treatments, tests, X rays, laboratory fees, prescriptions for senior citizens, hospitalization, and surgery costs. In some provinces, additional services are also covered, such as chiropractic visits, physical therapy, and dental care for children. Private insurance is allowed for certain noncovered services only, such as private or semiprivate hospital rooms, pharmacy costs, and some nursing home care.

The Canadian program differs from national health care systems in other countries. The system depends heavily upon tax subsidy payments rather than insurance premiums, although small premiums are collected from citizens in two of the provinces. The program generally provides for prepayment of services rather than for reimbursement to the patient for covered expenses. It is designed so that only a bare minimum of noncovered expenses is paid for by patients. Unlike many other systems, there is no limit on physician visits or number of days in the hospital which are covered. One of the advantages of the program is "portability." Canadians who move from one province to another, for example, may claim benefits immediately.

Most physicians are paid under the program on a fee-per-service basis, the rate schedule of which is negotiated with the provincial governments. In 1984, the Canada Health Act established stronger federal government controls on provincial health plans. The act, for example, discouraged a practice known as "extra billing," wherein physicians practicing outside the national health care program determined their own fees, rather than receiving the fees negotiated by the medical association with the provincial government. The practice of "extra billing" allowed the physician to charge the patient an amount in excess of the government-approved rates. In addition, in some provinces, user fees were being charged to hospital patients. The 1984 act provided the provinces with strong disincentives against allowing user fees and extra billing charges by threatening to withhold a certain amount of federal funding from provinces that permitted these practices.

The 1984 act set off a physician strike in Ontario and created conflict between the government and doctors, who feared loss of professional autonomy. The 1984 act was passed because of public support for a key feature of Canada's health insurance plan—accessibility to all regardless of ability to pay. The principle of equal public access to medical care was emphasized by the 1984 act and is a major attribute of the system.

Impact of Event

Canada's health care system is sometimes criticized but remains one of the most popular of the nation's social programs. The system is based on the assumption that health care is an essential service that should be widely available to citizens regardless of ability to pay. The situation may be compared with the United States, where it is estimated that thirty-seven million United States citizens did not have health insurance in the early 1990's. The Canadian system ensures that medical coverage will be provided for those who are unable to pay, including the unemployed and the working poor. It also provides coverage for those who may have difficulty obtaining insurance at a reasonable cost; for example, persons with preexisting medical conditions who find it difficult to obtain coverage under private insurance systems. In addition, in cases in which a person experiences catastrophic illness, under a system of public health insurance, income potential and existing assets are not threatened as severely, since insurance is guaranteed.

The Canadian system offers coverage on a universal basis. Because the system is regulated by the state, health care resources are subject to collective control, rather than control by the marketplace, where ability to pay becomes a major determinant of access to expensive treatment and surgery. Among the benefits cited by public regulation are control over expenditures, the number of physicians, and the number of hospital beds. Physicians' overhead is lower in Canada as compared with the United States because Canadian physicians pay less to collect fees, for liability costs, and for accoutrements such as office furnishings.

Critics cite certain problems with the system, however, including the difficulty of maintaining control over costs, particularly with political demand for increased services, such as coverage for nursing home care, dental care, optometric and chiropractic services, and physical therapy. In addition, Canada's population is aging, putting additional strain on the health care system since older people tend to require more medical care. The system is also strained by unexpected costs, particularly in view of the AIDS (Acquired Immune Deficiency Syndrome) crisis, although some proponents of national health care point out that the costs of treating AIDS patients are more evenly spread among the population under a state-run system rather than concentrated on those who develop AIDS.

Perhaps the most common criticism of the Canadian system stems from the infamous waiting lists for surgery. Canadians report that the wait for ordinary medical care is very brief, but limits on hospital beds and equipment prevent some who need surgery, particularly open-heart surgery, from receiving it immediately. Patients in need of such surgery are put on waiting lists based upon severity of illness. Supporters of the Canadian system point out that some research has claimed that United States physicians perform too much open-heart surgery, whereas Canadian physicians take a relatively conservative approach. They further point out that rationing of medical services in the United States occurs because of ability to pay, whereas Canadian patients receive preference based upon severity of illness.

The per-capita cost for health care in the Canadian system was considerably lower than in the United States in 1990. Canada also had a higher life expectancy and a lower mortality rate than the United States. Even with its advantages, the Canadian health care system may not be appropriate for other countries. It is difficult to transplant policies from one political system to another and to expect them to work equally well. Each nation has different political cultures, operative beliefs, population size, and distribution of wealth. Although the Canadian system of national health insurance may or may not work well elsewhere, it is a source of pride in Canada, ostensibly attracting widespread popular support.

Bibliography

Andreopoulos, Spyros, ed. *National Health Insurance: Can We Learn from Canada?* New York: John Wiley & Sons, 1975. Contains several chapters by health care experts which may be of interest to those looking for a national health care insurance model for the United States to emulate. Has sections on the historical perspective, economic perspectives, the public interest and the medical profession, and implications for the United States. A number of statistical tables and charts are included.

Glaser, William A. "Canada." In *Health Insurance Bargaining: Foreign Lessons for Americans.* New York: Gardner Press, 1978. Includes chapters on national health insurance in eight nations other than the United States. The work focuses on the way in which physicians are paid and organized in each nation. The chapter on Canada includes a brief historical overview and discusses some of the major controversies surrounding the program. Similar chapters on other nations are intended to offer lessons for the United States. Tables.

Globerman, Judith. "Free Enterprise, Professional Ideology, and Self-Interest: An Analysis of Resistance by Canadian Physicians to Universal Health Insurance." *Journal of Health and Social Behavior* 31 (March, 1990): 11-27. The author surveyed Toronto physicians representing four specialties to determine the basis for opposition by organized medicine to state-operated programs. She found that many physicians resisted the system because of conservative beliefs, economic self-interest, and a desire for professional autonomy. Bibliography.

Naylor, C. David. *Private Practice, Public Payment: Canadian Medicine and the Politics of Health Insurance 1911-1966.* Kingston, Ontario, Canada: McGill-Queen's University Press, 1986. Naylor focuses on physicians as an interest group with a strong stake in Canadian health insurance policies. He argues that physicians represented by the CMA have been more open-minded about state-regulated health programs than their American counterparts, but that organized medicine is nevertheless an important, self-interested organization that has occasionally opposed changes that threatened the economic or social interests of members. Tables.

Taylor, Malcolm G. *Health Insurance and Canadian Public Policy.* Montreal: McGill-Queen's University Press, 1978. This thorough, detailed history chronicles the development of the Canadian health insurance system. Taylor considers the factors that contributed to adoption of national health insurance as well as obstacles to the system. Relies on primary documents, interviews with participants, and first-hand knowledge. This book is thorough, but Taylor's recent publications are more accessible for most readers. Tables.

_____. *Insuring National Health Care: The Canadian Experience.* Chapel Hill: University of North Carolina Press, 1990. Examines development on Canada's national health insurance program and considers the major problems confronting the system. Includes a chapter on the Canadian political process. The author contends that United States political officials could learn from Canada's system, but that Canadian officials could also benefit from exposure to the United States system of health care delivery. The volume is condensed from a more comprehensive work by Taylor, *Health Insurance and Canadian Public Policy: The Seven Decisions That Created the Canadian Health Insurance System and Their Outcomes* (Montreal: McGill-Queen's University Press, 1988). Most readers will find the condensed work to be sufficiently detailed and preferable to the longer work.

Mary A. Hendrickson

Cross-References

The World Health Organization Proclaims Health as a Basic Right (1946), p. 678; Congress Passes the Occupational Safety and Health Act (1970), p. 1585; The Declaration of Tokyo Forbids Medical Abuses and Torture (1975), p. 1829; WHO Sets a Goal of Health for All by the Year 2000 (1977), p. 1893; An International Health Conference Adopts the Declaration of Alma-Ata (1978), p. 1998; Commission Studies Ethical and Legal Problems in Medicine and Research (1980), p. 2090; The U.N. Principles of Medical Ethics Include Prevention of Torture (1982), p. 2169.

THE NATIONAL ORGANIZATION FOR WOMEN FORMS TO PROTECT WOMEN'S RIGHTS

Categories of event: Women's rights
Time: 1966
Locale: The United States

NOW was an outgrowth of the burgeoning women's movement of the 1960's and of the Civil Rights Act of 1964, which initially did little to protect the rights of women

Principal personages:

BETTY FRIEDAN (1921-   ), the author of *The Feminine Mystique* (1964), the first president of NOW, and an important spokesperson for the women's movement in the 1960's and 1970's

MARTHA GRIFFITHS (1912-   ), a congresswoman from Michigan who played a crucial role in the adoption of Article 7 of the 1964 Civil Rights Act

GLORIA STEINEM (1934-   ), an early leader of NOW and the National Women's Political Caucus; founding editor of *Ms* magazine

BELLA ABZUG (1920-   ), a congresswoman and leader of the women's movement, also a member of the Carter Administration

Summary of Event

The formation of the National Organization for Women (NOW) was an important development in the rise of the feminist movement in the 1960's. In this, the third major feminist movement in the United States since the mid-nineteenth century, American women sought to achieve full equality. While no event in itself can be credited with the rebirth of a feminist movement in the 1960's, a few important developments should be noted. Betty Friedan's book, *The Feminine Mystique* (1964), deserves credit for its role in raising women's consciousness about their roles and status in American society. The Equal Pay Act of 1963, which called for equal pay for equal work, and the Civil Rights Act of 1964, Article 7 of which required equal employment opportunities for women and minorities, were landmark pieces of legislation. These developments played an important role in the genesis of NOW and of a revitalized women's movement.

Although the struggle for women's working rights had been pursued, with partial success, since World War II, a broadly based movement to ensure full equality for women in the workplace, and in society generally, did not exist. The President's Commission on the Status of Women strongly endorsed the principle of equal pay for women. The commission strongly supported the Equal Pay Act of 1963,,a law which to some degree paved the way for the inclusion of women under the protection of the Civil Rights Act of 1964. The Civil Rights Act of 1964 was principally designed to protect black Americans and other minority groups. Congress included women among protected groups because of significant lobbying by a few women's organizations. Some have argued that inclusion of women under the protection of the act was an attempt to weaken the emphasis on black Americans. Support by women for the inclusion of women under the act was not universal because there was fear, on the part of women in government and other groups, that the new law might signify the end of special protective legislation for women workers.

The 1964 Civil Rights Act applied only to enterprises which were engaged in interstate commerce and had at least twenty-five employees. Enforcement was through the newly formed Equal Employment Opportunity Commission (EEOC). Little was done initially to enforce the law on behalf of women, and a few members of the EEOC expressed their sense of helplessness in dealing with the problems. A special concern at that time was the EEOC's failure to prohibit job advertisements that discriminated against female applicants. Congresswoman Martha Griffiths, a leading spokesperson for women in Congress and supporter of the legislation, advocated stricter enforcement. Implementation of the new law was largely left in the hands of the state commissions on the status of women. During a June, 1966, meeting of the National Council of State Commissions on the Status of Women, it was recognized that little could be done to combat job discrimination if enforcement were left to the individual states. Some of the concerned members of the state commissions present joined with a few prominent women to form the nucleus of the group later called the National Organization for Women (NOW), whose initial purpose was to promote the enforcement of Article 7 of the Civil Rights Act. In October, 1966, NOW was officially established, with Betty Friedan as its first president.

In its early days, NOW campaigned for enforcement of Article 7 and brought several cases to the courts for resolution. In particular, NOW argued in favor of abolishing protective legislation for female workers which had the unintended side effect of removing women from consideration for lucrative jobs. In the 1970's, persuaded by NOW and other groups, Congress amended Article 7 to extend coverage to firms in the private sector with at least fifteen employees. The EEOC could bring lawsuits against employers violating the Civil Rights Act. In the early 1970's, the Equal Employment Opportunity Act corrected many of the problems involved in the implementation of Article 7 of the 1964 Civil Rights Act.

NOW expanded its program beyond implementation of equal employment opportunities for women. The organization held its first convention in October, 1967, at which time it published an eight-point women's bill of rights. Among the most important concerns in the new, broadly based program were an Equal Rights Amendment, equal opportunity in employment, child care, and reproductive freedom. As the organization grew at the state and local levels, its focus was harder to maintain. NOW had five hundred chapters by 1973. For some women, NOW was too radical; for others, too conservative. This led to splintering and the establishment of other groups. The abortion issue was an especially divisive one. When NOW became identified with a strongly prochoice position, some members left. On the other hand, NOW moved too slowly for the more radical women, who formed leftist feminist organizations, including Redstockings.

As NOW grew, it was recognized that there was a need for special purpose organizations. Those most interested in the pursuit of women's legal and economic rights formed the Women's Equity Action League (WEAL) in 1968. In 1971, some members of NOW interested in promoting women's active involvement in politics formed the National Women's Political Caucus (NWPC). Friedan, Bella Abzug, and Gloria Steinem were NOW leaders who played a role in developing the NWPC. Gloria Steinem, a journalist and NOW activist, established the well-known magazine *Ms* in 1971 as an outgrowth of the work of NOW.

NOW was a strong advocate of the Equal Rights Amendment. Despite organized lobbying in the states, the ERA failed to be ratified. This was perhaps NOW's most notable failure and its single most intense battle. Congress' second attempt in the 1980's to pass an equal rights amendment also fell short of the required two-thirds majority.

Abortion rights have been another area of long-term involvement for NOW. NOW was an important supporter of the Supreme Court's decision in *Roe v. Wade* (1973), which permitted abortion under women's right to privacy. NOW became one of the leaders of the prochoice position in the United States in 1973. Since the mid-1970's, NOW has also been identified with defense of the rights of gays and lesbians in society. More recently, some NOW leaders called for the establishment of a separate women's party, a strategy which does not have universal support.

From its origins as a small group united to implement Article 7 of the Civil Rights Act of 1964, NOW grew to become an organization of more than fifty thousand members by the early 1970's. NOW brought together concerned women from various segments of society. Most of its members, however, tended to be middle- and upper-class, urban, well-educated women. Rural women, factory workers, and the urban poor were perhaps underrepresented in the organization. From its narrow beginning, NOW expanded its work to many areas of American political, economic, and social life.

Impact of Event

NOW is important as the first broadly based feminist organization, arising from the women's movement of the 1960's. It could rightly be called the "mother" of most of the other women's groups formed since the late 1960's. Its efforts in advocating the implementation of the Civil Rights Act of 1964 led to significant improvements for women in the workplace. Without such efforts, the implementation of Article 7 might have been neglected for some years. As an organization, NOW's interests expanded into most areas of American life, and its early leaders, like Abzug, began to play important roles in the political arena during the 1970's.

NOW, as an organization occupying a liberal position, failed to satisfy moderate and conservative women, on one hand, and radical women, on the other. Over the years, as the organization grew and its leadership and membership evolved, NOW attained a reputation of leaning toward liberal or even radical feminism.

After the successes achieved by NOW and other groups in promoting women's rights, the early fervor and unity of the women's movement largely evaporated. Where once Betty Friedan spoke of a malaise affecting American women, women began speaking of a malaise affecting women's organizations. NOW continued its work in defense of reproductive freedom and other perennial issues, but, like numerous other women's groups, did not emerge with a clear agenda for the future. After the defeat of the ERA, feminists no longer felt the pressure to present a united front. As a result, there has been debate and discussion about which specific measures would best help women.

NOW's work in the mid-1960's in the struggle of women to obtain equal opportunity in the workplace was an important step in the struggle for women's human rights. Women are no longer perceived as auxiliary workers willing to tolerate poor conditions and smaller salaries. Women are now found in almost all jobs, earning salaries commensurate with their work. Although the struggle has not had complete success, great progress has been made in achieving equal opportunity for women in the workplace.

Bibliography

Deckard, Barbara Sinclair. *The Women's Movement: Political, Socio-Economic, and Psychological Issues.* New York: Harper & Row, 1975. This history of the women's movement gives an interesting account of the context in which NOW was conceived. Much of the book deals with radical women's movements, rather than with mainstream groups such as NOW.

Friedan, Betty. *The Feminine Mystique.* New York: Dell, 1964. This is an important book in the diagnosis and definition of women's malaise in the 1960's. It played a significant role in raising women's consciousness about their plight. Friedan attempted to identify the deeply rooted discontent that afflicted American women.

Gelb, Joyce. *Feminism and Politics: A Comparative Perspective.* Berkeley: University of California Press, 1989. Gelb provides a good chapter on the mobilization of feminists in her comparative study of feminist politics in the United States and the United Kingdom. NOW's central role is analyzed as Gelb provides a brief history of the feminist movement and the organization.

Katzenstein, Mary Fainsod, and Carol McClurg Mueller, eds. *The Women's Movements of the United States and Western Europe: Consciousness, Political Opportunity, and Public Policy.* Philadelphia: Temple University Press, 1987. In this serious work, the women's movement in the United States is compared and contrasted with other women's movements. Katzenstein provides a comparative overview and other authors detail specific case studies involving consciousness, political strategies, and issues in Europe and the United States.

Mansbridge, Jane J. *Why We Lost the ERA.* Chicago: University of Chicago Press, 1986. In this highly respected work, Mansbridge chronicles the struggle of the ERA. Significant attention is given to the role of NOW and other groups in attempting ratification. Mansbridge's reflections on the lessons to be learned and on the women's movement after the ERA movement are very interesting.

Randall, Vicky. *Women and Politics.* New York: St. Martin's Press, 1982. Randall uses a generally comparative approach in discussing women and politics and women's movements, but most of her focus is on the United States and the United Kingdom. She provides a brief history of the women's movement in the United States, helpful in putting NOW into historical perspective.

Staggenborg, Suzanne. "Stability and Innovation in the Women's Movement: A Comparison of Two Movement Organizations." *Social Problems* 36 (February, 1989): 75-92. A case study of the Chicago NOW organization, which was founded in 1969. Staggenborg compares the Chicago NOW group, which continued to exist at least until 1989, with the more radical Chicago Women's Liberation Union (CWLU), also established in 1969 but dissolved in 1977.

Stetson, Dorothy McBride. *Women's Rights in the U.S.A.: Policy Debates and Gender Roles.* Pacific Grove, Calif.: Brooks/Cole, 1991. One chapter traces the origin of the National Organization for Women in the implementation of the EEOC provisions. This important book focuses on legal issues and rights affecting women in the workplace, the family, and society.

Norma C. Noonan

Cross-References

The Pankhursts Found the Women's Social and Political Union (1903), p. 19; The League of Women Voters Is Founded (1920), p. 333; The Nineteenth Amendment Gives American Women the Right to Vote (1920), p. 339; Franklin D. Roosevelt Appoints Perkins as Secretary of Labor (1933), p. 486; The Equal Pay Act Becomes Law (1963), p. 1172; Congress Passes the Civil Rights Act (1964), p. 1251; Congress Passes the Equal Employment Opportunity Act (1972), p. 1650; The Equal Rights Amendment Passes Congress but Fails to Be Ratified (1972), p. 1656; *Roe v. Wade* Expands Reproductive Choice for American Women (1973), p. 1703; Congress Votes to Admit Women to the Armed Services Academies (1975), p. 1823; A U.N. Convention Condemns Discrimination Against Women (1979), p. 2057; O'Connor Becomes the First Female Supreme Court Justice (1981), p. 2141.

THE CHINESE CULTURAL REVOLUTION
STARTS A WAVE OF REPRESSION

Category of event: Political freedom
Time: 1966-1976
Locale: People's Republic of China

Mao Tse-tung's ideology motivated millions of Chinese youths to revolt against the bureaucracy, which in turn helped Mao to regain political prominence at the cost of thousands of lives

Principal personages:

MAO TSE-TUNG (1893-1976), one of the founders of the Chinese Communist Party (CCP), instrumental in the overthrow of Chiang Kai-shek and the Nationalists (1949)

LIN BIAO (1908-1971), Mao's handpicked minister of defense and the de facto head of the People's Liberation Army, the key promoter of Maoist policies and propaganda

JIANG QING (1914-1991), Mao's third wife and a member of the Gang of Four

YAO WENYUAN (1930-   ), a member of the Gang of Four

WANG HONGWEN (1936-   ), a member of the Gang of Four

ZHANG CHUNQIAO (1917-   ), a member of the Gang of Four

DENG XIAOPING (1904-   ), the dominant figure in Chinese politics after Mao's death and the demise of the Gang of Four in 1976

Summary of Event

In 1966, in an effort to restore the revolutionary spirit to the Chinese people and to prevent China's departure from socialism, Mao Tse-tung motivated millions of Chinese youths to challenge authority and capitalist tendencies—"to make revolution." He called for the masses to challenge authority by removing reactionary elements from Chinese society. These vague objectives only invited abuse, and, as in Mao's Great Leap Forward debacle, the initial ideological euphoria soon gave way to the reality of mass chaos and societal disarray. After the Great Leap failure, Mao had found himself on the outside of the political power structure. He would find a new power base not in the traditional political arena but in the ranks of the visionary youth—soon dubbed "Red Guards." These militants, mostly young teens, violently disbarred many authority figures and ushered in a state of chaos, the first stage of the Great Proletarian Cultural Revolution, Mao's direct attack on the very party he helped to found.

Most historical accounts identify the Wu Han case as the beginning of the Cultural Revolution, when in reality this case only set the stage. Although Wu's play *The Dismissal of Hai Rui from Office* (1961) ostensibly depicted Ming politics, it clearly reflected the errors of the contemporary Chinese Communist Party (CCP) cabinet, and, by inference, of Mao himself. Wu's character of the "average official" did not "dare to oppose anything even though he knew it was bad," and his monarch was "self-opinionated and unreceptive to criticism." Subsequently, Mao and his allies began a campaign against antisocialist literature and any "anti-socialist poisonous weeds" found in the Chinese cultural garden. Mao had criticized the Ministry of Culture in Beijing for its fascination with ancient history and suggested that the ministry be renamed "the Ministry of Foreign Mummies," "the Ministry of Talents and Beauties," or "the Ministry of Emperors, Kings, Generals, and Ministers." The Maoist People's Liberation Army (PLA) vowed to help "destroy blind faith in Chinese and foreign classical literature." Lin Biao, Mao's rising star and military leader, asserted that "if the proletariat does not occupy the positions in literature and art, the bourgeoisie certainly will. This struggle is inevitable."

The arts struggle interested Mao because it was a plausible pretext for revolution. Mao and his confidants soon signaled an attack on the "four old" elements within society—old customs, old habits, old culture, and old thinking. Unabashedly, Mao expected every Communist Chinese to be a revolutionary. Those who were uneducated or inexperienced could be taught and shown the personal value of revolution. China's youth, who had been called on to lead lives of restraint and obedience, readily absorbed lessons of violence. While combating political ostracism, Mao publicized legitimate weaknesses in the Communist central committee and planned a radical avenue back to political potency. He would rise on the backs of millions of youths who would follow his visionary teachings, canonize his homilies, and attack authorities at every turn. Mao was fulfilling his public promise made in 1958, when the committee had seriously questioned the Great Leap Forward policies, then only a few months old; Mao had informed his obstinate colleagues that he could "go to the countryside to lead the peasants to overthrow the government." He threatened, "If those of you in the Liberation Army won't follow me, then I will go and find a Red Army, and organize another Liberation Army." History substantiated the fears of the acquiescing CCP cabinet, for in 1927, a much younger Mao had predicted that "In a very short time . . . several hundred million peasants will rise like a mighty storm, like a hurricane, a force so swift and violent that no power, however great, will be able to hold it back." Two decades had been a very short time for the world's most durable civilization to wait, but Mao's bold 1958 threat would be realized in just eight years.

Following Mao's pyrrhic victory via the Red Guards (1966-1968) came the second of the revolution's three stages, dominated not by the Red Guards but rather by the PLA—the stabilizing force between the Red Guards and the Chinese workers. By August of 1968, Mao had organized the Worker-Peasant Mao Tse-tung Propaganda Teams to disband the Red Guards, which by then were plagued with factional fighting and anarchy. Mao's vague tirade against "reactionary" elements was permission enough for the Red Guards to wreak violence on nearly 10 percent of the Chinese population (bureaucrats, those with foreign connections, and unpopular professors were particularly targeted). Suicides (after Red Guard harassment), public humiliations (for example, the cutting of girls' long hair, the forcing of public retractions, and the wearing of dunce caps), and murders became commonplace. By 1969, Mao had halted the excesses of the revolutionaries by sending them all home or to the fields to work with the peasants. With the assistance of his wife, Jiang Qing, and her associates, Mao launched the Campaign to Purify Class Ranks (1967-1969). Liu Shaoqi and Deng Xiaoping had already been removed from the highest ranks of the CCP, paving the way for its restructuring.

After a period of intense calculated transition and the suspicious death of Lin Biao (1971), the final stage of the revolution ensued, led by Jiang Qing and her associates, collectively dubbed the "Gang of Four." The Four became the dominant political force, having assumed investiture duties, and by 1974 they were also solidly in charge of economics. This oligarchy was short-lived, however, and the Gang of Four's rule abruptly ended with the death of Mao in 1976. The Chinese masses blamed the four for manipulating the aging Mao into starting the misguided revolution and subsequently usurping the dying leader's power. The trial and conviction of the Gang of Four brought an ugly end to an uglier era, but at least there was closure.

Although the secrecy of Chinese communism discredited any definitive explanation of the revolution's causes, two factors loomed large: Mao's radical revolutionary vision and his political aspirations. His revolution was based on ideological incentives, a scheme that would fail not only economically but also diplomatically. Perhaps worst of all, the Cultural Revolution would invoke more humanitarian needs than it could solve. As it had in the 1958-1960 disaster, Mao's ideology paled in the face of pragmatic policies. Volunteerism supplanted planning. Besides the political and social chaos that ensued during "the ten bad years" (1966-1976), a generation of teens later referred to by their fellow Chinese as the "lost generation" would lose as many years of education. At least twenty thousand others lost their lives because of Mao's ill-conceived revolution. Mao's visionary ideology, underlying both the Great Proletarian Cultural Revolution and the Great Leap Forward, had the flaw of lacking any sense of realism. In the span of just eight years (1958-1966), Mao instituted such radical measures to protect and propagate his anticapitalist ideology that more than fifty million people would die because of his disregard for social, demographic, and economic realities. His guiding principle was that the quickest route to full communism was revolution. Mao sincerely believed that the Chinese Communist Party (CCP) should be preoccupied with creating a new kind of individual, one committed more to the country than to personal gain. China, Mao thought, needed to be totally self-sufficient, not like the capitalist countries, which would ultimately be swallowed up by communism when their colonial exploitation ceased to be profitable. In 1966, some CCP members, according to Mao, had acquired by design some curious capitalist bedfellows.

Impact of Event

The political motivation for the revolution seemed straightforward. Mao and his wife most likely felt disregarded; real political power had obviously shifted to others. A study of the Cultural Revolution is, in large part, a study of Mao's rise in power and popularity and most certainly his fall from political prominence in the early 1960's. As a revolutionary with an ardent belief in involving the masses in revolution, Mao had the singular ability to motivate the Chinese to action. The legendary Long March of 1934 had made him a folk hero, a national symbol for constructive change—a legitimate avenue to reform. Only someone of Mao's prominence could reemerge to national prominence after a mistake as grandiose and costly as the Great Leap Forward.

Slogans and scars would survive past the early 1960's, and it would take the Cultural Revolution to put Mao back at the political helm. Even then, the economic scars would persist for at least another generation. Between 1958 and 1965, famine and near-famine touched all of China. Demographic data confirmed that starvation and malnutrition claimed the lives of between twenty and thirty million Chinese between 1959 and 1962. Obviously, Mao's plan to revive the economy had failed. What at first appeared to be an acceptable retreat, a possible prelude to progress, became a glaring economic leap in the wrong direction. Mao was still chairman of the CCP in 1960 but could not prevent its senior members, led by Liu Shaoqi and Deng Xiaoping, from reversing most of his policies. While his political opponents took aggressive steps to alleviate the food shortage, Mao found himself relegated to the role of a revered ancestor; consultations with Mao were only polite gestures. Thus, the Cultural Revolution was a golden political opportunity, or so it seemed.

After Mao's death in 1976, the most common Chinese reassessment of their great statesman found him responsible for twenty years of misguided policies. Inherent within his system was "the fundamental policy to guide the peasants to accelerate socialist construction, complete the building of socialism ahead of time, and carry out the gradual transition to communism." These boasts were not only visionary but looked at the human condition through clouded ideological glasses. The conditions of life and basically all human rights of the peasants were being ignored. Deng Xiaoping was rehabilitated in 1977 and quickly invoked pragmatic policies. The "Four Modernizations" campaign was launched, emphasizing science and technology, industry, agriculture, and the military.

For Mao, the achievement of full communism justified the certain loss of some lives and the possible loss of millions. At the outset of the Cultural Revolution, the Soviets had long since effaced Joseph Stalin for such faulty logic (later, even the Lenin colossi disappeared). By 1958, Mao asserted that the interests and needs of the Chinese masses could be met only in the context of Maoist, not Marxist-Leninist, socialism. One of the main charges against the Gang of Four was their idealism. They cogently argued for a strict adherence to the Communist principles of Marx, Lenin, and Stalin and a plan for world communism, yet they would risk any and all of the gains of the revolution. After the revolution, China was left without any strong belief system. While China looked to the West for modernization assistance, materialism, freedom, capitalism, individualism, and other Western values entered an already vacillating Chinese society.

Bibliography

Chen, Jo-hsi. *The Execution of Mayor Yin and Other Stories of the Great Proletarian Cultural Revolution.* Bloomington: Indiana University Press, 1978. Firsthand accounts (short stories) of life during the revolution highlighting the plight of Chinese intellectuals.

Chia-Cheng, Beda Liu. "Political and Economic Reforms in Post-Mao China." *America* 162 (June 9, 1990): 572-574. A quick survey of China's steps in dealing with the fallout of Mao's ideological decisions. The main emphasis is the late 1980's.

Frolic, B. Michael. *Mao's People: Sixteen Portraits of Life in Revolutionary China.* Cambridge, Mass.: Harvard University Press, 1980. Vivid portrayals of sixteen different types of people in China in the Maoist era.

Hayhoe, Ruth, ed. *Contemporary Chinese Education.* Armonk, N.Y.: M. E. Sharpe, 1984. These six essays give insight into the radical Cultural Revolution system of education and contrast it with the later reformist model of Deng Xiaoping.

Heng, Liang, and Judith Shapiro. *Son of the Revolution.* New York: Vintage Books, 1984. A look at the Cultural Revolution by ex-Red Guards.

MacFarquhar, Roderick, Timothy Cheek, and Eugene Wu, eds. *The Secret Speeches of Chairman Mao: From the Hundred Flowers to the Great Leap.* Cambridge, Mass.: Harvard University Press, 1989. An important contribution of primary sources prefacing Mao's actions during the Cultural Revolution.

Ogden, Suzanne. *Global Studies: China.* 4th ed. Guilford, Conn.: The Dushkin Publishing Group, 1991. A concise account of the Great Leap Forward, with interesting details, that relies almost entirely on primary sources. The section on the People's Republic of China includes twenty-seven articles from leading journals.

Pye, Lucian W. *China: An Introduction.* 4th ed. New York: HarperCollins, 1991. This text places the modern political crises of China in historical and cultural context. Pye poignantly chronicles the Great Leap Forward with nuggets of Maoist quotations. The last three chapters serve as good overviews of the aftermath of the Great Leap Forward, covering "The Leadership of Deng Xiaoping," "China's Bold Effort at Reforms Under Deng Xiaoping," and "China's Future Domestically and Internationally."

Spence, Jonathan D. *The Search for Modern China.* New York: W. W. Norton, 1990. An excellent account of China's history that chronicles the key events that have factored significantly in the state of affairs in China. Spence also includes resourceful footnotes, complemented by an extensive topical bibliography.

Warsaw, Steven. *China Emerges: A Concise History of China from Its Origin to the Present.* 7th ed. Berkeley, Calif.: Diablo Press, 1990. The chapter on "Communism in China" serves as a useful outline of Mao's rise and fall from power. The last two chapters provide a useful outline of the various factors giving rise to open criticism of the CCP. The eleven indexes are filled with both primary sources and research data.

Jerry A. Pattengale

Cross-References

The Boxer Rebellion Fails to Remove Foreign Control in China (1900), p. 1; Sun Yat-sen Overthrows the Ch'ing Dynasty (1911), p. 116; Students Demonstrate for Reform in China's May Fourth Movement (1919), p. 276; Khrushchev Implies That Stalinist Excesses Will Cease (1956), p. 952; Mao Delivers His "Speech of One Hundred Flowers" (1956), p. 958; Mao's Great Leap Forward Causes Famine and Social Dislocation (1958), p. 1015; China Publicizes and Promises to Correct Abuses of Citizens' Rights (1978), p. 1983; Demonstrators Gather in Tiananmen Square (1989), p. 2483.

CONGRESS REQUIRES CIGARETTE WARNING LABELS

Categories of event: Health and medical rights; consumers' rights
Time: January 1, 1966
Locale: Washington, D.C.

The United States Congress responded to demands for regulation against the tobacco industry in general, and cigarette manufacturers in particular, by requiring health warning labels on cigarette packages

> *Principal personages:*
> LYNDON B. JOHNSON (1908-1973), the president of the United States from November, 1963, to January, 1969
> WARREN G. MAGNUSON (1905-   ), a Democrat from Washington State, served as chair of the Senate's Commerce Committee
> EARLE C. CLEMENTS (1896-1985), a former senator from Kentucky, the paid lobbyist for the six major cigarette manufacturers and the creator of the tobacco industry's legislative strategy
> MAURINE B. NEUBERGER (1907-   ), a Democrat from Oregon with an antismoking legislative agenda
> LUTHER L. TERRY (1911-   ), the surgeon general of the United States

Summary of Event

From the time it emerged as the economic salvation of the Virginia colony in the early seventeenth century until the latter half of the twentieth century, tobacco prompted arguments over the possibility of harmful health effects and its capacity to addict its users. Because of the popularity of tobacco generally, and cigarettes specifically, little governmental action was proposed to limit smoking until the middle of the 1960's. At that time, a broad coalition capitalized upon a landmark governmental report and succeeded in passing the first piece of legislation designed to decrease the use of tobacco products by making smokers aware of the potential health risks they faced.

By the beginning of the 1960's, the rate of cigarette consumption among all Americans over eighteen years of age had hit its peak. In 1963, the average American smoked 4,345 cigarettes. At about this time, an increase in the number of cases of several serious diseases, most particularly lung cancer, was reported by statisticians. In March, 1962, Senator Maurine B. Neuberger (D-Oreg.) introduced legislation calling for the formation of a presidential commission to study the relationship between smoking and health. In June of that year, U.S. Surgeon General Luther L. Terry announced the formation of a group of experts who would study the existing scientific literature to determine whether a link did, in fact, exist between tobacco and various health measures. In fairness to those who supported smoking, one-half of the panel did smoke, and the Tobacco Institute, the industry's umbrella organization, was allowed to veto any committee members it found objectionable.

In spite of the balance of the committee, its conclusions were unanimous and striking. In a two-volume report that was released on a Saturday (when the stock markets were closed, so that the potential for a negative reaction against the stocks of the tobacco companies would be limited), the Surgeon General's Advisory Committee concluded that cigarette smoking constituted a health hazard of proportions significant enough to warrant direct governmental action. The reaction to the report by various groups reflected their varied attitudes toward smoking in general. The Tobacco Institute disputed the existence of any causal link between smoking and cancer, while the American Cancer Society declared that the reduction of cigarette smoking represented the greatest possibility for the prevention of cancer, other serious illnesses, and premature death. In the House of Representatives, thirty-one separate bills were introduced in response to the report. Most of them called for further study of the supposed link between smoking and ill-health.

While Congress considered its next step, the Federal Trade Commission (FTC) prepared new regulations and scheduled public hearings on the proposal to require all cigarette packages to carry a specific health warning. By January, 1965, the FTC had two separate warnings under consideration: "CAUTION: CIGARETTE SMOKING IS A HEALTH HAZARD: The Surgeon General's Advisory Committee on Smoking and Health has found that cigarette smoking contributes substantially to mortality from certain specific diseases and to the overall death rate," and a more direct one, "CAUTION: cigarette smoking is dangerous to health. It may cause death from cancer and other diseases."

Prior to the announcement of the FTC's plan to require the warning labels, the tobacco industry prepared its own strategy to minimize the negative impact of any governmental action. The most important aspect of the plan was the employment of Earle C. Clements as a registered lobbyist on behalf of the industry. In addition to all of his contacts as a former Senate majority whip in the late 1950's, Clements had been one of Lyndon Johnson's most trusted aides while both served in the Senate. Further, Clements' daughter, Bess Abell, was then employed as the social secretary of "Lady Bird" Johnson, the president's wife. Clements developed the successful strategy that the tobacco interests pursued to limit the damage to their business. Realizing that a warning label was unavoidable, Clements urged the corporate leaders of the six major cigarette manufacturers to ask Congress for legislation requiring labels, rather than allow the FTC to control the issue. Clements' logic rested on the knowledge that the tobacco interests could lobby for the least intrusive labeling requirements possible by dealing with an elected body, Congress, rather than an appointed one, the FTC.

Clements' plans directly conflicted with the proposals of Senator Neuberger, whose husband had died of cancer. A devoted opponent of smoking, she had carried on her husband's crusade against the tobacco companies after his death, when she was elected to fill his unexpired Senate term. She proposed a strict warning on cigarette package labels in addition to a requirement that all cigarette advertising carry the

health warning. She also suggested barring advertising of cigarettes and other tobacco products from radio and television.

The battle between these two positions was fought principally in the Senate Commerce Committee, where Warren Magnuson worked to achieve the most fair bill
possible. Although not as devoted to the antismoking cause as Maurine Neuberger,
Magnuson was committed to reducing the number of tobacco-related deaths in the
United States. The Commerce Committee first debated the possibility of a total ban
on the advertisement of cigarettes and other tobacco-related products. After a long
fight, the Senate committee settled on a four-year moratorium on any actions by the
FTC to ban advertising. Although this disappointed many health advocates, the tobacco interests had been pushing hard for a moratorium in perpetuity. The Commerce
Committee then turned its attention to the wording, size, and other specific requirements for the package warning. After much debate, the compromise called for a
statement that read, "CAUTION: Cigarette Smoking may be Hazardous to Your Health."

After minimal debate, the full Senate approved the bill by a vote of seventy-two to
five in July, 1965. Attention then turned to the White House and the question of how
President Johnson would respond to the bill. A former three-pack-a-day smoker before a severe heart attack forced him to give up the practice, Johnson understood the
hazards of smoking as well as the difficulty many experienced when they tried to
quit the habit. Although there was a small movement within his administration to
veto the bill because the warning was not as explicit as it could have been, Johnson
signed Senate Bill 559 into law on July 27, 1965. As Public Law 89-92, it took effect
on January 1, 1966.

Impact of Event

The consequences of the first cigarette labeling law were many and far-reaching.
On one hand, the bill represented another in a long string of victories for the tobacco
companies. The warning on the packages was significantly less severe than it could
have been, given the findings in the Surgeon General's Advisory Committee report.
A complete medical consensus did not exist, however, on the connection between
smoking and ill-health. The prestigious American Medical Association did not endorse the conclusions of the original report, and many members of Congress used
that lack of an endorsement to bolster their calls for further study of the problem.

Over time, the FTC's and Maurine Neuberger's original recommendations became law. One of the clauses of PL 89-92, included as a result of the Senate Commerce Committee's deliberations, was the requirement that both the FTC and the
Department of Health, Education, and Welfare submit annual reports to Congress
evaluating the effectiveness of the law and the current nature of cigarette advertising.
These reports discussed current themes in print, radio, and television ads such as
brand loyalty and never failed to mention that any negative aspects of smoking or
tobacco addiction were absent from the ads.

As the four-year moratorium on action against cigarette advertising passed, the
FTC and then Congress held hearings on tougher warning labels, the inclusion of

these new warnings in all print advertising, and a total ban on any radio or television advertising. On April 1, 1970, President Richard M. Nixon signed the Public Health Cigarette Smoking Act of 1969, which barred television and radio ads for cigarettes. Cigarette advertising appeared in the electronic media for the final time on January 1, 1971.

Perhaps the most important aspect of PL 89-92 was that its evolution marked the first time that cigarette manufacturers recognized that a relationship between smoking and ill-health did exist. In spite of its protests to the contrary, the Tobacco Institute's lobbying for the passage of this bill signified an acceptance of the validity of the growing medical evidence documenting the link. As time has passed, the bulk of this evidence has increased. Each time the surgeon general releases a report examining the relationship between smoking and health, the conclusion becomes less ambiguous. These later reports have become the basis for more recent legislation restricting smoking in public facilities and have lent considerable support to the nonsmokers' rights and antismoking movements in the United States and elsewhere.

Bibliography

Diehl, Harold S. *Tobacco and Your Health: The Smoking Controversy.* New York: McGraw-Hill, 1969. Written during the height of the early battles, this book offers a convincing, if occasionally polemical, examination of smoking as a public policy question. A fine choice for the general reader. Contains a glossary, an index, and five appendices.

Drew, Elizabeth B. "The Quiet Victory of the Cigarette Lobby: How It Found the Best Filter Yet—Congress." *Atlantic Monthly* 216 (September, 1965): 75-79. A contemporary account of the wrangling in Congress, this article offers readers both a strong understanding of the compromises involved in the law's passage and an evaluation of the process used to achieve it. An outstanding selection. Offers no reference features.

Patterson, James T. "Smoking and Cancer." In *The Dread Disease: Cancer and Modern American Culture.* Cambridge: Harvard University Press, 1987. Located in a scholarly study of cancer in American society, this chapter is both freestanding and extremely engaging. While discussing the broad relationship between cancer and tobacco, the chapter thoroughly examines the cigarette advertising question. The volume contains a thorough index and references.

Price, David E. "The Commerce Committee in Action." In *Who Makes the Laws? Creativity and Power in Senate Committees.* Cambridge, Mass.: Schenkman, 1972. An examination of the legislative division of labor between the president and Congress in 1965-1966, an especially active period for domestic legislation in America. A separate twelve-page section addresses the Cigarette Labeling Act specifically. A good choice for readers with a strong desire to understand the broader political forces at work at this time. Contains a comprehensive index and thorough annotations.

Troyer, Ronald J., and Gerald E. Markle. *Cigarettes: The Battle over Smoking.* New

Brunswick, N.J.: Rutgers University Press, 1983. A social monograph, this book focuses on the cultural evolution of the smoking habit, specifically its progress from immorality to proof of social sophistication to a deviant behavior. Considerable attention is devoted to the powerful groups, with vested interests, that attempted to destigmatize smoking. Although highly technical in some spots, this is a valuable resource. Complete annotations and index.

E. A. Reed

Cross-References

The Pure Food and Drug Act and Meat Inspection Act Become Law (1906), p. 64; The World Health Organization Proclaims Health as a Basic Right (1946), p. 678; Cigarette Advertising Is Banned from American Television and Radio (1970), p. 1527; WHO Sets a Goal of Health for All by the Year 2000 (1977), p. 1893; An International Health Conference Adopts the Declaration of Alma-Ata (1978), p. 1998; A. H. Robins Must Compensate Women Injured by the Dalkon Shield (1987), p. 2342; Canada Passes the Tobacco Products Control Act (1988), p. 2376; A Jury Awards Monetary Damages to the Estate of a Smoker (1988), p. 2381; The U.S. Surgeon General Reports on Tobacco and Health (1989), p. 2455.

MIRANDA V. ARIZONA REQUIRES POLICE TO TELL ARRESTED PEOPLE THEIR RIGHTS

Category of event: Accused persons' rights
Time: June 13, 1966
Locale: United States Supreme Court, Washington, D.C.

The U.S. Supreme Court decided in Miranda v. Arizona *that arrested persons must be informed of their rights to remain silent and to counsel before police interrogation may begin*

Principal personages:

EARL WARREN (1891-1974), the chief justice of the United States from 1953 to 1969 and author of the Court's opinion

JOHN MARSHALL HARLAN (1899-1971), the author of the principal dissenting opinion in *Miranda v. Arizona*

BYRON WHITE (1917-   ), the author of a dissenting opinion in *Miranda v. Arizona*

TOM C. CLARK (1899-1977), the author of a separate dissenting opinion

ERNESTO MIRANDA (1940-1976), an accused rapist and kidnapper, the defendant in the case

Summary of Event

Miranda v. Arizona was one of a series of landmark Supreme Court cases of the mid-1960's establishing new guarantees of procedural fairness for defendants in criminal cases. The Court's decision in *Miranda* sprang from two different lines of precedents under the Fourteenth Amendment.

One of these lines was the right-to-counsel cases: *Powell v. Alabama* (1932), in which the Court held that indigent defendants had to be afforded counsel in capital cases; *Gideon v. Wainwright* (1963), which extended the right to counsel for indigent defendants to all felony cases; and *Escobedo v. Illinois* (1964), in which the Court held that a confession obtained from a defendant who had asked for and been denied permission to speak to an attorney was inadmissible. By 1964, the right to counsel had expanded to include mandatory representation for indigents at trial in all felonies and also gave potential defendants the right to representation during questioning while in custody if they requested it.

The second line of cases culminated with *Malloy v. Hogan* (1964), in which the Court had held that the privilege against self-incrimination applied to the states. Moreover, prior to the *Miranda* case, a long series of Supreme Court decisions had established that neither physical coercion nor certain forms of psychological coercion could be used by police to obtain confessions from accused persons. Thus, on the eve of *Miranda*, constitutional rules barred the admission of confessions which had been coerced through either physical or psychological pressures or which had been obtained from an in-custody defendant who had requested the attendance of an attorney. By then it was also clear that the entire body of the Fifth Amendment's self-incrimination clause was to be applied to the states through the due process clause of the Fourteenth Amendment. Like the other cases mentioned, *Miranda* rests on the due process clause of the Fourteenth Amendment, which requires that criminal procedure in state courts be fundamentally fair.

Ernesto Miranda's case involved a confession to rape and kidnapping which was elicited from him in a police interrogation room after his arrest. In addition to his oral admissions to the investigating officers, Miranda wrote out by hand a short statement, which he signed. The questioning, by two Phoenix detectives, involved neither physical nor psychological coercion as these had been defined in the earlier cases. The transcript of Miranda's interview showed that he answered the officers' questions freely, and that after an initial denial, he readily admitted abducting the victim and raping her. The entire interrogation and the preparation of Miranda's written statement took less than two hours. At trial, Miranda's oral admissions and his written statement were admitted into evidence over his objection; the victim testified against him as well. The jury found Miranda guilty of rape in the first degree and kidnapping, and he was sentenced to prison for a term of twenty to thirty years. He appealed to the Supreme Court of Arizona. After losing in that court, he appealed to the United States Supreme Court, which decided to hear the case in 1965. *Miranda* and three companion cases were argued February 28-March 2, 1966. On June 13, 1966, the Court decided in Miranda's favor by a 5-4 vote.

Chief Justice Earl Warren wrote for the majority, which consisted additionally of Justices Hugo Black, William O. Douglas, William J. Brennan, Jr., and Abe Fortas. Warren's opinion focused on the coercive elements present in any custodial interrogation. He argued that an accused person is isolated from friends, family, and his or her attorney and is often fearful of the police. The police, as contemporary textbooks on interrogation showed, were schooled in a variety of tricks and techniques which are designed to overbear the will of an arrested person and induce confession. These techniques, according to Chief Justice Warren's opinion, skirt the edge of improper physical or psychological coercion and demonstrate that custodial interrogation is inherently coercive. Consequently, an accused person does not have a free opportunity to use the Fifth Amendment right not to incriminate himself or herself or the Sixth Amendment right to counsel. Accordingly, the Court held that before any custodial interrogation can take place, an arrested person must be given a fourfold warning—what has become known as the "Miranda warning." Under this rule, a suspect in custody has to be informed of the right to remain silent, of the potential use of his or her words in evidence against him or her, of the right to consult an attorney before questioning, and of the right to an assigned attorney if he or she is indigent. Any statement elicited by the authorities is inadmissible at trial unless the defendant has been given the warning and has freely and knowingly waived these rights. Moreover, if during questioning the defendant has asked at any point that interrogation cease or that he or she be allowed to consult an attorney, any subsequent statements obtained by the police are also inadmissible.

Justice John Marshall Harlan's dissenting opinion in this case argued that the Court was searching for a kind of "utopian" voluntariness. The dissenters believed that Miranda's statement had been voluntarily given. No physical brutality or discomfort had been visited upon him, nor did the investigating officers use any special psychological tricks or deceptions. The record showed that Miranda freely gave a statement about the crimes of which he was accused. By the standards of 1963, the Phoenix police had acted properly. Harlan argued that the admissibility of Miranda's confession was supported by precedent; moreover, in Miranda's brief interrogation, there was "a legitimate purpose, no perceptible unfairness, and certainly little risk of injustice." Justices Byron White and Potter Stewart adhered to Harlan's opinion; Justice Tom Clark submitted a separate dissenting opinion.

The immediate result of *Miranda v. Arizona* was to reverse Miranda's conviction for kidnapping and rape. The Arizona authorities persevered in the prosecution, and in 1969, at his second trial, Miranda was again convicted. Although the confession was not introduced against him this time, the victim's testimony alone was enough to persuade the jury of his guilt. In consequence of this conviction he served a prison term from which he was paroled in 1972.

Ernesto Miranda was killed in a barroom fight in 1976; ironically, the man who stabbed him to death was given the "Miranda warning" when arrested.

Impact of Event

The larger consequence of this controversial case was to require police officers all over the United States to provide themselves with "Miranda cards" which embodied the warning required by the Supreme Court. Once a person has been detained, no questioning may take place unless the detainee has been given the warning and has waived the rights to silence and to consult counsel before responding to questions. If a detainee does request the assistance of an attorney, interrogation must stop until he or she has had the opportunity to consult with a lawyer. Treatment of arrested persons changed significantly after *Miranda v. Arizona*. Because the Court's decision placed on the state the burden of demonstrating knowing and voluntary waiver of the right to silence, police must persuade the defendant to agree if they wish to elicit a statement. The atmosphere in which an arrested person finds himself or herself in the crucial moments after arrest has changed substantially as a result of the Court's decision.

There has been much discussion of the impact of this rule on American law enforcement. In most criminal cases, the defendant's words constitute a significant part of the case against him or her. Police and prosecutors feared that the Court's holding in *Miranda* would cripple their efforts; they argued that the new rule would make it impossible for investigators to get the kinds of inculpatory statements necessary to obtain criminal convictions. Once a defendant had consulted counsel, they believed, no further statements of any kind would be forthcoming, since any competent lawyer would immediately urge silence on the client.

Despite these fears, which were shared by large portions of the public, *Miranda* does not seem to have crippled the work of the police and criminal courts. There have been a number of empirical studies of the behavior of arrested persons. Most criminal defendants do give statements—often incriminating statements—even after receiving the Miranda warning. Moreover, there have been as many successful prosecutions in relation to the number of arrests after the *Miranda* case as before.

Miranda also accomplished something else very important to the protection of the rights of arrested persons. There are signs that since *Miranda* the incidence of brutal or abusive police practices has diminished. Most observers of law enforcement practices in the United States believe police brutality is much less common than before this case. One strong indication is the rarity of claims of coerced confession in trials where the "coercion" involves police practices more abusive than violations of the Miranda rule itself. In the largest sense this is the real significance of *Miranda*: By forcing the police to attend to a rigid technical requirement which respects the defendant's rights, the opportunity for abusive behavior is lessened. Moreover, the increased professionalism of police that has resulted from *Miranda* and the other cases of the 1960's has benefited both police and prosecutors in preparing good cases. In this light, *Miranda* represents an important step toward actualizing the rights of accused persons regardless of whether it achieves Chief Justice Warren's stated aim, which was "to assure that the individual's right to choose between silence and speech remains unfettered throughout the interrogation process."

Bibliography

Baker, Liva. *Miranda: The Crime, the Law, and the Politics.* New York: Atheneum, 1983. Excellent essays about the *Miranda* case, blending the legal and political issues raised.

Hook, Sidney. *Common Sense and the Fifth Amendment.* New York: Criterion, 1959. Argument *against* the privilege against self-incrimination. Hook argues that one can correctly infer guilt from a defendant's silence most of the time. Written in the context of the red scare of the 1950's.

Israel, Jerold, and Wayne LaFave. *Criminal Procedure.* 3d ed. St. Paul, Minn.: West Publishing, 1980. Good discussion of the rules for police interrogation and a summary of empirical evidence regarding the efficacy of the Miranda rule in giving potential defendants a free choice whether or not to speak.

Jacobs, Robert. "*Miranda*: The Right to Silence." *Trial* 11 (March/April, 1975): 69-76. An analysis and critique of the logic underlying the Court's decision in *Miranda* as well as a discussion of the psychology of confession.

Kamisar, Yale. *Police Interrogation and Confessions: Essays in Law and Policy.* Ann Arbor: University of Michigan Press, 1980. Kamisar, a professor of law, presents this series of essays which emphasize the actualities of police questioning.

Levy, Leonard. *Origins of the Fifth Amendment: The Right Against Self-Incrimination.* New York: Oxford University Press, 1968. Discussion of the historical purposes and original meaning of the Fifth Amendment.

Lewis, Anthony. *Gideon's Trumpet*. New York: Random House, 1964. A study of the case of Clarence Earl Gideon, whose handwritten appeal to the Supreme Court resulted in the decision entitling all indigent defendants to assigned counsel. This book is particularly strong on Supreme Court procedure and on the issues raised by Gideon's appeal.

Medalie, Richard, Leonard Zeitz, and Paul Alexander. "Custodial Interrogation in Our Nation's Capital: The Attempt to Implement *Miranda*." *Michigan Law Review* 66 (1968): 1347. Empirical study of interrogations in Washington, D.C., subsequent to the Court's decision in *Miranda*.

Mendelson, Wallace. *The American Constitution and Civil Liberties*. Homewood, Ill.: Dorsey Press, 1981. This text has a strong chapter on constitutional theory and practice as applied to criminal procedure.

United States. Supreme Court. "*Miranda v. Arizona*." *United States Reports* 384 (1966): 436. Any study of this landmark case begins with the arguments made by the justices of the Supreme Court of the United States. Chief Justice Warren's opinion for the majority and John Marshall Harlan's dissent are both cogent and powerful.

Robert Jacobs

Cross-References

The American Civil Liberties Union Is Founded (1920), p. 327; *Gideon v. Wainwright* Establishes Defendants' Right to an Attorney (1963), p. 1182; The Supreme Court Extends Protection Against Double Jeopardy (1969), p. 1474; The United Nations Issues a Conduct Code for Law Enforcement Officials (1979), p. 2040; Race Riot Breaks Out in Miami, Protesting Police Brutality (1980), p. 2101.

THE BLACK PANTHER PARTY IS ORGANIZED

Category of event: Racial and ethnic rights
Time: October 15, 1966
Locale: Oakland, California

Originally founded to protect the African-American community from police brutality, the Black Panthers evolved into a communist group espousing violence to achieve social change

Principal personages:
  STOKELY CARMICHAEL (1941-   ), the chairman of the Student Non-
    violent Coordinating Committee
  MALCOLM X (1925-1965), a leading spokesman for the Black Muslims
  HUEY P. NEWTON (1942-1989), the cofounder and minister of defense for
    the Black Panther Party
  BOBBY SEALE (1936-   ), the cofounder and chairman of the Black
    Panther Party

Summary of Event

The Black Panther movement was born out of frustration. In the 1950's and 1960's, poor urban blacks led a treadmill existence in the United States. Without adequate education, they found it almost impossible to secure employment. Because the primary concern of many was surviving from one day to the next, most were not motivated or not able to get an education. Many became disillusioned with the reforms of Lyndon Johnson's "Great Society," because few of the benefits filtered down to their level. In the mid-1960's, the black protest movement became fragmented because of the leaders' conflicting ideologies. Many poor urban blacks believed they were being denied the advantages of being Americans.

The seething discontent that was fostered in the ghettos made retaliatory violence appear to be the only option. This course of action was first espoused in the 1930's by the Black Muslims, who encouraged blacks to end white domination by opposing the "slavemasters." In the early 1960's, small groups of Marxist-nationalists began to appear, the most notorious of which was the Revolutionary Action Movement (RAM) founded by Robert F. Williams. Even though these groups existed primarily on the fringes of the black protest movement, their philosophy was increasingly embraced by the more radical members of nonviolent organizations such as the Student Nonviolent Coordinating Committee (SNCC). The revolutionary dogma of radical leaders such as H. Rap Brown and Stokely Carmichael received considerable media coverage and appealed to the underprivileged sectors of society. Even though the riots of 1964 and 1965 cannot be linked directly to the influence of these individuals and groups, it became clear that more and more African Americans were angered by the disparity that existed between the expectations that had been raised by the Civil Rights movement and the day-to-day reality of being poor and black in the United States.

The growth of the Black Power movement and the decline of the Congress of Racial Equality (CORE) and the SNCC also spurred the emergence of the Black Panther Party. Black power, which was always more of a mood than a program, was precipitated by the shooting of James Meredith, a civil rights leader who had earlier been the first black student at the University of Mississippi, during the June, 1966, freedom march through Mississippi. Stokely Carmichael resumed the march and electrified the crowd with his cries of "Black Power." He told the crowd that the only way for blacks to become truly free was to take over. In the subsequent months, the Black Power movement not only stressed racial unity but also promoted militant violence, including the justification of guerrilla warfare, armed rebellion, and looting and arson in ghetto riots.

The Black Power movement was given a boost by the failure of CORE and the SNCC to make fundamental changes in the life of the masses. Instead of urging integration, as these weakened organizations had done, the proponents of black power favored black nationalism, a separatist philosophy that was eventually adopted by such Marxist-oriented revolutionary movements as the Black Panthers.

The leaders of the Black Panthers, like most revolutionaries, were poor. Both Huey Newton and Bobby Seale attended Merritt College on the fringes of the Oakland ghetto. At the time, Merritt was an incubator of black nationalism, and Newton and Seale often went to coffeehouses to talk about black revolution. While they were at Merritt, they joined the Afro-American Association but dropped out because they believed that it offered only cultural nationalism. After leaving Merritt, Newton considered becoming a Black Muslim but was put off by Malcolm X's religious beliefs. Newton's political beliefs solidified after he was sentenced to the county jail for one year on an assault-with-a-deadly-weapon conviction. The prison experience made Newton more militant toward the white world.

Once he was released from jail, Newton immediately reconciled himself with Seale and discussed with him the need for a revolutionary black party that would represent the ghetto youth who had no voice in the other civil rights groups. Newton and Seale viewed African Americans as a colonial people and believed that they needed to arm themselves to free themselves from the colonial power that was oppressing them. They also wanted weapons because the enforcers of the laws of white society, the police, were armed.

Newton and Seale were shocked into action by San Francisco's Hunters Point riot in the summer of 1966. Dismayed by the disorganized attempts of black youths to fight the police, Newton and Seale arrived at the conclusion that a new strategy was needed. They began talking to black youths after the riots to hear suggestions regarding what was needed. The best way to fight the police, they decided, was to revive the Black Panthers, an abortive party that had been sponsored by SNCC in Lowndes County, Alabama, in an effort to give control of the central cities to blacks.

On October 15, 1966, Seale met with Newton at a poverty center in North Oakland to write the platform for the Black Panthers. The ten-point program that came out of the meeting was articulated by Newton with the help of Seale, who made suggestions. The program, couched in class-conscious revolutionary rhetoric, included the following points. The program asked for freedom and the power to determine the destiny of the black community; full employment for black people; an end to the "robbery by the capitalists" of the black community; decent housing, fit for shelter of human beings; education for black people that would expose the true nature of "decadent American society" and teach a true history of African Americans and their role in present-day society; exemption of African Americans from military service; an immediate end to police brutality and murder of black people; freedom for all black men held in federal, state, county, and city prisons and jails; trials of black people accused of crimes by juries of their peer group or people from their black communities; and land, bread, housing, education, clothing, justice, and peace. As part of the final points, the program asked for a United Nations-supervised plebiscite to be held throughout the "black colony" in which only "black colonial subjects" would be allowed to participate, for the purpose of determining the will of black people as to their national destiny. To enforce their platform, Newton and Seale encouraged the use of guns, for both self-defense and retaliation. They believed that the greatest weapon that the police had was fear, and this fear could be removed if blacks had guns.

Newton and Seale then set about building their movement upon the grim reality of police brutality. They began recruiting members by forming "defense patrols." When a police car ventured into a ghetto, a car containing four Panthers armed with shotguns would follow close behind. The Panthers would observe the police if a black person was questioned and would try to raise bail if the person was arrested. After members were recruited, they were instructed in those points of law concerning search and seizure, the right to bear arms, and arrest procedure. Recruits were also introduced to the works of Malcolm X, Frantz Fanon, W. E. B. Du Bois, Marcus Garvey, and Mao Tse-tung. This indoctrination was geared to remind the recruits that their organization had a larger goal beyond that of confronting the police with equal force. The ultimate goal of the Black Panthers in 1966 was to change society by uniting blacks against their white oppressors.

Impact of Event

The Black Panthers' belief in arming the people in the ghettos inevitably led to highly publicized confrontations with police. In early May, 1967, a group of eighteen armed Black Panthers descended on Sacramento, read a statement of protest in the state capitol, and left. After leaving the capitol, they were arrested at a gas station for disrupting the state legislature and for conspiracy to disrupt the legislature. In a more violent episode in Chicago, a fourteen-man police detail, armed with sidearms, shotguns, and a machine gun, knocked on the door of the apartment of Fred Hampton, the Black Panther chief in Illinois, in the early morning hours of December 4, 1969. A few minutes later, Fred Hampton and another Black Panther, Mark

Clark, were dead, and four more Panthers were taken to the hospital with multiple gunshot wounds. By the end of the year, the Black Panthers claimed that twenty-eight of their members had been killed by police in New York and Chicago.

The trials that resulted from some of these confrontations demonstrated that the American legal system did not really know how to deal with this new breed of black revolutionaries. For example, the trial of thirteen Black Panthers in New York City in 1971 on bombing and conspiracy charges, the longest trial in the history of the state's criminal courts, resulted in the acquittal of all the defendants in May, 1971, because the prosecution did not have a sound case. In a separate trial in New Haven, Connecticut, a month later, Bobby Seale and Panther organizer Ericka Huggins were released because the jury could not reach a verdict. Both these trials revealed how difficult it was to convict a person on conspiracy charges. To prove conspiracy, pros-ecutors had to rely on the testimony of infiltrators and turncoats, evidence that most juries believed was unreliable. In addition, the cost of prosecuting the Panthers even-tually proved to be prohibitive. The New Haven trial, for example, cost $1.5 million. Almost the only thing that trials such as these accomplished was to raise doubts about the viability of the judicial system as a social arbiter.

Ironically, the Black Panthers' goal of uniting the black community was achieved, if only to a small extent, through their persecution by police and the resulting trials. The shooting of Fred Hampton, for example, resulted in the creation of a twenty-five-member independent commission composed of members of the National Asso-ciation for the Advancement of Colored People, the Urban League, the Conference of Black Elected Officials, the Southern Christian Leadership Conference, and the American Civil Liberties Union. For the first time in years, the entire black public in Chicago was aroused and united because of its outrage at the shooting. A similar phenomenon had occurred a year earlier in Oakland after the conviction of Huey Newton on murder charges. In the end, the "David and Goliath" image that the Black Panthers' confrontations created in the minds of the public gave them a larger boost than any of their self-serving strategies.

Bibliography

Baruch, Ruth-Marion, and Pirkle Jones. *The Vanguard: A Photograph Essay on the Black Panthers.* Boston: Beacon Press, 1970. This biased history of the first four years of the Black Panther Party is useful primarily because of the illustrations, which reveal the human side behind the Panthers' grim exterior. Although the listing of the high points of the growth of the movement is sketchy, the author does include the rules of the party as well as its ten-point platform.

Chevigny, Paul. *Cops and Rebels: A Study of Provocation.* New York: Pantheon Books, 1972. Chevigny recounts the evolution of four young men—Alfred Cain, Jr., Ri-cardo De Leon, Wilbert Thomas, and Jerome West—into Black Panthers. Written by the lawyer who defended them in court, this book illustrates how politics and justice were often confused during the turbulent 1960's.

Churchill, Ward, and Jim Vander Wall. *Agents of Repression: The FBI's Secret Wars*

Against the Black Panther Party and the American Indian Movement. Boston: South End Press, 1988. The first one hundred pages of Ward and Wall's book is a revealing look at the attempts of the Federal Bureau of Investigation (FBI) to infiltrate and destroy the Black Panthers through its counterintelligence programs. The authors, however, tend to place too much blame on the FBI for the disintegration of the Black Panthers.

Meier, August, and Elliott Rudwick, eds. *Black Protest in the Sixties.* Chicago: Quadrangle Books, 1970. Most of the articles included in this volume create a sense of immediacy because they were written during the 1960's. Meier's introduction explains the complex social setting that produced the Black Panthers. The book also contains Sol Stern's excellent "The Call of the Black Panthers," which originally appeared in *The New York Times Magazine.*

Seale, Bobby. *Seize the Time.* New York: Random House, 1970. Seale's book, written from his San Francisco County Jail cell is a fascinating firsthand account of the growth of the Black Panthers. The book suffers, though, from Seale's dated slang and his tendency to pontificate.

Shakur, Assata. *Assata: An Autobiography.* Westport, Conn.: Lawrence Hill, 1987. Shakur's book-length effort to explain why she joined the Black Panthers is a vivid account of the racism that permeated America in the first half of the twentieth century. The book is less convincing in its claim that Shakur's persecution and shooting by the police in 1973 is typical of the way the U.S. government has responded historically to individuals that it sees as political threats.

Alan Brown

Cross-References

The Congress of Racial Equality Forms (1942), p. 601; CORE Stages a Sit-in in Chicago to Protest Segregation (1943), p. 618; Race Riots Erupt in Detroit and Harlem (1943), p. 635; Parks Is Arrested for Refusing to Sit in the Back of the Bus (1955), p. 947; The SCLC Forms to Link Civil Rights Groups (1957), p. 974; Greensboro Sit-ins Launch a New Stage in the Civil Rights Movement (1960), p. 1056; Meredith's Enrollment Integrates the University of Mississippi (1962), p. 1167; Civil Rights Protesters Attract International Attention (1963), p. 1188; African Americans Riot in Watts (1965), p. 1301; Race Rioting Erupts in Detroit (1967), p. 1376.

THE U.N. COVENANT ON CIVIL AND POLITICAL RIGHTS IS ADOPTED

Category of event: Civil rights
Time: December 16, 1966
Locale: United Nations, New York City

When the U.N. General Assembly adopted the Covenant on Civil and Political Rights, a significant milestone was reached in providing international guarantees for human rights

Principal personages:
> ELEANOR ROOSEVELT (1884-1962), the chair of the U.N. Human Rights Commission
> RENÉ CASSIN (1887-1976), a member of the U.N. Human Rights Commission from 1946 to 1972
> CHARLES H. MALIK (1906-1987), a member of the U.N. Human Rights Commission from 1947 to 1954

Summary of Event

The unanimous adoption of the International Covenant on Civil and Political Rights by the U.N. General Assembly on December 16, 1966, represented a significant step toward the creation of a world in which human rights are protected and guaranteed by governments. The covenant itself does not guarantee that human rights will be promoted and preserved, but it did break new ground in encouraging governments to respect such rights. It represented an evolutionary rather than a revolutionary improvement over preexisting mechanisms for the promotion of human rights at the global level. Although many believed that the covenant did not go far enough, in actuality it went about as far as it could in promoting human rights without alienating the governments whose cooperation was essential.

Nearly two decades of discussion and debate about the role of human rights in a system of sovereign states preceded the actual adoption of the covenant. The U.N. Charter of 1945 specifically identified the promotion of human rights and fundamental freedoms as a principal purpose of the United Nations. This emphasis on human rights rested on well-established notions of natural rights developed during the eighteenth century Enlightenment, on the growth of legal remedies for aliens and minorities in the nineteenth century, and on the almost universal revulsion in the twentieth century toward the crimes committed by governments during World War II against innocent and helpless populations. The U.N. Charter represented an effort to lay groundwork for a more humane future in which respect for human rights would characterize global society. The charter contained a specific provision for the creation of a Human Rights Commission by the Economic and Social Council (ECOSOC).

Together, ECOSOC and the commission were charged with the task of proposing ways to encourage greater respect for human rights. In the U.N. Charter, governments obligated themselves to work separately and jointly with the United Nations to attain this end.

By January of 1947, the Human Rights Commission, including such notable members as René Cassin, Charles H. Malik, and Eleanor Roosevelt, held its first session in New York. Discussion ensued about how best to proceed with the creation of a universal bill of human rights. These discussions resulted in a twofold strategy that involved the promulgation of a nonbinding Universal Declaration of Human Rights, which was approved by the General Assembly in 1948, and the negotiation of two legally binding covenants, one on civil and political rights and the other on economic and social rights. Predictably, negotiations on the covenants took far longer to conclude than did those on the Universal Declaration of Human Rights.

Even though the Universal Declaration was more a statement of moral aspiration than a legally binding document, it did enumerate the panoply of rights individuals should, in principle, enjoy. The fact that many governments later incorporated provisions of the declaration into their constitutional and legal systems advanced the cause of human rights and paved the way for a binding covenant on civil and political rights.

Eighteen years of discussion and debate finally resulted in the adoption of the international covenants. These two conventions were drafted by the Human Rights Commission in consultation with national governments, the U.N. General Assembly, ECOSOC, and various nongovernmental organizations. The Human Rights Commission, in 1954, submitted drafts of the Covenants to the General Assembly for its further consideration. More than a decade of deliberation on the drafts then ensued in the General Assembly's Third Committee for Social, Humanitarian, and Cultural Affairs. Debate centered on a number of controversial issues, including such questions as which rights should be included under the rubric of civil and political rights or that of economic and social rights, whether governments could exclude themselves from the provisions of either covenant, and whether, in times of exigency, governments could ignore their obligations under the covenants.

By far the most significant question concerned the type of enforcement measures to be adopted to ensure that governments abided by their commitment to observe human rights. Some wanted effective enforcement measures included in the covenants. Others opposed this, believing that few governments would consent to direct infringements on their sovereignty. Some proposed that a separate optional protocol be negotiated which would include more significant enforcement mechanisms, including the right of individual appeals. Others believed that governments should be required only to submit periodic reports on the progress they made in implementing the covenants. Still others believed that only appeals by governments against the human rights behavior of other governments should be permitted, not individual appeals.

It was decided that the Covenant on Civil and Political Rights (hereafter, the covenant) would include a provision requiring governments to make periodic reports to a Human Rights Committee regarding measures adopted by the governments to further attainment of the rights enumerated in the covenant. A provision made it possible for governments to bring complaints against each other for human rights violations, provided that both states agreed to recognize the competence of the Human Rights Committee to hear such complaints. Provisions for conciliation of state-to-state complaints were also included in the covenant. These enforcement mechanisms did not compromise state sovereignty to any significant extent. Governments remained free not to recognize the Human Rights Committee's competence to hear state-to-state complaints. In addition, compliance of a state with human rights goals was in no way guaranteed by that state's report to the Human Rights Committee.

Stronger enforcement provisions were contained in a separate optional protocol, which states could choose to ratify if they desired to submit to more extensive external scrutiny and investigation. The optional protocol provided that individuals claiming to be victims of a violation, by a state party to the covenant, of any rights enumerated in the covenant, may, after exhausting all locally available legal remedies, alert the Human Rights Committee to the violation. Such violations are subject to further investigation and to an eventual report of findings by the committee.

The General Assembly, by adopting the covenant in 1966, recognized the sensitivity of states to infringements on their sovereignty but also provided measures which could be endorsed voluntarily to publicize human rights violations, and presumably to deter their frequency. The covenant further underscored the duty of contracting parties to protect the right to life and to eliminate torture, inhuman punishment, and slavery. No person, it held, should be imprisoned because of an inability to fulfill a contractual obligation, be judged guilty of crimes in an *ex post facto* situation, or be denied the right to recognition everywhere as a person before the law. Everyone, the covenant asserted, has a right to freedoms of thought, conscience, and religion. All of the provisions just enumerated were considered exempt from state derogation; that is, even during times of national emergency, a state was obligated to recognize the covenant's rights and principles.

Other provisions of the covenant could be qualified in time of national emergency. These included such areas as rights to privacy, liberty, and security of person; separation of juvenile from adult offenders when incarceration is necessary; and freedoms of expression, peaceable assembly, association, and political activity. States availing themselves of derogation from standard behavior in relation to these rights were required to give notice and to explain the circumstances necessitating the derogation.

Impact of Event

The immediate effects of the adoption of the covenant were not particularly impressive. A decade passed before the thirty-five ratifications that were necessary for the covenant to enter into force were deposited with the U.N. secretary-general. The covenant and the optional protocol both entered into force in March of 1976, the protocol having been ratified by ten states. The sluggishness of governmental response can be attributed to concerns about how the covenant and protocol might impinge on domestic policy discretion, especially in view of the requirement that the domestic legislation of parties to the covenant should be brought into compliance with the covenant's provisions. Many governments preferred to review their domestic legislative and constitutional situations prior to ratification to ensure that problems of noncompliance would not arise.

Once the covenant took force, the pace of ratifications increased. By 1980, the number of ratifications had nearly doubled to sixty-five. By the same year, twenty-five states had ratified the optional protocol. As of March, 1991, ninety-five countries had ratified the covenant and fifty-two had ratified the protocol. In addition, more than half of the parties to the covenant had accepted the Human Rights Committee's competence to accept state-to-state complaints.

In effect, more than half of the world's states were bound by the covenant, although many had reservations restricting their obligations or had failed to recognize the capacity of the Human Rights Committee to hear state-to-state complaints. Many people live in democratic countries where respect for human rights is already well developed. For them, the covenant represents further protections. For many other people, however, significant violations of rights continue to occur, especially in the context of civil wars, where brutal actions by governments and opposition forces limit the capacity of individuals to enjoy their human rights. Nor have states party to the covenant been aggressive in pointing out the failures of other states, perhaps out of concern that they too might be subject to closer external scrutiny. All this suggests that the goal of the covenant, that there should be a universal and genuine respect for human rights, has yet to be realized in full.

Progress has been made. The number of ratifications of the covenant has grown steadily. Numerous governments not party to the covenant, such as that of the United States, nevertheless respect the vast majority of the provisions contained in the covenant. Moreover, the Human Rights Committee, the Human Rights Commission, and a Human Rights Center at the United Nations continue to press for state awareness of human rights issues. Numerous specific human rights treaties have built on the covenant's foundations, including the Helsinki Agreement and other agreements concerning racial discrimination, religious discrimination, the rights of children, and the rights of migrant workers. The International Covenant on Civil and Political Rights was thus a milestone in the evolution of human rights law at the international level.

Bibliography

Buergenthal, Thomas. *International Human Rights in a Nutshell.* St. Paul, Minn.: West, 1988. This handy reference source describes the essential contents of regional and international human rights agreements, ranging from the U.N. Charter to European, inter-American, and African documents on human rights. Included is a section on the Covenant on Civil and Political Rights. Excellent for understanding the place of the covenant in the broader field of human rights. Includes an index.

Donnelly, Jack. *Universal Human Rights in Theory and Practice.* Ithaca, N.Y.: Cornell University Press, 1989. This philosophical inquiry into the meaning of human rights and the policy contexts in which human rights operates is not recommended for the casual reader. Students of international relations will find its theoretical discussion useful. Contains a list of references and a brief index.

Eide, Asbjörn, and August Schou, eds. *International Protection of Human Rights.* New York: Interscience, 1968. This somewhat dated but still useful collection of essays is drawn from the Proceedings of the Seventh Nobel Symposium, held in Oslo in 1967. Topics cover regional efforts to attain human rights, the natural law tradition, and implementation schemes for human rights covenants. Some individual selections contain references. No bibliography or index.

Falk, Richard. *Human Rights and State Sovereignty.* New York: Holmes & Meier, 1981. A prominent proponent of human rights takes on the central issue in effective enforcement of human rights agreements, that of sovereignty. Often innovative and provocative, the argument is also highly theoretical and thus not always accessible to the casual reader. Contains several useful illustrations, tables, and maps, as well as footnotes and an index.

Forsythe, David. *Human Rights and World Politics.* Lincoln: University of Nebraska Press, 1983. A nicely written and readable treatment of the political context of human rights. Covers both domestic politics and international relations. Includes numerous illustrations and tables, endnotes, a bibliography, an appendix, and an index.

Henkin, Louis, ed. *The International Bill of Rights: The Covenant on Civil and Political Rights.* New York: Columbia University Press, 1981. This collection of uniformly excellent essays on human rights probes various aspects of the covenant, including legal analysis of its provisions and historical assessment of its negotiation and implementation. Useful for more serious students of human rights. Includes extensive notes, copies of the Universal Declaration of Human Rights and the Covenant on Civil and Political Rights and its optional protocol, and an index.

Henkin, Louis. *The Rights of Man Today.* Boulder, Colo.: Westview, 1978. A very readable and reasonably compact treatment of the historical development and current significance of human rights. Accessible to a general audience, it is written in a very plain and direct style, making what can be an esoteric subject easy to understand. Contains footnotes but no bibliography or index.

Robert F. Gorman

Cross-References

The United Nations Adopts Its Charter (1945), p. 657; The Declaration on the Rights and Duties of Man Is Adopted (1948), p. 755; The United Nations Adopts the

Universal Declaration of Human Rights (1948), p. 789; The European Convention on Human Rights Is Signed (1950), p. 843; The United Nations Sets Rules for the Treatment of Prisoners (1955), p. 935; The Inter-American Commission on Human Rights Is Created (1959), p. 1032; The Helsinki Agreement Offers Terms for International Cooperation (1975), p. 1806; The OAU Adopts the African Charter on Human and Peoples' Rights (1981), p. 2136.

A GREEK COUP LEADS TO A MILITARY DICTATORSHIP

Categories of event: Revolutions and rebellions; civil rights
Time: April 21, 1967
Locale: Athens, Greece

Colonel George Papadopoulos led a right-wing military coup against the govern-ment of Panayiotis Kanellopoulos and established a dictatorship that limited politi-cal and civil liberties

Principal personages:
GEORGE PAPADOPOULOS (1919-   ), the right-wing military leader of
the coup
KING CONSTANTINE (1940-   ), the monarch of Greece, sympathetic to
the conservatives
PANAYIOTIS KANELLOPOULOS (1902-1986), the prime minister of Greece
at the time of the coup, a leader of the conservative National Radical
Union
GEORGE PAPANDREOU (1888-1968), the leader of the left-of-center Center
Union, the most popular party at the time of the coup
ANDREAS PAPANDREOU (1919-   ), the son of George, also led the Cen-
ter Union and was popular at the time of the coup

Summary of Event

The history of Greece in the twentieth century is one of turmoil and political struggle. Divided by regionalism, ideology, and economic class, the country has endured war and revolution, occupation and dictatorship. During World War II, Germany, Italy, and Bulgaria conquered and divided the country among themselves. Guerrilla resisters, most of whom opposed both the king and the occupiers and many of whom were communists, believed that they had earned the right to rule the country. After the war, however, the Western-sponsored monarch, George II, returned to the throne. A long civil war, lasting from 1944 until 1949, ensued. The civil war became a struggle between communist forces, backed only half-heartedly by Moscow, and the monarchist supporters, backed whole-heartedly by Washington. Republican noncommunists made their peace with the king.

After King George II died in 1947, his brother King Paul reigned until 1964 and was succeeded by his ineffectual son, King Constantine. In the meantime, Greece, one of the poorest countries in Europe, underwent an economic and political revival with help from the United States and Western Europe. Constitutional government and popular institutions were restored and strengthened, although the United States Department of State preferred and favored the conservative parties to those of the left and center. Washington particularly distrusted George Papandreou, the leader of the popular Center Union, even though he had been one of the first republican leaders to announce support for the monarchy during the war.

In the 1960's, Greek politics once again became chaotic. The slow pace of modernization and gradually rising standard of living produced struggles between town and countryside, the capital and the provinces, and rich and poor. The left, which included labor unions, Marxists, anarchists, and intellectuals, challenged the conservative elements of Greek society—the monarchy, the right-wing politicians, and the church. The right, for its part, incessantly proclaimed the danger of communism, even though by then such danger had largely disappeared.

In 1963, the misnamed National Radical Union, a conservative party led by Panayiotis Kanellopoulos and Constantine Karamanlis and backed by Washington, surrendered power after eight years in office. George Papandreou's Center Union took over. Papandreou's son, Andreas, an American-educated economist and flamboyant politician, played a major role in the new government. In 1964, a new election returned Papandreou with an even larger mandate.

The one policy upon which left and right agreed was the claim for irredenta and the insurance of national homogeneity. Greeks wanted the lands of southern Albania and the island of Cyprus incorporated into their territory. Furthermore, although Greece in the 1960's became more and more democratic in fact as well as in law, one area of significant oppression remained—the right to choose national identity. Greeks traditionally claimed that Albanian and Slavic speakers in the north whose forefathers had belonged to the Greek Orthodox confession were Albanophonic and Slavophonic Greeks, not Albanians or South Slavs. Using a carrot-and-stick policy, the authorities encouraged and pressured inhabitants in the north to "acknowledge" their Greek nationality and to adopt Greek ways, including the use of the Greek language.

The Cyprus question was of greatest concern to the Greeks. The island of Cyprus, while mostly Greek, nevertheless had a minority of 15 to 20 percent Muslim Turks. Furthermore, although Turkey was the traditional enemy of Greece, both countries now belonged to the North Atlantic Treaty Organization (NATO). Greece also hoped to associate with the European Common Market, and for this reason the Greek governments, whether the National Radical Union or the Center Union was in control, did not push for the incorporation of Cyprus into Greece, but were content to leave it as a separate Greek state.

Not content with this solution, the left-wing military circle *Aspida* (the shield), with the encouragement of Andreas Papandreou, aided and supported those on the island who favored union with Greece. Right-wing military officers disliked George Papandreou's military policies, particularly those governing promotions and appointments within the armed forces. Their fear of *Aspida*'s strength led to further conflicts. Papandreou tried to remove his minister of defense, who supported the right, and assume the post himself. Against custom, King Constantine intervened and prevented the change. In July, 1965, Papandreou protested by resigning. Constantine further confused issues by refusing to grant him a new mandate, even though the Center Union still retained its large majority in Parliament.

This "July Crisis" led to a weakening of the Center Union, as renegade members broke with Papandreou in order to preserve their own positions. In the fall, the king appointed a prime minister from the ranks of the right, but he lasted only a few weeks. Indeed, in the period from July, 1965, to April, 1967, five prime ministers served in Greece, but none could muster sufficient force to govern effectively.

In the meantime, Center Union leadership fell to Andreas Papandreou, who began to assume power once held by his aging father. His youth and vigor as well as his nationalism made him a popular figure. Greeks viewed the American-educated Papandreou as a national version of the recently martyred and much-venerated John F. Kennedy.

In the fall of 1966, a trial began of a group of *Aspida* officers charged with treason for their involvement with the Cypriot union movement. The government sought to try Andreas Papandreou as well, but he enjoyed parliamentary immunity. Guilty verdicts against the officers and rumors concerning the arrest of the popular Papandreou led to demonstrations and some outbreaks of violence. The king, desperately seeking a more stable government, consulted with all leading politicians at the end of March. After failing to come up with a solution, Prime Minister Panayiotis Kanellopoulos dissolved Parliament and called for new elections in May. With Parliament dissolved, the government could arrest Andreas Papandreou, but fear of violence as well as the possibility of intervention from the right led the elder Papandreou and Kanellopoulos to agree to extend parliamentary immunity during the campaign. The military right-wing acted anyway. They had already choreographed a move against the expected popular demonstration which would come with the arrest of Andreas Papandreou. To legitimize their coup, they claimed that Papandreou was involved in a communist conspiracy and that the existing politicians could not govern. On the morning of April 21, 1967, coup leaders—mostly colonels, not generals—drove their armored vehicles into Athens. There they arrested the leading politicians and pressured the king into acknowledging their deed. Later in the day, Constantine issued a decree suspending the civil liberty provisions of the constitution. Colonel George Papadopoulos soon emerged from the background to become the chief leader of the coup and assumed the premiership.

Impact of Event

Despite some infractions against constitutional and democratic government in the years preceding the coup, the Greek monarchy could be classified as a government generally adhering to modern standards of jurisprudence and civil and political liberties. In contrast, the South American term *junta* soon caught on as descriptive of the coup and as carrying a connotation of contempt. Immediately following the coup, the colonels arrested leading politicians who opposed them, but over the next few months released the most prominent. The *junta* also arrested opposition military officers and forced those who refused to cooperate to resign. This enabled the colonels to move themselves and their friends into the higher ranks, one of the chief goals of the takeover. The *junta* also carried out a purge of the civil and educational establishments, forcing out opponents and replacing the higher ranks with retired military officers. They appointed commissioners in every college, university, and institute and assigned them the tasks of checking curricula and uncovering "subversive" individuals and ideas. The colonels introduced a new constitution that severely limited political and civil liberties. Even the church was purged. The new government dissolved trade unions, even those with right-wing leanings, and appropriated their assets. The new leaders also closed dozens of other organizations which they found distasteful. They forbade gatherings of more than five even in private homes.

The *junta* extended its regulations into the daily lives of the Greek people. They forbade long hair on men and short skirts on women. Church attendance became compulsory. Censors banned hundreds of books and the playing of the works of the leftist composer and poet Mikis Theodorakis, one of the country's most prominent international figures. Newspapers found themselves under strict censorship as well, mitigated only by a limited freedom for foreign journalists, whose papers were still sold in Greece and who could be quoted to an extent by the Greek press. The government closed many newspapers and arrested journalists or hounded them into exile.

The colonels treated offenses against the martial law regime with draconian rigor. One well-known diplomat was imprisoned for having a group larger than five in his home. Many ordinary citizens as well as prominent opponents of the regime were detained without fair trial and subjected to torture and abuse. Papadopoulos attempted to give his government a populist appearance, but despite some superficial acts, such as the forgiving of some peasant indebtedness, the masses of Greeks fared no better than they had in the past, and with regard to civil liberties were far worse off.

Active and passive resistance to the *junta* expanded both inside the country and abroad, but this opposition, even with foreign support, could not oust the colonels. The king tried to organize a countercoup at the end of 1967, but the colonels foiled it and drove him from the country. In the fall of 1973, some of the dictator's own associates removed him from power, although the *junta* remained intact. Eight months later, in July, 1974, the military leaders resigned and democratic government was restored. The main catalyst for the change in 1974 was the Cyprus issue, over which the Turks and Greeks were in open conflict. When Turkey invaded the island and the *junta* could not respond effectively, the government resigned within a few days. Ironically, that same issue, Cyprus, had played a major role in sparking the coup of 1967.

Bibliography

Andrews, Kevin. *Greece in the Dark: 1967-1974.* Amsterdam: Adolf M. Hakkert, 1980. A narrative accounting the crimes and violations of human rights by the colonels' regime. Contains interviews, statements, and documents, some in the original Greek with English translation. Documentation, no bibliography or index.

Becket, James. *Barbarism in Greece: A Young American Lawyer's Inquiry into the Use of Torture in Contemporary Greece, with Case Histories and Documents.* New York: Walker, 1970. A collection of case histories, documents, and statements about the violations of human rights by the *junta.* Appendices contain lists of resistance movements and of persons killed and tortured.

Clogg, Richard, and George Yannopoulos. *Greece Under Military Rule.* New York: Basic Books, 1972. A collection of essays written by British and Greek scholars about the military government that then ruled. Although well-researched and analyzed, the book is clearly a polemic against the government. Documentation and bibliography. No index.

Danopoulos, Constantine P. *Warriors and Politicians in Modern Greece.* Chapel Hill, N.C.: Documentary Publications, 1984. A narrative and analysis of the Greek military before and after the coup. Excellent bibliography. Illustrations, documentation, and index.

Papandreou, Margaret. *Nightmare in Athens.* Englewood Cliffs, N.J.: Prentice-Hall, 1970. A personal account of the coup and of the succeeding events, by the American-born wife of Andreas Papandreou. The author describes the effects of the coup on her family and friends and gives some background from Papandreou's perspective. Castigates Washington for unfairly supporting conservative governments in Greece. Valuable as a primary source. Contains a list of the fates of some persons mentioned in the text. Index, no bibliography.

Rousseas, Stephen. *The Death of a Democracy: Greece and the American Conscience.* New York: Grove Press, 1967. An indictment of the colonels' regime for ending the Greek parliamentary democracy. Rousseas, a friend of Andreas Papandreou, to whom he dedicates the book, accuses the American Central Intelligence Agency of supporting the colonels in their coup. Contains much about an assassination attempt on the younger Papandreou. Documentation, no bibliography or index.

Schwab, Peter, and George D. Frangos, eds. *Greece Under the Junta.* New York: Facts on File, 1970. A short (147-page) collection of news reports compiled from the *Facts on File* archives on Greece, covering the coup and its aftermath. Contains a brief introduction. Illustrations and index.

Theodorakis, Mikis. *Journal of Resistance.* Translated by Graham Webb. New York: Coward, McCann & Geoghegan, 1973. A diary written by the prominent Greek composer, poet, and author of the years he spent in prison under the colonels. Contains some of his poetry and polemics against the *junta.* Translated from French. Contains a chronology and glossary. No index or bibliography.

Woodhouse, C. M. *The Rise and Fall of the Greek Colonels.* London: Granada, 1985. A well-researched, authoritative account of the *junta's* regime by a leading scholar of modern Greek history. Although the author is generally unsympathetic to the colonels, his work maintains the highest standard of scholarship and was written long enough after the events to provide perspective. The best single work on the subject. Illustrations, references, bibliography, and index.

Young. Kenneth. *The Greek Passion: A Study in People and Politics.* London: Dent, 1969. A narrative and analysis of the coup and its aftermath placing it in historical context. Also contains commentary on Greek life and the changes modernization has brought. Somewhat more sympathetic to Papadopoulos than other works. Directed to British readers. Index, bibliography, and maps. Little documentation.

Frederick B. Chary

Cross-References

Soviets Take Control of Eastern Europe (1943), p. 612; Cyprus Gains Independence (1960), p. 1084; Greek and Turkish Inhabitants of Cyprus Clash over Political Rights (1963), p. 1218; A United Nations Peace Force Is Deployed in Cyprus (1964), p. 1236; A Medical Group Helps Gather Evidence of Torture in Greece and Chile (1974), p. 1747.

THE SECESSION OF BIAFRA STARTS A NIGERIAN CIVIL WAR

Category of event: Indigenous peoples' rights
Time: May 30, 1967-January 15, 1970
Locale: Eastern Region, Nigeria

The secession of Biafra and the Nigerian civil war posed a human rights dilemma for the Nigerian and other governments

Principal personages:
YAKUBU GOWON (1934-   ), the Nigerian head of state
CHUKWUEMEKA ODUMEGWU OJUKWU, leader of the secessionist Ibo Eastern Region
OLUSEGUN OBASANJO (1937-   ), a military leader who facilitated the surrender of Biafrans and later became Nigerian head of state
PHILIP EFFIONG, replaced Ojukwu in the final days of the Biafran fighting and ordered the cease-fire of the Biafran armed forces

Summary of Event

On May 30, 1967, the Eastern Region of Nigeria, populated by more than nine million Ibo ethnic Nigerians, declared itself the sovereign state of the Republic of Biafra. Lieutenant Colonel Chukwuemeka Odumegwu Ojukwu charged that continuous violations of Ibo human rights by other Nigerians, particularly the Hausa ethnic group in the Northern Region, dictated the need for a separate Ibo state. The federal government of Nigeria vowed to prevent the dismantling of the Nigerian state. A civil war ensued that lasted more than two years.

In 1960, when Nigeria gained its independence, its major ethnic and religious groups competed for political control of the new state. The dominant and populous Northern, Muslim Hausa and the Eastern, Christian Ibo formed an uneasy alliance that effectively excluded the Western Yoruba from power. The new government, however, was unable to rule without recurring challenges to its legitimacy.

Following widespread allegations that the 1963 census and the elections of 1964 and 1965 were corrupt, Nigerians experienced outbursts of political unrest. Some Western political leaders were imprisoned by the federal government, allegedly for initiating a Western secession movement. In January, 1966, young Ibo army officers revolted and murdered the minister of finance, the prime minister, and other ranking Northerners. The Ibo officers insisted that their revolt was an anticorruption, profederation coup attempt and not an ethnically based action to advance the power of Ibos. Most Northern Hausa rejected this claim, however, because no Ibos had been murdered during the coup attempt. Moreover, the murdered prime minister was viewed as one of the federal government's anticorruption stalwarts.

Lieutenant Colonel Yakubu Gowon, a Northern officer from a small Christian ethnic group, organized government troops to respond to the revolt. Major General J. T. U. Aguiyi Ironsi also responded, and a few days after the coup, Ironsi assumed political power as supreme commander and Nigeria's head of state. Ironsi attempted to replace Nigeria's federal system with a unitary national government. In protest, many Nigerians rioted and used the opportunity to attack Ibos, who were given no government police or military protection. Many Ibos were beaten and killed in three days of rioting. A few weeks later, in late July, 1966, Ironsi was overthrown and murdered by military officers who, observers say, opposed altering the structures of the federal state of Nigeria. Gowon replaced Ironsi.

Gowon attempted to win support of Nigeria's disparate ethnic groups by reinstating the federal system while accommodating some of the demands of the West and the East. Gowon freed a popular political prisoner from the West, Chief Awolowo, and removed northern federal troops from the Eastern Region when Ibo Governor Ojukwu demanded their removal. Ojukwu, however, refused to recognize Gowon as Nigeria's executive authority, illustrating the Ibo's discontent with their lot in Nigerian politics.

On September 29, 1966, Nigerians once again attacked Ibos, slaughtering tens of thousands. The Ibo responded in the East by slaughtering Hausa and Fulani. It was estimated at this time that about one million Ibos fled Nigeria or returned to the Eastern Region for safety. Many of these Ibo were forced to live in refugee camps, and in the ensuing civil war many died from malnutrition and other health-related causes.

In March, 1967, Ibo Governor Ojukwu retained all taxes collected in the Eastern Region. Gowon warned Ojukwu not to attempt any secessionist effort. Western Region officials also began to talk of seceding, and Gowon tried to placate them by removing some federal troops from the West. Some observers have suggested that this effort to ease tensions was interpreted as a sign of weakness.

On May 27, 1967, Ojukwu and a number of Ibo chiefs declared the Eastern Region independent of Nigerian authority. In response, Gowon issued a decree to restructure the existing regions into twelve districts, including five in the East, which would allow non-Ibos in the East to exercise some political influence. On May 30, 1967, Ojukwu announced the secession of the East and declared that region the Republic of Biafra.

Gowon initiated an economic boycott of the East and began a military campaign against Ojukwu and his Biafran army. The French assisted Biafra militarily, and the civil war raged. Food in the East was in short supply. International Biafran relief committees formed and demanded the right to send food and health supplies to the isolated Ibo. Nigeria's federal government opposed relief efforts, arguing that the civil war would end more quickly if the economic boycott were allowed to continue without disruption, forcing the Ibo to surrender. Through the boycott, the federal government hoped to prevent arms, food, and medical supplies from reaching Biafra and to prevent petroleum from being exported by the Biafrans. This would prevent them from earning international foreign currency with which to purchase supplies.

Ojukwu and the Biafrans appealed to the international community for help on the principle of self-determination, argued that the Christian Ibo were victims of religious persecution by Northern Muslim zealots, and charged that the Nigerian federal government was pursuing a policy of genocide against the Ibo through military and economic warfare. Biafrans argued that Nigeria's recent history demonstrated that there was no hope of peaceful coexistence among the contending ethnic and religious groups.

The Biafrans made available to leading Western media officials detailed, well-argued political position papers and photographs of starving Biafrans. Biafran officials claimed that five thousand Ibos a day were dying from malnutrition and that the federal government's air attacks were killing thousands of civilians. The Nigerian federal government obstructed efforts by international aid organizations, such as the International Red Cross, and newly initiated organizations of Western cultural artists seeking to help relieve the famine in Biafra. Reluctantly, Gowon finally agreed to permit a land corridor through which supplies could pass. The Biafrans, however, demanded air relief.

Despite pressures from Western governments for a negotiated settlement, the Nigerian federal government delayed negotiations of a ceasefire, hoping that Biafra would be forced to sue for peace, thus preventing a negotiated compromise that would undermine Nigeria's central government. The federal government also argued against any foreign assistance to Biafra on the grounds that under the rules of the Organization of African Unity (OAU), no foreign power could aid efforts to redraw the boundaries of an African state. Member countries of the OAU, however, were divided in their support of the federal government and the Biafrans. The federal government of Nigeria accused the leaders of the new Biafran state of creating a civil war and a great human tragedy to advance their own careers. Gowon repeatedly pledged to protect the physical security of Biafrans if they would relent in their secessionist efforts.

After two and a half years of fighting, with thousands of federal soldiers who had been killed, millions of Ibos who had suffered and died, and millions more Ibos who were displaced from their homes, the federal government inflicted a major military loss on the Ibo. In January, 1970, with food and ammunition low, the Biafrans were militarily defeated when Colonel Olusegun Obosanjo captured the important town of Owerri. Shortly thereafter, Ojukwu and his family fled to the Ivory Coast. On January 13, 1970, Lieutenant Colonel Philip Effiong, who replaced Ojukwu as the major Biafran authority, surrendered to the federal government. Biafran decisionmaking bodies were dissolved, and the Ibo waited anxiously for the next actions of the federal government.

Impact of Event

Immediately, the federal government found itself responsible for distributing the much-needed aid that international donors pledged to provide. Nigeria's government would not allow distribution of food and medicine by any international agency that had aided Biafra during the civil war. While the federal government handled thousands of tons of food a week, it could not meet the needs of the Biafrans immediately after the cease-fire.

The fears of massacres and retaliation against Ibos that had provided some of the motivation for support of Biafra never materialized. Gowon enforced a national policy of reconciliation, and observers marveled at the speed and ease with which Ibos were reabsorbed into government and private Nigerian life. Some Ibos who had served in low-level federal government positions and fled to the East seeking safety now returned to their former posts with the federal government. Many leaders of the secessionist movement, however, were not reabsorbed. The ability to reabsorb the Ibo as an ethnic group has been attributed by some observers to the economic boom Nigeria experienced from oil price increases in the early 1970's. These increases provided expanding revenues from which it was possible to distribute resources to Nigerians of many ethnic backgrounds. Although economic discrimination did not fuel Nigeria's ethnic strife in the 1970's, Nigeria's civil war had entrenched military rule; a return to democratic civilian government would elude Nigerians for years. The civil rights that accompany democratic civilian government also eluded Nigerians for years. Union strikes were banned, political movements that the government designated as appealing to secessionist impulses were outlawed, journalists worried about censorship, and academics were restrained from criticizing the government freely. When the oil boom collapsed in the mid-1980's, Nigerians faced economic dilemmas as well.

In the years following the Biafran secession, Nigerians have had to cope with many of the problems that plagued other late-industrializing states. There has not been, however, any repeat of the atrocities and ethnic conflict on the scale of the 1960's. By the 1990's, Nigeria was struggling with issues of democratization and development, not with extraordinary human rights violations motivated by ethnic rivalry.

Bibliography

Africa Contemporary Record, 1968/1969-   . This annual publication, in its chapters on Nigeria, provides an excellent synopsis of the important developments, domestic and international, that affected the course of the war.

Dudley, Billy J. *An Introduction to Nigerian Government and Politics.* Bloomington: Indiana University Press, 1982. This is a classic text on Nigerian politics. In addition to offering insights on the policy-making of an African state, Dudley attempts to apply basic political science concepts in the African context.

Kirk-Greene, Anthony H. M., and Douglas Rimmer. *Nigeria Since 1970.* New York: Africana, 1981. Covers the time period from the aftermath of the Nigerian civil war to the election of Nigeria's first, short-lived, post-civil-war democratic government in 1979. The authors examine the 1970's as a decade of expanding oil profits for Nigeria and explore the alternative schemes for development and democratization. Separate chapters discuss agriculture, petroleum, industrialization, infrastructure, public finance, external trade, and development planning.

Legum, Colin. "The Tragedy in Nigeria." In *African Politics and Society*, edited by Irving Leonard Markovitz. New York: Free Press, 1970. Legum contends that the magnitude of the tragedy in Nigeria may never be known fully and suggests that failure to disclose information may be part of a strategy to prevent additional violence.

Stremlau, John. *The International Politics of the Nigerian Civil War, 1967-1970.* Princeton, N.J.: Princeton University Press, 1977. Stremlau offers a richly researched study of the foreign policies of the Nigerian federal government, the Biafrans, and other countries and international organizations that became involved in the Nigerian civil war.

Eve N. Sandberg

Cross-References

The Sudanese Civil War Erupts (1955), p. 941; Ghana Gains Independence (1957), p. 980; The Nonaligned Movement Meets (1961), p. 1131; Algeria Gains Independence (1962), p. 1155; The Organization of African Unity Is Founded (1963), p. 1194; Zimbabwe's Freedom Fighters Topple White Supremacist Government (1964), p. 1224; Civil War Ravages Chad (1965), p. 1273; The Amin Regime Terrorizes Uganda (1971), p. 1600; Burundi's Government Commits Genocide of the Bahutu Majority (1972), p. 1668; Revolution Erupts in Ethiopia (1974), p. 1758; Hunger Becomes a Weapon in the Sudanese Civil War (1988), p. 2354; The Kenyan Government Cracks Down on Dissent (1989), p. 2431.

THE KERNER COMMISSION EXPLORES
THE CAUSES OF CIVIL DISORDERS

Categories of event: Civil rights; racial and ethnic rights
Time: July, 1967
Locale: Washington, D.C.

The Kerner commission's report portrayed a nation divided along racial lines and recommended a plethora of antidotes to cure the maladies of hatred and violence besetting American society

Principal personages:
> LYNDON B. JOHNSON (1908-1973), the president of the United States (1963-1969), appointed the National Advisory Commission on Civil Disorders
> OTTO KERNER (1908-1976), the chair of the National Advisory Commission on Civil Disorders
> JOHN V. LINDSAY (1921-   ), the vice chair of the commission and mayor of New York City
> ROY WILKINS (1901-1978), a member of the commission and executive director of the NAACP

Summary of Event

The National Advisory Commission on Civil Disorders, also known as the Kerner Commission, was appointed by President Lyndon B. Johnson as an immediate response to racial disorders in American cities during the summer of 1967. The most devastating riots occurred in Newark and Detroit, within a two-week period in July. President Johnson established the commission to try to discover what had happened, why it had happened, and what could be done to prevent it from happening again.

Both President Johnson and the commission gave priority to the maintenance of law and order in the affected cities and to determining if a conspiracy had existed that created a chain reaction of riots. It was important to the president and to the members of the commission to determine the historical factors which caused the riots of 1967. It was this question that provided the commission with the opportunity to focus on systemic problems of racism in American society. The paramount observation of the commission was tersely stated: "Our nation is moving toward two societies, one white, one black—separate and unequal."

President John F. Kennedy, and his brother, Robert F. Kennedy, had shown much compassion in committing the United States to eliminating segregation in schools and public facilities. The Kennedy Administration was short-lived, but it did inspire a helpful political mood for government action against the more conspicuous forms of racism. President Johnson, as Kennedy's successor, pledged to continue the battle for civil rights for minorities.

In July, 1967, President Johnson appointed the commission, giving it a mandate to investigate the origins of the recent disorders in American cities. The president pledged to use national resources to remedy historical racism and social injustice. In typical folksy prose, President Johnson beseeched Americans to pray for the day when "mercy and truth are met together; righteousness and peace have kissed each other." He pledged to work for better jobs, housing, and education for black Americans.

Otto Kerner, the governor of Illinois, was selected by President Johnson to chair the National Advisory Commission on Civil Disorders. John V. Lindsay, the mayor of New York City, was appointed vice chair. The other members represented a cross-section of American politics, leaning toward moderates. Exceptions to this tendency were Roy Wilkins, Executive Secretary of the National Association for the Advancement of Colored People (NAACP) and Fred Harris, U.S. senator from Oklahoma, whose work on behalf of Native Americans had sensitized him to the pains of racism.

A starting point for the commission was to examine racism in its historical framework. The causes of the 1967 riots, concluded the report issued by the commission in February, 1968, were inherent in the structure and dynamics of American society which established the pattern of interracial relations. Black Americans had always struggled for equality in law and in social life. Some blacks, particularly at the end of the nineteenth century and beginning of the twentieth, supported separatism and self-help. Black Power proponents of the 1960's, such as Stokely Carmichael and H. Rap Brown, revitalized this philosophy, originally championed by Booker T. Washington. Black Power supporters were actually promoting many of the objectives of white racism through their emphasis on black history, separatism, and racial solidarity, the commission noted.

A group of blacks, in the early years of the twentieth century, had organized to challenge Booker T. Washington's program of political accommodation to white racism. Washington was convinced that blacks could earn the respect of white society through hard work. Political rights, such as the franchise, could wait for an undetermined future date. W. E. B. Du Bois and Monroe Trotter began and led the Niagara Movement which rejected separatism, condemned Jim Crow laws, and took up protest and agitation for racial equality in law and in social life. The Niagara group placed the responsibility for black poverty and violence on white racism and demanded the abolition of all distinctions based on race and color.

Booker T. Washington fought back. He had the support of southern whites and many conservative northern philanthropists who wanted to preserve the racial status quo. Nevertheless, Washington failed to subdue Du Bois and his followers. In 1909 and 1910, Du Bois was able to enlist a small group of white liberals, some of whom could trace their ancestry back to the abolition movement of the nineteenth century, and socialists to form the National Association for the Advancement of Colored Peo-

1372 Great Events from History II

ple. Du Bois became the editor of *The Crisis*, a semiofficial journal of the NAACP which was adamant in its condemnation of white racism and in its demand for full equality for blacks.

The NAACP aimed its protest against the whole nation, insisting on the right to vote, equal protection under the law, equal pay for equal work, and the dismantling of segregation in public accommodations, in schools, and in the armed forces. A variety of tactics was used by the NAACP, including boycotts, publicizing lynching (while pressing for antilynching legislation) and other atrocities against blacks, and bringing lawsuits.

It was in these early years that the NAACP prepared the groundwork for *Brown v. Board of Education* (1954), with cases pertaining to white colleges and universities and their refusal to admit blacks to their graduate and professional schools. In 1936, Thurgood Marshall, counsel for the NAACP, successfully contested before the courts the exclusion of blacks from the law school at the University of Maryland. Two years later, the Supreme Court declared unconstitutional a Missouri plan that banned blacks from the University of Missouri law school as violating the "separate but equal" doctrine.

The federal government ignored the plight of blacks in northern cities and in the countryside of the southern states. Southern congresspeople, in fact, were able to expand de facto segregation in the District of Columbia, although they failed to enact Jim Crow laws. The nation's capital became another bastion and an important symbol of Jim Crowism and the subordination and segregation of Blacks in virtually every segment of society.

White prejudice and the frequent use of extralegal violence, violence often sanctioned by the larger community, by whites against blacks who broke social or political norms were principally responsible for black riots in the twentieth century. White racism, according to the commission's report, created a pattern of failures among blacks. The commission referred to pervasive racism and segregation, black migration from the South to the North, and the black ghettos, implicating white institutions for creating the ghettos. The commission urged the American people to commit themselves to the elimination of the ghettos through massive and sustained action, backed by the will and resources of the richest nation on earth.

The goals of society, according to the commission, needed to focus on creating a single American identity, a single society in which race and color would not determine a person's dignity or limit the choice of job, residence, or even partner in marriage. To reach these goals, the commission recommended the elimination of all forms of racial segregation in the United States by giving to blacks the right to choose their jobs, where they would live, and what schools they would attend. The commission proposed the formation of grass-roots institutions based in the ghettos and in rural areas, thereby making government more responsive to citizens on the local level. The commission insisted on destroying not merely the legal status of racism but also the legacy of racism by devising an array of programs to integrate American society.

Impact of Event

The assault by the National Advisory Commission on Civil Disorders on institutionalized racism was a comprehensive proclamation which indicted white racism while condemning black violence and committing the nation to build a single, nonracial society. The impact of the commission's report was felt by blacks and other minorities in many ways. Black Americans in general, but especially the young, began to see the federal government as compassionate and committed to eradicating legal and de facto racism throughout America.

In the area of employment, the commission proposed a comprehensive program to meet the needs of the unemployed and the underemployed through active recruitment, job training, affirmative action in the public and private sectors, and stimulating public and private investment in poverty-stricken areas, both in the cities and in rural communities. The commission recommended the creation of two million jobs through a combination of government and private efforts over a three-year period.

Education in a democratic society is necessary to provide citizens with the capacity to participate in the political process and to enjoy fully the fruits of their collective endeavors. Schools in the northern ghettos and segregated schools in the South and West had failed to discharge their obligations to educate blacks adequately. The commission recommended scores of reforms to remedy this failure. Many of the rioters in 1967, the commission observed, were high school dropouts. It also cited the disparity in educational achievement between blacks and whites in the same grades. Public schools were not teaching blacks basic verbal skills. The commission cited results of the Selective Service Mental Test showing that during the period between June, 1964, and December, 1965, 67 percent of black candidates but only 19 percent of whites failed the examination. To rectify the failure to educate blacks and other minorities, the commission supported the elimination of de facto school segregation, which was connected with residential segregation in the North; increased funding for schools in the inner cities; improving community-school relations; greater expenditures on early childhood education; enforcement of Title VI of the 1964 Civil Rights Act, which prohibited giving federal financial aid to any program which discriminated against blacks; year-round education for disadvantaged students; and expanded opportunities for higher education and vocational training for blacks and other disadvantaged groups.

The commission made other comprehensive proposals, addressing almost every conceivable segment of social life. It recommended a national system of income supplements, eliminating discrimination in housing, the construction of smaller housing projects (that is, "scattering") to break-down racial isolation, an expansion of the rent supplement program and an ownership supplement program, and the opening up of areas outside of ghetto neighborhoods to black occupancy. Many of the commission's recommendations became law. Its greatest impact, however, was perhaps in beginning the process of attaining racial equality.

Bibliography

Clark, Kenneth Bancroft. *Dark Ghetto: Dilemmas of Social Power.* New York: Harper & Row, 1965. Describes the psychology of racial inferiority and self-hatred of African Americans. The author shows how the larger society shapes and warps the ghetto.

_____. *Negro Protest.* Boston: Beacon Press, 1963. Views of three leading figures in the civil rights struggle are given: Martin Luther King, Malcolm X, and James Baldwin. An interesting ideological contrast among the three is provided.

Finch, Minnie. *The NAACP: Its Fight for Justice.* Metuchen, N.J.: Scarecrow Press, 1981. Attention is given to the legal struggles of the NAACP from its inception through the 1960's.

Franklin, John Hope. *From Slavery to Freedom.* New York: Alfred A. Knopf, 1947. A recounting of Negro history from 1619 to the twentieth century. The author, unfortunately, concentrates on too many trifles.

Franklin, Robert Michael. *Liberating Visions: Human Fulfillment and Social Justice in African American Thought.* Minneapolis, Minn.: Fortress Press, 1990. W. E. B. Du Bois' vision of African Americans stood the test of time. This brilliant, though often unsuccessful, agitator and conscience of the nation is described here.

Harlan, Louis. *Booker T. Washington: The Making of a Black Leader, 1856-1901.* New York: Oxford University Press, 1972. Washington is depicted as paternalistic and self-centered. His philosophy is presented as convoluted. Washington himself is portrayed as more interested in controlling his empire than in battling segregation.

Rose, Arnold Marshall. *An American Dilemma: The Negro in America.* New York: Harper & Row, 1948. This work shocked America by unabashedly condemning American racism and exposing its hypocrisy. This was an important work in shaping American sociology in the post-World War II era.

Wilkins, Roy. *Standing Fast: The Autobiography of Roy Wilkins.* New York: Viking Press, 1982. Wilkins is an articulate and consistent advocate of racial equality. He gives much insight into many of the major triumphs of the NAACP, especially its Legal and Education Fund.

Woodward, C. Vann. *The Strange Career of Jim Crow.* New York: Oxford University Press, 1955. Explodes the myths of a gentle and benign South following Reconstruction. The author revises history to tell the truth about segregation and racism in the United States.

Claude Hargrove

Cross-References

The American Civil Liberties Union Is Founded (1920), p. 327; Roosevelt Outlaws Discrimination in Defense-Industry Employment (1941), p. 578; The United Nations Adopts the Universal Declaration of Human Rights (1948), p. 789; *Brown v. Board of Education* Ends Public School Segregation (1954), p. 913; The Civil Rights

Act of 1957 Creates the Commission on Civil Rights (1957), p. 997; Congress Passes the Civil Rights Act (1964), p. 1251; African Americans Riot in Watts (1965), p. 1301; Race Rioting Erupts in Detroit (1967), p. 1376; The Civil Rights Act of 1968 Outlaws Discrimination in Housing (1968), p. 1414.

RACE RIOTING ERUPTS IN DETROIT

Category of event: Racial and ethnic rights
Time: July 23-30, 1967
Locale: Detroit, Michigan

The most devastating race riot in U.S. history set off riots in other major cities and showed that reforms of the 1960's had neglected a sizable segment of the black population

Principal personages:
JEROME PATRICK CAVANAGH (1928-), the mayor of Detroit from 1961 to 1968
RAMSEY CLARK (1927-), the attorney general of the United States from 1967 to 1969
LYNDON B. JOHNSON (1908-1973), the thirty-sixth president of the United States
GEORGE ROMNEY (1907-), the governor of Michigan from 1963 to 1969
CYRUS VANCE (1917-), the U.S. deputy defense secretary from 1967 to 1968

Summary of Event

On the surface, Detroit, Michigan, in 1967 was one of the success stories of President Lyndon Johnson's "Great Society." Under the administration of Mayor Jerome Patrick Cavanagh, Detroit had prospered, and so had many of its blacks. Many blacks commanded high wages in Detroit's factories and occupied high positions in the United Auto Workers union. Consequently, approximately 40 percent of the city's 555,000 blacks owned or were buying houses, many of which were in integrated neighborhoods. Mayor Cavanagh had also attempted to reach out to the underprivileged in his city through his federally funded antipoverty agency, Total Action Against Poverty, which provided $200 million for jobs, job training, education, and recreation.

Blacks in Detroit had also attained a share in political power. The director of Total Action Against Poverty, the chief civilian assistant to the police commissioner, and two of the seven members of the board of education were black. In addition, Detroit in 1967 was the only city in the United States that had two black members of Congress. Because of his sensitivity to the political needs of minorities, Mayor Cavanagh was very popular with many blacks in his city.

Beneath the surface, though, Detroit was a city in turmoil. The unemployment rate among blacks was 11 percent; this was double the national average. The rate of unemployment was even higher among black youths; one out of every four young black males in Detroit, most of whom were the products of broken homes and inadequate schools, ended up on the streets after high school graduation, if indeed they graduated. The best future that most of them could hope for was work at poverty wages. In an eight-block area of Twelfth Street, the west side ghetto strip where the riot erupted, only 17 percent of the residents owned their own homes, compared to 60 percent in the city as a whole.

Poverty was not the only problem with which many inner-city blacks had to deal. A survey taken just prior to the riots indicated that 91 percent feared being robbed and 93 percent wanted to move. Holdups were so common in downtown Detroit that they often went unreported. Even small children stole on Twelfth Street, where pawn shops thrived and the streets were clogged with litter and abandoned cars. White property owners contributed to the problem by taking money from prostitutes who worked in buildings that the owners had declared vacant.

Ironically, the improved economic conditions that some blacks were enjoying only served to aggravate the situation in the ghettos. The advances that African Americans had made in Detroit and in other major cities since the Civil Rights Acts of 1960 and 1964 and the Voting Rights Act of 1965 had raised the expectations of many underprivileged blacks. When these hopes were not quickly realized, frustration set in, prompting many young blacks to listen to the revolutionary rhetoric of such "Black Power" advocates as H. Rap Brown and Stokely Carmichael.

Like the Newark, New Jersey, insurrection a few days earlier, the Detroit riot began as the result of a minor police incident. On July 23, 1967, at 4:00 A.M., police raided a "blind pig"—an after-hours bar—on Twelfth Street. While the police arrested eighty people inside the building, a crowd of blacks gathered outside, cursing and throwing rocks and bricks, one of which broke a police car window. Instead of confronting the mob or pulling out altogether, the police followed Mayor Cavanagh's "walk soft" strategy by doing nothing.

As a result, the violence escalated. People began to smash windows and loot stores, setting fires as they went along. The rioters spread through the ghetto and far beyond, growing in numbers until they outnumbered the city's four thousand police. In an almost carnival-like atmosphere, blacks took luxury goods that they believed had been unfairly denied them—color television sets, stereos, and expensive liquor.

After taking a tour of the ruins the next morning, Governor George Romney decided that a show of force would be more effective than Mayor Cavanagh's efforts to contain the rioting. Romney proclaimed a state of emergency, set a 9:00 P.M. curfew, and called in state troopers and National Guardsmen. The use of force, however, only made matters worse. As was the case in Watts and Newark, the National Guard in Detroit had little training in crowd control and tended to fire at anything that moved. In an effort to escape the bloodshed, thousands of blacks clogged the available refugee centers. As the riot raged through the rest of the day, offices, banks, stores, and hotels closed, leaving the city virtually paralyzed.

The situation was complicated by governmental red tape. On the morning of July 25, Governor Romney began an eight-hour telephone conversation with Attorney General Ramsey Clark to sort out the legalities involved in making a formal request for federal troops. When President Johnson finally received Romney's formal request, he ordered the Pentagon to start airlifting "Task Force Detroit," which consisted of forty-seven hundred paratroopers from Fort Bragg, North Carolina, and Fort Campbell, Kentucky, to Selfridge Air Force Base in Detroit. The troops, however, were forced to stay on the base for several hours, until an investigation of the problem was made by the president's field team, headed by Deputy Defense Secretary Cyrus Vance. Because Vance's team concluded that no troops were needed, nothing was done until one of Detroit's black congressmen, Charles Diggs, Jr., personally called the White House to demand troops. Vance finally shuttled troops to the ghetto at 1:30 A.M. on July 26. During the nearly twenty-four hours that had elapsed between the time Romney requested the troops and the time the troops took up positions in the city, the riot had spread over fourteen square miles of the city, reaching dangerously close to the exclusive Grosse Pointe suburbs.

Instead of stopping the riot, though, the arrival of federal troops only shifted the riot back to Twelfth Street, where the violence had started. Because the west side was populated by the poorest and angriest of Detroit's citizens, the riot was transformed into guerrilla warfare. Snipers shot at firefighters and assaulted a police station. A white woman who was watching from her window was shot and killed by a sniper. Altogether, there were about one hundred snipers.

When the police and the National Guard retaliated against the snipers, they also placed innocent lives in jeopardy. In midmorning, the crew of an M-48 tank pummeled a building where a sniper had been sighted, only to discover twenty-five minutes later that the sniper had vanished; the only occupants were a terrified family of four who were cowering under the front porch. Several hours later, the police strafed the Algiers Hotel, where another sniper was reputed to have been hiding. When the shooting ceased, the police found three dead African Americans but no guns. In a similar incident, a dozen National Guards and policemen shot at a white Chevrolet convertible, resulting in the death of another unarmed black man.

The rage that had fueled the violence in the early days of the riot died out by the weekend. When the authorities were finally able to assess the damage, the cost in both property and lives was found to be tragically high. Property damage exceeded that of any other riot in the United States up to that time—more than $45 million. So many people had been arrested—more than four thousand—that some had to be detained in buses. More than a thousand people were injured, and forty-three people died. The dead included looters, snipers, a policeman, and a fireman, as well as many innocent people who had been caught in the cross fire. Only eight of the dead were white, and three of those were looters who were shot by police. Without a doubt, the African Americans of Detroit paid the highest price for the riot.

Impact of Event

Even before the Detroit riot had ended, "Black Power" advocates began to capitalize on the turmoil. Insurrections soon followed in other Michigan cities, including Pontiac, Saginaw, Kalamazoo, and Grand Rapids. Throughout July and August, the cry "Burn, Baby, Burn" was heard in cities across the entire United States as well. By the end of the summer, more than seventy U.S. cities had experienced race riots, including Rochester, New York; Chicago, Illinois; Toledo, Ohio; and South Bend, Indiana. For the bitter, downtrodden residents of the ghettos, the war cries of dissidents such as H. Rap Brown rang louder than those of the advocates of peaceful change. Indeed, Martin Luther King, Jr., recognized this point when he refused to go to Detroit during the riot. "I am not a fireman," he said. "My role is to keep fires from starting."

Even President Johnson felt the fallout from the Detroit riots. Within a week after the violence in Detroit, a statement issued by the Republican Coordinating Committee blamed the president for vetoing the 1966 District of Columbia Crime Bill. The president was also criticized for waiting so long to send federal troops to Detroit.

On the positive side, the Detroit riot made many members of Congress aware of the need for legislative action to improve life in U.S. cities. Shortly before the riot, Johnson had been forced to cut expenditures for model cities, the Teacher Corps, and aid to education in order to fund the Vietnam War. After the riot, Johnson's "safe streets" bill, which provided $50 million for support for local police, had easy passage through Congress. Advocates of gun control also received considerable support for their cause after the riot.

On the other hand, the Johnson Administration's view of the problem destroyed any hope that social legislation would receive a boost from the riot. Essentially, President Johnson viewed the riot as a law-enforcement problem. He believed that funneling more money to the black ghettos would be construed by many people as rewarding the rioters. Consequently, little important social legislation was passed during the remainder of Johnson's term in office.

The Detroit riot can also be credited with generating an atmosphere of paranoia across the nation for the rest of the year, and the prospect was raised of white backlash. Hundreds of whites living in major cities across the United States began buying guns for protection. Even some government officials succumbed to the notion that the nation's underprivileged posed a real threat. Even though the Justice Department insisted that there was no real threat of a conspiracy, both J. Edgar Hoover of the Federal Bureau of Investigation and the Michigan Crime Commission attributed the violence to planned efforts by organized groups. Some military analysts went so far as to blame China and Cuba for the trouble in Detroit.

The most important lesson to come out of the Detroit riot, however, was the realization that the disenfranchised factions of society could disrupt any city in the United States. The revolt in Detroit, like all revolutions, was born out of hope, not despair. By taking over Detroit, the rioters demonstrated to whites and middle-class blacks that the reforms instituted by King and Johnson had not filtered down to the poorest members of society. After the riot, the nation as a whole was forced to face a startling fact: If a riot could occur in a model city like Detroit, it could happen anywhere.

Bibliography

Bernstein, Saul. *Alternatives to Violence: Alienated Youth and Riots, Race, and Poverty.* New York: Association Press, 1967. Even though this book was published just before the Detroit riot, it sets the stage for the turmoil in Detroit by examining the discontent that precipitated the riots that preceded it. The book also provides solutions for change in the end.

"City at the Blazing Heart of a Nation in Disorder." *Life* 63 (August 4, 1967): 16-24. This probes the mystery of the riot by beginning with the progress that Mayor Cavanagh had made toward achieving racial harmony. The color photographs that accompany the account of the riot underscore the horrors of mob rule.

Dotson, J. "An American Tragedy." *Newsweek* 70 (August 7, 1967): 18-26. This day-by-day record of the unfolding of the Detroit riot of 1967 is the best available account of that event. This well-illustrated article personalizes the riot by providing eyewitness anecdotes.

Isenberg, Irwin, ed. *The City in Crisis.* New York: H. W. Wilson, 1968. This anthology of articles pertaining to race riots in the United States is noteworthy for the inclusion of three articles: a condensed version of "An American Tragedy, 1967—Detroit" (*Newsweek*), "The Hard-Core Ghetto Mood" (*Newsweek*), and Ronald G. Shafer's "Rebuilding Detroit" (*Wall Street Journal*).

Widick, B. J. "Motown Blues." *The Nation* 205 (August 14, 1967): 102-104. Written by a shop worker in a Detroit auto plant, this article is valuable because it analyzes the causes and effects of the riot from a black perspective.

"A Young Mayor Seeks an Answer in the Ashes." *Life* 63 (August 11, 1967): 21-22. This article makes an interesting contrast between the idealism of Mayor Cavanagh's liberal vision for his city and the harsh reality of the riot. The color photographs graphically illustrate the aftermath of the riot.

Alan Brown

Cross-References

CORE Stages a Sit-in in Chicago to Protest Segregation (1943), p. 618; Zoot-Suit Riots Exemplify Ethnic Tensions in Los Angeles (1943), p. 624; Race Riots Erupt in Detroit and Harlem (1943), p. 635; CORE Stages the "Journey of Reconciliation" (1947), p. 718; Eisenhower Sends Troops to Little Rock, Arkansas (1957), p. 1003; Greensboro Sit-ins Launch a New Stage in the Civil Rights Movement (1960), p. 1056; Meredith's Enrollment Integrates the University of Mississippi (1962), p. 1167; Civil Rights Protesters Attract International Attention (1963), p. 1188; Martin Luther King, Jr., Leads a March from Selma to Montgomery (1965), p. 1278; African Americans Riot in Watts (1965), p. 1301; The Kerner Commission Explores the Causes of Civil Disorders (1967), p. 1370.

MARSHALL BECOMES THE FIRST BLACK SUPREME COURT JUSTICE

Category of event: Racial and ethnic rights
Time: October 2, 1967
Locale: Washington, D.C.

President Lyndon Johnson appointed the nation's leading civil rights lawyer, Thurgood Marshall, to become the first black justice of the Supreme Court

Principal personages:
THURGOOD MARSHALL (1908-   ), an associate justice of the Supreme Court, the leading civil rights lawyer in the United States during the twentieth century
LYNDON B. JOHNSON (1908-1973), the president of the United States (1963-1969), oversaw the enactment of groundbreaking civil rights legislation
STROM THURMOND (1902-   ), a United States senator from South Carolina, led opposition to civil rights laws

Summary of Event

The justices of the United States Supreme Court are responsible for defining and defending the Bill of Rights in the Constitution. The meanings of freedom of speech, freedom of the press, equal protection, and other rights are determined by the nine individuals who don black robes and preside over the highest court in the land.

Because the justices are human beings who must confront difficult social problems, their decisions inevitably are shaped by their personal attitudes, values, and experiences. The Supreme Court's decisions tend to reflect the dominant societal values of each era. While racial prejudice against African Americans was accepted in many parts of the United States, the justices declared that cities and states could segregate blacks into separate schools, neighborhoods, and public facilities. When women were excluded from professions because of societal attitudes about their proper roles as wives and mothers, the Supreme Court declared that state laws could prevent women from working as lawyers or as bartenders and in other occupations. The Supreme Court determines the extent to which women, racial minorities, and others are protected by the Constitution, yet before 1967 only white males served as justices and participated in these decisions.

There were few opportunities for alternative viewpoints and experiences to be represented in the Supreme Court's deliberations, because only politically well-connected white men were appointed by presidents to serve on the highest court. In order to serve as a justice, a lawyer must be appointed by the president and confirmed by a vote of the United States Senate. Presidents have frequently reserved appointments for prominent, like-minded political allies. As a result, members of groups within society that have been hampered by discrimination have had little chance to gain political prominence and thereby become eligible for federal judicial appointments.

Because the membership of the Supreme Court has been unrepresentative of the diversity within American society, critics of the Court have argued that constitutional rights have been interpreted to favor the interests of the narrow group of individuals, namely affluent white men, who comprise the Supreme Court justices. The court began to interpret the Bill of Rights to protect corporations' property in the 1890's, and it was not until 1925 that it began significantly to protect individuals' free speech and other civil rights against infringement by state and local governments. Critics also note that although the Fourteenth Amendment to the Constitution, added in 1868, required state governments to provide equal protection for all people, the justices of the Court did not use those words to protect blacks from widespread discrimination until 1954, in the case of *Brown v. Board of Education.*

Although the Supreme Court gained a reputation during the 1960's for being the guardian of powerless individuals, such as racial minorities, criminal defendants, and women, the Court rarely used the words of the Bill of Rights to protect individuals prior to that decade. As a result, blacks and women were victimized by discrimination in voting, education, and other aspects of American life. Some critics have argued that the white men who comprised the justices of the Supreme Court demonstrated little sensitivity to the problems faced by others in society.

The Supreme Court, and American society generally, began to change during the 1950's and 1960's. The justices on the Court increasingly made decisions that struck against racial discrimination. When President John F. Kennedy was assassinated in 1963, the new president, Lyndon B. Johnson, was able to use the wave of national political sympathy in order to push antidiscrimination legislation through Congress.

As Johnson oversaw the implementation of the most comprehensive American laws ever initiated against racial discrimination, he turned his attention to the Supreme Court. It was well known that Johnson wanted to make a significant symbolic gesture in support of equality for blacks by appointing a black lawyer to the Supreme Court.

When Justice Tom Clark retired, President Johnson appointed Thurgood Marshall to fill the vacancy. In selecting Marshall to be the first black justice, Johnson chose a lawyer who had such vast experience as a litigator, government attorney, and federal judge that it was nearly impossible for civil rights opponents to claim that Marshall lacked the proper qualifications to be a justice.

Marshall's great-grandfather had been a slave. The future justice grew up in Baltimore as the son of a schoolteacher. Marshall was an honors graduate of Lincoln University, a college for blacks in Pennsylvania. Many top law schools were closed to blacks at that time. Marshall attended law school in Washington, D.C., at Howard University, an institution founded to educate black students. He graduated at the top of his law school class in 1933.

After graduation from law school, Marshall embarked upon a career as a civil rights lawyer for the National Association for the Advancement of Colored People (NAACP). For more than twenty-five years, he traveled throughout the United States pursuing lawsuits on behalf of black people who wished to utilize the courts in order to fight against racial discrimination. He developed a reputation for thinking quickly on his feet in the courtroom because he grew accustomed to facing openly hostile judges in Southern courthouses. Marshall was the chief architect of the series of cases challenging racial segregation in education that culminated in the Supreme Court's landmark 1954 decision against school segregation in *Brown v. Board of Education.* Prior to appointment to the highest court, few justices have ever been so experienced in preparing and presenting arguments before the Supreme Court. Marshall argued thirty-two cases before the Supreme Court, and he won twenty-nine of them.

In 1961, President Kennedy appointed Marshall to be a judge on the United States Court of Appeals in New York City. He faced heated opposition from southern senators opposed to civil rights, and it took a year for him to gain confirmation from the Senate. In 1965, President Johnson appointed Marshall to be Solicitor General of the United States. The Solicitor General represents the United States government in front of the Supreme Court. The position gave Marshall the opportunity to build his already impressive reputation and experience as an advocate before the highest court in the land.

After Johnson appointed him to serve on the Supreme Court, Marshall's confirmation by the Senate was delayed for several months. Southern opponents of civil rights attempted to prevent the nation's most famous champion of racial equality from serving. During lengthy hearings before the Senate Judiciary Committee, Senator Strom Thurmond from South Carolina attempted to derail the nomination by asking dozens of questions about obscure aspects of legal history in the hope that Marshall would stumble in answering. Ultimately, Marshall's appointment was confirmed overwhelmingly by the Senate, with only one senator from outside the South among the eleven opposing the nomination. Marshall was sworn in as the first black justice on October 2, 1967.

Impact of Event

By becoming a justice of the Supreme Court, Thurgood Marshall broke the color barrier in one of the most powerful institutions in American society. Symbolically, his appointment demonstrated to American society that rigid racial discrimination was no longer socially acceptable. For black Americans, Marshall's appointment demonstrated that the old obstacles to professional advancement were being reduced. Black children could aspire to become lawyers, doctors, and judges without facing the absolute barriers to professional careers that had prevented so many bright, ambitious black people from pursuing their career goals prior to the 1960's. For Marshall's generation and preceding generations, racial discrimination and segregation had been so pervasive throughout American society that very few blacks could hope to attend college or compete with whites for professional jobs. Marshall's appointment to the Supreme Court was a visible sign of the broadening of opportunities for succeeding generations.

Marshall became a powerful liberal voice on the Supreme Court, especially when cases concerning discrimination were under consideration. Marshall was the first justice to have experienced firsthand the harassment and humiliation of racial discrimination. Because he traveled throughout the rural South as a litigator for the NAACP during the 1930's and 1940's, Marshall had witnessed and experienced the severest problems of racial prejudice in American society. In fact, Marshall was once nearly murdered by a lynch mob of Tennessee police officers who opposed his advocacy of civil rights and racial equality.

Just as other justices' views are shaped by their attitudes and experiences, Marshall's experiences as a victim of racial discrimination gave him great sensitivity to the plight of powerless people within American society. For the first time in history, the other justices on the Supreme Court could benefit from the insights of a colleague who had personal experience with the harsh realities of racial discrimination.

The new perspective contributed by Marshall helped to generate many opinions during the 1960's and 1970's which demonstrated a heightened concern for protecting the constitutional rights of all Americans. Marshall's concerns for civil rights were evident beyond issues of racial discrimination, including attention to the constitutional rights of poor people, women, and criminal defendants. Until the addition of several new justices moved the Supreme Court's decisions in a conservative direction during the late 1980's, Marshall was a key member of a liberal Court majority that protected and expanded individuals' civil rights to unprecedented lengths.

Marshall announced his retirement from the Supreme Court in 1991.

Bibliography

Abraham, Henry J. *Justices and Presidents: A Political History of Appointments to the Supreme Court.* 2d ed. New York: Oxford University Press, 1985. Detailed description of every appointment to the Supreme Court, including Thurgood Marshall's. Provides the best description of the political considerations that motivate every president's decisions regarding Supreme Court appointments. Gives a complete, concise discussion of the Marshall appointment.

Bland, Randall W. *Private Pressure on Public Law: The Legal Career of Justice Thurgood Marshall.* Port Washington, N.Y.: Kennikat Press, 1973. Biographical description of Justice Marshall's career up through his early years on the Supreme Court. Marshall's career extended well behind the time frame of this early volume.

Cox, Archibald. *The Court and the Constitution.* Boston: Houghton Mifflin, 1987. Presents a thorough, readable history of the Supreme Court and its decisions, including the era of Thurgood Marshall's service on the Court. Discusses how justices' decisions reflect the historical era in which they live. Provides the general audience with analysis of most important areas of constitutional law.

Kluger, Richard. *Simple Justice: The History of Brown v. Board of Education and*

Black America's Struggle for Equality. New York: Alfred A. Knopf, 1976. Detailed discussion of civil rights lawyers' efforts to win Supreme Court decisions against racial discrimination in education. Provides extensive details on Thurgood Marshall's work as a civil rights lawyer over the course of two decades. Considered the definitive history of civil rights litigation.

Nieman, Donald G. *Promises to Keep: African-Americans and the Constitutional Order, 1776 to the Present.* New York: Oxford University Press, 1991. Discussion of racial discrimination in the United States. Provides a thorough history of ways in which the courts and other government institutions failed to provide African Americans with the rights guaranteed by the words of the Constitution.

O'Brien, David M. "LBJ and Supreme Court Politics in Light of History." In *Lyndon Baines Johnson and the Uses of Power,* edited by Bernard J. Firestone and Robert C. Vogt. New York: Greenwood Press, 1988. Discussion of President Johnson's motivations in selecting appointees for the Supreme Court, including Thurgood Marshall. Discusses the reactions of Supreme Court justices and leading political figures to Johnson's choice of Marshall for the Supreme Court. Includes discussion of controversy surrounding Johnson's other appointee, Abe Fortas.

_____. *Storm Center: The Supreme Court in American Politics.* 2d ed. New York: W. W. Norton, 1990. Thorough, readable discussion of the Supreme Court's procedures and role in the American governing system. Provides many anecdotes about the justices' personalities and interactions. Includes references to Thurgood Marshall's participation in specific cases.

Christopher E. Smith

Cross-References

Brandeis Becomes the First Jewish Member of the Supreme Court (1916), p. 172; The American Civil Liberties Union Is Founded (1920), p. 327; The Congress of Racial Equality Forms (1942), p. 601; *Brown v. Board of Education* Ends Public School Segregation (1954), p. 913; Eisenhower Sends Troops to Little Rock, Arkansas (1957), p. 1003; Congress Passes the Civil Rights Act (1964), p. 1251; Discrimination in Accommodations Is Forbidden by the U.S. Supreme Court (1964), p. 1262; The Supreme Court Endorses Busing as a Means to End Segregation (1971), p. 1628; O'Connor Becomes the First Female Supreme Court Justice (1981), p. 2141; Jackson Becomes the First Major Black Candidate for U.S. President (1983), p. 2209; Wilder Becomes the First Elected Black Governor (1989), p. 2517.

THE ZERO POPULATION GROWTH MOVEMENT SPURS ENVIRONMENTAL CONSCIOUSNESS

Categories of event: Reproductive freedom; health and medical rights
Time: November, 1967
Locale: The United States

Amid the Vietnam conflict and domestic demonstrations in the United States, "zero population growth" jumped into the American vocabulary and became both a political and an environmental cause

Principal personages:

KINGSLEY DAVIS (1921-   ), the maverick demographer who coined the phrase "zero population growth" in an article in *Science* magazine

PAUL EHRLICH (1936-   ), the author of *The Population Bomb* (1968)

GARRETT DE BELL (1942-   ), a ZPG lobbyist who in 1970 spearheaded the first environmental "teach-in" called "Earth Day"

SUSAN WEBER (1939-   ), the executive director of the Zero Population Group movement

Summary of Event

In 1968, during the social and political unrest in the United States brought on by the Vietnam conflict, zero population growth came of age. It was a new movement with slogans of Stop at Two and Onlies Are Okay. The movement joined forces with other human rights movements of the day such as those pursuing civil rights, women's rights, and environmental protection. It became part of the ferment of the times. That year, as the baby-boomers were beginning to come of age, marked the founding of the "Zero Population Growth" movement.

The term was first used by scientist and demographer Kingsley Davis late in 1967. Writing in *Science* magazine, he declared: "Most discussions of the population crisis lead logically to zero population growth as the ultimate goal, because any growth rate, if continued, will eventually use up the earth." It took Paul Ehrlich and his persuasive book, *The Population Bomb* (1968), to ignite the movement. Paul Ehrlich was the founder of Zero Population Growth (ZPG) and coordinated his efforts in publishing the book with the Sierra Club. The book met with resounding success and went through twenty-two printings in just three years. It is considered a classic work on the subject of overpopulation. By the end of 1968, ZPG was incorporated as a national membership organization, and within the next year chapters had sprung up all over the United States.

The Vietnam War, women's rights, and the environmental movement all fueled ZPG. The media grabbed on to the movement: *Life* magazine ran a cover feature, and *Newsweek* and *Time* magazines devoted cover stories to the future of the planet. Concern climaxed with the "teach-in" on Earth Day celebrated at hundreds of universities nationwide on April 22, 1970. Several months later, in December, the Environmental Protection Agency was established.

When ZPG was founded, the fertility rate for American women was 2.5 children. There was no federal program supporting family planning. Because of religious beliefs and lack of an overall strategic plan, contraceptives of any type were neither well received nor disseminated. Abortion was a major issue of the time. More than eighteen out of every hundred thousand women who risked abortion did not survive the operation. Childbirth also carried great risks, with more than sixteen maternal deaths out of every hundred thousand live births. Improvements in health-care services, technical breakthroughs, greater access to birth control information and technology, and qualified family planning programs have yielded change for the better. By 1990, the fertility rate in the United States had fallen to approximately 1.7 children.

ZPG was closely linked with pollution concerns and the Clean Air Act of 1970. Greater understanding of the environment revealed that there are complex interactions occurring in nature. The 1970's brought recognition of and concern about acid rain. Scientists soon discovered acid snow, fog, and other deposits that sweep across state and national boundaries damaging crops, forests, lakes and streams, and wildlife. In the first two decades that these phenomena were studied, millions of acres of estuaries and productive farmland were destroyed, billions of tons of topsoil washed into America's waterways, and hundreds of species of plants and animals became endangered.

When Ronald Reagan campaigned for the U.S. presidency, one of his themes was "Morning in America." ZPG translated this to mean that America needed to pay attention to its own population problem instead of focusing entirely on that of the Third World. ZPG perceived Americans as having a blind spot; this is why the major objective of ZPG is to increase public awareness.

Economic growth commonly is believed to be the cure for poverty, unemployment, international debt, inflation, pollution, crime, drug addiction, and even the population explosion. Herman Daily, an economist with the World Bank, defined this phenomenon as "growthmania." There are also "no-limits-to-growth" theorists who contend that through technological fixes and human ingenuity, problems can be resolved so that growth and prosperity can continue forever. They maintain that population growth was a major contributor to the rising levels of prosperity and growth after the middle of the twentieth century. One economist who reinforced this concept was Julian Simon, who stated "We are able to support five billion people healthily . . . where only one hundred years ago we could only keep a billion alive." In his view, the population explosion is "the most incredible triumph of humanity."

The Zero Population Growth movement believes that the environment, human welfare, and economics are unavoidably linked. Development specialists began to realize that economic growth does not necessarily mean growth in human progress and that applying economic principles of strictly material production is not a cure-all to environmental and social ills. Much of the focus has been on the concept of "sustainability." One common definition is "the ability to meet the needs and aspirations of present generations without compromising the ability of future generations to meet their needs." Herman Daily has written extensively on the concept of a "steady state" economy and proposes it as a healthy alternative to "growthmania." His fundamental point is that if Earth's physical resources are finite, civilization cannot be sustained indefinitely, no matter how efficient and ingenious technology becomes. Human population growth must stop at some point to achieve a state of equilibrium.

The ZPG movement's major cause is family-planning projects in Third World countries, which exhibited extraordinarily high birth rates at the end of the twentieth century. With the exception of Japan, however, industrialized nations decreased their level of financial assistance for family-planning programs in developing nations. In 1991, the United States and other industrialized nations combined spent less money annually to help deliver family planning services to the developing world than U.S. consumers spent on cosmetics. Curbing the population growth in less developed countries (LDCs) would be a difficult activity even if financial resources were available. The most important constraint is the age composition of the countries. Many of the LDCs have high proportions of young people, so to halt rapid growth, the sizes of families must drop well below replacement levels (two children per couple) for some time. This is difficult to achieve in LDC societies, where the average family size is often as high as eight.

Children are highly valued as economic contributors in LDC families. This is also a major factor in and a barrier to family planning success. In the absence of a social security system in many of these countries, strong sons and daughters are an important hedge against starvation in the family structure. Children, in effect, provide a form of pension or old-age insurance.

The most important objective of the ZPG movement has been the development of practical guidelines and reasonable actions which an average citizen can adopt to help avoid the consequences of an overpopulated earth. The most important factor one should consider is not to have too many children. ZPG encourages couples to have one child, or two at most. As lifespans increase over time, population growth would result even if couples on average had two children each. Another critical conservation practice is to be aware of one's consumption habits. Choices can slow or accelerate global warming, acid rain, and other global problems. For example, driving fuel-efficient cars and keeping thermostats turned down are two obvious choices to save the environment.

Impact of Event

World population, 5.3 billion in 1991, could stabilize at 8 billion by the year 2050. If current trends continue, however, global numbers will continue to grow, and population could nearly triple to 14 billion.

Certain demographic indicators improve one's understanding of population growth. The birthrate is defined as the average number of children born per thousand people in a population per year. In 1989, the world's population of 5.2 billion produced about 144 million children, or an average of 28 children per thousand people. The counterpart of the birthrate is the death rate. In 1989, about 51 million people died, giving a death rate of 10 per thousand. The growth rate of the human population is simply the difference between the birthrate and death rate, or 18 per thousand in 1989. The world's growth rate in 1989 was therefore 1.8 percent. That rate of growth would result in a doubling of the world's population in about forty years.

Less developed countries accounted for about 85 percent of the world's population growth at the end of the twentieth century. Those countries had about one-third of their populations under fifteen years of age, a figure that translates into more than a billion more adults who would soon be searching for food, shelter, and clothing. Much of the world already lived at a subsistence level. Continued deforestation, abuse of available water resources, and pressure on the land meant living standards that would fall even lower.

In the rich industrialized countries, high consumption levels and population growth combined to place unsustainable demands on the earth's resources. Between 1900 and 1990, world population rose by a factor of four, but consumption of fossil fuel increased by a factor of twelve. Although Americans composed only 5 percent of the world's population, they used 25 percent of the world's commercial energy in 1990. The average American consumed as much energy as 385 Ethiopians and ate enough grain, directly or through other food products, to feed 370 people in Bangladesh. Clearly, choices made by Americans would affect resource availability in the future.

The most explosive population growth was expected to occur in Africa and southern Asia. The ZPG movement raised the collective consciousness of the world's leaders to do something about the need for family planning. Universal access to contraceptives and family planning services would have a tremendous impact on population growth. Governments, however, faced a dilemma of paying for the services required to substantially lower growth while still providing health services to the current population.

The ZPG movement served an important function in focusing the world's attention on the concept of sustainability. Population growth, as well as consumption and production choices, would have to be considered carefully as policy issues in order to provide for the welfare of future generations.

Bibliography

Daily, H. E. *Steady State Economics.* San Francisco: W. H. Freeman, 1977. A very good book describing the finiteness of the world's resources and dispelling economic myths.

The EarthWorks Group. *The Next Step: Fifty More Things You Can Do to Save the Environment.* Kansas City, Mo.: Andrews and McMeel, 1991. The authors include overpopulation as one of fifty environmental problems. Unfortunately, the authors are timid in their recommendations, not even mentioning limiting family size as one of the things to do.

Ehrlich, Anne H., and Paul R. Ehrlich. *Earth.* New York: Franklin Watts, 1987. A broad, nonquantitative overview of the conflicts and relationships among population, resources, and the environment. Color illustrations.

Ehrlich, Paul R. *The Population Bomb.* New York: Ballantine, 1968. The first cult book on major population and environmental issues.

Ehrlich, Paul R., and Shirley Feldman. *The Race Bomb: Skin Color, Prejudice, and Intelligence.* New York: Quadrangle/New York Times Book Co., 1977. Explodes the myth that there are genetically superior groups of people that should be encouraged to breed and genetically defective ones that should be discouraged.

Scarf, Judith S. *The Mother Earth Handbook.* New York: Continuum Books, 1991. This book is an "action guide" alerting people to environmental problems which accompany overpopulation. It goes beyond traditional calls to recycle and urges citizens of the earth to adopt fundamental life-style changes.

United Nations. *Population Bulletin of the United Nations*, 1983-   . A series of publications on studies commissioned by the United Nations' Population Division of the Department of International Economic and Social Affairs.

Zero Population Growth. *The Population Challenge.* Washington, D.C.: Author, 1990. Describes how unchecked population growth threatens the world's life-support systems. Discusses how individual actions can help restore and maintain a balance among people, resources, and the environment.

John Dorman

Cross-References

Sanger Opens the First Birth-Control Clinic in the United States (1916), p. 184; Sanger Organizes Conferences on Birth Control (1921), p. 356; Nevada and Montana Introduce the Old-Age Pension (1923), p. 373; Congress Passes the Clean Air Act Amendments (1970), p. 1561; The Family Planning Services Act Extends Reproductive Rights (1970), p. 1579; A U.N. Declaration on Hunger and Malnutrition Is Adopted (1974), p. 1775; WHO Sets a Goal of Health for All by the Year 2000 (1977), p. 1893; An International Health Conference Adopts the Declaration of Alma-Ata (1978), p. 1998.

THE UNITED NATIONS ISSUES A
DECLARATION ON EQUALITY FOR WOMEN

Category of event: Women's rights
Time: November 7, 1967
Locale: United Nations, New York City

After two decades of work, the United Nations adopted a declaration on the rights of women which reiterated the principles of the Universal Declaration of Human Rights and gave men and women equal rights

Principal personages:
> U THANT (1909-1974), the secretary-general of the United Nations (1961-1972)
> HELVI SIPILA (1915-   ), the chair of the Committee on the Status of Women (1967) and secretary-general of the International Women's Year Mexico City Conference (1975)
> MILAN KLUSAK (1923-   ), the president of the U.N. Economic and Social Council

Summary of Event

The Declaration on the Elimination of Discrimination Against Women has a long history. At the 1945 San Francisco conference which established the United Nations, the Brazilian delegation suggested the establishment of a committee on the status of women, but the United States and other countries questioned the need for a special committee, and the conference took no action. At the first session of the United Nations Economic and Social Council (ECOSOC), a subcommittee on the status of women was formed. This subcommittee's first report to ECOSOC recommended that the group be elevated to the rank of a full committee. ECOSOC approved this recommendation in June, 1946. The Committee on the Status of Women reports to ECOSOC, and occasionally to the Committee on Human Rights, on issues regarding the Universal Declaration of Human Rights and its covenants, adopted December 10, 1948.

Political rights were viewed by the Committee on the Status of Women and ECOSOC as being the cornerstone for equality of rights in economic, cultural, and social arenas. In June, 1946, ECOSOC requested that the U.N. secretary-general prepare a detailed study of political conditions for women. Questionnaires were sent to member states for five years. Data from them were analyzed and became the backbone for the committee's subsequent recommendations. In 1949, a Mexican representative proposed a U.N. convention on political rights of women; again, the United States and other countries questioned the need for a convention. Finally, in 1952 the U.N. General Assembly adopted the Convention on the Political Rights of

Women as a result of the committee's efforts.

The committee's work on a convention on the nationality of married women began in 1948. Data were collected by the secretariat on the conflicting laws of member states, and eventually, over objections of U.S. delegates, a draft was approved by
the General Assembly in 1955. The convention itself was adopted by the Assembly
in 1957. In 1962, the Convention on a Minimum Age at Marriage, Free Consent to
Marriage, and the Registration of Marriage was adopted.

During the 1960's and 1970's, more U.N. agencies began examining the status of
women within the context of their own agencies. The United Nations Educational,
Scientific, and Cultural Organization (UNESCO) was interested in discrimination
against women and girls in education; the Food and Agriculture Organization (FAO)
focused on the plight of rural women; and Planned Parenthood International, a
nongovernmental organization (NGO) with consultative status in the United Nations, collected data on family planning and services. The Declaration on the Elimination of Discrimination Against Women emerged from this background and was
adopted by the General Assembly in 1967. Various U.N. world conferences convened
during the 1970's on women's issues as well as on energy, the environment, population, housing, and other topics quickly demonstrated the inadequacy of a mere
declaration. The committee began working on a convention, which carries more
force.

During the 1960's and 1970's, more of the world's countries began to look at
human rights issues within their own countries. In the United States, extensive legislation was passed during the 1960's protecting women's rights. In Africa, the Banjul
Charter, finally adopted at the Nairobi Summit in 1981, gave women full rights in all
African countries, but only if these rights did not conflict with local custom and law
("clawback clauses").

Eventually, the idea for an International Women's Year and a United Nations Decade for Women, which would spotlight women's issues and problems, was pushed by
women's organizations with consultative status with the committee. Both of these
ideas were adopted by the General Assembly. During the Decade for Women (1975-
1985), three global conferences were held in Mexico City (1975), Copenhagen (1980),
and Nairobi (1985). These conferences adopted documents in accordance with the
U.N. Charter's preamble and the Universal Declaration of Human Rights. Data were
collected, the Convention on the Elimination of All Forms of Discrimination Against
Women was signed (1979), and goals and strategies were set for the year 2000. The
Convention on the Elimination of All Forms of Discrimination Against Women is an
international bill of rights for women and incorporates all of the principles contained in the earlier declaration on the same topic, plus many more.

Thus, through gradual, piecemeal work on various women's issues within the
United Nations, data were collected and support was secured. Particularly important
were the efforts of less developed countries (LDCs), women's organizations represented by the Committee on the Status of Women, and U.N. agencies such as the
United Nations Children's Fund (UNICEF) and FAO for a declaration, and then a

convention, on women's rights.

A U.N. declaration is a statement adopted by the General Assembly regarding specific principles on which the member states agree. The U.N. Charter and the Universal Declaration of Human Rights, the first international bill of rights in human history, both have served as keystones for various committees, declarations, and conventions. The language in declarations must be open to interpretation (for example, the phrase "work of equal value") because of the requirement that the United Nations respect all members' cultures and not intervene in a state's internal affairs. Declarations have no legal force: They are nonbinding agreements.

The United Nations Declaration on the Elimination of Discrimination Against Women focused on the need for equality for men and women in the political sphere, in civil law, in economic and social life, and in all levels of education. It called for the abolition of all laws and customs that discriminate against women and of all practices based on the idea of female inferiority. Child marriage and betrothal before puberty were prohibited. It requested measures to combat the traffic in women and the exploitation of prostitution. Certain rights were also enumerated for women: A woman can freely choose her husband, a married woman can retain her nationality, and women are to have equality of treatment with men with respect to work of equal value.

Various groups perceived a need for a stronger statement of women's rights and equality than this nonbinding declaration. In 1974, work began on the Convention on the Elimination of All Forms of Discrimination Against Women. A convention is a document containing certain agreed-upon principles which is then submitted to governments for action. Nations can support conventions in one of two ways. They may simply sign it; this means they agree with the stated principles and pledge not to contravene them. A state may instead ratify, or accede to, the convention. In this case, the government takes on the obligation to pursue the necessary actions to effect the convention's principles. This also means that the convention has become an international treaty and is therefore enforceable.

The guarantee of basic human rights for all and behavior based on the rule of law are U.N. goals. The difference between *de jure* (of law) and *de facto* (of fact) situations, however, creates problems in achieving U.N. goals. Thus, laws are needed to change situations. As people adapt to the new laws and situations, their attitudes change, and as attitudes change, a more positive atmosphere is created for the changing of even more laws. The understanding of this process by the Committee on the Status of Women and allied groups became the basis for the drafting, adoption, and ratification of the declaration, the convention, and other documents on elimination of discrimination against women.

Impact of Event

At the beginning of the twentieth century, only New Zealand had suffrage for women. By the time the United Nations was established, thirty-one countries allowed women the vote. The initial work of the Committee on the Status of Women focused on extending political rights of women even further. During this process, other problems materialized. The most serious problems were the lack of data specific to women and the lack of comparable data for within-country as well as cross-country comparisons: Women were statistically invisible. In addition, definitions of concepts as basic as "economic activity" varied from country to country, furthering the difficulties of making comparisons. A collateral problem was that economic development was a first priority in most countries after World War II. Rights of women, equality, and human rights issues in general were put on hold. For example, the idea of an equal rights amendment was introduced in the U.S. Congress in 1923, but little action was taken on the idea until the 1960's. The amendment did not pass Congress until 1972, and even then failed to be ratified.

With the demise of colonialism, beginning in earnest in the 1950's, it became apparent that Western concepts of human and civil rights were different from those in the nonindustrialized world. In the "new" countries, human rights were associated with the colonial imposition of Western government forms and constitutions.

The global spread of modern hygiene and medical technologies after World War II also caused the world's population to grow rapidly. Women, particularly in the LDCs, were affected more than were men. Their poverty, morbidity, and mortality rates increased, as did their rate of illiteracy. The welfare of children was also at risk.

Many countries in the 1970's and 1980's recognized the need to reduce the inequality experienced by women, but few did anything substantive about it unless pushed by women's groups. By the early 1970's, more people realized that both planned and unplanned development programs in the LDCs had the potential for adverse effects on women. There are wide global patterns, but accumulating research demonstrated that neither female subordination nor a patriarchal system withered with industrialization. Rather, patriarchal control expanded as a result of factors such as women's decreasing access to resources, the devaluation of unpaid work, low wages in insecure jobs, and male control of female sexuality.

It is within these contexts that the impact of the Declaration on the Elimination of Discrimination Against Women must be assessed. The declaration served notice that women's rights are important. Governments could not achieve their goals for economic development and political stability if both men's and women's rights as citizens of their own countries were not acknowledged. To achieve self-reliance, countries must provide leadership and equal access to basic institutions for both men and women. The declaration highlighted what in the 1990's is being accepted as a truism, but what in the turbulent postwar years was considered to be both radical and unnecessary.

Bibliography

Editorial Research Reports. *The Rights Revolution.* Washington, D.C.: Congressional Quarterly, 1978. An unbiased series of articles and reports on various social movements in the United States during the 1960's and 1970's. Written for the layperson. The factual presentation of contemporary historical events is centered on civil rights. References are provided.

Fraser, Arvonne S. *The U.N. Decade for Women: Documents and Dialogue.* Boulder, Colo.: Westview Press, 1987. Excellent overview and history of the decade of women's conferences. College level reading. References and abridged documents are provided.

Green, James Frederick. *The United Nations and Human Rights.* Washington, D.C.: Brookings Institution, 1958. Excellent history of early U.N. activities. Unbiased and factual. College level reading. References are provided.

Momsen, Janet Henshall, and Janet Townsend, eds. *Geography of Gender in the Third World.* Albany: State University of New York Press, 1987. Excellent collection of articles (research and theory) dealing with development in the Third World. Written for academics and upper division college students. References are provided.

National Commission on the Observance of International Women's Year. "*. . . To Form a More Perfect Union . . .*": *Justice for American Women.* Washington, D.C.: Government Printing Office, 1976. A data-based government document written by the commission appointed by President Gerald Ford. Easy to read. Good for historical perspective of problems in the United States. References are provided.

Staudt, Kathleen A., and Jane S. Jaquette, eds. *Women in Developing Countries: A Policy Focus.* New York: Haworth Press, 1983. A collection of articles on the difficulties of development projects and their adverse impact on women and children. College level reading. References are provided.

Tinker, Irene, ed. *Persistent Inequalities: Women and World Development.* Oxford, England: Oxford University Press, 1990. This book originated from the realization that all the studies and data produced for the U.N. Decade for Women had very little impact on development economists or women's studies scholars in universities. Designed for the academic community. Authors are advocates, practitioners, and scholars in development. Extensive bibliography.

U.N. Chronicle 22, no. 7 (1985). This is a magazine published by the United Nations. Various issues contain major speeches, data, interviews, and assessments of conferences. This issue discusses the end of the U.N. Decade for Women. College level reading.

Welch, Claude E., Jr., and Ronald I. Meltzer, eds. *Human Rights and Development in Africa.* Albany: State University of New York Press, 1984. A series of papers originally presented at a State University of New York, Buffalo, conference. College level reading. The African human rights charter and other documents are in the appendix.

Wylie, Eunice. "Women in the Picture." *World Health* 37 (June, 1984): 14-15. *World Health* is a World Health Organization publication written for the general reader. Contains excellent, short, data-based articles on health. This article deals with mortality, access to services, sexism, and other topics.

Dixie Dean Dickinson

Cross-References

CONGRESS ENACTS THE
AGE DISCRIMINATION IN EMPLOYMENT ACT

Category of event: Older persons' rights
Time: December 15, 1967
Locale: Washington, D.C.

After acting against racial and other forms of discrimination, Congress acted to protect older Americans by passing the Age Discrimination in Employment Act

Principal personages:
JOHN H. DENT (1908-1988), a member of the House of Representatives who worked to pass legislation against age discrimination
WILLARD WIRTZ (1912-   ), the secretary of labor under presidents John F. Kennedy and Lyndon B. Johnson from 1962 to 1969
LYNDON B. JOHNSON (1908-1973), the president of the United States (1963-1969)

Summary of Event

For most of American history, society demonstrated little concern about age discrimination. This lack of concern stemmed from several important influences. First, only racial discrimination was recognized as a serious social problem prior to the twentieth century. Other forms of discrimination that denied opportunities to people because of their gender, ethnicity, physical disabilities, or age were presumed to be natural components of the social order. Although northern legislators' awareness of racial discrimination led to several ineffective remedial enactments by Congress as early as the 1860's, there remained significant disagreement within American society even about the seriousness of racial discrimination and about the need for government efforts to eradicate it.

Second, until the late nineteenth century, the United States was primarily an agrarian society. People generally worked throughout their lives on farms or in small towns that provided services to farmers. Problems of age discrimination in employment did not become noticeable until industrialization, urbanization, and immigration transformed the American labor market into a competitive sector that periodically produced problems of unemployment.

Third, Americans' life expectancy increased during the twentieth century in conjunction with advances in medical science, sanitation, and occupational safety. Problems of age discrimination developed as people began to live longer and to remain active in the labor force for longer periods of time. Because the problem of age discrimination was not recognizable until the twentieth century, there was little government action directed toward the problem until American society's overall sensitivity to various forms of discrimination was heightened during the 1950's and 1960's. During the 1950's, decisions by the U.S. Supreme Court, protest marches, and sit-ins by African-American demonstrators and their supporters helped to raise the national consciousness about the problems of discrimination in American society. Television news coverage of protesters being beaten by law enforcement officers and attacked by police dogs gave middle-class white Americans greater awareness of the systematic victimization of African Americans in the South. Relatively little changed in the lives of many African Americans, however, because the Supreme Court decisions that ordered the dismantling of segregated schools were generally not implemented until the mid-1960's and thereafter.

Members of Congress shared this heightened concern about the existence of discrimination in American society, and many civil rights laws were proposed during the 1950's and 1960's. Because of the structure of the committee system within Congress, however, southern senators and representatives controlled many key committees. These southern legislators succeeded in blocking congressional consideration of antidiscrimination legislation even as public support for such legislation grew.

In the aftermath of the 1963 assassination of President John F. Kennedy, his successor, President Lyndon Johnson, asked Congress to pass civil rights legislation as a means of honoring the deceased president. Johnson, previously a leading member of the U.S. Senate, also applied his substantial legislative contacts and political skills to encourage passage of antidiscrimination laws. With momentum from the Kennedy assassination and encouragement from Johnson, members of Congress were finally able to gain sufficient votes to break the stranglehold of southern committee chairs who had been blocking legislation. Congress passed the Civil Rights Act of 1964 that forbade discrimination in public accommodations, employment, and government programs.

The initial civil rights legislation was designed to redress discrimination on the basis of race, color, religion, and national origin. As Congress finally addressed the problems of discrimination in American society, it gained a heightened awareness of other kinds of discrimination, such as gender discrimination, that served to prevent people from obtaining employment and otherwise enjoying the benefits of life in American society. One part of the Civil Rights Act of 1964 demonstrated the increased congressional concern about various kinds of discrimination by mandating that the secretary of labor undertake a study of the problems of employment discrimination experienced by older Americans.

Secretary of Labor Willard Wirtz conducted this study and found substantial problems throughout American society. In his 1965 report to Congress, Wirtz noted that half of all private job openings were barred to individuals age fifty-five and over. One-quarter of all private job openings were barred to people over age forty-five. When people lost their jobs after they had reached their forties or fifties, they frequently experienced great difficulties in finding employment, despite studies demonstrating that older workers often exceeded younger workers in skills and dependability. As a result of this age discrimination, more than one-half of all families in poverty were headed by individuals age forty-five and older. Older people throughout the country were suffering dire economic consequences because of the prevalence of age discrimination in employment. If they lost their jobs, they had an especially difficult time providing food, shelter, medical care, and the other necessities of life for their families.

Secretary Wirtz suggested that Congress consider enacting remedial legislation that would protect older people from age discrimination in employment in the same manner that people were protected against discrimination by race and other categories. The impetus for congressional action ultimately came when President Johnson addressed the problems of older Americans in January, 1967. In a message to Congress, Johnson urged the legislators to enact a law to prevent the unjust and arbitrary denial of employment opportunities for older people.

A primary sponsor of the resulting antidiscrimination legislation was Representative John H. Dent of Pennsylvania. As the chair of the Subcommittee on Labor of the House Committee on Education and Labor, Dent presided over hearings that examined the problems of age discrimination and attempted to fashion workable legislation to address those problems. Dent's subcommittee heard testimony about age discrimination from Secretary Wirtz and from representatives of various organizations concerned with the rights of older Americans. The subcommittee also heard testimony from flight attendants and others who were subjected to mandatory firing upon reaching ages as young as thirty-two.

The U.S. Chamber of Commerce was among the groups that objected to the proposed legislation and argued that the problem could be solved through voluntary initiatives involving education and public relations. A majority of senators and representatives, however, believed that age discrimination was sufficiently serious to deserve stronger action on behalf of victims. Congress passed the Age Discrimination in Employment Act (ADEA) in 1967 to permit lawsuits by employment discrimination victims between the ages of forty and sixty-five. In subsequent years, the law was amended to permit suits by anyone age forty or over, with no upper age limit.

The ADEA actually gave older workers greater ability to hold discriminating employers accountable than did other civil rights laws aimed at employment discrimination. Unlike the federal statute concerning race and gender discrimination, in which the claims are heard by a judge only and financial awards are limited to back pay, the ADEA permits older workers to have jury trials and to seek financial damages that punish employers found guilty of wrongful discrimination as well as compensating the workers for damages. Although relatively few older workers had any awareness of the ADEA until the 1980's, the law represents an important tool to combat employment discrimination.

Impact of Event

The passage of the ADEA marked a significant moment in the history of American civil rights. For the first time, national policymakers recognized the harms endured by older people in the job market and took strong action to redress the problems of age discrimination. Prior to the passage of the ADEA, some states had limited statutes designed to provide remedies for older people victimized by employment discrimination. The state laws represented a patchwork pattern that provided protection for older people in some states but left discrimination victims in other states completely unprotected. The ADEA provided uniform national protections for older people in every state.

As a result of the ADEA, people age forty and older can initiate legal actions to challenge unfair discrimination by employers. This is a useful means of attacking age discrimination in employment and represents a policy declaration by the federal government that places employment discrimination against older persons on the same footing as employment discrimination against other groups of people. Thousands of people have made use of the ADEA to challenge discriminatory actions that previously had harmed older workers and had unfairly barred them from earning a fair living and contributing to the national economy. During congressional debates about mandatory retirement age legislation, people became more aware of the ADEA, and the number of cases filed steadily increased. For example, there were only fifty-four hundred cases filed with the Equal Employment Opportunity Commission in 1978, but there were fifteen thousand cases filed in 1984.

Although the ADEA represents a significant step against age discrimination, it has not eliminated employment discrimination against older workers, for several reasons. The law protects older workers, but it does not prevent age discrimination against workers under the age of forty. The law permits employers to utilize bona fide occupational qualifications, such as physical fitness tests for some jobs, which may disproportionately eliminate older people from specific jobs. Many workers remain unaware that they are protected by federal laws. The long process of filing claims with the federal Equal Employment Opportunity Commission can discourage some discrimination victims from pursuing claims. Likewise, the long and expensive process of civil litigation can deter people from pursuing their claims through the court system. In addition, it is often difficult to gather sufficient proof to succeed in court, even when discrimination actually exists.

Despite the fact that the ADEA shares the same practical limitations as other antidiscrimination laws, it represents a symbolic and practical statement of federal policy. The statute heightens the awareness of employers about the problems of age discrimination and serves to pressure employers to treat older workers fairly. Although age discrimination problems continue to exist, the ADEA gave older persons a valuable tool for battling against a kind of discrimination that was pervasive throughout the American labor market until 1967.

Bibliography

Brown, Robert N. *The Rights of Older Persons.* Carbondale: Southern Illinois University Press, 1989. Provides readable descriptions of the various government laws and programs that specifically affect older Americans. Historical background is given for the relevant legislation. One chapter is devoted to discussion of the Age Discrimination in Employment Act.

Kalet, Joseph E. *Age Discrimination in Employment Law.* Washington, D.C.: Bureau of National Affairs Books, 1986. This book provides the most complete and readable description of the history and details of the Age Discrimination in Employment Act. Includes descriptions of the enforcement procedures, involving the Equal Employment Opportunity Commission.

Kendig, William L. *Age Discrimination in Employment.* New York: AMACOM, 1978. A brief description of the history and details of the ADEA. Written to inform business executives about how the statute operates.

Northrup, James P. *Old Age, Handicapped, and Vietnam-Era Antidiscrimination Legislation.* Philadelphia: University of Pennsylvania Press, 1977. Describes events leading to the passage of the ADEA. Includes statistics that describe the composition of older workers within the American work force.

Scheingold, Stuart A. *The Politics of Rights: Lawyers, Public Policy, and Political Change.* New Haven, Conn.: Yale University Press, 1974. This well-known book provides description and analysis of the development of Americans' consciousness about "rights." Discusses how various groups and individuals attempt to shape government policy by seeking to attain protections and entitlements that they believe they should possess.

Christopher E. Smith

Cross-References

Nevada and Montana Introduce the Old-Age Pension (1923), p. 373; Social Security Act Establishes Benefits for Nonworking People (1935), p. 514; The Civil Rights Act of 1957 Creates the Commission on Civil Rights (1957), p. 997; The Equal Pay Act Becomes Law (1963), p. 1172; Congress Passes the Civil Rights Act (1964), p. 1251; Congress Passes the Equal Employment Opportunity Act (1972), p. 1650; Congress Responds to Demands of Persons with Disabilities (1973), p. 1731.

CONGRESS ENACTS THE BILINGUAL EDUCATION ACT

Category of event: Educational rights
Time: 1968
Locale: Washington, D.C.

Congress in the late 1960's moved to provide federal assistance to schoolchildren of limited English-speaking ability

Principal personages:
RALPH W. YARBOROUGH (1904-　　　), the liberal Democratic senator from Texas who authored the original bilingual amendments to the Elementary and Secondary Education Act
LYNDON B. JOHNSON (1908-1973), the Democratic president (1963-1969) from Texas who reluctantly embraced bilingual education
JAMES H. SCHEUER (1920-　　　), the liberal Democratic representative from New York who expanded the act to include all children of limited English-speaking ability

Summary of Event

Although hailed as the world's melting pot, for most of its history the United States has been a nation of one language and culture. This conformist ethic maintained that as immigrants came to the United States they should give up their native customs and languages and assimilate as quickly as possible into the Anglo-American mainstream. Underlying this drive toward conformity was the unwritten rule in both Anglo and immigrant communities that to succeed, immigrants must bend to American culture instead of expecting American culture to bend to them.

Although ethnic neighborhoods and enclaves did exist and in some areas even flourished, the mainstream of American society was one of English-derived Anglo tradition. It was believed by many educators that the best way to prepare the children of immigrant parents for life in this culture was to immerse them in the English language and customs as quickly as possible. In this process of immersion, it was thought that the children who could learn would; those who could not were obviously of inferior mental abilities and therefore were not capable of obtaining the American dream. This philosophy, besides confirming the prevailing notion of Anglo-American superiority, also fit well with the notion of social Darwinism popular in the late nineteenth century.

The reality for most immigrant children in the late nineteenth and early twentieth centuries was that they were much more likely to sink than swim. In 1908, 13 percent of immigrant children enrolled in New York City schools at age twelve were likely to go on to high school, as opposed to 32 percent of the native-born. This trend was mirrored across the country, as non-English-speaking immigrant children, not understanding the language of instruction, fell further and further behind their native-born classmates.

While English dominance remained the rule across most of the United States in the years preceding World War I, certain areas of the country were forced by circumstance to provide limited native-language instruction. These areas included parts of Louisiana, where French was the language of the majority of the population, and the Northeast and Midwest, where there were substantial German-American populations. These areas, as well as several Native American reservations, provided instruction in the language of the non-English-speaking population.

With the advent of World War I, an intense wave of nationalism swept the country. It reinforced the negative reaction of many Americans to the large wave of immigration that had begun in the 1890's. Among the first casualties of this increase in "nativism" were programs for instructing schoolchildren in any language other than English. By 1925, thirty-seven states had passed laws requiring instruction in English no matter the dominant culture of the region. This trend continued into the 1950's. By the end of that decade, however, there were growing indications that more and more students with limited English proficiency were falling through the cracks of the educational system and thereby becoming trapped in language-induced poverty and despair.

For those children who attempted to stay in school, the outcome was often little better than if they had dropped out. During this period, the preferred method of dealing with those who spoke little or no English was to tag them as mentally retarded or learning impaired. Once so characterized, these children were placed in remedial instruction programs, where they were constantly reminded how different they were from their native, English-speaking classmates. For those who managed to avoid being tagged as retarded, the most likely educational track was vocational, foreclosing access to higher-paying professional occupations.

Demographics began to force a change in the attitudes of many public officials by the early 1960's. As immigrant populations began to flood into the schools of the South, districts were forced to consider alternative means of instruction. The first to do so was Coral Way, Florida. After the Cuban revolution of 1959, waves of Cuban refugees entered South Florida. Responding to the demand for quality bilingual instruction, the Coral Way school district implemented the first state-supported program to instruct students in their native language, thereby easing their transition to English. Since there was no U.S. precedent for the school district to draw upon, it turned to the American schools in Ecuador and Guatemala, which sought to develop fluency in both languages. The bilingual program was implemented for the first three grades of Coral Way schools and provided all students, Anglo and Cuban, instruction in both Spanish and English. Given the middle- to upper-class background of much of the early Cuban immigrant population, there was no need for a compensatory component to the program to care for general language or learning deficiencies.

With the success of the Coral Way project, the precedent for state and local government involvement in language assistance was set. By the mid-1960's, there were indications that the federal government was ready to become involved as well. As the national government began to investigate poverty and discrimination, several pieces of legislation were enacted that paved the way for the eventual adoption of the Bilingual Education Act. Of these, the two most important were the 1964 Civil Rights Act, specifically Title VI barring discrimination in education, and the Elementary and Secondary Education Act of 1965, which established the precedent for federal involvement in aid to impoverished and educationally deprived students. In 1968, the Elementary and Secondary Education Act would be the vehicle by which Congress funded bilingual education.

By the time the Ninetieth Congress opened in 1967, bilingual education had become a popular topic. More than thirty-five bills on the subject were introduced during the session, as many members of Congress became aware of the injustice of forcing immigrant children to struggle to learn lessons in what was to them a foreign language. Of these bills, Senate Bill 428, introduced by Ralph W. Yarborough, was typical. It proposed amending the Elementary and Secondary Education Act to create a new section, Title VII, providing bilingual education for those students speaking Spanish at birth or whose parents had originated in either Mexico or Puerto Rico. The Yarborough bill thus was not universal in scope but rather a concession to the Hispanic community—by far the nation's largest non-English-speaking minority and a group that was increasingly vocal. Mexican Americans were of growing importance in Yarborough's home state of Texas.

Yarborough's approach was immediately attacked by both the White House and members of Congress. President Lyndon B. Johnson had portrayed the Elementary and Secondary Education Act as the hallmark of his war on poverty and saw no need to modify it. Commissioner of Education Harold Howe II formalized this position when he proposed that instead of creating a new Title VII, additional monies could be appropriated under the existing Title I of the act. This section earmarked funds for language programs in economically impoverished areas, although it did not require schools to use languages other than English in order to receive funding.

In Congress, numerous members rose in opposition to the bill's limitation of bilingual education to one ethnic group, no matter how potentially powerful that group might be. It was argued that targeting one group for aid would unconstitutionally deny equal protection to myriad other ethnic groups and language minorities scattered across the country.

Representative James H. Scheuer of New York proposed a compromise that would provide funding for bilingual education to school districts with substantial non-English-speaking populations residing in economically disadvantaged areas. To receive funding, districts would be required to provide instruction in a student's native tongue until the child could demonstrate competence in English. Although Senator Yarborough resisted the expansion of the act's scope, he relented when the White House gave its grudging approval. With this political hurdle cleared, President Johnson signed the amendments adding Title VII to the Elementary and Secondary Education Act on January 2, 1968. Although no money was appropriated for 1968, $7.5 million was appropriated for 1969, enough to fund bilingual education for some twenty-seven thousand students.

Accompanying the political battle over the number of language groups to be served was a deeper philosophical struggle concerning the goals of bilingual education. Congress knew that it had to do something, but the "how" of bilingual education was unclear. The Bilingual Education Act created a framework for federal aid to schools with students of limited English ability but said little about whether the goal of the program should be a rapid transition to instruction in English or a slower approach allowing the maintenance of the child's native language and customs. The act's only significant stipulation was that to obtain federal aid a district had to use native languages in instruction. This lack of clarity contributed to the creation of an ideological conflict that lasted into the 1990's and brought the overall impact and effectiveness of bilingual education into question.

Impact of Event

The federal government's commitment to bilingual education grew into the hundreds of millions of dollars by the mid-1970's. Reauthorizations in 1972 and 1974 broadened the scope of the legislation and provided additional programs. These efforts were aided by both the federal courts and the Office of Civil Rights (then a part of the Department of Health, Education and Welfare).

In 1974, the Supreme Court ruled in *Lau v. Nichols* that school districts with a substantial number of non-English-speaking students must take steps to overcome language difficulties. This provided the Office of Civil Rights with the backing needed to force recalcitrant school districts to initiate bilingual education plans. These Lau plans greatly expanded the number of native-language instructional programs available across the country. They also set standards for when students qualified for inclusion in a program and when they could be allowed (or forced) to exit. During this period, test scores repeatedly showed that students exiting from well-designed and well-implemented programs consistently performed at or above grade level and thus were on a par with their native English-speaking classmates.

By the 1980's, the ambiguities in the goals of bilingual education had begun to engender resentment in parts of the Anglo population. Some believed that the aim of bilingual education was not to speed immigrants into the mainstream but rather to maintain their culture through state-sponsored ethnic programs. Fueling this attack were several studies showing that some bilingual programs were allowing students to remain in bilingual classes longer than the three-year maximum and were not teaching them sufficient English to function in mainstream classrooms.

With the election of Ronald Reagan to the presidency, the federal government began to retreat from aggressively promoting native-language instruction and instead encouraged districts to choose their own methods to develop capability in English. The 1984 reauthorization for the first time saw federal monies available for methods of instruction that did not utilize a student's native tongue but rather allowed for English immersion or submersion. Although this funding was limited in 1984, it was expanded in 1988. This change was amplified by a major retreat on the part of the

Office of Civil Rights in its enforcement of Lau remedies. Under the Reagan Administration, a school district was one-ninth as likely to be reviewed by the Office of
Civil Rights as under the administrations of either Gerald Ford or Jimmy Carter.

This change in government philosophy, while not signaling the end of bilingual
education, did have a significant impact. By the mid-1980's, several studies, including an influential one by the General Accounting Office, had shown that while there
were problems in the implementation of some programs, the philosophy of instruction in students' native languages during the transition to English not only worked
but allowed students to obtain grade-level standing much more quickly than English-
only programs. Correspondingly, as the English-dominant approach became the program of choice for many districts, the performance of limited-English students once
again declined.

As with any attempt to expand the rights of the few, the Bilingual Education Act
was politically charged and buffeted by ideological storms. What was indisputable,
however, was that the leap of faith that Congress undertook in 1968 was aimed at the
future—a future in which the dominant Anglo-American culture would be forced to
adapt to an increasingly diverse population. In creating the Bilingual Education Act,
Congress attempted to bend the will of the many to the needs of the few and provide
a chance for the children of all people to share in the American dream.

Bibliography

August, Diane, and Eugene E. Garcia. *Minority Education in the United States:
Research, Policy, and Practice.* Springfield, Ill.: Charles C Thomas, 1988. A fairly
analytical work, this book provides a thorough discussion of the theoretical ground-
ings of bilingual education as well as federal and state attempts to implement
these programs. Well-indexed and referenced. Includes a particularly well-written
chapter on specific types of bilingual education programs.
Crawford, James. *Bilingual Education: History, Politics, Theory, and Practice.* Trenton, N.J.: Crane Publishing, 1989. Written from a lay perspective, this book presents a good summary of the competing educational and political philosophies that
characterize the debate over bilingual education. Although somewhat unsophisti-
cated, the book touches on all aspects of bilingual education: political, practical,
and philosophical.
Grant, Joseph H., and Ross Goldsmith. *Bilingual Education and Federal Law: An
Overview.* Austin, Tex.: Dissemination and Assessment Center for Bilingual Education, 1979. As its name implies, this book summarizes and comments on the
various federal laws pertaining to bilingual education. A particular strength is the
author's excellent weaving together of the often conflicting priorities of the Congress, the president, and the courts to show how bilingual education has been
affected.
Leibowitz, Arnold H. *The Bilingual Education Act: A Legislative Analysis.* Rosslyn,
Va.: InterAmerica Research Associates, National Clearing House for Bilingual
Education, 1980. Provides a compact history both of the original 1968 amend-

ments to the Elementary and Secondary Education Act that created the Title VII bilingual provisions and of the 1974 reauthorization. The discussions of the statutory provisions of each are thorough, but there is little discussion of impacts.

Porter, Rosalie Pedalino. *Forked Tongue: The Politics of Bilingual Education.* New York: Basic Books, 1990. A fascinating presentation of the arguments opposed to bilingual education. Using both theoretical discussions and historical examples drawn from twenty years of bilingual practice, the author builds the argument that bilingual education has failed both the students it is supposed to help and the society that is paying for it.

Sandoval-Martinez, Steven. *How Much Bilingual Education? Educational vs. Legislative Considerations.* Los Alamitos, Calif.: National Center for Bilingual Research, 1984. A very short work, this paper is nevertheless useful for its discussion of the implications of legislative standards on bilingual program exit criteria. In looking at these criteria, the author demonstrates how standardized exit requirements are incongruent with the educational needs of most students.

Skutnabb-Kangas, Tove. "Multilingualism and the Education of Minority Students." In *Minority Education: From Shame to Struggle,* edited by T. Skutnabb-Kangas and J. Cummins. Philadelphia: Multilingual Matters, 1988. In keeping with the theme of the book, this chapter looks beyond the minority education problems in the United States and takes a more global perspective. The author investigates the impact that a multilingual population has on a society and the demands this imposes on the educational system to integrate language minorities into the mainstream.

Stein, Colman Brez, Jr. *Sink or Swim: The Politics of Bilingual Education.* New York: Praeger, 1986. Provides a good history of bilingual education policy from its modern inception in Coral Way, Florida, through the 1984 reauthorization. Contains a substantial discussion of state initiatives and how they worked to support or undermine federal programs.

Christopher H. Efird

Cross-References

Intellectuals Form the Society of American Indians (1911), p. 121; Congress Establishes a Border Patrol (1924), p. 377; Spanish Becomes the Language of Instruction in Puerto Rico (1949), p. 801; *Brown v. Board of Education* Ends Public School Segregation (1954), p. 913; The United Nations Adopts the Declaration of the Rights of the Child (1959), p. 1038; Cubans Flee to Florida and Receive Assistance (1960's), p. 1044; Chávez Forms Farm Workers' Union and Leads Grape Pickers' Strike (1962), p. 1161; Congress Passes the Civil Rights Act (1964), p. 1251; Head Start Is Established (1965), p. 1284; Congress Passes the Equal Employment Opportunity Act (1972), p. 1650; Congress Enacts the Education for All Handicapped Children Act (1975), p. 1780; The United Nations Adopts the Convention on the Rights of the Child (1989), p. 2529.

THE BREZHNEV DOCTRINE BANS
ACTS OF INDEPENDENCE IN SOVIET SATELLITES

Category of event: Political freedom
Time: 1968-1989
Locale: Moscow, Union of Soviet Socialist Republics

Under the Brezhnev Doctrine, the Soviet Union exercised the right of direct inter-vention to restore order anywhere among its satellites that it deemed socialism to be threatened

Principal personages:
LEONID ILICH BREZHNEV (1906-1982), the general secretary of the Com-munist Party and the leader of the Soviet Union
MIKHAIL GORBACHEV (1931-   ), the president of the Soviet Union who renounced the Brezhnev Doctrine in 1989
NIKITA S. KHRUSHCHEV (1894-1971), the first secretary of the Communist Party and premier of the Soviet Union who formulated the policy of the Brezhnev Doctrine
ALEXANDER DUBČEK (1921-   ), the first secretary of the Czechoslovak Communist Party who oversaw the liberalization of the "Prague Spring" in 1968
IMRE NAGY (1896-1958), the Hungarian Communist premier who led the revolt against the Soviet Union in 1956
TITO (1892-1980), the Yugoslav Communist leader who helped to sepa-rate his country from the Soviet empire in 1948

Summary of Event

As a victorious Ally and in direct violation of the provisions of the Atlantic Char-ter (1941) against territorial aggrandizement at the expense of the enemy, after World War II the Soviet Union came to inherit an empire larger than the old Romanov, Hohenzollern, and Habsburg empires combined. This diverse, multinational new empire consisted of an expanded Soviet Union plus numerous satellite states sur-rounding its Eurasian frontiers, and it reflected the Soviet Union's status as an emerg-ing superpower in the vacuum left by the total defeat of the Axis by the Allied Powers. The founding of this communist empire through the victories and subse-quent occupation by the counterattacking Red Army after the Battle of Stalingrad (1942-1943) also marked a beginning of the post-World War II Cold War between the Soviet Union and its Western allies.

The Brezhnev Doctrine was a policy evolved by the Soviet Union for the main-tenance of its empire against the right and forces of national self-determination. Under this coercive and punitive program, the Soviet Union assumed the right to intervene directly anywhere in its sphere—from East Germany, Hungary, and Czechoslovakia to Afghanistan—where it deemed "socialism" to be threatened. It was specifically enunciated by Leonid Brezhnev in his "Speech to the Fifth Congress of the Polish United Workers Party" in Warsaw on November 12, 1968, in connection with the Soviet-Warsaw Pact invasion of Czechoslovakia on August 20-21, 1968, to suppress the moves toward greater independence during the so-called Prague Spring. The policy's foundations actually were laid in the late 1940's.

With the split of Yugoslavia under Josip Broz Tito from the Soviet Empire in 1948 and the success of the communists in China in 1949, new centers of communism in addition to Moscow began to arise in Belgrade, Beijing, and elsewhere, threatening Soviet hegemony. World communism was becoming polycentric and multinational communism with the appearance of Titoism, Maoism, and other forms. Nationalism began to express itself through communism as well as affecting the nature of communism.

Events in Eastern Europe mirrored these changes in the Soviet Empire and communist ideology. In the early 1950's, continued repression and deteriorating economic conditions led to worker unrest in Poland and East Germany, culminating in a Soviet military intervention to put down strikes in East Germany in 1953. This invasion to suppress German worker and national aspirations was the first application of the Soviet policy later to be dubbed the Brezhnev Doctrine. In 1956, Nikita Khrushchev similarly ordered the Soviet Army to crush the Hungarian uprising under Imre Nagy. The Hungarian situation was seen as much more severe than the earlier ones in Poland and East Germany. After initially trying to reform communism in Hungary, the revolutionaries had quickly moved toward discarding it and adopting national independence. Consequently, the Soviet reaction also was much more severe, earning Khrushchev, the real author of the Brezhnev Doctrine, the nickname "the butcher of Budapest."

Thereafter, East Germany and Hungary stood as clear examples to the peoples of the Soviet Empire dreaming of national rights and freedoms. During the 1960's and 1970's, any moves toward the realization of these dreams had to be carried out carefully so as not to bring down the full force of Soviet power. Over the next two decades, for example, Romania slowly moved toward greater independence, Hungary gradually established a more Western national economy, and Albania broke away from the Soviet Empire under Chinese sponsorship. As part of this process, liberalization came to Czechoslovakia under Alexander Dubček in 1968. Brezhnev and the Soviet leadership watched these events closely and periodically issued warnings to the Czech leadership. Once again, when the situation deteriorated too far for the Soviet Union, it declared socialism in danger in Czechoslovakia and interfered, with the Brezhnev Doctrine as its justification.

The invasion of Czechoslovakia demonstrated the Soviet Union's commitment to maintaining its hegemony, and internationally this event had significant negative ramifications for the Soviet Union. For example, the process of Soviet-American détente was set back at least five years, the Soviet-Yugoslav rapprochement was halted, and the Soviet Union generally lost prestige abroad. Despite these consequences, the policy was not abandoned, and late in 1979 the Soviet Union intervened again, this time in Afghanistan to prop up and finally to replace a faltering communist regime. This intervention precipitated prolonged Western-supported resistance and a civil war which became the Soviet Union's Vietnam.

The Brezhnev Doctrine not only put pressure on the various satellites to remain loyal and to conform to the Soviet ideology but also was used to intimidate the subject nationalities of the Soviet Union. The message was clear: If the Soviet leadership was willing to use whatever force necessary in East Berlin, Budapest, Prague, or Kabul, it certainly would not hesitate to do so in Vilnius, Kiev, Yerevan, or Tashkent to stifle any national aspirations or disorders. The Soviet "socialist peace" was maintained until 1985 and the coming of Mikhail Gorbachev.

Enforcement of the Brezhnev Doctrine, especially in the case of the costly war in Afghanistan, contributed greatly to the decline of the Soviet economy. Gorbachev inherited this economy, which was on the verge of collapse. Like the Russian Empire before it, the Soviet Union was not only economically bankrupt but ideologically bankrupt as well. Gorbachev's eventual response was sweeping reform, and the more democratic era of *glasnost* (openness) and *perestroika* (restructuring) was initiated. With this liberalization of the Soviet system came the demise of the Brezhnev Doctrine.

From the time of the founding of the opposition Solidarity trade union at the Lenin Shipyard in Gdansk in 1980, Poland was in danger of running afoul of the Brezhnev Doctrine. The Soviet Union did not respond as in the past, in part because of the sorry state of the Soviet economy and the war in Afghanistan and in part because of the instability of top leadership after the death of Brezhnev. Under Gorbachev, the Soviet Union withdrew from Afghanistan in 1989, and with Poland and Yugoslavia leading the way, Eastern Europe also began to liberalize.

In the waning weeks of 1989, Gorbachev indicated on several occasions, such as during an official visit to Finland, that the Soviet Union would no longer intervene in the internal affairs of its satellites and, thereby, that the Brezhnev Doctrine was dead. Thereafter, Poland and the other Central and Eastern European satellites quickly asserted their national independence from the disintegrating Soviet Empire. Following their lead, other republics and peoples in the Soviet Union began to assert their national rights and identities.

The Brezhnev Doctrine, as it became known in the West, was never proclaimed publicly as such by the Soviet Union, which even denied that such a policy existed. From its real inception under Khrushchev through its practice and justification by Brezhnev to its passing under Gorbachev, it was a major foundation for the centralized control exercised from Moscow throughout the Soviet domains.

Impact of Event

For four decades, the Brezhnev Doctrine helped to restrict severely the human rights of the Eurasian peoples under Soviet domination. For example, in forcing the adherence of Hungarian, Polish, or Lithuanian Catholics, Jews, Volga Germans, and Crimean Tatars to the Soviet state and its Stalinist ideology, the Soviet Union deprived these peoples of rights of national self-determination and tried to destroy their national cultures, aspirations, and identities and replace them with artificial and alien Soviet substitutes. The Brezhnev Doctrine was nothing more than a brutal policy of Stalinist imperialism and totalitarian control.

In these years, Soviet power rested largely on the use of force, force which the Soviet Union readily exercised to control its satellites and to bully its own citizens into submission. Partially under the auspices of the Brezhnev Doctrine, the Soviet Union tried in vain to substitute material progress and hollow superpower prestige for national and individual freedoms. It succeeded only in stifling real leadership and productivity, initiative, and creativity.

While somewhat dampened perhaps, the fires of nationalism were not so easily extinguished. In 1989, once the oppression of communism began to lift through Gorbachev's reforms and abandonment of the Brezhnev Doctrine, the blossoms of national rights quickly began to bloom again. One by one, Soviet satellites moved toward national self-determination and took on its challenges. Civil war persisted in Afghanistan, but without foreign involvement, indicating that the country would find its own solutions to its problems. Germany was reunited, and Poland, Czechoslovakia, and Hungary moved rapidly toward democracy. Romania, Bulgaria, and Mongolia moved more slowly, but all took steps toward independent and more democratic futures.

The abandonment of the Brezhnev Doctrine was part of a general Soviet pullback internationally. Consequently, settlements to problems became more readily achievable in areas of former Soviet involvement from the Middle East, where the curtailment of Soviet aid to Syria, Libya, and the Palestine Liberation Organization brought a regional peace agreement closer, to southern Africa, where Soviet moderation brought an end to the Angolan civil war and a greater willingness of the African National Congress to cooperate with reform efforts in the Republic of South Africa, and to Central America, where the new Soviet stance helped force the Sandinista government to grant free elections and left Cuba effectively isolated. Even in tiny Albania, the Soviet moves contributed to the breakdown of Stalinist isolationism and to democratic changes.

On the other hand, in the Soviet Union itself, the resultant resurgence of nationalism, inspired in part by events and changes in Central and Eastern Europe, brought major problems. It also speeded the drastic political and economic restructuring by fostering democratization and the transition to a free market system as well as the national realignment of the Soviet Union. The Brezhnev Doctrine was a major impediment to human rights and progress in the Soviet Empire and ultimately was symptomatic of its political, economic, social, and ideological weaknesses. Its renunciation contributed substantially to a dynamic for momentous change in the Soviet Union and elsewhere by ending the Cold War and encouraging international cooperation.

Bibliography

Dawisha, Karen. *Eastern Europe, Gorbachev, and Reform: The Great Challenge.* 2d ed. Cambridge, England: Cambridge University Press, 1990. A contemporary evaluation of the era of *glasnost* and *perestroika.* Offers an understanding of the reasons for and consequences of the Soviet renunciation of the Brezhnev Doctrine by Gorbachev.

Edmonds, Robin. *Soviet Foreign Policy 1962-1973: The Paradox of Super Power.* New York: Oxford University Press, 1977. A year-by-year review of Soviet foreign policy for the early period of the Brezhnev Doctrine. Very good in pointing out the negative ramifications as well as the positive returns of the policy for the Soviet Union.

Gati, Charles. *The Bloc That Failed: Soviet-East European Relations in Transition.* Bloomington: Indiana University Press, 1990. A good study of contemporary Soviet-European relations. Deals with the formulation and impact of the Brezhnev Doctrine as well as the current outcomes of its abandonment by the Soviet Union under Gorbachev. A factual and well-written account.

Hamsik, Dusan. *Writers Against Rulers.* New York: Random House, 1971. A detailed discussion of the coming of the Prague Spring by a leading Czech intellectual and participant. Chapter 8 deals specifically with the Soviet-Warsaw Pact intervention, the Czech reaction to it, and the Brezhnev Doctrine. Written from the Czech point of view.

Hutchings, Robert L. *Soviet-East European Relations: Consolidation and Conflict 1968-1980.* Madison: University of Wisconsin Press, 1983. A concise history of post-1968 Soviet-East European relations, stressing the impact of the Brezhnev Doctrine on foreign policy. Internal as well as external factors shaping the policy are examined. Includes a good bibliography.

Jelavich, Barbara. *St. Petersburg and Moscow: Tsarist and Soviet Foreign Policy, 1814-1974.* Bloomington: Indiana University Press, 1974. A history of Russian-Soviet foreign relations. Offers the longer view of the continuity of Russian-Soviet foreign policy toward Central and Eastern Europe for a fuller understanding of the formulation and exercise of the Brezhnev Doctrine.

Nogee, Joseph L., and Robert H. Donaldson. *Soviet Foreign Policy Since World War II.* 3d ed. New York: Pergamon Press, 1988. A standard history of contemporary Soviet foreign policy. Puts the emergence of the Brezhnev Doctrine in the broader perspective of post-World War II Soviet international relations. Chapter 7 concerns the events surrounding the formation and executions of the policy.

Staar, Richard F. *USSR Foreign Policies After Détente.* Stanford, Calif.: Hoover Institution Press, 1987. Social-science analysis of Soviet foreign policy and its making in the years since Khrushchev and Brezhnev. The impact of the Brezhnev Doctrine, its deterioration, and its reversal are aptly discussed in a wider context. Somewhat dated but still very good for the basics of policy-making.

Stokes, Gale, ed. *From Stalinism to Pluralism: A Documentary History of Eastern Europe Since 1945.* New York: Oxford University Press, 1991. These edited primary sources put the Brezhnev Doctrine into the broader historical perspective of post-World War II Eastern Europe. Part 2 concerns the formulation of the policy and contains the actual speech by Brezhnev of November 12, 1968, enunciating it.

Terry, Sarah Meiklejohn, ed. *Soviet Policy in Eastern Europe.* New Haven, Conn.: Yale University Press, 1984. A collection of twelve essays examining virtually every aspect of Soviet policy toward Eastern Europe in the early 1980's. Centers on the events unfolding in Poland. Also quite good on Czechoslovakia and Hungary. Thorough and very detailed.

Dennis Reinhartz

Cross-References

Soviets Take Control of Eastern Europe (1943), p. 612; A Hungarian Uprising Is Quelled by Soviet Military Forces (1956), p. 969; Soviets Invade Czechoslovakia (1968), p. 1441; The Helsinki Agreement Offers Terms for International Cooperation (1975), p. 1806; Soviets Invade Afghanistan (1979), p. 2062; Solidarity Leads Striking Polish Workers (1980), p. 2112; Gorbachev Initiates a Policy of *Glasnost* (1985), p. 2249; Hungary Adopts a Multiparty System (1989), p. 2421; Soviet Troops Leave Afghanistan (1989), p. 2449; Poland Forms a Non-Communist Government (1989), p. 2500; Soviet Troops Withdraw from Czechoslovakia (1990), p. 2570.

THE CIVIL RIGHTS ACT OF 1968
OUTLAWS DISCRIMINATION IN HOUSING

Categories of event: Racial and ethnic rights; civil rights
Time: March-April, 1968
Locale: Washington, D.C.

The Civil Rights Act of 1968 was designed to reduce discrimination in the purchasing, renting, and leasing of housing by members of ethnic and racial minorities

Principal personages:

LYNDON B. JOHNSON (1908-1973), the president of the United States, the moving force behind the major civil rights legislation of the 1960's
MARTIN LUTHER KING, JR. (1929-1968), the major civil rights leader in the United States
EVERETT DIRKSEN (1896-1969), the Senate minority leader who initially opposed the Civil Rights Act of 1968

Summary of Event

Residential segregation became a staple of American society in the late nineteenth century and continued into the twentieth. It began in southern cities, in compliance with the "Jim Crow" principle of the inappropriateness of close social contact between the races. Residential segregation became the vehicle to separate blacks from whites. It was accomplished through a combination of real estate practices, intimidation, and legal regulations. As black Americans migrated to the North and West, residential segregation spread to those areas as well.

In the North, the real estate industry led in the drive to create segregated housing. Real estate boards adopted regulations prohibiting their members from renting or selling property in predominantly white areas to nonwhites. Members usually complied with the rules, since they could be expelled for noncompliance. Agents steered Asians, African Americans, and other racial minorities away from white preserves. Violence and harassment were frequently aimed against minorities brave enough to venture into white areas.

Residential segregation was also institutionalized by law. States, beginning with Virginia in 1912, authorized cities and towns to designate neighborhoods as either black or white. Urban localities enacted ordinances which designated individual blocks as available to only whites or blacks. Many Southern urban areas were already racially integrated, and problems developed in drawing up the necessary laws. Some cities defined the right to a block on the basis of which race constituted the majority. Members of a minority group did not have to move, but no more of its members could move into the block.

In 1917, in *Buchanan v. Warley*, the U.S. Supreme Court prohibited government-mandated residential segregation. It is noteworthy that the Court based its decision in property rights, not civil rights—that is, on the grounds that such ordinances denied owners the prerogative of disposing of their property as they wished. Even after the *Buchanan* decision, restrictive racial covenants, policies, and practices of real estate organizations perpetuated residential apartheid. Racially restrictive covenants, which were more prevalent in the North than in the South, bound property owners in a particular neighborhood to sell only to other "members of the Caucasian race." In *Corrigan v. Buckly* (1926), the Supreme Court ruled that such covenants constituted private agreements and therefore were not prohibited by the Fourteenth Amendment to the Constitution. Two decades later, in *Shelley v. Kraemer* (1948), the Court, in a unanimous opinion, ruled that even though restrictive covenants were private agreements, enforcement of them through the use of state courts constituted state action and therefore violated the Fourteenth Amendment. In a companion decision, *Hurd v. Hodge* (1948), the Court held that judicial enforcement of restrictive covenants in the District of Columbia violated the Civil Rights Act of 1866 and was also inconsistent with the public policy of the United States.

Actions by the real estate industry after those decisions illustrated the entrenched nature of racial exclusion in housing. In 1924, seven years after the *Buchanan* decision, the National Association of Real Estate Boards (NAREB) revised Article 34 of its official code of ethics to forbid Realtors from assisting sales to members of any race or nationality or to any individual "whose presence will be detrimental to property values" of the neighborhood. Shortly after the *Kraemer* and *Hurd* decisions, a NAREB leader expressed doubt whether those Supreme Court decisions would "mitigate in any way against the efficacy of Article 34." Although NAREB and most local real estate organizations eliminated mention of race from their codes during the 1960's, Realtors resorted to the clandestine exclusion of cultural and racial minorities. During President John F. Kennedy's administration, those regulations which authorized residential segregation in federally funded housing were removed, and many municipalities adopted open housing laws. Even then, there was very little movement toward housing desegregation. Real estate agents continued to steer whites to predominantly white neighborhoods and blacks to correspondingly black neighborhoods. Financial institutions continued to discriminate in providing mortgages to minorities.

Because residential segregation contributed to school segregation and trapped blacks and Hispanics in economically depressed inner-city neighborhoods, a strong federal fair housing law became an urgent priority for civil rights leaders. In 1966, as Martin Luther King, Jr., campaigned against segregation in the Chicago area, President Lyndon B. Johnson proposed a fair housing law. It presented a dilemma for liberals. The coalition which had successfully steered major civil rights legislation through Congress in 1964 and 1965 fractured. Fearful of "white backlash," Northern liberals were unwilling to act against discriminatory practices. A badly divided House of Representatives passed an open housing bill in 1966. Support by some Republicans ensured its passage, even though the House Republican leadership, including Minority Leader Gerald R. Ford, opposed it. The bill died in the Senate. The next year, the House passed the Civil Rights Bill of 1967, proposed by

President Lyndon B. Johnson largely to protect civil rights workers and to reduce discrimination in jury selection.

This bill became the Civil Rights Act of 1968. The Senate push for a strong open housing statute was led by Democratic senators Philip A. Hart of Michigan and Walter F. Mondale of Minnesota and Republicans Edward W. Brooke of Massachusetts and Jacob K. Javits of New York. Until the final days of the debate on the bill, Senate Republican leaders opposed any open housing legislation, ostensibly because federal action would usurp prerogatives of the states. Explaining his conversion, Senate Minority Leader Everett McKinley Dirksen of Illinois told the Senate that only twenty-one states had open housing laws. He expressed a fear that it might take fifteen or twenty years for the other twenty-nine states to enact similar laws. In reality, he and other conservative opponents of open housing were won over by a compromise which added what they claimed were "tough sanctions against rioters and provocateurs of racial violence." The Senate approved the bill on March 11, 1968.

Immediate consideration of the bill in the House was blocked by opponents of fair housing laws. Many of them wanted to delay consideration of the bill until after the "poor people's march" which Martin Luther King, Jr., had planned to begin in Washington on April 22. They reasoned that the march would annoy enough members to doom the bill. King's death, however, created a groundswell of support for the bill. The House of Representatives adopted the Senate's version without amendment on April 10, 1968, one week after King's assassination. Reminding the nation that he had waited three years for the bill, President Johnson signed it the next day.

The Civil Rights Act of 1968 applied to about 80 percent of the nation's housing. It reduced racial barriers, in three stages, in about 52.6 million single-family dwellings. When it became fully operational on January 1, 1970, the law prohibited discrimination on the basis of color, race, religion, or national origin in the sale or rental of most apartments and homes. The only dwellings exempted were single-family homes sold or rented without the assistance of a Realtor and small apartment buildings with resident owners. The law also prohibited discriminatory lending practices by financial institutions. It also provided severe federal penalties for persons convicted of intimidating or injuring civil rights workers and blacks engaged in activities related to schooling, housing, voting, registering to vote, jury duty, and the use of public facilities. The act also extended the Bill of Rights to Native Americans living on reservations under tribal government and made it a federal crime to travel from one state to another or to use radio, television, or other interstate facilities with intent to incite a riot.

Impact of Event

It is difficult to determine the impacts which resulted from the passage of the 1968 Civil Rights Act. The act cannot be assessed in isolation. It was but one of a series of statutory actions to integrate minorities, especially blacks, into American life. Moreover, decisions of the Supreme Court on the issue of open housing carried far-ranging potentials.

The fair housing law did little to alleviate the problem of housing discrimination, as its enforcement provisions were weak. The Department of Housing and Urban Development was empowered to investigate complaints and to negotiate voluntary agreements with those found guilty of discrimination. If this conciliatory approach failed, the attorney general was authorized to bring lawsuits, an expensive and time-consuming process. Because the act failed to afford timely redress, victims of discrimination largely ignored it. Fewer than fifteen hundred complaints were filed during the first two years that the act was in effect. A 1974 study of real estate practices in major cities by the U.S. Commission on Civil Rights and another at the University of Michigan in 1976 showed that housing discrimination was widespread but subtle. Steering remained a common practice.

The Civil Rights Act of 1968 was amended on September 13, 1988, to eliminate defects. The amendments provided the Department of Housing and Urban Development with authority to forward class-action cases to the Department of Justice for prosecution, empowered the Department of Justice to initiate class-action suits on its own initiative, and increased monetary penalties.

A noticeable decline in residential segregation has occurred since the bill was enacted. Segregation in the twenty-five cities with the largest black populations declined 1 percent between 1960 and 1970 and 6 percent between 1970 and 1980. The decline for Asians and Hispanics was much greater. Preliminary statistics suggest that the decline in segregation accelerated for all groups between 1980 and 1990.

Court decisions also advanced the cause of open housing. In 1967, a year before the Civil Rights Act of 1968 finally became law, the Supreme Court invalidated California's Proposition 14, which had been adopted by voters in 1964 to negate a fair housing bill enacted by the legislature. In ruling against Proposition 14, which gave property owners an absolute right to dispose of their property as they saw fit, the Court, in *Reitman v. Mulkey*, held that although the state was not obligated to enact nondiscriminatory housing legislation, it could not enact provisions which had the effect of encouraging private discrimination. Much more significant, a few weeks after enactment of the new civil rights law, the Supreme Court made open housing a legal reality with the decision in *Jones v. Alfred H. Mayer Co.* That decision resurrected a provision of the 1866 Civil Rights Act. Codified as Section 1982, the provision reads that "All citizens of the United States shall have the same right, in every State and Territory, as is enjoyed by white citizens thereof to inherit, purchase, lease, sell, hold, and convey real and personal property." The resurrection of Section 1982 made the heart of the Civil Rights Act of 1968 dispensable.

Bibliography

Bell, Derrick A., Jr. *Race, Racism, and American Law.* Boston: Little, Brown, 1980. The premier text on racism in the legal system. Appears in the standard law school format. It is punctuated with manufactured examples designed to stimulate discussion.

Brooks, Roy L. *Rethinking the American Race Problem.* Berkeley: University of

California Press, 1990. This work merges the questions of race and class and suggests that self-help offers the best mechanism for improving conditions in the black community.

Clark, Thomas A. *Blacks in Suburbs: A National Perspective.* New Brunswick, N.J.: Rutgers University, Center for Urban Policy Research, 1979. This sociological work places black suburbanization in the context of class development, urbanization, and migration.

Farley, Reynolds, and Walter R. Allen. *The Color Line and the Quality of Life in America.* New York: Russell Sage Foundation, 1987. One of the best works on deprivations caused by racism. Also examines the continued existence of discrimination in this age of alleged equality.

Feagin, Joe R., and Clairece B. Feagin. *Discrimination American Style: Institutional Racism and Sexism.* 2d ed. Malabar, Fla.: Robert E. Krieger, 1986. Focuses on racial and sexual discrimination and argues that discrimination has causes other than bigotry and prejudice. Modern discrimination, according to the authors, is subtle and difficult to combat.

Nieman, Donald G. *Promises to Keep: African-Americans and the Constitutional Order, 1776 to the Present.* New York: Oxford University Press, 1991. Although rather brief, this work is an excellent source on the evolution of legal rights for blacks. It is especially strong on developments in the twentieth century.

Ashton Wesley Welch

Cross-References

Roosevelt Outlaws Discrimination in Defense-Industry Employment (1941), p. 578; The Civil Rights Act of 1957 Creates the Commission on Civil Rights (1957), p. 997; Congress Passes the Civil Rights Act (1964), p. 1251; Discrimination in Accommodations Is Forbidden by the U.S. Supreme Court (1964), p. 1262; FBI and CIA Interference in the Civil Rights Movement Is Revealed (1971), p. 1595.

MARTIN LUTHER KING, JR.,
IS ASSASSINATED IN MEMPHIS

Categories of event: Atrocities and war crimes; civil rights
Time: April 4, 1968
Locale: Memphis, Tennessee

The greatest voice for interracial peace and understanding, Martin Luther King, Jr., was shot to death while campaigning for civil rights

Principal personages:

MARTIN LUTHER KING, JR. (1929-1968), a civil rights leader whose nonviolent protest work influenced key American social and political changes

JAMES EARL RAY (1928-   ), a drifter and small-time criminal who was convicted of King's assassination

RALPH ABERNATHY (1926-1990), King's closest friend and confidant, succeeded him as president of the Southern Christian Leadership Conference

ROSA PARKS (1913-   ), an Alabama seamstress whose defiance of segregated bus-seating patterns inspired the 1955 Montgomery bus boycott

EUGENE "BULL" CONNOR (1897-1973), the Birmingham police chief whose brutal tactics against peaceful black protesters in 1963 led to national outrage

Summary of Event

The Civil Rights movement of the 1950's and 1960's proved to be one of the most consequential social and political episodes in American history. Dedicated activists effectively worked to eliminate racial barriers that had denied millions of black people basic citizenship rights in the Jim Crow South. The movement produced numerous leaders, but none was more identifiable than Martin Luther King, Jr., a highly educated and articulate Baptist minister from Atlanta, Georgia. For more than a decade, his name was synonymous with the struggle for blacks' civil rights in the United States.

King, a charismatic figure, encountered little difficulty in rallying support around his causes and leadership style. Influenced by the teachings of Morehouse College president Benjamin Mays, India's Mahatma Gandhi, and the German philosopher Friedrich Hegel and by the social gospel of Walter Rauschensbusch, he developed a protest philosophy that blended religion with issues of justice, human and civil rights, and a vision of an ideal American society.

King was the Civil Rights movement's greatest exponent of nonviolent mass civil disobedience. He rose to national prominence in 1955 as the leader of the Montgomery (Alabama) Improvement Association's boycott against the city's racially segregated bus line. Black passenger Rosa Parks precipitated the boycott with her arrest for refusing to surrender her seat to a white rider. The boycott successfully desegregated the buses. It also helped initiate a period of mass protest that not only challenged Southern segregation and black disenfranchisement but also influenced human rights issues in foreign countries.

Many of the subsequent campaigns that affected Southern life were led by King through his own Southern Christian Leadership Conference (SCLC). An occasional failure, such as the SCLC's 1961-1962 Albany, Georgia, initiative to eliminate segregation ordinances and discriminatory hiring practices, did not discourage King. A foray in Birmingham, Alabama, in the spring of 1963 produced more tangible results. King, ably assisted by Ralph Abernathy, his closest friend and handpicked SCLC successor, resolved to change downtown hiring practices and to escalate the pace of court-ordered desegregation in schools and public facilities. Unlike in Albany, King employed the tactic of passive resistance with telling effect, as the demonstrators defied local law and taxed the patience of police chief Eugene "Bull" Connor. On national television news, Americans watched with abhorrence the acts of police brutality against the protesters, many of whom were children; they were similarly outraged over King's and Abernathy's solitary confinement in the Birmingham jail. The demonstrations eventually helped to win major advances for Birmingham blacks.

King utilized the Birmingham campaign to raise the national consciousness about the morality of civil rights causes. In the process, he enhanced his own prestige and leadership position. That stature was further strengthened by his August 28, 1963, "I have a dream" speech during the March on Washington campaign. Addressing 250,000 persons assembled at the Lincoln Memorial as well as a national television audience, King expressed his continuing faith in America's ideals. Speaking in his characteristic rhythmic cadence, he stirred the nation with his "dream" of an America free of racial prejudice and bigotry. The address was perhaps King's finest hour as an orator. King continued to garner national and international acclaim for his work. By the end of 1964, he had won *Time* magazine's prestigious Man of the Year award and had been honored as a Nobel Peace Prize recipient. Both recognitions further solidified his position as the United States' preeminent leader in the struggle for blacks' civil rights.

Sensitized national leaders reacted to King's and other black leaders' efforts with concrete legislation. The comprehensive 1964 Civil Rights Act outlawed discrimination and segregation in key aspects of American life. In the same year, King's Selma, Alabama, campaign for black voting rights provoked savage white police reaction against demonstrators similar to that in Birmingham. Congress responded to incidents in Selma and to black voting demands with an extensive law effectively enfranchising Southern blacks, the 1965 Voting Rights Act.

Before 1965, King had confined his civil rights activities primarily to the segregated South. Such efforts, however, did not preclude a concern for oppressed people worldwide. Almost from the outset of his activism, he linked America's black struggle to human rights issues elsewhere, particularly in Africa. He spoke boldly against South African apartheid and supported the move to end colonialism across the continent. His attendance at Ghana's independence celebrations in Ghana in 1957 and Nigeria in 1960 helped to endear him to citizens of those emerging Third World nations.

Increasingly after 1965, King's attention turned to opposing America's Vietnam involvement and to the problems of African Americans and poor urbanites in Northern cities. These initiatives produced considerably less than the desired results. His antiwar stance cost him important white Northern support, and his efforts in cities such as Chicago won blacks few substantive gains in better housing and employment. Nevertheless, King's internationalism and his inclusion of human rights and economic justice in a broadened civil rights agenda inspired plans for a major campaign to encourage massive federal spending to fight poverty rather than war. He would not, however, have the opportunity to lead this ambitious Poor People's March on Washington.

King's urban concerns took him to Memphis, Tennessee, in the early spring of 1968. His purpose there was to support striking municipal sanitation workers seeking recognition of their recently formed union. A demonstration planned on their behalf for March 28, 1968, ended violently when youthful members of a local black gang fought with police and vandalized stores along the route. Discouraged, King canceled the demonstration and promised to return to lead another march that would adhere to his nonviolent philosophy. In the late evening of April 4, 1968, several days before the scheduled second march, King was mortally wounded by a sniper while standing on the balcony near his room at Memphis' Lorraine Hotel.

King's meteoric rise to international prominence clearly had not occurred without challenges and personal dangers. A 1958 stabbing in New York by a mentally disturbed black woman had made clear the grave risks that accompanied public stature and recognition. It was the nature of his activism that provoked the greatest opposition and made him a logical target of racial extremists. King was acutely aware of this; death threats and bomb scares constantly reminded him of it. An emotional speech to a church audience the night before his assassination was so interspersed with veiled references to dying that it makes credible his aides' suggestions that King saw his death as imminent.

If King readily envisioned his own death, it seemed not to trouble his lieutenants. They, too, fully understood the dangers inherent in his role, but they had witnessed his preoccupation with death before and were not overly concerned with his latest mood. King's assassination was certainly unexpected, and it generated a range of emotions from close associates, but few of them seemed truly surprised that such an event could happen.

After one of the nation's most intensive manhunts ever, James Earl Ray, an escaped Missouri felon with decidedly antiblack racial views, was captured, tried, convicted, and sentenced to life imprisonment for King's murder. In many black communities, however, suspicion surfaced that Ray did not act alone. Long after the trial, charges were rampant of a King conspiracy that implicated the Federal Bureau of Investigation (FBI) and the Central Intelligence Agency (CIA). No conspiracy evidence was ever substantiated in King's murder, however.

Impact of Event

The reaction to King's death was universal. The international community memorialized him and recognized his impact on human rights developments beyond the United States. American leaders praised his commitment to nonviolence and acknowledged his role in influencing many of the social and political changes affecting American life, especially in the South. Even King's militant rivals lamented his passing and predicted dire national social consequences because of it.

Such predictions resulted largely from the violence that the assassination triggered in many American communities. Rioting struck Memphis almost immediately, as black youths vented their anger and frustration over yet another fallen symbol. In Washington, leaders pleaded for calm, but the national capital and 130 other cities could not be spared from violent disturbances in the emotional wake of the assassination. The disorders caused forty-six deaths and property damage exceeding $100 million.

This violent response hardly represented the vast black majority, who memorialized King in more traditional and peaceful ways. Nevertheless, the consequences of the riots were far-reaching. King's death virtually assured congressional passage of the 1968 Civil Rights Act providing for open housing, legislation that King had long supported. That act was the last major civil rights legislation of the era. A growing conservative white backlash concerned about law and order stiffened its resolve against further minority demands.

Civil rights leaders seemed unable to reverse the trend. Before King died, the movement had already splintered badly over the issues of nonviolence and Black Power. It continued to founder after his death. Historians have debated whether King and his enlarged agenda of human rights, economic justice, and international peace could have stemmed the reversal, but his SCLC successor could not. Despite renewed fears of violence, in June, 1968, Abernathy led King's Poor People's Campaign in Washington peacefully; however, it accomplished little. Lacking both King's charisma and his leadership qualities, Abernathy soon fell from power and sank into relative obscurity.

King was not the first leader-activist felled by white racism. In the five-year period before his death, America had anguished over the loss of several others, including Medgar Evers, James Chaney, and Viola Liuzzo. To many blacks, however, King was not merely another beloved figure victimized by racism. For most, he embodied their hopes and aspirations to enjoy the full benefits of American citizenship. He spoke for them, articulating their demands in a way that, it seemed, only he could. In life, he symbolized the black struggle, and in the years following his death no leader emerged who was capable of mobilizing the masses as he did.

In death, King's image became even more powerful, taking on new meaning and symbolism. In the nation's cumulative memory of King's work and vision, he was transformed from martyr to virtual demigod. A national holiday was declared to honor his life, and annual King celebrations were inaugurated in several West African countries. Long after his death, he continued to represent the idealism of the 1950's and 1960's civil and human rights struggle.

Bibliography

Abernathy, Ralph D. *And the Walls Came Tumbling Down: An Autobiography.* New York: Harper & Row, 1989. A controversial memoir of King's dearest friend and civil rights associate. It gives a good account of the inside strategies and operations behind the SCLC's campaigns. It is particularly valuable for its revealing portrait of the nonpublic part of King's life. Pictures, appendix, and index.

Ansbro, John J. *Martin Luther King, Jr.: The Making of a Mind.* Maryknoll, N.Y.: Orbis Books, 1982. An interesting study of King's nonviolent resistance strategy that examines doctrines and insights of the many thinkers who influenced him. In some ways, this study criticizes King as a person who appropriated the ideas of others. Includes references and index.

Bishop, Jim. *The Days of Martin Luther King, Jr.* New York: G. P. Putnam's Sons, 1971. Written for a popular audience, this readable volume is primarily the story behind King's assassination and the responses of those close to him. Includes a bibliography and index.

Branch, Taylor. *Parting the Waters: America in the King Years, 1954-1963.* New York: Simon & Schuster, 1988. A comprehensive study dealing with an important period of King's life. This prize-winning book is superbly written and is especially valuable because of its focus on King from the context of his origins in the larger black religious culture, a base from which other civil rights leaders also originated. Includes notes and index.

Frank, Gerold. *An American Death: The True Story of the Assassination of Dr. Martin Luther King, Jr., and the Greatest Manhunt of Our Time.* Garden City, N.Y.: Doubleday, 1972. The subtitle suggests this volume's basic content. The book is valuable for its extensive research and coverage of James Earl Ray and his trial and for Frank's attempts to answer the questions that suggested a conspiracy in King's murder. Includes notes and index.

Garrow, David. *Bearing the Cross: Martin Luther King, Jr., and the Southern Christian Leadership Conference.* New York: William Morrow, 1986. This massive book comes from the scholar who has most thoroughly studied King and his civil rights role. A Pulitzer Prize winner, the volume ends rather abruptly with King's death. It has vast references and an extensive bibliography.

King, Coretta Scott. *My Life with Martin Luther King, Jr.* New York: Holt, Rinehart and Winston, 1969. An intimate account of the Kings' life together. It depicts the impact of King's work on the leader himself and on his family. Pictures and a useful index.

King, Martin Luther, Jr. *Why We Can't Wait.* New York: New American Library, 1964. One of several books authored by King. It provides his personal prescription for progress in the civil rights struggle. Considered a classic by King scholars, it includes his protest and reform philosophy and is an appropriate beginning for understanding King's thoughts and motivations.

Miller, William Robert. *Martin Luther King, Jr.: His Life, Martyrdom, and Meaning to the World.* New York: Weybright and Talley, 1968. This book appeared in the immediate aftermath of King's death. The title suggests much about Miller's presentation. It contains sound conclusions about King's legacy. Bibliography and index.

Oates, Stephen B. *Let the Trumpet Sound: The Life of Martin Luther King, Jr.* New York: Harper & Row, 1982. The work of an accomplished biographer, this study is comprehensive, absorbing, and well written but notably reverent of its subject. Oates taps previously unused sources. Contains references and an index.

Robert L. Jenkins

Cross-References

Parks Is Arrested for Refusing to Sit in the Back of the Bus (1955), p. 947; The SCLC Forms to Link Civil Rights Groups (1957), p. 974; The Civil Rights Act of 1957 Creates the Commission on Civil Rights (1957), p. 997; Civil Rights Protesters Attract International Attention (1963), p. 1188; Martin Luther King, Jr., Delivers His "I Have a Dream" Speech (1963), p. 1200; Congress Passes the Civil Rights Act (1964), p. 1251; Martin Luther King, Jr., Wins the Nobel Peace Prize (1964), p. 1257; Martin Luther King, Jr., Leads a March from Selma to Montgomery (1965), p. 1278; Congress Passes the Voting Rights Act (1965), p. 1296; The Civil Rights Act of 1968 Outlaws Discrimination in Housing (1968), p. 1414.

LEFTISTS REBEL IN FRANCE

Categories of event: Revolutions and rebellions; political freedom
Time: May-June, 1968
Locale: Paris, France

In 1968, a leftist rebellion by students and workers fundamentally questioned the political order and prosperity of Charles de Gaulle's Fifth French Republic

Principal personages:
 DANIEL COHN-BENDIT (1945-   ), a key leader of the student militants at Nanterre
 CHARLES DE GAULLE (1890-1970), the president of France at the time of the rebellion
 ALAIN GEISMAR (1939-   ), the general secretary of SNESUP, the *Syndicate national de l'enseignement supérieur* (National Union of University Teaching Personnel), in 1968
 GEORGES POMPIDOU (1911-1974), the premier of France at the time of the rebellion
 GEORGES SÉGUY (1927-   ), the secretary general of the CGT, the *Confédération générale du travail* (General Confederation of Labor), in 1968

Summary of Event

The "events of May," as the leftist rebellion in France in 1968 came to be known, were as unexpected as they were momentous. In the years after World War II, French society had become increasingly stable and prosperous and, after the rise of General Charles de Gaulle to power in 1958, politics in the Fifth Republic (which de Gaulle inaugurated) had also appeared to stabilize under his firm leadership. During the 1960's, de Gaulle had led France back to a position of importance in European and world affairs. To many, France had become a model of an emerging affluent, technocratic, postindustrial society.

Yet in May and June, 1968, the prosperity and national grandeur of de Gaulle's France was challenged by a series of uprisings that came close to a revolutionary upheaval. The initial explosion in France was triggered by militant students dissatisfied with the overcrowded classrooms, irrelevant curricula, and unresponsive faculty that they considered characteristic of the French university system in the 1960's.

The first protests occurred at the Nanterre campus of the University of Paris in November, 1967, when sociology students opposed the introduction of a reform plan by the minister of education. This "Fouchet Plan" responded to some student complaints, but what especially aroused student resentment was the refusal of the Ministry of Education and the deans of the faculties at Nanterre to include them in the discussions concerning the proposed changes. Student demands for participation in determining curricular change and for more socially relevant curricula won over many younger faculty members at Nanterre to the idea of reform of the educational system.

Although the initial protest at Nanterre failed, over the course of the next several months student and younger faculty radicals became more and more vocal around four major issues: student freedom, opposition to Gaullism, university reform, and protest against the Vietnam War. Daniel Cohn-Bendit, a radical sociology student at Nanterre, emerged as the most vigorous leader of the dissidents. For Cohn-Bendit, the repressive atmosphere of French universities reflected the alienation and repression of bureaucratic capitalist society as a whole. Radicals like Cohn-Bendit saw the transformation of the university system as inseparable from broader social and political transformation.

An attempt by university officials to expel Cohn-Bendit escalated the conflict, and when leaders of the protest against the Vietnam War were arrested at Nanterre on March 22, 1968, students occupied the administration building. From that date on, the Nanterre campus witnessed a rapid collapse of traditional academic relationships, as numerous student and student-faculty groups critically discussed the Vietnam War, the structure of French universities, the potential revolutionary relationships between radical students and workers, and the repressive character of French social and political life. On May 2, the dean at Nanterre decided to close the university; this move shifted the focus of radical activity to the centerpiece of French university life, the Sorbonne in Paris, and the "events of May" began.

On May 3, left-wing students, including many of the Nanterre militants of what became known as the "March 22 Movement," met at the Sorbonne to discuss their future course of action. The university rector, fearing violence, called in the police, the first time since 1791 that police in Paris had entered any university grounds. The jailing of student activists revealed the repressive face of the French state and spurred increasing sympathy for them not only among fellow students but also from other groups within French society, especially young workers.

Until May 13, the upheaval was limited primarily to students, as ever-larger numbers of demonstrators clashed with police in the streets of the Latin Quarter. The government refused to listen to students' demands, and confrontations continued; the more students were injured and jailed, the more popular their insurrection became. The night of May 10-May 11—the "Night of the Barricades"—witnessed an estimated thirty thousand students demanding the removal of police from the Sorbonne. During the night, the students erected barricades on major Latin Quarter streets that were then attacked by the police. Large numbers of injuries and arrests occurred, but the battle ended with a victory for the students. They occupied most of the Latin Quarter, and the police withdrew from the area at the request of Premier Georges Pompidou, who returned on May 11 from a state visit to Afghanistan and Iran.

The student protest spread to the working classes, and over the course of the next several weeks French society came to a virtually complete halt. The major French trade unions were invited to call a one-day general strike for Monday, May 13. On that date, some seven hundred thousand people demonstrated in Paris. Neither the French Communist Party nor the CGT, usually dominated by the Communists, was eager to see a close association of students and workers, but the CGT leaders were aware that events appeared to be moving beyond their control and complied with the decision to strike.

Wildcat strikes spread across France beginning on May 14, and by May 17 close to ten million workers had struck across the nation. Young workers in large numbers joined students in protest demonstrations. By May 20, most normal activity in France had either halted or been seriously impaired: Workers at Sud-Aviation, Renault, and other major state-owned companies were on strike, railways, airlines, and the postal services were at a standstill, and a large segment of the private sector was affected.

This massive show of worker unrest forced the Communist and Socialist Parties to support labor's demands for reforms. On May 25, the major unions met with the government and arrived at the Grenelle agreements, which gave the workers unprecedented material gains. When Georges Séguy, the secretary general of the CGT, met with the striking workers at Renault on May 27, however, they resoundingly rejected the Grenelle accords. On the same day, a demonstration took place at Charléty stadium in Paris, and some fifty to sixty thousand people took part. Both François Mitterand, the leader of the Socialist Party, and ex-Premier Pierre Mendès-France offered to head provisional governments. The two weeks of extraordinary events gave many of the student and worker protesters ample reason to think that the government was collapsing and that France was on the brink of revolution.

Up to that point, Charles de Gaulle had been uncharacteristically indecisive in responding to the rebellion. In a speech on May 24, he had called for a referendum on whether he would have a mandate to engage in the reconstruction of France. This speech detonated the worst episode of violence in Paris since the outbreak of revolt three weeks before, but the continued opposition of the Communist Party and CGT leadership to the most radical activists' schemes coupled with the complex divisions among the many leftist groups gave de Gaulle sufficient breathing space to recover his nerve and act decisively.

He left Paris mysteriously on May 29, secretly flying to Germany to assure himself of the loyalty of French military commanders there. On May 30, he delivered a radio address appealing to supporters of law and order, dissolved the National Assembly to prepare for new elections, and presented himself as the sole bulwark against either anarchy or Communist rule. A mass demonstration of a million people in support of de Gaulle occurred after his speech. The traditional leaders of the French left, the Communist Party and the CGT, refrained from any attempts to assume leadership of the radical movement and refused to countenance the use of force. In the ensuing weeks, the theater of confrontation in France moved from the streets to the ballot box, where in elections on June 23 and June 30 de Gaulle and his supporters won an impressive majority in the National Assembly.

Impact of Event

The impact of the crisis of May-June, 1968, on France was profound. De Gaulle's personal victory was short-lived; within a year he had resigned from office. The government made a series of concessions to the protest groups, both student and worker: a university reform bill, better wages and working conditions, and some concessions to militant workers' demands for joint management of the enterprises in which they worked. Despite these significant institutional changes, the hopes and visions of the radicals for a dramatically changed France were extinguished with the Gaullist victory.

What did not disappear so easily were the discontents that underlay the extraordinary mélange of social critiques and utopian programs that the "events of May" produced. Students and young workers spoke for and acted in the name of rights and values—self-expression, comradeship, spontaneity, antiauthoritarianism, self-management—that they hoped would be the basis for radically changing the consumption-oriented, technology-driven, repressive society of post-World War II France. They argued that a democratic yet authoritarian government had shown its repressive face in the streets of Paris during the month of May. Affluence produced alienation in their vision of modernity; advanced capitalism was capable of integrating within itself even self-described opposition movements, as the behavior of the Communist and Socialist parties and of the CGT had demonstrated.

Drawing from a complex intellectual and political heritage—Karl Marx, Vladimir Ilich Lenin, Leon Trotsky, Mao Tse-tung, Che Guevara, Rosa Luxemburg, Jean-Paul Sartre, surrealism, and Dadaism—the leftist rebels sought to develop new principles for reorganizing society and new modes of action to effect that reorganization. Their successes were often at the same time a reason for their failures. For example, student action committees proliferated across France in May. Radically democratic, without overall direction, these committees saw themselves as the nuclei for change in the workplace, in government, and in the provision of social needs such as child care. Their very diversity and radical democratic organization prevented them from becoming the basis for an organized nationwide left-wing assault on the bastions of power, something that the older forms of leftist political practice in France were also unable to provide.

The leftist rebels in 1968 did not make a revolution. The student-worker movement did, however, reveal the conflicts and contradictions that lay beneath the prosperous society of 1960's France. The upheaval in May was a symptom both of the emergence of what many commentators called a "postindustrial" society and of new forms of political action that would emerge to seek change within that society. Together with the uprising against Soviet hegemony in Prague in the same year, the "events of May" revealed discontents that would not go away and aroused hopes that would not disappear. The political culture of Europe had been changed irrevocably.

Bibliography

Aron, Raymond. *The Elusive Revolution: Anatomy of a Student Revolt.* New York:

Praeger, 1969. Incisive analysis of the student revolt by one of France's leading twentieth century political thinkers; very critical of the student movement.

Hoffmann, Stanley. *Decline or Renewal? France Since the 1930s.* New York: Viking Press, 1974. A series of important reflections on French political life by a leading American expert. Contains an excellent chapter on the May events.

Katsiaficas, George. *The Imagination of the New Left: A Global Analysis of 1968.* Boston: South End Press, 1987. Interesting comparative discussion of the worldwide insurrectionary events of 1968. Important for placing French events in broad perspective.

Larkin, Maurice. *France Since the Popular Front: Government and People, 1936-1986.* Oxford: Clarendon Press, 1988. Solid analytical history of France since the 1930's; places the events of 1968 in broader historical perspective.

Poster, Mark. *Existential Marxism in Postwar France: From Sartre to Althusser.* Princeton, N.J.: Princeton University Press, 1975. Broad-ranging intellectual history of postwar France that provides ample discussion of the intellectual background of the ideas of the 1968 militants.

Schnapp, Alain, and Pierre Vidal-Naquet, eds. *The French Student Uprising, November 1967-June 1968: An Analytical Record.* Boston: Beacon Press, 1971. Essential compilation of a wide range of documents concerning the "events of May"; Vidal-Naquet's introductory essay provides an excellent overview by a historian who was active in the movement.

Touraine, Alain. *The May Movement: Revolt and Reform.* New York: Random House, 1971. A sympathetic analysis of the May movement by a sociologist who taught at Nanterre at the time of the insurrection; compare with Aron. Touraine has been one of the leading proponents of the thesis of the emergence of a postindustrial society.

Michael W. Messmer

Cross-References

Jouhaux Is Awarded the Nobel Peace Prize (1951), p. 873; Soviets Invade Czechoslovakia (1968), p. 1441; Four Students Are Killed at Kent State by the National Guard (1970), p. 1532; FBI and CIA Interference in the Civil Rights Movement Is Revealed (1971), p. 1595; Vietnam Releases United States Prisoners of War (1973), p. 1691.

THE PROCLAMATION OF TEHERAN
SETS HUMAN RIGHTS GOALS

Category of event: International norms
Time: May 13, 1968
Locale: Teheran, Iran

The International Conference on Human Rights adopted the Proclamation of Teheran, setting priorities for the future human rights work of the United Nations

Principal personages:

PRINCESS ASHRAF PAHLAVI (1919-　　), the elected president of the conference, wife of the ruling shah of Iran

MARC SCHREIBER (1915-　　), the director of the United Nations' Division of Human Rights; executive secretary of the conference

U THANT (1909-1974), the secretary-general of the United Nations who presented the opening address to the conference

C. K. DAPHTARY (1893-　　), the representative of India and chair of the drafting committee

Summary of Event

In December, 1963, the United Nations General Assembly proclaimed 1968 as the International Year for Human Rights. In connection with this celebration, the International Conference on Human Rights met in Teheran, Iran, from April 22 through May 13, 1968. The meeting was seen as an occasion for detached stocktaking and long-term planning, as Secretary-General U Thant put it in his address to the conference, in an environment of recently renewed international human rights activity.

The adoption of the Universal Declaration of Human Rights in December, 1948, was followed by more than a decade of little progress in U.N. human rights activity. Like most other issues in international relations, human rights became subordinated to Cold War rivalry. Each bloc focused its attention on violations in the other and raised issues of human rights primarily as a matter of ideological struggle. In such an environment, even the further development of international human rights norms became problematic. For example, drafting of the international human rights covenant, which attempted to give binding legal force to the rights proclaimed in the Universal Declaration, was largely complete by 1953. Nevertheless, the covenant was tabled because of insuperable ideological rivalry over the status of economic and social rights.

By the mid-1960's, however, the political context began to change. A large part of the explanation lies in the one area of human rights in which the United Nations had been active, that of self-determination and decolonization. In 1945, when the United Nations was founded, most of Africa and Asia were Western colonial possessions. That situation began to change with the independence of Indonesia and India in

1947. The process of decolonization took off dramatically, with the active support of the United Nations, in the late 1950's and early 1960's. By 1970, more than 99 percent of the world's people lived in independent states.

The Afro-Asian bloc became the largest voting bloc in the United Nations during the 1960's. These countries, which had suffered under colonial rule, had a special interest in reviving the issue of human rights. They also found a sympathetic hearing from at least some Western European and Latin American countries. There was thus a renewed flurry of activity, beginning in 1960, when the General Assembly adopted resolution 1514, the Declaration on the Granting of Independence to Colonial Countries and Peoples. In 1961, the Nonaligned Movement (NAM) first met on a formal basis, in an attempt to organize the political power of what became known as the Third World.

The political subordination of colonialism was usually associated with pervasive discrimination against indigenous people of color. Therefore, it is not surprising that racial discrimination was another high-priority item for the new states of Africa and Asia. In 1963, the General Assembly adopted a Declaration on the Elimination of All Forms of Racial Discrimination, and in 1965 it completed work on the International Convention on the Elimination of All Forms of Racial Discrimination.

The momentum generated by these new initiatives on self-determination and racial discrimination spread into the general human rights work of the United Nations. In 1966, the International Human Rights Covenants were finally completed. The Teheran Conference reflected this reinvigoration of international human rights activity.

The Teheran Conference was the largest intergovernmental human rights conference ever held. Eighty-four states participated, along with representatives or observers from fifty-seven nongovernmental organizations, seven other U.N. bodies and specialized agencies, and four regional organizations. In addition to the Proclamation of Teheran, a statement of human rights priorities for the international community, the conference adopted twenty-six substantive resolutions on a great variety of human rights issues.

The operative paragraphs of the Proclamation of Teheran begin by stressing the importance of states fulfilling their human rights obligations as laid out in the Universal Declaration of Human Rights. The goal of human rights activity should be "the achievement by each individual of the maximum freedom and dignity." In pursuit of this goal, freedoms of expression, information, conscience, and religion, as well as the right to participate in political, economic, cultural, and social life, are proclaimed to be particularly important.

The proclamation also gives specific attention to apartheid and racial discrimination; self-determination; international cooperation to avoid aggression and war; the widening gap between rich and poor countries; the special importance of economic, social, and cultural rights and economic and social development; illiteracy; women's rights; the rights of families and children; the rights and contributions of youth; scientific and technical developments; and disarmament. It concludes by urging "all peoples and governments to dedicate themselves to the principles enshrined in the Universal Declaration of Human Rights and to redouble their efforts to provide for all human beings a life consonant with freedom and dignity and conducive to physical, mental, social and spiritual welfare."

The fact that the Proclamation of Teheran covers so much ground in just a few pages suggests its extreme generality. For the most part, each topic receives only a short paragraph that reiterates general and often-expressed principles and aspirations. There is little that is innovative, but the special priorities of the conference and the proclamation do reflect changes in the makeup of the international community in the twenty years after the Universal Declaration of Human Rights.

Much the same is true of the resolutions of the conference, most of which are short and very general. In addition to the topics covered in the proclamation, the conference adopted resolutions on human rights in Israeli-occupied territory, Nazism and racial intolerance, opponents of racist regimes, nondiscrimination in employment, model rules of procedure for human rights bodies, cooperation with the United Nations High Commissioner for Refugees, rights of detainees, family planning, legal aid, human rights education, an International Year for Action to Combat Racism and Racial Discrimination, publicity for the Universal Declaration of Human Rights, and sporting boycotts of South Africa.

Article 4 of the proclamation noted that considerable progress had been made in the elaboration of international human rights standards but that much remained to be done in the area of implementing these rights. Likewise, Secretary-General U Thant, in his opening address to the conference, noted that it "must find new means of carrying out the continuing struggle for the recognition and enjoyment of human rights." In this endeavor, however, the International Conference on Human Rights achieved little or nothing. It made no suggestions for new international institutions or procedures to implement internationally recognized human rights. In fact, the conference did not even vote on, let alone adopt, draft resolutions by Haiti and the Ivory Coast suggesting the creation of an international human rights court.

Impact of Event

The lack of both substantive and procedural innovation in the products of the International Conference on Human Rights might suggest that it was of ephemeral importance. Nevertheless, it (along with the completion of the International Human Rights Covenants in the fall of 1966) marks an important turning point in international action on behalf of human rights.

By the mid-1960's, there was a growing recognition that if the United Nations was to continue to contribute significantly in the field of human rights, it would have to move into new areas of activity. Through 1966, the principal human rights work of the United Nations was focused on creating international norms, supplemented by efforts to publicize and promote these norms. The United Nations simply did not have the power to require states to implement internationally recognized human rights.

If there was to be major progress in international action on behalf of human rights after 1966, it would have to come primarily in the area of implementing, or monitoring the implementation of, these standards. In the late 1960's, the United Nations did launch a number of new initiatives that attempted to monitor national human rights performance. In 1967, the Commission on Human Rights was given the authority to discuss human rights violations in particular countries. In 1968, a special committee of investigation was created to consider human rights in the territories occupied by Israel after its war with its Arab neighbors in 1967. In the same year, the Security Council imposed a mandatory blockade on the white minority regime in South Rhodesia. The 1965 racial discrimination convention, which was the first international human rights procedure that required states to submit mandatory periodic reports on implementation, came into force in 1969. In 1970, Economic and Social Council Resolution 1503 authorized the Commission on Human Rights to conduct confidential investigations of communications (complaints) that suggested "a consistent pattern of gross and reliably attested violations of human rights and fundamental freedoms."

None of these new initiatives appears to have been directly influenced by the International Conference on Human Rights. They do, however, reflect the human rights concerns of the new Third World majority in the United Nations. As the place at which these concerns were first given international prominence, the Teheran Conference almost certainly had some indirect influence.

The other major objective of the conference was to emphasize economic, social, and cultural rights and the linkage between human rights and economic and social development. This was an attempt to redress a serious imbalance in past U.N. work. Efforts to redress the imbalance began in the early 1960's. They were given a significant boost by the International Conference on Human Rights and the Proclamation of Teheran. Paragraph 13 of the proclamation states: "The achievement of lasting progress in the implementation of human rights is dependent upon sound and effective national and international policies of economic and social development." Critics have contended that in the 1970's, the U.N. majority, rather than establish a balance between civil and political rights and economic, social, and cultural rights, in fact attempted to subordinate civil and political rights to the pursuit of economic development and struggles for a new international economic order. Whatever the validity of such claims, it is clear that the Teheran conference was a significant event in the rising prominence of economic, social, and cultural rights in international human rights discussions. This was probably the most important contribution of the International Conference on Human Rights. Issues of race and colonialism had already been placed at the center of international human rights agendas prior to the conference. After, and partly as a result of, the International Conference on Human Rights, economic, social, and cultural rights also had prominent places on the U.N. human rights agenda.

The International Conference on Human Rights was an important event in the genesis of the human rights policies and priorities of the United Nations in the 1970's. It effectively marked the close of the period of norm creation and Western domination of the human rights work of the United Nations and the opening of a new phase that would be politically dominated by the Third World, with the support of the Soviet bloc. Much of the human rights work of the United Nations in the 1970's reflected the priorities of the Proclamation of Teheran and the political processes that shaped it.

Bibliography

Development, Human Rights, and the Rule of Law. Oxford, England: Pergamon Press, 1982. This is a report of a conference held in The Hague, April 27-May 1, 1981, convened by the International Commission of Jurists. Although the link between human rights and development was a central theme at Teheran, little was done until the early 1980's. This book, and the conference that it records, were important first steps toward concrete action on this central objective of the Teheran Conference.

Final Act of the International Conference on Human Rights. New York: United Nations, 1968. The Final Act includes a brief review of the organization and operation of the conference along with the texts of the Proclamation of Teheran and the resolutions adopted by the conference.

Ganji, Manouchehr. *The Realization of Economic, Social, and Cultural Rights: Problems, Policies, Progress.* New York: United Nations, 1975. This U.N. study represents the first major effort to inject issues of economic, social, and cultural rights into the mainstream of U.N. human rights work.

Moskowitz, Moses. *International Concern with Human Rights.* Dobbs Ferry, N.Y.: Oceana, 1974. A good general introduction to the evolution of international action on behalf of human rights. Provides a useful discussion of the context in which the Teheran Conference took place.

Van Dyke, Vernon. "Self-Determination and Minority Rights." In *Human Rights, the U.S. and World Community.* New York: Oxford University Press, 1970. A useful contemporary overview of self-determination, which was both a central theme at the Teheran Conference and one of the principal political factors that led up to it.

Jack Donnelly

Cross-References

The United Nations Adopts the Universal Declaration of Human Rights (1948), p. 789; The Nonaligned Movement Meets (1961), p. 1131; The United Nations Issues a Declaration on Racial Discrimination (1963), p. 1212; The U.N. Covenant on Civil and Political Rights Is Adopted (1966), p. 1353; The OAU Adopts the African Charter on Human and Peoples' Rights (1981), p. 2136.

CONGRESS PASSES THE
ARCHITECTURAL BARRIERS ACT

Category of event: Disability rights
Time: August 12, 1968
Locale: Washington, D.C.

The Architectural Barriers Act of 1968 represented the first federal legislation calling for the removal of barriers that prevented the access of handicapped people to publicly owned buildings

Principal personages:
> LEON J. CHATELAIN, JR. (1902-   ), head of the National Commission on Architectural Barriers from 1966 to 1968
> WILBUR J. COHEN (1913-1987), secretary of the Department of Health, Education and Welfare from 1968 to 1969
> LYNDON B. JOHNSON (1908-1973), the president of the United States from 1963 to 1969

Summary of Event

Architectural barriers sometimes physically bar the access of disabled people to post offices, museums, houses of worship, concert halls, and other public buildings. Although the number of physically disabled people is large, the efforts to remove barriers have been slow. These efforts were first advocated by a few organizations and concerned individuals, then supported by local and state laws and later federal laws. Compliance has been lackluster, and the problem of architectural barriers has only slowly entered the public conscience.

In 1957, Hugo Deffner, a disabled man from Oklahoma City, was named the Handicapped American of the Year for his one-man crusade against unnecessary barriers. Ironically, because there were steps leading to the building where he was to receive his award, two Marines had to carry him to the stage in his wheelchair. Four years later, the American National Standards Institute, in cooperation with the National Easter Seal Society for Crippled Children and Adults, issued American National Standards Specifications for making buildings and facilities accessible to and usable by the physically handicapped (the A117.1 ANSI standards). These set forth minimal requirements for sixteen aspects of building design, including grading, parking lots, walks, entrances, doors, doorways, and rest rooms. These standards, although groundbreaking, are generally considered to have been incomplete and minimal because they contained few descriptive drawings, were too nonspecific, and did not cover residential buildings.

These standards were distributed to all the offices of the Department of Housing and Urban Development (HUD) and incorporated into the construction manual of the Department of Health, Education and Welfare (HEW), which made the standards applicable to all new construction under its responsibility. A national education program was also undertaken to ensure that state and local governments adopted the standard. As a result of public education, a small number of important structures, such as New York City's Philharmonic Hall and LaGuardia Airport and University of California campuses at Davis and Riverside, were built to accommodate the physically disabled.

By 1965, thirty-four states had some legislation describing the removal of barriers, but most laws were not comprehensive and lacked enforcement provisions. Few buildings were built in compliance to these laws. In November of that year, the first federal law designed to further the removal of architectural barriers was passed. Congress amended the Vocational Rehabilitation Act (Public Law 89-933), establishing a National Commission on Architectural Barriers. The commission's objective was to determine the extent to which architectural barriers impeded the access of handicapped people to public buildings, to determine what was being done by public and nonprofit organizations to remove these barriers, and to prepare a proposal for further action.

After two years of study, the National Commission on Architectural Barriers presented its findings to Wilbur J. Cohen, the secretary of HEW. The commission, headed by Leon Chatelain, Jr., who was also president of the National Society for Crippled Children and Adults, found that the single greatest obstacle to the employment of the handicapped was the design of the buildings in which they would work. The commission also presented shocking evidence that the public was generally unaware of and unconcerned with the problem of architectural barriers, despite the education programs. Sixty-four percent of Americans polled did not even realize that architectural barriers were a problem because they had not thought about the issue. Of 709 architects surveyed, 251 were not even aware of the ANSI standards. Only three of seven national building materials suppliers were familiar with the ANSI standards, and none had any policies to meet them. There were still no standard specifications for accessible transportation.

The problems of inaccessibility mostly involved curbs and steps; inaccessible elevators; steep and narrow walks; gratings in walkways; doors that were too narrow, revolved, or were hard to open; lack of parking spaces for the handicapped; lack of accommodations for wheelchairs; aisles that were too narrow; public toilet stalls and telephone booths that were too small; and telephones, drinking fountains, vending machines, light switches, and fire alarms that were too high. Among the worst offenders were, ironically, Social Security offices in small towns, usually located on the second floor of a building without an elevator.

In light of the lack of public concern, the commission recommended that federal legislation be enacted requiring all new public buildings funded by the government to be designed for accessibility to the elderly and handicapped, that all federal agencies plan and budget for architectural changes to existing buildings to improve accessibility, that similar laws be passed on the state level, that building codes be revised, and that a government agency be established to administer this new legislation. These recommendations substantially were adopted by the House of Representatives as legislation H.R. 6589 in the summer of 1968. A committee then set out to resolve the slight differences between this bill and a similar one passed in the Senate (S. 222). An agreement was reached, and the Architectural Barriers Act of 1968 (Public Law 90-480) was signed into law by President Lyndon B. Johnson on August 12, 1968. Sections authorized the head of the General Services Administration (GSA) and the secretaries of the departments of HUD and Defense, in consultation with the secretary of HEW, to issue standards for public buildings. The heads of these agencies were given authority to waive the standards on a case-by-case basis and authorized to undertake surveys and investigations to determine general compliance. The jurisdiction of the law included buildings and facilities constructed or altered by, or on behalf of, the United States government; buildings leased after alterations in accordance with the law; and buildings funded by government grants and loans. The act was amended in 1970 as Public Law 91-205, making it applicable to the District of Columbia metro facilities but not to the trains themselves.

The month before the Architectural Barriers Act was passed, William A. Schmidt, commissioner of the Public Buildings Service of the General Services Administration, had warned building owners and operators that unless they provided for easy access for physically handicapped people they would risk losing government agencies as tenants. Schmidt noted that this was no small matter. At the time, government agencies as a group were one of the nation's biggest tenants, occupying 6.5 percent of the space in buildings owned and managed by members of the National Association of Building Owners and Managers. Schmidt said that more than 10 percent of the people in the United States, or twenty-two million, were handicapped, including those in wheelchairs and the elderly. He demanded that these people be given equal opportunity for gainful employment and other normal activities from which they had been barred, literally, by the design and construction of government buildings.

Noting the lack of a program to ensure compliance with the Architectural Barriers Act, Congress enacted the Rehabilitation Act of 1973 (Public Law 93-112). This law created the Architectural and Transportation Barriers Compliance Board (A&TBCB), which was conceived to be the primary force to ensure the full implementation of the earlier laws. Modified by an amendment to the 1973 law, the A&TBCB was made up of the heads of the departments of HEW, Transportation, HUD, Labor, the Interior, and Defense and the heads of the GSA, Postal Service, and Veterans Administration.

Impact of Event

In 1975, the General Accounting Office (GAO), responding to a request from Congress, determined the effectiveness of the Architectural Barriers Act. The GAO inspected 314 federally financed buildings and architectural plans for buildings, all of which were built, altered, leased, or designed after the 1968 act was implemented.

None of them fully complied with the law, and most buildings showed halfhearted compliance. For example, wheelchair ramps were constructed, but they were too long, slick, or steep; doors were built wide enough for wheelchairs but were blocked by ledges. The GAO's report also cited inconvenient elevator controls and controls for heat, air conditioning, and lighting in bathrooms; high curbs; and water fountains that were too high. Although the government, private contractors, and building designers all agreed that the cost of incorporating accessibility features into new buildings was as low as one-tenth of 1 percent of total construction costs, little was being done. It was clear that the 1968 act had fallen short of its goals: It delegated authority too much, allowing different government agencies the discretion of implementing proper action, performing surveys, and waiving standards case by case. It also did not cover privately owned residential structures leased for public housing.

David R. Williamson, executive director of National Paraplegia, noted that when the Post Office was reorganized in 1970 and taken out of government surveillance, it was also (perhaps inadvertently) exempted from the 1968 law. When Williamson went to his local post office in Chicago, he could get into the front door but no further, because steps blocked his path to the main area of business. Usually, he had to request that a passerby go to a window to get an employee's attention for him. If no passersby were around, he would yell. The longer he waited, the louder he would yell. The entire process was frustrating and demeaning.

Progress since 1975 has been slow but visible. The Center for Independent Living, established in 1972 as a workshop and growth center for the disabled in the San Francisco area, became a model for changing the environment to meet the needs of disabled people. After much time and effort was spent, the ANSI standards were revised in 1980. Descriptions of curb ramps, bathrooms, and kitchens were added, as were more figures and mandatory specifications. These additions corrected earlier deficiencies of this standard. Many reports, studies, and books have been published, so public awareness has increased. Many physical barriers have been removed. State legislation has improved, and the United Nations even had a special year to highlight the problem.

Bibliography

Bednar, Michael J., ed. *Barrier-Free Environments.* Stroudsburg, Pa: Dowden, Hutchinson and Ross, 1977. An international encyclopedia containing sections on the history of American barrier-removal legislation; the Fokus Housing system in Sweden, built with the rights, freedoms, and responsibilities of disabled people in mind; a case study for creating a barrier-free environment for the elderly and handicapped in Moline, Illinois; the Center on Environment for the Handicapped, an advisory and information service in London; and provisions for the handicapped in Denmark.

Developmental Disabilities State Legislative Project, Commission on the Mentally Disabled, Public Service Activities Division, American Bar Association. *Eliminating Environmental Barriers.* Washington, D.C.: Government Printing Office,

1979. Although rather technical in nature, this guide contains information, broken down by state, on various topics, including enforcement provisions, waiver provisions, administrative authority, design and construction standards, and tax incentives (for example, a 1977 Oregon law that allows the entire cost of renovating a building to remove barriers to be subtracted from taxable income). Also contains a model act designed to be used by local governments to implement legislation on the removal of barriers.

Lifchez, Raymond, and Barbara Winslow. *Design for Independent Living.* Berkeley: University of California Press, 1979. Provides useful information on construction and design of accessible environments such as kitchens. The beauty of this book lies in the portrait of the disabled as people. Photographs show disabled people dancing, feeding their babies, working out, cutting a wedding cake, making love, studying computer science, and even pushing a stalled car.

Robinette, Gary O., ed. *Barrier-Free Exterior Design: Anyone Can Go Anywhere.* New York: Van Nostrand Reinhold, 1985. An architectural handbook, including dimensions of small and large wheelchairs, minimum turning spaces, and the like. Includes diagrams and photographs of what had been done in the previous decade, how it was done, and what still needs to be done in terms of ramps, curbs, stairs, and railings.

Spock, Benjamin. *Caring for Your Disabled Child.* New York: Macmillan, 1965. In this very practical guide, the renowned child psychologist tells parents of handicapped children how to talk to their children about their disabilities; how to deal with guilt, fear, and loneliness; and how to be otherwise helpful and supportive.

U.S. Architectural and Transportation Barriers Compliance Board. *Resource Guide to Literature on Barrier-Free Environments.* Washington, D.C.: Government Printing Office, 1980. A guide to publications on various topics related to architectural barriers. Lists the civil and legal rights of the disabled. Describes litigation and court cases involving barriers, including a case wherein plaintiffs were denied the right to vote due to physical disabilities that prevented access to polls. Also contains sections on aids and devices to assist the disabled (including joystick-controlled vehicles), travel guides, and recreational facilities.

U.S. Congress. Committee on Public Works and Transportation. *Effectiveness of the Architectural Barriers Act of 1968.* Washington, D.C.: Government Printing Office, 1976. The transcript of 1975 hearings presided over by Representative Jim Wright, containing descriptions of the GAO report to Congress. Notes that people in wheelchairs could neither look out the windows of the Washington Monument nor view the Constitution. The hearings describe how poorly the 1968 legislation was enforced.

Frank Wu

Cross-References

The United Nations Declares Rights for the Mentally Retarded (1971), p. 1644; Congress Responds to Demands of Persons with Disabilities (1973), p. 1731; Congress Enacts the Education for All Handicapped Children Act (1975), p. 1780; Congress Passes the Americans with Disabilities Act (1990), p. 2595.

SOVIETS INVADE CZECHOSLOVAKIA

Category of event: Political freedom
Time: August 21, 1968
Locale: Czechoslovakia

Soviet and Warsaw Pact forces entered Czechoslovakia to suppress the independence movement popularly known as the "Prague Spring"

Principal personages:

ALEXANDER DUBČEK (1921-   ), the first secretary of the Czechoslovakian Communist Party and the architect of the Prague Spring reforms

LEONID BREZHNEV (1906-1975), the general secretary of the Soviet Communist Party and leader of the Soviet Union from 1964 to 1982

ANTONIN NOVOTNY (1904-1975), the president of Czechoslovakia from 1957 to 1968

LUDVIK SVOBODA (1895-1979), the president of Czechoslovakia from 1968 to 1975,whose popularity was tied to his support for the Prague Spring reforms

Summary of Event

In 1963, Czechoslovakia began to emerge from the severe political and cultural repression imposed by the Czechoslovakian Communist Party in the early 1950's. The moderation of restrictions corresponded with an economic upswing that created an atmosphere of confidence and optimism in the government of Antonin Novotny, who was also chair of the Czechoslovakian Communist Party. Novotny believed the time had come to appease Czechoslovakian intellectuals, who had complained for years about government censorship. A more permissive policy was introduced that allowed cultural exchanges with the West and the publication of essays that questioned the Soviet Union's domination of Czechoslovakia. In 1967, Novotny, under pressure from Soviet leader Leonid Brezhnev, reestablished censorship. By that time, however, Czechoslovakia had gained international recognition for its writers, filmmaking, and theater. In response to renewed censorship, the Czechoslovakian Writer's Union, on June 27, 1967, issued a vigorous protest.

The position taken by the writer's union in 1967 came at a time when some leaders within the Czechoslovakian Communist Party were disillusioned with President Novotny's economic policies and his unwillingness to show greater independence from Moscow. Opposition to Novotny was acute in Slovakia, where the president's policies were viewed as heavily favoring the Czech majority. Although the Slovak Communist Party had remained loyal to the government in Prague, in 1967 the leader of the Slovak Party, Alexander Dubček, openly criticized Novotny for failing to address the country's economic and political problems effectively.

Dubček's assault on Novotny seemed to galvanize those who were dissatisfied with the president's performance. Novotny received little help from Brezhnev, who resented the fact that the Czech president had remained loyal to the previous Soviet leader, Nikita Khrushchev. In the autumn of 1967, it was apparent that Novotny was finished. There was surprise, however, when the Czechoslovakian Communist Party announced in January, 1968, that Dubček would succeed Novotny as first secretary of the Party. Dubček was not well known outside the Slovakian bureaucracy; moreover, he was a notoriously poor speaker with a benign personality. There is some reason to think, as William Shawcross noted in his 1970 biography of Dubček, that Brezhnev may have intervened on his behalf.

Early in 1968, Dubček began to discuss a "new model" for socialist Czechoslovakia, one that would bring Communists and non-Communists together. The Communist Party would retain its leading role, but it would permit the full range of freedoms associated with a democratic society. Aided by dissident Party members who agreed with him, Dubček incorporated his ideas into what became known as the "Action Program." The Action Program was published on April 9, 1968, and quickly gained the attention of Soviet authorities in Moscow. The program called for personal freedoms, significant political reform, a new constitution for the Slovak peoples, and economic liberalization.

Over the next three months, Dubček's reforms came under increasingly heavy attack from Moscow. The Soviet press criticized Dubček for trying to undermine the unity of the Warsaw Pact countries. The Czechs had become, according to Moscow, apologists for the bourgeois system. In Czechoslovakia itself, there was widespread support for Dubček's Action Program.

Three times between May and August, Dubček and other Czechoslovakian Communist Party leaders were called to meetings with Soviet officials, including Brezhnev. At each of these gatherings, the most important of which was held at Bratislava on July 30, Dubček insisted that he had no intention of destroying Communist unity. He remained convinced that Communism and political freedom were completely compatible. That, he contended, was what Karl Marx and Friedrich Engels had believed. Brezhnev, however, made it clear that he had no interest in allowing the Prague Spring to set an example for other Eastern European Communist regimes.

When the Bratislava conference ended, a tepid statement, the Bratislava Declaration, was released in which both sides agreed to carry on mutually advantageous relations. In early August, a succession of Eastern European leaders visited Prague to warn of possible Soviet intervention. Dubček and recently selected Czechoslovakian president Ludvik Svoboda seemed unconvinced that Brezhnev would unleash Soviet power against the popular reforms.

The warnings of Soviet intervention became fact on the night of August 20. Soviet planes and equipment began to arrive at Prague's Ruzzone airport. At dawn, tanks rolled toward the center of the capital. By the next night, some three hundred thousand troops from East Germany, Poland, Hungary, Bulgaria, and the Soviet Union had crossed the Czechoslovakian border. There was no significant armed opposition.

Dubček asked the residents of Prague to go to their workplaces as usual. At first, the citizens of Prague tried to convince the invading soldiers to turn back, and, when that tactic failed, they turned to passive resistance. They refused to provide troops with food and water, they removed street signs and house numbers, they published clandestine newspapers, and they displayed huge pictures of Dubček and President Svoboda.

The events of August stunned the Western world. There were expressions of support for Czechoslovakia from many countries, including the United States, but no help was forthcoming. The United States, at the time heavily involved in Southeast Asia, condemned the Soviet intervention while saying that it intended to abide by the terms of the Yalta agreement. The Yalta accord, signed at the conclusion of World War II, had, in effect, given Moscow dominion over Eastern Europe.

Shortly after the intervention began, Dubček and several other Czech officials were arrested and taken to Moscow. Several days later, President Svoboda also was summoned to the Soviet capital. Svoboda and Dubček realized that they would have to compromise in order to preserve even a small amount of the independence Czechoslovakia had claimed. They returned to Prague subdued and talking of a needed accommodation with the Soviet Union. There were some who felt betrayed by Dubček and Svoboda, but the reality was that the Czech leaders had no choice. By early September, the situation in Czechoslovakia was much as it had been prior to the publication of the Action Program, and the occupying forces had begun to withdraw. Dubček continued to hope that some portion of the April reforms could be preserved, but, in fact, the Prague Spring had come to an end.

Impact of Event

The Soviet intervention caught world leaders by surprise, especially in the West. The Cold War, which had appeared to be winding down in the mid-1960's, was not quite finished after all. Soviet leaders were not ready to relinquish Moscow's stranglehold over Eastern Europe. Western officials, who had been encouraged by the Nuclear Test Ban Treaty of 1963 and by the seeming insouciance of Leonid Brezhnev, were now required once again to condemn the actions of the Soviet Union. It was clearly a setback for those in the West who had hoped for continuing progress toward détente.

For those in Eastern Europe who sought greater independence from Moscow and greater political freedom, the intervention was even more crushing. National Communist leaders understood that the Kremlin would not allow them to chart their own course. Some of them, particularly Romanian president Nicolae Ceausescu, openly upbraided the Soviet leadership, but all had received Moscow's clear message.

In Czechoslovakia, the disappointment was acute. Within a year of the intervention, Soviet officials had forced local Communist Party leaders to reimpose restrictions on political and cultural freedom. Dubček was gradually removed from a position of power in the Party until, in June, 1970, he was expelled from the Party. Those most negatively affected by the Soviet action were the artists, writers, and intellectuals who had enjoyed a brief period when they could express their ideas as they wished. The end of the Prague Spring meant the stifling of what had been a major cultural renaissance in the mid-1960's. Still, Czechoslovakia's intellectual community did not surrender easily. In January, 1969, Jan Palach, a university philosophy student, inspired a violent demonstration by burning himself to death as a protest against censorship. Many writers, particularly Václav Havel, maintained a stream of protests. Dubček, while under surveillance, continued to offer his opposition. Lesser-known intellectuals who lacked international support were dismissed from their academic and cultural posts or sent to prison.

Although the Prague Spring had been repressed, the ideas that inspired it lived on. When Soviet president Mikhail Gorbachev introduced his policies of *glasnost* (openness) and *perestroika* (restructuring) in 1985, the spirit of the Prague Spring was revived throughout Eastern Europe. In Czechoslovakia, all the reforms promised in the Action Program were restored. Dubček returned to political prominence in 1989 and was chosen to lead the Czechoslovakian parliament. In December, 1989, the parliament selected Václav Havel to be president of the country. After more than twenty years, Czech reformers had eased the effects, if not the memory, of the Soviet invasion in August, 1968.

Bibliography

Chapman, Colin. *August 21: The Rape of Czechoslovakia.* Philadelphia, Pa.: J. B. Lippincott, 1968. A reporter's account of the arrival of Warsaw Pact forces and the reaction of residents in Prague and in some smaller villages. Highly readable; contains a few dramatic photographs of the city during the invasion. Chapman was foreign news editor for the *Sunday Times* (London), and the book features on-the-spot accounts from reporter Murray Sayles.

Czerwinski, E. J., and Jaroslav Pielkalkiewicz, eds. *The Soviet Invasion of Czechoslovakia: Its Effects on Eastern Europe.* New York: Praeger, 1972. Accounts, many of them firsthand, of the reaction to the invasion in each Eastern European country. The effectiveness of the book is reduced by the fact that the editors and contributors were emotionally involved in the events. E. Bennett Warnstrom's chapter on Romania is naïve, particularly his gushing praise for President Ceausescu.

Golan, Galia. *The Czechoslovak Reform Movement.* Cambridge, England: Cambridge University Press, 1971. Golan is an expert on Czechoslovakian affairs, and this book can be read with great profit by students and the general public. Highly recommended. Index and bibliography.

Kusin, Vladimir V. *Political Grouping in the Czechoslovak Reform Movement.* New York: Columbia University Press, 1972. This is an account of the creation of reform political organizations from the post-World War II era through 1968. It is essential background information for understanding the Prague Spring. Recommended for serious students. Bibliography and index.

Schwartz, Harry. *Prague's 200 Days.* New York: Praeger, 1969. Schwartz takes a close look at the first two hundred days of 1968 in Czechoslovakia. A readable, and generally reliable, account. The chapters dealing with the invasion itself and the reaction of the Czech people are especially compelling. Index.

Shawcross, William. *Dubček.* New York: Simon & Schuster, 1970. The principal biography of Dubček in English. Shawcross, a journalist, has produced a detailed and surprisingly balanced study òf Dubček's career. Written within two years of the main events in Dubček's life, the biography lacks the necessary perspective and cannot be considered definitive. It is, however, well written and informative.

Skilling, H. Gordon. *Czechoslovakia's Interrupted Revolution.* Princeton, N.J.: Princeton University Press, 1976. Skilling's work provides excellent information on all aspects of the Prague Spring. There are superb insights into Dubček's behavior during 1968 and an excellent discussion of relevant scholarship on the events of 1968 published in the early 1970's. Bibliography and index.

Valenta, Jiri. *Soviet Intervention in Czechoslovakia, 1968: Anatomy of a Decision.* Baltimore, Md.: The Johns Hopkins University Press, 1979. In this most interesting book, Valenta discusses how the decision to invade Czechoslovakia was made by Soviet leaders. He also explains the negative impact the invasion had on the Soviet position in world politics. Bibliography and index.

Ronald K. Huch

Cross-References

The Berlin Wall Is Built (1961), p. 1125; The Brezhnev Doctrine Bans Acts of Independence in Soviet Satellites (1968), p. 1408; Solidarity Leads Striking Polish Workers (1980), p. 2112; Gorbachev Initiates a Policy of *Glasnost* (1985), p. 2249; Hungary Adopts a Multiparty System (1989), p. 2421; Solidarity Regains Legal Status in Poland (1989), p. 2477; Poland Forms a Non-Communist Government (1989), p. 2500; Ceausescu Is Overthrown in Romania (1989), p. 2546; Soviet Troops Withdraw from Czechoslovakia (1990), p. 2570; Lithuania Declares Its Independence from the Soviet Union (1990), p. 2577.

CHICAGO RIOTS MAR THE DEMOCRATIC CONVENTION

Categories of event: Political freedom; atrocities and war crimes
Time: August 24-30, 1968
Locale: Chicago, Illinois

The Democratic National Convention in Chicago in 1968 was marred by riots and police violence representative of one of the most tumultuous years in mid-twentieth century American political history

Principal personages:

LYNDON B. JOHNSON (1908-1973), the thirty-sixth president of the United States (1963-1969), involved in escalating the war in Vietnam

HUBERT H. HUMPHREY (1911-1978), the vice president of the United States under Lyndon B. Johnson and the Democratic nominee for president in 1968

EUGENE MCCARTHY (1916-   ), a U.S. senator from Minnesota and antiwar candidate for the Democratic presidential nomination in 1968

RICHARD DALEY (1902-1976), the mayor of Chicago and head of the Illinois Democratic political machine at the time of the convention

RENNIE DAVIS (1941-   ), an antiwar activist and cofounder of the National Mobilization to End the War in Vietnam

DAVID DELLINGER (1915-   ), an antiwar activist and cofounder of the National Mobilization to End the War in Vietnam

TOM HAYDEN (1939-   ), a New Left political organizer and founder of Students for a Democratic Society (SDS)

ABBIE HOFFMAN (1936-1989), an author, political activist, and cofounder of the Youth International Party (Yippies)

Summary of Event

By all measures, 1968 was one of the most tumultuous years in twentieth century American political history. The Vietnam War increased in intensity, escalating American casualties and citizen disillusionment with the conflict. Racial tensions exploded into riots in many cities, particularly after the assassination of Martin Luther King, Jr. Demonstrations on college campuses against the war brought students into conflict with police who were often called to maintain order. Lyndon B. Johnson, who had been elected president with one of the largest pluralities in history four years earlier, responded to the turmoil by deciding not to run for a subsequent term in office.

Frustrations with the political process mounted on both the Left and the Right. Left-wing thinkers attributed problems to the underlying causes of the demonstrations, notably the continuing war in Vietnam and the government's failure to address racial and social inequities quickly enough. These individuals often argued for radical change in the political, judicial, and executive systems. Right-wing politicians argued that the demonstrators themselves were the problem and blamed the confrontations on indulgent political officials who failed to use sufficient force to suppress protests. George Wallace ran for the presidency as an Independent candidate, demanding "law and order"—a catchphrase that became synonymous with the repression of political dissent.

Most American citizens fell somewhere between these two extremes. There was a growing feeling that the government's Vietnam policy was not working and that many social injustices went unaddressed. Most citizens also feared the increased polarization of the society and hoped that the conflicts would be worked out within the confines of the present political system. Many young people who opposed the war expressed this hope by working on Eugene McCarthy's or Robert Kennedy's campaigns for the Democratic presidential nomination. Both candidates enjoyed success in the Democratic primaries by taking a stance against Johnson's war policies; Eugene McCarthy continued this crusade after Robert Kennedy's assassination. Many McCarthy delegates perceived the Democratic National Convention as a forum for challenging the administration's Vietnam policy and its candidate, Vice President Hubert H. Humphrey. The Democratic National Convention, for several reasons, proved a suitable place for the conflict between left- and right-wing extremists to boil over into violent confrontations.

First, the city was run by Mayor Richard Daley, an old-style political boss who controlled the state Democratic Party system with unchallenged authority. Daley viewed disruptive demonstrations and calls for more participation in the choice of presidential candidates as a direct affront. He made this position clear during disturbances following the death of Martin Luther King, Jr., and during a peace march in Chicago in April, 1968. When police acted with restraint in the first case, they were chastised by Daley, who had issued a command to "shoot to kill arsonists and shoot to maim looters." When police attacked demonstrators, bystanders, and media personnel in the second case, the mayor's office ignored the violence.

Second, several groups planned to organize demonstrations against the war and called upon supporters to join them in Chicago for the convention. Four of the main groups were the National Mobilization to End the War in Vietnam, led by David Dellinger and Rennie Davis; the Yippies, led by Jerry Rubin and Abbie Hoffman, who attempted to combine the counterculture life-style of the hippies with a political statement against the war; Students for a Democratic Society (SDS), a campus antiwar group led by Tom Hayden; and the Coalition for an Open Convention, led by Martin Slate, which attempted to bring together antiwar and anti-Humphrey forces in the Democratic Party. Some McCarthy supporters also came to Chicago, despite the senator's warning to stay away. The first four groups officially intended to demonstrate and rally but avoid disrupting the convention. Rumors and careless statements by some group leaders, and the presence of more militant minor groups, undermined these peaceful intentions. All four groups applied unsuccessfully for permits for marches, rallies, and access to the public parks for sleeping. The seemingly inevitable public assemblies were therefore illegal from the start, increasing the potential for confrontation.

Finally, the Chicago convention became a symbolic forum for the conflict between "old" and "new" politics. For many demonstrators, Humphrey's presidential candidacy represented a continuation of the back-room politics which ignored public dissent on Vietnam and other issues. They viewed the convention as a confrontation between traditional machine politics, represented by Daley and the Democratic Party's old guard, and the new (and often idealized) politics of increased citizen participation, represented by McCarthy supporters and young protest leaders.

As expected, the city's prohibition of demonstrations was only partially successful in stopping protesters from arriving in Chicago. Group leaders' early estimates of the number of participants proved to be overly optimistic, but approximately five thousand protesters had gathered in Lincoln Park by the Sunday evening before the convention was to begin. The first confrontations between demonstrators and law enforcement officials occurred following a peaceful afternoon march. The police, enforcing a ban on overnight camping in the park, randomly attacked protesters, bystanders, and media personnel, chasing them into the city's Old Town district.

This pattern was repeated on August 28, following a legal rally in Grant Park, across from the Hilton Hotel where a number of delegates were staying. The rally was attended by SDS, Yippie, National Mobilization, and Open Convention protesters in addition to a number of older, nonviolent demonstrators, including disillusioned McCarthy supporters. Altercations began at a flagpole, where an American flag was lowered. Police attacked Rennie Davis when he attempted to restore order by assembling rally marshals between the protesters and the police. The rally concluded and the demonstrators marched out with unclear objectives, eventually joining a legal march by the Southern Christian Leadership Conference (SCLC). Approximately seven thousand people eventually massed in front of the Hilton, where television cameras were present. Police allowed the SCLC marchers to pass but began clearing other protesters from the site.

Suddenly, several police stormed the crowd and began indiscriminately attacking protesters and innocent bystanders with clubs, mace, and fists. A few protesters fought back with rocks and other projectiles. The violence continued for about three hours in front of the hotels occupied by Hubert Humphrey, George McGovern, and Eugene McCarthy. Television cameras recorded the entire confrontation despite police attacks on media personnel. The antiwar protesters retreated back to Grant Park for an all-night rally just as Humphrey received the Democratic nomination for president. Humphrey's victory was to be remembered for the clashes between police and demonstrators which were televised as the final convention votes were tallied.

Impact of Event

The immediate impact of the events in Chicago were felt within an already divided Democratic Party. There was an upsurge of support for the "law and order" stances of George Wallace and, in a milder version, Richard Nixon. Humphrey's standing in the polls suffered accordingly, even though he regained most of his support and lost the November election to Nixon by only .7 percent of the vote.

Longer-term effects involved the way in which the public regarded the press and its role in covering political upheavals. The Federal Communications Commission answered many complaints about the media's coverage of the violence. The National Commission on the Causes and Prevention of Violence held public hearings in late 1968 to evaluate whether the press contributed to such confrontations in Chicago and other cities. The press was cleared of complicity, but arguments about the impact of mass media on protest activity were to continue for years to come.

Also charged with complicity in the Chicago violence were Rennie Davis, Tom Hayden, David Dellinger, Bobby Seale, Abbie Hoffman, Jerry Rubin, and Mobilization officials Lee Weiner and John Froines. These individuals became known as the Chicago Seven after Seale was removed from the courtroom and tried separately. All were charged with conspiracy to riot by Attorney General John Mitchell, even though most had never even met one another until the convention. By this action, Nixon signaled his intolerance of protests and demonstrations. He made attacks on protesters one cornerstone of his 1972 presidential campaign, adapting George Wallace's hard-line "law and order" stance to a more moderate audience.

Perhaps the farthest reaching effects of the Chicago demonstrations, however, were the changes they prompted in the procedures for choosing presidential candidates. The unrest was interpreted as one sign that the back-room selection of candidates for office needed to be opened up to wider citizen participation. By 1972, the rules governing selection had been changed dramatically, providing for an expanded primary system and a selection process for delegates to the Democratic convention including significant numbers of women, young people, and racial minorities. In a final ironic footnote, the Daley delegation to the 1972 convention failed to meet the national party quotas for women and minorities and was not seated.

The changes in the presidential selection process cannot, of course, be traced solely to the events in Chicago in 1968. The clashes, however, remained a major symbol of the conflict between the old and new politics, a conflict which redefined the direction and agenda of American politics for the following two decades.

Bibliography

Farber, David. *Chicago '68*. Chicago: University of Chicago Press, 1988. This work was published in part to commemorate the twentieth anniversary of the Chicago Convention. The work's strongest point is that its author, a political scientist, was a resident of Chicago during the riots and knows its people and geography well. Its weakest point concerns the author's attempts to explain the Yippie movement within a philosophical context. At best, this book serves as a supplemental text, to be used primarily for its close-up views of many of the major personages in the drama. Includes an index and notes.

Hayden, Tom. *Trial*. New York: Holt, Rinehart and Winston, 1970. This book was written by the founder of Students for a Democratic Society, one of the defendants in the Chicago Seven trial. Although the expected biases are present, Hayden does attempt to link the events in Chicago, and the subsequent trial, to the broader political and social confrontations in American society at the time. Hayden's analysis presents the New Left critique of American society in a clear and doctrinaire fashion. No index or notes.

Lukas, J. Anthony. *The Barnyard Epithet and Other Obscenities.* New York: Harper & Row, 1970. The book presents a journalist's perspective on the Chicago Seven conspiracy trial; the author was a reporter for *The New York Times* magazine section. Lukas carefully combines the trial transcripts with relevant news stories and commentaries by politicians and citizens to describe the atmosphere in the United States following the convention violence. He concludes that American institutions, including the courts, may have had difficulty withstanding the confrontations represented by the clashes at the convention. No notes or index.

United States Congress. House Committee on Un-American Activities. *Subversive Involvement in Disruption of 1968 Democratic National Party Convention.* Washington, D.C.: Government Printing Office, 1968. This book records the investigations of the House Un-American Activities Committee into the violence at the Chicago Democratic National Convention. The hearings were clearly designed more for political grandstanding than investigation but do represent the confrontation between left- and right-wing forces which characterized the Chicago violence. Taken as a historical document, the testimony of David Dellinger before the committee underscores the degree of polarization between the two sides during this period. Includes notes.

Walker, Daniel. *Rights in Conflict.* New York: Bantam Books, 1968. This book is a transcript of the report submitted to the National Commission on the Causes and Prevention of Violence. It represents the most comprehensive study of the events surrounding the confrontations in Chicago, summarizing more than twenty thousand pages of testimony. The author sometimes strains to show both sides of the issue in the confrontations, but his straightforward analysis makes this book a critical resource for students of these events. No notes or index.

Frank Louis Rusciano

Cross-References

Civil Rights Protesters Attract International Attention (1963), p. 1188; Martin Luther King, Jr., Delivers His "I Have a Dream" Speech (1963), p. 1200; The Black Panther Party Is Organized (1966), p. 1348; The Kerner Commission Explores the Causes of Civil Disorders (1967), p. 1370; Martin Luther King, Jr., Is Assassinated in Memphis (1968), p. 1419; The U.S. Voting Age Is Lowered to Eighteen (1970), p. 1521; Four Students Are Killed at Kent State by the National Guard (1970), p. 1532; Lieutenant Calley Is Court-Martialed for the Massacre at My Lai (1970), p. 1555; FBI and CIA Interference in the Civil Rights Movement Is Revealed (1971), p. 1595; The United States Grants Amnesty to Vietnam War Draft Evaders (1974), p. 1769.

CHISHOLM BECOMES THE FIRST BLACK WOMAN ELECTED TO CONGRESS

Categories of event: Women's rights; racial and ethnic rights
Time: November 5, 1968
Locale: New York Twelfth District, centered in Bedford-Stuyvesant

Shirley Chisholm, the first black woman elected to Congress, opposed all forms of discrimination and supported vigilantly the interests of blacks, women, children, Puerto Ricans, and other minorities

Principal personages:

SHIRLEY CHISHOLM (1924-   ), a specialist in early childhood education whose parents were from Barbados

WESLEY MCDONALD HOLDER (1896-   ), Chisholm's political mentor, whose lifetime goal was to see a black person elected to Congress

JAMES FARMER (1920-   ), Chisholm's Republican opponent in 1968, a former national director of the Congress of Racial Equality

WILLIAM COLERIDGE THOMPSON (1924-   ), a black lawyer and state senator, later a justice of the supreme court of New York State

THOMAS R. JONES (1913-   ), a black lawyer and founder of the Unity Club, later a justice of the supreme court of New York State

THOMAS R. FORTUNE (1917-   ), a politician, assembly district leader, and Unity member who supported Chisholm in 1968; elected to the New York Assembly to replace Chisholm

Summary of Event

The political education of Shirley Chisholm began in the Seventeenth Assembly District (AD) Club of Brooklyn and continued in the Bedford-Stuyvesant Political League. Decorating cigar boxes used to hold raffle tickets was one of Chisholm's first political jobs. Women did this work to raise money for the AD Club, but this work, according to Chisholm, was unsupported financially and unappreciated by the men of the club. She demanded money to pay the women and to cover the costs of supplies, tickets, and prizes, costs that the women had been paying. She got seven hundred dollars. In time, Chisholm became a member of the board of directors of the AD Club, and even though she was both a woman and a black, became a vice president of the club while still in her twenties.

Chisholm was introduced to Wesley McDonald (Mac) Holder during her senior year in college. Holder was to be the seminal political influence in Chisholm's life. She described him as the "shrewdest, toughest, and hardest-working black political animal in Brooklyn." In 1953, she joined Holder in a campaign to elect a black municipal court judge. The Bedford-Stuyvesant Political League grew out of that campaign. It was the Unity Club, of which she was a founding member, that was most important to her political future. Its goal was to gain political control of the Seventeenth District and end white rule there. Unity offered candidates for election in 1960, including its leader, Thomas R. Jones. Unity's campaign attracted the support of both Eleanor Roosevelt and Harry Belafonte, but its candidates lost. In preparation for 1962, Unity expanded its membership, held voter registration drives, and conducted political education seminars. It petitioned for the appointment of more blacks and Puerto Ricans to city jobs and called for better health care; improved housing, transportation, and lighting; integrated schools; and expanded youth services. It demanded that both blacks and Puerto Ricans be granted political representation equal to their numbers. Jones was elected, thereby ending white political rule in Bedford-Stuyvesant in 1962.

In 1964, Jones became a judge on the civil court in Brooklyn, opening the way for Chisholm to run for the New York legislature from the Seventeenth District with the support of Unity. With limited financial support, augmented by four thousand dollars of her own money, she won the Democratic nomination, then defeated Republican Charles Lewis, 18,151 to 1,893. She was neither the first black woman to seek office in Brooklyn—Maude B. Richardson had in 1946—nor the first black woman elected to the New York legislature—Bessie Buchanan had earlier represented Harlem. Chisholm's election in 1964 was the year after the Supreme Court handed down its decision in *Gray v. Sanders*, "one person, one vote." Reapportionment of districts that resulted from this decision aided in the election of eight blacks to the New York legislature in 1964, six to the assembly and two to the senate.

Chisholm maintained that her years in the assembly were productive despite the fact that she was a political maverick. Legislation she introduced created the Search for Evaluation, Education, and Knowledge (SEEK) program that enabled black and Puerto Rican students without adequate academic training to enter the state universities. She proposed legislation to promote day-care centers and provide unemployment insurance for domestic workers. Another measure protected female school teachers from losing tenure as a result of interruptions in employment related to pregnancy. She strongly opposed the use of state money for church-run schools because it would erode support for public education. Another bill she proposed would have required police officers to complete successfully courses in civil rights, minority problems, and race relations. The Associated Press judged her to be one of the two most militant and effective black members of the assembly, along with Percy Sutton.

Court-ordered reapportionment in 1968 created a new Twelfth District in Brooklyn. The new district was eighty percent Democratic and seventy percent black and Puerto Rican. Chisholm saw the district as ideal for her and announced her candidacy for Congress. Of eight AD leaders in the Twelfth District, only Thomas R. Fortune supported Chisholm; four supported William C. Thompson, a black lawyer. Chisholm used that support to define Thompson as the candidate of the political bosses, adopting a campaign slogan of Fighting Shirley Chisholm—Unbought and

Unbossed. The third candidate was Dollie Lowther Robinson, a lawyer and former labor leader and official in the Kennedy Administration's Labor Department.

A tenacious, outspoken campaigner, Chisholm enjoyed the support of the Unity Club and Mac Holder. With a sound truck, a caravan of cars, and a small army of volunteers, many of whom were women, she carried her campaign to the people— to housing projects, parks, churches, and even street corners. At each stop, Chisholm manned the sound truck while her volunteers fanned out in all directions, loaded with shopping bags stuffed with campaign literature. Her contact with Puerto Ricans was particularly effective because of her fluent Spanish (her college minor).

The political pundits predicted a Thompson victory in the Democratic primary, but the votes provided by the United Club in Bedford-Stuyvesant produced a victory by almost eight hundred votes. After the primary, Chisholm faced the Republican candidate, James Farmer, who actually lived in Manhattan. Both candidates stressed jobs, housing, and education, and both opposed the Vietnam War. Farmer's campaign suggested the need for a "strong male image" in Washington, an issue that unnecessarily raised the question of sex, in Chisholm's estimate. Actually, as Holder discovered, the district had more than twice as many female as male voters, making the issue of sex a liability for Farmer. Chisholm found discrimination against women in politics particularly unjust. "Of course we have to help black men," she conceded, "but not at the expense of our own personalities as women. The black man must step forward, but that does not mean *we* have to step back."

Farmer failed to receive the support of the Brooklyn chapter of the Congress of Racial Equality. Some local Republicans, who resented the fact that he was an interloper, also withheld support. Furthermore, Farmer refused to support the Richard Nixon-Spiro Agnew presidential campaign (although he later accepted a position as assistant secretary of health, education, and welfare in the Nixon Administration). Chisholm's strongest support came from the Puerto Rican community. She beat Farmer 34,885 to 13,777, with Conservative candidate Ralph J. Carrane receiving 3,771 votes. After her election in 1968, she was returned to the House of Representatives, with majorities in excess of eighty percent, in every election through 1980.

In the Ninety-first Congress, Chisholm requested a committee assignment consistent with her experience and education, preferably on the House Education and Labor Committee. Instead, she was appointed to the Agriculture Committee and its subcommittee on forestry and rural villages. She railed against the system as "petrified"; the seniority system, she said, should be called the "senility" system. Ultimately she took her case to the Democratic caucus. Even there, seniority prevailed and Chisholm was ignored. Finally, she simply walked down the aisle and stood in the well, waiting to be recognized. "For what purpose is the gentlewoman from New York standing in the well?" Wilbur Mills asked. Chisholm maintained that since there were only nine black congressmen (feminist terms such as "congresswoman" or "congressperson" were trivial in her opinion, especially given the problems of black women)—an underrepresentation relative to black population—the party was under a moral obligation to make the most effective use of them. Subsequently she was assigned to the Veterans' Affairs Committee, and in the Ninety-second Congress received appointment to the Education and Labor Committee.

Impact of Event

In her maiden speech, Chisholm responded to President Richard Nixon's reduction in funding of Head Start, an education program, in order to fund the antiballistic missile (ABM) program. She vowed to vote against any funding bill for the Department of Defense that came up in the House until the administration rethought its "distorted, unreal scale of priorities." Like the ABM program, however, the Vietnam War depleted national resources and energy needed to resolve domestic problems.

The legacy of the Civil Rights movement of the 1960's was little more than unenforced laws. More legislation was not the answer; proper enforcement was, she claimed. She was suspicious that integration was intent upon refashioning blacks in the image of whites. The War on Poverty was a failure, too; it had been created by white middle-class intellectuals. She rejected the resort to violence that some militants advocated—even though she defined herself as a militant—because violence made blacks victims of their own actions. The power structure of society resided with a few whites, she argued, so blacks, browns, yellows, reds, and even whites must unite in common cause, within the system, to secure justice.

In 1971, she joined members of the congressional black caucus in presenting sixty demands to President Nixon. Earlier they had formed a shadow cabinet to oversee federal enforcement of civil rights laws. They asked the president to commit himself unequivocally to the goal of equality for all Americans, as had the National Advisory Commission on Civil Disorders appointed by President Johnson in 1967. The government lacked both the will and the staff to address civil rights effectively and meaningfully, according to that commission's report. The pervasiveness of white racism, chronic discrimination, and segregation in employment, education, and housing had appalling effects on the ghetto life of blacks, particularly youths, men, and the hard-core disadvantaged. The conscience of the whole nation needed to be aroused to oppose racism against blacks and sexism against women, Chisholm contended.

Chisholm concluded that abortion had no relevancy to law, as no one should be forced to have or not have an abortion. She accepted the honorary presidency of the National Association for the Repeal of Abortion Laws, the goal of which was the repeal of all laws restricting abortion. She supported the Equal Rights Amendment in 1971; she had from the beginning in 1969 sponsored a House resolution calling for equal rights for men and women. Chisholm subscribed to the proposition that women were not inherently anything, only human. "In the end," she wrote, "antiblack, antifemale, and all forms of discrimination are equivalent to the same thing—antihumanism."

Because black political strategists could not agree among themselves regarding the presidential election in 1972, Chisholm decided to seek the Democratic nomination, thereby becoming the first woman ever actively to seek the presidential nomination of a major political party. She could not win, but she could pioneer the way for others. She denied that she was the candidate of black Americans, even though she was black and proud of it, or the candidate of women, even though she was a woman and equally proud of that. "I am the candidate of the people," she said. Only two members of the congressional black caucus, Ronald Dellums and Parren Mitchell, were at her side when she announced her candidacy on January 25, 1972. The National Organization for Women did not endorse her because it would have lost its tax-exempt status, but feminists Betty Friedan and Gloria Steinem ran as Chisholm delegates for the Democratic convention in Manhattan. They lost. Militant Gay Liberation members joined her campaign in Boston. She defended their rights, too. She welcomed the support of Bobby Seale and the Black Panthers, to the chagrin of some of her advisers. An extraordinary cross-section of Americans supported her campaign, but most conspicuous in the absence of their support were black male politicians—not all, but most.

The use of busing to correct racial imbalances in public schools was one of the most controversial issues of the campaign. For Chisholm, open housing was the real solution to the problem, but lacking that, busing was an expedient alternative.

With only 151 delegate votes at the convention, Chisholm was obviously unable to influence its deliberations on behalf of the issues of importance to blacks and other minorities, women, children, and the less fortunate. In that she failed, but in Congress she had championed the cause of job training, child welfare programs, open housing, urban development, and consumer affairs. Her work on behalf of educational opportunity programs was exemplary. She helped abolish the House Committee on Un-American Activities. She called for a national holiday in honor of Dr. Martin Luther King, Jr., and a study commission on Afro-American history and culture. Her voice was heard across the land, and the courage of her conscience served to remind the nation of its birthright of equality and justice for all.

Bibliography

Brownmiller, Susan. "This Is Fighting Shirley Chisholm." *The New York Times Magazine* (April 13, 1969): 32-102. Based on an interview with Chisholm. Contains information relating the congressional candidates in 1968 to the presidential candidates.

Chisholm, Shirley. *The Good Fight.* New York: Harper & Row, 1973. Essentially an account of the presidential campaign in 1972. To some degree, it relates the campaign to the other candidates, but it is primarily focused on the issues and conficts in the state primaries. Limited scope is given to the machinations of the convention. A number of position papers are included in the appendix.

_____. *Unbought and Unbossed.* Boston: Houghton Mifflin, 1970. An autobiography that begins with her Barbadian background, of which she is particularly proud. The focus is on her election to Congress in 1968 and her opinions on a number of issues, including the Vietnam War, coalition politics, abortion, and black politicians.

Duffy, Susan, comp. *Shirley Chisholm: A Bibliography of Writings by and About Her.* Metuchen, N.J.: Scarecrow Press, 1988. An extensive compilation of sources, indispensable to the serious student. Many of the citations are widely available.

Kuriansky, Joan, and Catherine Smith. *Shirley Chisholm, Democratic Representative from New York.* Washington, D.C.: Grossman, 1972. Emphasis on Chisholm's Congressional actions, with some analysis of her voting record and with comments by Chisholm.

Romero, Patricia W., ed. *In Black America 1968: The Year of Awakening.* New York: Publisher's Company, 1969. Of general value, it provides the broad racial and political setting for understanding the context within which Chisholm launched her congressional career.

Jimmie F. Gross

Cross-References

Rankin Becomes the First Woman Elected to Congress (1916), p. 190; HUAC Begins Investigating Suspected Communists (1938), p. 550; The Equal Pay Act Becomes Law (1963), p. 1172; Head Start Is Established (1965), p. 1284; Congress Passes the Voting Rights Act (1965), p. 1296; The Black Panther Party Is Organized (1966), p. 1348; The Kerner Commission Explores the Causes of Civil Disorders (1967), p. 1370; Congress Enacts the Bilingual Education Act (1968), p. 1402; Martin Luther King, Jr., Is Assassinated in Memphis (1968), p. 1419; Riots Against Police Harassment Launch the Gay Rights Movement (1969), p. 1479; The Supreme Court Endorses Busing as a Means to End Segregation (1971), p. 1628; The Equal Rights Amendment Passes Congress but Fails to Be Ratified (1972), p. 1656; *Roe v. Wade* Expands Reproductive Choice for American Women (1973), p. 1703; Congress Extends Voting Rights Reforms (1975), p. 1812; Congress Requires Bilingual Elections to Protect Minority Rights (1975), p. 1817; Jackson Becomes the First Major Black Candidate for U.S. President (1983), p. 2209.

THE STATUTE OF LIMITATIONS IS RULED NOT APPLICABLE TO WAR CRIMES

Category of event: Atrocities and war crimes
Time: November 26, 1968
Locale: United Nations, New York City

The United Nations General Assembly ratified the Convention on the Non-Applicability of Statutory Limitations to War Crimes and Crimes Against Humanity

Principal personages:
> U THANT (1909-1974), the secretary-general of the United Nations (1962-1971)
> LUDWIG ERHARD (1897-1977), the West German chancellor from 1963 to 1966
> KURT WALDHEIM (1918-   ), the Austrian diplomat who served as secretary-general of the United Nations (1971-1981)

Summary of Event

War crimes tribunals have been used throughout history to compel states to follow existing laws of warfare. The war crimes tribunals in Nuremberg and Tokyo and the 1949 Geneva Conventions were examples of international efforts to expand the scope of international law after World War II. The tremendous suffering of both combatants and civilians during the war clearly aroused international interest in protecting human rights. Statements of the Allied leaders at Yalta and Potsdam clearly indicated that the Allied Powers intended to pursue individuals responsible for war crimes and crimes against humanity. In its preamble, the United Nations Charter stated that the protection of fundamental human rights and justice were fundamental goals of the organization. The barbarous actions of Germany in its persecution of European Jews were an indication that rules of state and individual conduct in war had to be strengthened.

Unable to establish an international criminal court of justice after the war, the United Nations gave states jurisdiction to prosecute in municipal courts individuals charged with war crimes. The 1949 Geneva Convention for the Protection of Civilian Persons in Time of War required each signatory to search for persons alleged to have committed, or to have ordered to be committed, war crimes, and to bring such persons, regardless of their nationality, before its own courts. The origins of the 1968 U.N. convention can be found in the efforts of the Polish delegation to the U.N. Commission on Human Rights. The Polish delegation introduced resolutions that drew attention to the debate in the Federal Republic of Germany (West Germany) over the applicability of statutes of limitations for persons accused of war crimes.

In 1965, the West German Bundestag passed a resolution that excluded the period from May, 1945, to December, 1949, from statute-of-limitations protections for all persons accused of serious crimes. The 1965 resolution extended the period in which persons accused of crimes could be prosecuted by the German government. The Polish delegation expressed concern that under German law, all legal proceedings against accused war criminals would be stopped in December, 1969. This was troubling to many states in 1965 because it was estimated that although sixty-one hundred individuals had been convicted in West German courts for Nazi war crimes since 1945, as many as eighteen thousand individuals suspected of war crimes remained at large.

To many member states of the United Nations, the application of statute-of-limitations protection to accused war criminals appeared to contradict the intent of the 1946 genocide convention. The General Assembly declared in a 1946 resolution that genocide is always a crime under international law. The efforts of the Polish delegation led the Commission on Human Rights to ask U.N. Secretary-General U Thant to begin examining laws that would hinder the prosecution of accused war criminals. The report of the secretary-general and the efforts of the Economic and Social Council culminated in a draft proposal of the convention on the nonapplicability of statutory limitations to war crimes and crimes against humanity in 1968.

The convention adopted the definition of war crimes established during the military tribunal at Nuremberg in 1946 and affirmed in the Geneva Conventions of 1949. The Nuremberg Principles adopted by the General Assembly stated that "any person who commits an act which constitutes a crime under international law is responsible therefor and liable to punishment." Article 6 of the Charter of the International Military Tribunal at Nuremberg had previously defined war crimes as violations of the laws or customs of war. Such violations included murder, ill treatment, or deportation to slave labor of civilian populations in occupied territory; murder or ill treatment of prisoners of war; killing of hostages; plunder of public or private property; wanton destruction of cities, towns, or villages; or devastation not justified by military necessity.

Although some United Nations members expressed reservations about incorporating the Nuremberg Principles into the 1968 convention, attempts to alter the definition of war crimes were strongly opposed by many members of the General Assembly. Article 1 of the convention also included the United Nations definitions of crimes against humanity defined in the Nuremberg Charter. The United Nations had accepted these definitions in the 1946 genocide convention. The only addition to the category of crimes against humanity was the addition of the United Nations resolution condemning apartheid, the policy of racial discrimination by the government of South Africa.

While there was general agreement that statutory limitations clauses existing in municipal law should not shield individuals from prosecution, a number of states strongly objected to provisions of the U.N. draft proposal. The four-year debate in the United Nations over the wording of the convention symbolized the tremendous differences in opinion a number of states had concerning the eleven articles of the convention. One of the most fundamental issues surrounding the convention was whether the exemption of statutory limitations to war criminals already existed in international law.

The United Kingdom and the United States took the position that the nonapplicability of statutes of limitations for war criminals already existed in international law. The Soviet Union and its allies rejected this position and lobbied to strike any language from the convention that would have established that existing international law had addressed this issue. As the debate over the convention continued, many in the West began to characterize the convention as an attempt by Eastern European states and the Soviet Union to embarrass the Federal Republic of Germany by insinuating that it had not vigorously pursued individuals linked to atrocities during World War II.

The Convention on Non-Applicability of Statutory Limitations to War Crimes and Crimes Against Humanity was adopted by the General Assembly in 1968 with more opposing votes than any previous human rights convention: fifty-eight states approved its adoption, seven opposed, and thirty-six abstained. Israel, Czechoslovakia, Poland, and the Soviet Union were some of the states that supported the convention. The United States, the United Kingdom, and South Africa voted against the convention. Argentina, Bolivia, Brazil, Uruguay, and Venezuela were among the states that abstained from voting.

Impact of Event

The 1968 convention was important in the history of international law because, for the first time, an international convention clearly stated that crimes against humanity by individuals had no statute of limitations. The 1968 convention's treatment of the issue of retroactivity has been criticized because it failed to address the rights of individuals accused of war crimes and crimes against humanity. The United States opposed the convention because of concerns about what it saw as political rather than legal objectives in not clearly addressing how the convention would address existing laws of various states.

The convention's effect on international human rights is difficult to assess because of the nature of the offenses that the convention addresses. While it is a fundamental tenet of criminal law that a defendant is entitled to full protection under the laws of the state, critics of the convention have questioned whether individuals accused of crimes during war were provided the same rights as persons accused of other types of crime. The convention's main provisions required all states party to the convention to eliminate all legal statutes that provide statutory limitations protection to individuals accused of war crimes, crimes against humanity during peacetime, or acts related to the policy of apartheid.

Many have also expressed disappointment with international efforts to bring to justice individuals responsible for crimes against humanity. The provisions of the genocide convention have been used only two times in the postwar period. The inability to define genocide clearly has led to obstacles when national courts have attempted to punish individuals accused of international crimes. An example of this difficulty was the trial and execution of Marcias Nguema, the former leader of Equatorial Guinea. After murdering a number of individuals, he was overthrown and found guilty of genocide in 1979. A later report by the International Commission of Jurists found that although mass murder was clearly proven, Marcias was wrongly convicted of genocide because there was no compelling evidence to prove intentional destruction of racial, ethnic, or religious groups.

The absence of an international tribunal to prosecute war criminals after World War II made it possible for many to avoid prosecution by finding sanctuary in other countries. The number of individuals who actually have been put on trial for crimes against humanity did not significantly change after the adoption of the 1968 convention. The various resolutions adopted by the United Nations and the attention given to the apprehension and punishment of war criminals found in the 1968 convention has not been matched by U.N. actions to seek out individuals responsible for war crimes. Information about many of the individuals accused of Nazi war crimes has come from private individuals interested in bringing individuals to justice. The most prominent of these individuals was Simon Wiesenthal, who was instrumental in Israel's apprehension, trial, and execution of one of the principal planners of the persecution of European Jews, Adolf Eichmann. Kurt Waldheim, the secretary-general of the United Nations from 1971 through 1981, has himself been accused of Nazi collaboration during World War II. Many of the states that objected to the language of the original resolution have refused to become signatories to the 1968 convention. Because universal acceptance of the convention has not occurred, the effect of this convention on national and international law since 1968 has been limited.

Bibliography

Best, Geoffrey. *Nuremberg and After: The Continuing History of War Crimes and Crimes Against Humanity.* Reading, England: University of Reading, 1984. A short account of how the principles established at Nuremberg have been incorporated into international law. Includes notations.

Clausnitzer, Martin. "The Statute of Limitations for Murder in the Federal Republic of Germany." *International and Comparative Law Quarterly* 29 (April-July, 1980): 473-479. Examines the debate in Germany over the thirty-year limitation for murder in Germany and its effect on Nazi war criminals still at large. Includes notations.

Falk, Richard, Gabriel Kolko, and Robert Jay Lifton, eds. *Crimes of War.* New York: Random House, 1971. A collection of essays and documents that examine the legal framework of various laws of war. Includes index.

Green, Leslie C. "Human Rights and the Law of Armed Conflict." In *Essays on the Modern Law of War.* Dobbs Ferry, N.Y.: Transnational Publishers, 1984. A very readable account of the historical development of laws of warfare. Although it does not specifically address the 1968 resolution, it is a valuable introduction to the subject of human rights and warfare.

"Human Rights-Actions of the Third Committee." *U.N. Monthly Chronicle* 5 (November, 1968). A brief account of the debate in the Social, Humanitarian, and Cultural Committee over the draft convention on the nonapplicability of statutory limitations on war crimes. Includes text of the resolution and individual countries' votes on the convention.

Kuper, Leo. *The Prevention of Genocide.* New Haven, Conn.: Yale University Press, 1985. An examination of the United Nations and its implementation of the 1948 genocide convention. Includes notations, appendices, bibliography, and index.

Miller, Robert H. "The Convention on the Non-Applicability of Statutory Limitations to War Crimes and Crimes Against Humanity." *American Journal of International Law* 65, no. 3 (1971): 467-501. An excellent treatment of the subject written by a former United Nations official. One of the best sources on the origins of and United Nations debate over the 1968 convention. Includes notations.

Tolley, Howard, Jr. *The U.N. Commission on Human Rights.* Boulder, Colo.: Westview Press, 1986. A comprehensive history of the United Nations Commission on Human Rights and its impact on international politics after World War II. Includes notations, tables, illustrations, appendices, bibliography, and index.

United Nations Department of Public Information. *The United Nations and Human Rights.* New York: United Nations, 1984. An account of United Nations efforts to encourage the protection of human rights. Includes appendix and index.

Lawrence Clark III

Cross-References

Nazi Concentration Camps Go into Operation (1933), p. 491; Japanese Troops Brutalize Chinese After the Capture of Nanjing (1937), p. 539; The United Nations Adopts a Convention on the Crime of Genocide (1948), p. 783; The United Nations Sets Rules for the Treatment of Prisoners (1955), p. 935; The Iraqi Government Promotes Genocide of Kurds (1960's), p. 1050; Eichmann Is Tried for War Crimes (1961), p. 1108; The Amin Regime Terrorizes Uganda (1971), p. 1600; The United Nations Issues a Declaration Against Torture (1975), p. 1847; The Argentine Military Conducts a "Dirty War" Against Leftists (1976), p. 1864; Barbie Faces Charges for Nazi War Crimes (1983), p. 2193; Israel Convicts Demjanjuk of Nazi War Crimes (1988), p. 2370.

CASSIN IS AWARDED THE NOBEL PEACE PRIZE

Categories of event: Peace movements and organizations; civil rights
Time: December 10, 1968
Locale: Oslo, Norway

In recognition of decades of work toward uniting the nations of the world in the fight to establish global standards for human rights, René Cassin received the Nobel Peace Prize

> *Principal personages:*
> RENÉ CASSIN (1887-1976), a French delegate to and primary force behind the U.N. Commission on Human Rights
> ELEANOR ROOSEVELT (1884-1962), the wife of U.S. president Franklin Delano Roosevelt and chair of the U.N. Commission on Human Rights
> CHARLES DE GAULLE (1890-1970), a French general and president of the Fifth Republic
> AASE LIONÆS (1907-   ), the chair of the Nobel Committee of the Norwegian Parliament

Summary of Event

In November of 1968, the Nobel Committee of the Norwegian Parliament announced the selection of René Cassin as recipient of the Nobel Peace Prize. Cassin's was not a household name; few outside the realm of international human rights work or the United Nations knew of him. His work over the previous decades, culminating in 1966 with the ratification of the U.N. Commission on Human Rights's two International Covenants after nearly twenty years of debate, constitutes a major contribution to the promotion of human rights.

Cassin was born in 1887 to a Jewish mercantile family in Bayonne, France. He earned degrees in humanities and law at the University of Aix-en-Provence and a doctorate in juridical, economic, and political science at the Faculty of Law at Paris. He was called up to serve in the infantry in World War I and in 1916 suffered a severe abdominal wound from German shrapnel. His life was saved by a stunning coincidence: His mother was a nurse at the field hospital for hopeless cases to which he was taken, and she convinced the doctors to attempt surgery on her son.

From the war, Cassin gained a keen sense of human suffering, of the destruction of families and the randomness of tragedy. In World War I, the advent of aerial warfare and technological advancements in ammunition, including chemical weapons, had expanded the dimensions of wartime suffering, and millions across the face of Europe were killed, maimed, widowed, orphaned, or displaced.

After the war, Cassin began to fight on behalf of its victims. He called for compensation for personal damages incurred in national service, artificial limb banks, professional retraining programs, small business loans, and provisions for the welfare and education of orphans. In 1918 he formed the Union Fédérale des Associations des Mutilés et d'Anciens Combattants (the Federal Union of Associations for Disabled War Veterans) and served as its first president. He also served as vice president of the Conseil Supérieur des Pupilles de la Nation (High Council for Wards of the Nation). In 1921, he arranged conferences of war veterans from Italy, Poland, Germany, and Czechoslovakia, and in 1926 he established an international organization of disabled veterans. Working with these groups made the price of war clear but also gave hope that unity among war's victims— soldiers, workers, average men and women, and their families—could become an international peace force.

The League of Nations, founded in 1919 in the aftermath of World War I, was the first organization to bring together the nations of the world to promote cooperation and the peaceful resolution of conflict. Cassin was a French delegate to the League from 1924 to 1936. It was through the League's International Labor Organization that he encouraged veterans who fought on opposing sides to demonstrate together for the Disarmament Conference of 1932.

Disarmament was not to come. Despite the growth of international organizations and the activities of individuals such as Cassin, Adolf Hitler armed Germany and established concentration camps to incarcerate, torture, and exterminate undesirable persons systematically. In 1938, Germany annexed the Sudetenland; the invasion of Poland the following year sparked World War II. After France fell in 1940, Cassin joined Charles de Gaulle in London to serve as minister of justice in the French government-in-exile. Cassin drafted the agreement between de Gaulle and Winston Churchill that became the charter of the French Free Forces.

With the Allied victory and the war's end in 1945, the world became aware of the atrocities perpetrated in Hitler's Germany. As the League of Nations had been disbanded, the leaders of the world drafted the charter for a new organization, the United Nations, calling for a Commission on Human Rights to examine human rights conditions throughout the world and to formulate policies for their improvement. This effort represented the first time that a supranational organization would focus on sovereign nations' treatment of their citizens. Eleanor Roosevelt, widow of the late U.S. President Franklin Delano Roosevelt, was chosen to chair the commission. Its other members were an impressive and diverse group of statespeople, scholars, and jurists, including Cassin as vice chair.

The commission decided first to formulate a general declaration on human rights as a statement of principle and then to draft conventions regarding specific standards, implementation, and enforcement. These were no simple tasks, for the gap was wide between the ideals and the realities of political repression and conflict across the globe. Not all statespeople agreed on what constituted human rights, how they should be defined, where national authority should defer to the United Nations, and how to effect cooperation from belligerent or repressive regimes. From the beginning, Cassin mediated between the Western emphasis on civil and political rights and the Eastern concern for economic, social, and cultural rights. He suggested that two conventions be drafted reflecting these two viewpoints.

The work of the commission was slow and arduous, with annual meetings of five to eight weeks. In January of 1947, a drafting committee was appointed consisting of Eleanor Roosevelt, P. C. Chang of China, and Charles Malik of Lebanon. Complaints about the lack of regional representation led to expansion of the committee to include European and Latin American delegates. Cassin was asked to review the U.N. Secretariat proposals; his recommendations were central to the drafting process. The text of the Universal Declaration of Human Rights was sent to the General Assembly in 1948, after two years of formulation. It included assertion of the universal rights to life; personal security; equality before the law; freedom of conscience, religion, expression, and assembly; work at a fair wage; reasonable working hours; and free education.

Two months, seven meetings, and more than one thousand proposed amendments later, the declaration was adopted by the General Assembly in Paris on December 10, 1948. The vote was forty-eight in favor and none opposed, with eight abstentions (the Soviet bloc, Saudi Arabia, and South Africa). The commission then turned to the covenants. The means of enforcement and controversy over encroachment on national sovereignty posed the greatest problems. Cassin, concerned over limiting the covenants' breadth, expressed concerns to the U.N. Economic and Social Council and attempted unsuccessfully to meet with Secretary-General Dag Hammarskjöld.

Ultimately, the commission took six years to submit the two covenants to the General Assembly, and it took the General Assembly thirteen years to consider them. They were finally approved in 1966 with substantially weakened enforcement provisions. Ironically, the last original Economic and Social Council member to ratify the covenants was France, in 1974.

Cassin's work on the commission was the cornerstone of his career and a primary reason for his Nobel Prize two years after the passage of the covenants, but it was only one of his achievements. In the years preceding his award, Cassin was an author of the charter of the United Nations Educational, Scientific and Cultural Organization (UNESCO). He was a professor of fiscal and civil law at the University of Paris from 1929 through 1960. In the 1960's, he served as president of the French branch of the World Federation of International Jurists, the French National Overseas Center of Advanced Studies, the Society of Comparative Legislature, and the International Institute of Diplomatic Studies and Research. From 1950 to 1960, Cassin was a member of the Court of Arbitration at The Hague, and from 1965 to 1968 he presided over the European Court of Human Rights at Strasbourg. Thus, his Nobel Prize came at the culmination of a long and distinguished career.

Impact of Event

The immediate impact of Cassin's Nobel Peace Prize was to give him much-deserved recognition. At the age of 81, Cassin was among the prize's oldest recipients. Mrs. Aase Lionæs, chair of the Nobel Committee of the Norwegian Parliament in 1968, had been a Norwegian delegate to the United Nations when the General Assembly first considered the formation of the Commission on Human

Rights. She was personally familiar with Cassin and his work and, in her presentation speech on December 10, 1968, on the twentieth anniversary of the General Assembly's adoption of the Universal Declaration of Human Rights, recognized the difficulty of defining human rights in an intercultural context and congratulated Cassin for his primary role in that achievement.

Along with the honor of the Nobel Prize, Cassin received a cash award of earnings from Alfred Nobel's original bequest. He fulfilled a longtime hope by establishing the International Institute of Human Rights at Strasbourg as a center for human rights documentation, communication, and research. During 1968, Cassin and his supporters had promoted his candidacy for the prize with founding the institute as a primary objective.

More important, Cassin's prize focused attention on the Universal Declaration of Human Rights and on international human rights efforts in general. The declaration was a lofty, idealistic, carefully framed document that had endured twenty years. Human rights violations had by no means ceased by 1968, the International Human Rights Year, but the declaration had formed the basis for a growing international dialogue setting uniform standards and attempting to effect enforcement or, at the least, to influence the behavior of sovereign governments.

The work of the commission continued and expanded. In the late 1960's, the members of the Nonaligned Movement, which was founded in 1961 to ensure the integrity of nations outside the Eastern and Western blocs, became more active in focusing commission attention on issues of self-determination, racial discrimination, and economic rights. Through their encouragement, a more defined system was developed for implementing commission determinations. This system included promoting positive goals through communications and resolutions, initiating investigations of suspected offenses, and punishing guilty regimes through economic and diplomatic isolation and prosecution in the World Court. The impetus for enhanced enforcement derived greatly from African and Asian member concerns over South Africa's apartheid policies and Israel's treatment of residents in lands occupied in the Six-Day War in 1967.

Through the 1970's, South Africa, Israel, and Chile were a chief focus of commission activities, but they were by no means the only nations criticized or investigated. The commission sent telegrams, for example, to Guatemala to resolve a murder case, to Malawi to spare a political dissident, and to the Sudan, Cyprus, and Nicaragua over suspected violations. Resolutions were passed regarding the status of East Timor and the Tamil separatist movement in Sri Lanka. Self-determination was studied in the cases of Palestine, Namibia, Kampuchea, the Western Sahara, Grenada, and Afghanistan. In the 1980's, the commission investigated political disappearances and government-sponsored kidnappings in Latin America: In 1985, more than ten thousand complaints were received and answered regarding such disappearances worldwide. Unfortunately, only six percent of those cases were clarified. Throughout the commission's history, ineffectiveness was a constant criticism. In addition, controversy persisted over the partisan issues of political double standards and selective enforcement along lines of East versus West, political versus economic, and developed nations versus the Third World.

Nevertheless, the commission continued to be an outspoken proponent of human rights. In addition to the Universal Declaration and its subsequent Covenants, the commission sent five other declarations and six other conventions to the General Assembly for passage. The commission worked closely with the General Assembly, the Secretariat's Centre for Human Rights, the U.N. High Commissioner for Refugees, and other international organizations to coordinate the fight for human rights. Promotional activities including seminars, fellowships, advisory services, publications, and studies, many of which were developed during Cassin's tenure, helped to disseminate information and raise awareness.

In general, identification, investigation, and publication of violations has provided great spiritual support to oppressed individuals everywhere. In 1985, Senator Alberto Zumaran of Uruguay spoke to the commission about his nation's recently replaced military regime:

> The Commission had handed down innumerable decisions on individual cases, all of which had been consistently disregarded by the dictatorship but had nevertheless greatly boosted the people's morale. . . . The work accomplished by the UNCHR during these years had been simply stupendous; many Uruguayans owed their life and freedom to that agency.

Bibliography

Cassese, Antonio, ed. _U.N. Law/Fundamental Rights: Two Topics in International Law._ Alphen van den Rijn, The Netherlands: Sijthoff & Noordhoff, 1979. This volume contains fifteen essays by internationally diverse scholars of international law. The outlook is realistic, factual, and unrelentingly objective.

Commission to Study the Organization of Peace. _The U.N. and Human Rights._ Dobbs Ferry, N.Y.: Oceana Publications, 1968. Issued the year of Cassin's award, this official report includes documents from the canon of U.N. law and a supplementary history by a member of the commission's executive committee. The discussion of the draft committee under Roosevelt depicts the tension between the lofty ideals and practical challenges of human rights work.

Frankel, Marvin E., with Ellen Saideman. _Out of the Shadows of Night: The Struggle for International Human Rights._ New York: Delacorte Press, 1989. Written by two human rights attorneys, this is an empirical study of individuals and groups worldwide facing human rights violations and efforts taken on their behalf. Appendices include international covenants and a listing of human rights organizations.

Holleman, Warren Lee. _The Human Rights Movement: Western Values and Theological Perspectives._ New York: Praeger, 1987. This is a short theoretical discussion of human rights in the context of modern Western policymaking. Holleman views history in terms of ideological movements and conflicts: West versus East, individual versus collective, national versus global, and secular versus religious.

Luini del Russo, Alessandra. _International Protection of Human Rights._ Washington,

D.C.: Lerner Law Books, 1971. A legalistic approach to the implementation of human rights enforcement, this book discusses the U.N. Commission and the European Court, including specific cases. Appendices include relevant documents.

Nickel, James W. *Making Sense of Human Rights: Philosophical Reflections on the Universal Declaration of Human Rights.* Berkeley: University of California Press, 1987. In this extended philosophical discussion, Nickel demonstrates a deep appreciation of the events and individuals that have shaped thought about human rights and its expression as well as the Declaration of Human Rights and its interpretation. The prose is dense and formal.

Sherwood, Robert, ed. *Peace on Earth.* New York: Heritage House, 1949. This volume consists of articles by eleven figures from the United Nations' formative years. A short piece by Eleanor Roosevelt is idealistic and rhetorical, reflecting her hope for speedy ratification of the covenants. Appendices include documents and biographical notes.

Tolley, Howard, Jr. *The U.N. Commission on Human Rights.* Boulder, Colo.: Westview Press, 1986. This is a definitive work on the commission from its establishment through 1986. Tolley clearly delineates the commission's goals, functions, activities, and accomplishments, and provides generous statistical information on national participation.

Barry Mann

Cross-References

The League of Nations Is Established (1919), p. 270; The International Labour Organisation Is Established (1919), p. 281; The United Nations Adopts the Universal Declaration of Human Rights (1948), p. 789; The European Convention on Human Rights Is Signed (1950), p. 843; The European Court of Human Rights Is Established (1950), p. 849; The United Nations Issues a Declaration on Racial Discrimination (1963), p. 1212; The U.N. Covenant on Civil and Political Rights Is Adopted (1966), p. 1353; The Proclamation of Teheran Sets Human Rights Goals (1968), p. 1430; The United Nations Votes to Suppress and Punish Apartheid (1973), p. 1736; The Helsinki Agreement Offers Terms for International Cooperation (1975), p. 1806; The United Nations Issues a Declaration Against Torture (1975), p. 1847.

BRAZIL BEGINS A PERIOD OF INTENSE REPRESSION

Category of event: Political freedom
Time: December 13, 1968
Locale: Brasilia, Brazil

The suspension of the congress and the promulgation of Institutional Act Number Five signaled the tightening of control over Brazilian citizens by the military government

Principal personages:

ARTUR DA COSTA E SILVA (1902-1969), the president of Brazil from 1967 to 1969

EMÍLIO GARRASTAZÚ MÉDICI (1905-1985), the head of the Brazilian intelligence service under Costa e Silva and president of Brazil from 1969 to 1974

HUMBERTO DE ALENCAR CASTELO BRANCO (1900-1967), the first military president of Brazil following the 1964 coup

ANTONIO DELFIM NETO (1928-   ), the minister of finance under Costa e Silva and Médici

Summary of Event

Industrial growth in Brazil, already significant in the 1930's and accelerating after World War II, changed the nature of politics in that country. As urban workers became an important voting group, politicians courted their support. The nationalist, populist tone of such politicians became troubling after the Cuban revolution of 1959. The Brazilian military, steeped in anticommunist ideology, watched warily as João Goulart, president of Brazil from 1961 to 1964, appeared to lean ever more dangerously toward the left.

The Brazilian economy suffered under Goulart's administration. Foreign businesses, fearing nationalization, either invested more cautiously or pulled out completely. Inflation soared, and prices nearly doubled in 1963. Workers organized strikes to protest the erosion of their purchasing power. Peasants in the rural areas of the northeast clamored for land reform. Even the lower ranks of the military talked about forming unions to promote their interests.

Political ferment among the lower classes came to an abrupt end on April 1, 1964, when the military deposed João Goulart. The president fled into exile in Uruguay and was replaced by General Humberto de Alencar Castelo Branco. During Castelo Branco's administration, a new constitution was written, political parties were abolished and replaced by a government party and an opposition party, and attempts were made to stabilize the economy in order to attract investment and resume growth. Many of the stabilization policies, while bringing inflation under control, also eroded workers' salaries. At the same time, however, they gave middle- and upper-class Brazilians hope that the uncertainty of progress during the Goulart years was gone. As investments increased, better jobs were indeed created for those with higher levels of education. Meanwhile, the military silenced opposition to its regime, by force when necessary.

When Castelo Branco passed the presidency to General Artur da Costa e Silva in 1967, Brazilians believed that the new president would ease the country back to democracy. Costa e Silva appeared less rigid than his predecessor, giving many Brazilians confidence to voice their opposition to military dictatorship. As vocal opposition grew, a "hard-line" faction within the military became convinced that the country was not yet ready to see the resumption of direct citizen participation in government. Those who argued that the military should take a stronger hold on power pointed to the violence of student demonstrations and the emergence of an urban guerrilla movement in 1968 as evidence that chaos would replace repression. Many believed economic growth would come only in a context of law and order.

By early 1968, more and more Brazilians were protesting visibly against the military government. Workers struck for higher pay. Students sponsored large protest rallies in Brazil's major cities, sometimes with tragic results. On March 28, 1968, police fired into a group of protesters, killing a young secondary school student. The outpouring of support for the students, manifested in the huge turnout for the dead student's funeral and memorial mass, strengthened the resolve of those hard-liners who believed that such demonstrations should not be allowed.

At the same time, discontent surfaced in the national congress as well. One congressman in particular, Márcio Moreira Alves, made several speeches urging Brazilians to show that they did not support the violence and repression. He even suggested in jest that Brazilian women keep sexual favors from military men until police brutality ended. This enraged many in the military, who called for the suspension of Moreira Alves's congressional immunity so that he could be expelled from the congress and tried for crimes against the regime. On December 12, 1968, a congress in which the majority of the members belonged to the official government party voted to refuse to suspend their colleague's immunity. At that point, the president realized that he needed to act.

On the evening of December 13, 1968, Institutional Act Number Five was passed. The congress was dissolved indefinitely, strict censorship was instituted, and habeas corpus was suspended. Instead of returning the country to democracy, the Costa e Silva Administration had succumbed to the pressure of the hard-liners. The military was determined to maintain its control of the country as long as necessary to destroy what it perceived as the destabilizing opposition.

Dissent, albeit illegal and pushed underground, grew during the first months of 1969. Clandestine political parties of the left, including the Brazilian communist party, trained guerrillas for urban and rural warfare against the regime. The army and the police diligently sought out these groups, imprisoning and torturing members of those they uncovered. The forces of the right and of the left polarized. Guerrillas robbed banks to fund their training programs while death squads eliminated leftist suspects.

On August 28, 1969, President Costa e Silva suffered a debilitating stroke that left him partially paralyzed. It quickly became apparent that he was not capable of conducting the affairs related to his office. In the debate over how to proceed with the presidential succession, the hard-liners prevailed. The constitutional succession procedure by which the civilian vice president, Pedro Aleixo, would become chief executive was not acceptable to the hard-line faction because Aleixo had opposed the severe curtailing of civil and political rights in late 1968. Instead, the hard-liners selected a new military president to replace the ailing general. This man, Emílio Garrastazú Médici, had been chief of the intelligence service under Costa e Silva and commander of the Third Army in the south of Brazil. Convinced that it was his military duty to keep the country from falling into chaos, Médici accepted the appointment.

In the days following Costa e Silva's stroke, but before Médici assumed office, one of the guerrilla factions carried out a startling action as a means of getting attention and as a source of pressure for the release of political prisoners. On September 4, 1969, guerrillas kidnapped Charles Burke Elbrick, United States ambassador to Brazil. Their demands for radio time and for the release of prisoners were met, and Ambassador Elbrick was released on September 7. In the following months, guerrillas would kidnap other important foreign officials. The government usually gave in to most of their demands.

The Médici government combined intense repression with a determination to accelerate the economic growth begun under Costa e Silva. Antonio Delfim Neto, minister of finance in the Costa e Silva Administration, was kept on by General Médici. He presided over a period of remarkable economic growth that was dubbed the "Brazilian Economic Miracle." Between 1968 and 1973, Brazil's gross national product (GNP) grew at an annual rate of around 10 percent. The miracle came at great cost to the Brazilian poor. Real wages dropped precipitously, while the ban on protests and strikes meant that demonstrating discontent could be very dangerous. While the majority of the workers suffered, managers did rather well. Many in the middle and upper classes strongly supported the military policy. Brazil, during the miracle years, became the eighth industrial power in the Western World.

The economic boom, however, proved ephemeral. With the increase in oil prices after 1973, the bill for Brazilian industry grew astonishingly. Highly reliant on oil imports, the military administrations sought alternative fuel sources at the same time that they increased exploration for oil off their large coast and in the interior of the country. As inflation climbed once again, the large blue-collar work force felt the pinch. By the late 1970's, protests and strikes had resurfaced. This time, however, the military met popular criticism with a promise to open up the political system. Saddled with a huge foreign debt that had skyrocketed during the 1970's, Brazilians faced a difficult economic future. The military was blamed for the financial mess. By 1985, protests culminated in demands for the free election of a civilian president.

That year, however, a congress controlled by the government party once again selected Brazil's president. This time, popular opinion was so strongly against the regime that Congress selected the opposition party's candidate. Only in 1989 would Brazilian citizens finally elect their president.

Impact of Event

The dissolution of Congress in December, 1968, marked the inauguration of the worst period of repression during the military regime that spanned the period from 1964 to 1985. Strict censorship of the media was enforced, and criticism of the government became grounds for arrest. The fear that "subversive" elements would take advantage of an open political system in order to promote Marxist revolution caused the generals to become overly suspicious of their fellow citizens. Those believed to sympathize with the left were arrested and sometimes tortured. Prisoners were often held without being charged. Universities were purged, and many professors lost their jobs. Fear spread among those who had earlier believed that they could pressure the government to demonstrate concern for the Brazilian poor.

The intensification of guerrilla activity following Costa e Silva's stroke was met by increasingly harsh repression. Many Brazilian students and intellectuals fled into exile rather than risk imprisonment. When guerrillas arranged the release of political prisoners in exchange for their kidnap victims, those prisoners had to agree to perpetual exile from Brazil. Exiled Brazilians, while abroad, published information about the excesses of the military regime, but within Brazil, silence continued to be enforced.

The state coupled its censorship concerning human rights abuses with a program designed to increase the patriotism of Brazilian citizens. Students at all levels, from primary school through the university, were required to take a civics course every semester they attended classes. These courses, taught by individuals who had been certified by the state, denounced the dangers of communism in the region and were meant to inspire support for the regime. During the early 1970's, in their struggle against "subversion" in the hemisphere, Brazilians provided logistical and financial support to highly repressive military coups in Bolivia, Uruguay, Chile, and Argentina. A massive public relations campaign was also mounted, to convince Brazilians that their country was on the way to international greatness. Grandiose projects such as the construction of the trans-Amazon highway signaled Brazil's entry into the developed world at the same time that they often destroyed important elements of Brazil's past, in this case a delicate environmental balance as well as a fragile and rapidly declining Indian population.

The developmental thrust of finance minister Delfim Neto meant continued need for low working-class salaries. Real wages dropped. Strikes were banned, so that discontented workers had no recourse for venting their frustrations and pressuring for salary hikes. Despite impressive economic performance, some members of the Brazilian elite also grumbled. Their complaint was against the state's use of violence against their sons and daughters who participated in protest movements.

Widespread opposition to the military dictatorship surfaced only after the economic miracle soured. Repression, some believed, might be the necessary price to pay for long-term national benefits. A break in the economic boom, however, removed this justification for violence, and the military began to be called to task even by its supporters. The oil shocks of 1973 and 1979 would mark a new era of widespread discontent with the military and would eventually lead Brazil back to a tenuous rule of law.

Bibliography

Bruneau, Thomas. *The Political Transformation of the Brazilian Catholic Church*. New York: Cambridge University Press, 1974. An important account of the role of the Catholic church in the years leading up to the 1964 coup and then in opposition to the military regime.

Dassin, Joan, ed. *Torture in Brazil*. New York: Vintage Books, 1986. Based on records kept by the Brazilian military and clandestinely photocopied by a group of lawyers and clergy, this work documents the routine use of torture against political prisoners during the military years. An excellent introduction to the period is provided by the editor.

Dulles, John W. F. *President Castello Branco: Brazilian Reformer*. College Station: Texas A&M University Press, 1980. The most thorough English-language study of the first presidential administration after the 1964 coup. The author admires Castelo Branco and was given access to his papers to produce this biography. Bibliography and index.

Langguth, A. J. *Hidden Terrors*. New York: Pantheon Books, 1978. The story of Dan Mitrione, a North American who trained police in several South American countries and was killed in Uruguay by the Tupamaro guerrillas. This work by a former reporter for *The New York Times* provides good material on Brazilian guerrillas, and on Mitrione's activity in Brazil before being assigned to Uruguay. Notes and index.

Marighella, Carlos. *For the Liberation of Brazil*. London: Penguin Books, 1971. Written by the most important Brazilian guerrilla fighter of the late 1960's, this work provides the view of the left. Includes Marighella's "Handbook of Urban Guerrilla Warfare," explaining how to participate in the struggle against the dictatorship.

Moreira Alves, Márcio. *A Grain of Mustard Seed: The Awakening of the Brazilian Revolution*. Garden City, N.Y.: Doubleday Anchor Press, 1973. Written by the Brazilian congressman whose speeches against the regime brought about the dissolution of Congress, this is a personal view of the 1964 revolution and of the role of Christians in opposition to the state. Provides a firsthand account of the repression along with strong criticism of the military regime.

Quartim, João. *Dictatorship and Armed Struggle in Brazil*. New York: Monthly Review Press, 1971. A good description of the social divisions within Brazil during the 1960's as well as of the significant divisions within the Brazilian left. Explains the tactics and strategies of the urban guerrillas.

Skidmore, Thomas E. *The Politics of Military Rule in Brazil, 1964-85.* New York: Oxford University Press, 1988. The best and most comprehensive account of the military years, organized around the individual presidential administrations. Especially good at explaining the transitions among the generals and the importance of the nation's economic performance. Good footnotes and index, but no separate bibliography.

Joan E. Meznar

Cross-References

Perón Creates a Populist Political Alliance in Argentina (1946), p. 673; Castro Takes Power in Cuba (1959), p. 1026; The Inter-American Commission on Human Rights Is Created (1959), p. 1032; An Oppressive Military Rule Comes to Democratic Uruguay (1973), p. 1715; Allende Is Overthrown in a Chilean Military Coup (1973), p. 1725; A Medical Group Helps Gather Evidence of Torture in Greece and Chile (1974), p. 1747; The Argentine Military Conducts a "Dirty War" Against Leftists (1976), p. 1864; Carter Makes Human Rights a Central Theme of Foreign Policy (1977), p. 1903; Argentine Leaders Are Convicted of Human Rights Violations (1985), p. 2280.

THE SUPREME COURT EXTENDS PROTECTION AGAINST DOUBLE JEOPARDY

Category of event: Accused persons' rights
Time: June 23, 1969
Locale: United States Supreme Court, Washington, D.C.

The Supreme Court ruled that the protection against double jeopardy, guaranteed at the federal level, also applied at the state level

Principal personages:
THURGOOD MARSHALL (1908-   ), the Supreme Court justice who wrote the majority opinion
JOHN DALMER BENTON, the accused person whose case led to the Supreme Court decision
JOHN MARSHALL HARLAN (1899-1971), a Supreme Court justice who dissented from the majority opinion
POTTER STEWART (1915-1985), a Supreme Court justice who dissented from the majority opinion

Summary of Event

Protection against double jeopardy is widely regarded in Western culture as one of the most basic of an individual's legal rights, equal in importance to the right to a trial by jury. The term refers to the principle that no person should be at risk twice—that is, be put in "double jeopardy"—for one alleged criminal act. So basic is this concept that its roots can be traced back to Greek, Roman, and canon law. In the United States, this principle is incorporated in the Fifth Amendment to the Constitution, stating that no one is to "be subject for the same offence to be twice put in jeopardy of life and limb."

Theoretically, this protective principle is a humane acknowledgment of the discrepancy in power between an ordinary citizen and the government. Private individuals, with limited resources, are protected from harassment by the ubiquitous and mightier powers of the government, which, with its greater resources, could continue to investigate and charge any person for any crime any number of times over an indefinite period were it not for this protection against double jeopardy. This protection also allows an accused person to be given a final judgment, eliminating the anxiety and uncertainty that could be caused if an accusation of criminal wrongdoing could be levied repeatedly. Finally, it acknowledges that the verdict delivered after the due process of the law must be allowed to stand, even if the evidence would seem to indicate a different result.

In practice, such a balance between the individual's rights and the government's need to maintain law and order is difficult either to identify clearly or to administer consistently. It is an area of the law so fraught with practical problems that several aspects of the definition of double jeopardy have had to be tested and judged repeatedly. So many issues have had to be determined on a case-by-case basis in court that the set of standards has been left unclear.

Understanding the significance of any one specific case, therefore, requires keeping in mind that the practice of double jeopardy has evolved over many years. In the United States, history illustrates the power of the Supreme Court in directing the course of human rights. From the beginning, for example, there arises the question of when an accused person might be placed in double jeopardy. Logically, it would seem clear that a person who has been tried initially and found not guilty could claim "double jeopardy" if he or she were to be tried again. It took a Supreme Court decision in 1978 (*Crist v. Bretz*) to determine that the initial jeopardy attaches when a jury is sworn in, not necessarily upon completion of a trial. On the other hand, what happens in the case of a mistrial? In a landmark case (*Perez*) in 1824, the Court ruled that a person cannot claim double jeopardy on the second trial if the judge in the first trial correctly declared a mistrial.

Other seemingly basic definitions have been subject to court rulings. Legal and scholarly debate has tried, for example, to determine what constitutes the "same offense," because one criminal act could be construed to break several laws. The Court has ruled that the same criminal action could involve several different offenses, so that a person could be charged several times and not be in double jeopardy.

One of the major decisions in the history of double jeopardy protection and the United States Supreme Court came in 1969, in the case of *Benton v. Maryland*. Appreciation of the significance of this one specific decision requires understanding of an old conceptual problem, that of dual sovereignty. In the United States, the Constitution and the first ten amendments to it—the Bill of Rights—were framed with the federal government in mind. While an individual is protected against the danger of being tried twice for the same offense by a federal prosecutor, if the same criminal offense also breaks a state law, a person may be tried by the state. Many but not all states had evolved their own codes protecting an individual from double jeopardy, but the standards tended to differ from state to state and were not always consistent with federal standards. In an important case in 1937 (*Palko v. Connecticut*), the Supreme Court had declared that the Fourteenth Amendment's due-process clause did not guarantee double jeopardy protection in state actions.

In August, 1965, John Dalmer Benton was tried in the state of Maryland on charges of larceny and burglary. He was convicted of burglary, but the jury found him not guilty of the larceny charges. Benton was given a ten-year sentence. He filed an appeal in the Maryland Court of Appeals. Meanwhile, in another case, the same court had ruled that the section of the state constitution requiring jurors to swear their belief in the existence of God was invalid. Because the jurors in Benton's trial had been asked to so swear, he was given the option of asking for a reindictment and retrial, which he did. Benton appealed the charge of larceny, however, claiming that he had been found not guilty of that charge in the first trial and to be tried again would put him in double jeopardy. This appeal was denied, and Benton was tried again on both burglary and larceny charges.

Ironically, this time the jury found him guilty of both offenses, and he was given fifteen years for burglary and five years for larceny. Benton's case was appealed to the Maryland Court of Special Appeals on the double jeopardy claim, but it was rejected. When the case reached the Supreme Court in 1968, the Court decided to hear the case to the extent of asking two questions. First, is the double jeopardy clause of the Fifth Amendment applicable to the states through the Fourteenth Amendment? Second, if double jeopardy applies to states as well as to federal prosecutions, was Benton put in double jeopardy?

On the merits of the case, the Supreme Court ruled, on June 23, 1969, that the double jeopardy clause of the Fifth Amendment is applicable to the states through the Fourteenth Amendment. Benton's conviction for larceny was reversed. Writing the majority opinion for the Court, Justice Thurgood Marshall rejected the opinion of the *Palko* case that basic constitutional rights could be denied by the states as long as the totality of the circumstances does not result in a denial of "fundamental fairness." Instead, once it is decided that a particular Bill of Rights guarantee is fundamental to the American scheme of justice, the same constitutional standards apply against both the state and federal governments. Justices John Marshall Harlan and Potter Stewart dissented from the majority opinion, objecting to the continuing incorporation of the Bill of Rights into the due process clause.

Impact of Event

The exact origin of the concept of an individual's protection against double jeopardy remains unclear. Even a brief sampling of the historical development of the practice of this ideal suggests how much the political and social environments influence the nature of human rights, such as protection against double jeopardy, in any one country in any one time period. In the 1969 case of *Benton v. Maryland*, the Supreme Court clarified at least one very important aspect in the United States system of government, that double jeopardy protection, previously limited to federal prosecution, also extends to state prosecution.

In the broader historical context, the impact of this decision can be seen as analogous to the situation in England in the twelfth century. Considerable tension resulted from the skirmishes between the head of the state, Henry II, and the representative of the church in England, the Archbishop of Canterbury, Thomas Becket. To protect clerks from being tried and punished by both the ecclesiastical and the king's courts, the protection against double jeopardy was sometimes cited. The framers of the American Constitution included this protection in the Bill of Rights in 1789. Although the relationship between the states and the federal government is nowhere near as adversarial as the reference to twelfth century English politics might suggest, the two were conceived and remain as separate sovereignties. Thus the Fourteenth Amendment declares, ". . . nor shall any State deprive any person of life, liberty, or property, without due process of law." The Fifth Amendment, referring only to the federal government, explicitly protects against double jeopardy.

That the Court ruling linking these two amendments came in the 1960's may also provoke some reflections on the fragility of any human right. During the 1960's, the nation as a whole put great faith in the power of the federal government to undertake the responsibility of finding solutions to national social problems and protecting the rights of individuals. Such an attitude was a considerable change from the historical view of the federal government.

It is dangerous to overstate the importance of the *Benton* case. Dual sovereignty still exists—the states and the federal government are separate entities, with their own rights to prosecution. In practice, both are leery of wasting effort on prosecuting twice and tend not to do so. What was clarified in 1969 was the basic human right to be judged by some uniform standard by both sovereignties.

The practice of the ideal of double jeopardy protection remains riddled with confusion, inconsistencies, and questions. Progress toward smooth implementation of this ideal has been, and will no doubt continue to be, rocky. The *Benton* case, no matter how technical the victory may seem, was a symbolic step toward protecting an individual from getting lost in the battle between two much more powerful entities.

Bibliography

Kirchheimer, Otto. "The Act, the Offense, and Double Jeopardy." *The Yale Law Review* 58 (March, 1949): 513-544. A scholarly analysis of one specific aspect of double jeopardy, the difference between a single criminal act and the many categories of law one such act may violate. Discusses the potential dangers of this dichotomy and the differences between legal substance and legal procedures. Notes.

Parker, Frank J. "Some Aspects of Double Jeopardy." *St. John's Law Review* 25 (May, 1951): 188-202. A discussion by a state's attorney of some of the issues in double jeopardy cases. Uses specific cases to illustrate the problems of dual sovereignty when a state as well as a federal law has been violated; the issue of closely related offenses which may be tried separately; and the problem of retrials when the first is terminated. Notes.

Schulhofer, Stephen J. "Jeopardy and Mistrials." *University of Pennsylvania Law Review* 125 (January, 1977): 452-539. Detailed discussion of the issues involved when mistrials occur. A brief summary of the double jeopardy concept is followed by an analysis of a landmark decision, the *Perez* case in 1824, as well as other specific cases of mistrials. Classification of the kinds of mistrials that may occur. Notes.

Sigler, Jay A. *Double Jeopardy: The Development of a Legal and Social Policy.* Ithaca, N.Y.: Cornell University Press, 1969. Traces the history and development of double jeopardy as a legal and social policy, both federal and state, in the United States. Includes comparisons of the policy with practice in other nations and a discussion of the possibilities for doctrinal reform. An often-cited study, particularly useful for its extensive bibliography of both primary and secondary sources. Index.

Slovenko, Ralph. "The Law on Double Jeopardy." *Tulane Law Review* 30 (April, 1956): 407-430. A discussion of the law on double jeopardy with specific reference to one state. Although it refers to aspects of the criminal code of Louisiana, it provides a brief overview of basic concepts, such as the tests for determining double jeopardy, and is useful as a supplementary reference for the general reader.

Westen, Peter, and Richard Drubel. "Toward a General Theory of Double Jeopardy." *The Supreme Court Review* (1978): 81-169. An often-cited article in the discussion of double jeopardy. Argues that the shifts and inconsistencies in double jeopardy applications are a result of flaws in the fundamental theory. Addresses three distinct issues: finality, double punishment, and acquittal against evidence. Specific court cases are analyzed as illustrations.

Shakuntala Jayaswal

Cross-References

Supreme Court Disallows a Maximum Hours Law for Bakers (1905), p. 36; The European Convention on Human Rights Is Signed (1950), p. 843; Government Policies Seek to End the Special Status of Native Americans (1953), p. 897; *Gideon v. Wainwright* Establishes Defendants' Right to an Attorney (1963), p. 1182; *Miranda v. Arizona* Requires Police to Tell Arrested People Their Rights (1966) p. 1343; Marshall Becomes the First Black Supreme Court Justice (1967), p. 1381; The Supreme Court Abolishes the Death Penalty (1972), p. 1674.

RIOTS AGAINST POLICE HARASSMENT LAUNCH THE GAY RIGHTS MOVEMENT

Category of event: Gay persons' rights
Time: June 27-July 2, 1969
Locale: Greenwich Village, New York City

Homosexuals patronizing the Stonewall Inn in New York City spontaneously rebelled against a police raid; the incident inspired gay pride and sparked the gay rights movement

Principal personages:
SEYMOUR PINE, a deputy inspector of the New York City Police Department
DAVE VAN RONK, a well-known folk singer and participant in the Stonewall riots
HOWARD SMITH, a reporter for *The Village Voice* who was alongside the police during the riots
DICK LEITSCH, the executive director of the Mattachine Society of New York
ALLEN GINSBERG (1926-   ), a poet known for homosexual verse; a leading homosexual figure
LUCIAN TRUSCOTT IV, the reporter who covered the Stonewall riots for *The Village Voice*

Summary of Event

In New York City in 1969, the rights of homosexually oriented individuals to congregate and to express their homosexuality in public were at best tentative. The reigning social morality disapproved of homosexuality, and the law and law enforcement agencies tolerated the existence of homosexuals but used various means to limit their visibility and freedom.

Every major city of the United States had a small population of male homosexuals and lesbians, and a number of bars and private clubs where they gathered. Police would occasionally stage impromptu raids in search of illicit behavior, and violators would be arrested. The frequency of such raids varied according to the visibility of the homosexual community, the current level of societal disapproval, and the proximity of specific events. As local elections approached, incumbents often increased enforcement of antihomosexual statutes to appear tough on crime and immorality; in 1964 and 1965, Operation New Broom, initiated to improve New York's image for the 1966 World's Fair, included closings of gay bars.

Such practices resulted in a tenuous relationship between the homosexual community and the police. In San Francisco in 1960-1961, a tactical battle occurred when gay bar owners revealed they had been bribing police to prevent raids; the police retaliated with mass roundups of homosexual patrons and bar closures. The bar owners ultimately formed a Tavern Guild as a united front against harassment. A 1967 campaign against gay bars in Los Angeles led to a rally on Sunset Boulevard calling for organized resistance.

In general, however, the struggle for gay rights through the 1950's and 1960's was intermittent. The Mattachine Society, America's first gay rights organization, was founded by Harry Hay in Los Angeles in 1951 and over the years developed affiliate groups in other cities. The Daughters of Bilitis, a lesbian group established in San Francisco in 1955, did the same, but neither organization ever claimed more than a few hundred members. ECHO, the East Coast Homophile Organizations, was founded in 1965 and sponsored public demonstrations at government buildings in Washington, D.C., and Philadelphia, but never established momentum.

Thus, in New York City in June, 1969, it was not unusual that several gay bars—the Snake Pit, the Sewer, Checkerboard, and Tele-Star—were raided and closed for a period of three weeks. The Sixth Precinct had come under a new commanding officer who initiated the crackdown. One bar that had been ignored was the Stonewall Inn, a club at 53 Christopher Street, just off of Sheridan Square in the heart of Lower Manhattan's Greenwich Village. The Stonewall Inn was frequented by young, mostly African-American and Hispanic homosexuals, many of whom were drag queens or runaways. Its youthful, flamboyant, and ragged clientele was not particularly welcome even in other gay bars. There were also scantily clad young dancers—"go-go boys"—for entertainment. The Stonewall Inn was rumored to have ties with organized crime, and the establishment did not have a liquor license.

It was on suspicion that alcoholic beverages were being dispensed illegally that two plainclothes detectives from the Sixth Precinct entered the Stonewall Inn just before midnight on Friday, June 27, 1969. They presented management with a search warrant, confiscated cases of liquor, announced the closure of the bar, called for police reinforcements, and began expelling the club's two hundred or so customers. Deputy Inspector Seymour Pine, head of the public morals section, supervised the evacuation of the club with his force of eight officers. Police paddy wagons arrived to haul away the bartender, the doorman, and assorted others, including "queens" in full drag. As patrons were herded into the streets, they began to chant. The crowd taunted and jeered at the police, attracting attention and swelling in numbers as friends and passersby, also young, nonwhite homosexuals, joined in. Police headquarters ordered partial riot mobilization.

The last customer to be guided out, a lesbian, put up a struggle. As the police subdued her, the crowd grew unruly and then virtually exploded into rebellion. A rain of coins was released on the police. Beer bottles were thrown. Cobblestones were pulled out of the street and thrown in all directions. The eight police officers, grossly outnumbered, sought refuge in the empty bar; reporter Howard Smith, of *The Village Voice*, was with them. At one point, Pine grabbed a man whom he had seen throwing a beer bottle. He turned out to be Dave Van Ronk, a popular folk singer who had wandered over from another bar. The police locked the front doors, but protesters uprooted a parking meter and used it to batter them down. The police used a fire hose from inside the bar to deter the crowd. With the door battered down, they pulled their guns and threatened to shoot any rioter who entered the building. It was then that helmeted Tactical Patrol Force units arrived and began dispersing the crowd. Many of the rioters disappeared into buildings and alleys but continued the protest. They got inside the Stonewall Inn, and soon the building erupted in flames.

Eventually, the police gained control over the neighborhood and got the fires extinguished. Thirteen men were arrested on charges of harassment, disorderly conduct, and resisting arrest, including Van Ronk, who was accused of assault and paroled on his own recognizance. Four police officers were injured in the melee; the most serious injury was a broken wrist. The riot itself began shortly after 3:00 A.M. and lasted about forty-five minutes.

The following evening, Saturday, June 28, throngs of young men congregated at the site of the burned-out bar to read a condemnation of police behavior. Graffiti on the boarded-up windows read "Support Gay Power" and "Legalize Gay Bars." Groups gathered on street corners and spoke and chanted loudly. As the night progressed, tensions mounted. By midnight, several hundred were gathered, and the protest resumed. Protesters threw bottles and set small fires. A sack of wet garbage was heaved into one patrol car; on Waverly Place, a concrete block landed on another, and protesters descended on the vehicle.

Police from the Charles Street Station House were unable to control the riot, and Tactical Patrol Force units again poured into the area, shortly after 2:00 A.M. They broke through a line of protesters and, linking arms in a line of their own, swept up and down Christopher Street between Sixth and Seventh Avenues to control and disperse the gathering. The police line broke, and helmeted officers charged the crowd. Estimates of the number involved in the disturbance were as high as four hundred police and two thousand rioters. Eventually, the crowd dispersed. The police withdrew at approximately 4:00 A.M. Three men were arrested on charges of harassment and disorderly conduct.

Tensions remained high on Christopher Street through the week. Milling on street corners, taunting by both gays and police, and sporadic violence, looting, and trash fires persisted. By Wednesday night, much of the activity involved outsiders, people not directly involved in the gay or Greenwich Village communities. The initial eruption at the Stonewall Inn had died down, but a movement was born. For the first time in their history, homosexuals had rebelled in numbers and with force against the systematic oppression that society imposed on them.

Impact of Event

Those few nights outside the Stonewall Inn set in motion the movement for gay liberation that would continue for decades. The impulse for homosexuals to fight for equal rights in American society had been strong but latent; the Stonewall rebellion was a catalyst that created an immediate and extensive response.

On Sunday, June 29, New York's Mattachine Society, led by Dick Leitsch, began disseminating leaflets calling for organized resistance to police and societal harassment of the homosexual community. Many contacted the society, as the leading gay rights organization at the time. By Tuesday, July 1, a Gay Liberation Front was organized and meeting in spaces provided by New York's Alternative University. Allen Ginsberg, a noted poet, arrived and participated in meetings, providing practical and spiritual leadership. Ginsberg's "Howl," with explicit references to homosexuality, had gained him fame in the larger homosexual community.

The rioting received cursory coverage in the interior pages of *The New York Times* on Sunday and Monday, June 29 and 30. The coverage there and in *The Village Voice* fueled awareness and commitment among the gay community and all of New York. The following Sunday, an East Village bar called the Electric Circus invited gays and straights to mingle in a setting free from "raids, Mafia control, and checks at the front door."

The gay rights movement developed with rapid speed. Gay Liberation Fronts were established and organized in New York and San Francisco, and branches were soon founded in major cities and universities not only in the United States but in Canada, Europe, and Australia as well. The groups engaged in a variety of activities: letter writing, picketing, distributing propaganda, and seeking media exposure. Gay dances were held openly in New York, Chicago, and Berkeley. Gay newspapers appeared everywhere: the *Advocate* in Los Angeles, the *Fag Rag* in Boston, the *Gay Liberator* in Detroit, and *Body Politic* in Toronto, to name a few.

Acts of discrimination met with organized response. In San Francisco, activists picketed a steamship company that had fired an openly gay man. In Queens, New York, they demonstrated in a park in which trees had been cut down to prevent homosexual liaisons. The Gay Liberation Front put pressure on Delta and Western airlines regarding employment of gays, and on *The Village Voice*, the *San Francisco Examiner, Harper's*, and *The Dick Cavett Show* for better coverage of homosexuals. By November, 1969, the movement had grown so large that a splinter group, the Gay Activist Alliance, was founded to pursue an even more radical agenda. The new group forced the mayor of New York to address gay issues in front of television and opera audiences.

Within the gay community, a new era had begun. Along with activism was self-awareness, manifested in consciousness-raising groups to nurture pride, openness, and mutual support. In 1970, Carl Wittman published his "Gay Manifesto," a treatise to define and integrate the themes and forces of the new movement. On June 28, 1970, the first anniversary of the riots, an estimated five to ten thousand people marched in the Christopher Street Parade to commemorate Gay Liberation Day. Hundreds attended similar parades in Chicago and Hollywood. On the second anniversary, public celebrations were added in Boston, New Orleans, San Francisco, San Jose, and elsewhere.

Over the next few years, the spiritual and political transformation within the homosexual community was reflected in society at large. Huey Newton, leader of the radical Black Panthers, declared support for the gay movement. Gay Liberation Front groups attended conventions in San Francisco, Chicago, and Los Angeles on psychiatry and behavior modification. The National Association of Mental Health called in 1970 for decriminalization of homosexual conduct between consenting adults, and laws to that end were passed in Colorado, Connecticut, and Oregon in 1971. In 1972, the National Association of Social Workers rejected the medical model of homosexuality as a disease. Between 1970 and 1975, gay and lesbian caucuses were formed among librarians, linguists, psychologists, psychiatrists, historians, sociologists, and public health workers. In 1973, after three years of intense lobbying, the American Psychiatric Association deleted homosexuality from its official diagnostic manual of mental disorders. With this development, the scientific and academic basis for much of the institutionalized oppression and discrimination had been erased.

To be sure, American society did not wholeheartedly embrace homosexuality or even acknowledge the equal rights of those whose sexual preference deviated from the majority. The riots at the Stonewall Inn in June of 1969, however, permanently changed the way that homosexuals cope with and confront societal attitudes and, by extension, the way that society understands and accepts homosexuality.

Bibliography

Adam, Barry D. *The Rise of a Gay and Lesbian Movement.* Boston: Twayne, 1987. Adam traces the history of homosexual community and politics from medieval times through the 1980's, including both "civilized" and "primitive" societies. Concise, well developed, and exhaustively referenced.

Bullough, Vern L. *Homosexuality: A History, from Ancient Greece to Gay Liberation.* New York: New American Library, 1979. Bullough examines the history of homosexuality not chronologically but through relevant topics such as religion, law, education, politics, literature, and transvestism. Ambitious in scope. The material is developed clearly if broadly.

D'Emilio, John. *Sexual Battles, Sexual Communities: The Making of a Homosexual Minority in the United States, 1940-1970.* Chicago: University of Chicago Press, 1983. D'Emilio focuses on the emergence of homosexual personal identity and culture. The prose is slow-moving, and the approach is deep in sociological theory. The book has a small index and no bibliography.

Miller, Neil. *In Search of Gay America: Women and Men in a Time of Change.* New York: Atlantic Monthly Press, 1989. Miller set out to find, "twenty years after the Stonewall riots, if gay pride and progress had finally begun to trickle down to the grass roots." He traveled through small towns across America meeting, interviewing, and observing gays, activists, and others. The resulting volume is an intimate, reflective, and fascinating travelogue.

Teal, Donn. *The Gay Militants.* New York: Stein & Day, 1971. This is the most comprehensive treatment available on the Stonewall riots and the emergence of the gay liberation movement in the year that followed. Teal provides names, dates, and events with an appreciation of press reaction and contribution to the movement. Teal's is an insider's view. The prose is rich, fast moving, even frenetic at times. The book lacks an index.

Warren, Carol A. B. *Identity and Community in the Gay World.* New York: John Wiley & Sons, 1974. This is a cultural profile of the gay community in the early 1970's. A true ethnographer, Warren examines gay languages, milieux, rituals, customs, and social patterns. Thorough but intentionally timebound, this small volume avoids historical and political perspectives.

Weiss, Andrea, and Greta Schiller. *Before Stonewall: The Making of a Gay and Lesbian Community.* Tallahassee, Fla.: Naiad Press, 1988. This is a companion volume to the authors' acclaimed documentary film of the same name about gay life before 1969. Its eighty-six pages include a discussion guide, reading list, and list of organizations in addition to ample photos, posters, news clippings, cartoons, and quotes drawn from the film.

Barry Mann

Cross-References

The American Civil Liberties Union Is Founded (1920), p. 327; The Wolfenden Report Recommends Decriminalizing Homosexual Acts (1957), p. 991; The Civil Rights Act of 1957 Creates the Commission on Civil Rights (1957), p. 997; Congress Passes the Civil Rights Act (1964), p. 1251; The Black Panther Party Is Organized (1966), p. 1348; A NIMH Task Force Recommends Legalizing Homosexual Behavior (1969), p. 1497; Homosexuality Is Removed from the APA List of Psychiatric Disorders (1973), p. 1741; The Civil Service Decides That Gays Are Fit for Public Service (1975), p. 1801; Race Riot Breaks Out in Miami, Protesting Police Brutality (1980), p. 2101; Government Mandates Collection of Data on Crimes Against Homosexuals (1988), p. 2364.

BRITISH TROOPS RESTORE ORDER IN NORTHERN IRELAND

Category of event: Civil rights
Time: August, 1969
Locale: Londonderry and Belfast, Northern Ireland

In response to increasing violence between segments of the Catholic and Protestant communities, the British government sent military units to Northern Ireland to restore and maintain order

Principal personages:

JAMES CHICHESTER-CLARK (1923-   ), the prime minister of Northern Ireland who requested British troops in August, 1969

HAROLD WILSON (1916-   ), the prime minister of Great Britain who authorized sending British troops

JAMES CALLAGHAN (1912-   ), the British home secretary directly responsible for Northern Irish relations

JACK LYNCH (1917-   ), the prime minister of the Republic of Ireland who advocated Irish unification

IAN PAISLEY (1926-   ), a Protestant minister who strongly supported the union between Northern Ireland and Great Britain and was opposed to Catholic influence

TERENCE O'NEILL (1914-1990), the prime minister of Northern Ireland whose moderate reforms alienated many on both extremes; resigned in 1969

Summary of Event

The often tragic relations between Britain and Ireland go back hundreds of years, but the late 1960's saw an intensification of the troubles in Northern Ireland. In 1921, six of the nine counties of the old Irish province of Ulster were given home rule by Great Britain. Shortly after, the other twenty-six counties achieved dominion status as the Irish Free State, which severed all ties with the British Commonwealth and became the independent Republic of Ireland in 1948. Northern Ireland, however, remained an integral part of the United Kingdom, with its own parliament having responsibility for domestic issues.

The population of the six counties of Northern Ireland was divided by culture, history, and religion. The Protestant majority was unionist in politics, committed to maintaining the union with Great Britain. One-third of the population was Catholic. Many in this minority community wished to unite the six counties with the largely Catholic Republic of Ireland. This was anathema to most members of the majority community, whose Protestant ancestors had come from England and Scotland in the seventeenth century.

What the two Northern Ireland communities had in common was fear—fear that the other wished to deprive it of religious freedom, national and cultural identity, and economic rewards. Because the majority Protestant community had been in power since home rule had been granted in 1921, it was the Catholic community that had faced economic, political, and social discrimination. The administrative bureaucracy was overwhelmingly Protestant, as was most industrial employment. Local government was gerrymandered so that even where Protestants were in the minority, as in the city of Londonderry, they still controlled. Public housing was often allotted to Protestants rather than to more needy Catholic families. The police and security forces were overwhelmingly Protestant and had a reputation for anti-Catholic activities. In the past, there had been violence in the six counties, but by the early 1960's those troubles apparently were over.

Northern Ireland's industrial base declined in the 1960's. Increased trade between the Republic and Northern Ireland was seen as a possible solution, but it would be workable only if tensions between Catholics and Protestants were reduced. These economic difficulties led some to hope that class-based politics might unite Protestants and Catholics by class and break down the traditional barriers which had long divided the communities. Harold Wilson became prime minister of Great Britain in 1964. Many members of his Labour Party were sympathetic to the plight of the Catholic minority, and Wilson himself discussed the necessity to end discrimination against Catholics. Within the Catholic community, there was an increasing demand for equal economic and political rights, a demand symbolized by the formation of the Campaign for Social Justice in 1964.

In 1963, Terence O'Neill became prime minister of Northern Ireland. He attempted to build bridges to the Catholic minority in Northern Ireland and to the government of the Republic. In reality, "O'Neillism" involved mostly symbols rather than substantive change: He continued to envision the Protestant unionist majority retaining their position, although with less obvious discrimination than in the past. Over time, he lost support. Many Protestant unionists feared he had gone too far in reconciling Catholics and nationalists, but the latter claimed he had not gone far enough. Under O'Neill's tenure, discrimination against the minority community was not ended, but the issue had come to the fore. In 1967, inspired by the American Civil Rights movement, the Northern Ireland Civil Rights Association was founded to end discrimination against Catholics. A countermovement developed among elements in the Protestant community, notably under the leadership of Ian Paisley, an evangelical fundamentalist minister who was adamantly opposed to Catholicism and even to politicians such as O'Neill and other Protestants who were, he believed, overly sympathetic to Catholic aspirations.

The Catholic minority's demand for equal rights was complicated by another issue: the choice between continued union with Great Britain or unification with the Irish Republic. Many Protestants claimed that the demand for civil rights by the Catholic community was only a preliminary step: The real objective of the civil rights movement was to join the six counties to the Republic. Many leaders of the civil rights movement were indeed nationalists, but for most, the issue of civil rights was a sincere concern.

Eventually, civil rights advocates organized protest marches. The first was on August 28, 1968. The demonstration against housing discrimination was peaceful but resulted in countermarches and demonstrations by radical Protestant groups. The Royal Ulster Constabulary, the Northern Irish police force which was overwhelmingly Protestant, was more sympathetic to the counterdemonstrators than to the civil rights marchers. In Londonderry, on October 5, 1968, a civil rights march banned by O'Neill's government ended in violence when the police resorted to indiscriminate force against the demonstrators. Seventy-eight civilians and eighteen police officers were injured. A radical student organization, People's Democracy, soon formed at Queen's University, Belfast. The members of People's Democracy, like those of student groups elsewhere in the 1960's, were often more willing to seek confrontation with the police than were the moderate reformers who began the movement. In late November, O'Neill promised both more equitable treatment in housing and local government representation.

Some civil rights advocates were willing to give the government time to implement its pledges, but the People's Democracy movement was not. In January, 1969, a protest march from Belfast to Londonderry encountered considerable violence, some at the hands of Protestant extremists and some from the police. Catholics living in the Bogside neighborhood of Londonderry were also attacked. In reaction, many in the Catholic community turned to the radicals for leadership. Many members of the Protestant community also became radicalized, but on the other side, criticizing O'Neill's leadership for its seeming pro-Catholic orientation. Reverend Ian Paisley was jailed for leading an unlawful assembly. An outlawed Protestant group caused a series of explosions in March and April at several public utility facilities. This violence contributed to O'Neill's decision to resign in late April, 1969. The new prime minister, James Chichester-Clark, O'Neill's cousin, promised to continue O'Neill's reforms, including proportional representation and the end to gerrymandering in local elections, but it was too little, too late.

The summer of 1969 saw more violence in Northern Ireland. Some occurred on July 12, the anniversary of the victory of the Protestant William of Orange over James II, deposed Catholic monarch of England, in 1690, in the Battle of the Boyne. The major conflict occurred in Londonderry on August 12. On that date in 1689, thirteen young Protestant apprentices had successfully shut the city's gates against James II. When the Protestant marchers approached Catholic Bogside, stones were thrown and bottles filled with gasoline were tossed. The police intervened, but the battle went on for many hours, ultimately leaving Bogside under Catholic control as the police were unable to end the violence. On August 13, Jack Lynch, prime minister of the Irish Republic, spoke on television and perhaps added to the tension, claiming that the people of the Republic would not stand for further violence in the six counties of Northern Ireland. He argued that the only lasting solution would be for Northern Ireland to join the Republic.

Violence spread throughout much of Northern Ireland. After it became obvious that the Royal Ulster Constabulary and other police units could not restore order, Chichester-Clark's government called for British troops. Prime Minister Harold Wilson and his home secretary, James Callaghan, had been urging reforms on the Northern Ireland government and immediately authorized the use of troops on August 14. Radical elements in the Protestant community, particularly the outlawed Ulster Volunteer Force, took action against Catholics in Belfast. On the night of August 14, about ten civilians were killed, approximately 150 were injured, and hundreds of Catholic residences were burned. More troops were sent. By early September, there were six thousand British soldiers in Northern Ireland. As a result of the escalating violence, some of it at the hands of unionist forces, the use of the British army seemed necessary to return peace to the six counties.

Impact of Event

Initially, the Catholic community in Northern Ireland was relieved at the intervention of British troops. From the minority's viewpoint, the British army was the protector that could stand between them and the radical Protestant unionists. In a short time, however, the position of the British army became controversial. Even the Protestant unionist majority in the six counties became alienated by the intervention of the government of the United Kingdom.

The presence of the British army gave renewed impetus to the Irish Republican Army, which had originated during the struggle against British rule during and after World War I. The IRA's activities had led the government of the Irish Republic to ban the organization, and in Northern Ireland the IRA had been defeated during the late 1950's. Events in the late 1960's gave the IRA renewed life. They also caused a split in that organization. The official IRA remained committed to a socialist vision of a united Ireland, believing that it might be attained through peaceful political means. The provisional IRA argued that Irish unity was more important than any particular economic system and was willing to resort to force to achieve its aims. British forces in Ireland reawakened the IRA: The old enemy was back again.

Acts of violence multiplied in 1970 and 1971. The inability of the British army and the Northern Ireland government to control the violence led to an escalation by elements in both communities. Even though Wilson's British government had taken over the security system in Northern Ireland, there were 213 shootings in 1970 and 1,756 in 1971. A Ministry of Community Relations was established, property qualifications for local government voting were abolished, and proportional representation was instituted. Public housing allocations were taken out of the hands of local government. In 1971, Chichester-Clark was replaced as Northern Ireland's prime minister by Brian Faulkner, a Protestant unionist who included a Catholic in his cabinet, the first in Northern Ireland's history. Education was still largely segregated, but this resulted as much from desires of the Catholic community as from Protestants' wishes. By 1971, much of the segregation previously practiced in the six provinces had ended, but there was no peace. Faulkner banned demonstrations and urged the internment of suspected terrorists.

In an anti-internment march in Londonderry on January 30, 1972, thirteen civilians were killed by British soldiers. Finally, in March, 1972, the Conservative British government of Edward Heath took direct control in Northern Ireland, thus ending the home rule which had been established in 1921. The violence continued. In 1972 alone, there were 474 deaths. The British government attempted to work out a power-sharing arrangement between the two communities in Northern Ireland and to recognize that there was an all-Irish dimension to the continuing problems of the six counties. A strike by Protestant workers in 1974 ended hopes for a permanent peaceful settlement.

Sending troops to Northern Ireland in 1969 to restore order, however necessary in the short run, was in retrospect no solution to the troubles. The British were seemingly trapped, alienated from the Catholic and nationalist minority as well as from many in the majority community who resented their loss of power as the result of the British takeover. If some overt discrimination had ceased because of the greater British involvement, it did not solve the questions of how or by whom the six counties should be governed. Many believed that the presence of British troops contributed to the troubles in the six counties, while others argued that if the British troops were withdrawn, a civil war between the opposing communities in Northern Ireland would be inevitable. The search for compromise, for a middle way in the historical conundrum—between Catholic and Protestant and between nationalist and unionist—continued, but no solution seemed possible.

Bibliography

Bruce, Steve. *God Save Ulster: The Religion and Politics of Paisleyism.* Oxford, England: Oxford University Press, 1986. This study of Ian Paisley attributes Paisley's success and influence to his apt expression of the deepest beliefs and fears of the Protestant unionist majority. Includes a bibliography and index.

Buckland, Patrick. *A History of Northern Ireland.* Dublin: Gill and Macmillan, 1981. The author is one of the leading historians of Northern Ireland. This brief work is an excellent introduction to the history of the six provinces. Includes a bibliography and an index.

Callaghan, James. *A House Divided.* London: Collins, 1973. The author was British home secretary at the time troops were sent to Northern Ireland. His personal account, as one who had the responsibility of assuming control, is enlightening. Appendices and index, no bibliography.

Hull, Roger H. *The Irish Triangle: Conflict in Northern Ireland.* Princeton, N.J.: Princeton University Press, 1976. The author discusses a number of topics, including that of human rights, from the perspectives of Belfast, Dublin, and London and from the Protestant Unionist, Catholic Nationalist, and British government's points of view. Includes a bibliography and an index.

White, Barry. *John Hume: Statesman of the Troubles.* Belfast, Northern Ireland: Blackstaff Press, 1984. This is a sympathetic biography of the most important of the Irish civil rights leaders of the 1960's and after. A moderate, Hume was opposed to the IRA. Bibliography and index are included.

Wilson, Harold. *A Personal Record: The Labour Government, 1964-1970.* Boston: Little, Brown, 1971. Wilson was the British prime minister who sent troops into Northern Ireland in August, 1969. In this memoir, he claims that the British government was correct in making that decision but admits that it was a gamble. From his perspective, the gamble succeeded. Includes photographs, cartoons, and an index but no bibliography.

Eugene S. Larson

Cross-References

The Easter Rebellion Fails to Win Irish Independence (1916), p. 178; Ireland Is Granted Home Rule and Northern Ireland Is Created (1920), p. 309; The Statute of Westminster Creates the Commonwealth (1931), p. 453; India Signs the Delhi Pact (1931), p. 459; India Gains Independence (1947), p. 731; The Emergency Provisions (Northern Ireland) Act Is Passed (1973), p. 1720; Two Founders of Peace People Win the Nobel Peace Prize (1977), p. 1932.

AN AFRICAN CONVENTION EXPANDS
THE DEFINITION OF REFUGEES

Category of event: Refugee relief
Time: September 10, 1969
Locale: Addis Ababa, Ethiopia

African governments broadened the international refugee definition to include groups of people fleeing from generalized violence in all or part of their country of origin

> *Principal personages:*
> AHMADOU AHIDJO (1924-   ), the president of Cameroon and president of the OAU Assembly of Heads of State and Government
> JULIUS NYERERE (1922-   ), the president of Tanzania, a prominent advocate of refugee rights
> HAILE SELASSIE (1892-1975), the emperor of Ethiopia, an influential figure in OAU negotiations

Summary of Event

The adoption of the 1969 Organization of African Unity (OAU) Convention Governing the Specific Aspects of the Problem of Refugees in Africa was an important human rights event because it substantially broadened the legal refugee definition as it applied to millions of Africans. The narrower definition found in the 1951 U.N. Convention Relating to the Status of Refugees required individual refugees to demonstrate a well-founded fear of specific kinds of persecution. The African definition anticipated that groups of people, as well as discrete individuals, might have genuine fears of persecution. It extended refugee status to those who fled more general contexts of domestic disruption and civil war. To appreciate the importance of this event, we must understand the historical context from which it emerged.

Long before the countries of Europe set foot in sub-Saharan Africa to carve its vast territory into exclusive colonial domains, Africans had known the yoke of indigenous tyranny and the relief of flight. The arrival of the Europeans did not change historical migration patterns: Africans continued to move across the artificial colonial boundaries following traditional nomadic patterns, searching for seasonal employment, or fleeing from oppressive circumstances, regardless of who exercised overlordship.

Thus, when one African nation after another was born in rapid succession in the 1960's, it was no surprise that these new states almost immediately faced refugee problems. The boundaries bequeathed by the departing Europeans to the fledgling states of Africa often bore little resemblance to demographic realities: In some cases warring tribes were called upon to fashion national unity from hundreds of competing and often incompatible ethnic communities, while in other cases peoples were split in two, their loyalties divided between new, artificial, and often arbitrary sovereign entities. Tensions resulting from these challenges to the new African states often boiled over into conflict, as they did in Rwanda and Burundi in the late 1950's and early 1960's. In other parts of Africa, such as Algeria and Southern Africa, struggles by indigenous peoples to secure their independence from colonial or white minority regimes also led to the displacement of people. Neither in the struggle to gain independence nor afterward did Africa avoid the copious flow of refugees.

Thus, when the Organization of African Unity was founded in 1963, it was seized almost immediately with the question of how to protect and assist refugees. In response to the Rwanda and Burundi crises, the OAU Council of Ministers established a refugee commission to study the matter and suggest ways in which the refugee problem could be solved. In 1966, the committee of legal experts of this commission met at Addis Ababa, Ethiopia, headquarters to the OAU secretariat, to draft a refugee convention. From these discussions emerged the principles upon which the 1969 OAU convention on refugees would be based.

In the meantime, refugee problems were proliferating and intensifying across the continent. Three revolutions against Portuguese authority produced substantial refugee flows: Mozambicans fled into Tanzania, Angolans crossed over into Zambia, and Senegal received thousands from Guinea-Bissau. By 1966, nearly 100,000 Sudanese had fled into Uganda to escape civil war, while only a year later, Eritreans also began to flee into the Sudan from Ethiopia's civil war.

It was with a sense of some urgency, then, that the OAU convened in 1967 a conference on the legal, economic, and social aspects of African refugee problems. This important conference—under the able influence of the Tanzanian government, whose President, Julius Nyerere, was a stalwart champion of refugee interests—further strengthened momentum toward adoption by the OAU of a refugee convention. Tanzania presented the findings of the Conference to the OAU Council of Ministers meeting in 1968. The conference recommendation that the OAU should broaden the refugee definition beyond that contained in the 1951 U.N. Convention was approved by the ministers and was incorporated into the African convention on refugees. At Addis Ababa, the OAU Assembly of Heads of State and Government, with Ahmadou Ahidjo of Cameroon presiding, adopted the OAU refugee convention on September 10, 1969. Five years of deliberations had finally borne fruit, but it took another five years before the convention finally entered into force, on June 20, 1974.

The OAU refugee convention reemphasized several basic principles contained in the 1951 U.N. convention on refugees. It called upon member states to grant asylum to refugees and to permit their temporary settlement. The granting of asylum to refugees was characterized as a strictly humanitarian act, not a hostile or unfriendly one toward the country of origin. Governments were called upon to refrain from rejecting refugees at the border, and from expelling or involuntarily returning them to their country of origin, while at the same time acting aggressively to assist those refugees who requested repatriation. Where neither repatriation nor settlement in the country of first asylum was feasible, the OAU convention called upon member states to facilitate refugees' resettlement to a third country. Governments were required to refrain from discriminating against refugees and to issue travel documents so that refugees might be able to travel outside the territory of the country of asylum. All the foregoing principles were wholly consistent with obligations many African states already adhered to under the 1951 U.N. convention or 1967 protocol.

The most significant difference between the OAU and the U.N. conventions centers on the definition of the term "refugee." The OAU convention incorporates virtually verbatim the 1951 U.N. convention language identifying refugees as persons who have a well-founded fear of persecution, but the OAU convention carries the definition a very important step further. Paragraph 2 of Article I states that the term would also apply to people who, because of external aggression, occupation, foreign domination, or events seriously disturbing public order in either part or all of their country of origin or nationality, are compelled to leave in order to seek refuge in another place outside their country of origin or nationality.

This definition is significantly broader than the U.N. definition, which, narrowly construed, requires the individual to document a specific well-founded fear of becoming the target of governmentally sponsored religious, ethnic, racial, or political persecution. The OAU convention confers refugee status not only to such individuals but also to whole groups of people fleeing from colonial wars, foreign intervention, and civil disturbances in all or part of their home state. The vast majority of African refugees fall into this broader category. The OAU convention extends guarantees of protection and assistance to them.

This new and more generous standard established a legal basis by which African governments could guarantee the safety and welfare of dispossessed and distraught populations fleeing from a widening circle of conflicts in Africa. The United Nations High Commissioner for Refugees (UNHCR), acting under U.N. General Assembly auspices and with the support of the international donor community, readily accepted the broader OAU definition as being applicable to refugee situations in Africa. The UNHCR has been able to extend its protective functions and humanitarian endeavors to any and all persons African governments have granted asylum under the generous OAU standards. Whether one was a displaced Tigrean seeking to avoid a cross fire between Eritrean rebels and the Marxist Ethiopian government, or an Idi Amin supporter targeted for execution by the troops of Milton Obote in Uganda, or a member of the formerly banned African National Congress in South Africa, or a Mozambican fleeing from famine caused by rebel acts of sabotage against agricultural communities, one was, in Africa, a refugee deserving of protection and assistance not only from the host government but also from the UNHCR and the international community at large. Starving and destitute masses seeking safety and relief from civil wars and disruption together with politically persecuted individuals alike were embraced by the new OAU standard.

Impact of Event

At the time of the adoption and entry into force of the OAU convention, fewer than one million refugees resided in various African countries. Within a decade, that number tripled, and within two decades the total number of African refugees exceeded five million. The expanded OAU refugee definition fortunately encompassed the throngs of destitute, often sickly and starving, persons who sought refuge from the violence and turmoil of their home states. Instabilities in the Horn of Africa intensified throughout the 1970's and 1980's, sending millions of persons into exile, as Ethiopians, Somalis, and Sudanese fled persecution and civil war. Similar conflicts displaced nearly one million people from Mozambique and several hundred thousand from Uganda and Angola. A three-way battle for sovereignty in Liberia saw hundreds of thousands seek shelter in neighboring states during 1990. Countless smaller refugee movements have bedeviled as many as half of the OAU's member states.

The existence of a flexible legal instrument to deal with these massive and often overpowering migrations of desperately needy people has been a genuinely indispensable humanitarian tool. By reinforcing and expanding the U.N. definition, African governments have committed themselves to helping refugees survive and reestablish their lives. The fact that many of the hardest-hit African governments continued to abide by their legal obligations under the OAU convention, despite the fact that many are among the poorest countries in the world, is remarkable. The development needs of their own populations are often substantially hindered by these generous policies of asylum. It is an irony that the standards of assistance to African refugees fall well below those provided to refugees in other parts of the world, such as Central America and Southeast Asia, precisely because the host country nationals in Africa are themselves so poverty stricken. To give African refugees assistance equivalent to their counterparts in other regions would make them much better off than the surrounding host population, thus risking local resentments and possibly leading to less generous attitudes toward asylum.

Two international conferences held in the 1980's on the refugee problem in Africa sought to draw attention to the developmental implications of refugee flows on host countries. Wealthy donor countries have not responded as generously to the African countries' needs as the Africans have to the outcasts they received from their neighbors. That African countries continued to grant refuge to so many of their neighbors despite their own exigency is a tribute to the African spirit of brotherhood, a spirit that enabled African leaders to consider so broad a refugee definition as that contained in the OAU convention.

The OAU convention has not only benefited countless refugees in Africa proper but has also influenced legal developments in other parts of the Third World as well. The Cartagena Declaration, which more liberally defines refugees in the Latin American context, owes a substantial intellectual debt to the OAU convention. Little did African heads of state realize that they would contribute so greatly to the advance of humanitarian policy and refugee protection when they approved the OAU convention in 1969.

Bibliography

Brooks, H. C., and Yassin el-Ayouty, eds. *Refugees South of the Sahara.* Westport,

Conn.: Negro Universities Press, 1970. This dated collection of essays by several distinguished students of Africa, including academics and policymakers, provides an insight into the refugee situation as it stood when the African refugee convention was adopted. Some chapters contain footnotes. Several valuable documentary and statistical appendices and an index are included. No bibliography.

Gorman, Robert F. *Coping with Africa's Refugee Burden: A Time for Solutions.* Dordrecht, The Netherlands: Martinus Nijhoff with the United Nations Institute for Training and Research, 1987. This history of the Second International Conference on Assistance to Refugees in Africa (ICARA II) documents how governments, international agencies, and private organizations have responded in meeting not only Africa's refugee assistance needs but also the needs of host countries and populations whose economic and social welfare has been adversely affected by the presence of refugees. Includes an index and bibliography.

Greenfield, Richard. "The OAU and Africa's Refugees." In *The OAU After Twenty Years*, edited by Yassin El-Ayouty. New York: Praeger, 1984. This extensively documented chapter describes the African refugee situation as it has evolved by region since the early days of the Organization of African Unity. A brief but useful summary of events leading up to the OAU conference relating to the status of refugees is included. Other articles in this volume are also relevant to the refugee question. The volume contains an index but no bibliography.

Hamrell, Sven, ed. *Refugee Problems in Africa.* Uppsala, Sweden: Scandinavian Institute of African Studies, 1967. This monograph of readings explores various aspects of the refugee problem in Africa. Although dated, it provides insight into the pre-OAU convention situation in regard to refugees, including the political causes and consequences of refugee flows and the organizational responses meant to address them. No reference features.

Kibreab, Gaim. *African Refugees: Reflections on the African Refugee Problem.* Trenton, N.J.: Africa World Press, 1985. This trim volume, representing the sometimes unconvincing earlier views of a well-known African scholar, provides an iconoclastic interpretation of the role of tribalism and the notion of African hospitality toward refugees. Later chapters dealing with refugee flows as they relate to development are illuminating. Contains footnotes but lacks other reference features.

Timberlake, Lloyd. *Africa in Crisis: The Causes, the Cures of Environmental Bankruptcy.* Washington, D.C.: International Institute for Environment and Development, 1985. A readable analysis of the environmental underpinnings of contemporary African drought, famine, and refugee flows. The later chapters of this book show how the refugee problem and the development needs of the continent are directly tied to environmental degradation. Weak references and bibliography. No index.

Zolberg, Aristide R., Astri Suhrke, and Sergio Aguayo. *Escape from Violence: Conflict and the Refugee Crisis in the Developing World.* Oxford, England: Oxford University Press, 1989. This exhaustively documented book contains three chapters that directly focus on refugee problems in Africa as a whole and on various regional refugee-producing conflicts in the Horn of Africa and Southern Africa. Ethnic disputes, the weak development of the nation-state, ideological disputes, and external intervention are identified as primary causes of refugee flows in different areas. Extensive footnotes and an index are included. No bibliography.

Robert F. Gorman

Cross-References

The United Nations High Commissioner for Refugees Statute Is Approved (1950), p. 855; The U.N. Convention Relating to the Status of Refugees Is Adopted (1951), p. 867; The Sudanese Civil War Erupts (1955), p. 941; The Organization of African Unity Is Founded (1963), p. 1194; Zimbabwe's Freedom Fighters Topple White Supremacist Government (1964), p. 1224; The U.N. Covenant on Civil and Political Rights Is Adopted (1966), p. 1353; Burundi's Government Commits Genocide of the Bahutu Majority (1972), p. 1668; Revolution Erupts in Ethiopia (1974), p. 1758; The OAU Adopts the African Charter on Human and Peoples' Rights (1981), p. 2136; Nigeria Expels West African Migrant Workers (1983), p. 2180; Hunger Becomes a Weapon in the Sudanese Civil War (1988), p. 2354; Namibia Is Liberated from South African Control (1988), p. 2409.

A NIMH TASK FORCE RECOMMENDS
LEGALIZING HOMOSEXUAL BEHAVIOR

Category of event: Gay persons' rights
Time: October 10, 1969
Locale: Washington, D.C.

The National Institute of Mental Health's Task Force on Homosexuality issued a report recommending that legal penalties be removed against both homosexual and heterosexual behavior in private among consenting adults

Principal personages:
> STANLEY F. YOLLES (1919-   ), the director of the National Institute of Mental Health who appointed the Task Force on Homosexuality in September, 1967
> JEROME D. FRANK (1909-   ), a member of the task force and a professor of psychiatry at Johns Hopkins University School of Medicine
> PAUL H. GEBHARD, a member of the task force and director of the Institute for Sex Research, Inc., at Indiana University
> EVELYN HOOKER, a member of the task force and research psychologist at the University of California, Los Angeles
> ROBERT L. KATZ, a member of the task force and chair of the Department of Human Relations at Hebrew Union College
> JUDD MARMOR, a member of the task force and director of psychiatry at the Cedars-Sinai Medical Center, Los Angeles
> JOHN MONEY (1921-   ), a member of the Task Force and associate professor of medical psychology and pediatrics at Johns Hopkins University School of Medicine
> EDWIN SCHUR, a member of the Task Force and professor of sociology at Tufts University

Summary of Event

In 1955, a Model Penal Code was recommended to states by the prestigious American Law Institute. It suggested that all sexual practices not involving force, adult activity with minors, or public conduct be excluded from the criminal law. Illinois adopted the Model Penal Code of the American Law Institute, thereby becoming the first state to decriminalize homosexual acts between consenting adults in private. In 1957, a specially appointed study committee in Great Britain issued a report, known as the Wolfenden Report, recommending that private adult homosexual conduct be decriminalized. The National Mental Health Act of 1946 had created the National Institute of Mental Health (NIHM). The 1969 final report by the NIMH's Task Force on Homosexuality, concurring with the American Law Institute and the Wolfenden Report, was followed by a 1973 resolution passed by the American Bar Association urging states to repeal all laws that made criminal any form of consenting sexual conduct between adults in private.

It is worth noting that the task force's report was issued just a little more than three months after what many consider to be the birth of the modern-day gay rights movement. On the Friday night of June 27-28, 1969, New York City police raided a Greenwich Village gay bar called the Stonewall Inn. In the preceding three weeks, five well-known New York City gay bars had already been raided. What made the Stonewall a symbol of a new era of gay politics was the reaction of the bar patrons, who confronted the police first with jeers and then with a hail of coins, paving stones, and parking meters. By the end of the weekend, the Stonewall bar had been burned out, but the gay rights movement emerged out of the ashes.

In September, 1967, a Task Force on Homosexuality was appointed by Dr. Stanley F. Yolles, director of the National Institute of Mental Health. This group consisted of outstanding behavioral, medical, social, and legal scientists. Fifteen members were appointed to serve on the task force. One member, Judge David Bazelon, found it necessary because of the pressure of other commitments to resign prior to the completion of the group's deliberations. The mandate of the task force was to review carefully the current state of knowledge regarding homosexuality in its mental health aspects and to make recommendations for institute programming in this area.

The final report of the task force, issued on October 10, 1969, recommended the coordination of NIMH activities in the broad area of sexual behavior through the establishment of a Center for the Study of Sexual Behavior. The activities proposed for the center fell into two major areas, the first including the traditional activities of research, training and education, prevention, and treatment, while the second concerned questions of social policy with respect to sexual behavior. The members of the task force were unanimous in their support of the recommendations made in the first category. Three members of the task force, Drs. Clelland Ford, Henry R. Riecken, and Anthony F. C. Wallace, expressed reservations with respect to the recommendations on social policy. These members believed that there was a fundamental inconsistency between the first group of recommendations, with their emphasis on the lack of reliable information and need for further research, and the second section, proposing revision of social policy in the area. They maintained that consideration of social policy issues should have been deferred until further scientific evidence became available and that only by this approach could scientific knowledge be applied effectively and validly to social policy decisions.

The other members of the task force endorsed the recommendations in their entirety. While recognizing that there were many areas in which scientific knowledge was inadequate, these members believed that there was nevertheless sufficient evidence available to support a thorough review and possible alteration of at least some aspects of social policy with regard to sexual behavior.

The report itself consists of three sections: a short introduction, the longer recommendations section divided into five parts (research, training and education, prevention, treatment, and the somewhat controversial social policy), and a conclusion. The introduction begins by pointing out that human sexuality encompasses a broad range of behavior which is motivated by both internal and social forces. Turning to homosexuality, the introduction states that homosexuality represents a variety of phenomena and that homosexual individuals vary widely in terms of their emotional and social adjustments. The introduction concludes by observing that homosexuality presents a major problem for modern American society largely because of the amount of injustice and suffering entailed in it not only for homosexuals but also for those concerned about them. Individual homosexuals suffer in being isolated from much of society and from the fact that they live in a culture in which homosexuality is considered maladaptive and disgraceful. Their families suffer in feeling responsible and in adjusting to the problem. Society at large inevitably loses in a number of ways. For these reasons among others, efforts must be made at both the individual and social levels to deal with the problems associated with homosexuality.

The task force's detailed recommendations were subsumed under the more general recommendation for the establishment of a National Institute of Mental Health Center for the Study of Sexual Behavior. It was the consensus of the task force that for the development of a meaningful program it was essential that the study of homosexuality be placed within the context of the study of the broad range of sexuality, both normal and deviant. It was therefore strongly recommended that the proposed Center for the Study of Sexual Behavior be a multidisciplinary effort with representation from relevant disciplines and professions. Some of the primary goals of the Center for the Study of Sexual Behavior were to develop knowledge, generate and disseminate information, nullify taboos and myths, provide rational bases for intervention, and provide data to policymakers for use in their efforts to frame rational social policy.

The task force saw the center as necessary because too often in the past competent researchers and clinicians had failed to enter or had left this area because of the difficulties in obtaining support or because of the taboos associated with the field. Dissemination of current knowledge in the field was to be an essential function of the center. The task force report stated that comprehensive statements from an authoritative source within the government that would dispel myths and help to disseminate what is known could have a significant effect, both in terms of individual values and attitudes and in regard to social policy. Among prime targets of this information were community mental health centers, inasmuch as the task force considered them to be appropriate agencies to disseminate educational materials to schools and civic groups and because they can reach children, adolescents, and families at periods which are critical in psychosexual maturation.

Turning to social policy, the task force's report pointed out that although recommendations relating to social policies were not the primary focus of the activities of the NIMH, much of the institute's activity served to provide support for research and analyses which in themselves were of use to policymakers in the framing of rational and socially beneficial measures. Much of the homosexuality research that was needed related directly to issues of public policy. For this reason, the task force urged that policy-related research be an important component of the center's work.

The majority of the task force considered that it would be remiss if it did not express its serious misgivings about certain policy measures employed with respect to homosexual behavior. The task force report stated a belief that most professionals working in this area—on the basis of their collective research, clinical experience, and overall knowledge of the subject—were strongly convinced that the extreme stigma that society had attached to homosexual behavior, by way of criminal statutes and restrictive employment practices, had done more social harm than good and went beyond what was necessary for the maintenance of public order and human decency.

Changes in social policy were then discussed under two headings, legal changes and changes in employment policies and practices. With respect to legal changes, the task force's report noted that many homosexuals were good citizens, holding regular jobs and leading productive lives. The existence of legal penalties relating to homosexual acts meant that the mental health problems of homosexuals were exacerbated by the need for concealment and the emotional stresses arising from this need and from being in violation of the law. A number of eminent bodies, including the British Wolfenden Commission, the Ninth International Congress in Criminal Law, and the American Law Institute, had all recommended, after extensive studies, that statutes covering sexual acts be recast in such a way as to remove legal penalties against acts in private among consenting adults. A majority of the NIMH task force accepted and concurred with this recommendation and urged that the National Institute of Mental Health support studies of the legal and societal implications of such a change with respect to both homosexual and heterosexual behavior. Such a change would reduce the emotional stresses upon the parties involved and thereby contribute to an improvement in their mental health.

Impact of Event

There is absolutely nothing unlawful in the United States in being gay or lesbian, in and of itself. Homosexuality, that is, the condition of being sexually and emotionally oriented toward persons of the same sex, is a state of being. As such, it cannot constitutionally be considered a crime. All of the original thirteen states, however, had made sodomy a criminal offense when the Bill of Rights became part of the Constitution in 1791. As late as 1961, all fifty states had outlawed sodomy. Homosexual organizations played a quiet role in the initial lobby to repeal sodomy laws. In much of the country, private sexual conduct between consenting adults of the same sex became lawful.

In 1973, the American Bar Association passed a resolution urging states to repeal all laws that made criminal any form of consenting sexual conduct between adults in private. As of 1991, twenty-four states and the District of Columbia still criminalized consensual sodomy and various other sexual acts between consenting homosexual adults. The United States Supreme Court in its 1986 decision in *Bowers v. Hardwick*

(478 U.S. 186) held that statutes criminalizing consensual sodomy do not violate an individual's fundamental right to privacy. Among the groups that filed "friend-of-the-court" briefs with the Supreme Court in *Bowers v. Hardwick* were the American Psychological Association and the American Public Health Association, which filed a joint brief. This document included ninety-one citations to medical and social science literature. The brief noted that oral or anal sex was practiced by at least 80 percent of all married couples. In addition, the brief claimed, "there are great similarities among homosexual and heterosexual couples—in emotional makeup, significance of the relationship to the individual, and in the role sexuality plays in the relationship." Sodomy laws added nothing to campaigns against AIDS, the brief claimed. The brief argued that fear of prosecution for sodomy contributed toward "internalized homophobia," or self-hatred on the part of gays which might lead to rejection of "safe sex" efforts to curb AIDS.

According to a "fact sheet" put out by the Privacy Project of the National Gay and Lesbian Task Force, Maryland and Minnesota by the late 1980's were very close to repealing their statutes criminalizing consensual sodomy. The District of Columbia still had a maximum penalty of ten years' imprisonment. Michigan had a maximum penalty of life imprisonment for repeat offenders, and Rhode Island had a maximum penalty of twenty years. The following were considered to be "long-shots for reform" by the National Gay and Lesbian Task Force: Alabama, Arkansas, Georgia (with a maximum penalty of twenty years), Idaho (with a minimum penalty of five years), Louisiana, Mississippi (with a maximum penalty of ten years), North Carolina (with a maximum penalty of ten years), Oklahoma (with a maximum penalty of ten years), South Carolina, and Utah.

Bibliography

Adam, Barry D. *The Rise of a Gay and Lesbian Movement.* Boston: Twayne, 1987. Particularly helpful here is Adam's chapter on "Origins of a Homosexual People," in which he discusses the origins of society's attitudes toward sodomy as they developed in the medieval world and in the "Molly Houses" (gay meeting places in the 1700's).

Dynes, Wayne R., ed. *Encyclopedia of Homosexuality.* 2 vols. New York: Garland, 1990. See specifically Stephen Donaldson and Warren Johansson's article on "Movement, Homosexual" and Warren Johansson's article on "Sodomy." Donaldson and Johansson's article is especially helpful because in a section entitled "Law Reform" they place the efforts to legalize homosexual behavior between consenting adults in the broader context of the homosexual movement, which they date back to the Enlightenment of the eighteenth century.

Irons, Peter. *The Courage of Their Convictions: Sixteen Americans Who Fought Their Way to the Supreme Court.* New York: Penguin Books, 1990. Chapter 16 of this book, entitled "Michael Hardwick v. Michael Bowers," has two parts. Part 1, entitled "I Saw a Bedroom Door Partially Open," contains an excellent discussion of the Supreme Court case of *Bowers v. Hardwick*, including some background on sodomy laws in the United States as well as the arguments made by the attorneys and the opinions written by the justices in the case.

Marotta, Toby. *The Politics of Homosexuality: How Lesbians and Gay Men Made Themselves a Political and Social Force in Modern America.* Boston: Houghton Mifflin, 1981. This book places the efforts to legalize homosexual conduct between consenting adults in the broader context of the homosexual political movement between 1950 and 1980. Of special interest is a discussion of the efforts to decriminalize sodomy in New York State and in the Federal Republic of Germany (West Germany).

Yolles, Stanley F. "Final Report of the Task Force on Homosexuality: October 10, 1969." *SIECUS* (Sex Information and Educational Council of the U.S.) *Newsletter* 5 (December, 1970). The December, 1970, special edition of the *SIECUS Newsletter* made available the full report of the Task Force on Homosexuality, "hoping that in doing so," according to Mary S. Calderone, "professionals of the family-helping disciplines and, through them, the American public, may have the advantage of access to the thinking and recommendations of leading practitioners in these disciplines." Particularly helpful here is a listing of seven background papers prepared by members of the task force on the issues of homosexuality.

Gregory P. Rabb

Cross-References

The Wolfenden Report Recommends Decriminalizing Homosexual Acts (1957), p. 991; Riots Against Police Harassment Launch the Gay Rights Movement (1969), p. 1479; Homosexuality Is Removed from the APA List of Psychiatric Disorders (1973), p. 1741; The Civil Service Decides That Gays Are Fit for Public Service (1975), p. 1801; The U.S. Court of Appeals Affirms the Navy's Ban on Homosexuality (1981), p. 2124; Government Mandates Collection of Data on Crimes Against Homosexuals (1988), p. 2364.

THE INTER-AMERICAN COURT OF HUMAN RIGHTS IS ESTABLISHED

Category of event: Civil rights
Time: November 22, 1969
Locale: San José, Costa Rica

The Inter-American Court of Human Rights was given the task in 1969 of overseeing state compliance with the new American Convention on Human Rights

Principal personages:
> ANGEL MANFREDO VELÁSQUEZ RODRÍGUEZ, a Honduran student who was "disappeared" by the Honduran government
> MARCO GERARDO MONROY CABRA (1940-), the chair of the Inter-American Commission on Human Rights during the 1983 *Restrictions on the Death Penalty* case
> JIMMY CARTER (1924-), the United States president who signed the American Convention on Human Rights on June 1, 1977
> GENERAL EFRAÍN RIOS MONTT (1926-), a president (by coup) of Guatemala who used special courts to impose the death penalty without due process
> THOMAS BUERGENTHAL (1934-), a United States judge and later president of the Inter-American Court of Human Rights

Summary of Event

The American Convention on Human Rights (ACHR) was put before the Organization of American States (OAS) on November 22, 1969. The ACHR was a giant step forward for human rights because it was legally binding under international law, unlike its 1948 predecessor, the American Declaration on the Rights and Duties of Man. Moreover, the ACHR provided the crucial mechanism of independent judicial supervision through the Inter-American Court of Human Rights.

A specialized conference on human rights was convened in San José, Costa Rica, from November 7-22, 1969, at which the ACHR was put forward. Nineteen of the twenty-four OAS members were present, but only twelve signed the document at that time. Conspicuous by their absence were the "big four" in the OAS—the United States, Brazil, Mexico, and Argentina.

The ACHR is a unique document, achieving what neither the United Nations nor the Council of Europe attempted, the incorporation in a single instrument of both civil and political rights and economic and social rights, as well as provisions for enforcement procedures. It has three sections comprising eighty-two articles.

The first section specifies twenty-two civil and political rights and also recognizes the obligation of the states to achieve modern social and economic standards. This considerable listing is in sharp contrast to the 1953 European Convention on Human Rights, which modestly cited thirteen civil and political rights. Moreover, many rights are extensively elaborated in the ACHR. For example, Article 4, which protects the "right to life" in a region plagued by government-sanctioned death squads, also recognizes the right to life "from the moment of conception."

Section 2 provides the mechanisms of implementation, which are broadly patterned on the European Convention on Human Rights. Like the European system, it relies on two basic organs: the Inter-American Commission on Human Rights (created in 1959), and the (new) Inter-American Court of Human Rights. Unlike the European system, the inter-American system was designed to cope with widespread abuse of human rights.

The commission had already created a successful image of its ability to promote human rights within the OAS. Provisions in the ACHR established a "double mandate" for the commission: continued authority over OAS members regarding human rights and a new role over signatory states under the ACHR.

A unique aspect of protection under the inter-American system is its automatic authorization of the right of individual petition: The Commission is permitted to accept petitions alleging human rights violations from "any person or group of persons, or any nongovernmental entity" regarding any signatory. Other human rights treaties have reserved such a right of individual petition as an optional protocol, for the obvious reason that it creates a direct link between the international system and the individual in defiance of the states' domestic jurisdiction. The complainant, who is not even required to be the victim of the alleged violation, must first exhaust domestic remedies (so that states have the opportunity to correct the alleged violation in their juridical systems). States can also be petitioners against other states. Because interstate petitions are highly political, however, the authority of the commission to review them is not inherent but is instead reserved for an optional protocol.

The states must cooperate with the commission's efforts to gather information, including on-site investigations. The commission is to seek a friendly settlement between the parties when possible. If this is not achieved, the commission is either to compile a report based on its recommendations and state compliance or, when appropriate, to send the case on to the Inter-American Court of Human Rights.

The capstone of the enforcement machinery is the Inter-American Court of Human Rights. Only the European Court of Human Rights shares the same crucial, visible, and authoritative position as an independent international tribunal capable of supervising state compliance with a given human rights document. The court has two kinds of jurisdiction—contentious, or adjudicatory, and advisory. Because its advisory jurisdiction is intrinsic to the ACHR, the court itself came into existence when the ACHR entered into force with the required eleventh ratification on July 18, 1978. The court's advisory jurisdiction may be invoked by the request of any appropriate organ of the OAS or any signatory regarding the interpretation of the treaty. A state may also request an advisory opinion on the compatibility of its domestic legislation with the ACHR. What this anticipates, given the very active role of the commission and its wide scope for taking individual complaints, is a pattern of advisory opinions requested by the commission aimed at an authoritative identification and condemnation of the worst violations among the ACHR membership.

The court's accompanying compulsory jurisdiction—tantamount to a landmark breach of domestic jurisdiction—is not intrinsic to the document but is an optional protocol. States that accept Article 62 recognize "as binding . . . the jurisdiction of the Court on all matters relating to the interpretation or application of this Convention." (Costa Rica, which hosts the court in San José, was the only immediate adherent to Article 62.) Obviously, no state can pursue a contentious case or be required to respond to one unless both parties have accepted the optional protocol in Article 62.

The court may order compensation from the state for victims and authorize interim steps "in cases of extreme gravity and urgency." The latter is unusual, yet appropriate in light of the scope and seriousness of violations within its membership. State parties agree to comply with the judgment of the court in any case to which they are parties, and the court makes an annual report to the OAS regarding compliance. Only adhering states and the commission have standing before the court, and the commission is involved in every case. The court is composed of seven members (no two from the same OAS state) who serve in their individual capacity, not as representatives of their states. Five judges constitute a quorum.

The ACHR entered into force on July 18, 1979, with the requisite eleven adherents: Colombia, Costa Rica, the Dominican Republic, Ecuador, El Salvador, Grenada, Guatemala, Haiti, Honduras, Panama, and Venezuela. Ten more states had subsequently joined the ACHR by 1990—Argentina, Barbados, Bolivia, Jamaica, Mexico, Nicaragua, Paraguay, Peru, Suriname, and Uruguay. The prerogative to reach through domestic jurisdiction and act upon the most sensitive areas of state sovereignty on behalf of the human rights contained in the ACHR had been accepted by ten states as of 1990. Argentina, Colombia, Costa Rica, Ecuador, Guatemala, Honduras, Peru, Suriname, Uruguay, and Venezuela joined the optional protocol in Article 62 and therefore recognized the compulsory jurisdiction of the Inter-American Court of Human Rights.

As noted, the United States did not sign the treaty at the close of the San José conference. The United States has long evidenced an ambivalent attitude toward the ACHR, as well as other human rights treaties. That is, the United States championed human rights as an abstract ideal and as a useful bulwark against communist expansion, yet the United States has rejected nearly every human rights treaty as an unacceptable infringement upon its sovereignty. President Jimmy Carter, widely known as a supporter of human rights who was willing to confront repressive regional allies such as Argentina and Chile, signed the treaty (with several reservations) on June 1, 1977, and sent it on to the Senate (which had not ratified it by 1991).

Impact of Event

The Inter-American Court of Human Rights has had to function quite differently from the European Court of Human Rights. Virtually all of the Western European adherents to their court had established domestic systems in which basic human rights were routinely protected. Thomas Buergenthal, later to be a judge on and president of the Inter-American Court, noted that in much of Latin America, "immense poverty, vast illiteracy, widespread corruption, economic exploitation and social backwardness" resulted in totalitarianisms in regimes on both the political right and left which were the "very antithesis of human rights." Nevertheless, the Inter-American Court found a way, in tandem with the commission, to use effectively the authority at its disposal, as illustrated in two highly publicized cases.

Honduras had accepted Article 62 in 1981. In 1986, it was brought before the court by the commission regarding the "disappearance" of a Honduran student, Angel Manfredo Velásquez Rodríguez. According to his family, Velásquez was violently arrested without a warrant on September 12, 1981, accused of political crimes, and later subjected to torture. When Velásquez was "disappeared" from detention, his family brought a complaint to the commission. The court ruled unanimously, on July 29, 1988, to uphold the commission's case: The Honduran government at least tolerated, and perhaps directed, "disappearances" of its political opponents from 1981 to 1984. The "disappearance" of Manfredo Velásquez was part of this pattern of abuse and therefore a violation of his rights under the ACHR. Although the case focused on one individual, Manfredo Velásquez, the commission and the court took the opportunity to widen the scope of the case to condemn pervasive violations in Honduras. Most of the testimony concerned the pattern of kidnappings and "disappearances" carried out by the Honduran armed forces from 1981 to 1984.

The second case concerned Guatemala, which had not accepted Article 62. The commission, therefore, used the court's advisory jurisdiction in 1983 to confront Guatemala in the *Restrictions on the Death Penalty* case, in which lives were at stake. After General Rios Montt came to power through a military coup in 1982, new courts of special jurisdiction were created under Decree Law 46-82, which also added to the list of crimes punishable by death. The courts began sentencing people to death. An on-site visit by the commission in September, 1982, revealed that the accused had no lawyers and were tried in military courts with evidence often obtained under torture. General Montt met with the commission under chairperson Marco Monroy Cabra. Montt noted to the commission that Guatemala had joined the ACHR with a reservation on the death penalty. On April 15, 1983, the commission asked the court for an advisory opinion about the legal issues, despite Guatemala's protest. As the court convened July 26, 1983, to hear Monroy Cabra introduce the commission's case, Guatemala informed the court that such executions were being suspended.

Although Latin American members of the ACHR continued to suffer from pervasive poverty and, in many instances, political violence, an extraordinary shift to democratic regimes took place after the ACHR and the court were realized in 1978. At that time, genuine democracies were the exception. By the end of the first decade of the inter-American system, democratic regimes (some troubled) were the rule.

Bibliography

Blaustein, Albert, Rogers Clark, and Jay Sigler, eds. *Human Rights Source Book.* New York: Paragon House, 1987. Contains all of the major international and regional human rights documents, including the American Declaration on the Rights and Duties of Man as well as the statute and rules of procedure of the Court of Human Rights. Also has selected constitutions, domestic legislation, and judicial decisions. Index and bibliography.

Buergenthal, Thomas, Robert Norris, and Dinah Shelton, eds. *Protecting Human Rights in the Americas: Selected Problems.* Strasbourg, France: International Institute of Human Rights, 1990. Buergenthal was a judge on the Court of Human Rights. This is the first English-language textbook on the Inter-American Human Rights system. The first edition won the 1982-1983 book award from the Inter-American Bar Association. Offers cases and materials on the commission and the court, using the problems approach. Index and bibliography.

Farer, Tom J., ed. *The Future of the Inter-American System.* New York: Praeger, 1979. The editor was a member of the commission, and this book was a special project for the American Society of International Law. It provides an excellent background of multiple aspects of the inter-American system, including economics and development, trade, military issues, nuclear proliferation, and human rights. One chapter is on "Human Rights in the Inter-American System." Index. No bibliography.

Farer, Tom J., and James P. Rowles. "The Inter-American Commission on Human Rights." In *International Human Rights Law and Practice*, edited by James Tuttle. Chicago: American Bar Association, 1978. Explanation of the composition and authority of the commission and how to bring a complaint before the commission, including a model complaint. An appendix contains the regulations of the commission regarding the communication of complaints.

Gros Espiell, Hector. "The Organization of American States." In *The International Dimensions of Human Rights*, edited by Karel Vasak. Vol. 2. Westport, Conn.: Greenwood Press, 1982. Gros Espiell's chapter highlights the American Convention on Human Rights. Most useful is his diagram comparing the implementation machinery of the European and inter-American systems. Index. Superb fifty-page bibliography on international human rights law.

Martz, John D., and Lars Schoultz, eds. *Latin America, the United States, and the Inter-American System.* Boulder, Colo.: Westview Press, 1980. Authors acknowledge the "love-hate" relationship between the United States and its Latin American neighbors. Three chapters specifically cover human rights and United States policies, mostly centered on Carter's years. Index, no bibliography.

Robertson, A. H. *Human Rights in the World.* New York: St. Martin's Press, 1982. Robertson, former director of human rights for the Council of Europe, has a chapter on the American Convention on Human Rights, including sections on the Inter-American Commission and Court. Material is densely informative yet lucidly written. Index, no bibliography.

Rubin, Barry M., and Elizabeth P. Spiro, eds. *Human Rights and U.S. Foreign Policy.* Boulder, Colo.: Westview Press, 1979. Contains twenty-one chapters in four sections: global context, U.S. foreign policy, hard cases, and policies. The approach represents a liberal point of view, endorsing the policies of President Carter. Most of the authors, including President Carter himself, are former members of the Carter Administration. No index or bibliography.

Nancy N. Haanstad

Cross-References

The Declaration on the Rights and Duties of Man is Adopted (1948), p. 755; The United Nations Adopts the Universal Declaration of Human Rights (1948), p. 789; The European Convention on Human Rights Is Signed (1950), p. 843; The European Court of Human Rights Is Established (1950), p. 849; The Organization of American States Is Established (1951), p. 879; The Inter-American Commission on Human Rights Is Created (1959), p. 1032; The U.N. Covenant on Civil and Political Rights Is Adopted (1966), p. 1353; Brazil Begins a Period of Intense Repression (1968), p. 1468; Allende Is Overthrown in a Chilean Military Coup (1973), p. 1725; The Argentine Military Conducts a "Dirty War" Against Leftists (1976), p. 1864; Indigenous Indians Become the Target of Guatemalan Death Squads (1978), p. 1972; The National Commission Against Torture Studies Human Rights Abuses (1983), p. 2186; Argentine Leaders Are Convicted of Human Rights Violations (1985), p. 2280; Voters in Chile End Pinochet's Military Rule (1989), p. 2540; Sandinistas Are Defeated in Nicaraguan Elections (1990), p. 2564.

THE INTERNATIONAL LABOUR ORGANISATION WINS THE NOBEL PEACE PRIZE

Category of event: Workers' rights
Time: December 10, 1969
Locale: Oslo, Norway

The ILO, a specialized agency of the United Nations, was awarded the Nobel Peace Prize for its fifty years of efforts to improve the condition of workers around the world, to protect human rights, and to foster social justice

Principal personages:
ALBERT THOMAS (1878-1932), the first director-general of the ILO, a Frenchman, served from 1919 to 1932
HAROLD B. BUTLER (1883-1951), the second director, an Englishman, served from 1932 to 1938
JOHN G. WINANT (1889-1947), the third director, an American, served from 1938 to 1941
EDWARD J. PHELAN (1888-1967), the fourth director, an Irishman, served from 1941 to 1948
DAVID A. MORSE (1907-   ), the fifth director, an American, served from 1948 to 1970

Summary of Event

The Nobel Peace Prize was a fitting reward to the International Labour Organisation (ILO) for fifty years of accomplishments on behalf of all laborers. These accomplishments included development of international labor standards to improve the conditions of workers regarding hours of work, compensation, vacations, and safety in the workplace; the protection of human rights such as freedom of association and freedom from discrimination; and the promotion of social justice.

The creation of the ILO by the Treaty of Versailles in 1919 was in many respects an unprecedented event: Issues of social justice, the condition of workers, and individual human rights had all been left exclusively to the care of each country. With the creation of the ILO, they became matters for international action. The ILO was also unprecedented in its innovative structure. Nations wanting to organize to attain a common objective normally create institutions composed of their own governmental representatives. The ILO departed from this classic model. It was structured to ensure the participation of labor and management as well as governments to permit a continuing dialogue among them. This was achieved with an unusual tripartite formula. Each member-country was to be represented by a delegation of four persons, two appointed by the government and one each by its leading employers' and workers' organizations. Government, employer, and worker delegates vote separately and caucus independently. Each group elects its own representatives to other tripartite ILO bodies.

The ILO has three principal organs. The International Labour Conference is the organization's policy-making body. Each of the member-states, numbering about 150 as of 1990, is represented by a tripartite delegation. The Governing Body is the executive council of the ILO, elected by the Labour Conference. It is composed of fifty-six members, twenty-eight representing governments, fourteen employers, and fourteen workers. Ten of the government representatives are always appointed by the states of chief industrial importance (Brazil, China, France, Germany, India, Italy, Japan, the Soviet Union, the United Kingdom, and the United States). The other eighteen government representatives and the employer and worker members are elected for three-year terms by the corresponding government, employer, and worker delegates sitting in the International Labour Conference. Committees are created to address specific issues such as problems of key industries. Resolutions adopted by these committees may call for further action by the ILO, or they may contain suggestions addressed to the United Nations, the other specialized agencies, or governments. They may also be intended for the guidance of employers' associations and trade unions in their collective bargaining.

The third principal organ is the International Labour Office, headed by a director-general. It is headquartered in Geneva, Switzerland, and has responsibility for carrying out the day-to-day operation of the organization. Three thousand officials and technical advisers from more than one hundred countries work in Geneva, in locations of ILO technical cooperation projects, or in its forty field offices. A liaison office is maintained at U.N. headquarters in New York. The ILO became, in 1946, the first specialized agency of the United Nations.

The director-general is in charge of this bureaucracy. Directors from the beginning of the ILO's existence have been leaders rather than quiet administrators and have used political skill to guide the organization and its membership toward the attainment of its goals, particularly in the protection of human rights and the furthering of social justice. The task is a difficult one. The director must energize the membership of sovereign states that have extremely different political cultures and often follow conflicting policies. Issues of human rights and social justice are frequently sensitive, if not explosive, in the member-states.

An important function of the ILO is the development of international labor standards to protect laborers and foster social justice. This is done by means of international agreements and recommendations. The agreements, called conventions, are adopted by the International Labour Conference and require ratification by individual member-states. Ratifying states undertake the obligation to incorporate the labor standards into their national legal system by means of legislation; they must report annually to the International Labour Office on how the conventions are applied. Recommendations adopted by the annual conference do not require ratification. They provide guidance for labor policy in a given field. Conventions and recommendations make up the International Labour Code. The ILO has developed investigative procedures to monitor implementation of the code. Many of its standards pertain to work conditions such as minimum wages, working hours, and occupational safety. Others pertain to basic human rights such as nondiscrimination, the right of free association, and collective bargaining.

The ILO's technical cooperation program provides means of helping workers in underdeveloped countries. A large variety of technical assistance projects carried out under this program are funded in large measure by the United Nations Development Program (UNDP). By 1990, there were more than eight hundred ILO experts working in 140 countries on projects geared to local needs such as improvement of work conditions and selection of appropriate technology. The technical cooperation program has grown rapidly and had a 1990 budget of $152 million.

The ILO is deeply involved in the development of human resources through training both workers and instructors. It provides assistance to improve management performance and to broaden the social role of managers through education in areas such as environmental protection and other social, as opposed to strictly business, areas. This work has led to much innovation and concrete results. In Pakistan, for example, the ILO contributed to improving the distribution of basic commodities to the poorest segments of the population.

In the area of vocational training, initiated in the early 1950's, the ILO program spread to eighty different countries, with about 160 projects under way in 1990. The ILO targeted some programs for special groups, including women, youth, migrants, and disadvantaged members of the population. In 1965, it established the International Center for Advanced Technical and Vocational Training in Turin, Italy. The center provides advanced training and retraining, and is also responsible for the organization and monitoring of the extensive ILO Fellowships Program. Every year, hundreds of fellows from developing countries are sent abroad for training under specific technical cooperation projects.

In 1969, the ILO launched its world employment program to increase employment opportunity, a project of critical importance for the alleviation of poverty. Developing nations received assistance in employment planning, economic restructuring, and other employment-related activities. A special program was developed concerning the issue of the large numbers of people who went abroad to find work.

The rapid growth of multinational corporations created new problems in the application of the ILO standards. The Tripartite Declaration of Principles Concerning Multinational Enterprises of 1977 provided a new framework to approach these issues. The Committee on Multinationals, created by the ILO Governing Body, monitors its application.

An extensive program of research and publication contributes significantly to the fulfillment of the ILO's mission. The organization collects a large array of data on labor issues, then publishes and disseminates it among the states and agencies that can use it. For example, a series on occupational safety and health included more than fifty monographs on such issues as occupational cancer prevention and the health risks of asbestos. An encyclopedia of occupational health and safety covered every aspect of workers' health. The ILO has created an international information center to collect, analyze, and distribute worldwide information pertaining to occupational safety. It has established an international occupational safety and health hazard alert system which provides scientific and technical information on newly identified occupational hazards to all ILO member-countries. There are now thousands of ILO publications in print, including a variety of reviews, journals, and yearbooks. More than one hundred new items are released each year.

The International Institute for Labor Studies, established in Geneva in 1960, is a center for the systematic study of labor problems around the world. It carries out its own research and publishes the results, organizes meetings and conferences of experts to study social questions and labor policies, and offers courses on labor issues for government executives working in the labor field, management, trade unions, academics, and labor institute personnel.

Impact of Event

The Nobel Peace Prize added to the ILO's stature, gave it more authority, and undoubtedly imparted to the staff an extra measure of zeal and commitment. It was also a kind of vindication, a token of validity and legitimacy for what had been done over a span of fifty years to improve the conditions of workers, protect human rights, and foster social justice. The Nobel Prize gave public recognition to the ILO's achievements and pursuit of goals many considered utopian or overly optimistic. The ILO had many achievements to its credit.

First and foremost was the Labor Code, internationally developed, promoted, and monitored. The task of standard-setting, however, is never done once and for all, particularly in a rapidly changing global environment. The ILO has kept pace, and by 1990 had promulgated 172 conventions and 179 recommendations touching virtually all problems affecting laborers. The standards, of course, were not universally applied, but the ILO's follow-up procedures, involving mandatory periodic reporting, monitoring, and public exposure of noncompliance, have produced results.

The ILO program of development assistance contributed to the reduction of poverty and fostered economic and social change. The program greatly increased in scope as a result of funding provided by the UNDP. In 1990, this agency contributed about $70 million. Other U.N. agencies and independent contributors added another $70 million. ILO research, publication, and information services are of enormous help to governments, whether they concern new methods of ensuring occupational safety, health protection, or the social security experiences of nations.

The difficult economic conditions experienced in many parts of the world in the 1990's made ILO members reluctant to provide additional funds to expand the ILO's programs. The organization began operating under a policy of a zero-growth budget. The 1990-1991 budget of $320 million appears remarkably small, considering the magnitude of ILO's mission. The ILO continued to be of enormous value for the protection of human rights, the betterment of the condition of workers, and the promotion of social justice. In short, it remained totally committed to the kind of work rewarded in 1969 with the Nobel Peace Prize.

Bibliography

Alcock, Antony. *History of the International Labor Organization.* New York: Octagon books, 1971. The ILO commissioned the preparation of this official history as a fiftieth anniversary project. A thorough, well-documented study. Shows clearly the diplomacy of ILO activities and the difficulty of working with governments whose policies frequently clash. This useful book gives insights into the accomplishments of the organization. Includes a comprehensive bibliography.

Cox, Robert W. "ILO: Limited Monarchy." In *The Anatomy of Influence: Decision Making in International Organization*, edited by Robert W. Cox and Harold K. Jacobson. New Haven, Conn.: Yale University Press, 1973. An excellent discussion of the inner workings of the ILO, its decision making process, and the power dynamics behind its programs. Extensive footnotes provide many additional sources of information on the functioning of the organization. A serious and useful study.

Galenson, Walter. *The International Labor Organization: An American View.* Madison: University of Wisconsin Press, 1981. A well-documented analysis of the work of the ILO, what it does, the problems confronting it, and the issues leading to clashes between states, viewed from an American perspective. Discusses the problems that the United States has experienced within the organization, dissent over structure and operations, and the U.S. decision to withdraw from and subsequently to return to the ILO.

International Labour Office. *Activities of the ILO, 1990.* Geneva: Author, 1991. Provides a convenient official survey (in forty-nine pages, plus tables) of the activities and accomplishments of the organization. Sufficiently detailed to give a good idea of the scope and depth of its work. Provides statistical information and a list of ILO publications issued in 1990.

Jenks, C. Wilfred. *Social Justice and the Law of Nations: The ILO Impact After Fifty Years.* New York: Oxford University Press, 1970. This small volume by one of the former ILO directors reviews the accomplishments of the organization upon its fiftieth anniversary and discusses how the ILO affected the course of social justice. Concise and informative. Provides a short bibliography.

Summaries of International Labour Standards. 2d ed. Geneva: ILO, 1991. A very useful summary of the main ILO conventions and recommendations, with a page or slightly more on each of them. Includes descriptions of documents adopted at the seventy-seventh session of the International Labor Conference (1990). Gives a complete chart of ratifications as of January 1, 1991, and a helpful guide to international labor standards according to substantive categories.

Weiss, Thomas George. *International Bureaucracy: An Analysis of the Operation of Functional and Global International Secretariats.* Lexington, Mass.: Lexington Books, 1975. Discusses the functioning of the secretariats of international organizations, the problems encountered, and the remedies available. Chapter 5 presents a case study focused on the ILO, showing the difficulties it has coped with. Includes a thorough bibliography on international administration.

Jean-Robert Leguey-Feilleux

Cross-References

Supreme Court Disallows a Maximum Hours Law for Bakers (1905), p. 36; The Bern Conference Prohibits Night Work for Women (1906), p. 75; Massachusetts Adopts the First Minimum-Wage Law in the United States (1912), p. 126; The International Labour Organisation Is Established (1919), p. 281; Great Britain Passes Acts to Provide Unemployment Benefits (1920), p. 321; The Wagner Act Requires Employers to Accept Collective Bargaining (1935), p. 508; Social Security Act Establishes Benefits for Nonworking People (1935), p. 514; Jouhaux Is Awarded the Nobel Peace Prize (1951), p. 873; The United Nations Adopts the Abolition of Forced Labor Convention (1957), p. 985; Congress Passes the Equal Employment Opportunity Act (1972), p. 1650.

BORLAUG RECEIVES THE NOBEL PRIZE FOR WORK ON WORLD HUNGER

Category of event: Nutrition
Time: 1970
Locale: Oslo, Norway

Norman Borlaug received the Nobel Peace Prize in 1970 for developing a disease-resistant strain of dwarf wheat that helped to relieve worldwide famine

Principal personages:

NORMAN BORLAUG (1914-   ), a plant pathologist known for his contribution to the "Green Revolution"

WILLIAM EARLE COLWELL (1915-   ), an agronomist who worked in the Mexican Agricultural Program with Borlaug

JACOB GEORGE HARRAR (1906-1982), the director of the Rockefeller Foundation's Mexican Agricultural Program (1943-1951) and president of the Rockefeller Foundation (1961-1972)

DOUGLAS MACARTHUR (1880-1964), the United States Army general who oversaw the rebuilding of Japan after World War II

THOMAS ROBERT MALTHUS (1766-1834), a British clergyman who predicted that world population would eventually exceed world food supply

PAUL MÜLLER (1899-1965), the Swiss scientist who developed DDT

HENRY A. WALLACE (1888-1965), a United States vice president (1941-1945) who recommended expanded agricultural research

Summary of Event

In 1944, under the auspices of the Rockefeller Foundation, thirty-year-old Norman Borlaug, two years out of a doctoral program in plant pathology at the University of Minnesota, joined a team of agricultural researchers led by J. George Harrar that had been working in Mexico for a year. The group's assignments were to help Mexico improve its agriculture, which for several reasons was producing far below its potential, and to help the Mexicans avoid famine. There was widespread hunger in Mexico, and much of the populace, particularly in rural areas, had little reason to hope that their lives could ever improve. Agriculture was held in low esteem as a vocation, and what revenues it produced found their way into urban rather than rural projects.

In the mid-1940's, Mexican farming was notoriously unproductive. Farms in the country averaged eight bushels of corn from each acre, as opposed to twenty-eight bushels in the United States. Wheat production per acre in Mexico was about 75 percent what it was on the farms of its northern neighbor. In order to feed its population, Mexico had to import 50 percent of its wheat, causing a crushing balance of payments deficit. By 1948, Borlaug's work had made it possible for Mexico to stop importing wheat.

When Borlaug arrived in 1944, the Rockefeller project was vastly understaffed, although agronomists and plant pathologists such as Harrar and William Earle Colwell were moving toward solutions. The political climate had been improved by U.S. vice president Henry A. Wallace's call for an increased emphasis on world agricultural development. Severe problems persisted, however, for the next two decades and beyond. The project's work was often impeded by bureaucratic regulation, both its own and that of the Mexican government agencies with which it worked. Borlaug, sensing some of the problems that hampered progress, put into effect a new set of criteria under which the project would operate.

To begin with, Borlaug established a set of priorities and saw to it that they were observed. The first priority was to focus on a single crop, wheat, and to focus even more narrowly on one major problem related to that crop, the growth of the rust fungus that attacked wheat and wiped out whole fields of the grain before it was mature. The ultimate aim of this priority was to feed large numbers of hungry Mexicans as quickly as possible. Borlaug further mandated that theoretical and applied science would be valued equally and that the project would emphasize whatever seemed most likely to help it achieve its stated priorities. In practice, Borlaug did not favor basic over applied science. He realized that a symbiotic relationship existed between the two, and he acted accordingly in his capacity as director. Finally, Borlaug saw to it that the scientists who were placed in charge of the project's various programs were hired as long-term researchers, not as experts who came into situations they knew little about, gave theoretical advice, and then departed before the actual program was functional, as had frequently been the practice.

Borlaug insisted that young natives who had a stake in the region be brought in as trainees. Those who excelled in their internships were given subsidies to pursue further study that would enable them eventually to run the project. The ultimate aim was to turn the entire operation over to well-trained Mexicans and to get the Rockefeller Foundation out of it.

Part of the challenge Borlaug and his colleagues faced was to increase production from soil that had in some cases been worked for almost two millenia without regard to replacing its nutrients. Fertilization was an obvious solution, but once it was instituted, it caused its own problems. Wheat grown in well-fertilized fields grew tall, and farmers were elated until rain and windstorms left the wheat prostrate in the mud before it could be harvested.

Borlaug had to work on this problem while simultaneously experimenting with crossbreeding of various strains of wheat to find one that was rust-resistant and that could be grown successfully in all of Mexico's varied climatic regions. His experiments involved growing two crops of wheat a year in four discrete climatic zones in Mexico.

When his crossbreeding, which involved as many as six thousand crosses a year, began to yield results, Borlaug had to find ways to disseminate his findings. He decided to hold a field day for local farmers, who were reputed to be resistant to change. Five skeptical farmers attended the first field day at the test plots in Valle de Yaqui in Sonora, northwest of Mexico City. Three years later, hundreds of farmers attended a similar field day, and, in less than a decade, the event attracted thousands from the whole of northern Mexico.

Illiterate Mexican farmers had been resistant to programs that offered them no practical outcomes. Once they realized that the seeds they obtained from Borlaug increased their yields substantially and reduced the invasions of the rust fungus that had previously destroyed their crops, they became cooperative—indeed, enthusiastic—followers of this down-to-earth leader.

Out of one test of five thousand crosses, Borlaug found two strains that could resist the rust fungus. This fungus, however, was insidious. It could undergo rapid mutations that enabled it to attack resistant strains, so no victory could be considered an immediate triumph.

Borlaug saw unfolding before him some of the problems Thomas Robert Malthus had identified two centuries earlier concerning explosive population growth. Mexico's population was doubling every twenty-five years, an increase that threatened to cancel the strides Borlaug's methods made possible. Borlaug stressed the urgency of controlling population if his work was to have any impact in eliminating hunger.

In an attempt to find better strains of wheat than were available to him, Borlaug looked to other parts of the world. In Japan during reconstruction after World War II, General Douglas MacArthur had assigned agronomists to work on the food problem. They had found that Japanese farmers were growing a dwarf wheat, Norin 10, previously unknown outside Japan. In 1946, the U.S. Agricultural Research Service made sixteen varieties of Norin wheat available to wheat breeders.

This strain used water and nutrients from the soil in a highly efficient manner to develop more leaves than stalk, making for a compact entity that produced more grains of wheat on each plant than Borlaug had ever dreamed possible. Norin, however, was not without its own problems. The wheat sprouted subhumously at the wrong time in the United States and Mexico. Researchers at the Agricultural Research Service in Washington worked on this problem and, by the late 1950's, had produced a strain, Gaines, that was insensitive to light, thereby overcoming the sprouting problem.

This was a major turning point for Borlaug. Here was a remarkably prolific strain of wheat that could be fertilized heavily, which was necessary in Mexico's depleted soil, but that would stand erect through various climatic exigencies. Borlaug began crossbreeding the Gaines strain with some of his Mexican strains and finally, by 1961, had two strains that were essentially disease resistant, compact, and adaptable to Mexico's different climates. Because of their light insensitivity, these strains could be grown in many parts of the world.

Even before this breakthrough, as early as 1957, Borlaug had crossbred strains of wheat that could resist the rust fungus. Production of wheat per acre in his test fields increased from 11.5 bushels to 20. Once Borlaug's crossbreeding reached optimal levels, however, through the increased use of fertilizer and insecticides, particularly DDT, which Paul Müller had developed in 1939, some farmers got as much as 105 bushels of wheat from an acre.

The "Green Revolution," mentioned when Borlaug received the 1970 Nobel Peace Prize, was now under way, and not only in Mexico: Borlaug's work had implications for the entire world. The hungry of the world had cause to hope that their hunger would be alleviated. Borlaug had to some extent defeated—or at least forestalled—Malthusianism.

Impact of Event

Hunger is not merely a result of low food production. Many other elements, most notably distribution, enter into alleviating hunger, particularly in Third World countries where inaction is often a way of life and where sometimes-impenetrable bureaucracies make change difficult.

In 1961, when Mexican farmers were able to plant Borlaug's considerably improved strain of dwarf wheat seeds, his research group, renamed the International Center for Maize and Wheat Improvement, began to gain worldwide recognition. Borlaug visited other Third World countries in the hope that he could extend his Green Revolution to them. Borlaug's expressed desire was to implement his program in countries that faced severe hunger problems and, within one year, to double their production of wheat, a realizable goal in light of the prolific crops his seeds could produce. Borlaug was impatient, because he realized that world hunger could not wait for creaking bureaucracies to implement the kinds of changes that would save human lives and would both restore dignity to human beings and give them the physical strength they needed to be productive and self-reliant.

It was at this point that Borlaug realized he had to become a statesman without portfolio. He quickly realized that if he could not budge recalcitrant governmental bureaucracies, human suffering and famine would continue, even though the means of averting it were within easy reach. Even as his efforts in countries such as India and Pakistan were progressing, the International Rice Research Institute in the Philippines was using Borlaug's model to produce semidwarf strains of rice. This research led to the spread of the Green Revolution throughout Southeast Asia. In addition, half a dozen Latin American countries and numerous countries in the Middle East were direct or indirect beneficiaries of Borlaug's programs. Because of them, thousands of humans were saved from the ravages of starvation.

In his acceptance speech when he was awarded the Nobel Peace Prize, Borlaug said that food was the first and most important priority for all human beings. Without it, he contended, social justice was not achievable. He went on to say that world peace was directly related to the alleviation of world hunger. Expressing his faith in the rationality of human beings, Borlaug noted that providing food for the people of the world was only a first step toward cultivating the sort of environment in which people could live fruitful existences. Adequate housing, sufficient clothing, good education, rewarding employment, and effective medical care were also vital components of any society in which human beings could live freely and happily.

Retired since 1979 from his International Wheat Research and Production Program directorship in Mexico, Borlaug remained active as a faculty member at Texas A & M University. He maintained an appointment as Whiting Professor-at-Large at Cornell and served on many committees connected with world hunger and human rights. He also served as an associate director of the Rockefeller Foundation and in 1983 was appointed a life member of the foundation.

Bibliography

Bickel, Lennard. *Facing Starvation: Norman Borlaug and the Fight Against Hunger.* New York: Reader's Digest Press, 1974. Biography of Norman Borlaug and his work. The author, a leading Australian scientific writer, has an accurate sense of what Borlaug tried to achieve; he writes knowledgeably about his subject. Easy for general readers; readily obtainable in libraries. No index or bibliography.

Brown, Lester R. *Increasing World Food Output.* Washington, D.C.: Government Printing Office, 1965. Brief overview of world hunger with proposed solutions, including those that are the direct result of Borlaug's activities as director of the International Wheat Research and Production Program. Much in this study is presented more accessibly in *Seeds of Change* (see below).

_____. *Seeds of Change: The Green Revolution and Development in the 1970's.* New York: Praeger, 1970. Mentions Borlaug fleetingly but provides an introduction to world hunger, helping to explain the Green Revolution in understandable terms and historical context. Its final section, "Preview of the 1970's," is interesting to read retrospectively. Index; minimal bibliography.

Cockrane, Willard W. *The World Food Problem: A Guardedly Optimistic View.* New York: Crowell, 1969. Much of Cockrane's guarded optimism stems from the kind of pioneering work Borlaug did in Mexico. Cockrane's emphasis is on production, which leads to optimism. Fails to acknowledge adequately the other major component of any solution to world hunger: distribution. Index and bibliography.

Freeman, Orville. *World Without Hunger.* New York: Praeger, 1968. A former secretary of agriculture presents an overview of world hunger, emphasizing the role the United States has played and will play in dealing with it. Freeman writes like an ideologue, but his information is worthwhile. Borlaug's contributions, both research and applied, are well explained.

Hardin, Clifford, ed. *Overcoming World Hunger.* Englewood Cliffs, N.J.: Prentice-Hall, 1969. Contains some of the best thinking on world hunger to 1968. It takes into account every important aspect of the problem. The contributors are experienced. A good starting point for anyone new to the field. Index and bibliography.

Kellerman, Mitchell. *World Hunger: A Neo-Malthusian Perspective.* New York: Praeger, 1987. Kellerman approaches the question of world hunger from an economic rather than an agricultural point of view. Provides a strong historical background. Gets quite statistical, but general readers can ignore the charts and tables. Minimal bibliography and slim index.

Paarlberg, Don. *Norman Borlaug: Hunger Fighter.* Washington, D.C.: Government Printing Office, 1970. Written for the U.S. Department of Agriculture, this twenty-page pamphlet, available in the documents sections of libraries, provides the best capsule summary available of Borlaug's career up to his winning the Nobel Peace Prize. Biographical details flesh out the summary of Borlaug's scientific contributions. Illustrations.

Stakeman, E. C., Richard Bradfield, and Paul C. Mangelsdorf. *Campaigns Against Hunger.* Cambridge, Mass.: Harvard University Press, 1969. The senior author, Stakeman, persuaded Borlaug to go into the field he entered and was his mentor at the University of Minnesota. Provides a comprehensive view of world hunger, focusing more on production than on distribution but addressing each. Comprehensive index and full, useful bibliography.

United Nations. Food and Agricultural Organization. *Agriculture: Toward 2000.* Rome: Food and Agricultural Organization, 1984. The prognostications in this report are grounded on solid information gathered from a broad variety of sources. The importance of work like Borlaug's is evident on nearly every page. Contains statistics for those who need them, but the general reader can ignore their details.

R. Baird Shuman

Cross-References

The First Food Stamp Program Begins in Rochester, New York (1939), p. 555; Mao's Great Leap Forward Causes Famine and Social Dislocation (1958), p. 1015; A U.N. Declaration on Hunger and Malnutrition Is Adopted (1974), p. 1775; The World Health Organization Adopts a Code on Breast-Milk Substitutes (1981), p. 2130; Hunger Becomes a Weapon in the Sudanese Civil War (1988), p. 2354.

THE U.S. VOTING AGE IS LOWERED TO EIGHTEEN

Category of event: Voting rights
Time: 1970-1971
Locale: Washington, D.C.

A combination of federal statute and the Twenty-sixth Amendment lowered the minimum voting age in the United States to eighteen, increasing the electorate by eleven million voters

Principal personages:
MIKE MANSFIELD (1903-   ), the majority leader of the U.S. Senate, a leading advocate of the vote for eighteen-year-olds
EMANUEL CELLER (1888-1981), the chair of the House Judiciary Committee, a leading opponent of lowering the voting age
HUGO L. BLACK (1886-1971), a Supreme Court justice who was the swing vote in the key case of *Oregon v. Mitchell*
RICHARD M. NIXON (1913-   ), the president of the United States, an advocate of lowering the voting age by constitutional amendment

Summary of Event

Twenty-one was the minimum voting age throughout most of American history. By the American Revolution, twenty-one was the minimum age for voting in all British colonies, as the colonies had adopted England's standard. The U.S. Constitution, adopted in 1787, left the definition of the elective franchise to the states, and all kept it at age twenty-one.

The electorate expanded vastly over the next century and a half: States gradually abolished property qualifications, the Fifteenth Amendment (1870) was intended to safeguard the voting rights of former slaves, and the Nineteenth Amendment (1920) enfranchised women. Although the latter two set precedents for federal definition of voting rights by constitutional amendment, Congress never considered a lower voting age. Nor, with one exception, did the states—the New York legislature voted down such a proposal in 1867. The country was apparently content with a voting age of twenty-one.

The first indication of a change in attitude came during World War II. Motivated by the belief that a person old enough to fight and die for his or her country ought to be old enough to vote, various members of Congress introduced proposed constitutional amendments to lower the voting age to eighteen. The proposals, however, received little serious consideration. State legislatures also began to take up the question. Interest peaked in 1943, when about thirty states considered lowering the voting age. Only in Georgia, however, were proponents of the change successful.

The Korean War saw a revival of interest in the question. Again the major momentum was a perceived connection between military service and voting rights. The

Senate voted thirty-four to twenty-four in favor of a proposed amendment, but this fell short of the necessary two-thirds majority. Thirty-five states considered changes during the early 1950's but only Kentucky lowered its voting age (to eighteen). In 1958, Alaska entered the union under a constitution that allowed nineteen-year-olds to vote, and Hawaii followed the next year with one enfranchising twenty-year-olds.

A more sustained revival of interest came in the late 1960's. The Vietnam War resurrected earlier arguments. This time another factor was at work as well: The baby-boom generation (those born between 1946 and 1964) was beginning to come of age. The population explosion that had followed World War II not only produced the largest demographic surge in modern American history but also made American society much more conscious of youth. Lowering the voting age had natural appeal to the maturing baby-boomers. It was no surprise that organizations such as the Youth Franchise Coalition formed to lobby for the change. Public opinion polls began to show a growing majority in favor of a lower voting age.

Congress began to react. The late 1960's saw the introduction of an increasing number of proposed youth suffrage amendments. In May, 1968, a Senate subcommittee opened hearings on the subject. Every president since Dwight D. Eisenhower had endorsed a lower voting age, and after 1968, the Nixon Administration showed signs of active support. In various states, there was also a flurry of activity.

The question received a thorough airing in the media, and a national debate took place. Proponents of a lowered voting age marshaled a number of arguments. The nation's young people were better educated than ever before, it was argued, and giving them the vote would encourage civic responsibility. The "old enough to fight, old enough to vote" argument was again offered. It had added strength because, by 1970, almost one-half of all Americans killed in Vietnam were under age twenty-one. Georgia and Kentucky were cited as examples to show that the change would not collapse the structure of politics. Others believed that lowering the voting age would be a step toward bridging the "generation gap" that was then a much-discussed topic.

There remained, however, vocal opposition to lowering the voting age. Those against the idea rejected the connection between military service and voting rights. Much of the opposition centered on the alleged immaturity of those in their late teens: It was argued that they lacked the life experience on which to ground political judgments. The young, some felt, would be more susceptible to manipulation either by their parents or by the increasingly sophisticated use of the media by politicians. Some conservatives feared that the young would vote as a liberal bloc.

It was in this atmosphere that Congress began, in 1970, to extend serious consideration to the issue. A Senate subcommittee chaired by Senator Birch Bayh (D-Ind.), a strong advocate of the vote for eighteen-year-olds, reopened hearings; however, the prospects of the proposed constitutional amendment were uncertain. The House Judiciary Committee would have to report on the measure, and its chairman, Emanuel Celler (D-N.Y.), was a staunch foe of lowering the voting age. Moreover, the amendment process itself presented a number of hurdles: Two-thirds majorities in both houses of Congress were required, to be followed by ratification by three-fourths of the state legislatures. Forty-six of the states had thus far refrained from amending their own constitutions on this subject—and three had recently rejected attempts to do so—so ratification was far from certain.

Mike Mansfield (D-Mont.), the Senate majority leader and one of the leading advocates of a lower voting age, devised an alternative strategy: Congress would simply legislate the vote for eighteen-year-olds. This would require only a simple majority of each house, provided that the president did not veto the measure, and would leave the states entirely out of the process. The constitutionality of such a course, however, would be open to challenge. Previous restrictions on state power to determine voting requirements were based on constitutional amendments that prohibited discrimination on the basis of race, sex, or failure to pay taxes. A law reducing the voting age would almost certainly meet a court challenge. Mansfield and others believed that recent court decisions, most notably in the case of *Katzenbach v. Morgan*, had expanded congressional power to regulate elections under the equal protection clause of the Fourteenth Amendment, so there was a chance that legislation could survive a court challenge.

Mansfield took the opportunity provided by the Senate's consideration of a renewal and expansion of the Voting Rights Act of 1965, one of the legislative landmarks of the Civil Rights movement. The version of the bill that had already passed the House came before the Senate in March, 1970, and Mansfield offered an amendment that lowered the voting age to eighteen for all elections, effective January 1, 1971. After considerable debate, the Mansfield Amendment was adopted, eighty-four to seven. The amended Voting Rights Act was then sent back to the House. Congressman Celler was one of the House's strongest supporters of civil rights legislation. He feared that if the House refused to go along with the Senate version the consequent reconsideration would weaken the act's ability to protect minority rights. He therefore went along with the Senate version, and it passed the House easily.

There was some question as to whether President Nixon would veto the bill. He had stated his opposition to lowering the voting age in this fashion, and his political advisers urged a veto on the grounds that much of the youth vote would go to his opponent in 1972. Nixon, however, signed the Voting Rights Act of 1970, Mansfield Amendment and all, on June 22, 1970. He also urged Congress to continue consideration of a constitutional amendment.

Expectations of an early court test were correct. In early August, 1970, the states of Oregon and Texas asked the Supreme Court to declare unconstitutional the lowered voting age provision of the act. On December 21, 1970, the court handed down its decision in the case of *Oregon v. Mitchell*. By a five-to-four majority it upheld the Mansfield Amendment so far as it applied to federal elections, but it declared unconstitutional its application to state and local elections.

The court was badly divided on the question, and the decision turned on the attitude of a single justice, Hugo L. Black, who wrote the majority opinion in the case. Four members of the court thought that the Mansfield Amendment was entirely unconstitutional, while four others believed that Congress could regulate all elections. Only Black believed the amendment to be valid in federal elections but not in others. The majority opinion reflected Black's views.

The decision in *Oregon v. Mitchell* threatened most of the country with electoral chaos. Unless states brought their voting age requirements into line with the new federal law, they would be forced to maintain separate electorates that might even require separate elections. Potential confusion and the certainty of greater expense loomed as the 1972 elections drew nearer. To many, a constitutional amendment lowering the voting age was now much more attractive. When Congress returned in January, 1971, Bayh's subcommittee resumed hearings, and a joint resolution proposing suffrage for eighteen-year-olds in all elections easily passed on March 23, 1971 (by votes of 94 to 0 in the Senate and 400 to 19 in the House). The states responded with dispatch: It took only 107 days for the requisite number of states to ratify the Twenty-sixth Amendment, the shortest ratification period in American history. People between the ages of eighteen and twenty-one now had the vote in every state.

Impact of Event

The major impact of the Mansfield-amended Voting Rights Act of 1970 and the Twenty-sixth Amendment was to increase the electorate. An estimated eleven million more Americans became eligible to vote. In this sense, the effect of the change ranks with the impacts of the Fifteenth and Nineteenth amendments in producing sudden and massive increases in the number of potential voters.

The political impact of the lowered voting age was less dramatic. Politicians, columnists, and political scientists produced a growing body of predictions on the likely effect of the youth vote, with particular regard to the upcoming presidential election of 1972. Some believed that the newly enfranchised would vote in smaller proportions than older voters, as those voters in their early twenties already did, and would follow the tendencies of their parents. Others, bearing in mind the razor-thin margins of the 1960 and 1968 elections, forecast that the youth vote in 1972 would be decisive. Many expected the new voters to be overwhelmingly aligned with the Democrats. At the local level, cities and towns with large student populations began to fear that older electorates would be swamped by the newcomers and that city halls across the country would be occupied by long-haired radicals.

As it turned out, the predictions of large-scale political change were wrong. The 1972 presidential election attracted only about 55.6 percent of potential voters, the lowest turnout since 1948, and a study by the Census Bureau revealed that only 48 percent of those enfranchised by the Twenty-sixth Amendment reported casting votes. The actual portion was thought to be even lower. The Democratic candidate, Senator George McGovern, had gone out of his way to attract the youth vote, and some had predicted that it could provide him with the margin of victory. The young, however, did not vote as a bloc and divided their votes equally between the two candidates. The lowering of the voting age did little to avert the Nixon landslide, and very few college and university towns elected campus activists, as some had predicted.

There was a marked decline in interest in studying the politics of the young after the 1972 election. Those who investigated the subject confirmed the failure of the lower voting age to alter drastically American politics. Voters aged eighteen to twenty-one typically have the lowest turnout rate of any age group, and their political choices are much more likely to be shaped by education, occupation, ethnic background, and other variables than they are by age.

Although obtaining the vote for eighteen-year-olds did not change the face of American politics, it was not without importance. In addition to a sizable expansion of the electorate, it marked a recognition of the importance of youth and may well have helped to secure other changes sought by the emerging baby-boom generation, such as lowering the drinking age (which proved to be temporary) and ending the draft. In the long run, the Twenty-sixth Amendment may be seen as one of the baby-boom generation's most enduring monuments.

Bibliography

Beck, Paul Allen, and M. Kent Jennings. "Lowering the Voting Age: The Case of the Reluctant Electorate." *Public Opinion Quarterly* 33 (Fall, 1969): 370-379. Based on a study of high-school seniors conducted in 1965. Finds a surprising lack of support for lowering the voting age at that time. Sees the major momentum for the change developing after 1965.

Carleton, William G. "Votes for Teen-agers." *Yale Review* 58 (October, 1968): 45-60. A political scientist's arguments against lowering the voting age. Carleton finds that eighteen-year-olds are not yet mature and would be too susceptible to the manipulative trends he contends already corrupt American politics.

"Congress and the Voting-Age Controversy." *Congressional Digest* 49 (May, 1970): 130-160. Provides a wealth of information on the topic, including a state-by-state summary of efforts to lower the voting age. Also includes Senate arguments on both sides of the Mansfield Amendment.

Evans, Rowland, Jr., and Robert D. Novak. *Nixon in the White House: The Frustration of Power.* New York: Random House, 1971. A political history of Nixon's first administration, stressing its inconsistencies in domestic policy. Contains an account of Nixon's decision, against the counsel of most of his advisers, not to veto the 1970 Voting Rights Act. No bibliography, but does have an index.

Jones, Landon Y. *Great Expectations: America and the Baby Boom Generation.* New York: Coward, McCann & Geoghegan, 1980. Although it contains a brief discussion of the consequences of lowering the voting age, this book's greatest value is in its overall social and political portrait of the baby-boom generation. Very helpful for putting the events of 1970-1971 in context. Bibliography and index.

Roth, Robert. "A Rapid Change of Sentiment: Lowering the Voting Age." *Annals of the American Academy of Political and Social Science* 397 (September, 1971): 83-87. Discusses the unanticipated collapse of opposition to lowering the voting age and speculates as to the effect it would have on American politics. Accurately predicted that the new voters would not vote as a bloc.

Seagull, Louis M. *Youth and Change in American Politics.* New York: New Viewpoints, 1977. A general treatment of the role of youth in American politics in the 1960's and 1970's, including consideration of the vote for eighteen-year-olds. Sees the resulting major change as a tendency for younger voters to be more independent and less inclined to have strong party identifications. Bibliography and index.

William C. Lowe

Cross-References

The Nineteenth Amendment Gives American Women the Right to Vote (1920), p. 339; The Twenty-fourth Amendment Outlaws Poll Taxes (1964), p. 1231; Congress Passes the Voting Rights Act (1965), p. 1296; Congress Extends Voting Rights Reforms (1975), p. 1812; Congress Requires Bilingual Elections to Protect Minority Rights (1975), p. 1817.

CIGARETTE ADVERTISING IS BANNED FROM AMERICAN TELEVISION AND RADIO

Categories of event: Consumers' rights; health and medical rights
Time: April 1, 1970
Locale: The United States

The Public Health Cigarette Smoking Act prohibited all cigarette advertising on television and radio under the FCC's jurisdiction

Principal personages:
LUTHER TERRY (1911-   ), the surgeon general of the United States from 1961 until 1965
JOHN BANZHAFF III (1940-   ), sued CBS in order to win equal time to present his views on cigarette smoking; became the founder of Action on Smoking and Health
MAURINE NEUBERGER (1907-   ), became a senator from Oregon (1960-1966) after the death of her husband from lung cancer
FRANK E. MOSS (1911-   ), a senator from Utah
JAMES C. CORMAN (1920-   ), a member of Congress and lawyer who spearheaded the congressional campaign against the tobacco industry

Summary of Event

Tobacco smoking was introduced to Western civilization upon the discovery of America. Native Americans taught European explorers the pleasures of smoking tobacco and other leaves at the same time Europeans introduced the drinking of liquor to the New World. The poisonous effects of smoking were not so immediate as to prevent its rapid introduction throughout the world. Cigarette smoking was a rather late development, first gaining wide popularity in the United States after the Civil War. Its success can be traced to the development of the White Burley leaf, the safety match, and the marketing and advertising techniques of James Duke, Richard Joshua Reynolds, and other late nineteenth century pioneers of the tobacco industry.

From the start, the sales of cigarettes were tied intimately to national advertising designed to overcome initial public skepticism. Advertising turned around the negative image of cigarettes as poor people's substitute for luxurious cigars to a habit associated with active people, with urban sophisticates, and later, after World War I, with women.

Every major war advanced the sale of cigarettes. The Civil War introduced Northerners to Virginia tobacco. During World War I, cigarette companies responded to patriotic appeals to donate their product for the benefit of the soldiers and reaped huge benefits when the soldiers continued their smoking in civilian life. In this period, per-capita cigarette consumption went from 134 in the four-year period from 1910 to 1914 to 310 in the period from 1915 to 1919. World War II repeated this marketing bonanza and gave the cigarette companies added profit when their product became the de facto currency of postwar Europe, replacing the virtually worthless local official scrip.

Although many were always skeptical about the health consequences of smoking, there was little systematic investigation until the generation of World War I started to reach advanced age. By the 1950's several health organizations had noticed and written about the statistical correlations between cigarette smoking and the incidence of lung cancer. Lung cancer had been gaining ground as a killer in these years. The public, however, was only starting to be aware of these allegations, largely through the continued reporting of *Reader's Digest* and a handful of other media outlets.

Several commentators have argued that the large amount of print advertising the tobacco industry paid for every year inhibited editors from publishing articles regarding the hazards of smoking. *Reader's Digest* could afford to be forthright in its condemnation of smoking since it contained no advertising. The anticigarette movement began to focus on the effects of broadcast advertising, claiming that television influenced young people, to an uncontrollable degree, to smoke.

The tobacco industry's response was defensive. Tobacco industry spokespersons insisted that no causal link had been established between smoking and cancer. The evidence was statistical and inductive, rather than a demonstrated deduction. The industry accepted Federal Trade Commission guidelines in 1955 that prohibited advertising from describing any positive physical effects from tobacco use. Companies also introduced filtered cigarettes to allay public fears and to increase brand diversification. Cigarette sales rebounded after an initial drop.

The pressure mounted, and President John Kennedy responded by directing Surgeon General Luther Terry to issue a report on the health consequences of cigarette smoking. The report came out in 1964 and created an immediate uproar. It stated that there was a direct relationship between cancer and smoking. Both the president and Congress were hesitant in acting against the cigarette industry because of its economic importance and the political clout of the tobacco-growing states. The logical step of banning cigarettes was not considered seriously, since everyone knew that the other great attempt to ban an ingrained American habit, drinking, had failed miserably in the Prohibition era.

Some wanted to continue the attack on the tobacco industry and its advertising. John Banzhaf III was a young New York lawyer who in 1966 requested that WCBS-TV give him the opportunity to present contrasting views on the subject of smoking, in response to cigarette ads. WCBS denied his request, but on June 2, 1967, the Federal Communications Commission (FCC) decided that his request must be honored under the "fairness doctrine." This doctrine had originated during the Hoover presidency and required radio and television stations to give equal access to any spokesperson who might oppose views already presented on the station. It was rescinded quietly by President Ronald Reagan, but at the time was still in force. The FCC agreed that it should apply to cigarette advertising. The networks objected, arguing that the doctrine could not apply to advertising since advertising presented no particular view which could be rebutted. The FCC ruled that after the surgeon general's report, cigarette smoking was a controversial issue and that its promotion could be opposed by antismoking forces. Networks countered that there would be a flurry of other product advertising subject to opposing points of view and that the whole economic structure of commercial broadcasting would be undermined if the networks had to give time to organizations campaigning against these products. The FCC essentially promised that cigarettes were a unique danger and that no other product would be subject to the fairness doctrine. It has held to this logic, frustrating efforts by Friends of the Earth and other groups to counter oil and automobile advertising.

The Federal Trade Commission had proposed warning labels on cigarette packets and on advertising. In various compromise efforts to get laws enforcing the health warnings, the tobacco industry accepted the packet warnings in exchange for a three-year moratorium against efforts trying to restrict its ability to advertise. Antismoking forces were outraged at the compromise, and as the three years drew to an end, Congressman James C. Corman of California introduced a bill banning all television and radio advertising of cigarettes and little cigars. On the Senate side, Maurine Neuberger and Frank Moss led the fight. The Public Health Cigarette Smoking Act passed Congress. It was signed into law by President Richard Nixon on April 1, 1970. Television and radio ads for cigarettes were forbidden as of January 1, 1971.

The Tobacco Institute and the television networks immediately tried to have the law declared an unconstitutional infringement on their right to free speech. They suffered a series of negative decisions as they appealed their way through the federal court system. The matter ended when the Supreme Court summarily affirmed the legality of the ban in a seven-to-two decision. Only Justices William Douglas and William Brennan wanted the Court to conduct a full-scale review.

Some analysts noticed that the tobacco industry did not fight passage with full vigor. An industry viewpoint was that television advertising was too expensive and that the only reason tobacco companies continued to advertise was to maintain par with the other companies. Therefore, a total ban was not altogether a bad thing. Profits from cigarettes continued to be high through 1977, although consumption of tobacco on a per-capita basis dropped, partly as a result of the use of nontobacco additives in cigarettes and partly because cigarette sales did not increase as rapidly as did the population. The tobacco companies increased their prices on the assumption that smokers would pay any reasonable price. Tobacco companies to a certain extent had allayed public fears in the first decade after the surgeon general's report and the ad banning through the development of low-tar and low-nicotine cigarettes. Health officials eventually made it quite clear that no smoking was safe. The industry's attempts to promote older forms of tobacco consumption, such as cigars, pipes, and snuff, were defeated when these forms were also declared unhealthy. According to the United States Agriculture Department, real declines in cigarette profits did not occur until the late 1970's. There was a steady attrition through the 1980's, but by then the various tobacco companies had protected themselves through diversification into other consumer products.

Impact of Event

The banning of nonprint cigarette advertising proved to be only the first step in the regulation of smoking. Both local and federal governments spent the succeeding decades promulgating laws concerning public smoking. The American public began to give up smoking, or never started smoking. The fraction of adults who smoked fell from 40 percent in 1964 to 29 percent in 1990. Tobacco farming, however, remained profitable. Television initially lost as much as one-tenth of its revenues as a result of the ban. The networks, however, quickly made up the loss.

The final analysis of the actual effect of the cigarette advertising ban is mixed. It is easier to correlate declines in per-capita cigarette smoking to tax increases and price hikes in the late 1970's than it is to show any statistical correlation with the 1971 advertising ban. Intuitively, it makes sense that the ban fostered the continuing legal assault on cigarette smoking, including local bans on smoking in public places. Further extending this trend, Representative Tom Luken (D-Ohio) introduced legislation to prohibit motion pictures from featuring specific cigarette brands. He claimed that such product placement is a circumvention of the television advertising ban. The tobacco companies responded by refraining from such placement, making the issue moot. Such an attempt to expand the original ban, however, is of a different philosophical status from the original, purely commercial-speech (advertising) prohibition.

The legal and policy questions lingered. Historically, the First Amendment was considered not to protect commercial speech. The Earl Warren Supreme Court changed this understanding by expanding the protection of commercial speech from government interference. It did not choose to do so in the case of the cigarette advertising ban. Many believe that the electronic media should be subjected to greater government interference than are the printed media. This is justified by the need to regulate use of the limited broadcast frequencies. It is a short step to propose that users be required to act in the public interest. There is also an assumption that the easier access to the printed media guarantees a free marketplace of ideas.

The cigarette advertising ban was allowed because of government's legitimate concern with both commercial and electronic speech. It is difficult to understand how this logic can be applied only to the cigarette industry, but the Supreme Court has done just so. It overturned an attempt by the state of Mississippi to restrict billboard advertising of liquor and specifically denied Mississippi's contention that the cigarette advertising ban had set the precedent for such an attempt.

Bibliography

Conrad, Mark. "Limiting the Pitch: Tombstone Ads for Coffin Nails." *Commonweal* 117 (August 10, 1990): 441-442. A current view of legal thought as it relates to commercial speech and attempts to further legislate cigarette ads.

Devol, Kenneth, ed. *Mass Media and the Supreme Court.* New York: Hastings House, 1976. A collection of extracts from Supreme Court and associated writings. It is rather interesting concerning the Warren Court and commercial and electronic speech but gives no specific reference to the tobacco industry.

Francois, William E. "Access to the Media." In *Mass Media Law and Regulation.* Ames: Iowa State University Press, 1990. An excellent source for placing the ad ban in the context of constitutional law.

Miles, Robert H., and Kim S. Cameron. *Coffin Nails and Corporate Strategies.* Englewood Cliffs, N.J.: Prentice-Hall, 1982. An overview of the antismoking campaign and the tobacco industry responses. The point of view is obvious from the title.

Sobel, Robert. *They Satisfy: The Cigarette in American Life.* New York: Anchor, 1978. The most complete history of the tobacco industry and its changing economics. The discussion of the political struggle is very dispassionate.

Taylor, Peter. *The Smoke Ring.* New York: Pantheon, 1984. Tends to focus on the antismoking campaign in the United Kingdom and the Commonwealth. Its discussion of the American struggle focuses on the actual ban and the personalities of the legislators and the lobbyists.

Tollison, Robert D., and Richard E. Wagner, eds. *Smoking and the State: Social Costs, Rent Seeking, and Public Policy.* Lexington, Mass. Lexington Books, 1988. A polemical attempt to defend cigarette smoking and to cast doubt on the altruistic motives of the antismoking movements. The absolutist interpretation of free speech is a classic statement of laissez-faire conservatism.

Frederick A. Wasser

Cross-References

The World Health Organization Proclaims Health as a Basic Right (1946), p. 678; Congress Requires Cigarette Warning Labels (1966), p. 1338; Canada Passes the Tobacco Products Control Act (1988), p. 2376; A Jury Awards Monetary Damages to the Estate of a Smoker (1988), p. 2381; The U.S. Surgeon General Reports on Tobacco and Health (1989), p. 2455.

FOUR STUDENTS ARE KILLED AT KENT STATE BY THE NATIONAL GUARD

Categories of event: Atrocities and war crimes; civil rights
Time: May 4, 1970
Locale: Kent State University, Kent, Ohio

Ohio National Guards called in to restore order following antiwar protests unexpectedly opened fire on students, killing four and wounding nine others

Principal personages:
RICHARD M. NIXON (1913-), the president of the United States (1969-1974)
JAMES A. RHODES (1909-), the governor of Ohio who ordered the Ohio National Guard to the KSU campus
ROBERT I. WHITE (1908-), the president of Kent State University at the time of the shootings
SYLVESTER DEL CORSO, the adjutant general of the Ohio National Guard
ROBERT H. CANTERBURY, the senior officer in command of the Ohio National Guard at KSU in May, 1970
JOHN MITCHELL (1913-1988), the attorney general of the United States at the beginning of the Nixon Administration

Summary of Event

The shooting at Kent State University left in its wake a complex controversy which may never be fully resolved, even though some of the facts are simple and relatively undisputed. On May 4, after dispersing a peaceful rally on the commons of the KSU campus, the Ohio National Guard unexpectedly opened fired on students. Four were killed and nine others were wounded, some seriously.

No one was convicted of any crime associated with the incident, and no satisfactory explanation was ever given as to why the Guard opened fire. Many theories have been put forward, all of which have some bearing on the appropriateness of the Guard's actions. Like the Kennedy assassination, the incident was photographed and filmed from several angles and was also recorded on audio tape. The accumulated evidence refutes some theories, but fundamental questions remain unanswered.

Growing opposition to the war had resulted in massive demonstrations nationwide in 1969. The government eventually responded to public pressure, and the war appeared to be winding down. Public opinion on the United States' involvement in the war in Vietnam was still divided in early 1970, and public resentment of the protest movement, which was strongest on college campuses, was high. Shortly before the Kent State shootings, President Nixon had made public statements which were highly derogatory toward those who opposed his Vietnam policy.

On Thursday, April 30, President Nixon announced that U.S. forces had invaded

Cambodian territory to search out and destroy enemy bases. The announcement triggered huge demonstrations on college campuses across the country the following day. At KSU, campus unrest coincided with the first warm night of the season (Friday, May 1) and the arrival of an out-of-town motorcycle gang. Rioting occurred in the streets downtown, and some property was damaged. On Saturday, the protests continued, and the University's Reserve Officer Training Corps (ROTC) building was burned down. This incident precipitated the calling of the Ohio National Guard to Kent.

A peaceful demonstration the following day (Sunday, May 3) was dispersed by the Guard, who used tear gas against the students. Several students were beaten and some were bayoneted by Guards, although no fatalities resulted. The confrontation on Monday began with the dispersal of the students on the commons and ended forty minutes later with a thirteen-second sustained volley in which at least sixty-seven rounds were fired.

Officials claimed at the time that the retreating Guards had fired in self-defense while being attacked by hundreds of students who had charged to within three or four yards of the Guard's position. Eyewitness accounts and analyses of films and photographs showed that this was not the case. The nearest shooting victim was sixty feet from the Guards who did most of the shooting. A photograph taken just an instant after the Guard opened fire clearly shows the victim standing with his middle finger upraised in an obscene gesture, for which he was shot twice (according to the Guard who shot him) and seriously wounded. The majority of the dead and wounded students were standing one hundred or more yards away. At least one of the fatally wounded students had not participated in the demonstration, and one was an ROTC student.

According to many observers and participants, the focus of the students' anger at the Monday rally was actually the presence of the Guard itself, not the Cambodian invasion that had initially triggered the demonstrations. The students were outraged over the use of tear gas, the beatings, and the bayoneting that had taken place the previous evening. Furthermore, students believed that their noon rally was legal and that the Guard was violating their constitutional rights to freedom of speech and freedom of assembly. Brigadier General Robert O. Canterbury, the senior officer in charge of the Guards, believed that the assembly was illegal and that he had the authority to disperse it. Governor James Rhodes, however, did not actually sign the martial law decree banning assemblies until May 5, and he then declared it retroactive to April 30. A federal court later ruled that the demonstration was illegal.

Because of the highly charged emotional atmosphere on campus, Guards were subjected to extreme verbal abuse by students after dispersing the rally on the commons. Military experts testified later that tactical orders issued during the confrontation had placed the Guards in an unnecessarily vulnerable position. Some rocks were thrown at them, and some of the tear gas canisters they fired into the crowd were thrown back. Moreover, they had just come from riot duty in Cleveland, where they had been shot at while trying to contain violence during a truckers' strike. They had neither eaten properly nor had much sleep during the several days preceding the incident.

A Justice Department study, parts of which were disclosed by the *Akron Beacon Journal*, found that the shootings were unnecessary and urged the filing of criminal charges against the Guards. The President's Commission on Campus Unrest (the Scranton Commission) also concluded that the shootings were "unnecessary, unwarranted, and inexcusable."

Despite the fact that two federal investigations found the Ohio National Guard to be at fault, public opinion in Ohio ran strongly against any form of punishment for soldiers who had participated in the shootings. A special state grand jury convened by Governor Rhodes exonerated the Guards but indicted twenty-five other individuals, most of whom were students, for various offenses before the shootings. The judge in that proceeding had refused to admit testimony given earlier by Sylvester Del Corso, adjutant general of the Ohio National Guard, in the Justice Department investigation. In that testimony, in response to questions, General Del Corso stated no less than sixteen times that the Guard had no reason to use lethal force.

Substantial evidence indicates that the Nixon Administration attempted to obstruct investigation of the case and prosecution of the Guards, apparently for political reasons. It was later disclosed that the Nixon Administration had authorized a covert policy of taking illegal measures against antiwar and civil rights groups. In 1971, Attorney General John Mitchell officially closed the case. The Watergate scandal of 1973 weakened Nixon's control of the Justice Department, and Elliot Richardson, who succeeded John Mitchell as Attorney General, reopened the Kent State case. The reopening of the case in 1973 was at least partially prompted by a 1971 report by Peter Davies, in which Davies alleged that several Guards had decided in advance of the shooting to "punish" the students. Photographs lend plausibility to the Davies theory, but none of the Guards was ever questioned on the point.

In March of 1974, a federal grand jury indicted eight Guards on charges that they violated Section 242 of the United States Code, depriving the rights of the students to due process by summarily executing them. In November, a federal judge dismissed the charges, saying that prosecutors had failed to prove their case beyond a reasonable doubt. After a three-month-long civil trial in 1975, a jury decided not to award damages to victims and survivors, but that decision was set aside in 1977. The victims settled out of court shortly after the beginning of the second civil trial in 1979. The out-of-court settlement included a statement of regret signed by the defendants. Some of the victims regarded the statement as an apology, but the defendants and their lawyers disagreed.

Impact of Event

A Gallup poll published in *Newsweek* a few weeks after the incident at KSU showed that fifty-eight percent of the American public thought that the shootings were justifiable and that the Guard was not at fault. This may reflect the success of early efforts by officials to manage the news and to portray the demonstrators as a violent mob. The Scranton Commission, which interviewed many KSU students as part of its investigation, reported that many parents had supported the shootings, even to the point of hypothetically condoning the shooting of their own children if the children had participated in the demonstrations.

In a public statement made the day before the shootings, Governor Rhodes had characterized the protesters as "the worst type of people that we harbor in America. . . . I think that we're up against the strongest, well-trained, militant revolutionary group that has ever been assembled in America. . . . We are going to eradicate the problem, we're not going to treat the symptoms."

The governor's statement, in retrospect, seems out of line in reference to the comparatively staid student body of Kent State. Even though KSU had been a fairly conservative campus, however, its students were substantially radicalized by the shootings, as demonstrated by their subsequent public statements and writings.

The search for a "larger meaning" to the tragedy has proved inconclusive for most of those who were involved. Some believe that it marked the beginning of the end for the war in Southeast Asia. In this view, the event marked a climax of repressive tendencies in the government and so appalled the public that it generated a strong momentum for change. To others, this view not only is erroneous but also represents a kind of romantic idealism. For the idealists, the gunfire brought an end to the belief that one could stand up to one's government in dissent and ultimately prevail against injustice. In support of this interpretation, they cite the virtual end to campus protest that followed. Still others claim that the decline of campus protests is more properly associated with the end of the draft in 1973. This perspective sees student protest as a matter of self-interest that became unnecessary when the Selective Service stopped conscripting students.

At the very least, the shootings marked a rare historical case in which American soldiers killed American civilians engaged in protest of government policy. The shootings also touched off an unprecedented student strike, which shut down more than two hundred colleges and universities nationwide and disrupted classes in hundreds more. Although the strike was also partially in response to shootings at Jackson State University, in which two students were killed on May 12, the Jackson State incident never resulted in the same degree of controversy and litigation. Many observers have since pointed out that the Jackson State students were African American and the victims at Kent State were white. Thus, the Kent State incident indirectly may have shed light into another dark corner of American life.

Bibliography

Bills, Scott L., ed. *Kent State/May 4: Echoes Through a Decade*. Kent, Ohio: Kent State University Press, 1982. A collection of articles, interviews, and essays which attempts to deal with the broader historical and contextual issues. Some photographs and an extensive annotated bibliography.

Davies, Peter. *The Truth About Kent State: A Challenge to the American Conscience*. New York: Farrar, Straus & Giroux, 1973. A very complete photo sequence. Good reportorial material, but the author's intense emotional involvement makes some areas of the text polemical. The Davies study on which the book is based has been credited with the reopening of the federal investigation. Bibliography.

Gordon, William A. *The Fourth of May: Killings and Coverups at Kent State.* Buffalo, N.Y.: Prometheus Books, 1990. Good photo section, extensive source notes, chronology, and annotated bibliography. A very even-handed treatment of the event, the participants, and the subsequent coverage.

Kelner, Joseph, and James Munves. *The Kent State Coverup.* New York: Harper & Row, 1980. Kelner represented the plaintiffs in the court case demanding damages. Includes a detailed chronology, May 1 through May 4, and itemized details of charges and litigants. Appendix includes pertinent information about the Ohio National Guard and logs of the legal proceedings.

Warren, Bill, ed. *The Middle of the Country: The Events of May 4th as Seen by the Students and Faculty at Kent State University.* New York: Avon Books, 1970. A collection of personal essays by KSU students and faculty, published within a few weeks of the shootings. Some of the essayists were present at the May 4 demonstration, but many were not. The book's historical value is that it records the response of the students and shows how the event radicalized a conservative campus.

L. B. Shriver

Cross-References

Chicago Riots Mar the Democratic Convention (1968), p. 1446; Lieutenant Calley Is Court-Martialed for the Massacre at My Lai (1970), p. 1555; FBI and CIA Interference in the Civil Rights Movement Is Revealed (1971), p. 1595; Vietnam Releases United States Prisoners of War (1973), p. 1691; The United States Grants Amnesty to Vietnam War Draft Evaders (1974), p. 1769; The United Nations Issues a Conduct Code for Law Enforcement Officials (1979), p. 2040.

CONGRESS RATIFIES THE NATIONAL COUNCIL ON INDIAN OPPORTUNITY

Category of event: Indigenous peoples' rights
Time: August, 1970
Locale: Washington, D.C.

The National Council on Indian Opportunity gave Native Americans unprecedented top positions in the U.S. government and, for the first time, a voice in the formulation of a new federal Indian policy in the late 1960's and early 1970's

Principal personages:
LYNDON B. JOHNSON (1908-1973), the thirty-sixth president of the United States (1963-1969)
HUBERT H. HUMPHREY (1911-1978), the vice president of the United States, served as the first chair of the NCIO
RICHARD M. NIXON (1913-   ), the thirty-seventh president of the United States (1969-1974)
SPIRO T. AGNEW (1918-   ), the vice president of the United States who chaired the NCIO during the reformulation of federal Indian policy

Summary of Event

Since 1824, management of Native-American affairs in the United States had fallen to the Bureau of Indian Affairs (BIA), which became a subdivision of the U.S. Department of the Interior in 1849. For generations, Native Americans were governed by a BIA bureaucracy that was at best well-meaning and paternalistic and at worst corrupt and incompetent. The BIA answered to the U.S. Congress, not to the Native Americans it governed; thus, Native Americans had little voice in the formulation of federal Indian policy. Discontent with the operation of the BIA and the management of Native-American affairs grew increasingly stronger through time among Native Americans. Unhappy as they were with the BIA, however, they also feared that funding and management of Native-American programs might be "terminated" by the federal government; that is, they would be turned over to state governments that were even more difficult to deal with.

By the middle of the twentieth century, Native-American distress, frustration, suspicion, and anger toward the federal government, particularly the BIA, had increased enormously. More than four hundred leaders from sixty-seven Native-American tribes met at the University of Chicago in June, 1961, and formulated a "Declaration of Indian Purpose." This document contained proposals for numerous policies and programs. More important, it argued for "self-determination," allowing tribal groups to govern themselves on their own federally protected lands with programs organized and managed by Native Americans. The help of outside specialists and outside funding would be provided only when requested.

Although this declaration had no immediate impact upon the BIA or general fed-

eral Indian policy, in 1964 Native Americans were included in the Economic Opportunity Act. This act allowed Native Americans to propose, plan, and administer
economic opportunity programs on their reservations. In general, however, they remained discontented with federal Indian policy and the BIA. BIA services were
extremely inadequate, living conditions were deplorable, and federal paternalistic
policies were preventing them from taking control over their own lives.

In the late 1960's, a few bodies within the federal government began to sympathize with the growing Native-American desire for self-determination. Consequently,
President Lyndon B. Johnson set up two governmental task forces to study Native-
American affairs. Their reports, delivered in 1967, contained many program suggestions, along with the advice to involve Native Americans in the formulation of educational and economic policy and programs relevant to them. The White House then
began reformulating Indian policy.

As part of this reformulation, President Johnson created the National Council on
Indian Opportunity (NCIO) through an executive order on March 6, 1968, when he
delivered his "Message on Indian Affairs." Although Johnson's message produced
little perceptible change for Native Americans, it created the first federal agency in
which Native-American leaders participated on an equal footing with top-ranking
federal officials to evaluate, create, and administer federal Indian policy and programs.

Vice President Hubert Humphrey was named head of the NCIO, which was placed
within the vice president's office. The council consisted of seven cabinet members
and six Native-American members, all appointed by the president to serve two-year
terms. Native-American members of the council were to be selected on the basis of
leadership and in order to obtain geographical and tribal diversity within the council. A non-Indian executive director and a small staff of non-Indians and Native
Americans performed the council's daily activities.

The NCIO's functions were to ensure that Native Americans received the maximum benefits from programs offered by different government departments, coordinate programs within the various government departments, bureaus, and agencies
that affected Native Americans, assess the impact and progress of federal programs
pertaining to Native Americans, propose improvements in federal programs used by
Native Americans, and involve Native Americans in the formulation of federal Indian policy and programs.

The reaction of Native Americans to the NCIO was mixed. Many believed it was
merely another federal bureaucratic organization that would not contribute significantly to improving their condition. Tribal representatives, however, found the NCIO
much more sympathetic and willing to listen to their grievances than the BIA had
been.

The NCIO was an innovative and promising response by the executive branch of
the federal government to the rising demand by Native Americans that they be allowed to participate in the formulation of policies and programs that would affect
their lives, both on and off the reservations. It gave them a means of communicating

directly with the highest members of the federal government instead of trying to funnel information up through the BIA. Between its creation in 1968 and its congressional ratification in 1970, the NCIO served as a forum for the exchange and discussion of bureaucratic and Native-American ideas about the nature and specific component parts of federal Indian policy.

When Richard M. Nixon was elected president of the United States, it appeared that his administration might inaugurate a new federal Indian policy. Nixon had indicated during his campaign that he would not impose termination on Native Americans without their consent. The formation of the NCIO and talk of policy changes made Native Americans somewhat optimistic when Richard Nixon took office as president in 1969. Even as late as 1969, little real change had taken place.

On the other hand, during the 1960's Native Americans had become militant. Paralleling the evolution of the African-American protest movement in the 1950's and 1960's, Native Americans began holding nonviolent direct action protests, such as "fish-ins" in Washington State. In November, 1969, seventy-eight Native Americans from a mixture of tribes nonviolently occupied the San Francisco Bay island of Alcatraz, which originally had been Native-American land, and created a settlement there as a symbol of Native Americans' intent to secure their rights. Organized protests occurred across the United States, all with the common theme that Native Americans wanted an end of paternalistic federal rule, self-determination, security for their land and resource rights, and fulfillment of promises made in earlier treaties.

During the first year and a half of Nixon's administration, studies of Native-American questions begun during the Johnson Administration were continued by various government authorities. These studies were submitted to Congress in preparation for Nixon's reformulation of federal Indian policy. By the fall of 1969, the NCIO work load had increased as Native Americans began bypassing the BIA and taking their problems directly to the NCIO. Later, the NCIO was called upon to help negotiate a successful resolution to the occupation of Alcatraz. Consequently, among the recommendations made to the Nixon Administration in early 1970 was that the NCIO had proved its value and should be continued.

In early 1970, Native Americans had hopes that the Nixon Administration's new federal Indian policy, scheduled for unveiling in July, 1970, would respond to the concerns they were voicing to the NCIO. To make these concerns clear and to recommend solutions, the Native-American members of the NCIO delivered a "Statement of the Indian Members of the National Council on Indian Opportunity" to Vice President Spiro Agnew and the cabinet secretaries during an NCIO meeting at the White House on January 26, 1970. In this statement, they described the suspicion Native Americans felt toward the federal government and the BIA; the poor Native-American physical, social, educational, and economic conditions; and the poor services they were receiving from the BIA. They emphasized that they wanted improved services, an end to BIA paternalism, and self-determination. Lastly, they outlined specific goals to be met in the areas of Native-American health care, housing, education, employment, agriculture, water and other natural resource rights, economic development, land titles and reparation, urban relocation, and participation in policy-making.

The presentation of the Native-American members of the NCIO generated Vice President Spiro T. Agnew's concern. This and other NCIO work between 1968 and 1970 thus appears to have influenced the reformulation of federal Native-American policy during the Nixon Administration. In his historic "Message to Congress on Indian Affairs" delivered in July, 1970, President Nixon showed that the executive branch had been listening to Native Americans, the NCIO, and the experts studying the state of Native-American affairs. In the new federal Indian policy Nixon's message unveiled, it was evident that he had considered the NCIO recommendations, had put some into action, and was planning to move Native Americans closer to self-determination. Calling on Congress to work with the administration to bring about Native-American self-determination, he charged the NCIO with studying the problem of Native-American education further and with sponsoring field hearings throughout the country to establish dialogue between the administration and individual Native Americans.

The National Council on Indian Opportunity, which had been in operation since its creation by executive order in 1968, was ratified by Congress in late August, 1970. At the same time, it was increased to eight Native-American members. The U.S. attorney general was also added to the council.

Impact of Event

The NCIO was created during a time of change in federal Indian policy. One facet of this policy change was to ensure that Native Americans were hired and appointed to top government positions, so that they could represent themselves instead of being represented by the BIA, as in the past.

Creation of the NCIO and appointment of Native Americans to its membership was one aspect of this new approach. It marked the first time that Native Americans had worked on an equal level with top government officials. Serving as a mediator between the administration and Native Americans, the NCIO enabled many Native-American activists to express their views about the formulation of the new, and very significant, federal Native-American policy. The NCIO also opened lines of communication between the federal government and the Native Americans occupying Alcatraz and helped bring a resolution to that protest movement.

Policy and legislative suggestions made by the NCIO also were realized during Nixon's administration. When Nixon described his policy in July, 1970, he specifically recommended adoption of many of the organizational and program changes that had been put forward by the NCIO in its January 26, 1970, statement.

Within the year, action was taken to follow through on the recommendations made by the NCIO and others with regard to Nixon's federal Indian policy. In addition to helping Nixon's staff prepare legislative bills, in one series of hearings the NCIO brought the bills to Native-American leaders around the country and asked for their input, revisions, and additions. In a second series, held from October through December, 1970, the NCIO gathered their reactions and suggestions for revisions and new proposals. Lastly, the NCIO helped introduce bills into Congress.

In the long run, the results of the work of the NCIO varied. Some concrete changes were made. For example, the NCIO helped develop a plan, which was implemented in December, 1970, to return the Blue Lake region to the Taos Indians in New Mexico. In addition, with input from the NCIO, the BIA undertook structural, procedural, and philosophic changes that improved service to Native Americans and allowed them to achieve self-determination. Some of the federal proposals suggested by the NCIO, such as the concept of the "Indian Desk," were implemented. In addition, the NCIO helped develop proposals for providing federal services to urban Native Americans. These changes, along with the bills proposed by the Nixon Administration with the input of the NCIO, set the stage for the realization of Native-American self-determination.

The NCIO was disbanded during Nixon's administration, but by 1975 Congress had enacted many of the programs it had suggested and reviewed during its existence. Then, in 1975, the "Indian Self-Determination Act" was passed by Congress, giving Native-American tribes the option of operating BIA and Indian Health Service programs under contract with the government. The NCIO thus had a hand in securing increased Native-American control over reservation life and tribal programs in the late 1960's and early 1970's.

Bibliography

Jackson, Curtis E., and Marcia J. Galli. *A History of the Bureau of Indian Affairs and Its Activities Among Indians.* San Francisco: R & E Research Associates, 1977. Chapter 17, "Indian Self-Determination," concisely describes the state of Native-American policy and self-determination at the beginning of the Nixon Administration, outlines Nixon's approach, and summarizes some of the results of his proposals in the areas of Native-American recruitment, education, finance, and land restorations.

Josephy, Alvin M., Jr. *Red Power: The American Indians' Fight for Freedom.* New York: American Heritage, 1971. A collection of sometimes-hard-to-find documents, addresses, essays, and other primary materials pertaining to the Native Americans' fight for self-determination in the late 1960's and 1970's. The excellent introduction and preface to each document help place the Native-American fight for self-determination and each selection in historical perspective. Several documents pertaining to the creation and activity of the NCIO are included.

Levitan, Sar A., and Barbara Hetrick. *Big Brother's Indian Programs—With Reservations.* New York: McGraw-Hill, 1971. Although it provides no specific information on the NCIO, this work contains good historical background and a wealth of information on the state of federal Native-American programs on the reservations in the early years of the Nixon Administration. It describes programs covering education, health, community organization, and natural and human resources of Native Americans.

Prucha, Francis Paul. *Documents of United States Indian Policy.* Lincoln: University of Nebraska Press, 1975. A very useful collection of documents pertaining to federal Native-American policy. Prucha's work contains excerpts from the texts of President Johnson's March 6, 1968, message to Congress on the problems of the American Indian as well as President Nixon's July 8, 1970, message on Indian affairs, among others relevant to termination, self-determination, and the NCIO.

Taylor, Theodore W. *The Bureau of Indian Affairs.* Boulder, Colo.: Westview Press, 1984. Provides a wealth of information on the BIA, the organization within whose grasp Native Americans lived, worked, and generally existed. The creation of the NCIO, its background and context, and the recommendations it made cannot be understood completely without understanding the BIA and its operations. Describes the programs that were put in effect after the change of federal Native-American policy and gives information on changes they have produced in Native-American life.

Martha Ellen Webb

Cross-References

Intellectuals Form the Society of American Indians (1911), p. 121; The Indian Reorganization Act Offers Autonomy to American Indians (1934), p. 497; U.S. Government Encourages Native Americans to Settle in Cities (1950's), p. 820; Government Policies Seek to End the Special Status of Native Americans (1953), p. 897; The Blue Lake Region in New Mexico Is Returned to the Taos Pueblo (1970), p. 1573; Native Americans Occupy Wounded Knee (1973), p. 1709.

CANADA INVOKES THE WAR MEASURES ACT AGAINST SEPARATISTS IN QUEBEC

Categories of event: Political freedom and civil rights
Time: October 16, 1970
Locale: Quebec, Canada

Canada, a nation with a nonviolent political tradition and democratic freedoms, confronted separatist terrorism by suspending civil liberties in its French-speaking province

Principal personages:
> PIERRE ELLIOTT TRUDEAU (1919-   ), the prime minister of Canada, a French-Canadian liberal-federalist opposed to separatism
> ROBERT BOURASSA (1933-   ), the premier of Quebec
> JÉRÔME CHOQUETTE (1928-   ), the minister of justice in Quebec's provincial government
> PIERRE LAPORTE (1921-1970), the minister of labor in Quebec's government, a terrorist kidnap victim
> JAMES CROSS (1921-   ), a British trade commissioner in Montreal, kidnapped by terrorists
> JEAN DRAPEAU (1916-   ), the mayor of Montreal

Summary of Event

Political violence and upheavals are very rare in Canadian history. In spite of the country's divisive tensions, generated by regionalism and by cultural and ethnic diversity, Canada has avoided the dramatic, bloody resolutions of conflict experienced by its neighbor, the United States. As a result, many Canadians have proudly referred to their country as "the peaceable kingdom." Canada's tradition of liberty, democratic stability, and tranquillity in the face of regional and cultural diversity was severely tested in October, 1970. Contributing factors to the October crisis were a rebellious trend associated with this historical period and the long-standing grievances of Canada's French-speaking community. Francophones, about 25 percent of Canada's population and largely concentrated in Quebec province, had always waged an uphill struggle against assimilation into the dominant Anglophone culture.

In spite of some gains by Quebec's French-Canadians in the 1960's, Anglophones, mainly based in Montreal and composing barely 20 percent of the province's population, still exercised disproportionate political and economic power. The phrase "white niggers of America" was employed by a Francophone radical in his famous autobiographical description of the oppression and social injustice felt by himself and many of his compatriots as second-class citizens in their own land.

Some Francophone nationalists abandoned the province's major political parties to form movements advocating much greater autonomy or independence for Quebec. In 1968, two of these groups organized the *Parti québécois* (PQ) under René Lévesque. The PQ soon became a major vehicle for achieving separatist-nationalist goals through the legal capture of political power. Small numbers of frustrated radicals chose the more extreme course of revolutionary terrorism.

In February, 1963, the *Front de libération du Québec* (FLQ) was founded. Inspired by Third World liberation struggles, the FLQ's long-term goals were socialist revolution and an independent Quebec. Canada's FLQ operated mainly in Montreal and probably never had more than a few dozen militants or about ten active terrorists at any given time. Ad hoc cells appeared and appropriated the name FLQ when militants came up with ideas for operations. There was little or no communication between them. From 1963 to 1970, FLQ groups conducted about thirty-three armed robberies and ninety bomb attacks against military installations and various symbols of Anglo imperialism. These actions caused seven deaths and forty-nine injuries. By 1970, more than twenty FLQ members were imprisoned on criminal, not political, charges. The FLQ's smallness and extremely diffuse nature made it a difficult target for police to eradicate; its constant reappearance following capture and elimination of entire cells gave the appearance of a much larger and well-organized hydra-headed conspiracy.

The period from 1968 to 1970 was one of growing unrest and violence in Montreal. An upswing in FLQ terrorism, several traumatic labor strikes, and some unruly demonstrations by political radicals had nervous Montreal city officials and provincial leaders feeling threatened and prone to exaggerate all rumors and signs of revolutionary activity.

On the morning of October 5, 1970, the FLQ moved beyond its previous tactics when it kidnapped British Trade Commissioner James Cross from his Montreal residence. The kidnappers demanded the release of twenty-three political prisoners and their safe passage to Algeria or Cuba. The October crisis was under way.

Quebec's government, under Liberal Premier Robert Bourassa, worked closely throughout the crisis with the federal government, headed by Pierre Trudeau. Militant Quebec nationalists and separatists had not welcomed the ascendency of Trudeau, a French-Canadian native of Quebec, to the post of prime minister in 1968. This intellectual, urbane politician was a dedicated liberal-federalist who viewed Quebec separatism as a reactionary, inward-looking course. From the start, Trudeau adamantly opposed any concession to terrorist blackmail.

Feeling strong pressure from Ottawa, Quebec's justice minister, Jérôme Choquette, basically rejected all FLQ demands on October 10. In exchange for Cross's release, Choquette offered only parole for five prisoners who were eligible and safe passage abroad for the kidnappers. Fifteen minutes after this statement was broadcast, a new FLQ group, acting independently, snatched Quebec Labor Minister Pierre Laporte from his suburban Montreal home.

The kidnapping of the second most important figure in Quebec's government personalized the crisis, creating fear and panic among many of his colleagues. Bourassa momentarily wavered on the issue of a prisoner-hostage exchange but held firm. Trudeau remained uncompromising throughout. He declared that a "parallel power" would never be allowed to dictate to Canada's elected government and denounced "weak-kneed bleeding hearts" afraid to take measures to defend freedom.

As the crisis reached a climax, there were pro-FLQ mass demonstrations in Montreal and some statements of sympathy for the FLQ's political manifesto. Ottawa officials believed that the situation in Quebec was becoming chaotic and that some definitive assertion of federal power was crucial. Mayor Jean Drapeau and other Montreal city officials warned Ottawa about a threatening, organized revolutionary conspiracy. According to these sources, a state of "apprehended insurrection" existed in Quebec, requiring extraordinary police powers and assistance from the national government. On October 14, Premier Bourassa requested that the Canadian armed forces be sent into Quebec.

On October 15, the federal government dispatched troops to Montreal and a few other localities to protect public buildings and prominent individuals. Trudeau had already deployed the army in Ottawa. Bourassa offered the kidnappers the same limited terms as had Choquette and demanded a reply by 4:00 P.M. on October 16. As soon as this deadline passed, the federal government invoked the War Measures Act, a relic of World War I which had last been used in World War II. The act gave the cabinet power to enact regulations allowing arrest, detention, censorship, and deportation in conditions of war, invasion, and insurrection. Under this authority, the cabinet introduced measures which banned the FLQ, making membership or evidence of association with that organization a retroactive offense. The Royal Canadian Mounted Police (RCMP) received extraordinary powers which overrode legal safeguards, permitting the search of premises without a warrant and arbitrary arrest on mere suspicion. The right of habeas corpus was suspended, allowing suspects to be held incommunicado without charges, legal counsel, or bail for up to twenty-one days. Two days after this act was proclaimed, Laporte's corpse was found in a car trunk.

Civil liberties were suspended in Quebec until April 30, 1971. Police raids hit every part of Quebec with more than forty-six hundred house searches involving confiscation of property, especially reading material. Around five hundred citizens were jailed. Armed with such broad, open-ended authority, police committed excesses. A federal cabinet minister's home was searched by mistake. No distinction was made between dissent and sedition on the RCMP's list of suspects. Many prominent persons were arrested solely on the basis of known or suspected political sympathies. More than 460 of those arrested were released, acquitted, or simply never prosecuted. Eighteen were convicted; sixteen of ordinary criminal charges (mostly for being linked somehow to Laporte's kidnapping or murder) and only two for an offense under the emergency provisions.

The act applied throughout Canada, and some arrests occurred outside Quebec. Freedom of expression was curtailed in British Columbia's schools. For individual Canadians, this was a tense period.

Impact of Event

The results and wisdom of the Trudeau government's actions are controversial subjects. Laporte's murder silenced vocal support for the FLQ in Quebec. Canadians, including Quebecers, immediately rallied behind Trudeau, who enjoyed hero status for his firmness and decisiveness in combating terrorist outrages. When the police closed in on Cross's five captors in early December, the kidnappers released him in exchange for a flight to Cuba. Within a few years, all but one had returned and received short prison terms. At the end of December, police found the hideout of Laporte's abductors, who got more severe sentences. Thereafter, FLQ activity tapered off and eventually disappeared. Canada returned to its normal status as one of the world's most tolerant and free societies.

On the negative side were the abuses of innocent persons' civil rights, the government's questionable political judgment in invoking unneeded and arguably excessive powers based on faulty intelligence, and its efforts to manipulate public opinion with misleading or exaggerated rumors. Police uncovered no evidence of an apprehended insurrection. Trudeau, whose early career was devoted to defending political dissidents, saw his reputation as a civil libertarian devastated.

The lives, employment, and families of innocent individuals were traumatically disrupted. No apology was ever made, and the public never held its leaders accountable. Angered by the Quebec situation, the majority applauded when their government took forceful action and turned a blind eye to the fact that no apprehended insurrection existed. In 1971, however, Quebec's ombudsman investigated complaints and awarded compensation in 104 cases involving police brutality, damage to property or reputation, and unjust conditions of confinement.

In Quebec, the crisis dealt a short-term setback to the separatist *Parti québécois*, which lost members. The PQ, however, gained over the longer term. The elimination of separatist terrorism in Quebec politics made the PQ a more respectable alternative. Furthermore, the fact that English-Canadians so zealously cheered the use of the War Measures Act against a French-Canadian movement, unpopular and tiny though it was, drove many intellectuals into the separatist fold. The PQ's support rose, and from 1976 to 1985, a PQ government under René Lévesque held power. In a 1980 referendum, Quebecers rejected the choice of negotiating a new relationship with the rest of Canada by a 60 percent to 40 percent margin. Nevertheless, by 1990, the separatist option had revived because of a dispute between Quebec and other provinces concerning Quebec's status in Canada's new constitutional setup.

A positive side effect of the 1970 events may be the political lessons which thoughtful Canadians have pondered and debated. Among the most important issues is the scope of powers a democratic government needs to defend its society and the proper use of this authority. The controversial War Measures Act remained in the government's arsenal. Still, the experience of 1970 likely influenced Trudeau's decision to place restrictions on its use by future governments in the Charter of Rights associated with his 1982 constitution. Lessons learned from the October crisis are important to the preservation of Canada's free society and are instructive to other democracies.

Bibliography

Auf der Maur, Nick, and Robert Chodos, eds. *Quebec: A Chronicle, 1968-1972.* Toronto: James Lewis and Samuel, 1972. A collection of six articles which deal with the crisis and events preceding and following it. Auf der Maur, an Anglophone radio journalist, was one of the approximately five hundred persons detained by police in Quebec. Left-of-center perspective. Includes appendices containing an annotated list of major individuals and organizations mentioned in the text and a useful chronology of events.

Berger, Thomas. "Democracy and Terror: October, 1970." In *Fragile Freedoms: Human Rights and Dissent in Canada.* Toronto: Clarke, Irwin, 1981. Berger, a distinguished Canadian academic, takes the position that invocation of the War Measures Act was not warranted by the circumstances. The author argues that the government was justified in responding firmly but could have relied on ordinary police powers and criminal law combined with a strong defense of civil liberty. Bibliography, index, and chapter endnotes.

Fournier, Louis. *F.L.Q.: The Anatomy of an Underground Movement.* Translated by Edward Baxter. Toronto: NC Press, 1984. This is the most complete study of the revolutionary terrorist organization which precipitated the October crisis. The author is a Quebec radio broadcast journalist who is sympathetic to some FLQ political goals while rejecting terrorist tactics. Includes photos, select bibliography, index, and list of names of organizations.

Gellner, John. *Bayonets in the Streets: Urban Guerrilla at Home and Abroad.* Don Mills, Ontario: Collier-Macmillan Canada, 1974. This monograph includes a useful analysis of the FLQ. Chapter 3 examines the FLQ before the crisis, and Chapter 4 deals with its role and the government's exaggeration of the threat it posed. Critical of the government's handling of the affair. Bibliography and index.

Gwyn, Richard. "Just Watch Me." In *The Northern Magus.* Toronto: McClelland and Stewart, 1980. This popular and fascinating biography of Prime Minister Pierre Trudeau discusses the October crisis and the prime minister's role in the controversial affair in an even-handed style. Gwyn notes the positive and negative consequences Trudeau experienced due to his firm handling of the situation. Index.

Haggart, Ron, and Aubrey E. Golden. *Rumors of War.* Toronto: James Lorimer and Co., 1979. This work by two civil libertarians contains a detailed summary of events leading to the October crisis. The focus is on civil rights issues. The authors present their critique of the government in an objective, measured manner. Contains a thoughtful introduction by former Conservative Party leader Robert Stanfield. Illustrations, bibliography, and appendices with relevant documents.

Pelletier, Gerard. *The October Crisis.* Translated by Joyce Marshall. Toronto: McClelland and Stewart, 1971. One of the very rare defenses of the Trudeau government's invocation of the War Measures Act. Pelletier is a longtime political associate of Trudeau from Quebec and was secretary of state in the government during this affair. Pelletier voted to use this measure with great reluctance. Ulti-

mate blame for the unfortunate results is placed on the FLQ. Index.
Smith, Denis. *Bleeding Hearts, Bleeding Country: Canada and the Quebec Crisis.* Edmonton, Canada: Hurtig, 1971. A forceful and sometimes passionate condemnation of Trudeau's handling of the kidnappers and invocation of the War Measures Act. The author is a Canadian academic. Contains a useful analysis of the FLQ's political aims. Includes bibliography, footnotes, and index.
Tarnopolsky, Walter Surma. "The War Measures Act and the Canadian Bill of Rights." In *The Canadian Bill of Rights.* Toronto: Macmillan of Canada, 1978. A Canadian scholar provides a good discussion of the legal and civil rights issues raised by the October crisis. Provides useful background information on the War Measures Act and its few uses by Canadian governments since it originated during World War I. Includes chapter end notes, bibliography, and index.

David A. Crain

Cross-References

THE MOSCOW HUMAN RIGHTS COMMITTEE IS FOUNDED

Categories of event: Civil rights and political freedom
Time: November 4, 1970
Locale: Moscow, Union of Soviet Socialist Republics

The Moscow Human Rights Committee played a major role in monitoring and publicizing Soviet violations of civil and political rights

Principal personages:
VALERY CHALIDZE (1938-   ), a committee cofounder, physicist, and author
ANDREI SAKHAROV (1921-1989), one of the committee's founders, a leading nuclear physicist, and a Nobel Peace Prize recipient
ANDREI TVERDOKHLEBOV (1940-   ), a Soviet physicist, cofounder of the Moscow Human Rights Committee and of Moscow's Amnesty International chapter

Summary of Event

Under the rule of Leonid Brezhnev (1964-1982), numerous types of Soviet dissenters existed, religious groups, professional groups, and national groups among them. The Moscow Human Rights Committee came to play an important role in facilitating communication among the different activists and in publicizing incidents of Soviet repression to the West.

Committee initiator Valery Chalidze is a major chronicler of the human rights movement. He traces the origin of that movement to a December 5, 1965, demonstration in Moscow with two slogans: "Respect the Constitution, the Basic Law of the USSR" and "We Demand That the Sinyavsky-Daniel Trial Be Public." Andrei Sinyavsky and Yuri Daniel were authors brought to trial for writing work critical of the Soviet Union and for smuggling it to the West for publication. The trial was not public (although its procedural flaws were soon revealed). This trial, the convictions for "anti-Soviet agitation and propaganda" that followed, the Soviet invasion of Czechoslovakia, and further arrests of prominent dissidents served as catalysts for the intellectuals who formed the Moscow Human Rights Committee.

Two additional acts of dissent inspired the Moscow Human Rights Committee: the publication of the *Chronicle of Current Events*, an anonymously published journal of the Soviet human rights movement (beginning in April, 1968), and formation of the Initiative Group for the Defense of Human Rights in May, 1969, when fifteen citizens petitioned the United Nations regarding a wide range of civil rights violations.

The Moscow Human Rights Committee was set up as a "creative," "nonpolitical" organization, and pledged to operate within the laws of the Soviet Union. Its

"Statement of Purposes" expressed satisfaction with Soviet human rights achievements since 1953. It identified three aims: to consult with the state in developing human rights guarantees, to assist individuals interested in investigating "theoretical aspects" of the human rights question, and to conduct civic education regarding international and Soviet human rights guarantees. Chalidze acknowledged an additional function: The committee contributed to the exercise of rights in unaccustomed areas, often resulting in unlawful persecution by the authorities.

Formation of the committee (publicized through issuance of the "Statement of Purposes" and a November 11 press conference at Chalidze's apartment) extended its founders' human rights activities. They had issued appeals in behalf of General Pyotr Grigorenko (when, in 1969, he was incarcerated in a mental hospital for the second time) and Zhores Medvedev (a biologist who was confined in a mental hospital for a period in 1970). The committee reflected the contributions of its three leaders, all of whom were trained as physicists: Valery Chalidze, Andrei Sakharov, and Andrei Tverdokhlebov. Its activities ranged from sponsorship of symposia on human rights issues to publication of a typewritten journal (*Social Problems*) to issuance of detailed analyses of human rights issues. The committee's primary focus was on Soviet conditions, although it also came to the defense of American political prisoner Angela Davis.

The committee was Chalidze's idea, and it met in his apartment. Chalidze had an extensive record of human rights activity. He had a thorough knowledge of the Soviet procedural and criminal codes and provided legal assistance to the public, sometimes with the assent of other committee members but more often on his own. He assisted individuals seeking to emigrate from the Soviet Union, prisoners seeking to appeal incorrect sentencing, and religious communities seeking to acquire or change their legal status. The government made it increasingly difficult for Chalidze to pursue his career as a physicist, and he resigned from his institute in 1971. In September of 1972 he resigned from the committee. When he visited the West later that year to speak at Georgetown University, the Supreme Soviet took away his citizenship, forcing him into exile in the United States.

Sakharov provided the committee with legitimacy through his status as an academician and nuclear physicist. Sakharov's "turning point" occurred in 1967, when he wrote Leonid Brezhnev on behalf of dissidents Alexander Ginzburg, Yuri Galanskov, Alexei Dobrovolsky, and Vera Lashkova. For his protests, Sakharov lost his post as department head and received a reduction in salary. In October of 1970, Sakharov attended his first trial, in which Revolt Pimenov and Boris Vail were charged with circulating *samizdat* (typewritten or copied materials disseminated by dissidents). The hypocrisy affected Sakharov and brought him closer to Chalidze. For Sakharov, the committee served a valuable social function. He wrote in his *Memoirs* (1990) that "not having been spoiled by an abundance of friends in my life, I prized this opportunity for human contact." It was during a visit to Chalidze that Sakharov met Elena Bonner, whom he would later marry.

Tverdokhlebov was a physicist and the son of a former Soviet deputy minister of culture. In December of 1972, he left the committee. He later founded "Group 73" and served as secretary of the Soviet Amnesty International group. The indictment at Tverdokhlebov's 1976 trial summarized his human rights activities before, during, and after his work with the Moscow Human Rights Committee. In 1970, he signed a letter supportive of the Nobel Committee's award to Aleksandr Solzhenitsyn. He helped assemble documents about political uses of psychiatry and contacted officials of the World Psychiatric Congress and International League for Human Rights. The Soviet government described Tverdokhlebov's activities from 1970 to 1975 as criminal: "the drawing up [reproduction and distribution] of collective letters, declarations and appeals which contained libels against the Soviet system."

The three founders were later joined by geophysicist Grigory Podyapolsky and mathematician Igor Shafarevich, a Lenin Prize recipient and corresponding member of the Academy of Sciences. Shafarevich authored a 1972 report on religious legislation for the committee. Committee members differed somewhat in orientation. Chalidze emphasized law. Sakharov hoped that his influence could be used to pressure the government to reform. Sakharov and Shafarevich urged a focus on major issues (such as psychiatric abuse and religious persecution); they perceived that Chalidze and Tverdokhlebov were drawn to paradoxical and extreme legal points. Because the legal minds best understood the committee's bylaws, it was they who set the agenda.

The committee provided thorough analyses of human rights questions. They addressed the political uses of psychiatry and urged the World Psychiatric Association to take action. Chalidze prepared an opinion "On the Rights of Persons Declared Mentally Ill." This was used by the full committee in issuing a statement on July 3, 1971, that warned of "serious social danger in a broad interpretation of the concepts 'mental illness' and 'mental deficiency' while procedures for contesting application of these concepts are far from perfect." The committee was concerned that the state could use these concepts to restrict the rights of individuals or groups. Committee members were displeased by the hesitance of the international psychiatric community to recognize abuses. The committee (then composed of Podyapolsky, Sakharov, and Shafarevich) expressed its disappointment with the International Committee of Psychotherapists' inaction, claiming that the psychotherapists' desire for "rapprochement . . . should be contingent on the renunciation . . . of actions which outrage the conscience of mankind." Not acting was said to encourage expanded psychiatric repression and to betray inmates in psychiatric prisons. The World Psychiatric Association was also slow to respond to reports of psychiatric abuse.

Committee meetings included informative seminars. Topics included the right of the Tatars to return to their native Crimea from the republics to which they had been exiled in 1945, resettlement of the Mekshi (a Turkic people deported from the Georgian-Turkish frontier region), laws on "parasitism," the meaning of the term "political prisoner," and the right to legal defense. Often a committee member would draft a statement, and sometimes the statement would then be redrafted as a Committee document. The committee issued appeals to governments, to human rights organizations, and to world public opinion. These appeals usually addressed human rights in the Soviet Union (for example, the 1973 appeal protesting the arrest of dissident writer Andrei Amalrik) but occasionally dealt with events outside the Soviet Union (for example, a 1972 appeal concerning the imprisonment of Angela Davis in the United States). Committee appeals also publicized the existence of Russian Orthodox prisoners of conscience—the Orthodox church's close relationship with the Soviet government prevented it from doing so. The committee's emphasis on universal human rights was not the most common form of Soviet dissent. Most dissenters sought rights for their own national, religious, or social group. The committee's role was different: Its members sought a sweeping liberalization of Soviet society so that all citizens would be protected from arbitrary state action.

Impact of Event

The committee was small in number but powerful in impact. With other groups, it enhanced Moscow's central, coordinating role as nucleus of the Soviet human rights movement. Consequences of its activities included repression by the Soviet government, a mixed reception from Soviet citizens, and recognition by international human rights advocates. Leonid Brezhnev's Soviet government used an elaborate system of rewards and punishments to discourage dissent. Moscow Human Rights Committee members were subject to ostracism, harassment, imprisonment, economic sanctions, and exile.

KGB agents searched Chalidze's home, confiscating allegedly anti-Soviet materials. These included texts of United Nations documents and human rights journals. Chalidze was blacklisted as a physicist and put in a precarious financial position. When questioned by the KGB in 1972, Sakharov was told that his membership in the committee was in and of itself a slander against the state. He was told that he was "not morally sound," an ominous phrase that suggested the prospect of psychiatric treatment, used by Soviet authorities on several prominent dissidents. Solzhenitsyn was banished from the country in February of 1974.

The committee was ridiculed by some Soviet citizens for criticizing the Soviet government and condemned by some Soviet dissidents for its efforts to work within established legal channels. Sakharov indicated that Nobel laureate Solzhenitsyn, a corresponding member of the committee, came to see its formalistic approach as a "waste of time."

The Moscow Human Rights Committee's efforts were encouraged by a growing international human rights movement. In 1971, the International League for Human Rights (headquartered in New York) welcomed the committee as an affiliate. The committee established contact with many other groups, among them the International Institute for Human Rights, located in Strasbourg, France. The committee received extensive press coverage, surpassing its founders' expectations. The Voice of America, the British Broadcasting Corporation, and Deutsche Welle offered extensive reporting. Committee members enjoyed some protection from the authorities as a result of their status and were adept in attracting coverage from the Western press.

The lack of observable immediate effects only strengthened the resolve of committee members. The committee's founders did not end their human rights activities even after the committee drifted apart in 1974. Tverdokhlebov worked with Group 73 and Amnesty International until his trial in 1976. Sakharov continued to write and protest but declined to cosponsor the formation of the Moscow Helsinki Group in 1976. He preferred to be free of organizational constraints. Sakharov's continued public protests resulted in his exile to Gorky from 1980 to 1986. During that period, he spent 294 days alone in the hospital, only ten of them voluntarily. Chalidze continued his prolific writing on Soviet law and policy, edited the *Chronicle of the Defense of Human Rights in the USSR*, and received a prestigious MacArthur Foundation Award.

In the late 1980's and early 1990's, the Soviet Union liberalized and Sakharov was acclaimed as the "conscience of the nation." The thinking of the liberals who sought to protect the individual from arbitrary state action was now dominant. This was largely a result of the leadership of Soviet leader Mikhail Gorbachev, whose policy of *glasnost* (openness) generally reflected the principles of the Moscow Human Rights Committee. The committee stood for the proposition that it is ultimately an informed public, not solely the government, that promotes human rights and the rule of law.

Bibliography

Alexeyeva, Ludmilla. *Soviet Dissent.* Middleton, Conn.: Wesleyan University Press, 1985. This book is an excellent encyclopedic description of the many forms of Soviet dissent. The author was a founding member of the Moscow Helsinki Group and successfully distinguishes the goals and tactics of the Moscow Human Rights Committee from other groups. Index and photographs.

Chalidze, Valerii. *To Defend These Rights.* New York: Random House, 1974. Chalidze's book exemplifies his legalist approach to human rights. A well-written, readable argument that dissenters had the law on their side. Extensive appendices documenting the Soviet human rights struggle and an index.

Chronicle of Current Events. Soviet periodical of the human rights movement. A defiant, secretly written and self-published journal which gained a reputation for accuracy. Describes the activities and harassment of members of the Human Rights Committee and other groups. Published and disseminated in the West by Amnesty International.

Rubenstein, Joshua. *Soviet Dissidents: Their Struggle for Human Rights.* Boston: Beacon Press, 1985. This book offers a lively, very readable description of Soviet dissent. Index and bibliography.

Sakharov, Andrei. *Memoirs.* New York: Alfred A. Knopf, 1990. This book traces Sakharov's career and provides a sensitive description of Sakharov's interaction with other committee members. One chapter details the committee's founding; other parts shed light on differences among committee members. Index.

Saunders, George, Comp. *Samizdat: Voices of the Soviet Opposition.* New York:

Monad Press, 1974. This reader includes the text of the Human Rights Committee's "Statement of Purposes." It also includes documents from dissenters throughout Soviet history. The foreword by Saunders identifies distinct currents among the Soviet opposition. Index.

Shatz, Marshall S. *Soviet Dissent in Historical Perspective.* Cambridge, England: Cambridge University Press, 1980. Insightful comparisons among the Human Rights Committee members and previous dissidents in Soviet and Russian history. Discusses Sakharov as an exemplar of liberal dissent, in contrast with Medvedev and Solzhenitsyn. Notes the prominent role of natural scientists. Index.

Arthur Blaser

Cross-References

The United Nations Adopts the Universal Declaration of Human Rights (1948), p. 789; Amnesty International Is Founded (1961), p. 1119; Solzhenitsyn Is Expelled from the Soviet Union (1974), p. 1764; The Helsinki Agreement Offers Terms for International Cooperation (1975), p. 1806; Sakharov Is Awarded the Nobel Peace Prize (1975), p. 1852; Carter Makes Human Rights a Central Theme of Foreign Policy (1977), p. 1903; Soviet Citizens' Group Investigates Political Abuses of Psychiatry (1977), p. 1909; Misuse of Psychiatry Is Addressed by the Declaration of Hawaii (1977), p. 1926; Gorbachev Initiates a Policy of *Glasnost* (1985), p. 2249.

LIEUTENANT CALLEY IS COURT-MARTIALED FOR THE MASSACRE AT MY LAI

Category of event: Atrocities and war crimes
Time: November 17, 1970-March 29, 1971
Locale: Fort Benning, Georgia

William Calley was convicted of murdering twenty-two Vietnamese and was the only person convicted of any crime in the aftermath of the My Lai massacre

Principal personages:

WILLIAM L. CALLEY (1943-   ), a second lieutenant in command of a platoon of Company C at My Lai

FRANK A. BARKER (1928-1968), the commander of the unit that conducted the operation on My Lai

STEVEN K. BROOKS (1942?-1968), a second lieutenant in command of a platoon of Company C at My Lai

ERNEST MEDINA (1936-   ), a captain in command of Company C of Task Force Barker; immediate superior of lieutenants Calley and Brooks

WILLIAM R. PEERS (1914-   ), conducted the official Army inquiry of the My Lai incident

HUGH THOMPSOM (1947?-   ), a combat helicopter pilot involved in the assault on My Lai

SAMUEL W. KOSTER (1919-   ), the commander of the Americal Division

Summary of Event

The My Lai massacre occurred during the first hours of a March 16, 1968, operation carried out by a battalion-sized unit, code-named Task Force Barker, of the Americal Division of the U.S. Army. This unit, comprising three infantry companies (A, B, and C) supported by artillery, helicopters, and coastal patrol craft, was intended to sweep between two hundred and four hundred Viet Cong from a group of hamlets in the Son My subdistrict of Quang Ngai Province in South Vietnam.

Following the surprise Tet offensive launched by the Viet Cong on January 31, American commanders sought to reestablish control and to destroy known Viet Cong units. The Americal Division, including Task Force Barker, had been searching around Quang Ngai in February and March but encountered few Viet Cong.

On March 15, Lieutenant Colonel Frank A. Barker announced a three-day sweep against the Viet Cong 48th Local Forces battalion operating in and around a large, coastal fishing village, My Lai (1). This was the third such operation against this village since February. Barker planned to move his three infantry companies into place by helicopter about 8:00 A.M., following a short artillery barrage. Helicopters were to engage fleeing or fighting Viet Cong. Offshore, small Navy patrol craft blocked any escape through the eastern seaward end of the noose.

Company C landed at 7:30 A.M., just west of another hamlet, My Lai (4). Lieutenant William L. Calley's platoon of twenty-five men moved first through the hamlet's south section; Lieutenant Stephen Brooks's platoon went through the north. Lieutenant Larry LaCroix's platoon remained in reserve near the landing zone.

The men of Company C expected to encounter two armed Viet Cong companies. Captain Ernest Medina, commander of Company C, had instructed his officers to burn the houses and destroy the livestock, crops, and foodstuffs in My Lai (4). Several men from Company C later testified that Captain Medina, who stayed at the landing zone, had specifically instructed them to kill civilians found in the hamlets. Medina denied such statements.

Calley's platoon slaughtered two large groups of villagers sometime between 7:50 A.M. and 9:15 A.M. In one instance, more than twenty people were gunned down on a pathway; in another, around 150 were systematically slaughtered with machine gun and small arms fire in a ditch about one hundred meters east of the hamlet. Soldiers later testified that Calley ordered them to kill their civilian captives. Men from all three platoons of Company C committed murder, rape, and other atrocities that morning.

About 8:30 A.M. Brooks's platoon turned northward on Medina's command to recover the bodies of two Viet Cong killed by a helicopter gunship. Brooks's platoon then entered Binh Tay, a hamlet a few hundred meters away, where they raped and murdered villagers before rejoining Company C around 10:00 A.M.

While this killing was going on, Warrant Officer Hugh Thompsom, an experienced combat helicopter pilot, was flying close overhead in an armed observation craft. At various times from 8:00 A.M. to 10:00 A.M., Thompsom attempted to aid wounded South Vietnamese civilians he saw in the fields around My Lai (4), saw Medina kill a wounded Vietnamese woman in a field, and landed his craft near the ditch where so many defenseless people were shot. He urged members of Company C to stop the killing, but killings resumed after he left. Around 10:00 A.M. he landed again to protect a group of women and children who were being herded toward a bunker by men of Company C. Thompsom called in one of his gunships to evacuate some of the wounded civilians and then landed his own small helicopter to save one slightly wounded child from the heaps of bodies. In addition to his combat radio transmissions, Thompsom made reports upon his return to base to his commander about the slaughter.

The truth of these events was covered up within the Americal Division for a year, until a letter from a Vietnam veteran, Ronald Ridenhour, to Secretary of Defense Melvin Laird in late March, 1969, claimed "something very black indeed" had occurred at My Lai. Laird ordered an investigation. In September, 1969, William Calley was charged with murdering more than one hundred civilians at My Lai. The full dimensions of the massacre became public knowledge in mid-November, 1969, when newspapers carried Seymour Hersh's interviews with men from Company C, the *CBS Evening News* broadcast other interviews, and photographs of the massacred victims were printed in *Life* magazine.

Lieutenant General William R. Peers was assigned responsibility for conducting the official investigation of the incident. He learned that Hugh Thompsom's angry, but accurate, accusations of a civilian massacre, as well as reports by South Vietnamese officials of more than five hundred civilian deaths, were never properly investigated. Peers's report of March, 1970, contained detailed findings about what happened at My Lai and a recommendation that thirty individuals be held for possible charges.

The Army preferred charges against a total of twenty-five men: twelve for war crimes and thirteen for other military offenses. Four of the five men eventually tried on war crime charges were members of Company C. The fifth was Captain Eugene Kotouc, the staff intelligence officer of Task Force Barker. He was acquitted of torturing a prisoner. There was no evidence of any misdeeds by men from Company A, but Company B had been involved in killings of civilians at the hamlet of My Khe (4). Captain Earl Michles, in command of Company B, was killed in the same helicopter crash that killed Lieutenant Colonel Barker in June, 1968, so both of those men were beyond the reach of the law. Charges against Lieutenant Willingham of Company B were dismissed in 1970, in spite of evidence of between thirty-eight and ninety civilian deaths caused by his men in My Khe (4) on the morning of March 16.

Charges were brought in 1970 against thirteen officers in the Americal Division for various military offenses that were less than war crimes and did not involve murder or attempted murder. Charges were dismissed against several of the officers, and several had their cases resolved in other manners. Only four men were tried for the war crimes of murdering civilians, all members of Company C: Captain Medina, the company commander; Lieutenant Calley, in command of one of the company's platoons; Staff Sergeant David Mitchell, a squad leader in Calley's platoon; and Staff Sergeant Charles E. Hutto, a squad leader from Brooks's platoon. Lieutenant Brooks was killed in combat after the incident and so was not charged.

Initially, seven enlisted men from Company C had been charged by the Army with crimes including murder, rape, and assault. Charges against five were dropped and two men were tried. The first court-martial resulting from My Lai was that of David Mitchell, a career soldier; it began in October, 1970, at Fort Hood, Texas. Mitchell was acquitted of all charges. While Calley's trial was still in session, Charles Hutto was tried at Fort McPherson, Georgia, and found innocent. Medina's trial took place at Fort McPherson in August and September, 1971, after Calley's March, 1971, conviction. Medina was found not guilty of murder and assault.

Calley's trial was the most prominent of all the courts-martial. He had been identified from the start as ordering the shooting of women and children and was tried under article 118 of the Uniform Code of Military Justice for premeditated murder of more than one hundred Vietnamese. The trial at Fort Benning, Georgia, lasted about four months. On March 29, 1971, Calley was found guilty of three counts of murder by a panel of six officers. He was sentenced "to be confined at hard labor for the rest of [his] natural life; to be dismissed from the service; to forfeit all pay and allowances." Two days later, President Richard M. Nixon ordered Calley released from the stockade and returned to his quarters to serve his sentence. In August, 1971, the Army reduced Calley's sentence to twenty years, and in April, 1974, further reduced it to ten years. In the Army, prisoners become eligible for parole after one-third of their sentence is served. With Calley's punishment reduced to ten years, he became eligible in the fall of 1974 and parole was granted in November.

Impact of Event

The reactions both to the My Lai massacre and to Lieutenant Calley's conviction cover a tremendous range. Most Americans and many people around the world expressed horror and distress at the massacre itself; yet a great many considered Lieutenant Calley to be a scapegoat. To some, it was not Lieutenant Calley or the others who were tried in courts-martial, but the United States that was on trial for its Vietnam war.

The outcome of the courts-martial reveals that no one—not the Army, the president, Congress, or the American public—relished punishing American fighting men for their conduct in Vietnam. The Army backed away from a joint trial of the accused and did not carry through the stern spirit of justice that pervades the official Peers Report.

American official and popular statements from the time typically express outrage toward the massacre itself but suggest that it would be best to reserve judgment about Calley's or others' guilt. Some veterans and Army members believed that Calley was being punished for one of the inevitable tragedies of war. Still others believed Calley had done only what the Army had trained him to do: kill Communists. Many believed, in contrast, that since the United States was fighting to protect Vietnam from Communism, the Army should be saving, or at least protecting, Vietnamese civilians.

Immediately following Calley's conviction for murder, the White House and Congress received a strong wave of popular sympathy for him. It was believed that Calley's conviction condemned, by implication, all Americans who had fought in Vietnam. Others believed that what occurred at My Lai (4) were war crimes and that Calley, and others, should have been punished by death in the same way that German and Japanese war criminals were following World War II.

Beneath these opposing emotional calls for Calley's release or execution, the My Lai massacre and the subsequent courts-martial had a profound impact on the United States and the Army. Knowledge of the massacre came twenty-one months after the Tet Offensive, but it was additional confirmation that hopes for an American victory in Vietnam were unfounded. If U.S. troops were slaughtering the South Vietnamese, how could the people ever be won over to the side of the United States?

People also wondered if My Lai was only the first of many such massacres that would come to light. In fact, evidence of thousands of unnecessary and unwarranted deaths of South Vietnamese civilians caused by U.S. and other allied units have been documented, but nothing quite so horrible as that at My Lai (4).

Simply because of the questions raised about possible American atrocities in Vietnam, the whole discussion of the war itself took on a new color. The massacre gave proof to those antiwar protestors who called the war immoral and unjust. The atrocity marked an end, or at least a profound shock, to trust in American goodness and nobility of purpose.

In the 1970's, evidence of various hidden schemes and deadly plans by the U.S. government came to light, many of them completely unconnected with My Lai. The My Lai massacre remains a key incident that loosed the tide of self-doubt and questioning about the United States' purpose and moral stature that marked much of national life in the 1970's and 1980's. One of the most profound and lasting impacts of the My Lai massacre and the Calley court-martial was the coldness and distaste Vietnam veterans encountered after 1969 upon return to the United States. Many Americans treated all veterans as if they had joined with Company C to abuse and murder Vietnamese women and children. For those remaining in the military service, the vision of a unit running amok killing civilians in Vietnam's guerrilla war was one of several powerful forces that led to major reforms in Army military doctrine and the abandonment of the draft in favor of an all-volunteer armed services.

In the end, the accounts and photographs of the My Lai massacre make one think again of both the horror of war for those somehow caught in its grasp and the fragility of the rules by which civilized warfare is supposed to be conducted.

Bibliography

Calley, William. *Lieutenant Calley: His Own Story, as Told to John Sack*. New York: Viking Press, 1971. After interviewing Calley at length in 1969 and 1970, the author says he took Calley's words and feelings apart and put them back together as a continuous story. Revealing.

Gershen, Martin. *Destroy or Die: The True Story of Mylai*. New Rochelle, N.Y.: Arlington House, 1971. This book tries to explain why the men of Company C acted as they did on March 16, 1968. Portrays them as innocent infantrymen doing their job.

Hammer, Richard. *The Court-Martial of Lt. Calley*. New York: Coward, McCann & Geoghegan, 1971. Although highly unfavorable to Lieutenant Calley, this is a useful summary of the trial itself, containing large amounts of verbatim testimony from Calley and men of his unit.

Hersh, Seymour. *My Lai 4: A Report on the Massacre and Its Aftermath*. New York: Random House, 1970. Hersh won a Pulitzer Prize for his reporting about the My Lai incident. Here he brings together the early evidence of a massacre in a compelling way. The book is somewhat dated by the later courts-martial and the release of the Peers Report.

McCarthy, Mary. *Medina*. New York: Harcourt Brace Jovanovich, 1972. A riveting account by a writer who attended Medina's trial as a correspondent for *The New*

Yorker. McCarthy makes sense of this important trial, which attracted less attention than Calley's.

Peers, William R. *The My Lai Inquiry.* New York: W. W. Norton, 1979. Peers wrote this reflective, detailed book years after the official inquiry. A fascinating, readable summary of the massacre and its aftermath. Full of balanced, careful judgments. Indispensable.

Sim, Kevin, and Michael Bilton. *Four Hours in My Lai.* New York: Viking Press, 1992. Sim and Bilton, two British documentary filmmakers, reconstruct events leading up to the massacre, document the events, and report on the subsequent cover-ups and trials. Much of the material comes from interviews conducted in the 1980's and 1990's.

United States Department of the Army. *The My Lai Massacre and Its Cover-up: Beyond the Reach of Law? The Peers Commission Report: Goldstein, Joseph; Burke Marshall and Jack Schwartz.* New York: Free Press, 1976. In 1974, the Army released most of its official inquiry, commonly known as the Peers Report. This volume is the most convenient place to find the text of the Peers Report. Supplements deal with general war crime issues and some war crime matters relating to the Vietnam era. Be sure to distinguish between this official report and General Peers's own account.

David D. Buck

Cross-References

Legal Norms of Behavior in Warfare Formulated by the Hague Conference (1907), p. 92; Japanese Troops Brutalize Chinese After the Capture of Nanjing (1937), p. 539; Ho Chi Minh Organizes the Viet Minh (1941), p. 573; A Japanese Commander Is Ruled Responsible for His Troops' Actions (1945), p. 662; Nazi War Criminals Are Tried in Nuremberg (1945), p. 667; The Nationalist Vietnamese Fight Against French Control of Indochina (1946), p. 683; The United Nations Adopts a Convention on the Crime of Genocide (1948), p. 783; The Statute of Limitations Is Ruled Not Applicable to War Crimes (1968), p. 1457; FBI and CIA Interference in the Civil Rights Movement Is Revealed (1971), p. 1595; Vietnam Releases United States Prisoners of War (1973), p. 1691; The United States Grants Amnesty to Vietnam War Draft Evaders (1974), p. 1769.

CONGRESS PASSES THE CLEAN AIR ACT AMENDMENTS

Category of event: Consumers' rights
Time: December, 1970
Locale: Washington, D.C.

The U.S. government undertook an ambitious and aggressive regulatory role in an area previously left largely to the states and localities

Principal personages:

EDMUND MUSKIE (1914-   ), the Democratic senator from Maine who sponsored and promoted the bill's strongest portions

RICHARD M. NIXON (1913-   ), the Republican president (1969-1974) who accepted the strong bills

PAUL G. ROGERS (1921-   ), a Democrat from Florida who initiated the Clean Air Act Amendments in the House of Representatives

JOHN JARMAN (1915-1982), a Democratic (later Republican) representative from Oklahoma whose subcommittee handled the bill in the House

Summary of Event

The Clean Air Act Amendments of 1970, Public Law 91-604, revolutionized the federal government's efforts to control air contamination. The Clean Air Amendments, the National Environmental Policy Act (NEPA), and the Water Quality Improvement Act of 1970 constituted the core environmental measures of what President Richard M. Nixon called "The Year of the Environment." The 1970 clean air law amended and essentially absorbed previous efforts at air pollution regulation, particularly the 1963 Clean Air Act, the 1965 Motor Vehicle Air Pollution Control Act, and the Air Quality Control Act of 1967. Although the laws of the 1960's had initiated federal air pollution policies, the national government had made few efforts regarding pollution other than supporting state and local efforts. For example, only one prosecution had occurred under the 1963 Clean Air Act. The Department of Health, Education and Welfare (HEW) was still developing the implementation plan for the more demanding 1967 law when the 1970 law passed.

Adoption of the 1970 amendments was encouraged by several political conditions. First, President Richard Nixon sought to establish his environmental credentials in preparation for the 1972 elections. One of Nixon's strongest potential challengers was Senator Edmund Muskie (D-Maine), a key sponsor of the 1970 amendments who enjoyed a strong environmental image as a result of his activities as chair of the Senate Subcommittee on Air and Water Pollution in the 1960's. The president and his rival acted partially in response to the broad public concern about environmental issues at the time, strongly symbolized by the first Earth Day celebration of April 22, 1970. Action on air pollution policy was also favored by the impending expiration of earlier antipollution legislation.

Despite these favorable conditions, the costs that the 1970 amendments imposed on key organized interests, particularly the auto industry, generated strong debate. The bill's passage was a triumph of bipartisan cooperation and environmental politics, even though Nixon excluded Muskie from the signing ceremony. Many of the issues raised during the debates over the bill, such as provisions for citizen lawsuits to promote enforcement and the mandating of technology not yet developed, constituted continuing challenges in environmental policy.

In 1970, amendments to the Clean Air Act were proposed by the Nixon Administration, in the House of Representatives, and in the Senate. Senator Muskie initiated Senate action by submitting what was originally called the National Air Quality Standards Act of 1970. Muskie's original bill was much weaker than the other proposals. During the extensive subcommittee hearings chaired by Muskie in March and April, the bill became much stronger, probably pushed by the criticism of Muskie's earlier bills. A major criticism of the earlier laws was made in the book *Vanishing Air*, a Ralph Nader study group publication of 1970. The subcommittee's amended bill became the central framework for the final law. Hearings were also held in the Subcommittee on Energy, Natural Resources and the Environment of the Senate Commerce Committee in March. The bill, S. 4358, was approved by the Senate unanimously on September 22.

The Senate's bill was preceded by a House bill that incorporated most of the Nixon Administration's proposals. In the House, Florida Democrat Paul G. Rogers was particularly instrumental in placing the clean air issue on the agenda. He sought to respond in a timely manner to the scheduled expiration of the 1967 Air Quality Control Act on June 30, 1970. The most comprehensive House hearings took place in the Committee on Interstate and Foreign Commerce, Subcommittee on Public Health and Welfare, chaired by John Jarman (D-Okla.). The House bill, H.R. 17255, passed on June 10, 1970, with only one dissenting vote, but debate on it had been intense.

The House legislation differed from the Senate's final bill in that it did not mandate specific standards, provided less money for research and implementation of the law, and gave much more discretion to the secretary of Health, Education and Welfare (HEW). Most environmental programs were administered by HEW until the creation of the Environmental Protection Agency, or EPA, during 1970.

A conference committee was established to resolve the differences between the Senate and House bills. In conference, the biggest area of dispute was the Senate bill's specification that auto emissions for various pollutants be reduced by 90 percent by 1975, with a 1976 deadline for similar reductions in nitrous oxide emission from cars. The compromise bill favored the Senate position, although it allowed automobile manufacturers to apply for a one-year extension to the standards and reduced the warranty for the low emissions from the lifetime period favored by the Senate to a five-year or fifty-thousand-mile limitation. Senate provisions in the area of controlling fuel additives and concerning the creation and implementation of federal air quality standards were also kept in the final bill. The conference committee approved the bill on December 17, 1970. After limited debate, both the House and the Senate approved the conference bill on December 18 by voice vote.

As signed into law by Nixon, the Clean Air Act Amendments had four major components. First, the law required the administrator of the Environmental Protection Agency (EPA) to create a list of dangerous air pollutants within thirty days of the bill's enactment, and then to publish and enforce national ambient standards for these pollutants. The standards had two categories: primary, the levels that ensure that public health is protected; and secondary, which must be reached to promote other aspects of public welfare, such as reduced corrosion. The federal government controlled the establishment of primary standards while states were to formulate secondary standards. The EPA also could set emissions standards for specific hazardous air pollutants. A key concept in the law was that the EPA was to set emission standards for new pollution sources at a level matching what would be produced if the Best Available Control Technology (BACT) were used. In practice, this meant that the finest filtering systems would be required for all pollution producers, such as "scrubbers" for all coal-fired power plants.

A second element of the Clean Air Act was that states were responsible for developing and enforcing the standards and goals for designated air pollution regions within their borders. Each designated region was to meet or be below the standards set by the EPA for various pollutants. To facilitate this effort, the EPA was to provide extensive funds for state planning and implementation. If states failed to develop or implement plans adequately, the federal government could hold hearings within the state and ultimately impose federal plans. The failure of states to devise and implement air quality control plans according to the law's schedule was a major reason for the extensive reforms in air pollution laws in 1977.

The most controversial area of the bill was its third major component, involving automobile and fuel regulations. The Clean Air Act Amendments were very ambitious in that the 90 percent reductions mandated by 1975 (with the possibility of a one-year extension and an extra year for nitrous oxides) were asserted to be beyond the industry's existing technology. Among the opponents of this timetable were legislators from the automobile producing regions, such as Senator Robert P. Griffin (R-Mich.), and the Nixon Administration. Nixon thought that the schedule was too strict and that such specifics of implementation should be left to the executive branch, in this case the head of the EPA. An extension was in fact granted to the auto industry in April, 1973. Production and use of fuels or fuel additives which were dangerous or interfered with antipollution devices were also forbidden by the law. States were responsible for the development and maintenance of emissions testing programs.

The fourth component, the enforcement provisions, was also notable. The law granted the EPA the powers to use injunctions to prohibit or stop dangerous pollution and to punish resistant violators with fines up to $25,000 and a year in prison for each day of knowing violation or $50,000 and two years of imprisonment for repeat offenders. The bill also allowed for citizen lawsuits. Under the 1970 amendments, citizens or groups were granted the right to sue in federal courts both the administrator, for failing to perform required duties, or alleged violators, including government agencies. This clause was a highly controversial and important element. In essence, the law made citizens and environmental groups potential prosecutors of the law and theoretically created an important stick to drive the agency to implement the law forcefully. The bill also authorized the spending of $775 million for the period 1971-1973. Beyond these major elements, the law also mandated that the EPA administrator recommend legislation on noise pollution and regulate aircraft emissions and research. The signing of the bill by Nixon on December 31, despite his misgivings about the auto emissions sections, was a fitting end to 1970, which had been inaugurated by the signing of NEPA on January 1.

Impact of Event

The 1970 law was a major departure from past air pollution regulation. Although the 1967 law set forth ambitious goals, it lacked the mechanism for ensuring action. The 1970 amendments ensured action, but there were major controversies about the costs and organization of the program. Environmentalist Barry Commoner noted that pollution declined significantly in the United States after the mid-1970's, when consistent data became available. For example, annual lead emissions in the United States declined by 94 percent between 1975 and 1987, while emissions for particulates, sulfur dioxide, and carbon monoxide declined about 18 percent over the same period. Despite these results, Commoner criticized the 1970 law and its 1977 amendments for not going far enough and for their weak implementation. Some economists and other public policy analysts criticized the 1970 law and its implementation for inefficiency and inconsistent impacts. These facts and opinions reflect both the nature of the law and the different values of those who analyze or are affected by it.

Two major difficulties of the 1970 amendments deserve specific attention because they demonstrate the problems of fulfilling its goals. The first problem of the 1970 amendments was that their ambitious goals were unattainable without a major commitment by politicians and the general public. Because of the energy crisis of 1973, the Nixon Administration's philosophy about regulation, and the public's lack of continuing concern, the EPA was relatively unsupported in its implementation efforts. On June 15, 1975, the date when the national air quality standards were to be met, 102 of 247 regions were not in compliance. Twenty years after the law, 487 counties still did not consistently comply. In the area of auto emissions regulation, EPA administrator William Ruckelshaus was mandated to push automakers to produce a cleaner car, which they consistently maintained was impossible. In both cases, forcing compliance would have meant dramatic social and economic impacts, at least temporarily. The ambitious goals of the 1970 laws promoted action but had a counterproductive effect of forcing the EPA to negotiate about deadlines and standards, and sometimes abandon them. Not only were goals not reached, but regulations were not seen as absolute. Polluters with significant economic power delayed action, knowing that the agency would not enforce regulations as strictly as written since full compliance was impossible anyway. The EPA never enjoyed complete political support, and the missed deadlines and adjusted standards undermined its credibility with both environmentalists and industry.

The second problem associated with the 1970 clean air law was that of inefficiency, particularly in the case of the mandating of Best Available Control Technology (BACT) standards. Such technological requirements may not lead efficiently to environmental improvement, as the requirement of scrubbers in coal-burning facilities illustrates. In the 1970's, the EPA required new coal plants to install the costly scrubbers but allowed them to burn coal with high sulfur content when the use of low-sulfur Western coal and other less expensive cleaning processes would have produced cleaner power at lower cost. The net result of the 1970 law was that some technologies were encouraged and some environmental goals were served at the cost of foreclosing other options.

No law was likely to fulfill the goals of this legislation, given the size and complexity of the air pollution problem. The 1970 amendments initiated a sometimes troubled but ultimately progressive evolution of air pollution policy. Like many social problems, cleaning up the environment is far more complex than simply passing a law. This is particularly true when the extent of the problem is underestimated; later revelations about acid rain and the greenhouse effect indicate that the effects of air pollution were severely underestimated in the 1970's. In essence, the 1970 law can be seen as an experiment which yielded some success and some failure but is most important because it pointed the way to better future policies. The increased understanding of regulatory efficiency and effectiveness was reflected in the more sophisticated amendments of 1977 and 1990.

Bibliography

Ackerman, Bruce A., and William T. Hassler. *Clean Coal/Dirty Air.* New Haven, Conn.: Yale University Press, 1981. Although Ackerman and Hassler's book is concerned primarily with the 1977 Clean Air Act Amendments, the issues and political dynamics they describe reflect developments rooted in the 1970 act. A key idea they pursue is how the 1970 and 1977 amendments sought to push the EPA to act and thereby reduced its political independence. The net result was a less effective program dominated by the political concerns of legislators. Although complex, the notes are very interesting and provide some fine sources.

Jones, Charles O. *Clean Air.* Pittsburgh: University of Pittsburgh Press, 1975. This book is specifically devoted to air pollution control efforts in the Pittsburgh area but provides a fine view of the politics and implementation of clean-air policy in the late 1960's and early 1970's. One interesting aspect is the interaction of local, state, and federal concerns and laws. Some conclusions are made regarding the problems of establishing cleanup goals that are beyond the capability of the actors. Although dated, the book provides a superb review of the literature on air pollution and pollution policy in the 1960's and 1970's.

Miller, James. "Air Pollution." In *Nixon and the Environment*, edited by James

Rathlesberger. New York: Tarus Communications, 1972. The book is a contemporary critique of Nixon's environmental record, particularly of the implementation of environmental laws. Miller's conclusions are clearly directed at indicting Nixon on this account. He also gives an interesting view of the first years of implementation of the 1970 amendments. No useful references or bibliography.

Rosenbaum, Walter A. *Environmental Politics and Policy.* 2d ed. Washington, D.C.: Congressional Quarterly Press, 1991. This book is a general text on environmental politics. Its chapter on air and water pollution provides a straightforward account of air pollution regulation as it developed. The sections on standards and enforcement problems are particularly useful. Footnotes are not very useful, but a short suggested reading list is provided.

United States Senate. Subcommittee on Public Works. *A Legislative History of the Clean Air Amendments of 1970.* Washington, D.C.: U.S. Government Printing Office, 1974. Although this publication is lengthy and can be repetitive, there is no substitute for the original debates. This particular document is widely available. No bibliography but very fine primary documentation of the debates.

Yandle, Bruce. *The Political Limits of Environmental Regulation.* New York: Quorum Books, 1989. This book describes how environmental controls are typically devised by unlikely coalitions and therefore contain contradictions which limit their ultimate success. The most relevant chapter to the Clean Air Act Amendments of 1970 is Chapter 4, "The Rise of the Federal Regulator." Particularly interesting is Yandle's description of how the EPA's implementation of the Clean Air Act evolved toward a "pollution rights" position in the 1970's. Very good footnotes and bibliography.

Mark Henkels

Cross-References

The Pure Food and Drug Act and Meat Inspection Act Become Law (1906), p. 64; The Motor Vehicle Air Pollution Control Act Is Passed by Congress (1965), p. 1310; The Zero Population Growth Movement Spurs Environmental Consciousness (1967), p. 1386; Superfund Is Established to Pay for Hazardous Waste Cleanup (1980), p. 2084; New York State Imposes the First Mandatory Seat-Belt Law (1984), p. 2220.

CHÁVEZ IS JAILED FOR ORGANIZING
AN ILLEGAL LETTUCE BOYCOTT

Category of event: Workers' rights
Time: December 4, 1970
Locale: Salinas, California

César Chávez's jailing for his boycott against lettuce growers elevated him to the status of champion of the oppressed and the poor in the minds of Americans

Principal personages:
CÉSAR CHÁVEZ (1927-), a labor union organizer and founder of the United Farm Workers Organizing Committee
JERRY BROWN (1938-), the governor of California from 1975 to 1983
GEORGE MEANY (1894-1980), the first president of the American Federation of Labor-Congress of Industrial Organizations
ROBERT F. KENNEDY (1925-1968), the attorney general of the United States from 1961 to 1964; senator from New York from 1965 to 1968
JOHN LINDSAY (1921-), the mayor of New York City from 1966 to 1973

Summary of Event

Throughout the history of the farm labor movement in California, growers have relied on a cheap, dependable work force that has been composed primarily of minorities. The state's first farm workers were American Indians. The Native American population in the state was reduced from an earlier level of 300,000 to 30,000 in 1860 through disease and ill-treatment. Native Americans were replaced by Chinese, who had been brought over to America to help construct the Central Pacific and the Union Pacific railroads. The Chinese were eager to work in America, even though thousands succumbed to disease on the passage across the Pacific. When farmers replaced livestock and wheat with fruit and truck crops toward the end of the nineteenth century, even more Chinese "coolies" immigrated, until Congress suspended Chinese immigration in 1882. At almost exactly the same time that the Chinese labor supply was cut off, Japan relaxed its long-standing ban on emigration, and workers from Japan began to pour into California. By 1910, their numbers had swollen to more than forty thousand. Even though the Japanese were industrious, they were not ideal workers from the growers' viewpoint because they dreamed of owning land and becoming farmers in their own right. Agitation over the "yellow peril" and the "rising tide of color" in California culminated in 1924 in a new immigration act that ended Asiatic immigration.

Fortunately for the growers, the Mexican Revolution of 1910 opened another pool of foreign labor. Tens of thousands of rural families fled Mexico, and by 1920 the census reported nearly 100,000 Mexican nationals in California. Between 1942 and

1964, California received special dispensation to use Mexican contract workers. The influx of these braceros (literally, "arm-men") increased the Mexican population in the state by 100,000. For the most part, the growers welcomed the contract workers because they could be forced to work for whomever they were told under terms set by the growers. In addition to those who immigrated legally from Mexico, an untold number of "wetbacks" crossed the border illegally into the United States. In some ways, these workers were entirely at the mercy of employers and labor contractors. Except for a brief period during the 1930's, when thirty thousand Filipinos were imported to California, Mexicans provided the bulk of the farm labor force for most of the twentieth century. Unspoiled by normal American standards, Mexican immigrants fit the growers' concept of the perfect labor force because they did not aspire to land ownership or to fringe benefits.

For nearly one hundred years, agricultural employers beat back attempts to organize the work force. Prior to the 1960's, migrant workers had never won collective bargaining rights because they had not been highly motivated to organize. In addition, their itinerant lives made it difficult for them to weld into a solid group. Although the farm labor movement was active during the twentieth century, it was not very effective, primarily because leadership did not come from the groups that made up the work force. Leadership came from political groups (such as the Industrial Workers of the World), intellectuals (Ernesto Galarza), urban unionists (Norman Smith and Clive Knowles), and the clergy (Father Thomas McCullough).

César Chávez succeeded where his predecessors had failed partially because he worked in the fields as he organized and was trusted by the farm workers as no other leader had been. As the son of migrant workers, Chávez and his family had lived in their car or in tents without heat or light, had gone without shoes in the winter, and had eaten mustard greens to stay alive. César and his brothers and sisters attended segregated schools which provided little more than child-care service. Until his family learned the tricks of the labor contractors, they had worked hard harvesting fields only to be cheated by growers when the work was completed. There was no job security, and fringe benefits were few. The labor camps that they lived in periodically were a collection of nine-by-eleven-foot tin shacks which collected the heat of the summer sun and lacked indoor plumbing. Many of the conditions that Chávez's family and thousands of other Mexican families experienced were similar to those endured by the waves of Chinese, Japanese, Mexican, and Filipino workers who had preceded them.

Chávez became involved in the farm labor movement almost by accident. Like many second-generation Mexican Americans, he and his wife had left the migrant stream and probably would have left agricultural work altogether if Chávez had not spoken to Father Donald McDonnell. Father McDonnell got Chávez interested in the farm labor movement by telling him about Pope Leo XIII's endorsement of labor unions. Through Father McDonnell, Chávez met Fred Ross, a representative of the Community Service Organization (CSO) who had come to California to set up local chapters. In 1953, Chávez became a statewide organizer for the CSO and, with the help of his principal assistant, Dolores Huerta, built the CSO in California to twenty-two chapters.

After ten years, Chávez left the CSO because, unlike many CSO leaders, he believed that it would be better for his people to end the bracero system and upgrade farm work instead of fleeing to an uncertain future in the cities. He believed that farm labor organizing should be emphasized much more than it was. After withdrawing his life savings of $900 in April, 1962, Chávez and his family moved to Delano, where he founded the Farm Workers Association with no outside help.

The FWA's first big strike occurred in response to a cry for help in 1965 from the Filipino grape pickers in Delano. At that time, grape pickers in Delano received $1.20 an hour, which was $.45 less than the federal minimum wage. The pickers lived in shacks with no heating or plumbing. In addition, pickers were often accidentally sprayed with insecticides. At stake were the interests of 384,100 farm workers in California and 4 million agricultural workers in the United States.

To keep pressure on the table grape growers, Chávez decided in 1967 to stage a nationwide boycott against them. By 1968, with the support of the Roman Catholic church and such influential Americans as Robert Kennedy and John Lindsay, the boycott succeeded in lowering grape sales by 12 percent. Chávez's twenty-five-day fast in 1968 united California's farm workers behind him and established him as a hero. Victory was finally achieved in 1970 when the largest producer of grape growers in the United States, John Giumarra, signed contracts recognizing the existence of the union (known by this time as the United Farm Workers Organizing Committee or UFWOC), and agreeing to pay $1.80 an hour plus $.20 for each box of grapes. Chávez proved for the first time that field workers could force an entire industry— 85 percent of the grape growers in California—to sign a contract with their union leaders.

Fresh from the triumph of "La Huelga" (the strike), Chávez embarked on a much more ambitious crusade. This time the product was lettuce, picked by workers in California and Arizona. The lettuce growers not only had the support of corporations such as Purex, but they were also backed by the U.S. Defense Department, which had refused to buy any "union lettuce." The UFWOC's primary target was Bud Antle's huge ranch in the Salinas Valley. Antle was one of many growers in Salinas, King City, the Imperial Valley, and the San Joaquin Valley who had secretly signed contracts with the Teamsters in an effort to destroy the UFWOC.

On September 17, 1970, Chávez announced that the UFWOC was sending people to sixty-four cities in North America to organize a national boycott of lettuce. Chávez's announcement was in direct defiance of Superior Court Judge Anthony Brazil's decision the day before to grant permanent injunctions against picketing to thirty growers, on the grounds that this was a jurisdictional dispute which was illegal in California. Knowing full well of the publicity that would develop if he were jailed, Chávez continued the boycott against Antle and ordered that the following statement be given to the press on the day that he went to jail: "Boycott Bud Antle! Boycott Dow Chemical! And boycott the hell out of them! Viva!" Chávez's contempt-of-court trial was held on December 4, 1970. The presiding judge, Judge Gordon Campbell, sentenced Chávez to jail on each of two counts of contempt of court and ordered that he remain in jail until he notified all UFWOC personnel to stop the boycott against Antle. The judge also fined Chávez five hundred dollars for each of the two counts.

Chávez's jail sentence generated the attention that he had hoped for. While he was in the Salinas County Jail, Chávez's visits by Coretta Scott King (the widow of Martin Luther King, Jr.) and Ethel Kennedy were covered by both the national press and the major television networks. A week after Chávez was jailed, the State Court of Appeals denied a union petition that the Antle injunction be set aside. The UFWOC then appealed the decision to the California Supreme Court, which ordered Chávez's release twenty days after he was jailed. During a mass of thanksgiving that was held in the parking lot, Chávez told a crowd of about four hundred union supporters, "Jails were made for men who fight for their rights. My spirit was never in jail. They can jail us, but they can never jail the Cause."

Four months later, the California Supreme Court ruled that the UFWOC had the right to boycott Bud Antle.

Impact of Event

Chávez was correct in his assumption that the contempt-of-court trial and his subsequent jail sentence would bring "La Causa" (the farm labor movement) to national attention. Chávez's charismatic leadership, which was based on Mahatma Gandhi's philosophy of passive resistance, convinced many Americans that Chávez was the logical successor to Martin Luther King, Jr., and Robert Kennedy. The political ramifications of Chávez's jailing extended to both the union halls and the courts.

The Teamsters' fear that the court hearing would turn public opinion against them was well founded. In 1973, when the Teamsters called in one hundred or so "guards" at $67.50 per day to protect strike breakers from interference by Chávez's pickets, newspapers across the nation branded them as "goon squads." Convinced that the Teamsters and the growers were jointly seeking to destroy the farm workers, George Meany threw the full support of the AFL-CIO behind the grape and lettuce boycotts on April 8, 1974. Finally, in 1979, the Teamsters signed a peace treaty with the UFWOC that gave the field hands to the UFWOC and the canners, packers, and farm-truck drivers to the Teamsters. This was an amazing concession, considering that the Teamsters had already persuaded 50,000 of California's 250,000 agricultural workers to join them rather than the UFWOC. This uneasy alliance was primarily the result of the Teamsters' desire to repair the damage that their union's image had suffered through their dispute with the UFWOC.

Chávez's skill at persuading liberals to regard the boycotts of grapes and lettuce as a just cause eventually produced legislation that benefited the workers. Sensing that allying himself with the farm workers would help him to be elected governor, Jerry Brown made the creation of workable farm labor relations law one of his primary goals. In September, 1975, the Agricultural Labor Relations Act took effect. The main impetus of this law was the formation of the Agricultural Labor Relations Board, which gave labor organizers access to the fields. Although the ALRB was too poorly funded to be truly effective, its very existence testified to the belief of many lawmakers in California that the labor disputes were another manifestation of California's problem of interethnic relations between employers and workers. They interpreted Chávez's crusade as a struggle not simply for economic security but also for minority self-determination as well.

Of far more importance than Chávez's achievements is the way his nonviolent approach to social change carried over to other movements. He demonstrated through his deep emotional commitment to the UFWOC that people of various backgrounds, political persuasions, and faiths will come together for a common cause if it is morally correct. The truth of this statement is born out by the fact that the techniques developed by "La Causa" have been successfully applied by farm workers in other lands. Chávez also showed through his courage and hard work that individuals really can make a difference.

Bibliography

Levy, Jacques. *César Chávez: Autobiography of La Causa.* New York: W. W. Norton, 1975. This text should be considered the standard history of both César Chávez and the UFWA. Still, this is not a complete history of the movement because it traces Chávez's activities only through the first half of the 1970's.

"The Little Strike That Grew to 'La Causa.' " *Time* 102 (July 4, 1969): 16-22. This lengthy article does a fine job providing the background to Chávez's activities during the turbulence of the 1960's. It is much more objective than many other accounts of this period.

London, Joan, and Henry Anderson. *So Shall Ye Reap: The Story of César Chávez and the Farm Workers' Movement.* New York: Thomas Y. Crowell, 1970. Since this book covers only the first few years of the farm labor movement, it is more useful as a history of the movement in California than as an account of César Chávez's activities, which make up only the last two chapters. The authors assume that the reader is familiar with the problems faced by migrant workers in California.

Roberts, Naurice. *César Chávez and La Causa.* Chicago: Children's Press, 1986. Although this book was written for children, it still contains enough factual information to serve as a basic introduction to the man and the movement.

Taylor, Ronald B. *Chávez and the Farm Workers.* Boston: Beacon Press, 1975. This comprehensive history of César Chávez's farm movement is less personalized than Levy's book but is more objectively written. It portrays Chávez as a "man at odds with himself" who was better at organizing movements than he was at running unions.

Alan Brown

Cross-References

The British Labour Party Is Formed (1906), p. 58; The International Labour Organisation Is Established (1919), p. 281; Steel Workers Go on Strike to Demand Improved Working Conditions (1919), p. 293; A U.S. Immigration Act Imposes Quotas Based on National Origins (1924), p. 383; The Wagner Act Requires Employers to Accept Collective Bargaining (1935), p. 508; Social Security Act Establishes Benefits for Nonworking People (1935), p. 514; The Congress of Industrial Organizations Is Formed (1938), p. 545; Autoworkers Negotiate a Contract with a Cost-of-Living Provision (1948), p. 766; Jouhaux Is Awarded the Nobel Peace Prize (1951), p. 873; Chávez Forms Farm Workers' Union and Leads Grape Pickers' Strike (1962), p. 1161; The International Labour Organisation Wins the Nobel Peace Prize (1969), p. 1509.

THE BLUE LAKE REGION IN NEW MEXICO IS RETURNED TO THE TAOS PUEBLO

Category of event: Indigenous peoples' rights
Time: December 15, 1970
Locale: Taos Pueblo, northern New Mexico

From 1906, when parts of their traditional lands were incorporated into national forests, until a 1970 act of Congress, the Taos endured denial of part of their heritage

Principal personages:

THEODORE ROOSEVELT (1858-1919), the U.S. president when the Taos Pueblo's Blue Lake and its watershed were made part of the Carson National Forest

SEFERINO MARTINEZ, the Taos tribal governor who in 1955 sought congressional action in the Blue Lake controversy

PAUL BERNAL (1913-), the Taos' major spokesman and interpreter in dealing with Congress and other governmental bodies

OLIVER LA FARGE (1901-1963), an anthropologist who helped guide the Taos in their efforts to regain Blue Lake

CORRINE LOCKER, the Southwest director of the Association on American Indian Affairs (AAIA)

JOHN COLLIER (1884-1968), the U.S. commissioner of Indian affairs (1933-1945)

RICHARD M. NIXON (1913-), the president of the United States (1969-1974)

Summary of Event

In northern New Mexico, there are several long-established pueblos (villages) where Native Americans have lived in close communities for centuries. These pueblo peoples are descendants of aboriginals who lived in the American Southwest as long ago as 10,000 B.C. Situated just north of the town of Taos, New Mexico, is the northernmost of these pueblos. Taos Pueblo is believed to have been established in the fourteenth century. According to legend, it was founded by a great chief who, following an eagle, led his people to the foot of a huge mountain, where the eagle then dropped one of his feathers. There, on what is now known as the Rio Pueblo de Taos, at the foot of Pueblo Peak in the Sangre de Cristo Mountains of northern New Mexico, the Taos built their village. There they farmed, grazed their animals, fished, and hunted and trapped the wild game abundant in the thousands of adjacent forested mountain acres, which were accessible to them and to few others. The Taos felt connected to the land, its mountain streams and lakes, its forest and all its vegetation and wild life, to the sky, the wind, and all the other elements of nature. There is no word for "religion" in the native language spoken by the Taos. Perhaps this is a result of the fact that religion and religious ritual are not, to them, separate and apart from everyday thought and activity.

The Taos Pueblo is best known for its lovely, hand-built adobe dwellings, designed in stacked stories with each new story offset from the story just beneath it, creating what appears to be a staggered, random scheme but which is so aesthetically pleasing as to have been admired by visitors, including accomplished architects, from all over the world.

Equally deserving of admiration, yet certainly less recognized, was the long, patient struggle of the Taos to regain trust title to land containing what their supporters have termed "shrines"—elements of nature important in the practice of their private rituals. These lands had been removed, without tribal consultation, from the Taos reservation and made part of the U.S. national forest system in the early twentieth century.

The Taos had traditionally used an area that covered some three hundred thousand acres. Spaniards who began colonizing the Southwest in the late sixteenth century recognized the rights of the native peoples, granting each pueblo certain lands that were to be reserved for the exclusive use of the community. Under the Treaty of Guadalupe Hidalgo in 1848, the United States took over the entire territory but continued to recognize the Spanish land grants. The Taos grant covered approximately 17,400 acres. The area that includes and surrounds Blue Lake was a part of this grant, an area that is to the Taos the most important of what they have long considered to be their private ceremonial sites. For them, important stages of life—birth, transition to maturity, and even death—are symbolically associated with the waters of Blue Lake. As a practical matter, Blue Lake has also had great economic significance, as it is the primary source of water for this pueblo of farmers, who grow corn, various fruits, and beans, and raise cattle and sheep.

For a long time, few non-Indians ever went into the area of Blue Lake. Because of its elevation at almost twelve thousand feet and because it was accessible only on foot or horseback, requiring for most travelers a journey of two days from the Taos Pueblo, few were motivated to visit the lake. Toward the end of the nineteenth century, however, settlers began taking up residence on lands that were legally reserved for the pueblo peoples all along the upper Rio Grande. Fearing that their sacred places of prayer and ritual, as well as their water supply, would inevitably suffer intrusion, the Taos were somewhat relieved to learn in 1903, after having registered complaints with the U.S. government, that much of their land was soon to be included in protected national forests. This, they believed, would prevent any permanent settlement by persons who were not members of their small (then, four to five hundred members) pueblo. The Taos requested of the government that the lands and lakes (including Blue Lake) to the north of their pueblo be set aside for their sole use.

The tribal request was not honored. President Theodore Roosevelt, on November 7, 1906, signed an executive order that placed these lands and lakes in the Taos Forest Reserve, thereby bringing them under full and complete ownership and control of the federal government. An ardent conservationist, Roosevelt wished to secure the country's natural resources. Among his highest priorities was the conservation of forests, and he did not believe that the solution to this problem could be left entirely in private hands. He was quoted as having expressed the belief that Native Americans should no more have exclusive ownership of the vast territories that they had long considered their own than should any other individual or group be given ownership of land simply because they took up residence on it, or because they may have wandered it or hunted it for long periods of time.

Roosevelt was rightfully concerned for the nation's forests, which, by the year 1890, had been reduced by 75 percent. Settlers had treated the wild forests as if they were inexhaustible. For them, clearing the land was considered an important part of "civilizing" the West. Homesteaders, who were required to stay on their acreage for at least five years, meanwhile making the land productive, were perhaps equally unaware that timber might ever be in short supply. It was Roosevelt's intent to employ in the United States the sustained-yield methods that had protected the forests of Germany and France from destruction while allowing them to produce as much timber as had been harvested for centuries. It was of some concern to the Progressives, who advocated the use of federally controlled scientific methods, that the Taos might eventually sell or lease their land to loggers who could strip it of its timber and then move on.

It was feared by others that, were they to control Blue Lake and its watershed, the Taos might one day cut off the supply of water to those who were downstream. It was also argued that the tribe no longer needed the vast areas that they had once considered theirs, for the Taos had diminished from some twenty thousand in number when the Spaniards first arrived to fewer than five hundred. It was to become the task of the Taos to counter all such arguments.

In 1908, another executive order made the Taos Forest Reserve part of the Carson National Forest, administered by the recently established United States Forest Service. With these events, use of the traditional mountain lands and waters of the Taos became legally available to any and all who could make their way into these remote wilderness areas. Without assurance from the government of protection of their ritual sites and of their fishing, grazing, and hunting practices, the Taos began their attempt to regain trust title of Blue Lake and its watershed. Their early approach was to emphasize the economic necessity of their use and control of the water and land. It was much later that the significance to their religion of these areas was made a part of their formal argument to Congress.

In 1912, the U.S. commissioner of Indian affairs, pressured by the Indians and their supporters, recommended to the secretary of agriculture that 44,640 acres be set aside as reservation lands for the pueblos. This recommendation was rejected.

The Pueblo Lands Act of 1924, passage of which was advocated by various national Indian organizations, established the Pueblo Lands Board, which was to report to Congress on matters relating to claims to reservation lands by Indians and non-Indians and which could recommend compensation to tribes whose lands had been lost through the government's failure in its responsibilities. The Taos had for years claimed some of the land upon which the town (as opposed to the pueblo) of Taos had been built, for which the Pueblo Lands Board offered them compensation of $300,000. The Taos countered with a pledge to drop their claim and to decline the money offered in exchange for the return of Blue Lake and its watershed. The board had no authority to award land in lieu of money, and so the Taos received neither the land nor the money.

In recognition of the tribe's annual August pilgrimage to Blue Lake, the Forest Service, for the first time acknowledging the area's religious connection for the Taos, in 1927 granted the pueblo exclusive use of the sacred lands for their three cere-monial days. Also, the tribe was permitted nonexclusive year-round use of thirty-one thousand acres. (Congress ratified the Forest Service permit in 1933, and the Depart-ment of the Interior confirmed and amended it in 1940.)

The Indian Claims Commission was established in 1946. It was with this group that the Taos took the first step, in 1951, of a legal battle that would last for nineteen years. Filing a claim for the return to their pueblo of some three hundred thousand acres, they argued on the basis of their religion that it was not money but Blue Lake that they required. In 1965, their claim was approved, though the acreage was re-duced by amounts of land recognized as Spanish grants. Meanwhile, however, the Forest Service had made the area included in the claim open to recreational and economic development. The Taos came to recognize that in order for them to have exclusive control, they needed to have the Blue Lake area made a part of their reser-vation by an act of Congress.

Numerous bills to grant title of the watershed to the Taos were defeated between 1965 and 1970. Finally, in 1970, a bill designed to place forty-eight thousand acres in trust for the exclusive use of the pueblo was passed in the House of Representatives and was sent to the Senate, where it was debated in committee hearings in July of that year. Commercial and conservation lobbies worked to defeat it, but the Taos and their many supporters worked equally hard for passage of the bill. President Richard M. Nixon urged Senate passage, as did the secretary of the interior and other influential Taos friends. Full Senate debate took place on December 1 and 2, and passage occurred on December 2 by a vote of seventy to twelve. On Decem-ber 15, 1970, President Nixon signed the bill into law.

Impact of Event

For the first time, land was returned to Native Americans as the result of a claim argued on the basis that the land was necessary to the practice of their ancestral religion. The Taos had hesitated for years to approach the matter on the basis of religion, because earlier they had been urged strongly by Christian groups to abol-ish their "pagan" practices and had been intimidated by government authorities, who threatened to prohibit what some considered to be improper and immoral cere-monies. The tribe therefore had not dared to make an issue of the spiritual significance to them of the Blue Lake area. After the Taos had for years argued, to no avail, that it was economic need that motivated them, the fact that it was finally on the basis of their religious and spiritual needs that they obtained exclusive rights to the area was a significant and historic moment in relations between Native Americans and the U.S. government. Basing their claims, at least in part, on the Blue Lake decision, other Indian tribes had millions of acres returned to them after the signing of the Blue Lake law. President Nixon (referred to by the Taos religious leader as the tribe's greatest father) had promised to initiate other legislation that would make possible greater independence of action and decision making for Indians. The self-determination initiative finally did become law in November of 1975, and it perhaps did more to empower Indians than any other federal legislation.

At the Taos Pueblo, old and young alike were ecstatic with the news of the return of their sacred lands. Celebrations were held to give thanks. There were parades, chants, feasts, songs, and speeches. The long and painful process of battling the U.S. government for the right to practice their religious rituals at the traditional sites would not be forgotten, but the pain was somewhat diminished by the joy of knowing that that which had for centuries held them together would henceforth not suffer amendment or intrusion by the uninvited.

Bibliography

Bodine, John. "The Taos Blue Lake Ceremony." *American Indian Quarterly* 12 (Spring, 1988): 91-105. Includes the field notes of Matilda Coxe Stevenson, who in 1906 witnessed the Taos Blue Lake ceremony in its entirety. Bodine introduces Stevenson's narrative and follows it with verifications and changes that he obtained from interviews with Taos members. Bodine is certain that John Collier *(On the Gleaming Way)* did not witness the Blue Lake ceremony. With bibliography and notes.

Collier, John, "The Taos Indians' Sacred Wilderness." In *On the Gleaming Way.* Chicago: Sage Books, 1949. The author, U.S. commissioner of Indian affairs from 1933 to 1945, was in 1926 invited by the Taos to accompany them on their annual August trek to Blue Lake and to observe their ceremonies. Thus, Collier became one of the few outsiders ever to have witnessed, by invitation, any such sacred rites. Collier's resulting memorandum to Congress is included in the cited chapter.

Gordon-McCutchan, R. C. *The Taos Indians and the Battle for Blue Lake.* Santa Fe, N.Mex.: Red Crane Books, 1991. The author, a resident of the town of Taos, became a friend of the Taos Pueblo, having been for several years its tribal planner and having assisted in its interaction with the community at large. This book, with a foreword by Frank Waters, a noted novelist and student of the area and its native peoples, has value both to scholars and to others. It is indexed and has chapter notes.

Hecht, Robert A. "Taos Pueblo and the Struggle for Blue Lake." *American Indian Culture and Research Journal* 13, no. 1 (1989): 53-77. Details of the efforts of the Taos and their supporters (Oliver La Farge, Corrine Locker, John Collier, Frank Waters, and others) to regain Blue Lake for the pueblo. With notes.

Keegan, Marcia. *The Taos Indians and Their Sacred Blue Lake.* New York: Julian

Messner, 1972. A large-print book containing many photographs by the author. Of special interest and somewhat rare, perhaps, are quotes from various members of the Taos—elders, officials, and children—about their feelings for nature, their religion, and their reactions to the news of the return of Blue Lake and its watershed. With foreword by Frank Waters.

Morrill, Claire. "The Indian Is the Deer." In *A Taos Mosaic*. Albuquerque: University of New Mexico Press, 1973. This chapter, in a book full of interesting vignettes about tricultural (Spanish, Native American, and Anglo-American) Taos (the name for both the New Mexico town and the Native American pueblo), is devoted to little-known information about the pueblo, its people, its gods, and its struggle for control of its traditional lands and waters. The book contains a very good, though not annotated, bibliography. The author became a bookseller in Taos when she moved there from Michigan in 1947.

P. R. Lannert

Cross-References

Intellectuals Form the Society of American Indians (1911), p. 121; The Indian Reorganization Act Offers Autonomy to American Indians (1934), p. 497; U.S. Government Encourages Native Americans to Settle in Cities (1950's), p. 820; Government Policies Seek to End the Special Status of Native Americans (1953), p. 897; Congress Ratifies the National Council on Indian Opportunity (1970), p. 1537; Native Americans Occupy Wounded Knee (1973), p. 1709.

THE FAMILY PLANNING SERVICES ACT
EXTENDS REPRODUCTIVE RIGHTS

Categories of event: Women's rights and reproductive freedom
Time: December 28, 1970
Locale: Washington, D.C.

Birth control proponents, feminists, and social planners, after decades of advocacy, effected federal legislation making family planning services available to all American women

Principal personages:
MARGARET SANGER (1879-1966), the founder and leader of the American birth control movement
JOSEPH TYDINGS (1928-), a Democratic senator from Maryland and the initial Senate sponsor of the 1970 act
ERNEST GRUENING (1887-1974), the first senator from the state of Alaska
SHIRLEY CHISHOLM (1924-), the first African-American woman elected to Congress
JOHN D. ROCKEFELLER III (1906-1978), a businessman, philanthropist, and chair of the first Presidential Commission on Population and Family Planning
RICHARD M. NIXON (1913-), the thirty-seventh president of the United States, signed the act into law

Summary of Event

Since the beginning of the twentieth century, when the modern "birth control" movement emerged under the leadership of Margaret Sanger, feminists, social planners, and health care professionals have campaigned for public policy that would first acknowledge and then advance the legitimacy and importance of contraception and its practice. The Family Planning Services and Population Research Act of 1970 brought this effort to fruition by legislating a central agency to direct "population affairs" and by designating monies to support and extend family planning services to all Americans regardless of their ability to pay. The act advanced the opportunity for considerable numbers of American women, especially poor women, to have access to birth control information and reproductive health care. Viewed by supporters as a legislative watershed in advancing enlightened health care for women, as well as affording poor women the same opportunities or rights as the advantaged, the bill's most controversial elements, such as abortion, continued to be debated twenty years after its passage and implementation.

During the late nineteenth century and for the greater portion of the twentieth, information about contraception as well as contraceptive aids and procedures, including abortion, were banned in various ways on both the state and federal levels.

Feminists, beginning with Elizabeth Cady Stanton, advocated a woman's right to control the frequency of conception. This extremely controversial position contributed to divisions in the women's rights movement and was eventually abandoned by the mainstream of female suffrage reformers at the turn of the century.

The cause of legal contraception was revived in the twentieth century by the personality and activism of Margaret Sanger. A trained nurse and avowed socialist, Sanger educated herself about "birth control," as she was the first to call it, and then turned to the task of educating American society. She spoke of what she saw daily in New York City's lower East Side, of the women who worked in the sweatshop industries, and their ill health, fatigue, and desperate dread of frequent pregnancies. Sanger's graphic descriptions of these conditions and circumstances, especially the common resort to self-induced and often fatal abortion, awakened a growing number of Americans to the importance of legal birth control. For Sanger and her movement, which grew in size and effectiveness during the first half of the twentieth century, making legal the availability of birth control information, aids, and practice was more than a woman's right: It was essential to ensuring sound public health policy for women and children specifically, and for the American family generally.

During the 1930's, the courts' lifting of the federal ban on birth control combined with the actualities of the Depression to encourage policies that incorporated birth control counseling and reproductive health care into national and federally subsidized state programs. By the end of the decade, two pieces of legislation, Title V of the Social Security Act of 1938 and the Venereal Disease Control Act of 1939, designated several million dollars for maternal and child health services as well as the prevention of sexually transmitted disease. As administered by the Children's Bureau and the United States Public Health Service, these programs offered, to married women only, public health programs that recognized and advanced the legitimacy of birth control practice.

Attitudes about birth control and family planning shifted after the war. During this period of peace and prosperity, concerns about population growth diminished and the ethos of traditional family values prevailed, despite the ever-increasing number of women entering the labor market. Although the Truman and Eisenhower administrations rhetorically endorsed family planning research and reproductive health services, little actual progress was made until the 1960's, when Congress and the Kennedy and Johnson administrations turned national attention once again to issues of poverty and social welfare. In 1963, Senators Ernest Gruening and Joseph Clark introduced legislation calling on the president to increase family planning research programs within the National Institutes of Health and to make widely available the results of such efforts. Two years of extensive hearings followed, heightening public awareness and concern regarding reproductive health care, population growth, and declining resources.

Committed to making war on poverty, President Lyndon Baines Johnson promoted federally financed family planning services, and in his 1966 Message on Domestic Health and Education, endorsed the idea of each American's "freedom to choose the number and spacing of their children within the dictates of individual conscience." In 1967, he appointed a Presidential Committee on Population and Family Planning led by John D. Rockefeller III and Secretary of the Department of Health, Education, and Welfare (HEW), Wilbur Cohen. In the same year, as part of the Johnson legislative agenda, Congress passed amendments to the Social Security Act (Title V) and the Office of Economic Opportunity (OEO) Act, extending reproductive health care programs. Under Social Security, more monies were to be directed specifically to family planning, and all states were required to extend family planning services to any AFDC (Aid to Families with Dependent Children) recipient who requested such. In OEO, project grants for family planning became a special priority. The report of the presidential committee recommended an expenditure of $150 million by 1973 for family planning to reach all women who wanted but could not afford services, a consolidated "Center for Population Research," and appropriations of an additional $130 million for research in 1970 and 1971.

President Richard M. Nixon endorsed, in principle, the recommendations of the Rockefeller Commission, and in 1969, Senator Joseph Tydings and twenty-three cosponsors introduced the Family Planning Services and Population Research Act (S. 2108). The Tydings bill primarily sought to consolidate all extant family planning and population-related programs scattered throughout HEW in a National Center for Population and Family Planning which would also coordinate comparable programs in OEO and other departments, and report to Congress. In this regard, the bill responded to what many believed had been the slowness of HEW to implement the 1967 amendments. Testimony in hearings on the bill emphasized the persistent inadequacy of reproductive health care for poor and "near-poor" women in the United States. HEW's own surveys estimated that fewer than 800,000 of an eligible 5.4 million women were receiving family planning assistance, and Tydings argued that as of late 1969 "it was unlikely that any woman had yet received family planning services through Title V." The bill also specified monies, $89 million more than that recommended by the commission, to be spent in various project grants for family planning services, research, and training. The Nixon Administration introduced its own bill (S. 3219), which avoided any administrative reorganization, but also proposed the various project grants as amendments to the Public Health Services Act, although no appropriations were specified.

For most who supported the bill, the issue of federal family planning services was a matter of equal opportunity. They strongly believed that poor women should have the same "fundamental individual rights" as already enjoyed by the affluent. Allowing poor women to exercise their reproductive rights was understood as a way of attacking the poverty cycle as well. The bill was also designed to address the larger issue of "unwanted births," especially those resulting from ineffective contraception, which most agreed contributed to family instability for rich and poor alike. Not only did the bill encourage more aggressive research in the field of safe and effective contraception, but it tacitly responded to the arguments of a small group of feminists who held that women had an absolute right to control all phases of reproduction, including the option of medically advised abortion. Representative Shirley Chisholm, calling the laws prohibiting abortion "compulsory pregnancy laws," argued for the legalization of abortion and that it be recognized in the proposed legislation as an acceptable method of family planning. Neither Senate bill mentioned abortion, leaving the option open for its recognition.

The House received the Senate bills and, although enthusiastically supporting the Tydings version in principle, found reason to propose alternative legislation. The modifications concerned the authorization for the project grants, stipulating these as amendments to the Public Health Services Act at a significantly smaller dollar amount, and the provision that no federal monies used in the context of family planning be expended on abortion. Although the preponderant testimony before the House endorsed all aspects of the Tydings bill, the National Right to Life Committee, making its public debut, joined the traditional Catholic opposition and argued against any federal acknowledgment of abortion as legitimate. The House clearly did not want to have to defend the expenditure of tax money on this controversial and still, in all states, illegal practice of birth control. Nor did the Senate, which, after conferees met, agreed to the House version. On December 28, 1970, President Nixon signed into law the Family Planning Services and Population Research Act making contraception, excluding abortion, available to all American women as their right and as a vital means for improving the quality of life for all.

Impact of Event

With the passage of the Family Planning Services and Population Research Act, considerable amounts of money were directed to reproductive health care for the first time. In 1973, when Congress considered extending the bill for three more years, close to three million American women were receiving comprehensive family planning services under its provisions, although it was estimated that close to seven million women still remained to be served. Throughout the 1970's and 1980's, women's groups, public health leaders, and the Planned Parenthood Federation of America lobbied for increased appropriations, with minimal success. In 1991, federal grants to clinics administered by the Office of Population Affairs in the Public Health Service amounted to $144 million. Twenty years after the bill's passage, various family planning programs were conducted in four thousand voluntary clinics, community health centers, county health departments, and hospitals around the country, serving more than four million women. Most of the women served by these programs were poor or had low income; one-third were adolescents. As a result of the 1970 law, poor and unmarried women had access to the same reproductive health care available to the nonpoor and married.

From its inception, the most controversial aspect of the legislation was the role abortion should play in federally subsidized family planning services. After the Supreme Court's 1973 ruling in *Roe v. Wade*, the issue became particularly vexing for policymakers whose intent was to extend to poor women the same reproductive health care available to the nonpoor. As long as state law and court dicta recognized the legality of abortion as defined by the guidelines of *Roe*, poor women not served by public programs or whose contraception failed had little recourse in terminating unwanted pregnancies. In 1975, the Hyde amendment was passed, denying Medicaid reimbursements for elective abortions, and in 1977, Congress liberalized this restriction somewhat by allowing for Medicaid reimbursements only in cases of rape, incest, or endangerment of the woman's life. These restrictions left millions of poor women the choice of forced motherhood or "back-alley" abortion.

After 1973, prolife groups, primarily from the religious right, proliferated and increasingly put pressure on Congress and the courts to undermine and overturn the *Roe* decision. Public clinics often were targeted for protest demonstrations. By the 1980's, violent confrontation of this type was a common occurrence. Despite this activity and the modified Hyde amendment, the family planning programs operated during the first seventeen years under regulations that allowed clinic employees to provide information about abortion as well as about childbirth. Title X of the law was interpreted as referring only to abortions themselves, not to advice or information about abortion.

In 1988, the Reagan Administration openly embraced the right-wing agenda on reproduction and issued new regulations prohibiting federally financed family plan ning clinics from all discussion of abortion with their patients, even if the patient so inquired. Although never implemented because of various court challenges, on May 24, 1991, the Supreme Court upheld the regulatory prohibition in *Rust v. Sullivan* on the grounds that federal and state governments were not constitutionally required to pay for abortions, even if they chose to subsidize childbirth. Soon after the *Rust* decision, legislation was introduced in Congress to remove the restrictions of Title X. With the *Rust* decision and the conservative bent of the Reagan-Bush Supreme Court, family planning advocates and feminists expressed fear that the progress made since the 1960's on the front of women's and reproductive rights might be eroded seriously.

Bibliography

Berelson, Bernard. *Family Planning Programs: An International Survey.* New York: Basic Books, 1969. The introduction by John D. Rockefeller III and various chapters give a good composite of social planners' and policymakers' views concerning population control on the eve of the act's passage. Index only.

Cisler, Lucinda. "Unfinished Business: Birth Control and Women's Liberation." In *Sisterhood Is Powerful: An Anthology of Writings from the Women's Liberation Movement,* edited by Robin Morgan. New York: Random House, 1970. This article offers an excellent feminist analysis of the legal status and availability of contraception and abortion on the eve of the act's passage. Appendix includes bibliography and abortion counseling information.

Gordon, Linda. *Woman's Body, Woman's Right: Birth Control in America.* New York: Penguin Books, 1990. This volume is the definitive history of birth control in America. Chapters 13 through 16 offer excellent feminist analysis of birth control law and practice and activists' response to these during the period of the 1970 act. She makes no mention of specific federal laws during this period. Index but no bibliography. See also Linda Gordon and Allen Hunter, "Sex, Family, and the New Right," in *Radical America* 11 (Winter, 1977-1978): 9-25.

Hole, Judith, and Ellen Levine. "Origins and Development of the New Women's Movement" and "Abortion." In *Rebirth of Feminism.* New York: Quadrangle Books, 1973. These two chapters offer a good synthesis of the issue of reproductive rights with predominant attention given to abortion. Little discussion of legislative action. Chronology, historical documents, bibliography, and index.

Kennedy, David M. *Birth Control in America: The Career of Margaret Sanger.* New Haven, Conn.: Yale University Press, 1970. Focusing on Sanger's long career, Kennedy offers an excellent account of the birth control movement and the politics that led to liberalization of law and policy. Bibliographical essay and index.

McGlen, Nancy E., and Karen O'Connor. "Part III: Family and Lifestyle Rights." In *Women's Rights: The Struggle for Equality in the Nineteenth and Twentieth Centuries.* New York: Praeger, 1983. Although this chapter covers the broad spectrum of women's rights within the family, it offers an adequate, brief summary of reproductive rights. Of particular interest is the discussion of the impact of the "New Right" in the 1970's and 1980's. Index only.

Nancy A. White

Cross-References

Sanger Opens the First Birth-Control Clinic in the United States (1916), p. 184; Sanger Organizes Conferences on Birth Control (1921), p. 356; The National Council of Churches Supports Birth Control (1961), p. 1096; The Supreme Court Rules That State Laws Cannot Ban Contraceptives (1965), p. 1290; Chisholm Becomes the First Black Woman Elected to Congress (1968), p. 1451; *Roe v. Wade* Expands Reproductive Choice for American Women (1973), p. 1703; Prolife Groups Challenge Abortion Laws (1989), p. 2443; The National Organization for Women Sponsors an Abortion Rights Rally (1989), p. 2489.

CONGRESS PASSES THE OCCUPATIONAL SAFETY AND HEALTH ACT

Category of event: Workers' rights
Time: December 29, 1970
Locale: Washington, D.C.

Congress passed the Occupational Safety and Health Act in 1970 with the aim of correcting hazardous and unsafe working conditions through federal law

Principal personages:
JOSEPH LANE KIRKLAND (1922-   ), an AFL-CIO president, testified before Congress that the Occupational Safety and Health Act was beneficial to American workers
GEORGE MEANY (1894-1980), an AFL-CIO president and supporter of the Occupational Safety and Health Act
RICHARD M. NIXON (1913-   ), a business-backed U.S. president who recognized the need to protect working Americans

Summary of Event

In response to public concern over the human and financial toll exacted by workplace deaths and injuries, Congress enacted the Occupational Safety and Health Act (OSHA Act) in 1970. Although many business interests opposed this act, President Richard M. Nixon supported it in order to obtain working-class votes for himself and the Republican party and to secure better relations with American Federation of Labor-Congress of Industrial Organizations (AFL-CIO) president George Meany. During congressional consideration of the act, data presented to Congress indicated that 14,500 workers annually died of job related causes and an additional 2 million were injured. Most of the workers suffering job-related injury or death were working-class individuals employed in manufacturing.

Although some states attempted to regulate workplace safety, conditions varied widely. Congress decided that a national floor for workplace standards was needed. Although several earlier federal laws, such as the Walsh-Healey Act of 1936, had dealt with workplace safety, previous federal legislation in the area of workplace safety had been extremely limited. Miners had benefited from the Federal Coal Mine Health and Safety Act of 1969.

Using its authority to regulate interstate commerce, Congress stated in the OSHA Act that it desired "to encourage employers and employees in their efforts to reduce the number of occupational safety and health hazards at their places of employment." Reflecting Republican input and recognizing a joint employer-employee responsibility for workplace safety, Congress desired to spur private sector efforts to improve workplace safety. Accepting the limitations of private sector action, Congress also granted the secretary of labor authority to impose minimum safety standards and to support research in the field of occupational safety. A system of fines was set up to allow the Labor Department to enforce compliance with the standards it set. Advance notice to employers of workplace visits was expressly prohibited.

Within the Labor Department, the Occupational Safety and Health Act of 1970 (Public Law 91-596), provided the mandate for the creation of the Occupational Safety and Health Administration (OSHA). The OSHA Act charges OSHA to develop and promulgate safety and health standards, develop and issue regulations, conduct extensive job site investigations to determine the extent of workplace compliance with safety and health standards and regulations, and issue citations to employers and propose penalties for employers who fail to comply with standards and regulations. In addition to OSHA, the OSHA Act also created the Occupational Safety and Health Review Commission, which is an independent, quasijudicial agency known as the OSHRC. It is the responsibility of the OSHRC to rule on cases forwarded to it by the Department of Labor in which disagreement exists after occupational safety and health inspections. Employers may dispute alleged health and safety violations. The OSHA Act also established the National Institute for Occupational Safety and Health (NIOSH) as the research arm of federal regulation of worker safety. NIOSH became part of the Centers for Disease Control, which in 1991 were housed in the Department of Health and Human Services.

Many politically liberal and prolabor writers contend that the OSHA Act was an attempt at compromise between employer and worker interests that created an awkward administrative structure. This structure made enforcement of even minimal standards difficult, particularly in periods of limited funding and staffing for the Occupational Safety and Health Administration, which enjoyed no funding increases during the Reagan years and lost 20 percent of its staff in 1981. Even probusiness writers generally agree that the enforcement of OSHA standards declined dramatically during Ronald Reagan's presidency to an unfortunate extent. The Reagan Administration believed in a policy of minimal government intervention in the affairs of business, and Reagan appointed assistant secretaries of labor in charge of occupational safety and health who had strong ties to business and limited interest in federal safety standards.

Unfortunately for workers, OSHA produced only twenty-three health standards in its first twenty years, and these standards took six to eight years each to produce. Since approximately five thousand new substances are introduced into American workplaces each year, OSHA action consistently falls behind workplace realities. For this reason, most writers agreed that it was vital to have a secretary of labor dedicated to the enforcement of OSHA regulations and standards and a strong assistant secretary of labor for occupational safety and health. Weak Reagan-era assistant secretaries almost destroyed the agency, and several faced significant conflict of interest charges.

Authors sympathetic to worker rights and job safety point out that OSHA's actions in its first twenty years of existence resulted in the prosecution of only fourteen people by the U.S. Department of Justice for violating workplace health and safety regulations. Only one employer went to jail, with a sentence of forty-five days for workplace safety violations that resulted in two deaths. Under federal law, the government can file criminal charges against employers only when death occurs and evidence of willful violations exists. OSHA employed no criminal investigator as late as 1991. With some reason, critics can conclude that OSHA is a "paper tiger" that adopts existing industry standards as the basis for federal policy or uses business-dominated groups such as the National Safety Council to develop its new standards.

Because federal enforcement of the OSHA Act has produced limited results, state action in the field of workplace health and safety has assumed increasing importance. Section 18(a) of the act expressly permitted state regulation in areas where no federal standard exists. Section 18(b) of the OSHA Act allowed states to submit occupational health and safety standards to OSHA for approval under standards set forth under Section 18(c) of the OSHA Act. Advocates of strong state action in the field of occupational safety can also use the introductory text of the OSHA Act to support their views. The OSHA Act stated that Congress wished to continue "encouraging the States to assume the responsibility for the administration and enforcement of their occupational safety and health laws by providing grants to the states. . . ." The states were also promised grant funding to assist them in promoting greater occupational safety.

Court action related to occupational safety has focused on whether states may criminally prosecute employers responsible for unsafe health and safety conditions. Employers and employer groups have used the supremacy clause in the United States Constitution to contend that the OSHA Act preempts state action in this area. This employer viewpoint has had limited success in the courts, and employee advocates now often look to state action rather than OSHA action to protect workers, although some convincing statistical evidence exists that OSHA enforcement can have some teeth in larger, union shop workplaces.

Impact of Event

The history of the administration of the OSHA Act indicates that it has not created the essentially uniform national standard for workplace health and safety envisioned by its supporters in 1970. Increasingly, business groups turned to the OSHA Act to attempt to preclude tougher state action to protect workers and punish negligent employers. Despite the fact that the OSHA Act has not lived up in practice to the expectations of its supporters, it has established the principle that some national action is needed to protect worker health and safety. This represents an important gain for working people. Both union and nonunion groups sympathetic to worker interests must push for vigorous OSHA Act enforcement and adequate funding and staffing for OSHA. It is significant that Lane Kirkland, president of the American Federation of Labor-Congress of Industrial Organizations (AFL-CIO), credited the OSHA Act with at least some beneficial impact on worker safety and desired stronger enforcement of OSHA standards. Opinion in the early 1990's seemed to be reaching a consensus that stronger federal job safety enforcement efforts were needed, even if significant financial burdens would be imposed on the business community. Greater OSHA funding and staffing could produce more frequent federal inspection of unsafe workplaces, and it could also reduce the time required for OSHA to produce standards for handling dangerous materials such as asbestos.

To complement their support of strong OSHA enforcement, worker advocates sought vigorous criminal actions in state courts to impose criminal sanctions against employers responsible for unhealthy and unsafe working conditions. The high courts of Illinois, Michigan, and New York ruled that the OSHA Act does not preempt state criminal prosecution of negligent employers. In effect, the U.S. Supreme Court sustained the opinion (a conviction of the employer for aggravated battery and assault) in the *Chicago Magnet Wire Case* by declining to review it. Decisions in state courts have made employers criminally responsible when supervisory negligence contributes to worker death. State criminal sanctions for negligent employers in key occupational safety cases are more attractive means of inducing corrective action than fines, since wealthy corporations might include fines in their estimated cost of doing business and consider the payment of fines cost effective. Subjecting executives to criminal charges has significant potential for forcing corporate rethinking of safety practices, particularly in manufacturing enterprises dealing with dangerous chemicals and hazardous waste. The OSHA Act sees worker death as justifying only a maximum sentence of one year in prison and a $20,000 fine. State court criminal action can produce significantly tougher penalties.

Bibliography

Ballam, Deborah A. "The Occupational Safety and Health Act's Preemptive Effect on State Criminal Prosecutions of Employers for Workplace Deaths and Injuries." *American Business Law Journal* 26 (January, 1988): 1-27. Ballam contends that, given the U.S. Supreme Court's view of federalism at the time, the Court was unlikely to find that the OSHA Act prohibited state prosecution of employers for workplace deaths and injuries. Her view contrasts with that of Burstein and Cramer.
Bock, G. "Safety First?" *Common Cause* 15 (September/October 1989): 12. Bock contends that OSHA fines are good publicity for the agency but do little for workplace safety.
Burstein, James A., and Michael H. Cramer. "The Practical Labor Lawyer: A Split Among State Courts: Does the OSHA Act Preempt Criminal Prosecution of Employers for Workplace Injuries?" *Employee Relations Law Journal* 15 (Autumn, 1989): 307-313. In a proemployer view of the OSHA Act, Burstein and Cramer contend that there are strong arguments that the act preempts state criminal prosecution of employers for workplace hazards. They call for U.S. Supreme Court reversal of the Illinois Supreme Court's decision in the *Chicago Magnet Wire Case.*
Garland, Susan B. "This Safety Ruling Could Be Hazardous to Employers' Health." *Business Week* (February 20, 1989): 34. Garland briefly reviews the *Chicago Magnet Wire Case* and other decisions that deny OSHA preemption of state prosecu-

tion of employers for workplace safety violations.

Goldsmith, Willis J. "Current Developments in OSHA." *Employee Relations Law Journal* 11 (Summer, 1988): 700-707. Goldsmith discusses specific OSHA standards in varied fields. He also treats the role of the OSHA Review Commission.

Holzman, Sy. "The Occupational Safety and Health Act: Is It Time for Change?" *Northern Kentucky Law Review* 17 (1989): 177-193. Holzman considers the arguments for an overhaul of the OSHA Act. He contends that a full overhaul is less likely than administrative changes and adjustments.

Keehn, Holly Coates. "Bridging the Gap: The Problem of Uniquely Susceptible Individuals in the Workplace." *Tulane Labor Law Review* 64 (June, 1990): 1677-1708. Keehn describes how the OSHA Act and employment discrimination laws have failed to meet the needs of workers with more than the usual susceptibility to workplace hazards. Pregnant women are used as a prominent example. She recommends additional federal legislation in this area.

Mintz, Benjamin. *OSHA: History, Law, and Policy.* Washington, D.C.: B.N.A. Books, 1985. Mintz provides a general summary of the impact of the OSHA Act up to 1985.

Serrin, William. "The Wages of Work." *Nation* 252 (January 28, 1991): 80-82. Serrin finds OSHA ineffective and advocates a more direct worker role in policing workplace safety issues. He is not optimistic about the chances for improved worker safety.

Weil, David. "Enforcing OSHA: The Role of Labor Unions." *Industrial Relations* 30 (Winter, 1991): 20-36. Weil argues that unionized workplaces receive better OSHA enforcement than do nonunionized workplaces. He also holds that larger workplaces receive better OSHA enforcement than smaller firms.

Susan A. Stussy

Cross-References

The Congress of Industrial Organizations Is Formed (1938), p. 545; Jouhaux Is Awarded the Nobel Peace Prize (1951), p. 873; Chávez Forms Farm Workers' Union and Leads Grape Pickers' Strike (1962), p. 1161; The International Labour Organisation Wins the Nobel Peace Prize (1969), p. 1509; Chávez Is Jailed for Organizing an Illegal Lettuce Boycott (1970), p. 1567; Manville Offers $2.5 Billion to Victims of Asbestos Dust (1985), p. 2274.

SRI LANKANS PROMOTE NATIONALISM

Categories of event: Civil rights and indigenous peoples' rights
Time: 1971
Locale: Sri Lanka

The Sinhalese majority in Ceylon fomented a nationalist movement in 1971, resulting in a new constitution in 1972 and a renaming of the country as Sri Lanka

Principal personages:
SIRIMAVO BANDARANAIKE (1916-   ), the prime minister of Sri Lanka during the Sinhalese nationalist fervor
ROHANA WIJEWEERA (1942-   ), established the radical JVP Party in the 1960's and masterminded the revolt in April, 1971
COLIN DE SILVA, a highly renowned barrister in Sri Lanka who was a key member of the Constitutional Council

Summary of Event

The political and civil affairs of Sri Lanka reached a crisis in 1971. In that year, punctuated by the revolution of April, 1971, a number of discontented groups pressured the government to make changes in the structure of society, culminating in the adoption of a new constitution in 1972 and the renaming of the country, formerly known as Ceylon.

The events of 1971 manifested the political currents which had been building since the early 1950's, when Ceylon was a newly independent country. This country was almost unique among the panoply of emerging nations, since the nationalist movement was circumscribed by a constitutional framework and was hence exceptionally peaceful. Politics were dominated largely by the elite Tamil minority, who kept close ties to the language, education, and culture of their colonial power, England. Involvement of the "masses" in politics grew during the late 1950's, and a number of political groups were formed in addition to the dominant United National Party (UNP), composed of the Western-oriented elite. Most influential among these groups was the Sri Lanka Freedom Party (SLFP), largely Sinhalese Buddhists, led by Solomon Bandaranaike. In 1956, the Mahajana Eksath Peramuna (MEP, or People's United Front), composed of the SLFP, the Viplavakari Lanka Samasamaj (VLSSP, or Revolutionary Ceylon Equal Society), and the Sinhala Bhasha Peramuna (Sinhalese Language Front), won a great number of seats in an elected house. Members of the MEP began to put pressure on the UNP to sever colonial ties and end the rule by the elites, who still valued their cultural attachment to England. The coalition led by Bandaranaike represented the growing Sinhalese Buddhist nationalism. The parties favored indigenization and socialization in domestic affairs and nonalignment in foreign affairs. The system of two major parties, and competition between the UNP and the SLFP, thus began in 1956.

When Bandaranaike was assassinated in 1959, his widow, Sirimavo Bandaranaike, took over the SLFP. She was elected in 1960 and reelected in 1970. The 1970 election brought a dual-level polarization in the political system of the country, both at the center, between the two major parties and their affiliates, and between the center and the regions. Sinhalese-Buddhist sentiment strengthened and put enormous pressure on the government to change the fabric of Sri Lankan society and to recognize officially the Sinhalese-Buddhist nature of the culture. Great debates took place as to how to rewrite the constitution.

The Sinhalese-Buddhist coalition in government shifted its stance more toward the communist world to eliminate obvious connections to England. It vowed to establish a more egalitarian, socialist form of government, based on traditional values held by the majority in Sri Lanka.

Extreme demands were put on the government by radical groups touting their Buddhist heritage. An extreme leftist group, the Janattha Vimukthi Peramuna (JVP, or People's Liberation Front), established by Rohana Wijeweera in the late 1960's and comprising Sinhalese and Buddhists, started agitating against the government. Supported by students and poor Sinhalese youth, the party had voted for the SLFP and then planned to overthrow it. The group led an armed uprising in April, 1971, that resulted in the deaths of as many as ten thousand at the hands of government security guards. Historian K. M. de Silva called the 1971 JVP insurrection "perhaps the biggest revolt by young people in any part of the world in recorded history, the first instance of tension between generations becoming military conflict on a national scale." The JVP symbolized the aggregated aspirations of the younger and less-accommodated section of the Sinhalese masses and disenchantment with the alleged "centrist" character of the government. The uprising made apparent that the government was paying mere lip-service to the true economic needs of the poor.

The second constitution, adopted in 1972, was an attempt on the part of the SLFP-led United Front Coalition to create new political institutions reflecting more indigenous values than did the original constitution. Changing the name of the country from Ceylon to Sri Lanka, the constitution abandoned the notion of a secular state and designated Sinhala as the national language, replacing joint use of English, Sinhala, and Tamil. The constitution declared that the Republic of Sri Lanka would give to Buddhism the foremost place. It would be the duty of the state to protect and foster Buddhism while assuring religious freedom for non-Buddhists. The constitution established a republic devoted to the creation of a "socialist democracy."

The founding of the Civil Rights Movement of Sri Lanka in 1971 marked the beginning of a public consciousness regarding the rights of the citizens of Sri Lanka, as well as political detainees and prisoners, and served as an active check on the government's abuse of power. Composed mostly of lawyers and supported by the conservative United National Party (UNP), which had dominated politics before the SLFP obtained power, this group worked actively against the government's attempts to exploit its powers, recognizing that only an organized and articulate pressure group could act as a brake on the inroads into fundamental freedoms contemplated by the government. The group was one of many protective associations formed during the early 1970's to lobby against many aspects of the new constitution which they considered gave too much power to the government, failed to honor the rights of citizens, and leaned too far toward totalitarianism or communism. The Civil Rights Movement argued against the establishment of the Constitutional Court, which was to provide a final opinion on the constitutionality of the efforts of the government to implement its socialist policies and was thought to be a mere appendage of the government. The Civil Rights Movement presented evidence before the parliamentary select committee on the revision of the constitution, insisting that the functioning of the Constitutional Court did not inspire confidence in that institution. The Civil Rights Movement announced that it would never again appear before the court. The Civil Rights Movement also unsuccessfully attempted in the early 1970's to prevent Mrs. Bandaranaike from establishing a press council to control and censor the press in Sri Lanka.

The Civil Rights Movement also kept a vigilant eye on the operation of the supreme court, which was required to provide its opinion on bills "urgent in the national interest" within a period not exceeding three days. The group also provided free legal advice and aid to citizens who believed that their rights were not being safeguarded properly in the legal system, which had been established primarily to support the actions of the government, not the people. The Civil Rights Movement continued its work for decades, publicizing human rights abuses and writing monographs and books regarding mysterious deaths and torture of political prisoners.

Impact of Event

The nationalistic fervor which gained a strong political force in the early 1970's had both positive and negative impacts on Sri Lankan society. The positive impacts related to the indigenization of the Sri Lankan society and to the official recognition of the predominant Buddhist heritage. The society turned inward after breaking its colonial ties. The nationalist movement also succeeded in ending the domination of society by the minority Tamil elite who maintained their alliance with England.

The establishment of the Civil Rights Movement of Sri Lanka in 1971 heralded an enhanced consciousness of the rights of citizens in general, and of political prisoners and detainees in particular. It acted as an international window on the abuses of the government and mustered international support to pressure the government to conform to standards of just and humane treatment of such prisoners. The Civil Rights Movement, however, has been criticized as being an elite organization, commenting mostly on issues affecting the privileged and more affluent social groups.

The nationalist fervor of the early 1970's, although advancing an indigenous culture, also served to alienate the Tamils and to catalyze a radical reaction to the Sinhalese-Buddhist government which would create havoc, violence, and ethnic disputes into the 1990's. The government of the early 1970's established policies which discriminated against the Tamil minority, which had enjoyed a privileged position in Sri Lankan society. One such policy governed university admissions. Prior to the early 1970's, the Tamils were greatly overrepresented in the ranks of professional faculties at the university as a result of the fact that they generally had a higher educational level than the Sinhalese. For example, in 1969, 50 percent of the students in the faculties of medicine and 43 percent of all engineering students were Tamil, in spite of the fact that they represented only 12 percent of the overall population of the country. The government passed a preferential admissions system known as the "policy of standardization." This was a geographically based criterion, but because the two ethnic communities tended to be regionally segregated, such a policy increased Sinhalese enrollments. The scheme established quotas for 70 percent of university places on the basis of revenue districts, including a special allotment of 15 percent reserved for the educationally underprivileged. By the early 1980's, the result of such policies was striking: Only 22 percent of medical students and 28 percent of engineering students were Tamils.

These admissions policies also were reflected in the numbers of Tamils in the professional ranks of government. State-employed Tamil physicians declined from 35 percent in the 1966-1970 period to 30 percent in 1978-1979; engineers from a 38 percent average in 1971-1977 to 25 percent in 1978-1979; and clerical workers from 11 percent in 1970-1977 to about 5 percent in 1978-1979. By 1980, only 12 percent of employees in the public sector were Tamils.

The Sinhalese Buddhists also established a discriminatory hiring policy in the public sector, called the "chit system." Under this system, legislators had to write a memorandum or "chit" to personnel authorities recommending their candidate of choice. These favored the legislators' own supporters, who were by and large Sinhalese.

Government-sponsored settlement schemes also exacerbated the ethnic tensions. The government planned to resettle the Sinhalese in the northern or eastern parts of the island, which traditionally had been Tamil. For example, there was a scheme to settle thirty thousand Sinhalese in the dry zone of the northern province, giving each settler land and funds to build a house and each community armed protection in the form of rifles and machine guns. Tamils accused the government of a new form of "colonialism" and organized themselves into a United Front, which would become more powerful and aggressive during the following years.

Bibliography

Civil Rights Movement of Sri Lanka. *Death in Custody.* Colombo, Sri Lanka: Author, 1988. This report exposes the mistreatment of political detainees in Sri Lanka and some of their mysterious deaths.

Diamond, Larry, Juan J. Linz, and Seymour Martin Lipset, eds. *Democracy in Developing Countries.* 4 vols. Boulder, Colo.: Lynne Rienner, 1988-1989. Contains a very informative chapter on Sri Lanka, titled "Crises of Legitimacy and Integration," which discusses the unique strains on democracy in Sri Lanka.

Jayasuriya, D. C. *Mechanics of Constitutional Change: The Sri Lankan Style.* Sri Lanka: Asia Pathfinders and Booksellers, 1982. Jayasuriya discusses the constitutional changes in Sri Lanka, in particular the "Second Republican Constitution" enacted in 1972. Describes the emergence of civil rights movements in Sri Lanka.

Jupp, James. *Sri Lanka: Third World Democracy.* London: Frank Cass and Co., 1978. This book provides a very detailed and personal account of the development of democracy in Sri Lanka. The personalities involved in the various parties are explored in detail, as are the major influential families.

Kearney, Robert N. *The Politics of Ceylon (Sri Lanka).* Ithaca, N.Y.: Cornell University Press, 1975. Kearney describes the development of politics in Sri Lanka in great detail. The book was written during the period covered by this article and provides almost minute-by-minute coverage.

Rajanaygam, R. *Sri Lanka: Human Rights Violations—Extrajudicial and Arbitrary Killings.* London: Human Rights Council and Tamil Information Centre, 1987. This report describes the human rights abuses of Tamils in Sri Lanka and the way that political opponents were treated, without any regard for due process.

Ross, Russell, and Andrea Mattles Savada. *Sri Lanka: A Country Study.* Washington, D.C.: Library of Congress, 1988. This book, produced largely to brief foreign service officers on assignment to Sri Lanka, contains a very exhaustive analysis of the political situation as well as the civil rights movement and various political groups.

Rubin, Barnett R. *Cycles of Violence: Human Rights in Sri Lanka Since the Indo-Sri Lanka Agreement.* Washington, D.C.: Asia Watch, 1987. This report discusses the continued violations of human rights even after the Indian attempt to reach a peaceful settlement between Sinhalese and Tamils.

Saran, Parmatma. *Government and Politics of Sri Lanka.* New Delhi: Metropolitan, 1982. This study provides a critical study of the various aspects of government and politics in Sri Lanka, including the foundations of government, constitutional development, and party and group politics.

Randal J. Thompson-Dorman

Cross-References

The Tamil Federal Party Agitates for Greater Language Rights (1961), p. 1090; Zia Establishes Martial Law in Pakistan (1977), p. 1898; Zulfikar Ali Bhutto Is Hanged Despite Pleas from World Leaders (1979), p. 2018; Tamil Separatist Violence Erupts in Sri Lanka (1980's), p. 2068; Government-Supported Death Squads Quash JVP Insurrection in Sri Lanka (1987), p. 2315.

FBI AND CIA INTERFERENCE IN THE CIVIL RIGHTS MOVEMENT IS REVEALED

Categories of event: Civil rights; peace movements and organizations
Time: 1971-1974
Locale: The United States

Overstepping their traditional boundaries of investigation, the FBI and CIA attempted to disrupt and discredit various civil rights and peace movements in the 1960's

Principal personages:
J. EDGAR HOOVER (1895-1972), the director of the United States Federal Bureau of Investigation from 1924 to 1972
RICHARD HELMS (1913-   ), the director of the United States Central Intelligence Agency from 1965 to 1973
LYNDON B. JOHNSON (1908-1973), the thirty-sixth president of the United States (1963-1969)
RICHARD M. NIXON (1913-   ), the thirty-seventh president of the United States (1969-1974)
GERALD R. FORD (1913-   ), the thirty-eighth president of the United States (1974-1977)
RONALD REAGAN (1911-   ), the fortieth president of the United States (1981-1989)

Summary of Event

For many years, the United States Federal Bureau of Investigation (FBI) enjoyed a sterling reputation under the leadership of its longtime director, J. Edgar Hoover. In the later years of Hoover's administration, however, questions about overzealousness and abuse began to arise. Similar questions were raised about the United States Central Intelligence Agency (CIA) which always had been more controversial. Most of the CIA controversy focused on its foreign operations, for it was forbidden a domestic intelligence role. In the early 1970's, however, evidence emerged of illegal or improper domestic activity by both agencies, a significant part of it targeted against civil rights and anti-Vietnam War groups and individuals.

In 1971, a group calling itself the Commission to Investigate the FBI revealed a number of FBI documents which suggested that the agency had conducted intrusive, if not illegal, campaigns against a number of antiwar and New Left organizations. In October of the same year, the Committee for Public Justice and the Woodrow Wilson School of Princeton University sponsored a conference, "Investigating the FBI," which focused media attention on alleged FBI abuses in investigating civil rights and antiwar activities. Little evidence for these abuses could be produced, as the bureau closely guarded what it considered to be privileged information. After the death in

1972 of the FBI's powerful director, J. Edgar Hoover, and with the Watergate scandal in 1973 and 1974, public pressure mounted for further investigation. Finally, suits filed in December, 1973, and March, 1974, under the Freedom of Information Act resulted in publication of a number of FBI Counter Intelligence Program (COIN-TELPRO) files. The information in these files, coupled with documentation implicating the CIA in domestic intelligence abuses, prompted congressional investigation into the activities of both agencies. Although many FBI and CIA files had been destroyed or altered, the investigations revealed that both organizations had carried out a number of programs intended to undermine, discredit, or destroy civil rights and antiwar movements in the 1960's.

In 1964, following a number of race-related incidents, President Lyndon B. Johnson ordered the FBI to investigate the causes of racial unrest. In April, 1965, the bureau began investigating student antiwar groups for communist influence. When neither of these investigations found illegal or communist activity, Hoover intensified the programs. By 1968, the FBI had established two counterintelligence programs to gather data on black and student movements. COINTELPRO-Black Nationalist-Hate Groups extended to all forty-one FBI field offices authority for collecting information on civil rights groups. COINTELPRO-New Left attempted to undermine the activities of alleged campus radicals, with authority again given to all FBI field offices. Tactics included extensive wiretapping; planting listening devices in homes, hotel rooms, and meeting places of various organizations; infiltrating groups; and fabricating documents to create hostility within and among the organizations.

Specific evidence derived from the FBI's COINTELPRO files reveals that the bureau found certain individuals to be of particular interest. Martin Luther King, Jr., civil rights leader and recipient of the Nobel Peace Prize, was under intense FBI scrutiny from 1961 until his death in 1968. In 1964, shortly before King was to receive the Nobel Prize, the FBI sent him a tape of damaging information it had collected regarding his private life and threatened to make the data public if he did not commit suicide.

Leaders of the Black Panther Party (BPP) and the Student Nonviolent Coordinating Committee (SNCC) were also targets of FBI activity. When the two groups proposed a merger in 1968, the FBI engineered a rift between the groups. The rift contributed to decisions of high-ranking members of both groups, Stokely Carmichael of the SNCC and Eldridge Cleaver of the BPP, to go underground. The FBI accomplished this and other similar operations by fabricating stories and circulating them among members of targeted organizations. For example, the bureau leaked information that Carmichael was a CIA informant. It also telephoned his mother claiming that members of the BPP had threatened to kill Carmichael because of his alleged CIA affiliation. Carmichael left for Africa the next day.

FBI infiltrators at times encouraged illegal activities among groups which they had joined in order to create public disapproval of the organizations. These agents were known as provocateurs. One of the best-known provocateurs, Thomas Tongyai, traveled throughout western New York encouraging students to participate in violent activities such as bombing buildings and killing police.

The FBI's disruptive capabilities were enhanced by using local police and other federal agencies to collect data. For example, from 1968 through 1974, the FBI obtained confidential tax information from the Internal Revenue Service on 120 militant black and antiwar leaders. The CIA also became an important source of documentation and information for the FBI.

Although the CIA has no authority to gather information regarding domestic matters, that agency began collecting information on American citizens at the request of President Johnson. The agency's Special Operations Group, later known as CHAOS, was begun in August, 1967, to determine the role of foreign influence in the American peace movement. President Richard Nixon increased the demands on the CIA in 1970 by requiring that it became involved in evaluating and coordinating intelligence gathered on dissident groups. Some of the groups targeted for infiltration by the CIA included the SNCC, the Women's Strike for Peace, the Washington Peace Center, and the Congress of Racial Equality.

CIA Director Richard Helms was aware of the implications of the agency operating outside its jurisdiction. In a cover memo to a 1968 report on student revolutionary activities around the world, including the United States, Helms noted that "This is an area not within the charter of this Agency. . . . Should anyone learn of its existence it would prove most embarrassing for all concerned." The report concluded that student unrest was a product of domestic alienation, not of foreign manipulation, but the CIA continued to gather data on American citizens. By the early 1970's, the CIA had accumulated open files on more than 64,000 citizens and a computerized index of more than 300,000 individuals and organizations, all or most with doubtful connection to authorized CIA activities.

Impact of Event

Following the revelation of FBI and CIA abuses, there was a public outcry for curbs on both organizations. In 1975, President Gerald Ford ordered the creation of a special commission to establish the extent of CIA activities and to report findings and recommendations. The commission found that the CIA had indeed conducted improper investigations. Further, the commission recommended that the scope of CIA procedures be limited to foreign intelligence.

Also in 1975, a federal court awarded $12 million in damages to persons who had been arrested in Washington, D.C., while participating in antiwar demonstrations in May, 1971. The arrests were believed to have been a result of police coercion in which the FBI collaborated with local and national officials.

Since both the FBI and the CIA often deal with what is considered to be "sensitive" information, there has been a large amount of controversy over what the public has a right to know and what should be withheld to protect national security. In 1974, Congress amended the Freedom of Information Act (FOIA) to allow *in camera* review of documents by federal district courts in order to determine whether publication of information would pose a security risk. Although this amendment to the

FOIA resulted in the declassification of many COINTELPRO documents, in many instances text was deleted. The effect of the FOIA was further modified by President Ronald Reagan's Executive Order 12356 of April, 1983. The order allowed intelligence agencies more discretionary authority over documentation and appeared to make it more difficult for the courts to review files.

Revelations of CIA abuses led to increased congressional oversight of intelligence activities, but supporters of the CIA argued that the restraints dangerously weakened the agency. The requirements were modified in 1980 to reduce to two the number of congressional committees that had to be notified of intelligence operations. Other provisions, however, increased the likelihood of information reaching Congress. For example, legislation enacted in 1978 required a judicial warrant for most intelligence agency electronic surveillance conducted in the United States.

Participants in FBI and CIA abuses during the COINTELPRO era generally went unpunished. Richard Helms, former director of the CIA, was fined only $2,000. In 1980, the only two FBI personnel tried and found guilty of COINTELPRO abuses were pardoned by President Reagan. In 1981, the FBI settled a $100 million suit for abuses committed against former members of the Weathermen, a radical student group.

Changes have been made in leadership, administrative rules, and legislation, yet recurrences of abuses are not unlikely because of the natural tensions between individual civil liberties on one hand and the demands of national security and civil order on the other.

Bibliography

Blum, Richard H., ed. *Surveillance and Espionage in a Free Society: A Report by the Planning Group on Intelligence and Security to the Policy Council of the Democratic National Committee.* New York: Praeger, 1972. This compilation of works provides information on the historical background of surveillance, the abuses that were apparent before much had been revealed publicly, and policy recommendations for eliminating and preventing further abuses. An insightful work which foreshadowed events to follow.

Churchill, Ward, and Jim Vander Wall. *The COINTELPRO Papers: Documents from the FBI's Secret Wars Against Dissent in the United States.* Boston: South End Press, 1990. The authors provide a fascinating and frightening look at FBI files and show the pervasiveness of counterintelligence programs. Extensive documentation, notes, bibliography, and index.

Elliff, John T. *Crime, Dissent, and the Attorney General: The Justice Department in the 1960's.* Beverly Hills, Calif.: Sage Publications, 1971. Written prior to disclosure of the extent to which the FBI violated civil liberties, the book nevertheless conveys well the tension between protecting and violating rights. Especially good coverage of black militant groups and antiwar dissent. Includes notes and index.

Garrow, David J. *The FBI and Martin Luther King, Jr.: From "Solo" to Memphis.*

New York: W. W. Norton, 1981. This well-researched book provides detailed information on the FBI's relationship with King. Recommended for general readers for insight into the deviation from traditional law enforcement policies pursued by the FBI during the 1960's. Notes and index.

Morgan, Richard E. *Domestic Intelligence: Monitoring Dissent in America.* Austin: University of Texas Press, 1980. Morgan offers a somewhat different view from that taken by most of the other authors listed. Arguing that the accumulation of data on dissent in America is an important task of intelligence agencies, the author is concerned that agencies not become too restricted in the aftermath of scandalous activities. Contains notes and index.

Sorrentino, Frank M. *Ideological Warfare: The FBI's Path Toward Power.* Port Washington, N.Y.: Associated Faculty Press, 1985. Takes an intriguing look at the FBI's war on ideology. The thesis revolves around the bureaucratic use of intelligence, propaganda, and intimidation to maintain the status quo in political ideology. The emphasis on counterintelligence as ideology is useful. Indexed.

Theoharis, Athan. *Spying on Americans: Political Surveillance from Hoover to the Huston Plan.* Philadelphia, Pa.: Temple University Press, 1978. The author, an expert on intelligence, offers a comprehensive perspective of the various ways in which the government monitors the actions of American citizens. Includes notes and index.

United States Commission on CIA Activities Within the United States. *Report to the President.* Washington, D.C.: Government Printing Office, 1975. Commissioned by President Ford, this report includes a wealth of information on illicit CIA programs and recommendations for procedural and administrative changes. Appendices.

Laurie Voice
Robert E. Biles

Cross-References

THE AMIN REGIME TERRORIZES UGANDA

Categories of event: Civil rights; atrocities and war crimes
Time: January 25, 1971
Locale: Uganda

The military coup that brought Idi Amin to power in Uganda led to the creation of one of the bloodiest regimes in African history

Principal personages:
IDI AMIN (1925-   ), the man who ruled Uganda from 1971 to 1979
MILTON OBOTE (1924-   ), the man who was overthrown by Idi Amin in 1971
MUTESA II (1924-1969), the king of Buganda, whose conflict with the Obote regime in the 1960's led to the emergence of the military as a decisive political force in the country

Summary of Event

Like many Third World states, Uganda, a former British colony in East Africa, was an arbitrary creation of British economic, strategic, and political interests and late nineteenth century intra-European conflicts and compromises. It incorporated dozens of different linguistic and cultural groups that had previously lived separately, although some of them maintained various types of commercial as well as belligerent relationships. The indigenous political and social institutions included centralized monarchies in the southern part of the country, of which Buganda was the most important when the area that became Uganda was declared as a British protectorate (1894). Uganda also had small-scale, clan-based social and political systems. In some parts of the territory, a nomadic, pastoral style of life was predominant.

By the 1950's, elite groups that had emerged in various parts of the country were demanding the right to self-determination in the form of independent statehood. The anti-imperialist movement, however, was not unified. In Buganda and, to a lesser extent, in other kingdoms, there were strong autonomist and even secessionist sentiments arising from a desire to maintain special cultural institutions and distinct identities. Throughout the colony, the emerging African elites were divided by religious rivalry, especially that between the Roman Catholics, who were underrepresented in bureaucratic and politico-administrative positions, and the dominant Protestant Anglicans, who were overrepresented. The minority Muslims were also underrepresented but were somewhat peripheral to the rivalry within the Christian community.

On October 9, 1962, the British government granted political independence to the new state of Uganda. The government that acceded to power was a coalition dominated by the Uganda People's Congress (UPC), which was composed of elites from various parts of the country who shared a number of common aspirations and beliefs. They were mostly members of the Protestant Anglican church, many of them secular in outlook and desirous of eliminating the socioeconomic inequalities that had emerged over the years of colonial rule among their home districts and the more prosperous southern kingdoms, especially Buganda.

The UPC's coalition partner was the all-Buganda *Kabaka Yekka* ("The King Above All") movement, whose primary goal was the preservation of the monarchy and the political autonomy of Buganda. The only common element between this movement and the UPC was the Anglican religious identity of the leaders and most of the followers of the two organizations. The opposition Democratic Party essentially represented the aggrieved Roman Catholics.

Uganda started independent statehood under what was in essence a parliamentary democratic system of government. There was a directly elected parliament, a cabinet headed by a prime minister responsible to parliament and, after 1963, a ceremonial president elected by parliament. The first president was Edward Mutesa II, who was also the *Kabaka* (king) of Buganda. The administrative system provided for a large degree of autonomy for the four kingdom areas and a more centralized system for most of the country. The judiciary was independent, and the military and police forces were initially nonpartisan and not directly involved in politics.

Within four years, rivalries and tensions within the ruling coalition had led the country to the brink of civil war. In early 1966, Milton Obote, the prime minister, ordered the arrest of five of his ministers on charges of plotting against him. He subsequently accused Mutesa II of participating in the alleged conspiracy and deposed him from the office of president. Obote later assumed the post. In May, he ordered the Ugandan army, then commanded by Idi Amin, to attack the palace of the *Kabaka*.

The events of 1966 had several significant consequences that were to lay the foundation for the Amin regime. First and foremost, the military was used to intervene in the political process for the first time, thus brushing aside established constitutional procedures. Second, a large number of people lost their lives in the course of indiscriminate attacks by soldiers on unarmed civilians who were identified with the ethnic group of the *Kabaka*. This established a precedent for selective military repression of civilians, which was to be one of the more sanguinary aspects of the Amin regime. Third, from this time onward, maintaining the loyalty of the army was to be the most important determinant of the exercise of political power by Ugandan leaders.

Between 1966 and 1971, Milton Obote tried to create a one-party regime. He centralized administrative and political power in his hands and forced all opposition underground or into exile through imprisonment or denial of positions of influence in the state. In the process, the military, especially army commander Idi Amin, became more prominent on the Ugandan political scene. At the same time, personal and ethnic conflict between Idi Amin and Obote developed, culminating in efforts by Obote to remove Amin from control of the army in 1970. Amin successfully resisted and in January, 1971, pushed his resistance to the point of a *coup d'état* while

Obote was out of the country.

The Amin regime arose from a bloody revolt in which a number of the senior officers were either killed or forced to flee the country. During the first year, there were a number of purges of soldiers suspected of loyalty to the deposed regime. The most significant criterion used was ethnic identity. Thus, from the beginning, the Amin regime had genocidal tendencies.

In 1972, following an abortive invasion mounted by Obote loyalists from across the border in Tanzania, killings of opponents or suspected opponents of the regime spilled over into the civilian sector. People who had been senior officials of the UPC or belonged to the same ethnic group as Obote and his former military supporters became victims of brutal torture and murder. In the same year, Amin ordered the mass expulsion of citizens as well as resident aliens of Indian, Pakistani, or Bangladeshi origin. Many of them had been born in the country, and some families had lived there for several generations. Their property was taken from them without compensation and given to Amin's supporters and other Ugandans.

Impact of Event

During Amin's eight-year rule, thousands of Ugandans were killed for suspected opposition to the regime or because soldiers and members of other armed elements of the regime sought to dispossess them. Among the more prominent victims was the country's chief justice, Benedicto Kiwanuka, who was dragged from his chambers and never seen again, dead or alive. Other victims included numerous journalists, university professors, physicians, playwrights, military officers, police officers, senior civil servants, and members or former members of the regime who had fallen out of favor.

Millions of Ugandans suffered a drastic decline in their economic and social conditions. The economy rapidly deteriorated as a result of the disruption caused by the expulsion of the Asians, who had dominated commerce, and the climate of terror that discouraged investment and normal economic activities. Medical and educational services were hit hard as personnel fled the country to save their lives. Thousands of refugees fled to neighboring countries and beyond, some going as far as Europe and North America.

In late 1978, Amin sent units of his army across the border into Tanzania on the pretext that he was repelling an invasion. They killed and kidnapped civilians and looted property, thus spreading the violence and pain beyond the country's borders. The Tanzanian government decided to use this opportunity to rid Uganda and the region of the bloody tyrant. Beginning in December, 1978, the Tanzanian army, assisted by armed Ugandan exiles, steadily drove Amin's army out of Tanzania. They continued the pursuit until April, 1979, when Idi Amin and his regime were expelled from Uganda.

The impact of the eight-year rule of Idi Amin went beyond Uganda. The East African region and the African continent as a whole were affected. Apart from the thousands of lives lost or ruined, the Amin regime highlighted the enormity of the task facing countries like Uganda in creating stable, prosperous democratic states. At the regional level, Amin's often-belligerent attitude toward neighboring states led to the end of an attempt to create an East African Common Market linking Uganda, Kenya, and Tanzania.

At the continental level, the Amin regime became an embarrassment for African leaders, whose campaign against the apartheid regime in South Africa was robbed of some of its moral force by the excesses of one of their colleagues.

After the downfall of the Amin regime, Ugandans attempted to re-create civilian political institutions through multiparty elections in 1980 and a broad-based regime based on grass-roots direct participatory organizations. Obote was returned to the presidency in the 1980 elections. There is still, in the 1990's, a long way to go before the country creates stable, democratic institutions and a prosperous economy. The lessons of the Amin regime will undoubtedly continue to influence Ugandans as they look for solutions to their intricate political, economic, and social problems.

Bibliography

Gingyera-Pinycwa, A. G. G. *Apolo Milton Obote and His Times.* New York: NOK, 1978. This is a useful study of the goals and policies of Milton Obote, particularly in the period 1966-1971. It takes an overtly pro-Obote perspective.

Gwyn, David. *Idi Amin: Death-Light of Africa.* Boston: Little, Brown, 1977. Written under a pseudonym by a European or North American who worked in Uganda and gained intimate knowledge of the country and its people. This book combines careful analysis of the political background to the rise of the Amin regime with a passionate condemnation of its human rights outrages. One of the best works on the subject. Includes commentary in the form of an afterword. Historical chronology from the nineteenth century, maps, and appendix.

Karugire, Samwiri Rubaraza. *A Political History of Uganda.* Nairobi: Heinemann Educational Books, 1980. A good political history of Uganda that emphasizes the divisions and conflicts plaguing the country at the time of independence.

Kasfir, Nelson. *The Shrinking Political Arena.* Berkeley: University of California Press, 1976. This book focuses on the problem of interethnic and regional conflict in the period just before and following the attainment of political independence. This is an academic work. Maps, tables, selected bibliography, and index.

Kyemba, Henry. *A State of Blood: The Inside Story of Idi Amin.* New York: Grosset & Dunlap, 1977. The author served in both Milton Obote's and Idi Amin's governments. His is one of the few firsthand accounts of Amin's behavior and style. Maps, photographs, appendix, and index.

Mamdani, Mahmood. *Politics and Class Formation in Uganda.* New York: Monthly Review Press, 1976. This book analyzes the political history of Uganda up to and including the Amin regime, from a Marxist class perspective. Its analysis of the colonial period is excellent, but a rather rigid class framework renders the discussion of the postcolonial period unconvincing in many respects.

Smith, George Ivan. *Ghosts of Kampala.* New York: St. Martin's Press, 1980. Written in the form of a personal memoir by a former United Nations official, this book provides a good description of the Amin regime. It is, however, marred by some factual errors. Map and index.

Edward Kannyo

Cross-References

The United Nations Adopts the Universal Declaration of Human Rights (1948), p. 789; The Sudanese Civil War Erupts (1955), p. 941; Civil War Ravages Chad (1965), p. 1273; The U.N. Covenant on Civil and Political Rights Is Adopted (1966), p. 1353; The Secession of Biafra Starts a Nigerian Civil War (1967), p. 1365; Burundi's Government Commits Genocide of the Bahutu Majority (1972), p. 1668; Revolution Erupts in Ethiopia (1974), p. 1758; The United Nations Issues a Declaration Against Torture (1975), p. 1847; The OAU Adopts the African Charter on Human and Peoples' Rights (1981), p. 2136.

WOMEN IN SWITZERLAND ARE GRANTED THE RIGHT TO VOTE

Categories of event: Voting rights and women's rights
Time: February 7, 1971
Locale: Switzerland

Switzerland was the last independent Western democracy to grant women the right to vote in national elections

Principal personages:
ELISABETH BLUNSCHY-STEINER (1922-   ), the first woman elected president of the Swiss National Council (legislature), in May, 1977
GERTRUDE GIRARD (1913-1989), the president of the Swiss Association for Women's Suffrage
LISE GIRARDIN (1921-   ), the first female mayor of Geneva, Switzerland, and the first woman elected to the Swiss Council of States
LILIAN UCHTENHAGEN (1928-   ), an economist and financial expert who helped achieve woman suffrage in 1971
FRANCES E. WILLIS (1899-1983), the first female American career diplomat, appointed in 1953 as United States ambassador to Switzerland

Summary of Event

Universal suffrage is a cornerstone of democracy. The lateness with which Swiss women were granted the right to vote, then, is a paradox. Switzerland is a well-established democracy, yet it was the last Western democracy to extend the national suffrage to women. Until 1971, Swiss women did not possess the right to vote in national elections or to run for national office. A women's suffrage amendment was added to the Swiss constitution by referendum vote on February 7, 1971. It was approved by a margin of 621,403 to 323,596 votes.

The slowness in extending the franchise to women is difficult to reconcile with the emphasis in the Swiss political system on direct democracy and citizen participation. Changes to the Swiss constitution are subject to a compulsory referendum, whereby a majority of individuals and of the cantons (states) must vote affirmatively for amendments to be ratified. Other forms of direct citizen input include the popular initiative for legislation, in which people may by petition vote to add legislation, and facultative referendums, in which voters may petition to review certain types of laws. In addition, in some cantons, open-air town meetings (or *Landsgemeinde*) are held to debate and decide issues of local concern.

Switzerland is a multicultural nation. It has adopted three official languages (German, French, and Italian), and most of its people are members of two major religious denominations (Protestants and Roman Catholics in almost equal percentages). Peaceful coexistence among groups is fostered by strong local governments and by representation of major linguistic and religious groups in national government.

Switzerland is subdivided into twenty cantons and six half-cantons, many of which have distinct linguistic and religious identities. As in the United States, political rights not expressly granted in the constitution to the federal government are delegated to the cantons. For example, each canton determines its official language or languages, which then become the standard in public school instruction and government documents and regulations. Diversity is thus preserved through a commitment to strong cantonal rights.

In addition, a balance of major political and linguistic elements is maintained in the Federal Council (a seven-member cabinet, chosen by the legislature) and in the Federal Assembly, or legislative body. For example, the constitution provides that no more than one Federal Councillor may come from any one of the cantons (which reflect linguistic and religious groups), thus helping to maintain a representation of various groups. The stable working relationship developed in Switzerland among diverse groups has been cited as one explanation for resistance to the women's vote. Women's suffrage was viewed as potentially disruptive in a system in which group interests have been carefully balanced. Women's suffrage also met resistance because of the Swiss concept of the citizen-soldier. By practice and tradition, all Swiss men between the ages of twenty and fifty hold the responsibility for ongoing active military service. Swiss men must keep uniforms, arms, and ammunition in their homes. The Swiss policy of armed neutrality is linked to maintenance of a permanent army composed of the entire male citizenry. Historically, Switzerland's small size and vulnerable geographical position, amid powerful neighbors, created a need for an able defense. The close linkage between the role of citizen and soldier in the minds of the Swiss was thus an additional barrier to women's suffrage, since women do not serve in the military.

The Swiss are also reputed to hold traditional attitudes toward women's roles. A cross-national Gallup poll showed that, in the late 1970's, one-third of the Swiss respondents believed that men should be breadwinners while women should remain at home. When U.S. President Dwight Eisenhower announced his intention to appoint Frances Willis as ambassador to Switzerland in 1953, foreign diplomats speculated that the Swiss would not view positively the appointment of a woman to the position, given their views about women in politics. Even though women were given certain rights in Switzerland earlier than in most nations, such as the right to enter medical and law school in the 1890's, women's entrance into positions of authority in education, business, and politics lagged behind that of their counterparts in other Western democracies. The Swiss accepted the Willis appointment.

The campaign for women's suffrage occurred over most of the twentieth century. Periodically between 1918 and 1959, petitions were drawn up in support of women's suffrage. On several occasions, the Swiss national government considered the possibility of submitting a referendum to the voters, but rejected the idea each time. The first national referendum on the issue of granting the vote to women, held in

February, 1959, was rejected by a two-to-one margin (324,000 in favor and 655,000 against). Support for the amendment was greatest in French-speaking, urban, predominantly Protestant cantons, namely Geneva, Vaud, and Neuchâtel, where a majority voted in favor of the referendum. Rural, German-speaking cantons showed far less support.

Rejection of the referendum precipitated a protest by some women. On February 3, 1959, fifty female teachers from Basel Girls' School in Geneva organized a strike in protest of the referendum vote outcome. The strike was noteworthy since Swiss suffragettes generally did not adopt the bold methods of direct protest utilized in some countries. A representative of the Alliance of Swiss Women's Organizations was quoted as saying that women were "disappointed but not discouraged" by the negative vote. The alliance announced efforts to further penetrate political party organizations to deepen support for women's suffrage and to raise citizens' consciousness in a national information campaign.

A separate battle for women's suffrage occurred on the cantonal and national levels. The Swiss constitution permitted cantons to set their own voter qualifications. This required that women win the right to vote on the national as well as the cantonal level. Prior to 1959, about twenty-five initiatives aimed at granting women the right to vote on the cantonal level had been rejected. In 1958, the city of Basel was the first to grant women the right to vote on the local level. Following defeat of the 1959 national referendum, the French-speaking cantons of Vaud, Neuchâtel, and Geneva exercised their authority to give women the right to vote and seek office on the cantonal level. Local, cantonal voting rights in Switzerland are important because so much autonomy is granted to cantonal governments.

In May, 1968, Lise Girardin, former French professor at the University of Geneva, became Geneva's mayor, the first woman mayor in Switzerland's history. Girardin, an elected member of the Geneva Administrative Council, was appointed as mayor by her colleagues on the council. By September, 1970, eight of twenty-five cantons had granted women the right to vote in cantonal elections. In addition, three localities (in places where cantons had not granted the vote) had extended the vote to women.

In 1970, both houses of the national parliament granted unanimous approval for a vote, scheduled for 1971, on the suffrage issue. On February 7, 1971, Swiss males agreed to grant women the vote in national elections.

Impact of Event

While Swiss men seemed to fear the impact of women's suffrage on the political system, in the 1971 election women helped reelect the same stable party coalition that had been in office since the end of World War II. A number of women, however, were elected to the national parliament during the 1971 election. Women were elected to about five percent of seats in the Nationalrat, the lower house of the parliament. One woman, Lise Girardin, the former Geneva mayor, was elected to the forty-four-seat Council of States (similar to the United States Senate).

Women suffrage leaders, including Gertrude Girard, the president of the Swiss Association for Women's Suffrage, who failed to win a seat, expressed disappointment that more of the 263 female candidates for lower house seats were not elected. They pointed out that female candidates possessed a built-in disadvantage because men were acquainted with one another through their military service. Women, although outnumbering men, were not politically organized or members of clubs and groups. Involvement of this kind can be used by candidates to network with potential voters and to build name recognition and support.

Even though women gained the right to vote in national elections in 1971, they were not automatically granted the right to vote in cantonal and local elections. Votes cast against national women's suffrage in 1971 were clustered in rural cantons of east and central Switzerland. In one such half-canton, Appenzell Inner Rhoden, the men voted 1,141 to 574 against the national women's vote. Over time various cantons have granted women the right to vote; however, some cantons were especially resistant to change. Appenzell Inner Rhoden, where open-air town meetings (*Landsgemeinde*) were still held, maintained its traditional ways until forced to change. At the male-only town meetings, many men followed the tradition of attending the town meetings wearing ancestral swords, signifying their right to vote. Women, who were prohibited from participating, stood outside a roped area to watch the proceedings.

In 1990, the Swiss Federal Tribunal (similar to the United States Supreme Court) ruled that an equal rights clause in the constitution, passed in 1981 by the Swiss voters, overrode the constitutional provision giving each canton the right to decide its own voting requirements. With this decision, women were granted the right to vote in all elections on local, state, and national levels.

Since the vote was granted in 1971, Swiss women have made considerable progress in gaining election to political office. By 1979, women constituted about ten percent of members of the parliament, a level twice that of similar legislative bodies in the United States and Great Britain. In 1977, Elisabeth Blunschy-Steiner, an attorney who favored change in the patriarchal Swiss family law, was elected president of the Swiss National Council (the Swiss legislature). In December, 1983, Lilian Uchtenhagen was named the official candidate of the Social Democratic Party for one of two seats on the Federal Council (cabinet) that the party fills by custom. Uchtenhagen had served in parliament since 1971 and had been active in the women's suffrage movement. The parliament rejected her candidacy in favor of a male Social Democrat. In 1984, another woman, Elizabeth Kopp, was elected to the Federal Council. Following her election as vice president of the Confederation in 1989, she was forced to resign amid charges that she had breached confidentiality by revealing to her husband that a government investigation involving his company was going to take place.

Legal inequalities in the treatment of men and women have also been chipped away. In 1977, the Swiss federal court ruled that male and female civil servants must be paid equally. In 1981, an equal rights amendment to the constitution was adopted.

In 1971, husbands still retained rights over their wives' assets, and consent was legally required for women to take a job or obtain a passport. Divorce laws did not grant women an equal share of joint assets. In 1985, the women's vote was credited with passage of a referendum that transformed these and other marriage and family laws. For example, the new laws granted women authority over their own financial affairs and made it unnecessary for women to obtain permission from their husbands to open bank accounts or obtain jobs.

It might be argued that women have not obtained equal standing with men in politics in any nation, but Swiss women have made major inroads into a field that was almost completely dominated by men until the vote was granted to women in 1971.

Bibliography

Barber, Benjamin. "Participation and Swiss Democracy." *Government and Opposition* 23 (Winter, 1988): 31-50. This article describes the various institutions of Swiss government, and considers the philosophy of Swiss democracy and citizenship. It also includes a discussion of the various instruments of direct democracy adopted by the Swiss.

Barber, Benjamin, and Patrick Watson. *The Struggle for Democracy.* Boston: Little, Brown, 1988. This companion volume to the film series *The Struggle for Democracy* includes a chapter, "Citizens," that explores the role of women as citizens in several nations, including Switzerland. The discussion of citizenship is thoughtful, but some of the factual material is outdated.

Inglehart, Margaret. "Sex Role, Historical Heritage, and Political Participation in Switzerland." In *Switzerland at the Polls: The National Elections of 1979,* edited by Howard R. Penniman. Washington, D.C.: American Enterprise Institute, 1983. The author considers various factors that explain the extent to which Swiss women have become integrated into and involved in their political system. The first part of the chapter includes a brief history of women's suffrage and of women's political participation in Switzerland.

Norris, Pippa. "Women's Legislative Participation in Western Europe." In *Women and Politics in Western Europe,* edited by Sylvia Bashevkin. London: F. Cass, 1985. The author considers the relative influence of various factors on women's ability to obtain legislative seats in Western European nations, including Switzerland. Although only a portion of the article is devoted to the position of women in Switzerland, the article provides a comparative context within which to judge women's progress.

Schmid, Carol L. *Conflict and Consensus in Switzerland.* Berkeley: University of California Press, 1981. This book examines ways in which Switzerland manages its multicultural diversity. It discusses the role of Swiss political institutions, the political socialization of Swiss citizens, and the methods by which the Swiss handle certain difficult public policy issues.

Mary A. Hendrickson

Cross-References

Finland Grants Woman Suffrage (1906), p. 70; Parliament Grants Suffrage to British Women (1918), p. 247; The League of Women Voters Is Founded (1920), p. 333; The Nineteenth Amendment Gives American Women the Right to Vote (1920), p. 339; Women's Rights in India Undergo a Decade of Change (1925), p. 401; Japan Ends Property Restrictions on Voting Rights (1925), p. 417; French Women Get the Vote (1944), p. 646; The U.N. Convention on the Political Rights of Women Is Approved (1952), p. 885; The U.S. Voting Age Is Lowered to Eighteen (1970), p. 1521; A U.N. Convention Condemns Discrimination Against Women (1979), p. 2057.

CONFLICTS IN PAKISTAN LEAD TO
THE SECESSION OF BANGLADESH

Categories of event: Revolutions and rebellions; atrocities and war crimes
Time: March-December, 1971
Locale: East Pakistan and Bangladesh

East Pakistanis' perceptions of denial of political rights, especially the right of the Awami League to form a government after electoral victory, climaxed in secession through a civil war

Principal personages:
> MOHAMMED ALI JINNAH (1876-1948), a leader of the Muslim League, the founding father and the first governor general of Pakistan
> SHEIKH MUJIBUR RAHMAN (1922-1975), a leader of the Awami (People's) League and the founding father of Bangladesh, served as the first prime minister and as president of Bangladesh
> AGHA MOHAMMAD YAHYA KHAN (1917-1980), the chief martial law administrator and president of Pakistan between 1969 and 1971
> ZULFIKAR ALI BHUTTO (1928-1979), a leader of the Pakistan People's Party, the president (1971-1973) and then prime minister (1973-1977) of Pakistan
> INDIRA GANDHI (1917-1984), the prime minister of India

Summary of Event

In the wake of the British withdrawal in August, 1947, India and Pakistan emerged as two independent sovereign states following the bloody partition of the subcontinent. The demand for a separate state for Muslims was formulated by the leaders of the Muslim League, mainly between the 1920's and the 1940's. Self-rule became the main goal of the nationalist movement and was viewed as protection from the possible future tyranny of a Hindu-majority state. Initially, independent states were sought for the Muslim-majority areas in the northwestern and northeastern zones of undivided India. As the transfer of power from the British approached, the Muslim League, under Mohammed Ali Jinnah, negotiated for a single state for the Muslims of the two zones, which were a thousand miles apart.

From the beginning, the prospects of a strong national integration of Pakistan were bleak. Religion proved to be a weak bond of unity in comparison with cultural, linguistic, and other primordial loyalties of the peoples. Retrospectively, the East Pakistanis remained dissatisfied with the Muslim League's bargaining for a single state and apprehensive of playing second fiddle to the West Pakistanis, who dominated the national political, economic, and bureaucratic (civilian and military) circles. The geographical distance between the two zones, popularly known as the "wings" in Pakistan, posed a serious administrative challenge. There were gross cultural and linguistic differences between the Eastern Bengalis and the Western populations of Punjabis, Sindhis, and Pathans. The domination and unequal treatment by the national government of the East Pakistanis in the post-independence period paved the way for the civil war of 1971.

The long series of grievances of Bengalis against the national government began with the decision to make Urdu the official language of Pakistan in 1948. The strong reaction of Bengalis, who took great pride in their own language and literary tradition, was viewed as an unpatriotic act. Later, in 1956, Bengali was recognized as an official language along with Urdu only after rioting, police action, and bloodshed. By then, the Bengali grievances had been diverted to other issues.

Between the late 1950's and the late 1960's, the protests of East Pakistanis against the national government mounted sharply. They were proportionately underrepresented in the national political circles and in the civilian services despite their fifty-four percent majority in the general population. The appointment of a few Bengalis to top posts was viewed as symbolic only, as a show of Pakistani unity. Bengalis were appointed to the positions of governor general, prime minister, and president of Pakistan. In most cases, these appointees remained in office only as long as they were subservient to the Western Pakistani politicians and bureaucrats. Many resigned on their own. The top political and administrative positions in the provincial government in East Pakistan invariably went to the West Pakistanis.

The problem of Bengali underrepresentation was much more acute in military services, where they held only six percent of key positions. This underrepresentation was interpreted as a continuation of the British policy of treating Bengalis as a nonmartial race. Bengalis believed themselves to be defenseless in case of an attack from India, as their defense had to come from the West Pakistanis.

The industrialization of East Pakistan was totally neglected. Its role was mainly that of a supplier of raw materials and a consumer of finished products of Western industries. The Western Pakistani entrepreneurs also controlled the industries in the East. Moreover, an equitable share of the export earnings of Pakistan from the indigenous jute crop was denied to the East. West Pakistan also remained the sole beneficiary of economic and military aid received from allies in the Western world.

A strong Bengali political mobilization took place during the 1960's, under the Awami League. Its leader, Mujibur Rahman (Mujib), advanced his "Six Point" political and economic program in 1966. It became the mandate for the creation of Bangladesh in 1971. The six points had a dual objective of complete autonomy for East Pakistan within a loose confederation and the creation of a weak center, with power only over defense and foreign affairs. The center was to be dependent economically on the federating units. Mujib's proposal coincided with a general demand in both East and West for democratization of the political process. Later on, a Democratic Action Committee was formed of united opposition parties.

The political center's response to the changing political situation under both Mohammad Ayub Khan (1958-1969) and Agha Mohammad Yahya Khan (1969-1971) was to strengthen the powers of the national executive, appoint West Pakistanis to the top positions of administration in the East, imprison all opponents and leaders of opposition parties, and strengthen the role of the military in politics. In view of the rapidly deteriorating situation, Yahya Khan proposed the framing of a new constitution by a duly elected constituent assembly and showed willingness to broaden the base of autonomy and economic distribution for the East. Elections were to be held on the basis of a joint electorate and population. Yahya Khan, however, was committed to maintaining the authority of the central government and the unity of Pakistan.

The first general elections in Pakistan were held on December 20, 1970. In a 300-member House, the East won 162 seats and the West 138. In the provincial elections in the East, the Awami League under Mujib won 160 out of 162 seats. In the West, Zulfikar Ali Bhutto's Pakistan People's Party (PPP) won 81 out of 138 seats. The prospects of the Bengali, Mujib, in the prime minister's seat and of provincial autonomy for the East were in sight. The latter was totally unacceptable to Yahya Khan and the former to Bhutto, who had a personal ambition of being in power. The delay in the transfer of power to the Awami League aggravated Bengali apprehensions and hostility against the national government.

The course for separation was set as Mujib began to show rigidity that the new constitution must be based on the six points. Bhutto began to plead for unity of the nation. Several abortive attempts were made by Yahya Khan between January and April, 1971, to reconcile the stands of Mujib and Bhutto. The last in the series to be rejected was Mujib's proposal in March, 1971, that he be named prime minister of East Pakistan and Bhutto be made the prime minister of West Pakistan.

Between March and December, 1971, Pakistan's unity was maintained only by threats of violence. On March 1, 1971, Mujib called for civil disobedience and strikes to protest the indefinite postponement by Yahya Khan of the March 3 meeting of the National Assembly. Public demonstrations, looting, arson, and rioting were brought under control by the military only after three hundred people were killed and many more injured and left homeless. Military troops in the East were doubled in numbers to sixty thousand by the end of summer. At the time of independence for Bangladesh in December, 1971, their numbers were estimated at ninety thousand.

On March 15, 1971, Mujib took over the administration of *Bangladesh* (Bengali Homeland) on the basis of his electoral victory in 1970. A reign of terror was unleashed under orders from Yahya Khan, beginning on March 25. Mujib was arrested and sent to West Pakistan. Three military battalions, with a force of ten tanks, attacked the defenseless city of Dhaka. Universities were a special target of the army. Intellectuals, professors, and students were mowed down by firing squads. Genocide of the unarmed population as well as of armed guerrillas, both in cities and in the countryside, resulted in thousands of deaths.

Crowds of people were forced into buildings, which were then set on fire. Women were raped, maimed, and killed. In many cases, they were forced to drink the blood and eat the hearts of their children. By the end of the summer, the number of killings was estimated at 300,000. A substantial number of Bengali Hindus and Muslims, about ten million by December, 1971, fled to India as refugees. Many of them died there of epidemics.

The atrocities committed by the Pakistani army caused a militant twist in the secessionist movement. On April 11, 1971, a provisional government-in-exile in India was announced for the "independent, sovereign republic of Bangladesh," with Mujib as the president. Mukti Bahini, the liberation force organized under Colonel M. A. G. Osmani, began to counter the actions of Pakistani troops and the civilian militia recruited from among the non-Bengali, particularly the Bihari, populations. The Mukti Bahini freedom fighters received training and ammunition from neighboring India.

World public opinion began to turn in favor of the Bengalis as the horror stories of torture began to travel. Pakistani diplomats of Bengali origin began to resign from their posts abroad, and the anti-Pakistan campaign led by India and others at the United Nations focused the world's attention on atrocities in Bangladesh. Pakistan was on the defensive and began to mount military and diplomatic pressure against India.

Under immense pressure from its citizens, the alarming entry of refugees, and the perceived threat to its territorial security from the garrisoning of Pakistani troops on its borders, India decided to intervene militarily in the liberation movement for Bangladesh. The Indian intervention was decisive for the emergence of Bangladesh. The war between India and Pakistan, which was fought in both the eastern and the western sectors, lasted from December 4 to December 16, 1971. The new state of Bangladesh was born when the Pakistani armies surrendered. India became the first country to recognize Bangladesh on December 6, 1971.

Impact of Event

The prospect of war between India and Pakistan over Bangladesh brought about a realignment of regional and global forces. The Soviet Union moved closer to India through a twenty-year treaty signed in August, 1971, while China, a long-term adversary of both India and the Soviet Union, moved closer to Pakistan with a unilateral defense guarantee. The United States, under the Nixon Administration, sided with Pakistan even in the face of gross violations of political and human rights of East Pakistanis. The effect of having major powers on each side was that India could unilaterally intervene to liberate Bangladesh without any external interference.

India emerged as a regional power through its intervention, but its role as a "subimperialistic" state was to have an adverse impact on its future relations with the neighboring states, including Bangladesh. Soon after its emergence, Bangladesh made a series of allegations against India, including that the Indian troops stayed on for too long after the surrender of the Pakistani army and that no representative of the Bangladesh provisional government or of Mukti Bahini was present for the event.

Five days after the Pakistani army's surrender, Yahya Khan handed over his resignation and transferred powers to Bhutto. In January, 1972, President Bhutto unconditionally released Mujib from a Pakistan prison where he was held facing charges of treason and a death penalty. On January 10, 1972, Mujib arrived in Dhaka, the capital of Bangladesh, and was hailed as the father of the nation. He assumed the offices of president and, after two days, prime minister of Bangladesh.

The overthrow of Pakistani rule and the regime change did not lead to the freedom and prosperity to which the mass movement in Bangladesh had aspired. Problems of economic reconstruction and development, and the establishment of law and order following death, destruction, and the armament of civilians, proved to be the most serious challenges. On the political front, the new ruling elites did not prove to be very different from their predecessors.

After consolidating his power, Mujib viewed the consensus of people behind him as an excuse to establish an autocratic rule. He began to dispense patronage among his comrades, friends, and family members. He alienated a number of skilled bureaucrats and politically ambitious personalities. The economic situation worsened, with soaring prices, scarcity of goods, and uneven distribution. Famine and natural disasters added to the misery of the people. The superior treatment of the former Mukti Bahini guerrillas over the professional soldiers in the army, including the "repatriates" from West Pakistan, created low morale, resentment, and frustration among the latter.

In 1975, Mujib formally discarded everything for which Bangladesh had stood. He amended the constitution to concentrate powers in his own hands, abolished political parties, and suspended fundamental rights, including freedom of speech, the right to dissent, and equal opportunity of employment. On August 15, 1975, in a military coup known as the "Major's Plot," Mujib and several members of his family were assassinated.

Mujib's death initiated a period of political instability and power struggles. In the post-Mujib period, military rule was restored in Bangladesh. A series of coups and assassinations of the heads of state continued. The economic situation in Bangladesh remained gloomy even after two decades of independence. Poverty, disease, hunger, underdevelopment, overpopulation, and natural disasters remained the hallmarks of Bangladesh. Striking parallels of feudalism and capitalistic development, and of Islamic fundamentalism and leftist radicalism, continued to contend for their strongholds as the gap between the interests of the ruling elite and the struggling masses continued to widen.

Bibliography

Baxter, Craig. *Bangladesh: A New Nation in an Old Setting.* Boulder, Colo.: Westview Press, 1984. Deals with Bangladesh's preindependence past and makes a critical assessment of the postindependence period. The historical, social, political, and economic aspects are analyzed in depth. Relations of the new state with regional and global powers are examined.

Baxter, Craig, Yogendra K. Malik, Charles H. Kennedy, and Robert C. Oberst. *Government and Politics in South Asia.* Boulder, Colo.: Westview Press, 1987. This comprehensive volume provides a detailed and comparative review of the existing political systems in South Asia. It examines the transformation of the political process in Bangladesh from its democratic base into authoritarianism.

Franda, Marcus. *Bangladesh: The First Decade.* New Delhi, India: South Asian Publishers, 1982. Provides an account of the developments immediately surrounding the emergence of Bangladesh, the role of Indian intervention in its liberation, the phenomena of assassinations, coups, and countercoups, and the country's struggle for existence.

Khan, Mohammad Mohabbat, ed. *Bangladesh: Society, Politics, and Bureaucracy.* Dhaka, Bangladesh: Center for Administrative Studies, 1984. The volume is a collection of contributions of experts from many countries in various fields. They give a retrospective analysis of the first ten years of Bangladesh's existence. Originally, these papers were presented at a conference held at Harvard University.

O'Donnell, Charles Peter. *Bangladesh: Biography of a Muslim Nation.* Boulder, Colo.: Westview Press, 1984. The most complete and detailed work on the systematic developments, from 1947 to 1971, leading to the emergence of Bangladesh. The aftermath of secession from Pakistan and the problems of political control and economic reconstruction and development in Bangladesh, as well as the international relations of this new polity, are discussed at length.

U.S. Library of Congress. Federal Research Division. *Bangladesh: A Country Study.* Washington, D.C.: Author, 1990. This edited volume provides a complete analysis of the history, culture, society, and politics of Bangladesh. It is an excellent source for getting acquainted with the important personalities and processes of the society and politics in Bangladesh. Details of the geography and ecology of this country are outlined.

Indu Vohra

Cross-References

The Muslim League Attempts to Protect Minority Interests in India (1906), p. 87; Soldiers Massacre Indian Civilians in Amritsar (1919), p. 264; Gandhi Leads a Noncooperation Movement (1920), p. 315; Women's Rights in India Undergo a Decade of Change (1925), p. 401; Gandhi Leads the Salt March (1930), p. 447; India Signs the Delhi Pact (1931), p. 459; The United Nations Adopts a Convention on the Crime of Genocide (1948), p. 783; The U.N. Convention Relating to the Status of Refugees Is Adopted (1951), p. 867; Zia Establishes Martial Law in Pakistan (1977), p. 1898; Zulfikar Ali Bhutto Is Hanged Despite Pleas from World Leaders (1979), p. 2018; Indira Gandhi Is Assassinated (1984), p. 2232; Benazir Bhutto Becomes the First Woman Elected to Lead a Muslim Country (1988), p. 2403; Kashmir Separatists Demand an End to Indian Rule (1989), p. 2426.

GREAT EVENTS
FROM
HISTORY II

CHRONOLOGICAL LIST OF EVENTS

VOLUME I

VOLUME II

VOLUME III

VOLUME IV

VOLUME V